MW00723656

MODERN TANKS AND ARTILLERY

1945–PRESENT

MODERN TANKS AND ARTILLERY

1945–PRESENT

THE AUTHORITATIVE ILLUSTRATED HISTORY

MICHAEL E. HASKEW

METRO BOOKS
New York

METRO BOOKS
New York

An Imprint of Sterling Publishing
387 Park Avenue South
New York, NY 10016

METRO BOOKS and the distinctive Metro Books logo are trademarks
of Sterling Publishing Co., Inc.

© 2014 by Amber Books Ltd.

All rights reserved. No part of this publication may be reproduced, stored in a retrieval system
or transmitted in any form or by any means (including electronic, mechanical, photocopying,
recording, or otherwise) without prior written permission from the publisher.

The material in this volume has previously appeared in:
The Essential Vehicle Identification Guide: Postwar Armored Fighting Vehicles 1945–Present
and *The Essential Weapons Identification Guide: Postwar Artillery 1945–Present.*

Editorial and design by
Amber Books Ltd
74–77 White Lion Street
London N1 9PF
www.amberbooks.co.uk

Project Editor: Michael Spilling
Designer: Colin Hawes and Andrew Easton
Picture Research: Terry Forshaw

ISBN 978-1-4351-5705-7

For information about custom editions, special sales, and premium and corporate purchases,
please contact Sterling Special Sales at 800-805-5489 or specialsales@sterlingpublishing.com.

Manufactured in China

2 4 6 8 10 9 7 5 3 1

www.sterlingpublishing.com

Picture Credits
Art-Tech: 8, 10, 12, 14, 21, 31, 78, 90, 104, 106, 138, 170, 188, 194, 198,
216, 227, 247, 280–283 (all), 298, 299, 335, 339
Cody Images: 64, 81, 92–94 (all), 112, 115, 136, 196, 199, 244, 257
Corbis: 296 (Sygma/Christian Simonpietri), 312 (Reuters/Gil Cohen Morgan)
Press Association Images: 347 (Valery Levitin)
Rex Features: 351 (Sipa)
U.S. Department of Defense: 6/7, 11, 62, 140–153 (all), 177, 190/191,
192, 195, 254, 266, 269, 300, 328–332 (all), 345, 358

All **artworks** courtesy of Amber Books and Art-Tech/Aerospace

Contents

Volume One: Tanks & Armoured Fighting Vehicles

Introduction

During more than half a century of modern warfare, military strategists and tacticians have alternately praised and maligned the armoured fighting vehicle. With the advent of nuclear weapons, efficient anti-armour missiles and mines, it seemed at one time that the day of the tank had passed. However, armoured vehicle technology has advanced as well, and the role of the tank has been redefined to the battlefield of the twenty-first century and beyond. Through decades of warfare, the key attributes of firepower, speed and armour protection have guided the development and deployment of the tank. The armoured vehicle itself has been redesigned, fitted with futuristic equipment and armament, and integrated into the general battle plans of nations across the globe.

◀ **On manoeuvres**
US crew onboard their M60A2 Patton medium tank discuss strategy during winter exercises in West Germany. The M60 series remained in US service for almost 30 years, being replaced as the US Army's main battle tank by the Abrams M1 in the 1980s.

▲ **Armoured lion**

Based on its predecessor the Vijayanta, the Arjun (Lion) main battle tank has many excellent features, but its decades-long development has been dogged by technical problems. In trials in 2010, it performed well against the Russian T-90.

F OLLOWING THE CATACLYSM of World War II, a reassessment of the role of the tank and armoured fighting vehicle in warfare occurred. The division of labour among armoured forces inevitably gave way to a multi-purpose, powerful and highly mobile vehicle. Rather than the continued production of tanks to fit different functions – the lightly armed and armoured tanks for reconnaissance and rapid movement, medium tanks to engage enemy armour in tank versus tank combat, and heavy tanks to provide direct artillery and infantry support – the concept of the all-purpose, main battle tank emerged. This was typified in the Cold War era by the US Patton series, British-made Centurion and the Soviet-originated T-55 and its numerous upgrades and variants.

Offensive prowess

The effectiveness of the main battle tank has been demonstrated in combat and embodies continuing improvement in multiple aspects of design and tactical capacity. Heavier, more versatile platforms mount specialized turrets housing larger calibre guns capable of firing APFSDS (armour-piercing fin-stabilized discarding sabot) ammunition and, in some cases, anti-tank missiles. Stabilization systems allow main battle tanks to fire on the move with great accuracy, while laser rangefinding and infrared night vision equipment facilitate target acquisition and

compensate for atmospheric conditions in a variety of climates and weather conditions. Battlefield management systems allow the tracking of multiple targets simultaneously, assisting in the identification of both friendly and hostile vehicles, while advanced communications equipment coordinate operations on a grand scale. Increasingly powerful engines, such as the conventional diesel or innovative gas turbine types, provide speed, reliability and ease of maintenance.

Defensive demands

Defensive modernization includes the introduction of composite, modular and explosive reactive armour, isolated storage space for ammunition with blast doors to protect crew members and components designed to direct an explosion outwards in the event of penetration of the tank's hull or turret. Warning sensors designed to alert the tank crew to an imminent threat when the vehicle is 'locked on' by enemy laser equipment coordinate with appropriate countermeasures to minimize the likelihood of a direct hit.

Smoke grenade launchers are standard on the modern main battle tank, while machine guns remain a necessity for protection against low-flying aircraft or attacking infantry. NBC (nuclear, biological, chemical) defensive systems allow armoured vehicles to operate in such adverse conditions.

Modern low intensity combat has nevertheless constituted a persistent paradox for the armoured fighting vehicle. The confines of urban warfare often limit the capabilities of the tank during close-in fighting, while rudimentary improvised explosive devices (IED) and land mines remain hazards to even the latest in AFV technology. In response, defensive packages specifically designed for low intensity and urban survivability have been introduced.

New tactics

Along with the ever-improving technology, battlefield tactics have also been refined. Recent battlefield experience has confirmed the tank's ability to create and to exploit a breach in enemy lines, rapidly advance across favorable terrain and hold territory in cooperation with armoured infantry. These highly mobile ground troops ride into battle aboard armoured personnel carriers or infantry fighting

KEY TO TACTICAL SYMBOLS USED IN ORGANIZATION CHARTS

▷	Symbol for division or larger	Sig	Signals unit
▢	Symbol for regiment or brigade-sized formation	Hv	Heavy weapons unit
▷	Symbol for battalion or smaller unit	Bat	Battery
Arm	Armoured unit	Mot	Motorized infantry unit
Mec	Mechanized unit	Art	Artillery unit
Eng	Engineer unit	Rec	Reconnaissance
Inf	Infantry unit	AA	Anti-aircraft unit
		SP	Self-propelled gun unit

vehicles designed not only to provide transportation but also to add direct fire support with a variety of weapons from light machine guns to anti-tank missiles, chain guns and high-velocity cannon.

The main battle tank, its accompanying armoured fighting vehicles, self-propelled artillery and other types are destined to play active roles in ground warfare well into the future. As technology is continually refined, these versatile vehicles will serve as primary weapons systems in any armed conflict of great magnitude.

▼ **Stryker force**
US Army M1126 Stryker ICVs of the Stryker Brigade Combat Team kick up plumes of dust as they conduct a patrol near Mosul, Iraq, 2005. Infantry combat vehicles such as the Stryker provide a highly mobile platform from which to deploy infantry and firepower in reconnaissance operations and counter-insurgency warfare.

Chapter 1

Cold War Europe, 1947–91

Before the guns of World War II had fallen silent, the coalition that eventually defeated the Axis had begun to fracture. Ideological differences, which had simmered just below the surface, had come to the fore as sharply contrasting visions of the post-war world collided. In Europe, an historic battleground, the lines were again being drawn. This time, the force of armoured power was destined to project the will of the military planners who deployed their tanks only a few kilometres from those of their expected adversaries. The only sure trump card to an overwhelming mechanized land force was the potential use of nuclear weapons.

◀ **Amphibious manoeuvres**
Polish PT-76 amphibious tanks ford a river during a training exercise. Soviet tactical doctrine emphasized river crossings and amphibious outflanking manoeuvres.

Early Cold War

Germany lay defeated, and former Allies prepared to confront one another in an atmosphere of mutual distrust. The flashpoint of another world war, it seemed, would be in Europe, where tanks and troops were arrayed in readiness.

WITH THE SOVIET RED ARMY dominant in Eastern Europe, where its tanks had fought the largest armoured clashes in modern military history, and the British and American armies controlling the West, an uneasy peace settled across the continent, while the world watched the ebb and flow of political and military tension.

Acknowledging that the Soviet Union was intent on expanding communism around the world, the United States and Great Britain adopted a policy of containment during the early days of the Cold War. Such policy was predicated on the continued deployment of military assets in close proximity to the Soviets, particularly in Europe where armed confrontation, should it develop, was expected to take place; the predominance of the United States in the Pacific; and the simple fact that the US possessed the atomic bomb, its awesome destructive power demonstrated at Hiroshima and Nagasaki.

The Soviets, on the other hand, had extended their sphere of influence into Eastern Europe not only to spread their communist philosophy, but also to assuage their paranoia concerning another attack against their homeland from the west. Meanwhile, on the continent of Asia a civil war raged in China, and Marxist fervour tinged with nationalism had begun to create unrest in Indochina. Still, the power of the atomic bomb was expected to hold the Soviets in check, and the security of Western Europe was top priority.

By 1950, the United States and Britain were facing financial constraints, and military spending was one of those areas which bore the brunt of budget cuts. The armies of the United States and Great Britain

▼ **German M48**
West German Army tank formations were equipped with M48s at first, until enough Leopard tanks were available for frontline service.

consisted of veteran troops who had fought in World War II; however, the conditions of occupation duty and the inevitable relaxation of wartime readiness had degraded combat efficiency. The US military establishment reorganized its divisional make-up. On paper, a tank battalion and an anti-aircraft battalion were added to each infantry division, and an artillery battery was increased from four guns to six. Anti-tank companies were stricken from regimental rolls, and a tank company added. In practice, however, the needed equipment, men and supplies were not readily available. Military readiness in Europe was more of a notion than a fact.

For the West, the containment doctrine and the use of armour were defensive in nature and undergirded by the threat of nuclear arms should the Soviet Union initiate a military campaign. Containment meant the maintenance of a military ground force in Western Europe, face to face with the Soviet military. War was narrowly averted as early as 1948, when the Soviets blockaded Berlin and a massive American airlift of supplies caused them to finally relax their stranglehold on the German capital.

The year 1949 was indeed a Cold War watershed. The Soviet Union successfully tested its first nuclear device, well ahead of Western time estimates, while the communists of Mao Tse-tung gained control of mainland China. The Western powers established the North Atlantic Treaty Organization with 12 nations pledging that 'an attack against one or more of [these nations] shall be considered an attack against them all'. Obviously aimed at the Soviet Union, the NATO alliance further fuelled Soviet suspicions as to the intent of its former allies. Within months, war had erupted on the Korean peninsula.

A harbinger of things to come occurred on 7 September 1945, during an Allied victory parade in Berlin. Celebrating the defeat of Nazi Germany, infantry units marched first, with the Soviet IX Rifle Corps and Fifth Shock Army, the French 2nd Division, the British 131st Infantry Brigade and the US 82nd Airborne Division stepping out.

A large armoured display then passed in review. First, 32 M24 Chaffee light tanks and 16 M8 armoured cars of the US 705th Armored Battalion rolled forward. They were followed by elements of the French 1st Armoured Division, 24 Comet tanks and 30 armoured cars of the famed British 7th Armoured Division and then 52 brand new IS-3 heavy tanks of the Red Army's 71st Guards Heavy Tank Regiment. Western observers were taken aback by the number of new, modern Soviet tanks. The era of the arms race, posturing and global gamesmanship had begun.

Soviet Union
1947–69

Formed in 1955, the Warsaw Pact was a military alliance of the Soviet Union and its satellite states in Eastern Europe undertaken in response to NATO initiatives.

D IVIDED EAST AND WEST, Germany was considered the likely primary battleground between Red Army and Western land forces should a shooting war begin. The Federal Republic of Germany formally joined NATO on 9 May 1955, and less than a week later the Soviet Union formed the Warsaw Pact. Perhaps the most tangible perceived threat to Soviet security was a rearmed West Germany. With the Red Army the primary Warsaw Pact military force, the armies of Poland, East Germany and Czechoslovakia, which bordered the West, were also expected to supply men and arms, as were other client states to a lesser extent.

Of course, the strength of the Soviet alliance has been questioned from the start, and prime evidence of its tenuous nature was the short-lived Hungarian Revolt of 1956, when the Red Army deployed more than 1100 tanks, which rolled through the streets of Budapest and other Hungarian cities.

Warsaw Pact armoured doctrine of the Cold War years was in large part an extension of those tactics which proved successful in World War II – applying overwhelming force to a localized front, achieving a breakthrough and rapidly exploiting the breach in enemy lines. To complement the proven T-34

▲ **IS-2 Heavy Tank (1944 model)**

Soviet Third Guards Mechanized Army / East Germany, 1950

Designed in response to heavy German armour during World War II, the IS-2 heavy tank entered service with the Red Army in 1943. Soon, the Model 1944 incorporated the D25-T 122mm (4.8in) gun (faster-firing than its predecessor), a double-baffle muzzle brake and better fire control.

Specifications	
Crew: 4	Speed: 37km/h (23mph)
Weight: 46 tonnes (45.27 tons)	Range: 240km (149 miles)
Length: 9.9m (32ft 6in)	Armament: 1 x 122mm (4.8in) D-25T gun, plus
Width: 3.09m (10ft 2in)	3 x 7.62mm (0.3in) DT MGs (1 coaxial, 1 fixed in
Height: 2.73m (8ft 11in)	bow and 1 ball-mounted in turret rear)
Engine: 382.8kW (513hp) V-2 12-cyl diesel	Radio: 10R or 10RK

Soviet Independent Guards Heavy Tank Brigade, 1947

Most of the Soviet armoured formations that faced westwards during the early years of the Cold War were elite Guards units. With more than 60 tanks, the Red Army heavy tank brigade was organized into three armoured regiments and one mechanized infantry regiment that included supporting self-propelled assault guns.

HQ (3 x command vehicles)

1 Regiment (3 x command tanks, 21 x IS-2s)

3 Regiment (3 x command tanks, 21 x IS-2s)

2 Regiment (3 x command tanks, 21 x IS-2s)

Light SP Battery (3 x SU-76M)

**Support troops
(19 x M3 half-tracks)**

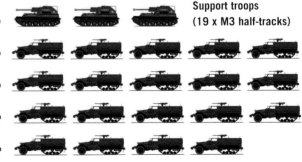

medium tank, the development of heavy tanks such as the IS-2 and IS-3 continued during the 1950s. While several improvements in heavy tank design did not extend beyond the prototype stage, the IS-2 went on to equip the standard Red Army heavy tank regiment of the early Cold War era (each fielded 21); the medium T-34 was deployed in large numbers as well.

In the 1960s, Soviet tank design made a significant leap forward with the T-64, which introduced an automatic loader, eliminating the need for a fourth crewman. The Soviets also refined tactics in the use of mechanized infantry, designating mechanized rifle divisions as light and heavy. The introduction of the BMP-1, the world's first purpose-built infantry fighting vehicle, and the wheeled BTR-40 and BTR-60 armoured personnel carriers, which had been in service since 1950, facilitated this adjustment.

As the Soviet armoured division's tanks advanced along the main front, the heavy mechanized infantry units were to follow in support, providing cover against enemy infantry and anti-tank units. The light mechanized infantry units were to fan out along

▲ IS-3 Heavy Tank

Soviet First Guards Tank Army / East Germany, 1952

Nicknamed the 'Pike' due to its distinctively pointed hull, the IS-3 formed the basis for Soviet heavy tank designs of the Cold War era. The turret of the IS-3 was rounded and flattened, resulting in a lower profile while sacrificing space for the crew.

Specifications

Crew: 3	Speed: 40km/h (25mph)
Weight: 45.77 tonnes (45.05 tons)	Range: 185km (115 miles)
Length: 9.85m (32ft 4in)	Armament: 1 x 122mm (4.8in) D-25T gun, plus 1
Width: 3.09m (10ft 2in)	x 12.7mm (0.5in) DshK HMG on AA mount and 1
Height: 2.45m (8ft)	x coaxial 7.62mm (0.3in) DT MG
Engine: 447kW (600hp) V-2-JS V12 diesel	Radio: 10RK

▲ T-10 Heavy Tank

Soviet First Guards Tank Army / East Germany, 1955

In 1948, the Soviet General Tank Directorate ordered a new heavy tank weighing approximately 50.8 tonnes (50 tons). Originally designated the IS-8, the final variant of the 'Josef Stalin' series underwent numerous modifications. With Stalin's death in 1953, the new tank, armed with a 125mm (4.9in) D-25TA gun, was at last named the T-10. Although manufacture ended in 1966, T-10s were not retired from reserve until 1996.

Specifications

Crew: 4	Engine: 522kW (700hp) V12 diesel
Weight: 49,890kg (109,760lb)	Speed: 42km/h (26mph)
Length: 9m (27ft 6in)	Range: 250km (155 miles)
Width: 3.27m (10ft)	Armament: 1 x 122mm (4.8in) gun, plus 2 x
Height: 2.59m (7ft 4.5in)	12.7mm (0.5in) MGs (1 coaxial and 1 AA
	Radio: n/k

the flanks of the advance, securing the main thrust against counterattacks that might threaten the rear of the offensive. In the West, the availability of tactical nuclear weapons to the Warsaw Pact forces was discounted despite the fact that intelligence could not confirm their presence or lack thereof. Conjecture persists as to whether the Soviets were prepared to use nuclear weapons of more than 10 megatons ahead of conventional offensive operations.

During the 1960s, a Soviet modernization programme was under way: the older T-54/55 tank, with its 100mm (3.9in) main weapon, was gradually replaced by the T-62, armed with a 125mm (4.9in) main gun, and subsequently the T-64, while the

BMP-1, BTR-40 and BTR-60 infantry fighting vehicle and armoured personnel carriers provided the rapid mobility necessary for successful operations against NATO forces. Self-propelled artillery, primarily the World War II-vintage SU-76, was organic to the Soviet armoured division as well.

In the autumn of 1962, the United States and the Soviet Union came closer to declared war than at perhaps any other time during the Cold War. The deployment of ballistic missiles to Cuba prompted the US to place its conventional and nuclear assets on high alert. Although war was averted, a telling aspect of the original Soviet commitment to Cuba was the intent to station four motorized regiments, two tank

▲ **T-54A Main Battle Tank**

Soviet Third Shock Army / IX Tank Corps, East Germany, 1956

The T-54/55 was produced in greater numbers than any other tank in history, and its service life extended to nearly half a century. The earliest of Soviet main battle tank designs, the T-54/55 proved relatively easy to modify, and production was not terminated until 1981.

Specifications

Crew: 4	Speed: 48km/h (30mph)
Weight: 36 tonnes (35.42 tons)	Range: 400km (250 miles)
Length (hull): 6.45m (21ft 2in)	Armament: 1 x 100mm (3.9in) D-10T gun, plus 1
Width: 3.27m (10ft 9in)	x 12.7mm (0.5in) DShK AA MG and 2 x 7.62mm
Height: 2.4m (7ft 10in)	(0.3in) DT MGs
Engine: 388kW (520bhp) V-54 12-cylinder	Radio: R-113

Specifications

Crew: 2	Speed: (road) 60km/h (37mph); (water) 10km/h
Weight: 9650kg (21,278lb)	(6mph)
Length: 9.54m (31ft 3in)	Range: 530km (330 miles)
Width: 2.5m (8ft 2in)	Armament: 1 x 12.7mm (0.5in) DShKM MG
Height: 2.66m (8ft 8in)	(optional)
Engine: 82kW (110hp) ZIL-123 6-cylinder	

▲ **BAV 485**

Soviet Third Guards Mechanized Army / East Germany, 1957

Similar to the US amphibious DUKW, the BAV 485 amphibious transport vehicle was based on the chassis of the ZiS-151 6X6 truck, which was also used in the BTR-152 armoured personnel carrier. Production began in 1952, and the BAV 485 was modernized and deployed by Warsaw Pact forces into the 1980s.

battalions equipped with T-55s and up to 51,000 troops on the Caribbean island.

Continuing Soviet tank development was evidence of the growing realization among the major powers that the well-defined division of labour among tanks was on the wane. The functions of light, medium and heavy tanks were being consolidated in the main battle tank, a new generation of weapon that would provide the best available combination of armour protection, firepower and mobility.

Soviet Medium Tank Battalion, 1961

By the 1960s, a complement of 32 T-54/55 main battle tanks were organized in two companies to comprise a Red Army medium tank battalion. The T-54/55 was the initial Soviet design to embrace the concept of the main battle tank. The T-54/55 was originally armed with the 100mm (3.9in) D-10T rifled cannon, which was soon upgraded to the D-10T2 with a bore evacuator located near the muzzle.

HQ (1 x T54/55 MBT, 2 x trucks)

1 Company (16 x T-54/55 MBTs)

2 Company (16 x T-54/55 MBTs)

Support Platoon (5 x trucks)

Specifications

Crew: 1 + 4

Weight: 2480kg (5470lb)

Length: 5.06m (16ft 7in)

Width: 1.74m (5ft 8in)

Height: 2.04m (8ft 6in)

Engine: 41kW (55hp) M-20 4-cylinder

Speed: 90km/h (56mph)

Range: 500km (310 miles)

Armament: None

▲ GAZ-46 MAV

Soviet First Guards Tank Army / East Germany, 1965

Patterned after the Ford GPA Seep amphibious vehicle, which had been supplied to the Soviets via Lend-Lease during World War II, the GAZ-46 MAV was intended as a light river-crossing and reconnaissance vehicle. It entered service in the 1950s and has been built under licence from Ford.

Specifications

Crew: 4

Weight: 15,500kg (15.25 tons)

Length: 6m (19ft 8in)

Width: 2.8m (9ft 2in)

Height: 2.1m 6ft 10in)

Engine: 179kW (140hp) V-6 diesel engine

Range: 260km (160 miles)

Armament: 1 x 85mm (3.4in) D-70 gun;

1 x 7.62mm (.3in) MG

▲ ASU 85 Tank Destroyer

Soviet 56th Guards Separate Air Assault Brigade / Tashkent, 1970s

The natural successor to the ASU-57, the ASU-85 was an air-transportable SP gun/tank destroyer that entered Red Army service in 1962. Used in airborne operations, its primary role was infantry support or assault, with limited anti-tank capability.

Specifications

Crew: 3 + 16

Weight: 15,100kg (33,300lb)

Length: 7m (22ft 11in)

Width: 3.22m (10ft 7in)

Height: 2.72m (8ft 11in)

Engine: 224kW (300hp) PV6 6-cylinder

turbo diesel

Speed: 60km/h (37mph)

Range: 460km (290 miles)

Armament: 1 x 7.62mm (0.3in) PKY MG and

other configurations

Radio: R-123M

▲ OT-62 Tracked Amphibious Armoured Personnel Carrier

Polish Army / 7th Coastal Defence Division, 1964

Based upon the Soviet-designed BTR-50 amphibious armoured personnel carrier, the OT-62 was capable of transporting 16 soldiers and was built jointly by Poland and Czechoslovakia under licence. Development began in 1958, and the first OT-62 entered service four years later.

NATO – France
1949–66

French armoured vehicle development was interrupted during World War II but regained its impetus rapidly after liberation. Within two years, French designers were developing the prototypes of several tanks.

EVEN DURING GERMAN OCCUPATION, French engineers had conducted a clandestine programme of armoured vehicle design, and by 1946 the *Atelier de Construction de Rueil* (ARL) had produced the ARL-44, a 54-tonne (53-ton) tank mounting a 90mm (3.5in) cannon. In 1953, the 503rd Tank Regiment of the French Army took possession of a few of these, but only 10 per cent of the initially ordered 600 were ever completed. Nevertheless, the French heeded the lessons of armoured combat during World War II and issued requirements for a new generation of armoured fighting vehicles.

The AMX-50 programme, named for the *Atelier de Construction* d'Issy-les-Moulineaux, where it was designed, incorporated a 90mm (3.5in) cannon along with features of successful tanks fielded during World War II and innovative design elements such as an oscillating turret that simplified the laying of the gun and the positioning of the hull in action. However, post-war financial constraints and the delivery of nearly 900 American-built M47 Patton tanks spelled the end of the AMX-50 programme. Meanwhile,

the light, airmobile AMX-13, armed initially with a 75mm (2.9in) gun and oscillating turret, entered production in 1952. The AMX-13 was produced steadily during the next quarter of a century and exported to over 25 countries.

French armaments manufacturers fully expected that West Germany would be allowed to rearm during the 1950s and promoted the production of a light tank which could be sold to the Germans. However, by 1956 a cooperative effort among several European nations endeavoured to come up with a suitable medium tank design to complement the British and American tanks that were deployed on the continent. With French and German designers in the lead, specifications were set forth in early 1957. Differing political and military priorities among the nations thwarted the cooperative effort, and French president Charles de Gaulle eventually withdrew his country from active participation in the NATO military organization in 1966.

In the same year, production of the French AMX-30, as the subsequent independent development project was designated, began in earnest. With the AMX-30, the French opted for a conventional turret and a 105mm (4.1in) rifled gun, and its designers decidedly favoured mobility over armour protection. At the same time as they developed the AMX-13 and AMX-30, the French designed numerous self-propelled artillery pieces and light armoured vehicles.

◀ **French MBT**
Around 3500 AMX-30 main battle tanks were built for France and for export.

Specifications

Crew: 4
Weight: 13,500kg (29,800lb)
Length (gun forwards): 6.15m (20ft 2in)
Width: 2.42m (7ft 11in)
Height: 2.32m (7ft 7in)
Engine: 149kW (200hp) Panhard 12-cylinder
petrol
Speed: 105km/h (65mph)
Range: 600km (370 miles)
Armament: 1 x 75mm (2.9in) or 1 x 90mm
(3.5in) gun, plus 2 x 7.5mm (0.295in) or
7.72mm (0.303in) MGs
Radio: n/k

▲ **Panhard EBR/FL-10 Armoured Car**
French Army / I Corps, Germany, 1960
Actually designed prior to World War II, the Panhard EBR did not go into production until after the war ended. More than 1200 were produced after 1954. Heavily armed for its size with a 75mm (2.9in) cannon, the vehicle was deployed in Europe and in former French colonies.

◀ **Panhard AML H-60 Light Armoured Car**
French Army / 2nd Armoured Division, Germany, 1965
The Panhard AML H-60 armoured car was developed during the 1950s to replace the ageing British Daimler Ferret armoured cars in service with the post-war French Army. Carrying a 60mm (2.4in) breech-loading mortar and light machine guns, the vehicle entered service in 1960.

Specifications

Crew: 3
Weight: 5.5 tonnes (5.41 tons)
Length: 3.79m (12ft 5.2in)
Width: 1.97m (6ft 5.5in)
Height: 2.07m (6ft 9.5in)
Engine: 67.2kW (90hp) Panhard Model 4 HD

4-cylinder petrol or 73kW (98hp)
Peugeot XD 3T, 4-cylinder diesel
Speed: 90km/h (56mph)
Range: 600km (373 miles)
Armament: 1 x 60mm (2.4in) low-recoil gun, plus
1 x 7.62mm (0.3in) MG
Radio: n/k

Specifications

Crew: 5
Weight: 13,500kg (29,800lbs)
Length: 6.15m (20ft 3in)
Width: 2.42m (7ft 11in)
Height: 2.32m (7ft 7in)
Engine: 149kW (200hp) Panhard 12-cylinder
petrol
Speed: 105km/h (65mph)
Range: 600km (370 miles)
Armament: 1 x 90mm (3.54in) gun,
plus 2 x 7.5mm (0.295in) MGs
Radio: n/k

▲ **Panhard EBR/FL-11**
French Army / II Corps, Germany, 1963
Differentiated from the EBR/FL-10 only by its turret, the FL-11 began life with a 75mm (2.95in) gun, which was upgraded to a 90mm (3.54in) gun in the 1960s.

▲ **Hotchkiss M201 VLTT**

French Army / II Corps, Germany, 1961

Based on the World War II-era American Jeep, the Hotchkiss M201 was the standard light transport vehicle used by the French army from 1946 until the 1980s.

Specifications

Crew: 1	Engine: 95kW (50 hp) Peugeot diesel engine
Weight: 1,880kg (4,140lb)	Speed: 105km/h (65mph)
Length: 3.37m (11ft)	Range: 400km (250 miles)
Width: 1.48m (5ft 10in)	Armament: n/a
Height: 1.3m (4ft 3in)	

NATO – West Germany
1955–69

With the creation of the Federal Republic of Germany, the pro-Western nation's rearmament was only a matter of time, and the *Bundeswehr* would soon embark on the design and deployment of its own armour.

SIX YEARS AFTER IT WAS CONSTITUTED AS A NATION, West Germany joined NATO and began a programme of rebuilding its armed forces. The direct German alignment with NATO was not without reservations. German leaders were well aware that their country would become the front line in the event of armed conflict with the Soviet Union. Therefore, it was critical to them that a NATO force commitment was substantial enough to defend against an attack by Warsaw Pact armies. In response, NATO adopted a forward defence strategy, which involved locating its forces quite near the national boundaries with the Warsaw Pact countries.

As West Germany rearmed, the US supplied M47 and M48 Patton tanks to the *Deutsches Heer*, or army. The Germans judged these tanks as rapidly becoming obsolescent, and by autumn 1956 German designers had embarked on a programme to develop their own world-class tank. The Leopard programme was under way when Germany and France entered into a joint venture to develop a common tank, known as the Europa Panzer, in the summer of 1957. While progress was made and prototypes were tested, the effort eventually failed, and both nations chose to pursue their tank development based on perceived priorities.

Production of the Leopard 1 began in 1965, and nearly 6500 of all variants were built. Emphasizing speed rather than armour protection, the tank was lighter than most of its contemporaries. Originally designated the Standard Panzer, the Leopard 1 bore some resemblance to the tanks of its lineage, namely the Tigers and Panthers of World War II, but was essentially a modern tank of 1960s design mounting the British Royal Ordnance 105mm (4.1in) L7A3 L/52 rifled gun. During the 1960s and 1970s, the Leopard 1 was exported to several countries.

By 1960, the Germans had also begun work on a new purpose-built infantry fighting vehicle. The Marder, however, did not make its debut until the early 1970s, and until that time the *Schützenpanzer lang*

HS.30, also known as the *Schützenpanzer* 12-3, was the principal such vehicle deployed by West German armoured formations.

From the outset, the Germans had disagreed with US doctrine that armoured personnel carriers were to serve only as 'battle taxis' to deliver infantrymen to the combat zone. US soldiers, transported in their M113s, were expected to dismount and fight. Only after practical experience in Vietnam demonstrated the value of the infantry fighting vehicle did this philosophy begin to change. In fact, battlefield conversions of many M113s were carried out to add firepower.

German designers considered the experience of their Panzergrenadiers, or armoured infantry, during World War II and decided to arm the *Schützenpanzer* 12-3 with a 20mm (0.79in) L/86 HS 820 autocannon

and a 7.62mm (0.3in) machine gun for use against enemy infantry. Up to five combat soldiers could be transported inside the vehicle and engage the enemy from inside or outside the troop compartment. The vehicle-borne troops were trained to work together and in coordination with tanks. Still, some German Panzergrenadier brigades incorporated truck and M113 transportation with the *Schützenpanzer* 12-3.

Although several German armoured divisions were constituted in the 1950s, field deployment departed from the pentagonal division structure of several NATO countries. Initially, armoured and infantry brigades were expected to form battle groups or task forces. Depending on the nature of the mission, additional armoured or infantry battalions could be added to this flexible structure as needed.

▲ **SPz lang LGS M40A1**

German Army / 10th Armoured Division / Mechanized Infantry Battalion 112, Germany, 1960

An infantry fighting vehicle developed in Germany during the 1950s, the SPz lang HS30 SP Gun was also produced in an anti-tank variant that mounted the 106mm (4.17in) M40A1 recoilless rifle along with the 20mm (0.79in) L/86 HS 820 autocannon. Another variant mounted an 81mm (3.2in) or 120mm (4.7in) mortar.

Specifications

Crew: 3 + 5
Weight: 14,600kg (32,200lb)
Length: 5.56m (18ft 3in)
Width: 2.25m (7ft 4in)
Height: 1.85m (6ft 1in)
Engine: 175kW (235hp) Rolls-Royce 8-cylinder petrol
Speed: 51km/h (32mph)
Range: 270km (170 miles)
Armament: 1 x 106mm (4.17in) M40A1 recoilless rifle, plus 1 x 20mm (0.79in) HS 820 autocannon

▲ **Jagdpanzer Kanone (JPK)**

German Army / 5th Armoured Division, Germany, 1968

Equipped with a 90mm (3.5in) main gun similar to that of the American M47 Patton tank, the light *Jagdpanzer Kanone* tank destroyer was deployed to German units in the mid-1960s and later exported to Belgium. Its lack of a turret limited traverse capabilities.

Specifications

Crew: 4	8-cylinder diesel
Weight (approx): 25,700kg (55,669lb)	Speed: 70km/h (43.5mph)
Length: 6.238m (20ft 5.6in)	Range: 400km (248.5 miles)
Width: 2.98m (9ft 9.3in)	Armament: 1 x 90mm (3.5in) gun, plus
Height: 2.085m (6ft 10in)	2 x 7.62mm (0.3in) MGs
Engine: 372.9kW (500hp) Daimler-Benz MB837	Radio: n/k

Specifications

Crew: 4	Speed: 65km/h (40.4mph)
Weight: 39,912kg (87,808lb)	Range: 600km (373 miles)
Length: 9.543m (31ft 4in)	Armament: 1 x 105mm (4.1in) gun, plus 2 x
Width: 3.25m (10ft 8in)	7.62mm (0.3in) MGs (1 coaxial and 1 anti-
Height: 2.613m (8ft 7in)	aircraft) and 4 x smoke dischargers
Engine: 619kW (830hp) MTU 10-cylinder diesel	Radio: n/k

▲ **Leopard 1 Main Battle Tank**

German Army / 1st Armoured Division / 1st Tank Battalion, Germany, 1969

The product of a lengthy development phase that had begun in the mid-1950s, the Leopard 1 main battle tank was the principal weapon of its kind deployed by the German Army for more than 20 years. Its main weapon was the British 105mm (4.1in) Royal Ordnance L7A3 L/52 rifled gun.

NATO – United Kingdom
1949–69

The British presence on the continent of Europe continued following the end of World War II, its infantry and armoured divisions constituting an occupation force in Germany, which soon became a major component of NATO defence.

AT THE END OF WORLD WAR II, Britain had been wracked by six years of war. Despite its commitment overseas to a slowly disintegrating empire, a financially strapped nation nevertheless recognized its obligation to participate in the defence of Western Europe against potential Soviet aggression. The British Army of the Rhine (BAOR) was subsequently established, and during the Cold War its strength ebbed and flowed from 25,000 to more than 60,000 troops. Economic constraints fostered the curtailment of men and equipment on the continent during the late 1940s, and at one time only the famed 7th Armoured and 2nd Infantry Divisions were present.

In 1950, the 6th and 11th Armoured Divisions arrived, and the four units formed the I British Corps, operating from bases in Lower Saxony and North Rhine Westphalia. Three infantry brigades were dedicated to anti-tank operations, while the three armoured divisions each consisted of three tank brigades, plus supporting motorized infantry, artillery and other ancillary formations.

The primary British tank of the early Cold War period was the Centurion, the product of a design effort undertaken in 1943 but not yet quite in production as World War II in Europe ended in the spring of 1945. The Centurion had originally been conceived as a counter to heavy German armour, which had taken a toll on the lighter M4 Sherman tanks supplied by the US and on the British tank designs deployed during the war.

The Centurion borrowed the basic suspension of the Comet tank, its predecessor, which remained in service with the British Army of the Rhine until the late 1950s. Its production began in November 1945; however, it was soon evident that the 76mm

(3in/17-pounder) and then the 84mm (3.3in/ 20-pounder) main cannon needed improvement. In 1953, the Centurion Mk 7 variant with a 105mm (4.1in) L7 main gun was placed in production, and this was to become the most prominent of the 24 Centurion configurations, including a variety of support vehicles, to see service.

While the Centurion successfully embodied the initial British endeavour into development of the main battle tank, another project, the Conqueror, was proceeding in the closing days of World War

II. Conceived in response to the heavy Soviet IS-2 and IS-3 tanks, the Conqueror may, in its own right, be considered a main battle tank. However, mounting an American-designed L1 120mm (4.7in) rifled gun, it was envisioned by some tacticians as a longer-range fire support system for the advancing Centurion. Both the Conqueror and the Centurion were components of the post-war effort to develop the 'universal tank'. As the Centurion progressed, the Conqueror waned, and fewer than 200 were built before production ceased in 1959.

▲ **Charioteer Tank Destroyer**

British Army of the Rhine / 7th Armoured Division, Germany, 1956

Designed during the 1950s to augment the firepower of British Army units deployed with NATO forces in Germany, the Charioteer tank destroyer mounted the Royal Ordnance QF 84mm (3.3in/20-pounder) gun atop the modified chassis of the World War II-vintage Cromwell tank.

Specifications

Crew: 4	Mks 1–3 12-cylinder petrol
Weight: 28,958kg (63,842lb)	Speed: 52km/h (32.30mph)
Length: 8.8m (28ft 10.4in)	Range: 240km (149 miles)
Width: 3.1m (10ft 2in)	Armament: 1 x 84mm (3.3in/20pdr) gun, plus 1 x
Height: 2.6m (8ft 6in)	7.62mm (0.3in) coaxial MG
Engine: 450kW (600hp) Rolls-Royce Meteor	Radio: n/k

▲ **Conqueror Heavy Tank**

British Army of the Rhine / 7th Armoured Division, Germany, 1964

The heavy Conqueror was designed concurrently with the better known Centurion main battle tank and considered primarily as long-range fire support for the latter. Shortly after the Conqueror entered production, the concept of the heavy tank was eclipsed by a refined 'universal tank' emphasis.

Specifications

Crew: 4	Speed: 34km/h (21.3mph)
Weight: 64,858kg (142,688lb)	Range: 155km (95 miles)
Length (gun forward): 11.58m (38ft)	Armament: 1 x 120mm (4.7in) rifled gun, plus
Width: 3.99m (13ft 1in)	1 x 7.62mm (0.3in) coaxial MG
Height: 3.35m (11ft)	Radio: n/k
Engine: 604kW (810hp) 12-cylinder petrol	

NATO armoured doctrine during the Cold War generally rested upon containment of a Warsaw Pact breach in the forward defensive positions of Western forces. The threat of tactical nuclear weapons, which might decimate an attacking Soviet formation, was considered a primary component of grand strategy and a counter to the overwhelming Warsaw Pact superiority in numbers. British armoured and mechanized infantry units would expect to slow a Soviet onslaught; however, prolonged combat would prove problematic. As the focus of British tank development shifted from Nazi Germany to the Warsaw Pact, the Centurion was upgraded to include heavier armour, advanced fire control systems and defences against nuclear, biological and chemical weapons.

During the early years of the Cold War, the Bren Gun Carrier, or Universal Carrier, which traced its origins to the 1920s, was widely used by British forces. Although it was the most highly produced vehicle of its kind in history, the versatile Universal Carrier had become obsolescent by the mid-1950s. In 1962, the FV 430 series was introduced, encompassing a variety of armoured vehicles serving as command, repair, ambulance and troop carrier platforms. The FV 432 armoured personnel carrier was capable of transporting up to 10 combat-ready infantrymen and was armed with a single 7.62mm (0.3in) machine gun. Its configuration complemented the prevailing NATO doctrine that infantry should dismount from 'battle taxi' transport to engage in combat.

▶ Saladin Armoured Car

British Army of the Rhine / 11th Armoured Division, Germany, 1967

The six-wheeled armoured car variant of the Alvis FV600 series of armoured fighting vehicles, the FV601 Saladin was designed in the late 1940s but did not enter service until 1958. Mounting a 76mm (3in) gun, it was originally intended to replace the ageing Daimler armoured car.

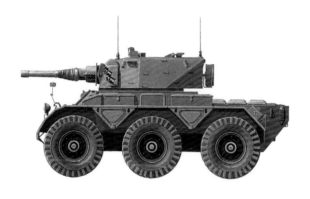

Specifications

Crew: 3
Weight: 11,500kg (25,300lb)
Length: 5.284m (17ft 4in)
Width: 2.54m (8ft 4in)
Height: 2.93m (9ft 7.3in)
Engine: 127kW (170hp) 8-cylinder petrol
Speed: 72km/h (45mph)
Range: 400km (250 miles)
Armament: 1 x 76mm (3in) gun, plus 2 x 7.62mm (0.3in) MGs (1 coaxial and 1 AA)
Radio: n/k

Specifications

Crew: 4
Weight: 16,494kg (36,288lb)
Length: 5.84m (19ft 2in)
Width: 2.641m (8ft 8in)
Height: 2.489m (8ft 2in)
Engine: 179kW (240hp) Rolls-Royce 6-cylinder diesel
Speed: 47.5km/h (30mph)
Range: 390km (240 miles)
Armament: 1 x 105mm (4.1in) gun, plus 1 x 7.62mm (0.3in) anti-aircraft MG and 3 x smoke dischargers
Radio: n/k

▲ Abbot SP Gun

British Army of the Rhine / 6th Armoured Division, Germany, 1969

Beginning in the late 1960s, the Abbot self-propelled gun was deployed to units of the Royal Artillery serving with NATO. Mounting a 105mm (4.1in) L13A1 gun, the Abbot featured an enclosed, fully rotating turret atop the modified chassis of the FV430 armoured fighting vehicle.

NATO – United States
1949–69

From the outset of the Cold War, the United States was to assume a leading role in the development of NATO and the defence of Western Europe against the forces of the Warsaw Pact.

B Y THE END OF THE 1940s, the US nuclear weapons monopoly had, for all practical purposes, disappeared. The Soviet Union had detonated a nuclear device, and the potential for a strategic exchange of catastrophic proportions appeared to be increasing. At the tactical level, the US and its NATO allies relied upon the strength of short-range nuclear weapons systems as a deterrent to Soviet aggression. Armoured and infantry forces would attempt to contain any offensive thrust.

During the mid-1950s, the 'forward defence' strategy developed, reassuring the West German government that its territory would be defended as close to the borders of the Warsaw Pact nations as possible. Among the first of the US divisions deployed along the tense frontier between the two alliances was the 3rd Armoured, which defended the strategically vital Fulda Gap, east of the German city of Frankfurt, a likely avenue of advance for any Soviet armoured offensive.

In October 1950, the role of US forces in Europe was changed from constabulary to combat-ready, and four divisions were committed. The pentomic structure of US divisional organization was reevaluated on several occasions and revolved around the flexible infantry brigade, which controlled two or three battle groups. Each brigade included infantry, armour and artillery as needed.

In the early 1960s, the doctrine of flexible response led to another reorganization of the US Army. Subsequently, the US armoured division consisted of six tank and five mechanized infantry battalions, while infantry divisions included two tank battalions supporting eight infantry battalions. US armoured battalions consisted of three companies, each with three platoons of five tanks, while two tanks were assigned to the company headquarters.

The US supplied the majority of equipment to the NATO forces during the early years of the Cold War. These included initially the M4 Sherman and

Specifications	
Crew: 5	Speed: 48km/h (30mph)
Weight: 41,860kg (92,301lb)	Range: 161km (100 miles)
Length: 8.61m (28ft 3in)	Armament: 1 x 90mm (3.5in) M3 gun; 1 x
Width: 3.51m (11ft 6in)	12.7mm (0.5in) AA HMG; 2 x 7.62mm (0.3in)
Height: 2.77m (9ft 1in)	MGs (1 coaxial, 1 ball-mounted in hull front
Engine: 373kW (500hp) Ford GAF V8 petrol	Radio: SCR508/528

▲ **M26 Pershing Heavy Tank**

US Army / 1st Infantry Division, Germany, 1948

With its 90mm (3.5in) M3 gun, the M26 Pershing was the heaviest US tank deployed during World War II. In Korea, it proved to be underpowered and was withdrawn. However, it served as the basis for the Patton series of the 1950s and 1960s.

M24 Chaffee tanks of World War II vintage. These were followed by the M26 Pershing heavy tank, developed late in the war and having seen minimal action, and the main battle tanks of the Patton series, the M47, M48 and M60. Like Great Britain, the United States also developed a heavy tank, the M103, in response to the Soviet IS-2 and IS-3, which would undoubtedly be encountered in the event of war; however, only one battalion of M103s was deployed. In the 1960s, the M113 armoured personnel carrier replaced the older armoured personnel carriers previously in service.

▲ M60A1 Main Battle Tank

US Army / 3rd Armored Division, Germany, 1963

Based on the M26 Pershing, the Patton main battle tank was developed in the United States during the 1950s. By 1957, the M60A1 emerged in response to a need for upgraded armour protection, better suspension and an improved turret shape. The M60A1 remained in service for more than 30 years.

Specifications

Crew: 4	1790-2A V12 turbo-charged diesel
Weight: 52,617kg (116,020lb)	Speed: 48km/h (30mph)
Length: 9.44m (31ft)	Range: 500km (311 miles)
Width: 3.63m (11ft 11in)	Armament: 1 x M68 105mm (4.1in) gun; 1 x
Height: 3.27m (10ft 8in)	12.7mm (0.5in) MG; 1 x 7.62mm (0.3in) MG
Engine: 559.7kW (750hp) Continental AVDS-	Radio: n/k

▲ M103 Heavy Tank

US Army / 4th Armored Group / 899th Tank Battalion, Germany, 1959

With its 120mm (4.7in) M58 main gun, the M103 was the heaviest tank in the US inventory until the 1980s. With the rise of the main battle tank concept, the M103 was produced in only small numbers. A single battalion was deployed to Europe.

Specifications

Crew: 5	Speed: 34km/h (21mph)
Weight: 56,610kg (124,544lb)	Range: 130km (80 miles)
Length: 11.3m (37ft 1.5in)	Armament: 1 x 120mm (4.7in) rifled gun, plus
Width: 3.8m (12ft 4in)	1 x 12.7mm (0.5in) anti-aircraft HMG and 1 x
Height: 2.9m (9ft 5.3in)	7.62mm (0.3in) coaxial MG
Engine: 604kW (810hp) Continental AV-1790-5B	Radio: n/k
or 7C V12 petrol	

Specifications
Crew: 3 or 4
Weight: 6930kg (15,280lb)
Length: 4.46m (14ft 7.5in)
Width: 2.33m (7ft 7.6in)
Height: 2.16m (7ft 1in)
Engine: 119kW (160hp) Chevrolet 283-V8
8-cylinder petrol
Speed: 58km/h (36mph)
Range: 440km (270 miles)
Armament: 1 x 20mm (0.79in) M139
or 1 x 12.7mm (0.5in) HMG;
1 x 7.62mm (0.3in) MG
Radio: n/k

▲ M114A1E1 Reconnaissance Carrier

US Army / 4th Infantry Division, 1963

Also known as the M114A2, a variant of the M114 armoured personnel carrier that entered service with the US military in 1962, the M114A1E1 reconnaissance carrier was heavily armed with a 20mm (0.79in) M139 gun mounted in a hydraulically powered cupola.

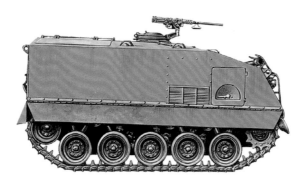

Specifications
Crew: 2 + 10
Weight: 18,828kg (41,516lb)
Length: 5.19m (17ft .36in)
Width: 2.84m (9ft 3in)
Height: 2.77m (9ft 1in)
Engine: 220kW (295hp) Continental AO-895-4
6-cylinder petrol
Speed: 71km/h (44mph)
Range: 185km (115 miles)
Armament: 1 x 12.7mm (0.5in) Browning
M2 HB HMG

▲ M75 Armoured Personnel Carrier

US Army / 1st Infantry Division, Germany, 1955

Based on the chassis of the T43 cargo carrier, the M75 armoured personnel carrier also shared suspension components with the M41 light tank and was developed in the autumn of 1946. Produced briefly from 1952 to 1954, it was replaced by the M59.

Specifications
Crew: 2 + 10
Weight: 19,323kg (38,197lb)
Length: 5.61m (18ft 5in)
Width: 3.26m (10ft 8in)
Height: 2.27m (7ft 5in)
Engine: 2 x 95kW (127hp) General Motors Model
302 6-cylinder petrol
Speed: 51km/h (32mph)
Range: 164km (102 miles)
Armament: 1 x 12.7mm (0.5in) Browning
M2 HB HMG

▲ M59 Armoured Personnel Carrier

US Army / 1st Infantry Division, Germany, 1959

Replacing the older M75 armoured personnel carrier, the amphibious and less expensive M59 entered service with the US military in 1953. It carried up to 10 combat infantrymen or one jeep, and more than 6000 were built by 1960.

Specifications

Crew: 2 + 11

Weight: 12,329kg (27,180lb)

Length: 2.686m (8ft 9in)

Width: 2.54m (8ft 4in)

Height: 2.52m (8ft 3in)

Engine: 205kW (275hp) Detroit Diesel 6V53T

Speed: 66km/h (41mph)

Range: 483km (300 miles)

Armament: 1 x 12.7mm (0.5in) MG

▲ **M113 Armoured Personnel Carrier**

US Army / 3rd Infantry Division, 1961

Entering service with the US Army in 1960, the M113 armoured personnel carrier is an iconic vehicle of the Cold War and Vietnam era. Its distinct boxlike silhouette was similar to its predecessors, the M59 and M75; however, its aluminium armour was much lighter and offered greater protection.

Late Cold War

As the Cold War intensified with armed conflict and proxy wars around the globe, the military establishments of NATO and the Warsaw Pact continued their programmes of armoured vehicle development.

A T THE DAWN of the Cold War's fourth decade, the strategic arms race was centre stage. Tensions between the superpowers had come to the brink of conventional, and then quite probably nuclear, conflict over access to West Berlin and during the Cuban Missile Crisis.

In the event of any armed confrontation between East and West, the role to be played by troops on the ground in Europe was likely to be only a prelude to global thermonuclear war. However, the wary adversaries maintained their armies in a state of readiness, weighing the economic cost and the immediate necessities to fulfil obligations elsewhere around the world. Until 1974, the United States was still directly involved in the Vietnam War, while the Soviet Union was supplying arms to client states in the Middle East and Southeast Asia.

At the same time, advancing technology contributed to the requirement for both NATO and Warsaw Pact nations to continually research and develop better weapons systems. Improved powerplants, armour protection and suspension systems were combined with computerized fire control, defences against nuclear, biological and chemical (NBC) weapons, a new generation of heavy guns and a variety of special purpose ammunition to encompass a modern main battle tank of extraordinary firepower, protection and mobility. The proving grounds for many of these innovations were the smaller, intense wars of the Middle East, Southeast Asia and Africa which occurred during the last 40 years of the twentieth century.

▲ **Show of force**

Soviet T-64 tanks take part in a parade in Moscow's Red Square.

Warsaw Pact
1970–91

Evolving Soviet nuclear and conventional arms doctrine diminished and then increased the significance of the tank and armoured fighting vehicle during the later years of the Cold War.

SOVIET AND WARSAW PACT military strategists never fully discounted the advantages of a preemptive nuclear strike against the West, but once nuclear parity with the NATO powers was achieved in the early 1970s, the Soviets considered an all-out nuclear war less likely. Weighing various scenarios, they envisioned a possible combined offensive strike, first by nuclear weapons and then followed by conventional forces, or possibly a conventional offensive alone – with the threat of Soviet nuclear capabilities dissuading NATO forces from launching a nuclear attack of their own in response.

Given these scenarios for war in Europe, the Soviets invested heavily in improving their conventional weapons systems. Further, the Brezhnev Doctrine asserted that the Soviet Union reserved the right to intervene militarily in neighbouring countries should the situation be deemed a threat to Soviet security. Tangible evidence of this posture occurred during the suppression of the 1968 revolt in Czechoslovakia and the invasion of Afghanistan in 1979.

Deep Battle theory

Advocated as early as the 1920s, the concept of Deep Battle was resurrected by Soviet military planners during the 1970s. The five major components of Deep Battle theory were the use of tactical formations to prosecute offensive operations; pressure across a large area to prevent an opponent from manoeuvring efficiently in response; deep penetration to shock enemy forces into inaction; coordinated firepower and manoeuvre leveraging technology to effect deep penetration of enemy defences; and a commander's holistic view of the battle – seeing the beginning of hostilities and the end game in total.

Speed was essential to the success of Deep Battle theory, preventing the enemy from regrouping and coordinating an effective defence. Combined infantry and armour would first find and fix the enemy. Then a strong armoured spearhead would attack on a narrow front and achieve the decisive breakthrough. Rapid exploitation of the breach would result in the continuous pursuit of the

Specifications	
Crew: 3	Speed: 75km/h (47mph)
Weight: 42,000kg (92,610lb)	Range: 400km (248 miles)
Length (hull): 7.4m (24ft 3in)	Armament: 1 x 125mm (4.9in) smoothbore gun,
Width: 3.64m (11ft 11in)	plus 1 x 12.7mm (0.5in) NSVT AA MG and
Height: 2.2m (7ft 3in)	1 x coaxial 7.62mm (0.3in) PKT MG
Engine: 560kW (750bhp) 5DTF 5-cylinder	Radio: R-123M
opposed diesel	

▲ **T-64 Main Battle Tank**

Soviet Army / Kiev Military District / 41st Guards Tank Division, 1967

An innovative Soviet design, the T-64 main battle tank equipped elite units of the Red Army in Eastern Europe and was never exported. Its 115mm (4.5in) gun was later replaced by a 125mm (4.9in) smoothbore. Expensive to produce, the T-64 was augmented by the cheaper T-72.

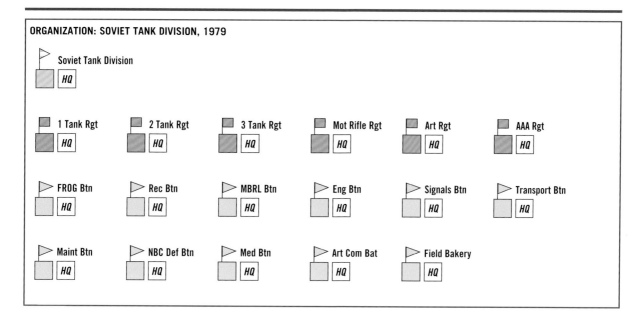

ORGANIZATION: SOVIET TANK DIVISION, 1979

Soviet Tank Division
HQ

1 Tank Rgt
HQ

2 Tank Rgt
HQ

3 Tank Rgt
HQ

Mot Rifle Rgt
HQ

Art Rgt
HQ

AAA Rgt
HQ

FROG Btn
HQ

Rec Btn
HQ

MBRL Btn
HQ

Eng Btn
HQ

Signals Btn
HQ

Transport Btn
HQ

Maint Btn
HQ

NBC Def Btn
HQ

Med Btn
HQ

Art Com Bat
HQ

Field Bakery
HQ

enemy, steadily degrading his armed forces and diminishing his will to resist. The outcome would be both militarily and psychologically debilitating to the enemy. By the 1980s, Soviet ground forces consisted of more than 200 infantry and armoured divisions, each of them mechanized, and more than 50,000 main battle tanks were in service.

Soviet tank divisions contained three tank regiments and one motorized rifle regiment, while the motorized rifle division consisted of three motorized rifle regiments and a single tank regiment. Such a configuration allowed supporting infantry to keep pace with the advance of armour and in turn allowed armour to mutually support accompanying infantry.

Armoured innovation

The deployment of the T-64 main battle tank in 1966 marked a significant advancement in Soviet tank design with the introduction of an

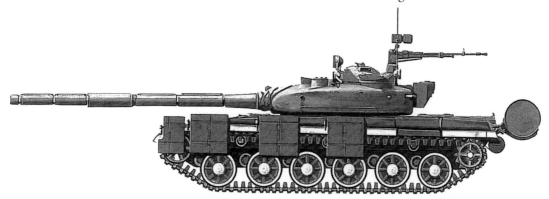

▲ T-72G Main Battle Tank

Polish Army / Silesian Military District, 1979

A licensed version of the T-72 main battle tank, the T-72G was manufactured in Poland and protected by thinner armour plating than T-72s built in the Soviet Union. The T-72G was provided to the armed forces of several Warsaw Pact nations.

Specifications

Crew: 3	Speed: 80km/h (50mph)
Weight: 38,894kg (85,568lb)	Range: 550km (434 miles)
Length: 9.24m (30ft 4in)	Armament: 1 x 125mm (4.9in) gun, plus
Width: 4.75m (15ft 7in)	1 x 12.7mm (0.5in) anti-aircraft HMG and
Height: 2.37m (7ft 9in)	1 x 7.62mm (0.3in) coaxial MG
Engine: 626kW (840hp) V-46 V12 diesel	Radio: R-123M

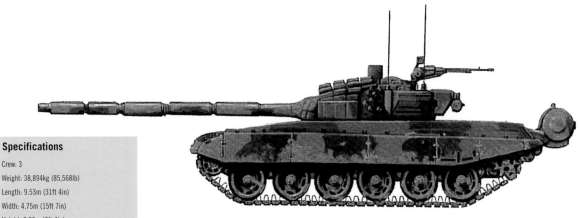

Specifications

Crew: 3
Weight: 38,894kg (85,568lb)
Length: 9.53m (31ft 4in)
Width: 4.75m (15ft 7in)
Height: 2.29m (7ft 4in)
Engine: 626kW (840hp) V-46 V12 diesel
Speed: 80km/h (50mph)
Range: 550km (434 miles)
Armament: 1 x 125mm (4.9in) 2A46M gun;
1 x 12.7mm (0.5in) anti-aircraft HMG and
1 x 7.62mm (0.3in) coaxial MG
Radio: R-123M

▲ T-72M1 Main Battle Tank

Czechoslovak People's Army / 1981

This export version of the Soviet T-72 was used by the Czechoslovak army until the end of the Cold War.
An upgraded version with some NATO components, called the T-72CZ M4, was developed by the Czech Army
following the split with the Slovak Republic in 1993.

Specifications

Crew: 2 + 11
Weight: 14,900kg (32,900lb)
Length: 7.47m (24ft 6in)
Width: 2.85m (9ft 4in)
Height: 2.42m (7ft 11in)
Engine: 164kW (220hp) YaMZ-238N 8-cylinder
diesel
Speed: 62km/h (39mph)
Range: 525km (330 miles)
Armament: 1 x 12.7mm (0.5in) DShK HMG or
1 x 7.62mm (0.3in) MG
Radio: R-123M

▲ MT-LB Armoured Personnel Carrier

Soviet Army / 35th Guards Motor Rifle Division, 1980

Utilized as a small armoured personnel carrier, ambulance, artillery tractor and in other roles, the amphibious MT-LB was
based on the chassis of the PT-76 light tank. The MT-LB was armed with a light machine gun and had entered service with
the Red Army by the early 1970s.

Specifications

Crew: 3
Weight: 14,000kg (30,800lb)
Length: 7.65m (25ft 25in)
Width: 3.14m (10ft 3.7in)
Height: 2.26m (7ft 4.75in)
Engine: 179kW (240hp) V-6 6-cylinder diesel
Speed: 44km/h (27mph)
Range: 260km (160 miles)
Armament: 1 x 76mm (3in) gun, plus
1 x 12.7mm (0.5in) AA HMG and 1 x coaxial
7.62mm (0.3in) MG
Radio: R-123

▲ PT-76 Amphibious Light Tank

Soviet Navy / Red Banner Northern Fleet / 63rd Guard Kirkenneskaya Naval Infantry Brigade, Baltic region, 1985

Originally a mainstay of the Soviet Red Army, the PT-76 provides amphibious support for attacking infantry formations.
First entering service in 1952, the PT-76 is still operated by Russian naval infantry today, although it is being gradually
phased out in favour of the T-80 MBT. More than 12,000 PT-76s have been built, of which 2000 were exported to Soviet
client states.

automatic loading system for the tank's 115mm (4.5in) main gun, which effectively reduced the size of the standard tank crew from four to three. Later variants of the T-64 were upgunned to a 125mm (4.9in) cannon and were capable of firing anti-tank missiles. Upgraded fire control systems and improved armour were included, and the T-64 was never exported to foreign countries. It equipped many of the elite guards units stationed opposite NATO forces in Eastern Europe and constituted the basis for the development of the T-80 main battle tank, which emerged in the mid-1970s.

New tanks

While the T-64 was originally intended to fill a perceived void created by the obsolescence of the IS-3 heavy tank of the early Cold War period, the T-72 main battle tank was in development concurrently with the T-64. The initial purpose of the T-72 was to equip the majority of Red Army armoured forces and to be exported to Warsaw Pact countries and arms purchasers around the world. Indeed, along with the T-54/55, the T-72 became an icon of the wars of the Middle East during the 1970s and served as the main battle tank for the armies of North Vietnam and several Arab states and of Soviet satellite countries during the 1970s and 1980s.

The T-72 combined elements of the T-62 and the T-64, entering production about 1970 and service with the Red Army in 1973. The T-72 maintained the characteristic 'frying pan' style turret of prior Soviet tank designs, sacrificing the comfort and operational efficiency of the crew by limiting space within but in turn diminishing the tank's silhouette. The T-72 was relatively inexpensive to produce compared with the T-64 and served as the primary Soviet main battle tank for the last 20 years of the Warsaw Pact.

The T-80, which was deployed to Red Army units in 1976 and was subsequently improved several times, marked the pinnacle of Soviet main battle tank design. Its most advanced variant was the T-80U, which included explosive reactive armour, improved target acquisition equipment and the 9M119M Refleks anti-tank missile system along with its 125mm (4.9in) 2A46-2 smoothbore gun. Its powerplant was similar to the turbine engine of the US Abrams main battle tank.

Improvements to infantry fighting vehicles continued as well, with the BMP-1 of the 1960s

ORGANIZATION: SOVIET TANK REGIMENT, 1989

Soviet Tank Regiment HQ		
1 Tank Btn HQ	2 Tank Btn HQ	3 Tank Btn HQ
Mot Rifle Btn HQ	Art Btn HQ	Air Def Battery HQ
Rec Coy HQ	Eng Coy HQ	

SOVIET TANK REGIMENT, 1989			
Type	Number	Vehicle	Strength
Headquarters	–	MBT	1
		BTR	2
		SA-7/14/16	3
Tank Btn	3	MBT	31
		BMP	2
Motorized Rifle Btn	1	BMP	43
		120mm mortar	8
		SA-7/14/16	9
		AGS-17	6
		BRDM-2	3
Artillery Btn	1	2SI	18–24
Air Defence Battery	1	SA-13	4
		ZSU-23-4	4
		BMP	3
Reconnaissance Coy	1	BRM	1
		BMP	3
		BRDM-2	4
		Motorcycles	3
Engineer Coy	1	MT-55	3
		TMM	4

giving way to the improved BMP-2 and BMP-3 of the 1980s, which were armed with 30mm (1.18in) autocannon, light machine guns and anti-tank guided missile systems. Capable of carrying up to seven combat infantrymen, the BMP-1 and BMP-2 were observed in large numbers during the Soviet invasion of Afghanistan.

Specifications

Crew: 2 + 10
Weight: 14,500kg (31,900lb)
Length: 7.44m (24ft 5in)
Width: 2.55m (8ft 4.4in)
Height: 2.06m (6ft 9in)
Engine: 134KW (180hp) Tatra V8 diesel
Speed: 94.4km/h (59mph)
Range: 710km (441 miles)
Armament: 1 x 14.5mm (0.6in) KPV HMG;
1 x 7.62mm (0.3in) PKT coaxial MG
Radio: R-112

▲ **SKOT-2A Wheeled Amphibious Armoured Personnel Carrier**

Polish Army / Silesian Military District, 1970

Known in the West as the OT-64C, this amphibious armoured personnel carrier was jointly developed by Czechoslovakia and Poland during the late 1950s and deployed to army units by 1963. The engine, transmission and other components were of Czech manufacture, while the hull and light machine gun armament were made in Poland. The SKOT-2A also included the turret from the BRDM-2.

▲ **DANA SP Howitzer**

Czechoslovak People's Army / 7th Mechanized Brigade, 1988

The world's first wheeled 152mm (6in) self-propelled artillery system to enter active service, the DANA howitzer was developed in Czechoslovakia during the 1970s and is similar to the Soviet 2S3 self-propelled gun-howitzer. The heavy weapon is mounted atop the 8X8 Tatra T815 truck.

Specifications

Crew: 4/5
Weight: 23,000kg (50,600lb)
Length: 10.5m (34ft 5in)
Width: 2.8m (9ft 2in)
Height: 2.6m (8ft 6in)
Engine: 257kW (345hp) V12 diesel
Speed: 80km/h (49.71mph)
Range: 600km (375 miles)
Armament: 1 x 152mm (6in) gun, plus
1 x 12.7mm (0.5in) HMG
Radio: n/k

Specifications

Crew: 3 + 8
Weight: 11,000kg (24,300lb)
Length: 7.22m (23ft 8in)
Width: 2.83m (9ft 3in)
Height: 2.7m (8ft 9in)
Engine: 2 x 104kW (140hp) 6-cylinder petrol
Speed: 95km/h (60mph)
Range: 500km (310 miles)
Armament: 1 x 14.5mm (0.57in) MG, plus
1 x 7.62mm (0.3in) PKT MG
Radio: R-113

▲ **TAB-72 Armoured Personnel Carrier**

Romanian Army / 1st Motorized Rifle Division, 1977

The Romanian TAB-72 armoured personnel carrier was a variant of the TAB-71, a licensed version of the Soviet-designed BTR-60. The vehicle design dates to the mid-1950s, and its deployment to the end of that decade. The TAB-72 had an improved turret, upgraded optical equipment and gun sights, and increased elevation angles for its machine guns for use in the anti-aircraft role.

Specifications

Crew: 3

Weight: 46,000kg (101,413lb)

Length: 9.66m (31ft 8in)

Width: 3.59m (11ft 10in)

Height: 2.2m (7ft 2in)

Engine: 932kW (1250hp) GTD-1250 multi-fuel
gas turbine

Speed: 70km/h (44mph)

Range: 440 km (273 miles)

Armament: 1 x 125mm (4.9in) smoothbore gun,
plus 1 x 12.7mm (0.5in) MG, 1 x 7.62mm (0.3in)
MG and 1 x 9K119 Refleks missile system

Radio: n/k

▲ T-80U Main Battle Tank

Red Army / 4th Guards Tank Division, 1990

The most advanced of Soviet main battle tanks, the T-80U was equipped with
the latest explosive reactive armour, target acquisition equipment and anti-tank
missile firing capability. Based on the original T-80 design of the mid-1970s, it
remains in service with forces of the Ukraine and the Russian Federation.

Specifications

Crew: 2 + 4

Weight: 7000kg (15,400lb)

Length: 5.79m (18ft 11in)

Width: 2.5m (8ft 2in)

Height: 1.91m (6ft 3in)

Engine: 75kW (100hp) Csepel D.414.44
4-cylinder diesel

Speed: 87km/h (54mph)

Range: 600km (370 miles)

Armament: 1 x 7.62mm (0.3in) SGMB MG

Radio: R-113 or R-114

▲ FUG-65 Amphibious Armoured Scout Car

Hungarian Ground Forces, 1985

The Hungarian FUG amphibious armoured scout car, based on the Soviet-designed BRDM-1, entered service in 1964 and
was deployed to the armed forces of at least six Warsaw Pact countries. Variants remain in service today.

Specifications

Crew: 2 + 6

Weight: 14,500kg (31,900lb)

Length: 7.44m (24ft 5in)

Width: 2.55m (8ft 4.4in)

Height: 2.06m (6ft 9in)

Engine: 134kW (180hp) Tatra V8 diesel

Speed: 94.4km/h (59mph)

Range: 710km (441 miles)

Armament: 1 x 7.62mm (0.3in) MG

Radio: R-114

▲ PSZH-IV Amphibious Armoured Scout Car

Czechoslovak People's Army / 7th Mechanized Brigade, 1980

Developed as an improvement to the FUG amphibious armoured scout car, the PSZH-VI incorporated a small turret mounting
a 14.5mm (0.57in) machine gun and a coaxial 7.62mm (0.3in) machine gun. It was capable of transporting six combat-
ready soldiers.

NATO – Canada
1970–91

A charter member of NATO, Canada contributed forces to the defence of Western Europe and championed the concept of United Nations peacekeeping during the Cold War.

THROUGHOUT THE COLD WAR PERIOD, the Canadian armed forces maintained two bases in West Germany under the auspices of Canadian Forces Europe. These were CFB Lahr and CFB Baden-Soellingen, and each supported armoured formations of the Canadian Army.

Canadian forces had supported the NATO alliance since 1951, when the 27th Infantry Brigade was deployed to Hanover. By the 1970s, the Canadian troop strength in Europe had diminished significantly. However, for much of the Cold War the 4th Canadian Mechanized Brigade Group was headquartered at Soest with its complement of Centurion and, later, main battle tanks, Ferret armoured cars and armoured personnel carriers, while at least a battalion of mechanized infantry was stationed at Baden-Soellingen along with light infantry formations. Among the units serving with the 4th Canadian Mechanized Brigade Group were Lord Strathcona's Horse, the Royal Canadian Dragoons, the 8th Canadian Hussars and the Fort Garry Horse,

as well as numerous mechanized infantry and horse artillery regiments.

Canadian tanks of the early Cold War era included British- and American-built models such as the Centurion and the M4 Sherman of the World War II period, during which a number of Sherman variants had been built under licence in Canada. In the late 1970s, Canada concluded the purchase of 127 Leopard C1 tanks from Germany. The Leopard C1 was equipped with laser rangefinding equipment similar to that of the German Leopard 1A3. Further improvements made by the Canadians included the addition of thermal night vision equipment, modular appliqué armour and improved fire control systems, and the upgraded Leopard was redesignated the C1A1.

Other Canadian armoured vehicles of the Cold War included the Cougar wheeled fire support vehicle, based on the Swiss-designed Piranha 6X6 fighting vehicle, which entered service in 1976, and the Lynx command and reconnaissance vehicle,

▲ **Cougar Gun Wheeled Fire Support Vehicle**

Canadian Army / Royal Canadian Dragoons, Germany, 1978

Fitted with the turret of the FV 101 Scorpion light tank, the Cougar fire support vehicle mounted a 76mm (3in) main gun. The Cougar entered service with Canadian forces in 1976 and was gradually replaced during the 1990s.

Specifications

Crew: 3	Engine: 160kW (215hp) Detroit Diesel 6V-53T
Weight: 9526kg (21,004lb)	6-cylinder diesel
Length: 5.97m (19ft 7in)	Speed: 102km/h (63mph)
Width: 2.53m (8ft 4in)	Range: 602km (374 miles)
Height: 2.62m (8ft 7in)	Armament: 1 x 76mm (3in) gun, plus
	1 x 7.62mm (0.3in) coaxial MG

similar in profile to the US M113 armoured personnel carrier. The Lynx was, in fact, built by the American FMC Corporation, which manufactured the M113, and the vehicle was supplied to the armed forces of Canada and the Netherlands. While US forces opted to purchase the M114 fighting vehicle in the early 1960s, Canada had deployed the Lynx by the middle of the decade as an amphibious reconnaissance and command platform.

Peacekeeping

Canada is often credited with advancing the concept of United Nations peacekeeping efforts during the half-century of the Cold War, and its troops and armoured assets have been deployed to the Middle East, the Balkans and other hotspots. Canadian troops were first deployed in such a role in 1957, patrolling along with the forces of several other nations in the Sinai Peninsula following the Suez Crisis that had erupted the previous year.

More than 100 Canadian personnel have been killed while fulfilling peacekeeping duties. The Royal Canadian Dragoons, an armoured regiment of the Canadian Army, has participated in peacekeeping efforts in the Korean demilitarized zone, in Kosovo in the Balkans and in Somalia on the Horn of Africa.

Canadian Reconnaissance Squadron

The Canadian reconnaissance squadron of Canadian Forces Europe included 10 Lynx armoured command and reconnaissance vehicles. Each Lynx had a crew of three – commander, driver and observer. The reconnaissance squadron was grouped into three troops, each fielding a complement of the Lynx vehicle. The combat support company of a Canadian infantry battalion included nine Lynxes.

Platoon (10 x Lynx APC)

Specifications

Crew: 3	Engine: 160kW (215hp) Detroit Diesel
Weight: 8775kg (19,300lb)	GMC 6V53 6-cylinder
Length: 4.6m (15ft 1in)	Speed: 70km/h (43mph)
Width: 2.41m (7ft 11in)	Range: 525km (325 miles)
Height: 1.65m (5ft 5in)	Armament: 1 x 12.7mm (0.5in) MG and
	1 x 7.62mm (0.3in) MG

▲ **Lynx Command and Recon (CR) Vehicle**

Canadian Army / Royal Canadian Regiment, Germany, 1971

In 1968, the Canadian Army procured the Lynx command and reconnaissance vehicle to replace its inventory of ageing Daimler Ferret armoured cars. The Lynx was armed with both heavy 12.7mm (0.5in) and light 7.62mm (0.3in) machine guns and was withdrawn from frontline units in the 1990s.

France
1970–91

Following its withdrawal from military participation in the NATO alliance in 1966, France continued its programme of armoured vehicle development and became a major exporter.

B Y THE 1970S, THE FRENCH AMX-30 main battle tank had matured as a weapons system. In production from 1966, the AMX-30 underwent several upgrades, including the installation of a stabilization system for its 105mm (4.1in) Modèle F1 main gun and the replacement of its coaxial heavy machine gun with a more powerful 20mm (0.79in) autocannon, an effective weapon against light armoured vehicles. Modernization was continued for the next 20 years and included the introduction of improved fire control systems, drive train elements and eventually laser rangefinding equipment and low light television targeting apparatus. The production of new AMX-30s was ongoing from 1979, while many of those already in service were upgraded. Numerous variants were also produced, including armoured recovery and bridgelaying vehicles.

From 1974 to 1984, the AMX-30 was also built under licence in Spain, while nearly 3000 examples of the main battle tank were produced for the

French military and the export arms market. The Spanish manufactured nearly 300 AMX-30s and deployed them with their army following an initial order of 19 placed in 1970. The primary reasons for Spanish interest in the AMX-30 were the reluctance of other nations to sell arms to the fascist regime of Generalissimo Francisco Franco and the attractive price point of the French system compared with others such the British Chieftain and the US M60. During the 1970s, such diverse nations as Saudi Arabia, the United Arab Emirates, Chile, Venezuela and Cyprus purchased the AMX-30. A delivery of 190 tanks was completed to Greece, the first nation to agree to purchase the French design.

Emerging Leclerc

A large number of AMX-30 variants remain in service around the world today, but by the 1980s it was apparent that the tank was inferior to the main battle tanks of other nations, including the American Abrams,

▲ **AMX-10 PAC 90 Light Tank**

French Army / 1st Armoured Division, France, 1984

Designed to complement the offensive capabilities of main battle tanks and infantry, the AMX-10 PAC 90 entered service with the French Army in 1979. The vehicle is also considered a self-propelled anti-tank weapon and is serviced by a crew of three. It also carries four infantrymen for defence or reconnaissance purposes.

Specifications

Crew: 3 + 4	115 V8 diesel
Weight: 14,500kg (31,967lb)	Speed: 65km/h (40.4mph)
Length: 5.9m (19ft 4.3in)	Range: 500km (310.7 miles)
Width: 2.83m (9ft 3.4in)	Armament: 1 x 20mm (0.79in) gun, plus
Height: 2.83m (9ft 3.4in)	1 x 7.62mm (0.3in) coaxial MG
Engine: 193.9kW (260hp) Hispano-Suiza HS	Radio: n/k

British Challenger, German Leopard and later Israeli Merkava. In light of the situation, French engineers reinvigorated the development of a new generation of main battle tank. Actually, research into a replacement for the AMX-30 had begun as early as the 1960s.

In a repeat performance of the 1950s fiasco, a joint venture with German designers had fallen apart by 1982, while France had also evaluated the main battle tanks offered for sale by other countries and decided against purchasing a foreign design. Meanwhile, the AMX-40 main battle tank, engineered purely for export sales, failed to gain orders and was cancelled. The high cost of the new Leclerc tank, with its 120mm (4.7in) main gun and a host of state-of-the-art systems, was offset somewhat by a partnership with the United Arab Emirates, who agreed to purchase more than 400 examples of the vehicle, and full production was begun in 1990.

▲ AMX-10RC Armoured Car

French Army / 2nd Regiment of Hussars, France, 1981

Developed in the early 1970s with full production commencing by 1976, the amphibious AMX-10RC served with the French Army in fire support and reconnaissance roles and is no longer in production. Heavily armed, it mounted a 105mm (4.1in) BK MECA L/48 main gun.

Specifications

Crew: 4	Speed: 85km/h (53mph)
Weight: 15,880kg (35,015lb)	Range: 1000km (620 miles)
Length: 6.36m (20ft 10in)	Armament: 1 x 105mm (4.1in) gun; 1 x 7.62mm
Width: 2.95m (9ft 8in)	(0.3in) coaxial MG; 2 x 2 smoke grenade
Height: 2.66m (8ft 8in)	launchers
Engine: 209kW (280hp) Badouin Model 6F 11	Radio: n/k
SRX diesel	

▲ ERC 90 F4 Sagaie

French Army / 31st Heavy Half-Brigade, Ivory Coast, 1982

The wheeled ERC 90 F4 Sagaie was developed by the Panhard Corporation as a light armoured vehicle capable of destroying Soviet main battle tanks such as the T-72. Its 90mm (3.5in) cannon was mounted in a turret manufactured by the government defence contractor GIAT.

Specifications

Crew: 3	Speed: 100km/h (62mph)
Weight: 8300kg (18,300lb)	Range: 700km (430 miles)
Length (gun forwards): 7.69m (25ft 2in)	Armament: 1 x 90mm (3.5in) gun, plus
Width: 2.5m (8ft 2in)	1 x 7.62mm (0.3in) coaxial MG and
Height: 2.25m (7ft 4in)	2 x 2 smoke grenade launchers
Engine: 116kW (155hp) Peugeot V6 petrol	Radio: n/k

Artillery

The most prominent of the French anti-tank vehicles produced during the latter years of the Cold War was perhaps the AMX-10 PAC 90, a variant of the AMX-10P infantry fighting vehicle. Mounting a 90mm (3.5in) rifled main gun, the AMX-10 PAC 90 entered service in 1979 and is sometimes classified as a light tank in its own right.

Armoured cars such as the AMX-10RC and the ERC 90 F4 came on line, while the heavy GCT 155mm (6.1in) self-propelled gun improved long-range fire support capabilities.

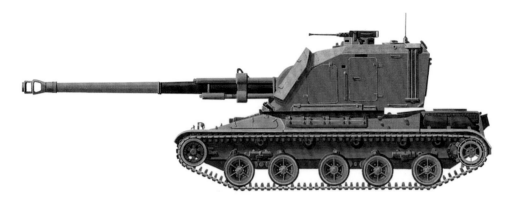

Specifications

Crew: 4	12-cylinder water-cooled multi-fuel
Weight: 41,949kg (92,288lb)	Speed: 60km/h (37mph)
Length: 10.25m (33ft 7.5in)	Range: 450km (280 miles)
Width: 3.15m (10ft 4in)	Armament: 1 x 155m (6.1in) gun, plus
Height: 3.25m (10ft 8in)	1 x 7.62mm (0.3in) or 12.7mm (0.5in) AA MG
Engine: 537kW (720hp) Hispano-Suiza HS 110	Radio: n/k

▲ **GCT 155mm SP Artillery**

French Army / 7th Armoured Brigade, France, 1980

Replacing the French Mk 3 155mm (6.1in) self-propelled gun, the GCT 155mm (6.1in) was developed in the 1970s and entered service with the armies of France and Saudi Arabia near the end of the decade. The gun was originally mounted on the chassis of the AMX-30 main battle tank.

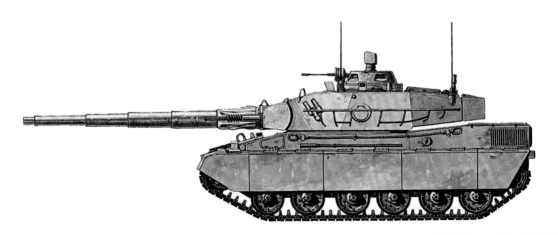

▲ **AMX-40 Main Battle Tank**

French Army, Undeployed, 1985

The AMX-40 main battle tank was designed specifically for the export market, mounting a 120mm (4.7in) smoothbore gun and a 20mm (0.79in) autocannon for use against aircraft and light armoured vehicles. By 1990, the project was scrapped due to lack of orders from foreign countries.

Specifications

Crew: 4	diesel
Weight: 43,000kg (94,600lb)	Speed: 70km/h (44mph)
Length: 10.04m (32ft 11.3in)	Range: 600km (373 miles)
Width: 3.36m (11ft 0.3in)	Armament: 1 x 120mm (4.7in) gun; 1 x 20mm
Height: 3.08m (10ft 1.3in)	(0.79in) gun in cupola; 1 x 7.62mm (0.3in) MG
Engine: 820kW (1100hp) Poyaud 12-cylinder	Radio: n/k

NATO – West Germany
1970–91

During the final decades of the Cold War, German tanks and armoured fighting vehicles gained a reputation as some of the finest of their type in the world.

WITH THE DEPLOYMENT of the Leopard 1 main battle tank in the 1960s, Germany established itself as a leading producer of armoured fighting vehicles. Employing some of the world's latest technology, the Leopard 1 was steadily improved through the mid-1970s; however, by the end of the decade its successor, the Leopard 2, was in production. The Leopard 2 was actually the product of joint research with the United States during the MTB-70 project of the late 1960s. While the German and US designers agreed on a number of points, the venture failed. A few years later, a second attempt was also cancelled following the shipment of a Leopard 2 prototype to the United States for evaluation against the XM-1 Abrams main battle tank prototype. Since the Germans favoured speed over armour protection and the Americans concentrated on tank survivability, each nation chose to pursue its own main battle tank independently.

The first order by the German government for the Leopard 2 was placed in 1977, and 1800 of the new main battle tanks were to be delivered in five batches. Mounting a 120mm (4.7in) Rheinmetall L55 smoothbore gun, acknowledged as the best weapon of its kind in the world, the Leopard 2 also incorporated modern protection against nuclear, biological and chemical weapons, state-of-the-art fire control and rangefinding systems and an 1109kW (1479hp) turbodiesel engine. A series of upgrades occurred during the 1980s, including the addition of improved radio equipment and automated fire and explosion suppression systems.

Belated export bonanza

During the 1980s, the export market was cool to the latest German main battle tank offering; however, by the 1990s the Leopard 2 was in high demand and being produced under licence in Switzerland, while Canada, Denmark, Greece, Sweden and Turkey were among its buyers. From 1991 to 1996, the Netherlands purchased nearly 450 examples of the German main battle tank.

Leopard 2 tanks have equipped the organic armoured units of the *Deutsches Heer* since the

▲ Luchs Armoured Reconnaissance Vehicle

German Army / 5th Armoured Division, Germany, 1977

An 8X8 wheeled amphibious reconnaissance armoured fighting vehicle, the *Spähpanzer Luchs* mounted a 20mm (0.79in) Rheinmetall MK 20 autocannon and a light 7.62mm (0.3in) machine gun. The amphibious vehicle replaced the SPz 11-2 *kurz* and entered service in 1975.

Specifications

Crew: 4	10-cylinder diesel
Weight: 19,500kg (42,900lb)	Speed: 90km/h (56mph)
Length: 7.743m (25ft 4.75in)	Range: 800km (500 miles)
Width: 2.98m (9ft 9.3in)	Armament: 1 x 20mm (0.79in) gun, plus
Height (with AA MG): 2.905m (9ft 6.3in)	1 x 7.62mm (0.3in) MG
Engine: 291kW (390hp) Daimler-Benz OM 403 A	Radio: n/k

1980s, facing the armour of the Warsaw Pact across the frontier between East and West. More than 400 Leopard 2 main battle tanks are estimated to be deployed with the German armed forces currently, and their service life has been extended by means of numerous upgrades.

In addition to the Leopard main battle tank, Germany's Marder armoured fighting vehicle also traces its development to the 1960s, and by 1971 it had entered production. It is capable of carrying up to seven combat infantrymen and mounts a 20mm (0.79in) autocannon and MILAN anti-tank guided missile launch system. More than 2100 Marders were produced. The vehicle was originally designed to work in cooperation with the Leopard 1, but several improvements have made it capable of keeping up with the latest Leopard 2 on the battlefield.

Since the end of the Cold War, the armed forces of the former East German People's Army have been integrated into the unified German armed forces.

▲ Marder Schützenpanzer

German Army / 10th Armoured Division, Germany, 1979

The Marder infantry fighting vehicle was the primary transport of the mechanized infantry formations of the West German Army. Numerous variants have been developed, and the vehicle mounts a 20mm (0.79in) autocannon as well as the MILAN anti-tank guided missile system. The Marder carries up to seven combat infantrymen.

Specifications

Crew: 3 + 6 or 7 troops	Ea-500 6-cylinder diesel
Weight: 33,500kg (73,855lb)	Speed: 65km/h (40.4mph)
Length: 6.88m (22ft 6.8in)	Range: 500km (310 miles)
Width: 3.38m (11ft 1in)	Armament: 1 x 20mm (0.79in) gun, plus MILAN
Height: 3.02m (9ft 10.7in)	ATGM launcher and 1 x 7.62mm (0.3in) MG
Engine: 447kW (600hp) MTU MB 833	Radio: n/k

Specifications

Crew: 4	8-cylinder diesel
Weight: 23,000kg (50,700lb)	Speed: 70km/h (43mph)
Length: 6.43m (21ft 1in)	Range: 400km (250 miles)
Width: 2.98m (9ft 9in)	Armament: 14 x SS-11 ATGWs, plus 2 x 7.62mm
Height: 2.15m (7ft 0.6in)	(0.3in) MG3 MGs
Engine: 373kW (500hp) Daimler-Benz MB 837A	

▲ Raketenjagdpanzer (RJPZ) 2 Anti-tank Vehicle

German Army / 5th Armoured Division, Germany, 1979

The tracked *Raketenjagdpanzer* (RJPZ) 2 anti-tank vehicle was designed to defeat Warsaw Pact armour with the Nord SS.11 anti-tank missile launcher system. Its development was begun in the 1960s, and it was deployed with armoured infantry brigades of the German Army, remaining in service until 1982.

▲ **Leopard 2A2 Main Battle Tank**

German Army / 10th Panzer Division, Germany, 1986

The latest generation of German main battle tanks, the Leopard 2 began its development during the 1970s. Replacing the Leopard 1 in frontline units of the German Army during the following decade, the tank mounts the 120mm (4.7in) Rheinmetall L55 smoothbore gun.

Specifications

Crew: 4	12-cylinder diesel
Weight (approx): 59,700kg (131,616lb)	Speed: 72km/h (45mph)
Length: 9.97m (32ft 8.4in)	Range: 500km (310 miles)
Width: 3.74m (12ft 3.25in)	Armament: 1 x 120mm (4.7in) smoothbore gun,
Height: 2.64m (8ft 7.9in)	plus 2 x 7.62mm (0.3in) MGs
Engine: 1119kW (1500hp) MTU MB 873 Ka501	Radio: SEM 80/90 digital

German Army, 23rd Panzer Battalion, 1989

As the Cold War came to a close, the German 23rd Panzer Battalion fielded 40 Leopard 2 main battle tanks, considered one of the finest weapons of its kind in the world, along with a complement of four M577 command vehicle variants of the M113 armoured personnel carrier and 12 M113s, transporting the battalion's mechanized infantry personnel.

(40 x Leopard 2 MBT)

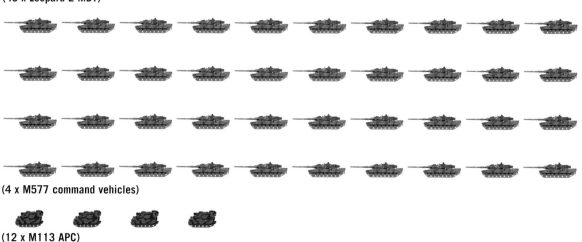

(4 x M577 command vehicles)

(12 x M113 APC)

▶ **M113 Green Archer**

German Army / 13th Mechanized
Infantry Division, 1990

The platform for mobile Green Archer
mortar and artillery locating radar
utilized by the German Army during the
latter years of the Cold War, the M113
Green Archer variant demonstrates
the versatility of the US-manufactured
armoured personnel carrier.

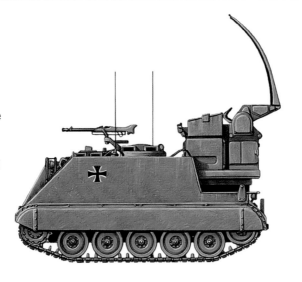

Specifications

Crew: 4
Weight: 11,900kg (26,200lb)
Length: 4.86m (15ft 11in)
Width: 2.7m (8ft 10in)
Height: 4.32m (14ft 2in)
Engine: 160kW (215hp) Detroit Diesel 6V-53N
      6-cylinder diesel
Speed: 68km/h (42mph)
Range: 480km (300 miles)
Armament: 1 x 7.62mm (0.3in) MG
Radio: SEM-80/90 digital

Specifications

Crew: 4
Weight: 25.5 tonnes (56,200lb)
Length: 6.61m (21ft 8in)
Width: 3.12m (10ft 3in)
Height: 2.55m (8ft 4in)
Engine: 1 x 373kW (500hp) Daimler-Benz
      MB837A 8-cylinder diesel
Speed: 68km/h (42mph)
Range: 400km (250 miles)
Armament: 1 x HOT ATGW system; 1 x 7.62mm
    (.3in) MG3 MG
Radio: SEM-80/90 digital

▲ **Jagdpanzer Jaguar**

German Army, 1990

The Jadgpanzer Jaguar 1 self-propelled anti-tank vehicle upgraded the Raketenjadgpanzer 2. It mounted the
Euromissile K3S HOT ATGW, a command-to-line-of-sight system with a range of 4000m (4374 yards), able to
penetrate modern explosive-reactive armour.

▲ **TPz 1A3 Fuchs NBC Reconnaissance Vehicle**

German Army, 1988

The Transportpanzer 1 Fuchs is an amphibious 6x6 vehicle, carrying 10 soldiers in a rear compartment. In water, it
reaches 10.5km/h (6.5mph) using twin propellers beneath the rear of the hull. Variants include an EOD vehicle and a
RASIT radar carrier.

Specifications

Crew: 2 + 10
Weight: 18.3 tonnes (40,350lb)
Length: 6.76m (22ft 2in)
Width: 2.98m (9ft 9in)
Height: 2.3m (7ft 6.6in)
Engine: 1 x 239kW (320hp) Mercedes-Benz
      OM402A 8-cylinder diesel
Speed: 105km/h (65mph)
Range: 800km (500 miles)
Armament: 1 x 7.62mm (0.3in) MG
Radio: SEM-80/90 digital

NATO – Italy
1970–91

Organic Italian armoured development during the latter years of the Cold War began with the influence of the German Leopard 1 main battle tank.

WHEN THE ITALIAN GOVERNMENT obtained licensing to produce a variant of the German Leopard 1 main battle tank in the early 1970s, Italian engineers were allowed to gain valuable insight into the design of the modern armoured fighting vehicle. In time, the Italians produced more than 700 of the licensed Leopard, which served as the impetus for a world-class main battle tank of Italian manufacture.

While the OF 40, designed by Otobreda and Fiat, may have incorporated numerous features of the Leopard 1, its performance proved unremarkable. Entering service in 1980, its original 105mm (4.1in) main cannon was not stabilized. Within a year, the OG 14 LR fire control system had been installed, improving its accuracy tremendously. Designated the OF 40 Mk 2, this improved version of the tank was subsequently purchased by the United Arab Emirates in the only recorded export sale of the tank. Still, the OF 40 offered no system of defence against nuclear,

biological and chemical weapons, and ammunition storage capacity was minimal.

During the 1980s, research continued on a new Italian main battle tank, and the Ariete was slated to enter production during the mid-1990s. The principal armoured personnel carrier of the Italian Army during the period was the VCC-1, a highly modified version of the US-designed M113 which was built under licence.

Artillery

Another Italian foray into the arms export market was the Palmaria 155mm (6.1in) self-propelled howitzer. Developed during the era of the superb US, German and British weapons of similar configuration, the Palmaria main weapon was mounted atop the chassis of the OF 40 main battle tank. Its development was undertaken in 1977, and the first prototype was tested in 1981. The former Italian colony of Libya was the first foreign country to purchase the

▲ **VCC-1 Armoured Personnel Carrier**

Italian Army / Folgore Mechanized Infantry Division, Italy, 1974

A licence-built and highly modified version of the American M113 armoured personnel carrier, the Italian VCC-1 featured sloped rear and side armour, firing ports for infantrymen, shields for its Browning 12.7mm (0.5in) machine guns and smoke grenade launchers.

Specifications

Crew: 2 + 7	Speed: 65km/h (40mph)
Weight: 11,600kg (25,578lb)	Range: 550km (340 miles)
Length: 5.04m (16ft 6in)	Armament: 2 x Browning 12.7mm (0.5in) MGs
Width: 2.69m (8ft 10in)	Radio: n/k
Height: 2.03m (6ft 8in)	
Engine: 156kW (210bhp) GMC V6 diesel	

Palmaria, followed by Nigeria and Argentina later in the 1980s. The system featured an automatic loader with a rate of fire of a single round every 15 seconds.

During the Cold War, the Italian Army was tasked with protecting its own borders against Warsaw Pact aggression. The *Ariete* Armoured Division and *Mantova* and *Folgore* Mechanized Infantry Divisions were deployed along the Italian northern frontier. The army also contributed to NATO operations around the world and to the efforts of United Nations peacekeeping forces.

Typical of the Italian Army's mobility was the *Aosta* Mechanized Brigade, its infantry regiments

equipped with numerous M113 armoured personnel carriers and variants of the Centauro infantry fighting vehicle. Cavalry formations fielded the wheeled Centauro tank destroyer, and artillery units the M109 self-propelled howitzer.

The *Ariete* Armoured Division, which traces its lineage to the fascist regime of Benito Mussolini during the 1930s, was redesignated a brigade in 1986 and included three tank regiments, an elite *Bersaglieri* regiment, and supporting artillery and engineers. The elite *Garibaldi Bersaglieri* Brigade was a mechanized infantry formation which included three infantry and one armoured battalions along with supporting artillery.

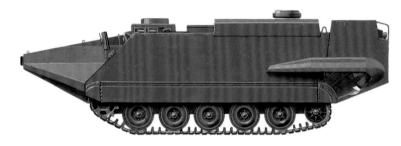

Specifications

Crew: 2 + 11
Weight (approx): 12,000kg (26,500lb)
Length: 6.87m (22ft 6.4in)
Width: 2.95m (9ft 8in)
Height: 2.05m (6ft 8.7in)
Engine: 160kW (215hp) Detroit 6V-53N
  6-cylinder diesel
Speed: 68km/h (42mph)
Range: 550km (340 miles)
Armament: 1 x 12.7mm (0.5in) Browning
  M2 HB HMG

▲ **Arisgator Amphibious APC**

Italian Army / Mantova Mechanized Infantry Division, Italy, 1975

A fully amphibious version of the American M113 armoured personnel carrier, the Arisgator was heavily modified by the Italian firm Aris. Readily identifiable due to its boat-shaped forward section, the Arisgator could carry a complement of up to 11 combat infantrymen.

▲ **Type 6616 Armoured Car**

Italian Army / Carabinieri, Italy, 1977

The wheeled Otobreda Fiat Type 6616 armoured car entered service with the Italian Army during the early 1970s and was made available on the export market as well. Capable of traversing water hazards, it featured a turret-mounted 20mm (0.79in) cannon and a light 7.62mm (0.3in) machine gun.

Specifications

Crew: 3
Weight: 8000kg (17,600lb)
Length: 5.37m (17ft 7in)
Width: 2.5m (8ft 2in)
Height: 2.03m (6ft 8in)
Engine: 119kW (160hp) Fiat Model 8062.24
  supercharged diesel
Speed: 100km/h (75mph)
Range: 700km (450 miles)
Armament: 1 x Rheinmetall 20mm (0.79in)
  Mk 20 Rh 202 gun, plus 1 x 7.62mm (0.3in)
  coaxial MG
Radio: n/k

NATO – Spain
1982–PRESENT

In May 1982, seven years after the death of fascist leader Generalissimo Francisco Franco, Spain joined the NATO alliance and initiated an effort to modernize its armoured force.

DURING THE EARLY YEARS OF THE COLD WAR, many Western nations refused to export arms to the fascist regime of Generalissimo Francisco Franco. One notable exception was France. Unable to purchase main battle tanks from other countries, the Spanish settled on the AMX-30, purchasing and producing under licence more than 300 examples of the French tank from 1973 to 1984.

By the mid-1980s, approximately 700 US tanks were also in the Spanish arsenal, including the venerable M41 Walker Bulldog light tank and the M47, M48 and M60 tanks of the Patton series. A number of the M41s, dating to the Korean War era, were reportedly updated as tank destroyers during the period. The Spanish Army fielded one armoured division, which included a pair of active armoured brigades and a reserve brigade. In addition to the array of tanks, it included armoured personnel carriers such as the American-built M113 and armoured cars such as the French AML-60 and AML-90. The Pegaso 3560 BMR armoured personnel carrier was a wheeled 6X6 vehicle that was produced in Spain from 1979

onwards. Several variants have been developed, and armament ranges from a 40mm (1.57in) grenade launcher to light machine guns and anti-tank guided missile systems. Nearly 700 of these vehicles have seen service with the Spanish military.

Armoured upgrade

The Spanish military establishment briefly considered the purchase of a new main battle tank during the early 1990s; however, that option was declined and the existing inventory of ageing AMX-30s was upgraded with explosive reactive armour, laser rangefinding equipment and high-performance diesel engines manufactured in Germany. Later, the Spanish Army acquired more than 300 of Germany's outstanding Leopard 2 main battle tanks. More than 100 of these were Leopard 2A4s previously in service with the downsizing German Army, while 219 were the brand new Leopard 2E, a variant of the 2A6 jointly manufactured by Germany and Spain and featuring greater armour protection than the domestic German tank.

Specifications	
Crew: 4	12-cylinder diesel
Weight: 35,941kg (79,072lb)	Speed: 65km/h (40mph)
Length: 9.48m (31ft 1in)	Range: 600km (373 miles)
Width: 3.1m (10ft 2in)	Armament: 1 x 105mm (4.1in) gun, plus 1 x
Height: 2.86m (9ft 4in)	20mm (0.79in) gun and 1 x 7.62mm (0.3in) MG
Engine: 537kW (720hp) Hispano-Suiza	Radio: n/k

▲ **AMX-30 Main Battle Tank**

Spanish Army / 1st Armoured Division, Spain, 1978

The AMX-30 main battle tank, purchased directly from France and also built in Spain under licence, served as the backbone of the Spanish Army's armoured forces for decades. Upgraded during the 1990s, a large number of the AMX-30s continue on active duty today.

The NATO-era Spanish armoured force includes four heavy armoured brigades and one cavalry brigade. Among the light armoured vehicles of the Spanish Army are at least 30 examples of the ASCOD Pizarro infantry fighting vehicle, which entered service in 2002 and is a product of the Austrian–Spanish Cooperative Development (ASCOD). The Pizarro carries a crew of three and up to eight combat-ready infantrymen. Its armament includes a turret-mounted 30mm (1.18in) cannon and a 7.62mm (0.3in) light machine gun. Functioning in battlefield cooperation with the Leopard 2 tank, the Pizarro has proven a capable replacement for the ageing M113 armoured personnel carrier in the Spanish inventory.

As the Cold War neared its end, the 1st *Brunete* Armoured Division of the Spanish Army was grouped within the IIF (Immediate Intervention Force), a corps-sized unit of the NATO armed forces. Among its components were the 11th Mechanized Brigade and the 12th Armoured Brigade which

Specifications

Crew: 5	Speed: 21km/h (13.5mph)
Weight: 46,500kg (102,533lb)	Range: 144km (90 miles)
Length: 12.3m (40ft 6.5in)	Armament: 1 x 76mm (3in) gun, plus 1 x
Width: 3.2m (10ft 8in)	12.7mm (0.5in) MG and 1 x 7.62mm (0.3in) MG
Height: 2.4m (8ft 2in)	Radio: n/k
Engine: 261.1kW (350hp) Bedford petrol	

▲ **M41 Walker Light Tank**

Spanish Army / 1st Armoured Division, Spain, 1982

The M41 light tank was a US design of the Korean War era, which replaced the M24 Chaffee during the early 1950s. The M41 initially mounted a 76mm (3in) M32 main gun. In addition to the M41, the Spanish Army had previously received a quantity of M24s.

▲ **Pegaso VAP 3550/1 Amphibious Vehicle**

Spanish Army / 1st Armoured Division, Spain, 1980

The Pegaso VAP 3550/1 amphibious wheeled vehicle was produced in Spain during the 1970s. It mounted a light machine gun for defence, and its crew rode in an enclosed cab, while combat troops or cargo were carried in its spacious rear compartment.

Specifications

Crew: 3 + 18	Engine: 142kW (190hp) Pegaso 9135/5
Weight: 12,500kg (27,550lb)	6-cylinder turbo diesel
Length: 8.85m (29ft 0.4in)	Speed: 87km/h (54mph)
Width: 2.5m (8ft 2in)	Range: 800km (500 miles)
Height: 2.5m (8ft 2in)	Armament: 1 x 7.62mm (0.3in) MG (export
	versions only)

included, as representative of its strength, the 11th Armoured Battalion with 27 AMX-30 main battle tanks, 14 French BMR 600 armoured personnel carriers licence-built in Spain, an 81mm (3.2in) mortar section, nine rifle squads and a pair of MILAN anti-tank guided missile launchers. The 11th Artillery Battalion fielded 18 M109 155mm (6.1in) self-propelled howitzers. The 2nd Motorized and 3rd Mechanized Divisions were also capable of rapid deployment.

Since the end of the Cold War, Spanish forces have participated with NATO in operations in Afghanistan, Lebanon, the Balkans, Iraq and other hotspots around the globe.

Specifications

Crew: 4	Speed: 48km/h (30mph)
Weight: 51.33 tonnes (50.5 tons)	Range: 500km (311 miles)
Length: 9.44m (31ft)	Bridge: length: (extended) 191.9m (63ft)
Width: 3.63m (11ft 11in)	(folded) 8.75m (32ft); span: 18.28m (60ft);
Height: 3.27m (10ft 8in)	width: (overall) 3.99m (13.1ft), (roadway)
Engine: 559.7kW (750hp) Continental AVDS-	3.81m (12.5ft); height: 0.94m (3.1ft); weight:
1790-2A V12 turbo-charged diesel	13.28 tonnes (13.07 tons)

▲ M60A1 AVLB

Spanish Army / 1st Armoured Division, Spain, 1993

Based on the M60 Patton chassis, the M60A1 AVLB is used for launching and retrieving an 18m (60ft) scissors-type bridge. The AVLB consists of three major sections: the launcher, the hull and the bridge. The launcher is mounted as an integral part of the chassis. The bridge, when emplaced, is capable of supporting most tracked and wheeled vehicles.

▲ M60A3E Patton Main Battle Tank

Spanish Army / 1st Armoured Division, Spain, 1993

The M60A3E Patton main battle tank featured an unusual turret configuration, with a small machine gun mount atop the main 105mm (4.1in) M68 gun turret. The Spanish Army acquired at least 50 of the M60A3E variant.

Specifications

Crew: 4	2 V12 diesel
Weight: 49 tonnes (48.2 tons)	Speed: 48km/h (30mph)
Length: 6.9m (22ft 9.5in)	Range: 500km (300 miles)
Width: 3.6m (11ft 11in)	Armament: 1 x 105mm (4.1in) M68 gun;
Height: 3.2m (10ft 6.5in)	1 x 12.7mm (0.5in) M85 MG; 1 x 7.62mm
Engine: 560kW (750hp) Continental AVDS-1790-	(0.3in) MG

Sweden and Austria
1970–91

An innovative Swedish armoured force has adopted the German Leopard 2 main battle tank while maintaining a willingness to experiment with radical designs of its own.

EARLY IN THE POST-WORLD WAR II PERIOD, the Swedish armed forces relied on the British Centurion as their primary tank. However, as Soviet tank designs progressed, a Swedish engineer proposed a departure from the expected: a turretless tank. The idea was not new, however. German armoured assault guns of World War II had been successful, their heavy weapons mounted within the hull.

The elimination of a turret would accomplish several things. The hull would provide a stable gun platform, potentially improving accuracy; the profile of the tank would be significantly lower, improving its ability to hide in revetments or fight from ambush; and the tank would be less expensive to manufacture. On the other hand, the tank would be at a distinct disadvantage in the hull-down position, and reorienting the main weapon would essentially mean moving the entire vehicle.

Nevertheless, the experiment went forward and the Stridsvagn 103 was developed. Beginning in the late 1950s, the prototype was tested, and by 1967 production was under way. The first unit was soon delivered to the Swedish Army, and production ceased at 290 units in 1971. During the late 1960s, the Stridsvagn 103, or S Tank as it came to be known, was tested against the Chieftain main battle tank of the British Army of the Rhine; and in 1975 trials were conducted in the US comparing the tank with the M60A1E3 Patton. In both cases, the S Tank came out favourably despite its inability to fire on the move.

Modern arms

Sweden sought a new main battle tank during the 1990s and has recently operated 280 German Leopard 2 tanks, 160 of which are the Leopard 2A4, designated the Stridsvagn 121; the remainder are the Leopard 2(S), or Stridsvagn 122. Since the early 1990s, Sweden has deployed the CV 90, or Stridsfordon 90, infantry fighting vehicle, designed by Hagglünds Bofors and built by BAE Land

▲ **Stridsvagn 103 Light Tank**
Swedish Army / Skaraborgs Regiment, Sweden, 1974
The turretless Stridsvagn 103 was an innovative main battle tank design and the only one of its kind deployed in large numbers. It mounted the 105mm (4.1in) L/62 rifled gun in the hull along with two light machine guns.

Specifications

Crew: 3	(490hp) Boeing 553 gas turbine
Weight: 38,894kg (85,568lb)	Speed: 50km/h (31mph)
Length (hull): 7.04m (23ft 1in)	Range: 390km (242 miles)
Width: 3.26m (10ft 8.3in)	Armament: 1 x 105mm (4.1in) gun, plus
Height: 2.5m (8ft 2.5in)	3 x 7.62mm (0.3in) MGs
Engine: 1 x 119kW (240hp) diesel; 1 x 366kW	Radio: n/k

Systems. The development of the CV 90 was begun in 1984, and testing of the prototype began four years later, successfully concluding in 1991. The first deliveries to the Swedish Army were made in 1993. The CV 90 carries a crew of three and a complement of seven combat infantrymen. More than 1000 CV 90s have been produced to date, and a variant was exported to Finland. The Swedish Army currently possesses three regiments of armoured and mechanized troops (*Pansartrupperna*).

Specifications

Crew: 2 + 8	Engine: 68kW (91hp) Volvo B18 4-cylinder diesel
Weight: 2900kg (6400lb)	Speed: 39km/h (24mph)
Length: 6.17m (20ft 2in)	Range: 400km (250 miles)
Width: 1.76m (5ft 9in)	Armament: None
Height: 2.21m (7ft 3in)	Radio: n/k

▲ **BV 202**

Swedish Army / Skaraborgs Regiment, Sweden, 1982

Developed by Volvo, the BV 202 troop carrier vehicle includes two Kegresse track units, with the crew and powerplant in the first and up to eight soldiers in the trailer. It was produced from 1964 to 1981 and last used by Swedish cavalry units, which perform training functions in the Swedish Army.

Specifications

Crew: 3	Engine: 1 x 238kW (320hp) Steyr 7FA / 6-cylinder
Weight: 17,700kg (38,580lbs)	diesel engine
Length: 5.58m (18ft 4in)	Speed: 65km/h (40mph)
Width: 2.5m (8ft 2in)	Range: n/k
Height: 2.88m (9ft 5in)	Armament: 1 x 105mm (4.13in) rifled gun, plus
	1 x 7.62mm (0.3in) anti-aircraft MG

▲ **Steyr SK 105 Kürassier light tank**

Austrian Army, 1974

Armed with a rifled 105mm (4.13in) gun in an oscillating turret, more than 700 of the SK-105 Kürassier light tank have been produced. The oscillating turret is similar to that fitted to the French AMX-13 light tank. The commander is seated on the left of the turret and the gunner on the right.

Switzerland
1970–91

The Swiss Army has rarely mobilized during the modern era. Nevertheless it maintains two armoured brigades in readiness for self-defence and to complement four brigades of infantry and three brigades of mountain troops.

THE SWISS ARMY maintains approximately 380 German Leopard 2A4 main battle tanks, designated the Panzer 87. In addition, more than 500 examples of the US-manufactured M113 armoured personnel carrier remained in service into the 1990s, while the APC 2000 variant of the Swedish CV 9030 infantry fighting vehicle was purchased early in the decade.

The Swiss MOWAG corporation has produced a series of armoured fighting vehicles, including the Roland and MR8 armoured personnel carriers of the 1970s and the Grenadier, an updated version of the Roland. Earlier, the Entpannungspanzer armoured recovery vehicle was designed by RUAG Land Company of Switzerland and entered service in 1970.

Specifications

Crew: 1 + 8
Weight: 6100kg (13,450lb)
Length: 4.84m (15ft 10in)
Width: 2.3m (7ft 6in)
Height: 2.12m (6ft 11in)
Engine: 150kW (202hp) MOWAG 8-cylinder
  petrol
Speed: 100km/h (62mph)
Range: 550km (340 miles)
Armament: 1 x 20mm (0.79in) cannon

▲ **MOWAG Grenadier**

Swiss Army / 11th Armoured Brigade, Switzerland, 1984

Mounting a 7.62mm (0.3in) light machine gun or the heavy 20mm (0.79in) M 2HB cannon in a small turret, the MOWAG corporation Grenadier infantry fighting vehicle was a modernization of the Roland fighting vehicle and entered service with the Swiss Army during the late 1970s.

Specifications

Crew: 5
Weight: 38,000kg (83,800lb)
Length: 7.6m (24ft 11in)
Width: 3.06m (10ft 4in)
Height: 3.25m (10ft 8in)
Engine: 525kW (704hp) MTU MB 837
  8-cylinder diesel
Speed: 55km/h (34mph)
Range: 300km (190 miles)
Armament: 1 x 7.5mm (0.295in) MG, plus
  8 x smoke dischargers
Radio: n/k

▲ **Entpannungspanzer**

Swiss Army / 1st Armoured Brigade, Switzerland, 1971

Fitted with a large winch, the RUAG Land Systems Entpannungspanzer armoured recovery vehicle was developed during the 1960s, with the first prototypes evaluated late in the decade and the initial deliveries to the Swiss Army in 1970.

NATO – United Kingdom
1970–91

As the Cold War dragged on, the British forces committed to NATO on the European continent continued to deploy more powerful and versatile armoured fighting vehicles.

DURING THE 1970s, the British Army of the Rhine maintained three divisions, increased to four by the end of the decade, each with considerable armoured strength. By the middle of the decade the Chieftain main battle tank had arrived in large numbers. Developed during the 1960s as a successor to the long-serving Centurion, the Chieftain was the most heavily armoured tank of its time and mounted the most powerful main weapon, the 120mm (4.7in) rifled L11A5 gun. The Chieftain crew was well protected, the tank provided firepower that was second to none and laser rangefinding gear was installed to replace a ranging machine gun.

The last Chieftain production model, the Mk 5, was also fully protected against nuclear, biological and chemical weapons. There was, however, a price to pay in speed and mobility. The question nagged as to whether the Chieftain was mobile enough to react swiftly to the onslaught of the latest Soviet-built tanks of the Warsaw Pact, namely the T-64 and T-72. A number of Chieftain variants were purpose built, including armoured recovery and bridging vehicles, and these served with NATO forces.

Flexible Response

Should the Warsaw Pact attack, the role of the British Army of the Rhine would be to halt the advance under the doctrine of Flexible Response, which basically dictated one of three courses of action. In the event of a Soviet attack other than a nuclear first strike, NATO forces would respond in kind.

The first response was called Direct Defence and involved stopping a Warsaw Pact conventional offensive with conventional forces. The second stage was Deliberate Escalation. It was fully expected that Warsaw Pact conventional forces would overwhelm NATO forces due to superior numbers. Therefore a response with tactical nuclear weapons would occur. Third, a General Nuclear Response would correspond to the 'mutually assured destruction' theory set out by Robert S. McNamara, US Secretary of Defense under President John F. Kennedy.

▲ **Alvis Saracen Armoured Personnel Carrier**

British Army of the Rhine / 3rd Armoured Division, Germany, 1978

The FV603 Alvis Saracen armoured personnel carrier was one of numerous armoured fighting vehicles produced by the Alvis Corporation during the 1960s and 1970s. It was armed with light machine guns for protection against enemy infantry and transported up to nine soldiers.

Specifications

Crew: 2 + 9	Engine: 119kW (160hp) Rolls-Royce B80 Mk 6A
Weight: 8640kg (19,008lb)	8-cylinder petrol
Length: 5.233m (17ft 2in)	Speed: 72km/h (44.7mph)
Width: 2.539m (8ft 4in)	Range: 400km (248 miles)
Height: 2.463m (8ft 1in)	Armament: 2 x 7.62mm (0.3in) MGs
	Radio: n/k

Specifications

Crew: 4

Weight: 54,880kg (120,736lb)

Length: 10.795m (35ft 5in)

Width: 3.657m (11ft 8.5in)

Height: 2.895m (9ft 6in)

Engine: 560kW (750hp) Leyland 6-cylinder
multi-fuel

Speed: 48km/h (30mph)

Range: 500km (310 miles)

Armament: 1 x 120mm (4.7in) rifled gun, plus 1
x 7.62mm (0.3in) coaxial machine gun and
12 x smoke dischargers

Radio: Twin Clansman VRC 353 VHF radio sets,
plus 1 x C42 1 B47 Larkspur VHF radio

▲ Chieftain Mk 5 Main Battle Tank

British Army of the Rhine / 7th Armoured Brigade, Germany, 1976

The Chieftain main battle tank combined the powerful 120mm (4.7in) L11A5 gun with the heaviest armour protection in the world. Its final production variant, the Mk 5, was equipped with defences against nuclear, biological and chemical weapons and had laser rangefinding equipment.

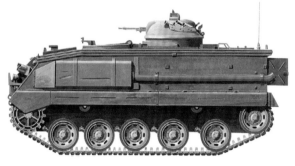

▲ FV432 Armoured Personnel Carrier

British Army of the Rhine / 2nd Division, Germany, 1975

The FV432 was developed in the 1960s and served as the primary armoured personnel carrier of the British Army for more than two decades. The vehicle was capable of transporting up to 10 combat infantrymen, and by the 1980s more than 2500 examples of the FV432 had been deployed.

Specifications

Crew: 2 + 10

Weight: 15,280kg (33,616lb)

Length: 5.251m (17ft 7in)

Width: 2.8m (9ft 2in)

Height (with machine gun): 2.286m (7ft 6in)

Engine: 170kW (240hp) Rolls-Royce K60
6-cylinder multi-fuel

Speed: 52.2km/h (32mph)

Range: 483km (300 miles)

Armament: 1 x 7.62mm (0.3in) MG

Radio: n/k

While speed was essential to the success of a deep penetration offensive according to Warsaw Pact doctrine, rapid response was equally significant in NATO plans to stem a Soviet-led tide of armour and infantry. In 1983, the British Army of the Rhine received yet another improved main battle tank, the Challenger 1. Integral in helping the British forces fulfil their charge in stopping a Warsaw Pact offensive, the Challenger 1 maintained the proven 120mm (4.7in) L11A5 rifled gun. However, it was considerably faster than the Chieftain with a top road speed of 56 km/h (37mph).

Although only 420 examples of the Challenger were actually built, the tank represented a great improvement in armour protection as well. Lighter Chobham armour, a ceramic and metal composite, was installed for the first time on the Challenger 1 and provided protection many times greater than that of rolled steel. Aside from serving with British forces in Europe, the Challenger 1 was the latest British main battle tank to see combat during Operations Desert Shield and Desert Storm in 1991, compiling an impressive record against Iraqi tanks. Even as the Challenger 1 was deployed during the mid-1980s,

British Army, 2nd Royal Tank Regiment, 1989

As the Cold War waned, the strength of the 2nd Royal Tank Regiment was typical of comparable armoured formations of the British Army of the Rhine. Its 56 Challenger tanks mounted heavy 120mm (4.7in) L11A5 main guns, while supporting infantry was transported aboard the ageing FV432 armoured personnel carrier. The Alvis Sultan and Scorpion vehicles, along with the venerable Daimler Ferret armoured car, provided command, reconnaissance and fire support structure.

Regiment (56 x Challenger, 4 x Sultan, 8 x Scorpion, 10 x FV432, 8 x Ferret)

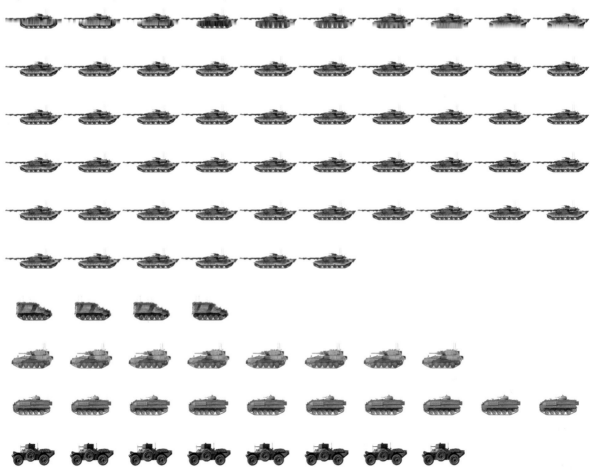

its successor, the Challenger 2, was on the drawing board. A radical departure from its predecessor, the Challenger 2 was scheduled to come on line by the end of the twentieth century.

Armoured fighting vehicles

During the 1970s, British armoured fighting vehicles such as the Alvis Saracen and the later FV101 Scorpion combat reconnaissance vehicle were utilized extensively in fire support and scouting roles. The FV432 armoured personnel carrier was capable of transporting up to 10 combat infantrymen and entered service during the 1960s.

Evaluating the capabilities of the Soviet-built BMP infantry fighting vehicles, British designers undertook the development of a comparable vehicle in 1972. Intended to replace the ageing FV432, the Warrior was designed for maximum cross-country speed and later to keep pace with the Challenger 1 and 2 tanks in Europe. An agonizingly slow development period led to the delay of the prototype until 1979. Further, the new vehicle did not enter service until 1987. Nevertheless, armed with a 30mm (1.18in) RARDEN cannon and 7.62mm (0.3in) machine guns, the Warrior has been proven effective, and long-range upgrade and sustainment programmes continued into the 1990s.

Specifications

Crew: 3

Weight: 8073kg (17,760lb)

Length: 4.794m (15ft 8.75in)

Width: 2.235m (7ft 4in)

Height: 2.102m (6ft 10.75in)

Engine: 142kW (190hp) Jaguar 4.2-litre petrol

Speed: 80km/h (50mph)

Range: 644km (400 miles)

Armament: 1 x 76mm (3in) gun, plus

   1 x 7.62mm (0.3in) coaxial MG

Radio: Clansman VRC 353

▲ **FV101 Scorpion CVR(T)**

British Army of the Rhine / 7th Armoured Brigade, Germany, 1984

One of seven Alvis-produced armoured vehicles, the FV101 Scorpion entered service with the British Army in 1973 and was deployed for more than 20 years. Serving in a reconnaissance role, it was originally armed with a 76mm (3in) cannon and upgunned to a 90mm (3.5in) weapon.

Specifications

Crew: 3 + 4

Weight: 8172kg (17,978lb)

Length: 5.125m (16ft 9in)

Width: 2.24m (7ft 4in)

Height: 2.26m (7ft 5in)

Engine: 142kW (190hp) Jaguar 6-cylinder petrol

Speed: 80km/h (50mph)

Range: 483km (301 miles)

Armament: 1 x MILAN ATGM launcher, plus 1 x

   7.62mm (0.3in) MG

Radio: Clansman VRC 353

▲ **FV120 Spartan with MILAN Compact Turret (MCT)**

British Army of the Rhine / 1st Armoured Division, Germany, 1977

The anti-tank version of the Alvis FV103 Spartan armoured personnel carrier, the FV120 mounted a two man turret with the MILAN anti-tank guided missile launching system. Two missiles were loaded to fire, while an additional 11 were transported.

▲ **FV106 Samson CVR(T) Armoured Recovery Vehicle**

British Army of the Rhine / 3rd Armoured Division, Germany, 1978

An armoured recovery adaptation of the FV120 Spartan, the FV106 Samson was equipped with a winch to remove vehicles that had bogged down or were damaged in combat. It carried a light machine gun for defensive purposes.

Specifications

Crew: 3

Weight: 8740kg (19,300lb)

Length: 4.78m (15ft 8in)

Width: 2.4m (7ft 10.4in)

Height: 2.55m (8ft 4.4in)

Engine: 145kW (195hp) Jaguar J60 N01

   Mk100B 6-cylinder petrol

Speed: 55km/h (34mph)

Range: 483km (300 miles)

Armament: 1 x 7.62mm (0.3in) MG

Radio: n/k

Specifications

Crew: 1

Weight: 2120kg (4664lb)

Length: 3.65m (12ft)

Width: 1.68m (5ft 6in)

Height: 1.97m (6ft 5in)

Engine: 30kW (51hp) 4-cylinder OHV diesel

Speed: 105km/h (65.6mph)

Range: 560km (350 miles)

Armament: None

Radio: n/k

▲ **Land Rover 4x4 Light Utility Vehicle**

British Army of the Rhine / 2nd Infantry Division, Germany, 1980

The modified military version of the Land Rover Defender series, the 4x4 light utility vehicle was a workhorse of the British military deployed in Europe. Excellent cross-country capability facilitated the rapid deployment of combat units.

NATO – United States
1970–90

US armour in service with NATO included the latest generation of main battle tank along with sophisticated weapons systems designed to defeat a Warsaw Pact ground offensive.

WHILE THE NATO TACTIC of Follow On Forces Attack had been standard procedure since the 1960s, the role of the alliance's ground defence component evolved from one of early warning or 'tripwire' involvement to one of defeat of the Warsaw Pact armour and infantry arrayed against it. In tandem with Flexible Response (outlined on page 131), the Follow On Forces Attack doctrine involved coordinated action against an enemy. The three elements of Follow On Forces Attack were Long-Range Attack, Immediate-Range Attack and Cross-Corps Support.

In Long-Range Attack, strikes would be conducted against Warsaw Pact marshalling areas, where troop and tank assets moving forward would be most vulnerable, concentrated for transport or choked in column along roads. Immediate-Range Attack involved identifying the most critical area requiring defence, concentrating forces and denying Warsaw Pact commanders an effective next move. Cross-Corps Support involved attacking long-range follow-on forces of the Warsaw Pact to diminish the strength of an attack against a specific sector.

Armour component

Into the 1980s, the Patton series remained a significant main battle tank for US forces, particularly the most advanced variant, the M60A3, which had resulted from an improvement programme undertaken in 1978 and included a 105mm (4.1in) main weapon, ballistic computer and turret stabilization system for improved accuracy.

However, it had become apparent to the American military establishment that a replacement for the Patton was needed. Following the failed MBT-70 project of the 1960s and an abortive joint tank development venture with West Germany, the research and development of the XM815, later known as the M1 Abrams main battle tank, was begun in about 1972. Eight years later, the first M1 Abrams tank entered service with the US Army. Mounting the M68 105mm (4.1in) rifled cannon, a licence-built version of the British Royal Ordnance L7 gun, the Abrams was later rearmed in the M1A1 upgrade with the M256 120mm (4.7in) smoothbore cannon developed by the Rheinmetall AG corporation of Germany for the Leopard 2 main battle tank. By

1986, the M1A1 had become the primary production model, and it was this version which was deployed during Operation Desert Storm.

The M1A1 Abrams was protected by a composite armour similar to the British Chobham and was powered by a 1120kW (1500hp) gas turbine engine, which later earned it the nickname 'Whispering Death'. Its pressurized nuclear, biological and chemical defence system increased survivability, and the advanced fire control system resulted in tremendous accuracy.

After a long delay in development, the M2/M3 Bradley Fighting Vehicle entered service in 1981 in both infantry and cavalry configurations. Mounting a 25mm (1in) M242 chain gun and the TOW anti-tank missile system, the Bradley was capable of carrying up to seven combat infantrymen. A significant requirement for the Bradley vehicle was that it keep pace with the M1 Abrams main battle tank under combat conditions while also providing protected transportation and direct fire support for infantry.

▲ **M1A1 Abrams Main Battle Tank**

US Army / 1st Armored Division, Germany, 1987

The M1A1 Abrams was the primary variant of the US main battle tank deployed during the mid-1980s. Its 120mm (4.7in) smoothbore gun, developed by Rheinmetall of Germany, was accurate up to a range of more than 2469m (2700 yards).

Specifications

Crew: 4	Speed: 67km/h (42mph)
Weight: 57,154kg (126,024lb)	Range: 465km (289 miles)
Length (over gun): 9.77m (32ft 3in)	Armament: 1 x 120mm (4.7in) M256 gun, plus 1
Width: 3.66m (12ft)	x 12.7mm (0.5in) MG and 2 x 7.62mm
Height: 2.44m (8ft)	(0.3in) MGs
Engine: 1119.4kW (1500hp) Textron Lycoming	Radio: n/k
AGT 1500 gas turbine	

▲ **M901 TOW APC**

US Army / 1st Infantry Division, Germany, 1987

Based on the M113A1 APC, the M901 entered production in 1978 and mounts 2 x M27 TOW anti-tank missiles. The M901 must come to a stop before it can fire, though it takes only 20 seconds for the TOW system to target and launch. Reloading takes around 40 seconds.

Specifications

Crew: 4 or 5

Weight: 11,794kg (26,005lb)

Length: 4.88m (16ft 1in)

Width: 2.68m (8ft 9in)

Height: 3.35m (10ft 11.8in)

Engine: 160kW (215hp) Detroit Diesel 6V-53N

  6-cylinder diesel

Speed: 68km/h (42mph)

Range: 483km (300 miles)

Armament: 1 x TOW 2 ATGW system

  (2 missles); 1 x 7.62mm (0.3in) MG

Radio: n/k

Specifications

Crew: 3 + 25
Weight: 22,837kg (50,241lb)
Length: 7.943m (26ft 0.7in)
Width: 3.27m (10ft 8.7in)
Height: 3.263m (10ft 8.5in)
Engine: 298kW (400hp) Detroit-Diesel Model
   8V-53T engine
Speed: 64km/h (40mph)
Range: 482km (300 miles)
Armament: 1 x 12.7mm (0.5in) M2HB HMG, plus
   optional 40mm (1.57in) Mk19
   grenade launcher
Radio: AN/VIC-2 intercom system

▲ **LVTP7 amphibious vehicle**

US Marine Corps / 31st Marine Expeditionary Unit, 1990

Currently the primary amphibious armoured personnel carrier of the US Marine Corps, the LVTP7 entered service
in the early 1980s. With a troop-carrying capacity of 25, it was armed with grenade launchers or a 25mm 1in) chain gun.

Specifications

Crew: 3
Weight: 25,191kg (55,420lb)
Length: 6.8m (22ft 4in)
Width: 2.92m (9ft 7in)
Height: 2.6m (8ft 6in)
Engine: 373kW (500hp) Cummings VTA-903
   turbo-charged 8-cylinder diesel
Speed: 64km/h (40mph)
Range: 483km (302 miles)
Armament: 2 x rocket pod containers,
   each holding 6 rockets
Radio: n/k

▲ **M270 Multiple Launch Rocket System (MLRS)**

US Army / 1st Infantry Division, Germany, 1989

The M270 Multiple Launch Rocket System entered service with the US Army in 1983. Mounting the M269 launcher module,
the system was capable of firing a variety of munitions at a rate of up to 12 per minute.

Specifications

Crew: 4
Weight: 50,803kg (112,020lb)
Length: 8.27m (27ft 1.5in)
Width: 3.43m (11ft 3in)
Height: 2.92m (9ft 7in)
Engine: 730kW (980hp) Continental
   AVDS-1790-2DR 12-cylinder diesel
Speed: 42km/h (26mph)
Range: 450km (280 miles)
Armament: 1 x 12.7mm (0.5in) Browning
   M2HB HMG
Radio: n/k

▲ **M88A1 Armoured Recovery Vehicle**

US Army / 1st Armored Division, Germany, 1985

Based on the M88, one of the heaviest armoured recovery vehicles in the world, the M88A1 medium armoured recovery
vehicle entered service with the US Army in 1977. Powered by a diesel engine, it also transported ammunition and supplies.

Chapter 2

The Korean War, 1950–53

When elements of the North Korean People's Army
crossed the 38th Parallel on 25 June 1950, communist
forces rapidly overwhelmed those of the South attempting
to stand against them. In the vanguard of the communist
offensive were Soviet-designed T-34 tanks, battle-tested
during World War II and considered among the finest
armoured fighting vehicles in the world. As United Nations
forces, primarily those of the United States and the British
Commonwealth, bolstered the South Koreans, a new
generation of Western tanks and armoured vehicles reached
the combat zones. The Korean War, therefore, became
a proving ground for tactical and technological
innovation – particularly in the role of the armoured
fighting vehicle on the modern battlefield.

◀ **US Marine armour**

US Marine M26 Pershing tanks roll through a village in Korea as a line of prisoners of war are marched into captivity,
September 1950.

Organization and armour

At the dawn of the Nuclear Age, senior military planners around the world grappled with redefining the nature of conventional warfare.

THE MOBILITY AND FIREPOWER of the modern tank were to take on added significance during the ebb and flow of the Korean War. The armoured fighting vehicle had come of age during World War II. The rapid advancement of technology and the unparalleled proving ground of the battlefield – particularly in the desert of North Africa, across the Western Front in Europe, and on the vast steppes of the Soviet Union in the East – had fostered a quantum leap in the development, deployment and doctrine of the armoured fighting vehicle. The tank was, without doubt, the mobile sledgehammer of a land army's combat arsenal. However, while the strength of an armoured formation was readily apparent, its shortcomings had been laid bare as well.

In the United States, the report of the War Department Equipment Board, popularly known as the Stilwell Board and presided over by General Joseph Stilwell of World War II fame, was published in January 1946. Its findings concluded that ground and air forces must cooperate fully in combat situations, while tanks could not operate without the support of infantry. The role of armour was defined as one of exploiting a breakthrough against the enemy on the ground.

Although the tank provided mobile firepower, it could not sustain the advantage indefinitely on its own. Therefore, the combined arms approach was deemed appropriate. The highest and best future use of the tank would be in concert with infantry and air assets. US infantry divisions were to be assigned their own organic tank battalions to facilitate the combined arms approach.

Furthermore, the United States Army would no longer field tank destroyer formations. The advent of the modern tank, with heavy firepower, rendered the tank destroyer obsolete. The M26 Pershing heavy tank, for example, fielded a 90mm

▲ **Tank destroyer**

First serving towards the end of World War II, the US-made M36 tank destroyer saw action in Korea. The M36 was later used in Indochina and the Indo-Pakistan War.

(3.5in) main gun and afforded crewmen better protection with a closed turret than the most recent tank destroyers of the World War II period had provided. Three types of tanks were recommended: the light tank for scouting, reconnaissance and the security of a defensive perimeter; the medium tank for combat assault and advance; and the heavy tank for further exploitation of a tactical advantage.

Development of the role of the modern tank in battle aside, the reality of a war-fatigued nation and the post-war budget constraints placed upon the military establishment resulted in the reduction of many battalion-sized tank formations within army divisions to mere company strength. Additionally, the manufacture of the M24 Chaffee light and M26 Pershing heavy tanks, and later the M46 Patton, was seriously curtailed and even suspended by the eve of the Korean War. Indeed, during the early days of the Korean War, the World War II vintage M4 Sherman was a mainstay.

Girding for war

While a financially strapped Great Britain wrestled with the lessons of the armoured experience during World War II as well, its Cromwell, Centurion and Churchill tanks were modified and field operations reassessed. However, as the chill of the Cold War settled in, Western defensive posture remained decidedly focused on the security of Western Europe. Although the security of its borders and the consolidation of its grip on the client states of Eastern Europe were paramount, the Soviet Union supported the build-up of arms in North Korea. The T-34 had been produced in staggering numbers during World War II, and its upgunned variant, the T-34/85, was made available in some numbers.

As North Korea prepared for war, its army consisted of eight full-strength infantry divisions, two more infantry divisions at partial strength, other independent units and an armoured brigade, the 105th. With an overall strength of 6000 men, the 105th was well trained and included 120 T-34s evenly distributed among three tank regiments and supported by a 2500-man mechanized infantry regiment. In contrast, there were no tanks organic to the eight infantry divisions of the South Korean Army in 1950.

Less than two weeks after the North Koreans crossed the 38th Parallel, a small, lightly armed

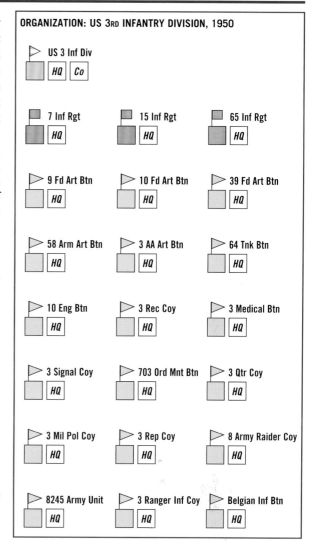

contingent of the US 21st Infantry Regiment, 24th Division, had been airlifted to Pusan and hurried north to confront the invaders. Spearheaded by T-34s, the North Koreans decimated Task Force Smith, named for its commander, Lieutenant-Colonel Charles B. Smith, and inflicted more than 150 casualties. By August, the 1st Provisional Marine Brigade and its M26s had reached Pusan, while army armoured units had also deployed, providing some measure of tenuous stability.

Armoured advantage

For several reasons, including the nature of the terrain, the real tactical value of the tank during the Korean War has been questioned. It may be reasoned that the presence of tanks directly affected the outcomes of numerous engagements; however, taken as a whole, their collective influence is open to conjecture. It has been estimated that total UN tank strength in Korea never exceeded 600 at any one time. Among these were many of the World War II-era Shermans, Cromwells and Challengers. The T-34/85 of the same vintage was by far the most prevalent tank employed by the North Korean forces. One Chinese armoured formation may actually have been fielded during the war but never engaged in any hostile action.

Korean proving ground

Still, the North Koreans had used the tank in its exploitative role, taking advantage of a breakthrough to rapidly advance southwards, while the arrival of UN armour had helped to avert total collapse, and armoured formations were again shown to be vulnerable to air attack. Even though large-scale armoured operations were few and tanks rarely engaged one another in significant numbers, the evolution of the main battle tank continued with the Korean War experience.

The Korean battlefield served as something of a narrow proving ground for the early tanks of the US Patton series, which was continually upgraded and

became the backbone of US armoured forces during the next 30 years. For Britain, the Centurion had already incorporated many of the lessons learned during World War II and included in the earlier Cromwell design. The improvements to later British tanks such as the Challenger and Chieftain were undoubtedly influenced. Furthermore, the Soviet Union was far from idle, continuing to develop its T-54/55 series of main battle tanks, which would eventually equip the armed forces of nations across the globe. Firepower, mobility and armour protection became the watchwords of the future. Bigger, stronger and faster tanks were on the horizon, and the perceived division of labour among light, medium and heavy tanks was beginning to noticeably wane. The Cold War demanded technology and treasure, while maintaining the balance of power and economic viability contributed to the development of the modern main battle tank.

Perhaps the influence of the Korean War on the development of the main battle tank has been underestimated. Regardless of opinion or perspective, the main battle tank of the twenty-first century has been, to some extent, shaped by the experience of both older designs and more innovative post-World War II features that were battle-tested in Korea.

Specifications

Crew: 5	Speed: 55km/h (34mph)
Weight: 18.28 tonnes (18 tons)	Range: 282km (175 miles)
Length: 5.49m (18ft)	Armament: 1 x 75mm (2.9in) M6 gun, plus 1 x
Width: 2.95m (9ft 8in)	12.7mm (0.5in) HMG on AA mount and
Height: 2.46m (8ft 1in)	2 x 7.62mm (0.3in) MGs (1 coaxial,
Engine: 2 x 82kW (110hp) Cadillac 44T24 V8	1 ball-mounted in hull front)
8-cylinder petrol	Radio: SCR 508

▲ **Light Tank M24**

Republic of Korea Army Training Center, Kwang-Ju 1953

The M24 Chaffee was lightly armed and armoured. Although quantities of both the Chaffee and the M4E8 Sherman had been promised by the US, the South Korean Army had no tanks when war broke out.

Pusan
AUGUST–SEPTEMBER 1950

The hard-pressed forces of the United Nations and the South Korean Army relied on armoured support to stem the North Korean tide and to defend the Pusan Perimeter.

B Y THE LATE SUMMER OF 1950, reinforcements had slowed the North Korean advance, which had followed a string of victories from Seoul to Osan and beyond. The defence of the Pusan Perimeter in the extreme southeast corner of South Korea was facilitated largely by the deployment of US armoured forces. As the Korean War intensified, many of the American M26 Pershing tanks had been slated for upgrade to the M46A1 Patton, primarily to address mechanical problems and improve engine performance and to implement a better suspension system. The 90mm (3.5in) main gun of the Pershing, however, remained in the M46A1 Patton and proved to be a potent weapon during the bleak early months in Korea. The sheer availability of the M4 Sherman variants, including the 'Firefly' with its 76mm (3in) high-velocity cannon, made these tanks instrumental in defensive operations.

More than half the North Korean complement of tanks were reported to be the improved T-34/85,

while the earlier T-34, with its 76mm (3in) main gun, nevertheless constituted a major threat. The numbers of Shermans, Pershings, Pattons, Centurions, Cromwells and Churchills increased over time. In tank-versus-tank combat, the United Nations armour proved at least equal to the prowess of the legendary T-34. On 3 September 1950, a platoon of US Marine M26 Pershings engaged three T-34s near Hill 117 during the Second Naktong Offensive, destroying all three.

More than 500 US medium tanks, mostly M26s and M4s, had reached the Pusan Perimeter by the end of August 1950, while a single battalion of M46s had been deployed. In contrast to the rapid offensive movement of North Korean infantry and armour during the opening weeks of the war, the defensive infantry support of these tanks proved a key element in the eventual breakout from the Pusan Perimeter and the concurrent amphibious landing at Inchon, far to the north, on 15 September.

▲ **M26 Pershing Heavy Tank**

Eighth United States Army / 1st US Marine Division / 1st Tank Battalion

The M26 Pershing tank was developed late in World War II and saw limited action. In Korea, its reputation for mechanical unreliability diminished its performance and hastened its withdrawal in favour of the improved M46 Patton.

Specifications

Crew: 5	Speed: 48km/h (30mph)
Weight: 41.86 tonnes (41.2 tons)	Range: 161km (100 miles)
Length: 8.61m (28ft 3in)	Armament: 1 x 90mm (3.5in) M3 gun,
Width: 3.51m (11ft 6in)	plus 1 x 12.7mm (0.5in) AA HMG and
Height: 2.77m (9ft 1in)	2 x 7.62mm (0.3in) MGs (1 coaxial and
Engine: 373kW (500hp) Ford GAF V8 petrol	1 ball-mounted in hull front)
	Radio: SCR508/528

The initial armoured engagements of the war had been fought between the North Korean T-34s and the light US-made M24 Chaffees, which mounted 76mm (3in) cannon of their own but proved inadequate against the communist tanks. The anticipated service life of the M24 with the US Army was drawing to a close, at least on paper. The new M41 was being developed; the 'Walker Bulldog' was named for General Walton Walker, killed in a jeep accident in Korea in December 1950.

As war wore on, armoured engagements became fewer and the role of the tank did gravitate towards infantry support; however, statistical analysis yielded some valuable information. An evaluation of 256 T-34s destroyed in US-controlled territory concluded that 97 had been knocked out by United Nations armour, including 45 by the M4 Sherman, 32 by the M26 Pershing, 19 by the M46 Patton and one by the M24 Chaffee. The T-34 was estimated to have claimed 16 per cent of the American armour lost.

▲ M45 Medium Tank

Eighth United States Army / 6th Tank Battalion

The close infantry support version of the US M26 Pershing heavy tank, the M45 mounted a powerful 105mm (4.1in) howitzer. Production was begun in the summer of 1945, and the M45 designation standardized after World War II. The 6th Tank Battalion fought in defence of the Pusan Perimeter in 1950.

Specifications

Crew: 5
Weight: 41.86 tonnes (41.2 tons)
Length: 8.61m (28ft 3in)
Width: 3.51m (11ft 6in)
Height: 2.77m (9ft 1in)
Engine: 373kW (500hp) Ford GAF V8 petrol
Speed: 48km/h (30mph)
Range: 161km (100 miles)
Armament: 1 x 105mm (4.1in) M4 howitzer,
    plus 1 x 12.7mm (0.5in) AA HMG and
    2 x 7.62mm (0.3in) MGs (1 coaxial and
    1 ball-mounted in hull front)
Radio: SCR508/528

▲ M46A1 Patton Medium Tank

Eighth United States Army / 7th Infantry Division / 73rd Heavy Tank Battalion

During the winter of 1950/51, the M46 Patton tanks of the 73rd Heavy Tank Battalion operated with elements of the 7th Infantry Division. The unit was commended for its eventual participation in six campaigns of the Korean War.

Specifications

Crew: 5
Weight: 44 tonnes (43.3 tons)
Length: 8.48m (27ft 10in)
Width: 3.51m (11ft 6in)
Height: 3.18m (10ft 5in)
Engine: 604kW (810hp) Continental AVDS-1790-
    5A V12 air-cooled twin turbo petrol

Speed: 48km/h (30mph)
Range: 130km (81 miles)
Armament: 90mm (3.5in) M3A1 gun;
    1 x 12.7mm (0.5in) AA HMG;
    2 x 7.62mm (0.3in) M1919A4 MGs
Radio: SCR508/528

◀ M29C Weasel

Eighth United States Army

Designed by the Studebaker company for use in snow, the M29 Weasel was utilized in Korea as a supply and personnel transport vehicle. The M29C was equipped with flotation tanks.

Specifications

Crew: 4

Weight: 3.9 tonnes (3.8 tons)

Length: 3.2m (10ft 6in)

Width: 1.5m (5ft)

Height: 1.8m (5ft 11in)

Engine: 48kW (70hp) Studebaker Model 6-170
   Champion

Speed: 58km/h (36mph)

Range: 426km (265 miles)

Specifications

Crew: 5

Weight: 33.7 tonnes (33.16 tons)

Length: 7.57m (24ft 10in)

Width: 3m (9ft 10in)

Height: 2.97m (9ft 9in)

Engine: 372.5kw (500hp) Ford GAA 8-cylinder
   petrol

Speed: 42km/h (26mph)

Range: 161km (100 miles)

Armament: 1 x 76mm (3in) M1A1 gun,
   plus 2 x 7.62mm MGs (1 coaxial and
   1 ball-mounted in hull front)

Radio: SCR508

▲ M4A3E8 Sherman Medium Tank

Eighth United States Army / 89th Tank Battalion

Although not as powerful as the Pershing or Patton tanks, the World War II-era Sherman was widely used in the Korean War by the US Army. The M4A3E8 Sherman and T-34/85 were comparable and could destroy each other when hit.

▲ M8 Armored Car

Republic of Korea (ROK) Army / 1st Capitol Division

At the beginning of the Korean War, the M8 Greyhound was the largest and most powerful armoured vehicle allocated to the Republic of Korea Army by the United States.

Specifications

Crew: 4

Weight: 8.12 tonnes (8 tons)

Length: 5m (16ft 5in)

Width: 2.54m (8ft 4in)

Height: 2.25m (7ft 5in)

Engine: 82kW (110hp) Hercules JXD 6-cylinder petrol

Speed: 89km/h (55mph)

Range: 563km (350 miles)

Armament: 1 x 37mm (1.5in) M6 gun, plus 1
   x 12.7mm (0.5in) AA HMG and 1 x coaxial
   7.62mm (0.3in) MG

Radio: SCR508

◀ GAZ 67B Command Vehicle
North Korean People's Army

The GAZ 67B was one of a series of multi-purpose Soviet-built vehicles of World War II which were provided to the North Korean armed forces. Inspired by the famous American jeep, the GAZ 67 was first produced in 1943.

Specifications

Crew: 1 driver	Engine: 37.25kW (50hp) 4-cylinder petrol
Weight: 1.32 tonnes (1.3 tons)	Speed: 90km/h (56mph)
Length: 3.35m (11ft)	Range: 450km (280miles)
Width: 1.685m (5ft 6in)	Radio: n/k
Height: 1.7m (5ft 7in)	

Specifications
Crew:
Weight: 5.1 tonnes (5 tons)
Length: 4.65m (15ft 3in)
Width: 2.1m (6ft 11in)
Height: 2.2m (7ft 3in)
Engine: 30kW (40hp) GAZ-A
Speed: 55km/h (34mph)
Range: 200km (124 miles)
Armament: 45mm (1.8in) 20-K gun;
  2 x 7.62mm (0.3in) DT MGs

▲ BA-6 Armoured Car
North Korean People's Army

The BA-6 armoured car was developed in the Soviet Union during the early 1930s and usually mounted a 45mm (1.8in) cannon atop a primitive turret. By the time of the Korean War, the vehicle was obsolescent.

▲ IS-2 Heavy Tank
Chinese People's Volunteer Army, 1953

According to Chinese accounts, Soviet-made IS-2 heavy tanks were committed to the Korean front. However, US and UN forces do not report encountering the powerful IS-2 in combat.

Specifications

Crew: 4	Speed: 37km/h (23mph)
Weight: 46 tonnes (45.27tons)	Range: 240km (149 miles)
Length: 9.9m (32ft 6in)	Radio: 10R
Width: 3.09m (10ft 2in)	Armament: 1 x 122mm (4.8in) D-25T gun, plus 3
Height: 2.73m (8ft 11in)	x 7.62mm (0.3in) DT MGs (1 coaxial, 1 fixed in
Engine: 382.8kW (513hp) V-2 12-cylinder diesel	bow, 1 ball-mounted in turret rear)

Seoul
July 1950 – September 1951

The war-torn city of Seoul endured four separate battles for control of the South Korean seat of government in a 10-month period during the Korean War.

CONTROL OF THE SOUTH KOREAN capital city changed hands several times during the first year of war in Korea. Within a week of the opening of hostilities, North Korean forces had captured Seoul; however, their hold was to be short-lived. By September 1950, United Nations forces under the command of General Douglas MacArthur had initiated the breakout from the Pusan Perimeter and brilliantly executed the amphibious end run at the port city of Inchon, and a bloody fight for the city ensued. In December 1950, the intervention of communist China sent the UN forces reeling, and Seoul was again under the control of invaders. The following spring, UN forces recaptured Seoul for the final time prior to stalemate, negotiation and armistice.

The arrival of American armoured units on the Korean peninsula in the autumn of 1950 had been critical in the stabilization of the front at Pusan, blunting the advance of the North Korean People's Army. The latter was spearheaded by columns of the battle-tested T-34 tank supplied by the Soviet Union and client states of the Eastern bloc and supported by self-propelled artillery such as the widely produced SU-76. Control of the air by UN forces was another essential element in the defence against communist armoured formations.

Although tanks were involved in most major battles of the Korean War, the mountainous and forested terrain that covered much of the country was not conducive to large-scale armoured operations. As the war continued, therefore, the number of tank battles declined. One of the larger concentrations of armoured units during the Korean War occurred during the second battle for Seoul in September 1950.

Inchon and beyond
Following the landing at Inchon on 15 September, the advance towards Seoul was slow and painful. UN air power took its toll on exposed North Korean

▲ **Light Tank M24**

Eighth United States Army / 25th Infantry Division / 79th Tank Battalion

Mounting 75mm (2.9in) main guns, the M24 Chaffee light tanks of the US Army's 79th Tank Battalion engaged the North Koreans in the summer of 1950 at the Han River during Operation Ripper, and in other offensive actions during the spring of 1951.

Specifications

Crew: 5	Speed: 55km/h (34mph)
Weight: 18.28 tonnes (18 tons)	Range: 282km (175 miles)
Length: 5.49m (18ft)	Armament: 1 x 75mm (2.9in) M6 gun, plus 1 x
Width: 2.95m (9ft 8in)	12.7mm (0.5in) HMG on AA mount and
Height: 2.46m (8ft 1in)	2 x 7.62mm (0.3in) MGs (1 coaxial,
Engine: 2 x 82kW (110hp) Cadillac 44T24	1 ball-mounted in hull front)
V8 petrol	Radio: SCR 508

T-34s operating in daylight. Successive North Korean counterattacks were beaten back, and the M26 gained a slight upper hand in tank-versus-tank actions. On the morning of the landings, American aircraft destroyed three North Korean T-34s with 227kg (500lb) bombs, while three more were destroyed by M26 Pershings of the US Marines.

The following day, Pershing tanks of D Company, 5th Marines destroyed five more T-34s, while a sixth was dispatched with bazooka fire. Only one Marine was wounded, while over 200 North Korean soldiers were killed in the engagement.

During the advance towards Seoul on 17 September, M26s of the 1st Marines destroyed four T-34s, and

Specifications

Crew: 5	Speed: 48km/h (30mph)
Weight: 28.14 tonnes (27.7 tons)	Range: 241km (150 miles)
Length: 6.15m (20ft 2in)	Armament: 1 x 90mm (3.5in) M3 gun,
Width: 3.05m (10ft)	plus 1 x 12.7mm (0.5in) AA HMG
Height: 2.72m (8ft 11in)	Radio: SCR610
Engine: 373kW (500hp) Ford GAA V8 petrol	

▲ 90mm Gun Motor Carriage, M36 Tank Destroyer
Eighth United States Army

Deployed late in World War II, the M36 tank destroyer, with its 90mm (3.5in) main weapon, was effective against enemy armour in Korea. Many of those deployed in Korea added a ball-mounted machine gun in the hull.

▲ Sherman M4A3 (76)W Dozer
Eighth United States Army / 3rd Engineer Combat Battalion (Hyzer's Tigers II)

This Sherman M4A3 (76)W Dozer operated with Hyzer's Tigers II, the US Army's 3rd Engineer Combat Battalion, during Operations Ripper and Killer in the spring of 1951. Note the tank's 76mm (3in) main cannon.

Specifications

Crew: 5	C1 petrol
Weight: 33.65 tonnes (33.1 tons)	Speed: 48km/h (30mph)
Length: 6.27m (20ft 7in) (with sandshields)	Range: 193km (120 miles)
Width: 3m (9ft 10in)	Armament: 76mm (3in) M1A1 gun; 1 x 12.7mm
Height: 2.97m (9ft 9in)	(0.5in) M2HB MG; 1 x 7.62mm (0.3in) M1919A4
Engine: 298 kW (400hp) Continental R975	coaxial MG
	Radio: SCR508/528/538

two days later elements of the 1st Marines struck again, wiping out a battalion of North Korean troops and five T-34s. In a small-scale tank battle, typical of those which occurred during the Korean War, tanks of B Company, 73rd Tank Battalion engaged a pair of North Korean T-34s, with each side losing a tank.

On 22 September, the US Marine vanguard of the UN forces entered the capital city, and Seoul was officially declared liberated three days later. Meanwhile, North Korean forces still engaged to the south near Pusan were rapidly in danger of being cut off. However, the UN objective of liberating Seoul took precedence and more than 30,000 North Korean soldiers were allowed to withdraw.

The UN advance continued to the Chinese frontier, and MacArthur appeared poised to cross the Yalu River, significantly widening the war. In December, the People's Republic of China launched a massive attack that drastically altered the military situation in Korea.

▲ OT-34/76 Medium Tank

North Korean People's Army

Supplied by the Soviet Union, the T-34/76 equipped the early armoured formations of the North Korean People's Army. First produced in 1940, the tank was revolutionary in its day, combining sloped armour for added protection with a powerful 76mm (3in) gun. The OT-34 was a flamethrower model, developed during World War II and first deployed in 1944. The OT-34 carried 200 litres (44 gallons) of fuel and could be effective up to a range of 90m (98 yards).

Specifications

Crew: 4
Weight: 26.5 tonnes (26.2 tons)
Length: 5.92m (19ft 5in)
Width: 3m (9ft 10in)
Height: 2.44m (8ft)
Engine: 373kW (500hp) V-2-34 V12 diesel
Speed (road): 53km/h (33mph)
Range: 400km (250 miles)
Armament: 1 x 76mm (3in) F-34 gun;
 1 x ATO-41 flamethrower (hull-mounted);
 1 x 7.62mm (0.3in) DT MG (coaxial)
Radio: 10R

Specifications

Crew: 5
Weight: 32 tonnes (31.5 tons)
Length: 6m (19ft 7in)
Width: 3m (9ft 10in)
Height: 2.6m (8ft 6in)
Engine: 372 kW (493hp) V-2 V12 diesel
Speed (road): 55km/h (33mph)
Range: 360km (223 miles)
Armament: 1 x 85mm (3.4in) ZiS-S-53 cannon;
 2 x 7.62mm (0.3in) DT MGs (1 in the bow and
 1 coaxial)
Radio: 10R

▼ Type 58 (T34/85) Medium Tank

Chinese People's Volunteer Army

The Type 58 was a Chinese copy of the Soviet T-34/85 Model 1944. The upgunned successor to the T-34/76, the T-34/85 medium tank mounted an 85mm (3.4in) cannon. In Korea the 85mm (3.4in) cannon was capable of knocking out the latest in United Nations tanks.

Imjin River
APRIL–MAY 1951

The Centurion tank stood tall while the British 29th Infantry Brigade achieved legendary status during an epic battle against overwhelming odds. A major Chinese offensive against Seoul was stalled in the process.

WHEN THE BRITISH ARMY'S 8th King's Royal Irish Hussars arrived at Pusan on 14 November 1950, they brought with them three squadrons of the heavy Centurion Mk 3 tank, equipped with 84mm (3.3in/20-pounder) main cannon. Although the Centurion had been developed during World War II as a counter-measure to the superb German PzKpfw V Panther medium and PzKpfw VI Tiger tanks, it gained lasting fame on the battlefield in Korea.

The 51.8-tonne (51-ton) Centurion had been developed too late to take on the German armour in Western Europe, instead emerging in late 1945 as the primary British battle tank of the early Cold War era. Intended to eventually supplant earlier designs such as the Churchill and the Cromwell, the Centurion was originally armed with a 76mm (3in/17-pounder) main weapon. By the time of its deployment to Korea, the Mk 3 variant included not only the heavier gun but also additional storage positions for track links on the glacis and a stabilizer for the main weapon. Powerful though it was, the

Centurion in the Korean War is best remembered for crucial infantry support rather than direct encounters with communist armour.

The earliest of 12 eventual Centurion marks, or variants, was powered by a 485kW (650hp) Rolls-Royce Meteor Mk IVB engine, and while the tank's limited range and relatively low speed were significant shortcomings, its overall performance was strong enough that some observers believed it capable of multiple roles as the 'universal tank' of the British Army.

Stand on the Imjin
On 22 April 1951, communist Chinese forces launched a spring offensive against the United Nations lines north of Seoul, the South Korean capital. The Chinese plan involved the quick exploitation of a breakthrough along the lower Imjin River, and powerful communist forces attacked positions held by the British 29th Infantry Brigade. A rapid breakthrough might have outflanked

▲ **Centurion Mk 3 Main Battle Tank**

British Commonwealth Occupation Force (BCOF) / 29th Infantry Brigade / 8th King's Royal Irish Hussars

During nearly two decades of production, more than 4400 Centurion tanks were produced in a dozen or so variants. The Mk 3 shown incorporated additional machine-gun mounts and was later upgunned to a 105mm (4.1in) main weapon.

Specifications

Crew: 4	Engine: 485 kW (650hp) Rolls-Royce Meteor
Weight: 51.8 tonnes (51 tons)	Speed: 34km/h (21mph)
Length: 7.6m (25ft)	Range: 450km (280 miles)
Width: 3.38m (11ft 1in)	Armament: 84mm (20pdr) gun, plus
Height: 3.01m (9ft 10in)	1 x 7.62mm (0.3in) Browning MG
	Radio: n/k

supporting United Nations units to the east and west, unhinged the enemy line and opened the way to Seoul. Through the course of the coming battle, British, Belgian, US, Filipino and South Korean troops engaged the Chinese.

Battling overwhelming odds, the British and Belgians suffered tremendous losses but slowed the Chinese advance. A combined force of Filipino M24 Chaffee light tanks and Centurions of the 8th Hussars attempted to relieve a nearly surrounded position held by the 1st Battalion, The Gloucestershire Regiment on Hill 235. However, the lead tank was destroyed by Chinese fire and the effort was halted 1830m (2000 yards) from the Glosters' position. As the remnants of the 29th Infantry Brigade retreated from a series of hills it had heroically defended for several days, the Centurions of the 8th Hussars covered the withdrawal and lost five tanks in the process, three of these to enemy fire.

Centurions in the thick of it

The sheer weight of Chinese numbers at times overwhelmed the British positions near the Imjin River, and repeatedly the tanks of the 8th Hussars braved enemy artillery fire to rescue pockets of trapped infantrymen. Although supported by their own infantry, the tanks were assailed by Chinese soldiers attempting to pry turrets and hatches open to drop grenades inside. Turning their machine guns on one another, the buttoned-up tanks mowed

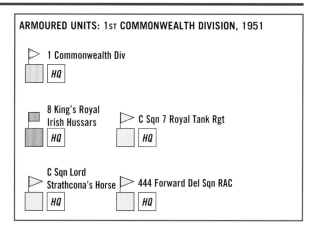

ARMOURED UNITS: 1ST COMMONWEALTH DIVISION, 1951

1 Commonwealth Div HQ

8 King's Royal Irish Hussars HQ

C Sqn 7 Royal Tank Rgt HQ

C Sqn Lord Strathcona's Horse HQ

444 Forward Del Sqn RAC HQ

down the Chinese infantrymen clinging to their hulls. One eyewitness remembered three platoons of Chinese soldiers emerging from a riverbed and being devastated by the guns of the Centurions. Major Henry Huth, commander of C Squadron, 8th Hussars, received the Distinguished Service Order (DSO) for his heroism at the Imjin River, and described the withdrawal of the 29th Infantry Brigade as 'one long, bloody ambush'.

The tanks of the 8th Hussars evacuated a large number of troops while under fire. One soldier remembered, 'We were told there was a chance that we wouldn't get through and that we'd be safer going up the hills, but anyway two or three of us took the chance and climbed up on the back of the tank. The Chinese were still running alongside the tanks,

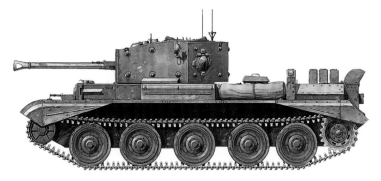

▲ **Cruiser Mk VIII Cromwell IV**

British Commonwealth Occupation Force (BCOF) / 29th Infantry Brigade /
8th King's Royal Irish Hussars

Developed in the early 1940s, the British Cromwell tank marked a comprehensive design effort to combine speed, firepower and armour protection in a single package. The Cromwell was largely outmoded by 1950.

Specifications

Crew: 5	V12 petrol
Weight: 27.94 tonnes (27.5 tons)	Speed: 64km/h (40mph)
Length: 6.35m (20ft 10in)	Range: 280km (174 miles)
Width: 2.9m (9ft 6in)	Armament: 1 x 75mm (2.9in) OQF gun,
Height: 2.49m (8ft 2in)	plus 2 x 7.92mm (0.31in) Besa MGs
Engine: 447kW (600hp) Rolls-Royce Meteor	Radio: Wireless Set No. 19

throwing grenades on to the tanks, trying to disable them. I mean we couldn't do a lot about it because we had nothing left, we just laid there quiet and still, watching them, listening to them actually being crushed by the tank tracks.'

Although the terrain near the Imjin was far from ideal tank country, the 8th Hussars had played a key role in facilitating the withdrawal of the 29th Infantry Brigade and sapping the strength of the Chinese offensive. One American officer noted, 'In their Centurions, the 8th Hussars have evolved a new type of tank warfare. They taught us that anywhere a tank can go is tank country, even the tops of mountains.'

The Chinese 63rd Army reportedly sustained more than 10,000 casualties during the Battle of the Imjin River and was withdrawn from combat. The 29th Infantry Brigade lost nearly 1100 killed, wounded and captured.

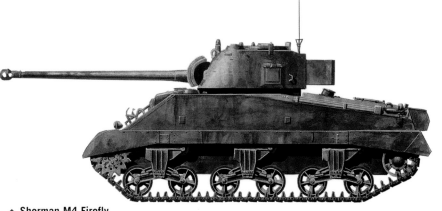

▲ **Sherman M4 Firefly**

British Commonwealth Occupation Force (BCOF)

A World War II British improvement to the original 75mm (2.9in) main armament version of the Sherman tank was known as the Firefly. Upgraded with the 76mm (3in/17-pounder) high-velocity gun for increased firepower, the Firefly was deployed to Korea as well.

Specifications

Crew: 4
Weight: 32.7 tonnes (32.18 tons)
Length: 7.85m (25ft 9in)
Width: 2.67m (8ft 9in)
Height: 2.74m (8ft 11in)
Engine: 316.6kW (425hp) Chrysler Multibank
  A57 petrol
Speed: 40km/h (24.8mph)
Range: 161km (100 miles)
Armament: 1 x 76mm (3in) 17pdr OQF,
  plus 1 x coaxial 7.62mm (0.3in) MG
Radio: Wireless Set No. 19

▲ **M4A3 Sherman Flail**

British Commonwealth Occupation Force (BCOF) / 7th Royal Tank Regiment / C Squadron

The M4A3 Sherman Flail was one of many variants of the World War II workhorse tank which continued in service throughout the Korean War. The flail apparatus mounted on the chassis was intended to detonate landmines.

Specifications

Crew: 5	Speed: 46km/h (29mph)
Weight: 31.8 tonnes (31.3 tonnes)	Range: 100km (62 miles)
Length: 8.23m (27ft)	Armament: 1 x 75mm (2.9in) M3 gun,
Width: 3.5m (11ft 6in)	plus 1 x 12.7mm (0.5in) AA HMG and
Height: 2.7m (9ft)	1 x 7.62mm (0.3in) MG
Engine: 373kW (500hp) Ford GAA V8 petrol	Radio: Wireless Set No. 19

▶ Daimler Scout Car

British Commonwealth Occupation Force (BCOF)

Produced throughout World War II by the British, the lightly armed and armoured Daimler Scout Car proved so successful that its service life was extended through the Korean conflict.

Specifications

Crew: 2
Weight: 3.22 tonnes (3.2 tons)
Length: 3.23m (10ft 5in)
Width: 1.72m (5ft 8in)
Height: 1.5m (4ft 11in)
Engine: 41kW (55hp) Daimler 6-cylinder petrol
Speed: 89km/h (55mph)
Range: 322km (200 miles)
Armament: 1 x 7.62mm (0.3in) MG
Radio: Wireless Set No. 19

HQ (1 x M10 tank destroyer)

Tank Destroyer Squadron, Lord Strathcona's Horse (Canada)

During and after the Korean War, from 1951 to 1954, A, B and C Squadrons of Lord Strathcona's Horse served in rotation with the 1st Commonwealth Division. A tank squadron was divided into five troops of three tanks each plus one tank as HQ vehicle. Initially equipped with the American M10 tank destroyer, the regiment later received the M4A3 Sherman tank. The 1st Commonwealth Division encompassed all British Commonwealth land units in Korea after July 1951, including troops from Britain, Canada, Australia, New Zealand and India.

Troop 1 (3 x M10 tank destroyer)

Troop 2 (3 x M10 tank destroyer)

Troop 3 (3 x M10 tank destroyer)

Troop 4 (3 x M10 tank destroyer)

Troop 5 (3 x M10 tank destroyer)

Chapter 3

The Vietnam War, 1965–75

For many observers, the employment of armoured forces during the Vietnam War might well deserve only a footnote to the overall prosecution of a conflict which raged, hot and cold, for more than 30 years. The attitudes of commanders were shaped largely by the combat experiences of World War II, Korea and the limited use of armour during France's ill-fated attempt to sustain its colonial empire in the Far East. In fact, the continued prosecution of the war in Vietnam led to improvisation and the eventual realization that armour could, in certain circumstances, prove to be decisive in combat.

◀ **Aussie armour**
Crew from the Royal Australian Armoured Corps (RAAC) service their Centurion tank. Between 1967 and 1970 the Australians employed 58 Centurions in Vietnam, mostly providing a fire base for infantry operations.

Introduction

The notion of mechanized combat in Vietnam was for many military strategists as remote as Asia itself as NATO and the Soviet Bloc were fully engaged in the throes of the Cold War.

DURING THE VIETNAM ERA, armoured doctrine for both the United States and the Soviet Union was decidedly centred on 'Battlefield Europe'. Surely, if armour were to be utilized on a grand scale, such events would occur in the West. Large tank formations had not participated in the liberation of islands across the Pacific during World War II, and the China–Burma–India theatre had not seen major clashes of armour.

As the US military presence in Vietnam gradually increased, the role of the tank was considered limited at best. During the Korean War, tanks had served a purpose; however, the perspective of time had not refined the contribution made to the United Nations effort there. Furthermore, the French experience in Vietnam had apparently offered a lesson in the use of armour in Southeast Asia. By the spring of 1954, the French armed forces in what was then Indochina included more than 450 tanks and tank destroyers along with nearly 2000 half-tracks, armoured cars and amphibious tracked vehicles. Much of this materiel had been acquired through American aid and consisted of the M24 Chaffee light tank, M4 Sherman and other vehicles of World War II vintage.

The French deployed a few tanks in the defence of the doomed airhead at Dien Bien Phu, and these had been unable to stem the communist Viet Minh assault. Aside from that disastrous defeat in the far north of Indochina, the debacle which befell a French task force known as *Groupement Mobile* 100 weighed heavily on Western armoured doctrine, or lack thereof, in Southeast Asia. *Groupement Mobile* 100, wrongly assessed as an armoured formation by many, actually included infantry, armoured and support units. Hastily evacuated from an exposed position, the French force was set upon and nearly annihilated by Viet Minh forces in the spring of 1954.

Terrain timidity

US military planners were wary of Vietnam's dense jungle, rice paddies and interior mountains of the Central Highlands, and General William Westmoreland, who would later command American troops in Vietnam, remarked matter-of-factly, 'Except for a few coastal areas …Vietnam is no place for either tanks or mechanized infantry units.'

Indicative of the US preoccupation with massive armoured assaults on the plains of northern Europe was the fact that in the early 1960s the US Army field manual for the operations of an armoured brigade included a single section of only 14 pages dealing with tactics in difficult terrain. Armoured formations, it said, should bypass such areas and allow infantry to clear them. The fatal flaw in such doctrine, which mirrored the failed French attitude, was that by definition armour would be vulnerable while confined to the few suitable roads. While the US military establishment asserted officially that the tank was 'not appropriate for counter-insurgency operations', combat conditions in Vietnam would eventually prove otherwise.

In addition to the hazards of jungle and mountain, the rainy season in Southeast Asia presented another obstacle to armoured operations. Certain geographic areas of Vietnam were actually designated off limits to tanks, armoured personnel carriers and other tracked vehicles during the months of the monsoon. However, a 1967 survey of the country by a group of US officers familiar with the capabilities of the frontline tanks in the American arsenal – particularly the M24 Chaffee, M41 Walker Bulldog and M48 Patton – indicated that nearly half of Vietnam was suitable for the use of armour during much of the year.

Increasing influence

By the time the communist Tet Offensive had been blunted in the winter of 1968, the concentrated firepower of the tank had proven itself a valuable weapon in Vietnam. Actually, the scope of the armoured vehicle had widened considerably as first South Vietnamese and then American and Australian troops adapted the M113 armoured personnel carrier into a true fighting vehicle with the addition of machine guns, a gun shield and even a small turret. Meanwhile, communist forces gained in armoured proficiency as the war dragged on. The growing number of North Vietnamese Army formations in the South included armoured units consisting of Soviet-built PT-76 amphibious tanks, T-34 variants and the later T-54/55 main battle tanks fielded by this well-trained communist army and to a lesser extent the insurgent Viet Cong.

In Vietnam, the anti-tank weapon came of age as well. The communists deployed their lethal shoulder-fired rocket-propelled grenade (RPG) in great numbers, and the US fielded the LAW and wire-guided TOW missiles. Powerful anti-tank mines took their toll and slowed the progress of armour considerably. Capable of destroying some tanks and lightly armoured vehicles or blowing the tread off a heavier tank, many of these were planted on roadways or rigged as booby traps.

Find and fix

Perhaps the greatest contrast to more than half a century of US armoured doctrine was the altered role of the tank in battle in Vietnam. Certainly, the tank's firepower in direct support of infantry operations was undeniable. Its mobility, albeit limited at times, was significant. Its psychological impact was notable.

However, in previous wars the tank had been envisioned and employed as the mailed fist which exploited the breakthrough of the enemy lines. Defined battle lines were seldom seen in Vietnam. The enemy often hit hard and then melted into the jungle or countryside. Therefore, to a great extent the tank became the 'fixer' of the enemy, joining battle, taking hold and pounding away with heavy weaponry. In conjunction with tanks and supporting infantry, the concept of airmobile warfare was implemented. Rather than the tank slashing through the enemy rear, combat infantrymen transported by helicopter could often serve as the enveloping force.

Although it must be acknowledged that Southeast Asia was far from an ideal proving ground for large tank formations to operate in, it was nevertheless indicative of the fighting which was to take place in other parts of the world as the superpowers fought proxy wars and avoided the direct confrontation for which they had so long prepared.

▲ **Light support**
French forces employed the versatile M24 Chaffee light tank in Indochina from the early 1950s. The tank proved ideal in the infantry support role, especially in mountainous and jungle terrain.

US/ARVN forces
1965–75

US and South Vietnamese forces came to rely on the armoured fighting vehicle in routine operations against an elusive enemy, although direct armoured confrontations were rare.

B Y THE SUMMER OF 1969, the United States had deployed more than 600 tanks and 2000 other armoured vehicles to combat areas in Vietnam. This was in sharp contrast to the initial belief among ranking military strategists that armour would be of little or no value in fighting a lightly armed insurgency. Possibly the American perspective changed as better trained and more heavily armed North Vietnamese Army units appeared in the South.

Regardless, the markedly changed point of view may be best illustrated by the directive of General William Westmoreland, a one-time opponent of armour in Vietnam, which followed the Tet Offensive of 1968. Westmoreland asserted that future reinforcements sent to Southeast Asia should be armoured, rather than infantry. Doubtless, he recalled that the first American tanks had arrived in Vietnam somewhat by accident when the organic armour of 3rd Platoon, Company B, 3rd Marine Tank Battalion arrived at Da Nang on 9 March

1965 with the Marine Battalion Landing Team. Apparently, some commanders already 'in country' had not realized that M48A3 Patton tanks were included in the force.

Another US Marine Battalion Landing Team came ashore in South Vietnam in August, and this was followed by the first US Army armoured units in Vietnam with elements of the 1st Infantry Division. In one of their first recorded actions during the Vietnam War, Marine tanks took part in Operation Starlite in the summer of 1965. During two days of heavy fighting, the tanks were instrumental in destroying numerous Viet Cong strongpoints, capturing a large number of weapons and killing 68 insurgents. Seven tanks were damaged in the fighting, and one was considered beyond repair.

Early in the war, US infantry brigades were often supported by a cavalry troop, which primarily consisted of the M114, and later the M113, armoured personnel carrier. Most of the heavy M48A3 tanks

▲ **M41A3 Light Gun Tank 'Bulldog'**

Army of the Republic of Viet Nam (ARVN)

In 1964 the M41 light tank was selected to replace the M24 Chaffee light tank, which the ARVN had inherited from the French. The first M41A3s arrived in January 1965, equipping five ARVN squadrons. The tanks entered combat in October 1965, when 15 M41s joined the relief force for the besieged Plei Mei Special Forces camp.

Specifications

Crew: 5	12-cylinder petrol
Weight: 46,500kg (102,533lb)	Speed: 21km/h (13.5mph)
Length: 12.3m (40ft 6.5in)	Range: 144km (90 miles)
Width: 3.2m (10ft 8in)	Armament: 1 x 76mm (3in) gun, plus 1 x
Height: 2.4m (8ft 2in)	12.7mm (0.5in) MG and 1 x 7.62mm (0.3in) MG
Engine: 261.1kW (350hp) Bedford	Radio: n/k

which had been deployed with the infantry were held out of the 'jungle fighting'.

Although some convincing was required, tanks were eventually allowed to join in combat operations. Chief among the proponents of armour in Vietnam was Major-General Frederick Weyand, commander of the US 25th Infantry Division, who demanded the deployment of his armoured units, which included the 3rd Squadron, 4th Cavalry; the 1st Battalion, 5th Infantry (Mechanized); and the 1st Battalion, 69th Armor.

In a classic example of the evolving armoured doctrine employed in Vietnam, Task Force Dragoon, consisting of Troops B and C, 1st Squadron, 4th

US Armoured Cavalry Squadron, 1969

The standard US armoured cavalry squadron of the Vietnam era packed substantial firepower, including the ACAV (Armored Cavalry Assault Vehicle) and infantry versions of the M113 armoured personnel carrier, which transported up to 11 combat-ready soldiers. The light M551 Sheridan tank was capable of being transported by air but proved a disappointment in combat. A company of four M48A3 Patton tanks mounted 90mm (3.5in) cannon, and a self-propelled M109 155mm (6.1in) howitzer provided heavy artillery support.

HQ (1 x M577 APC)

Armoured Cavalry Troop (3 x M113 ACAV, 2 x M551 Sheridans, 1 x M113 infantry combat team)

Armoured Cavalry Troop (3 x M113 ACAV. 2 x M551 Sheridans. 1 x M113 infantry combat team)

Howitzer Battery: 1 x M109 155mm SP howitzer

Armoured Cavalry Troop (3 x M113 ACAV. 2 x M551 Sheridans. 1 x M113 infantry combat team)

Tank Company (4 x M48A3 medium tanks)

Cavalry and Company B, 1st Battalion, 2nd Infantry, lured strong Viet Cong forces into a trap near An Loc in July 1966. M48A3 tanks and machine-gun-equipped M113s held onto the enemy while infantry converged from the flanks. At least two M113s were destroyed; however, more than 240 Viet Cong were killed.

Throughout the Vietnam War, the South Vietnamese Army (ARVN) was dependent upon the United States for arms. In the 1950s, ARVN armoured cavalry units were equipped with light tanks and armoured personnel carriers. By 1966, six armoured cavalry squadrons and units equipped solely with tanks were being added to ARVN infantry divisions. In 1969, two armoured brigades were constituted, equipped with tanks and other vehicles. In the spring of 1971, the 20th Tank Regiment was formed and equipped with the M48, and following the communist Easter Offensive the following year two more M48 tank regiments were added.

Specifications

Crew: 4	cooled petrol
Weight: 47,273kg (104,219lb)	Speed: 42km/h (26mph)
Length: 7.3m (23ft 11in)	Range: 216km (134 miles)
Width: 3.6m (11ft 11in)	Armament: 1 x 90mm (3.54in) gun, plus
Height: 3.1m (10ft 2in)	2 x 7.62mm (0.3in) MGs
Engine: 604kW (810hp) AV1790-7C V12 air-	Radio: n/k

▲ M48A1 Medium Tank

11th Armored Cavalry Regiment / 3rd Squadron / Company M

The M48A1 Patton medium tank featured the commander's cupola of the original M48, which allowed the M2HB 12.7mm (0.5in) anti-aircraft machine gun to function, including reloading, from inside the tank. Many early M48s were converted to the M48A3 and deployed to Vietnam.

▲ M48A2 Medium Tank

USMC / 3rd Tank Battalion

The M48A2 included an improved powrplant and transmission, redesigned rear plate, a modified commander's cupola and improved turret control.

Specifications

Crew: 4	Systems AVDS-1790 petrol
Weight: 49,600kg (109,350lb)	Speed: 42km/h (26mph)
Length: 6.95m (22ft 10in)	Range: 216km (160 miles)
Width: 3.6m (11ft 11in)	Armament: 1 x 90mm (3.54in) gun, plus
Height: 3.27m (10ft 9in)	3 x 7.62mm (0.3in) MGs
Engine: 620kW (845hp) General Dynamics Land	Radio: n/k

▲ **M578 Light Recovery Vehicle**

4th US Artillery / 8th Battalion

The M578 light recovery vehicle utilized the same chassis as the M110 203mm (8in) and M107 175mm (6.9in) self-propelled weapons. It was developed to facilitate the changing of the gun barrels, which experienced rapid wear during combat conditions.

Specifications

Crew: 3	Engine: 302kW (405hp) General Motors 8V-71T
Weight: 24,300kg (53,600lb)	8-cylinder diesel
Length: 6.42m (21ft .75in)	Speed: 55km/h (33mph)
Width: 3.15m (10ft 4in)	Range: 725km (450 miles)
Height: 2.92m (9ft 7in)	Armament: 1 x 12.7mm (0.5in) Browning
	M2 HB MG

North Vietnamese forces
1959–75

The armoured forces of the North Vietnamese Army began to take shape in the mid-1950s with the acquisition of armoured cars and half-tracks and the development of anti-tank tactics.

ALTHOUGH THE NORTH VIETNAMESE ARMY had established armoured vehicle units as early as 1956, it emphasized defence and acquired a number of towed anti-tank guns, including the Soviet 57mm (2.24in) and German Pak 40 75mm (2.9in) weapons. In 1959, the 202nd Armoured Regiment, the first tank unit in the North Vietnamese Army, was established. The unit received 35 T-34/85 tanks and 16 SU-76 self-propelled guns, and its designation referred to the 202 members of its command cadre who had been trained in the Soviet Union and China.

By 1965, a formal Armed Forces Directorate had been established to refine armoured doctrine and foster cooperative efforts among infantry, armour and artillery units. The 202nd Armoured Regiment had been expanded to include three battalions and fielded the modern T-54/55 main battle tank, the SU-76 and the PT-76 amphibious tank.

Acknowledging that its armoured assets were limited, reportedly fewer than 100 serviceable tanks, the North Vietnamese Army adopted a philosophy of limited use. Tanks were to be primarily deployed during offensive operations in order to reduce casualties, and only the minimum number of tanks necessary would be engaged at any one time. The close coordination of armour and infantry was deemed essential. It was not until late 1967 that North Vietnamese armour went into harm's way in appreciable strength.

Organization

Although the standard organization of armoured units was generally followed, it was not unusual for detached units to operate independently or for tank battalions to mix vehicle types liberally. A single tank battalion might, for example, include one or more companies of light PT-76 or heavier T-34/85 tanks, and one or more companies of BTR-50 armoured personnel carriers. A complete armoured battalion might include as many as 40 tanks or 35 armoured personnel carriers.

North Vietnamese armoured regiments were reorganized in 1971, and those formed subsequent to the 202nd Armoured Regiment were raised to three battalions, each including three companies of up to 12 tanks or 11 of the Soviet-built BTR-50PK or Chinese-manufactured K-63 armoured personnel carriers. By the 1970s, the People's Republic of China had begun to supply the North Vietnamese with its own Type 59 tank, a copy of the Soviet T-34, and the Type 63, which was quite similar to the amphibious PT-76. China also became the principal supplier of armoured personnel carriers with the K-63.

On those occasions when North Vietnamese armour ventured forward in force, the results were often predictable. US control of the air contributed to heavy losses during the Easter Offensive of 1972, and by mid-June more than 80 tanks had been destroyed. When the offensive ended, over 400 tanks and armoured personnel carriers had been lost. Anti-tank missiles and chance encounters with US and South Vietnamese M48s often left the lightly armoured PT-76 a smoking ruin.

Following the heavy losses of the Easter Offensive, the North Vietnamese replenished their armoured

NVA ARMOURED REGIMENT, 1971			
Type	Number	Vehicle	Strength
Headquarters	–	T34/85	1
Armoured Btn	3		
Headquarters	1	T34/85	1
Armoured Coy	3	T34/85	10
Reconnaissance Ptn	1	T34/85	3–5
Reconnaissance Btn	1		
Headquarters	1	BTR-40	1
Light Tank Coy	1	T34/85	7–10
Recce Coy	2	BTR-60PA	5
AA Battery	1	BTR-40A or ZSU-57-2	2

formations with more T-54/55s, T-34/85s and PT-76s supplied by the Soviets. Tactics were revised to include two offensive options, the sudden assault, which would shock the enemy and open the way for the deep thrust, which would then wreak havoc in the enemy rear.

On the eve of the decisive 1975 offensive against the ARVN, now fighting alone, the North Vietnamese Army could boast nine armoured regiments organized into 29 battalions with more than 600 tanks and 400 other armoured vehicles. The outcome of the final assault was a foregone conclusion, and the image of a T-54 crashing through the gate of the presidential palace in Saigon is an icon of the communist victory.

▲ **T-34/85M Medium Tank**

North Vietnamese Army / 202nd Armoured Regiment

The Soviet-built T-34/85 medium tank was a mainstay of the early armoured formations of the North Vietnamese Army. The T-34/85M, also known as the Model 1969, was developed in the late 1960s, with a V-54 engine, wide, T-55-style road wheels and several other modifications, including an improved radio set and an external fuel pump to ease refuelling.

Specifications

Crew: 5

Weight: 32 tonnes (31.5 tons)

Length: 6m (19ft 7in)

Width: 3m (9ft 10in)

Height: 2.60m (8ft 6in)

Engine: 433 kW (581 hp) Model V-55 12-cyl.

38.88-l diesel

Speed (road): 55km/h (33mph)

Range: 360km (223 miles)

Armament: 1 x 85mm (3.4in) ZiS-S-53 cannon; 2 x 7.62mm (0.3in) DT MGs (bow and coaxial)

Radio: R-123

NVA Armoured Regiment, 1971

At the height of the Vietnam War, the North Vietnamese armoured regiment fielded a complement of more than 90 tanks in three battalions, each comprising three companies, along with reconnaissance platoons and headquarters vehicles. Mechanized infantry was transported by up to 35 BTR-50 or K-63 armoured personnel carriers. By 1975, the North Vietnamese armoured strength had grown to nine regiments and was estimated at 600 tanks and over 400 armoured personnel carriers.

HQ

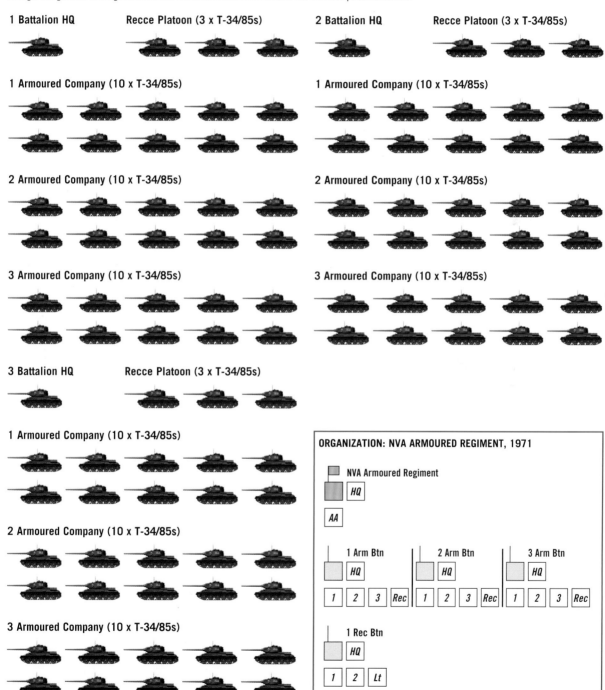

▲ Norinco Type 63 Amphibious Light Tank

NVA / 574th Armoured Regiment

The Chinese Type 63 amphibious light tank resembled the Soviet PT-76 and was first produced in 1963. In 1969, North Vietnam placed an order for 150 of the Type 63, and these tanks were delivered during the following three years.

Specifications

Crew: 4

Weight: 18,400kg (40,572lb)

Length: 8.44m (27ft 8in)

Width: 3.2m (10ft 6in)

Height: 2.52m (8ft 4in)

Engine: 298kW (400bhp) Model 12150-L V12

diesel

Speed: 64km/h (40mph)

Range: 370km (230 miles)

Armament: 1 x 85mm (3.4in) gun, plus 1 x 12.7mm (0.5in) HMG and 1 x 7.62mm (0.3in) MG

Radio: n/k

▲ BTR-40 Amphibious Armoured Scout Car

NVA / 198th Armoured Battalion

Indicative of the Soviet preference for wheeled armoured personnel carriers in the years following World War II, the BTR-40 was exported in large numbers to North Vietnam and also served as a command, reconnaissance and scout vehicle during the Vietnam War.

Specifications

Crew: 2 + 8

Weight: 5300kg (11,660lb)

Length: 5m (16ft 5in)

Width: 1.9m (6ft 3in)

Height: 1.75m (5ft 9in)

Engine: 60kW (80hp) GAZ-40 6-cylinder

Speed: 80km/h (50mph)

Range: 285km (178 miles)

Armament: 1 x 7.62mm (0.3in) MG

Specifications

Crew: 6

Weight: 28,100kg (61,820lb)

Length: 8.48m (27ft 10in)

Width: 3.27m (10ft 9in)

Height: 2.75m (9ft)

Engine: 388kW (520hp) Model V-54 V12 diesel

Speed: 50km/h (31mph)

Range: 420km (260 miles)

Armament: 2 x 57mm (2.24in) anti-aircraft guns

Radio: n/k

▲ ZSU-57-2 SP Anti-Aircraft Gun (SPAAG)

NVA / 201st Armoured Regiment

Its twin 57mm (2.24in) anti-aircraft cannon mounted atop the chassis of the T-34 medium tank, the ZSU-57-2 entered service in the mid-1950s and provided the North Vietnamese Army with mobile defence against enemy aircraft during the Vietnam War.

Tet Offensive/Battle for Hue
1968

Direct armoured combat was a rarity during the Vietnam War; however, the employment of the tank and the armoured personnel carrier was pivotal during numerous actions, particularly the defeat of the communist Tet Offensive.

O N 26 JANUARY 1968, less than a week before their commencement of the Tet Offensive, communist forces sent tanks into battle in the South for the first time. Assaulting South Vietnamese positions at Ta May, amphibious PT-76 tanks of the 3rd Company, 198th Armoured Battalion supported troops of the 24th Infantry Regiment, forcing the ARVN soldiers to abandon their position. Moving forward, the North Vietnamese attacked the US Special Forces position at Lang Vei, losing six PT-76s but overwhelming the garrison, which retreated to the US Marine base at Khe Sanh, which was under siege for months to come.

The majority of US and South Vietnamese armour losses in Vietnam were caused by anti-tank weapons such as the B-40 rocket launcher (RPG) and powerful landmines. As the war progressed, additional armour packages were installed on the undersides of many vehicles to minimize casualties and damage from mines. Tanks began to employ screens to detonate RPG rounds before they could directly impact hull or turret armour. North Vietnamese armoured vehicles often fell prey to both tactical and strategic bombers, as well as tank-killing Bell Huey Cobra gunships – heavily armed attack helicopters.

Tanks at Tet

When communist forces launched coordinated attacks throughout the South on 31 January 1968, to coincide with the new year celebration of Tet, regular army and guerrilla forces hit military and civilian targets, creating confusion and spawning a media event in the United States. Militarily, the Tet Offensive proved disastrous for the communists; however, images of fighting in the streets of Saigon, the South Vietnamese capital, and in the grounds of the US embassy provided a propaganda coup for the communists and hastened the US withdrawal from Vietnam.

When US and South Vietnamese forces brought armour to bear, the result was often successful. At

▲ **M706 Commando Light Armored Car**
Army of the Republic of Viet Nam (ARVN)

A multi-purpose light armoured vehicle, the M706 was used for both patrol and escort duties. It proved versatile in an anti-insurgency role, espcially when counter-attacking Viet Cong ambushes and hit-and-run raids.

Specifications

Crew: 3 + 2	Engine: 1 x 151kW (202hp) V-8 diesel engine
Weight: 9888kg (21,753lb)	Speed: 80km/h (50mph)
Length: 5.68m (18ft 8in)	Range: 643km (400 miles)
Width: 2.26m (7ft 5in)	Armament: 2 x 7.62mm (0.3in) MG
Height: 1.98m (6ft 6in)	Radio: n/k

▶ **M67 Flamethrower Tank**

A USMC M67 goes into action near Da Nang, 1969. Based on the M48 tank chassis, 109 M67 tanks were produced.

Quang Ngai City the concentrated firepower of South Vietnamese tanks and M113 armoured personnel carriers cleared the city of communist forces in about eight hours. During the two-day battle at the Pineapple Forest near Tam Ky, armoured cavalry units killed 180 Viet Cong and North Vietnamese soldiers.

Battle for Hue

The longest and most bitter battle during the Tet Offensive was the contest for the provincial capital of Hue, which lasted 26 days. Armoured cavalry and US Marine tanks, some of which mounted flame-throwers, rooted out communist soldiers who had occupied houses and administrative buildings within the walled 'Citadel'. The fighting was heavy, and US tank crews were rotated on a daily basis due to heavy contact, including multiple RPG hits on a single tank.

Although the Marines' M48s had not been intended for close, urban combat and were shown to be vulnerable to anti-tank weapons, their firepower was instrumental in the eventual recapture of Hue. Primitive urban combat tactics were developed, such as the tandem use of the M48 and the six-barrelled self-propelled 106mm (4.17in) Ontos recoilless rifle.

▲ **M48A3 Medium Tank**

1st Infantry Division / 4th Cavalry / 1st Squadron

The M48A3 was the most common type of Patton tank deployed in the Vietnam War. The A3 model included a diesel engine, which was also used by the new M60 tank.

Specifications

Crew: 4	AVDS-1790-2D 12-cylinder diesel
Weight: 48,987kg (107,998lb)	Speed: 48km/h (30mph)
Length: 9.29m (30ft 48in)	Range: 499km (310 miles)
Width: 3.6m (11ft 11in)	Armament: 1 x 90mm (3.4in) gun, plus
Height: 3.25m (10ft 7in)	3 x 7.62mm (0.3in) MGs
Engine: 1 x 558kW (750hp) General Dynamics	Radio: n/k

Several tanks were lost; however, the communists suffered more than 5000 killed and wounded.

Armour against armour

One of the few instances when opposing armour met in combat in Vietnam occurred when PT-76 tanks of the North Vietnamese 4th Armoured Battalion, 202nd Armoured Regiment met M48A3s of the US Army's 1st Battalion, 69th Armor at Ben Het on 3 March 1969. One M48 sustained a direct hit from a 76mm (3in) shell fired by a PT-76; however, the damage was slight. One PT-76 struck a mine and exploded, while two others were destroyed by 90mm (3.5in) fire from the M48s. The North Vietnamese had been surprised by the presence of heavier US armour and retreated.

During the Vietnam War, the US lost approximately 150 M48 and 200 M551 Sheridan tanks, while North Vietnamese armoured losses were known to be considerably higher.

▲ M551 Sheridan Light Tank

4th Armored Cavalry Regiment / 3rd Squadron / Troop A

Designed as a light, airmobile infantry support tank, the M551 Sheridan equipped many armoured cavalry units in Vietnam. The vehicle was susceptible to mines. Although its Shillelagh missile system was disappointing, the 152mm (6in) gun offered welcome firepower.

Specifications

Crew: 4
Weight: 15,830kg (34,826lb)
Length: 6.299m (20ft 8in)
Width: 2.819m (9ft 3in)
Height: 2.946m (9ft 8in)
Engine: 224kW (300hp) 6-cylinder Detroit
    6V-53T diesel

Speed: 70km/h (43mph)
Range: 600km (310 miles)
Armament: 1 x 152mm (6in) gun/missile
    launcher, plus 1 x 12.7mm (0.5in) anti-aircraft
    HMG and 1 x coaxial 7.62mm (0.3in) MG
Radio: n/k

▲ M113A1 Armoured Personnel Carrier

11th Armored Cavalry Regiment

The M113A1 armoured personnel carrier was introduced in 1964 and had the original petrol engine replaced with a reliable 158kW (212hp) diesel. Gun shields and additional machine guns were added, and the M113A1 was later designated ACAV (Armored Cavalry Assault Vehicle).

Specifications

Crew: 2 + 11
Weight: 11,343kg (25,007lb)
Length: 2.52m (8ft 3in)
Width: 2.69m (8ft 10in)
Height (to top of hull): 1.85m (6ft 1in)

Engine: 158kW (212hp) General Motors 6V53
    6-cylinder diesel
Speed: 61km/h (38mph)
Range: 480km (298 miles)
Armament: 1 x 12.7mm (0.5in) HMG
Radio: n/k

Chapter 4

Cold War in Asia

The Cold War and its influence were pervasive around the globe, and geopolitical wrangling, territorial disputes and religious fervour fuelled conflict throughout the twentieth century. With the end of World War II, the newly independent or reconstituted nations of the Far East and Central Asia grappled with national identity. Borders were drawn, and governments raised armies, alternately for defence and for conquest, often eagerly supplied by the superpowers. Spheres of influence emerged. Like no other symbol of military might, tanks and armoured fighting vehicles became the core elements of these armies and engaged in some of the largest clashes of armour since World War II.

◀ **Captured M47**

Indian civilians examine a knocked-out US-built M47 tank during the Indo-Pakistan War of 1965. Although the M47 was outdated by the early 1960s, it was still capable of taking on lighter opposition armour, such as the M4A3 Shermans employed by the Indian Army, as well as playing an infantry support role.

Introduction

The armoured formations of numerous Asian countries constituted the backbone of large armies and provided a proving ground for advancing technology, both in the modern design of the tank and in defence against it.

THE VAST CONTINENT OF ASIA, its oil-rich central region, the natural resources and raw materials in the southeast, its immense population and the preeminent colossi of its two communist powers – the Soviet Union and the People's Republic of China – often took centre stage in military conflict during the Cold War.

Exerting their influence throughout the region, the Soviet Union, China and the United States vied for preeminence in Asia, intent on protecting their supplies of oil, maintaining the security of national borders and blunting the perceived aggression of adversarial states. Simultaneously, there were scores to settle. Religious, ethnic, economic and political animosity simmered just below the surface and, on occasion, erupted in open war.

In December 1980, a report by the US Central Intelligence Agency (CIA) claimed that the Soviet Union had delivered nearly $7 billion in arms and military assistance to Third World countries during the previous year and that more than 50,000 Soviet military advisors were scattered across the globe. While the report may indeed have been accurate, the United States was also fully engaged in the worldwide arms trade. Other nations had joined in as well, including Great Britain, France and the nations of both the Warsaw Pact and NATO. The sale of weaponry provided hard currency to benefit teetering economies, extended spheres of influence and could potentially curb the territorial ambitions of aggressors. A by-product of the burgeoning arms sales bonanza was an illegal weapons trade, particularly in small arms, which resulted in billions of dollars in profits for black marketeers.

Since the 1950s, the United States had believed Pakistan to be a valuable buffer against potential

▲ **Soviet invasion**
Soviet BTR-60 APCs stop by the roadside during operations in Afghanistan, 1980. The BTR-60 proved vulnerable to shoulder-fired rocketpropelled grenades.

expansion into Central Asia. On the other hand, India and the Soviet Union maintained cordial relations. One of the world's poorest and most populous nations, India needed Soviet technology for its economic infrastructure and Soviet tanks to protect against its neighbouring enemy. Thus the inevitable clashes of arms that ensued pitted US tanks of the Patton series, particularly the M47 and M48, and the light M24 Chaffee against the Soviet-built T-54/55, T-62 and light amphibious PT-76.

Far East tensions

During the uneasy peace that followed the Korean War, the communist regime of North Korea continued a costly military build-up to the detriment of its overall economy, while the armed forces of South Korea were supported by US troops stationed in the country. North Korea modernized its armoured forces with tanks of both Soviet and Chinese manufacture and later embarked on its own programme of main battle tank development. In Vietnam, tanks were employed on a somewhat

limited basis, and the tactical deployment of armoured vehicles, their role in combat and their armour protection against a new generation of anti-tank weapons were tested in battle.

The People's Republic of China had long depended on the Soviet Union to equip its armoured units and produced its own version of the venerable T-34 medium tank, the Type 59. Subsequently, China began the development of its own armoured vehicles, including a modern main battle tank.

▶ **War trophy**

Indian troops sit atop a captured Pakistani T-55 after the cessation of hostilities during the Indo-Pakistan War of 1971.

India and Pakistan
1965–80

Heavy casualties and the largest tank battle since World War II failed to resolve a territorial conflict that has persisted into the twenty-first century.

SINCE THE PARTITION OF INDIA in August 1947, the primarily Hindu Republic of India and an Islamic Pakistan have clashed over the disputed border region of Kashmir and the emergence of the independent nation of Bangladesh (formerly East Pakistan). Each nation developed its own substantial armoured force with the assistance of the superpowers, India primarily through the acquisition of arms from the United States, Great Britain, France and later the Soviet Union, and Pakistan, as a counterweight to Soviet influence on the subcontinent, from the United States and the People's Republic of China.

In the mid-1950s, Pakistan and the United States had agreed that the armed forces of Pakistan would include capabilities substantial enough to maintain an uneasy balance with those of India. This included an armoured division and an independent armoured brigade, which would be equipped primarily with American arms. However, when war erupted in 1965, the Pakistani Army had already expanded beyond the limits of its agreement with the United States. This was reportedly in response to a major increase in Indian military strength during the early part of the decade.

The Pakistani 6th Armoured Division was formed less than a year prior to the opening of hostilities with

India in 1965 and included the 100th Independent Armoured Brigade. Subsequently, the United States declined to arm the new division, and existing assets were deployed. At the height of its strength, the 6th Armoured Division consisted of several armoured battalions, including the 10th Guides Cavalry, the 11th PAVO Cavalry, the 13th Lancers and the 22nd Cavalry which had been temporarily attached. The division's armour consisted of more than 160 M48 Patton tanks armed with 90mm (3.5in) main guns and a contingent of M36B tank destroyers, also with 90mm (3.5in) main weapons.

The Pakistani 1st Armoured Division included three armoured brigades, the 3rd, 4th and 5th, which were heavily engaged in the upcoming battle of Assal Uttar and included Patton tanks and motorized infantry. The M24 Chaffee light tank, with a 75mm (2.9in) main weapon, and the battle-tested M4 Sherman, some of which had been modernized, were also part of the Pakistani arsenal.

The Indian Army had at its disposal an array of ageing Sherman tanks, including several that had been upgunned with the high-velocity 75mm (2.9in) French CN 75 50 cannon; the British Centurion Mk 7 mounting the powerful 105mm (4.1in) Royal Ordnance L7 weapon; the French light AMX-13 tank with 75mm (2.9in) or 90mm (3.5in) cannon; and the World War II-vintage US-made M3 Stuart light tank.

When war broke out in 1965, the two Pakistani Army divisions fielded an estimated 15 armoured cavalry regiments, although some of these did operate independently. Each of the cavalry regiments included nearly 50 tanks divided into three squadrons. Along with their large number of M47 and M48 tanks, the Pakistanis were equipped with about 150 M24 Chaffees and 200 M4 Shermans.

By August 1965, Indian relations with the Soviet Union had warmed substantially, and the Indian 7th Light Cavalry received the first shipment to the Indian Army of the Soviet amphibious PT-76 tank, equipped with a 75mm (2.9in) cannon. Three Indian officers had travelled to the Soviet Union to train with Red Army tank crews.

The 1st Armoured Division was the pride of the Indian Army and its only organic armoured division. Some of its components traced their lineage to the early 1800s and the days of British colonial rule. These included the 18th Cavalry, 62nd Cavalry, 2nd Royal Lancers, 7th Light Cavalry, 16th Cavalry, 4th Hodson's Horse, 17th Cavalry and the Poona Horse. Both the 17th Cavalry and the Poona Horse were equipped with the upgunned M4 Shermans and heavy British Centurion tanks. In 1965, the Indian Army consisted of 17 cavalry regiments which included more than 160 AMX-13s, 188 Centurions and a large number of Shermans and Stuarts. The PT-76s were reported to have arrived only hours

▲ **Light Tank M24**

Pakistani Army / 1st Armoured Division / 12th Cavalry

Deployed in the reconnaissance regiments of the Pakistani 1st Armoured Division, the M24 Chaffee light tank was of US World War II-era manufacture. Its 75mm (2.9in) weapon remained potent, and its firepower was equal to that of Indian light armour.

Specifications

Crew: 5

Weight: 18.28 tonnes (18 tons)

Length: 5.49m (18ft)

Width: 2.95m (9ft 8in)

Height: 2.46m (8ft 1in)

Engine: 2 x 82kW (110hp) Cadillac 44T24
V8 8-cylinder petrol

Speed: 55km/h (34mph)

Range: 282km (175 miles)

Armament: 1 x 75mm (2.9in) M6 gun, plus 1 x
12.7mm (0.5in) HMG on AA mount and
2 x 7.62mm (0.3in) MGs (1 coaxial,
1 ball-mounted in hull front)

Radio: SCR 508

11th Prince Albert Victor's Own (PAVO) Cavalry (Pakistan)

A component of the Pakistani 6th Armoured Division, which was constituted early in 1965, the 11th PAVO Cavalry included two squadrons of modern US-manufactured M48A3 Patton tanks with 90mm (3.5in) cannon along with a squadron of M36B2 Jackson tank destroyers, also armed with 90mm (3.5in) weapons. The 6th Armoured Division was heavily engaged in the defeat of the Indian 1st Armoured Division at Chawinda.

HQ plus 2 x Squadrons (30 x M48A3 MBT)

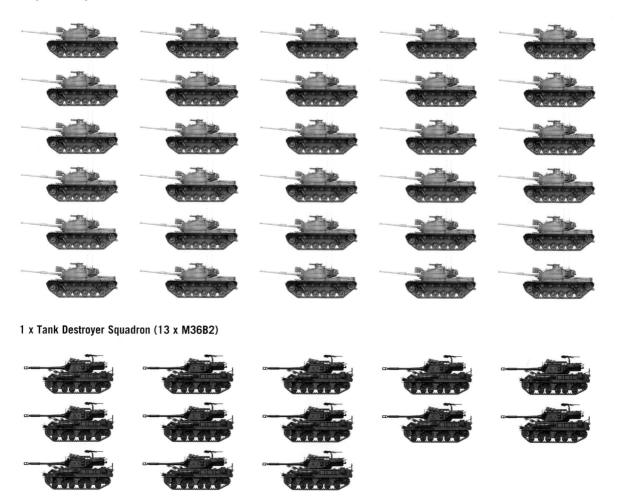

1 x Tank Destroyer Squadron (13 x M36B2)

before the opening of hostilities with Pakistan and were committed to battle without even having their guns properly bore-sighted.

Assal Uttar

During three days of intense combat, 8–10 September 1965, the largest tank battle since World War II occurred at Assal Uttar in the Indian state of Punjab. Estimates of the armoured strength involved vary widely; however, it is known that at least several hundred armoured vehicles took part.

Elements of the Pakistani 1st Armoured Division, including the 19th Lancers, 12th Cavalry, 24th Cavalry, 4th Cavalry, 5th Horse and 6th Lancers, blundered into a trap on 10 September, as three Indian armoured regiments, the 3rd Cavalry, Deccan Horse and 8th Cavalry, lay waiting in concealed positions that formed a defensive 'U' shape. The Indian force consisted of Shermans, AMX-13s and Centurions, a total of about 140 tanks, while approximately 300 Pakistani M47s and M24s advanced. Although the Pakistani tanks were more recent designs and possessed heavier armament than most of their Indian opponents, the ensuing action revealed glaring deficiencies in Pakistani tactics.

The Pakistanis advanced into an Indian artillery barrage, while the Indian tanks, concealed in a thick growth of tall sugar cane stalks, held their fire until the enemy was at near point-blank range. Failure to properly reconnoitre the prepared Indian defences was compounded by the inferior training of many of the Pakistani tank crews. Although the Pakistanis' weaponry may well have been superior to that of the Indians, it was rendered ineffective due to the operators' lack of proficiency.

The concentrated 75mm (2.9in) and 90mm (3.5in) fire from the Indian tanks destroyed nearly 100 Pakistani tanks, while dozens were abandoned. The Indians lost 32 tanks and blunted a Pakistani offensive in the process. Rows of destroyed and captured Pakistani tanks were displayed for months afterwards in Indian-held territory.

Chawinda

While the premier armoured force of the Pakistani Army was bloodied at Assal Uttar, the 1st Indian Armoured Division was also pounded during two weeks of fighting, 6–22 September, collectively known as the Battle of Chawinda. During the extended fighting, the 1st Division was severely

mauled, and the Indian Army lost more than 120 tanks, three times the losses of the Pakistanis. The Pakistani Air Force also accounted for some of the Indian tank losses. The fighting at Assal Uttar and Chawinda proved that the tank would be the primary future weapon of war on land, and the inconclusive strategic outcomes led to stalemate and negotiation between the warring nations.

Bangladesh at war

During only 13 days of war in December 1971, the Indian Army forced the surrender of Pakistani forces in East Pakistan. While a concentration of Indian armoured strength remained in the light AMX-13 or PT-76 tanks, which were relatively ineffective in tank-versus-tank fighting against Pakistani M47s and M48s, the tendency of the Pakistanis to deploy their tanks in troops of only two or three negated their superior firepower to an extent when confronted by an entire squadron of Indian light tanks that advanced to within 1000m (1094 yards) before opening fire. On those few occasions when Indian light tanks were caught in the open, the results were predictable, with even the heavily worn 75mm (2.9in) cannon of some Chaffee and obsolete Sherman tanks taking a toll on thinly armoured PT-76s.

The Indian-manufactured Vijayanta main battle tank, introduced in 1965 with a 105mm (4.1in)

▲ **M47 Patton Medium Tank**

Pakistani Army / 1st Armoured Division, 1965

Developed in the early 1950s, the M47 Patton was the US Army and Marine Corps primary tank, replacing the M46 and M4 Sherman tanks. After the tank was declared obsolete in 1957 by the US Army, hundreds of M47s were sold to Pakistan. Dozens were destroyed at the battle of Assal Uttar in September 1965.

Specifications

Crew: 5	1790-5B V12 petrol
Weight: 46 tonnes (45.3 tons)	Speed: 48km/h (30mph)
Length: 8.56m (28ft 1in)	Range: 129km (80 miles)
Width: 3.2m (10ft 6in)	Armament: 1 x M36 90mm (3.5in) gun; 2 x
Height: 3.35m (11ft)	12.7mm (0.5in) MGs; 1 x 7.62mm (0.3in) MG
Engine: 604.5kW (810hp) Continental AVDS-	Radio: n/k

L7A2 cannon, was based on the design of the Vickers Mk 1 and saw action in the 1971 war, while the number of Soviet- and Warsaw Pact-built T-54/55 tanks supplied to India grew steadily during the latter part of the decade. The Pakistanis were building their own version of the Chinese Type 59MII tank by 1979, while a limited number of T-54/55 tanks, along with upgraded M47 and M48 Pattons, remain in service. The Pakistani Army also fields a large number of BMP and M113 armoured personnel carriers.

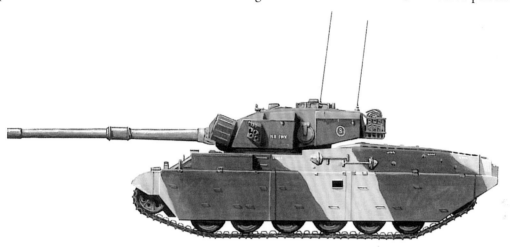

▲ Vijayanta Main Battle Tank

Indian Army / 66th Armoured Regiment, 1971

A licence-built version of the British Vickers Mk 1 main battle tank, the Vijayanta (Victorious) was developed in the early 1960s and participated in the 1971 war with Pakistan. It mounted a 105mm (4.1in) L7A2 gun. The last Vijayanta was withdrawn from active service in 2008.

Specifications

Crew: 4	6-cylinder multi-fuel
Weight: 39 tonnes (38.4 tons)	Speed: 48km/h (30mph)
Length: 7.92m (26ft)	Range: 480km (300 miles)
Width: 3.168m (10ft 6in)	Armament: 1 x 105mm (4.1in) gun; 1 x 12.7mm
Height: 2.44m (8ft)	(0.5in) MG; 2 x 7.62mm (0.3in) MGs
Engine: 484.7kW (650bhp) Leyland L60	Radio: Twin Clansman VRC 353 VHF

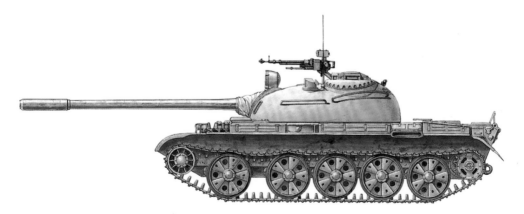

▲ T-55 Main Battle Tank

Indian Army / 72nd Armoured Regiment, 1971

During the 1971 Indo-Pakistani War, India operated T-55s around Chaamb, in the Western Theatre, against Pakistan's US-built M48 Patton and Chinese-built Type 59 tanks. The upgraded T-55 proved qualitatively superior to the T-54-based Type 59 when they met in battle.

Specifications

Crew: 4	Speed: 48km/h (30mph)
Weight: 39.7 tonnes (39 tons)	Range: 400km (250 miles)
Length (hull): 6.45m (21ft 2in)	Armament: 1 x 100mm (3.9in) D-10T gun;
Width: 3.27m (10ft 9in)	1 x 12.7mm (0.5in) DShK AA MG mounted on
Height: 2.4m (7ft 10in)	turret; 2 x 7.62mm (0.3in) DT MGs
Engine: 433kW (581bhp) V-55 12-cylinder	Radio: R-113

Soviet invasion of Afghanistan
1979

Committed to battle in order to support a pro-Soviet regime, the Red Army found that conventional tactics and heavy equipment were often ineffective against guerrilla fighters.

IN DECEMBER 1979, Soviet infantry and mechanized units crossed the border with Afghanistan in force. The nine-year military intervention that followed proved costly as the lives of more than 15,000 Red Army soldiers were taken and large quantities of materiel were destroyed, including nearly 150 tanks and more than 1300 armoured fighting vehicles and personnel carriers. The Soviet military commitment in Afghanistan increased rapidly, and by 1981 numbered more than 100,000 troops from an airborne division, four motorized rifle divisions and other units. More than 1800 tanks and 2000 armoured fighting vehicles had arrived.

Opposing the might of the Red Army were thousands of Islamic guerrillas, known as the Mujahideen. Ill-equipped and poorly trained, the guerrillas nevertheless waged an effective low-intensity war against the Soviets and their Afghan Army proxies. During the course of the conflict, the Mujahideen received substantial aid from the United States and other nations, as the Central Intelligence Agency viewed the conflict as the front line of the Cold War.

Anti-tank weapons were supplied, and the arrival of the US-made shoulder-fired FIM-92 Stinger surface-to-air missile was instrumental in making the air a dangerous place for Soviet aircraft.

Soviet commitment

The mountainous terrain of Afghanistan proved challenging for Soviet armoured operations. Hit-and-run tactics employed by the guerrillas and frequent attacks on population, communications and government centres, such as the Afghan capital city of Kabul, obliged the Soviets to commit armoured personnel carriers and tanks to urban environments. Furthermore, control of roads, power facilities and supply depots and the protection of convoys required the deployment of armoured assets most of the time.

By 1984, the United States was spending $200 million per year to supply the Mujahideen. Aside from financial assistance, the guerrillas received Type 69 RPGs (rocket-propelled grenades) and other small arms from the People's Republic of China, along with a limited number of the Chinese-made Type

▲ **BMD-1 Airborne Amphibious Tracked Infantry Fighting Vehicle**

Soviet Fortieth Army / 103rd Guards Airborne Division

Smaller and lighter than other infantry fighting vehicles, the BMD-1 was designed for deployment by air and entered service with Red Army airborne units in 1969. Armed with a 73mm (2.8in) semi-automatic main weapon, it also mounted machine guns and an anti-tank guided-missile launcher.

Specifications

Crew: 3 + 4	Range: 320km (200 miles)
Weight: 6.7 tonnes (14,740lb)	Armament: 1 x 73mm (2.8in) 2A28 'Grom'
Length: 5.4m (17ft 9in)	low- pressure smoothbore short-recoil gun,
Width: 2.63m (9ft 8in)	plus 1 x coaxial 7.62mm (0.3in) MG, 2 x front-
Height: 1.97m (6ft 6in)	mounted 7.62mm (0.3in) MGs and 1 x AT-3
Engine: 179kW (240hp) 5D-20 V6 liquid cooled	'Sagger' ATGW
Speed: 70km/h (43mph)	Radio: R-123

59 tank. Landmines, concealed explosives and even captured Soviet equipment were used against Red Army troops in Afghanistan.

Although the Soviets did have state-of-the-art technology at their disposal, it has been asserted that the Red Army did not deploy its T-72 and T-80 main battle tanks in large numbers. The majority of Soviet tanks deployed in Afghanistan were modified older T-54/55s and T-62s, which first rolled off assembly lines in 1959. In the spring of 1979, the Soviets had also delivered nearly 250 of these tanks to the Afghan Army. However, it must be understood that heavy armour is less effective than mobile, light armour in combat against guerrillas. Therefore, it is not surprising that an entire tank regiment was eventually

considered of no use in Afghanistan and returned to the Soviet Union by mid-1980. When the Soviets withdrew from Afghanistan, scores of armoured vehicles were abandoned. The rusting hulks of T-55 and T-62 tanks litter the landscape today.

The Soviets employed the ageing BTR-60, BMP-1 and BMD-1 armoured personnel carriers in Afghanistan, and the thin armour protection of these proved vulnerable to shoulder-fired projectiles, mines and shells of any calibre larger than small arms. Petrol engines were also a continual hazard, and a number of these vehicles were destroyed by igniting fuel tanks. Later, the diesel-powered BTR-70 and BTR-80 constituted a significant improvement in survivability.

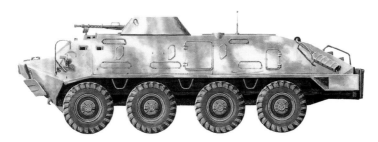

▲ **BTR-60PB Amphibious Armoured Personnel Carrier**

Soviet Fortieth Army / 108th Guards Motorized Rifle Division

Two decades old at the time of the Afghan invasion, the BTR-60 armoured personnel carrier was the first of several Soviet eight-wheeled fighting vehicles. Armed with a 14.5mm (0.6in) KPVT heavy machine gun, it entered service in 1959 and could carry up to 14 soldiers.

Specifications

Crew: 2 + 14	petrol
Weight: 10.3 tonnes (22,660lb)	Speed: 80km/h (50mph)
Length: 7.56m (24ft 9.6in)	Range: 500km (311 miles)
Width: 2.825m (9ft 3.2in)	Armament: 1 x 14.5mm (0.6in) KPVT HMG, plus 2
Height: 2.31m (7ft 6.9in)	x 7.62mm (0.3in) MGs
Engine: 2 x 67kW (90hp) GAZ-49B 6-cylinder	Radio: R-113

▲ **BTR-70 Armoured Personnel Carrier**

Soviet Fortieth Army / 5th Guards Motorized Rifle Division

With heavier armour plating and stronger tyres, the BTR-70 was originally intended as a replacement for the BTR-60 and entered service with the Red Army in 1972. Its troop capacity was scaled down to seven soldiers, and it was armed with 14.5mm (0.6in) and 7.62mm (0.3in) machine guns.

Specifications

Crew: 2 + 7	8-cylinder petrol
Weight: 11.5 tonnes (25,400lb)	Speed: 80km/h (50mph)
Length: 7.53m (24ft 8in)	Range: 600km (370 miles)
Width: 2.8m (9ft 2in)	Armament: 1 x 14.5mm (0.6in) KPVT MG, plus 1 x
Height: 2.23m (7ft 4in)	coaxial PKT 7.62mm (0.3in) MG
Engine: 179kW (240hp) ZMZ-4905	Radio: R-123

Soviet Tank Battalion, 1979

The standard Red Army tank battalion of the 1970s included three companies of three platoons each, a headquarters formation of a single tank and light transport, and a section of supply trucks. Its full complement of armour numbered at least 36 T-72 main battle tanks. Those Soviet heavy tanks which saw service in Afghanistan were often limited to main roads or the protection of facilities.

HQ (1 x T-72 MBT, 1 x command car, 1 x APC)

**Supply Section
(7 x trucks)**

1 Company, 1 Platoon (4 x T-72 MBT)

2 Platoon (4 x T-72 MBT)

3 Platoon (4 x T-72 MBT)

2 Company, 1 Platoon (4 x T-72 MBT)

2 Platoon (4 x T-72 MBT)

3 Platoon (4 x T-72 MBT)

3 Company, 1 Platoon (4 x T-72 MBT)

2 Platoon (4 x T-72 MBT)

3 Platoon (4 x T-72 MBT)

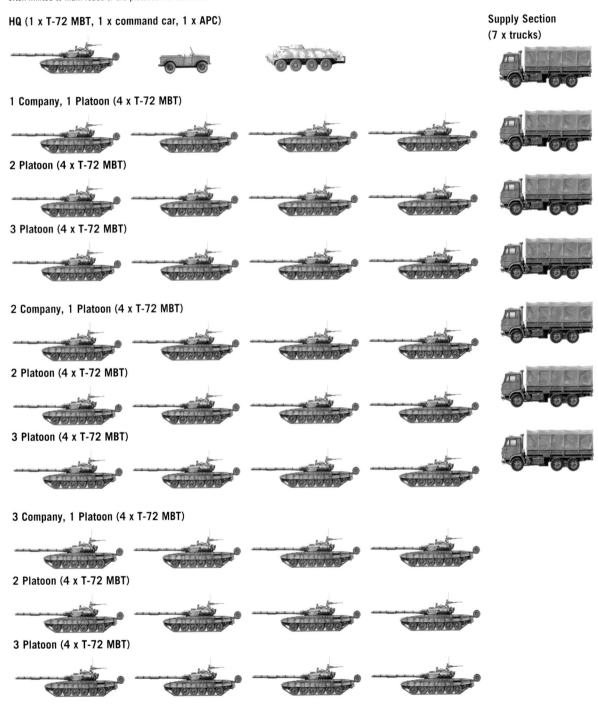

Disparate doctrine

Perhaps as challenging as the mountainous terrain and the determined enemy was Soviet armoured doctrine, which had been conceived to battle NATO forces in Europe. Further complicating the military situation was the simple fact that Soviet forces might take and hold territory, but destroying the Mujahideen in the field would require a vast military and financial commitment whose end was indefinite and could not be sustained. In the end, Soviet firepower was ineffective against a shadowy enemy.

Lieutenant-General Boris Gromov, 45, was the last high-ranking Soviet officer to leave Afghanistan. When he reached a bridge across from the Soviet frontier post at Termez, he climbed down from an armoured personnel carrier and walked the last few steps with his son. He was heard to say, 'I did not look back.'

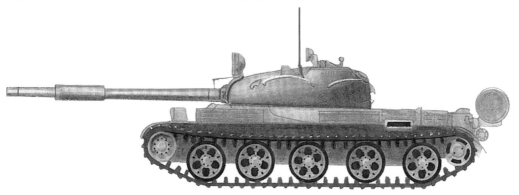

Specifications

Crew: 4	Speed: 60km/h (37.5mph)
Weight: 39.9 tonnes (87,808lb)	Range: 650km (404 miles)
Length: 9.34m (28ft 6in)	Armament: 1 x 115mm (4.5in) U-5TS gun, plus
Width: 3.3m (10ft 1in)	1 x coaxial 7.62mm (0.3in) MG
Height: 2.4m (7ft 5in)	Radio: R-130
Engine: 432kW (580hp) V-55-5 V12 liquid-	
cooled diesel	

▲ T-62 Main Battle Tank

Soviet Fortieth Army / 201st Motorized Rifle Division

Produced from 1961 to 1975, the T-62 main battle tank was originally intended to replace the older T-55; however, that tank also remained in production. The T-62 mounted a 115mm (4.5in) U-5TS smoothbore gun, and a number of them were reinforced with additional armour while in Afghanistan.

▲ T-72A Main Battle Tank

Soviet Fortieth Army / 5th Guards Motor Rifle Division

The T-72 main battle tank entered production in the Soviet Union in 1971 and has been in service since 1973. Although variants have been exported in large numbers, those deployed to Afghanistan were primarily of the original version, the Ural, with a 125mm (4.9in) 2A46M smoothbore gun.

Specifications

Crew: 3	Speed: 80km/h (50mph)
Weight: 41.5 tonnes (40.8 tons)	Range: 550km (434 miles)
Length: 9.53m (31 ft 3in)	Armament: 1 x 125mm (4.9in) 2A46M gun, plus
Width: 3.59m (11 ft 9in)	1 x 12.7mm (0.5in) NSVT anti-aircraft HMG and
Height: 2.37m (7ft 9in)	1 x coaxial 7.62mm (0.3in) PKT MG
Engine: 626kW (840hp) V-46 V12 diesel	Radio: R-123M

Far East

As the two Koreas faced one another on their troubled peninsula, the People's Republic of China maintained one of the largest land armies in the world.

ALTHOUGH THE CRADLE of the Cold War may indeed have been in Europe, the Korean peninsula was the scene of its first major armed conflict. Since the uneasy armistice that ended the shooting in 1953, the two sides have officially remained at war, staring warily at one another across the 38th Parallel. During the decades that followed, both Koreas increased their military preparedness – the communist North with paranoid intensity and the democratic South with stoic resolve to fend off aggression.

Meanwhile, the People's Republic of China embarked on its own programme of modernization and began transforming itself from being primarily a producer of clones of armoured vehicles designed in the Soviet Union to a sophisticated producer able to manufacture, deploy and export its own modern armoured vehicles.

North and South

The North Korean Army, known officially as the Korean People's Army, totalled approximately 400,000 troops in 1960. By 1990, its number was estimated at close to one million. Capable of both offensive and defensive operations on a large scale, the North Korean Army was originally organized in similar fashion to its early benefactors, the Soviet Union and the People's Republic of China.

During the 1960s, the army contained a single tank division of five armoured regiments, four with the Soviet T-54 and one with the older heavy IS-3. Self-propelled guns, primarily the Soviet SU-76, complemented the firepower of the armoured force. This was followed by the indigenous manufacture of a modified Soviet T-62 beginning in the 1970s.

Although the North Korean armed forces are shrouded in secrecy and much of the Western estimates of strength and equipment are based on sketchy intelligence, glimpses of military machinery are sometimes available during parades or special observances. Therefore it is known that the North Koreans added considerable modifications to the Soviet and Chinese tanks they had acquired during the 1950s and 1960s.

The 820th Armoured Corps and its 105th Armoured Division have long formed the backbone of the North Korean armoured forces. The officers of the 105th Division apparently formed the nuclei of several smaller armoured formations within the 820th Armoured Corps. By 1990, the North Korean armoured arsenal included more than 3000 tanks. The bulk of these were early Soviet T-54/55s, Chinese Type 59s and approximately 800 examples of the T-62, the primary Soviet tank of the 1960s. A number of mechanized units existed within the North Korean Army and operated about 2500 armoured personnel carriers and fighting vehicles.

During the early 1980s, the North Koreans embarked on a programme to improve their Soviet T62A main battle tanks. The result was the Chonma-ho, or Pegasus, which mounts either the 115mm (4.5in) 2A20 or 125mm (4.9in) 2A46 smoothbore gun. Since 1980, it is estimated that more than 1200 Chonma-ho tanks have been built, complementing a force that includes a diverse array of tanks such as the T-72, T-62, T-54/55 and the amphibious light PT-76.

◀ **Tanks on parade**
Chinese Type 59 tanks line up during a parade beneath portraits of Soviet communist leaders Lenin (left) and Stalin (right). China's first home-built main battle tank, the Type 59 was a simple copy of the Soviet T-54.

The army of the Republic of Korea (that is, the South Korean Army) had virtually no armour when the communists attacked in 1950. With the cessation of hostilities, the South Koreans began to organize a defensive armoured force with a core of US-built tanks of the Patton series, and for more than 20 years the M47 and M48 served as the frontline tanks. During the late 1980s, the core of Western tanks, including the improved M48A3K and M48A5K, was augmented with the purchase of a few T-80U main battle tanks from Ukraine. By 1987, each South Korean infantry division was supported by an attached armoured battalion or company. Mechanized infantry divisions included a cavalry battalion or one of nine armoured infantry battalions. In that year, the South Korean Army also began to deploy the K1 main battle tank. Designed by General Dynamics and produced in South Korea by Hyundai Rotem, the K1 mounts a 105mm (4.1in) KM68A1 cannon.

Myanmar militarism

In 1988, the government of Myanmar was overthrown in a coup d'etat carried out by the country's military. Since the 1960s, a total of 337 infantry and light infantry battalions had been supported by armoured reconnaissance and tank battalions which included the Chinese Type 63 light tank, the British Comet of World War II vintage and the Chinese Type 59. Later, Myanmar purchased T-72s from Ukraine and T-55s from India, which were being phased out of service, and began the licensed manufacture of Soviet-designed armoured personnel carriers. The army of Myanmar includes 10 armoured battalions in two divisions. Five of these are equipped with tanks, and five serve with armoured personnel carriers and infantry fighting vehicles, including the Soviet-designed BMP-1, the British Dingo, the Chinese Type 85 and the Brazilian EE-9.

Royal Thai Army

The Royal Thai Army has battled an insurgency for years while also remaining prepared to defend itself from attack by its neighbours. Its seven infantry divisions were initially supported by five organic armoured battalions, while an independent armoured division and an armour-equipped cavalry division completed its armoured forces. More than 300 M48A3 and M48A5 Patton tanks are included in its formations, along with about 100 of the Chinese Type 69II, an upgraded version of the older Type 59. Light tanks include the venerable M41 Walker Bulldog, the British Scorpion and the Stingray, an American design that mounts the 105mm (4.1in) L7A3 rifled gun and is only in use with the Royal Thai Army.

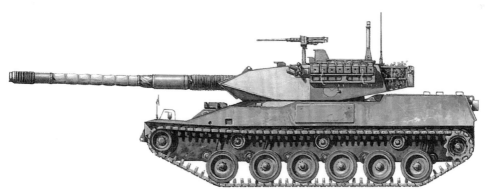

Specifications

Crew: 4	Speed: 69km/h (43mph)
Weight: 19.05 tonnes (41,912lb)	Range: 483km (300 miles)
Length: 9.35m (30ft 8in)	Armament: 1 x 105mm (4.1in) gun, plus 1 x
Width: 2.71m (8ft 11in)	coaxial 7.62mm (0.3in) MG and 1 x 7.62mm
Height: 2.54m (8ft 4in)	(0.3in) anti-aircraft MG
Engine: 399kW (535hp) Detroit Diesel Model	Radio: Long-range, directional
8V-92 TA diesel	

▲ **Stingray Light Tank**

Royal Thai Army / 1st Armoured Division, Thailand, 1990

Developed by Textron Marine and Land Systems during the mid-1980s, the Stingray light tank was originally intended for the US Army. However, it is currently deployed only by the Royal Thai Army. The Stingray mounts a 105mm (4.1in) L7A3 rifled gun.

China
1960–91

The modern People's Liberation Army of China, the largest land fighting force in the world, boasts mechanization of 40 per cent of its combat troops.

DURING ITS INFANCY, the People's Liberation Army fought a guerrilla war for control of the vast Chinese interior. Out of necessity, the communist military fought with small arms and propaganda, and later with tanks, armoured vehicles and artillery supplied by the Soviet Union. For years, the T-34 medium tank of World War II fame served as the backbone of a relatively small armoured corps. However, during the late 1950s, the Chinese military establishment came to the realization that armoured capability must be a component of its future armed forces.

China intervened in the Korean War, supplied weapons to North Vietnam during the 1960s, and during that time began to produce some of its own armoured vehicles, although the preponderance of these were clones or modifications of existing Soviet designs. For example, the Type 59 tank, armed with a 100mm (3.9in) main cannon, was a direct copy of the Soviet T-54A. The Type 62 light tank was another adaptation of the T-54A, which was then based on the Type 59. The Type 63 amphibious tank, which entered service in 1963, bore a striking similarity to the Soviet PT-76.

During the three decades from 1960 to 1990, the People's Liberation Army armoured force grew to roughly 10,000 tanks in 11 armoured brigades. Although efforts had been under way to develop indigenous Chinese tank designs, the bulk of Chinese armour, at least two-thirds, consisted of the clone Type 59 and Type 62 tanks. As these vehicles began to age, many were retired. Others, however, were continually upgraded as new technology became available. Likewise, approximately 2000 Type 63s remain in service, the recipients of numerous modernization packages.

Strained relations with both the Soviet Union and North Vietnam resulted in brief but sharp armed clashes in 1969 and 1979 respectively. Although the Chinese used tanks as mobile artillery support during these border clashes, the value of the armoured fighting vehicle on the battlefield was clarified. In

▲ **Show of strength**
Chinese Type 69 tanks parade at a military review outside of Beijing. The Type 69 was essentially an improved Type 59 with upgraded fire control systems and a more powerful gun.

addition, the Chinese military establishment became concerned that the survivability of its frontline tanks was substantially inferior to newer Soviet designs. The Tank Research Institute was created to begin work on new Chinese armoured vehicles. In 1977, the Communist Party Central Committee adopted a statement asserting that self-reliance in weapons design and production was a goal to be achieved during the sixth five-year plan for national defence.

Mechanized and modern

The People's Liberation Army of the 1980s received the Type 69 and Type 79 tanks, both of which were still based on the Soviet T-54A. Each did include some imported Western technology and an improved 100mm (3.9in) or 105mm (4.1in) rifled gun. They were, however, the first independently developed tanks in China's arsenal. Second generation tanks included the Type 80, which was revealed to Western journalists in 1987; the export Type 85, which was sold to Pakistan; and the Type 88. The experimental Type 90 was not adopted by the People's Liberation

Army; however, it was also sold to Pakistan and served as the basis for the MBT 2000 Al-Khalid, a joint venture between China and Pakistan.

In the 1980s, the People's Liberation Army also grew to 118 infantry divisions and 13 armoured divisions. Each armoured division included three regiments and fielded about 240 main battle tanks. However, mechanized transport and reconnaissance capabilities for accompanying infantry formations were still woefully lacking.

Modern Chinese armoured development since 1980 has been largely funded by China North Industries Corporation, NORINCO, a major defence contractor, heavy equipment manufacturer and producer of chemicals and other commodities. NORINCO has continued to produce copies of

Specifications

Crew: 7	Engine: 192kW (257hp) Deutz 6150L 6-cylinder
Weight: 15.4 tonnes (34,000lb)	diesel
Length: 5.65m (18ft 6in)	Speed: 56km/h (35mph)
Width: 3.06m (10ft)	Range: 500km (310 miles)
Height: 2.68m (8ft 9in)	Armament: 1 x 122mm (4.8in) howitzer

▲ Type 54-1 SP 122mm gun
People's Liberation Army / 6th Armoured Division, 1965

One of China's first internally designed self-propelled artillery pieces, the Type 54-1 mounts a 122mm (4.8in) howitzer similar to the Soviet M1938, which sits in an open-top turret. The chassis is a variant of the NORINCO YW 531.

▲ Type 63 (YW 531) Armoured Personnel Carrier
People's Liberation Army / 34th Motorized Division, 1974

Introduced by NORINCO in the late 1960s, the light armoured YW 531 carries a 12.7mm (0.5in) machine gun for defence against aircraft and is capable of transporting 10 combat troops, who enter and exit through a large door on the right rear of the vehicle.

Specifications

Crew: 2 + 10	Engine: 192kW (257hp) Deutz Type 6150L
Weight: 12.5 tonnes (27,600lb)	6-cylinder diesel
Length: 5.74m (18ft 10in)	Speed: 50km/h (31mph)
Width: 2.99m (9ft 9in)	Range: 425km (260 miles)
Height: 2.11m (6ft 11in)	Armament: 1 x 12.7mm (0.5in) MG
	Radio: Type 889

Soviet weaponry while developing new designs of its own, including the later Type 96 and Type 99 main battle tanks.

Armoured doctrine

Early People's Liberation Army armoured doctrine was based generally on Soviet techniques. However, the combined arms approach, with all elements of the ground and air forces working in concert, has become preeminent. The concept of the battle group emerged in the 1960s with emphasis on the infantry company and its subordinate platoons and squads. Each platoon would have its own artillery and armoured support. By the 1990s, the Chinese had

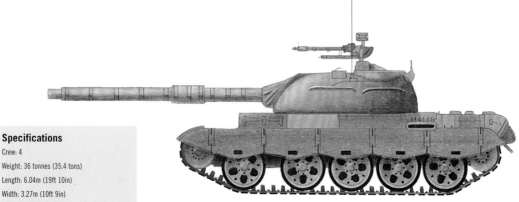

Specifications

Crew: 4

Weight: 36 tonnes (35.4 tons)

Length: 6.04m (19ft 10in)

Width: 3.27m (10ft 9in)

Height: 2.59m (8ft 6in)

Engine: 390kW (520hp) Model 12150L V12
    liquid-cooled diesel

Speed: 50km/h (31mph)

Range: 450km (280 miles)

Armament: 1 x 100mm (3.9in) rifled Type 69-II
    gun, plus 1 x Type 54 12.7mm (0.5in) AA MG
    and 2 x Type 59T 7.62mm (0.3in) coaxial MGs

Radio: Type 889

▲ **Type 59-I Main Battle Tank**

People's Liberation Army, 1980

A Chinese copy of the Soviet-designed T-54A tank, the Type 59 entered service with the People's Liberation Army in 1959. Originally mounting a 100mm (3.9in) rifled gun and later a 105mm (4.1in) weapon, it was produced for more than two decades. By the time the production finally stopped in the late 1980s, a total of 10,000 examples had been produced in a number of variants, with 6000 delivered to the PLA, and the rest exported to developing countries in Asia, Africa and the Middle East.

Specifications

Crew: 4	Speed: 60km/h (37mph)
Weight: 21 tonnes (20.7 tons)	Range: 500km (310 miles)
Length (including gun): 7.9m (25ft 11in)	Armament: 1 x 85mm (3.4in) Type 62-85TC rifled
Width: 2.9m (9ft 6in)	main gun, plus 2 x 7.62mm (0.3in) Type 59T
Height: 2.3m (7ft 6in)	MGs (1 coaxial and 1 bow-mounted)
Engine: 321kW (430 hp) 12150L-3 V12 liquid-	Radio: n/k
cooled diesel	

▲ **Type 62 Light Tank**

People's Liberation Army / 10th Armoured Division, 1965

Based on the Type 59, the Type 62 light tank entered service with the People's Liberation Army in 1963. Produced until 1989, upgraded and still an integral element of Chinese armoured forces, it mounts an 85mm (3.4in) rifled gun. It first saw combat during the Vietnam War, when China supplied Type 62 tanks to the NVA before the invasion of Kampuchea.

reengineered their battle groups to an extent, with these forces constituted in the divisional structure and facilitating the introduction of heavy armoured assets if needed. Adapting swiftly to battlefield conditions is paramount, and theoretically an armoured infantry unit could swiftly call in tank formations if enemy armour were encountered.

The Chinese government has charged the People's Liberation Army (PLA) with maintaining the authority of the communist party and securing national borders. In 2012, the PLA was estimated to number 1.6 million personnel, with another 500,000 reservists. This included more than 15,000 AFVs and self-propelled guns.

Specifications

Crew: 6
Weight: n/k
Length: 5.9m (19ft 7in)
Width: 3m (9ft 10in)
Height: 2.6m (8ft 6in)
Engine: 372kW (493hp) V-2 V12 diesel
Speed: 50km/h (31mph)
Range: 300km (186 miles)
Armament: 2 x 37mm (1.45in) Type
  63 AA guns, plus 1 x 7.62mm (0.3in)
  DT MG
Radio: None

▲ **Type 63 SP Anti-aircraft Gun**

People's Liberation Army / 13th Independent Armoured Brigade, 1966

The Type 63 self-propelled anti-aircraft gun included twin 37mm (1.45in) weapons mounted in an open-topped turret atop the hull of the obsolete Soviet T-34 medium tank of the World War II era.

Specifications

Crew: 4	Range: 440km (273 miles)
Weight: 36.7 tonnes (36.1 tons)	Armament: 1 x 100mm (3.9in) Type
Length: 6.24m (20ft 6in)	62-85TC rifled main gun, plus 2 x
Width: 3.3m (10ft 9in)	7.62mm (0.3in) Type 59T MGs (1 coaxial
Height: 2.8m (9ft 2in)	and 1 bow-mounted)
Engine: 430kW (580hp) diesel	Radio: Type 889
Speed: 50km/h (31mph)	

▲ **Type 69 Main Battle Tank**

People's Liberation Army / 10th Armoured Division, 1980

Although it was yet another Chinese tank based on the Soviet-designed T-54A, the Type 69 was the first tank developed solely within the Chinese arms system. Mounting a 100mm (3.9in) rifled cannon, it was followed by the Type 79 with a heavier 105mm (4.1in) weapon.

Japan
1965–95

Limited by its post-World War II constitution, Japan has developed and maintained armoured fighting vehicles for defensive purposes and entered the arena of the main battle tank.

ARTICLE 9 OF THE JAPANESE CONSTITUTION, framed during the occupation of the country by US forces after World War II, stipulates that the government is forbidden from 'settling international disputes [by the] threat or use of force'. When the Japanese deployed a contingent of armoured troops to protect a medical detachment and other specialized units in occupied Iraq in 2003, it was an historic moment. Japanese combat troops had not been deployed outside the country in more than half a century.

During the Cold War, the limited function of the Japan Ground Self-Defence Force (JGSDF) was to defend the northernmost home island of Hokkaido against attack by the Soviet Union and to provide a modicum of security against any aggressive military action by North Korea. A single Japanese armoured division, the 7th, exists today.

American cast-offs

Early Japanese post-war tanks were American M4 Sherman and M24 Chaffees. However, by 1955 the

▶ **SU 60 Armoured Personnel Carrier**

Japan Ground Self-Defence Force, 1973

A joint venture of the Mitsubishi and Komatsu companies, the SU 60 armoured personnel carrier entered service with the Japan Ground Self-Defence Force in 1959 and was produced until 1972. The SU 60 carried a complement of six infantrymen and mounted 12.7mm (0.5in) and 7.62mm (0.3in) machine guns.

Specifications

Crew: 4 + 6
Weight: 10.8 tonnes (26,000lbs)
Length: 4.85m (15ft 10in)
Width: 2.4m (7ft 9in)
Height: 1.7m (5ft 6in)
Engine: 164kW (220hp) Mitsubishi 8 HA 21 WT
   8-cylinder diesel
Speed: 45km/h (28mph)
Range: 300km (190 miles)
Armament: 1 x 12.7mm (0.5in) Browning
   M2 MG
Radio: n/k

Specifications

Crew: 3
Weight: 8 tonnes (17,600lbs)
Length: 4.3m (14ft 1in)
Width: 2.23m (7ft 4in)
Height: 1.59m (5ft 3in)
Engine: 89kW (120hp) Komatsu 6T 120-2
   6-cylinder diesel
Speed: 55km/h (34mph)
Range: 130km (80 miles)
Armament: 2 x RCL 106mm (4.17in) recoilless
   rifles, plus 1 x 12.7mm (0.5in) MG

▲ **Type 60 SP Recoilless Gun**

Japan Ground Self-Defence Force, 1980

For nearly 30 years, the Type 60 self-propelled recoilless gun served in a tank destroyer role with the Japan Ground Self-Defence Force. Mounting a 106mm (4.17in) recoilless rifle, it was produced from 1960 to 1977 and withdrawn from service in 2008. More than 250 were built.

Mitsubishi Company had begun design work on a main battle tank. The result was the Type 61 with a 90mm (3.5in) rifled main cannon, and 560 of these were built between 1961 and 1975. It was succeeded by the Type 74, which was produced until the late 1980s and carried a 105mm (4.1in) gun. The Type 90 main battle tank debuted in 1989, following more than a decade of research and development. Mounting a 120mm (4.7in) Rheinmetall smooth-bore gun, the Type 90 is similar in profile to the German Leopard 2. During the 1990s, development

began on a new main battle tank designated the Type 10.

The first armoured personnel carrier to serve with the JGSDF was the SU 60, which was developed in the late 1950s and carried up to six infantrymen. Variants included a self-propelled artillery weapon. A modern infantry fighting vehicle, the Mitsubishi Type 89, was developed during the 1980s and entered service at the end of the decade. Its primary weapon is a 35mm (1.38in) cannon, and its troop compartment carries seven soldiers.

Specifications
Crew: 8
Weight: 13,500kg (29,800lb)
Length: 5.72m (18ft 9in)
Width: 2.48m (8ft 1.6in)
Height: 2.38m (7ft 9.7in)
Engine: 227kW (305hp) Isuzu diesel
Speed: 100km/h (62mph)
Range: 500km (310 miles)
Armament: 1 x 12.7mm (0.5in) HMG, plus
   1 x 7.62mm (0.3in) MG
Radio: n/k

▲ **Type 82 Reconnaissance Vehicle**

Japan Ground Self-Defence Force / 7th Armoured Division, 1988

The Type 82 reconnaissance vehicle was manufactured by Mitsubishi for the Japan Ground Self-Defence Force beginning in the mid-1970s. The vehicle has not been offered for export, and approximately 230 have been produced. Manned by a crew of eight, it mounts machine guns for defence.

▲ **Mitsubishi Type 89 Infantry Fighting Vehicle**

Japan Ground Self-Defence Force, 1993

Armed with a 35mm (1.38in) cannon, the Type 89 Infantry Fighting Vehicle was introduced in 1989. However, fewer than 60 had been placed in service a decade later, and only about 70 were built as of 2005. The Type 89 carries a crew of three and seven combat-ready infantrymen.

Specifications
Crew: 3 + 7

Weight: 27 tonnes (26.6 tons)

Length: 6.7m (22ft)

Width: 3.2m (10ft 6in)

Height: 2.5m (8ft 2.5in)

Engine: 450kW (600hp) 6 SY 31 WA water-cooled
6-cylinder diesel

Speed: 70km/h (43mph)

Range: 400km (250 miles)

Armament: 1 x 35mm (1.38in) KDE cannon, plus
2 x Type 79 Jyu-MAT missiles and 1 x 7.62mm
(0.3in) coaxial MG

Radio: n/k

Chapter 5

The Middle East, 1948–90

The arid deserts of the Middle East have been
no strangers to military conflict. For centuries, wars of
empire, ethnicity and religion have wracked the region.
Modern warfare in the Middle East has been defined by
the power of the armoured fighting vehicle. In less than a
quarter of a century, the defenders of the nation of Israel
advanced from a vulnerable confederation of militia into
one of the world's most formidable advocates of armour.
The Arab states, faced with the burgeoning military might of
Israel, recognized both the offensive capabilities of the tank
and the urgent necessity of defending against it.

◀ **Show of strength**
Egyptian T-55 main battle tanks take part in a parade. A great deal of Soviet hardware was sold to countries of the
Middle East, especially Syria and Egypt.

National identity and nativism

The advent of the Jewish state spawned inevitable conflict with neighbouring Arab nations, frequently erupting in open warfare during the ensuing half-century, and with the tank serving as a primary weapon.

DESERT WARFARE has been likened to the manoeuvre of great fleets of warships across a trackless ocean, and is punctuated by sharp battles that alter the course of military and geopolitical fortune. Perhaps more than any other military venue, the vast expanse of the desert is the place where the tank is an icon of combat. The firepower, mobility and armour protection of the tank have become indispensable in efforts to control vast territories gained in battle and to secure national borders.

The tank achieved a place of preeminence among the armies of the Middle East in a relatively short period. Although the first Israeli armour consisted of a few 'armoured cars' jury-rigged by militia, the Jewish state has since achieved spectacular advances in modern technology and development of the main battle tank. Virtually from the beginning, the Israelis tinkered with what they had. The results were continuous improvements and upgrades.

Among these were the M-50/51 Super Sherman, similar to the British Sherman Firefly of World War II; the Sho't, an improved version of the British Mk 3 and Mk 5 Centurion with a 105mm (4.1in) cannon; the Tiran series of improvements to captured Soviet-made T-54/55 tanks; and the nation's own development of the Merkava – its first sole authorship in main battle tank design.

War surplus

Both Israel and the Arab nations initially remained dependent on the war surplus, abandoned or repaired equipment of the major powers that had battled in the region during World War II. Purchases were made through arms dealers, and at times the withdrawing armed forces of the former combatants simply looked the other way when their armour was appropriated.

Later, as allegiances to the superpowers became more polarized, the Arab states became dependent on the export variants of the T-54/55 and later models of main battle tanks designed and manufactured by the former Soviet Union and its client states, while Israel was supplied at first primarily by European benefactors, particularly France, and subsequently by the United States.

Throughout its existence, the Israeli military establishment has faced the challenges of maintaining a modern armoured force, including the stark reality of the political fallout that has accompanied open support of the armed forces, the relatively small population of the country and its limited technological base. During the last half-century, however, the proficiency of the Israeli Defence Forces (IDF) – the successors to the Haganah and other ad hoc militias that existed on the eve of the 1948 war – has been acknowledged worldwide.

The earliest known Israeli armoured vehicles were nothing more than fortified trucks with mounted machine guns and sheet metal protection attached in makeshift workshops. A few armoured cars of World War II vintage – especially the Marmon-Herrington, of South African design and adopted by the British – were available, and these were utilized by both the Israeli and Arab armed forces. The first true tanks in the Israeli arsenal were reported to have been about a dozen obsolescent Hotchkiss H-35 tanks, dating to the 1930s, which were located and purchased in France, according to some reports; or left to the Israelis by French colonial troops, according to others. Until the mid-1950s, France would continue as the primary supplier of armour to Israel, including the AMX-13 light tank, while the American-made Sherman and the British Cromwell – and later the Centurion – made up the majority of Israel's armour during the first decade of the nation's existence. A few American-built M3 half-tracks were also available.

During this period, the armoured cadre of the Israeli Defence Forces began to take shape; however, the majority of its equipment was ageing, and maintenance standards were low. The Suez Crisis of 1956 afforded the Israelis an opportunity to flex their limited armoured muscle and proved beneficial to future tactical operations and technological advances. In the aftermath of the Suez Crisis, France became more focused on its traditional colonial ties with the Arab regions of the Middle East and eventually discontinued its arms shipments to Israel. Thus the sense of urgency among the Israeli leadership to cultivate new sources of arms, upgrade their existing tanks and armoured vehicles, and begin their own programme of arms production was heightened.

Prior to the Six Day War of 1967, the United States responded to an appeal from the Israeli government and began direct shipments of armoured vehicles, including those of the Patton series, to Israel. Meanwhile, the Israelis had embarked on a programme of modernization and improvement of those tanks they had to hand or could purchase, while also developing a main battle tank of their own. By the mid-1970s, Israeli designers had begun to craft the prototype of the Merkava, which today has gained a reputation as a superb armoured vehicle and one of the best tanks in the world. The Merkava has been the backbone of the IDF's armoured contingent since the early 1980s and has itself undergone numerous improvements to its powerplant, fire control and armour protection packages.

Arab armour

Like their Israeli adversaries, the armed forces of the Arab nations arrayed against the Jewish state were limited in their armoured capabilities during the immediate post-World War II period. The armoured car served as the primary fighting vehicle of the Arab armies, while a hotchpotch of tanks, half-tracks and motorized infantry carriers were utilized. British, American, French and even German armoured vehicles were present in the armies of Egypt and

Syria, in the Trans-Jordanian Arab Legion, and to a lesser extent in the armies of Iraq and Lebanon. As the complex political posturing of the Cold War began to evolve, the superpowers exerted influence in the Middle East via cash, technology and arms. In 1955, the so-called Czech Arms Deal supplied the Egyptian Army with the Soviet-designed IS-3 heavy tank, the T-34 medium tank and the SU-100 self-propelled gun. This influx of arms from the Soviet Bloc complemented approximately 450 armoured vehicles of Western design already in the Egyptian inventory. Other Arab countries, particularly Syria, were armed with tanks and armoured fighting vehicles manufactured in the Soviet Union, Czechoslovakia or other Eastern European countries.

As the Arab nations gravitated towards the Soviet sphere of influence during the 1960s and 1970s, the T54/55 and later the T-62 and T-72 main battle tanks became the standard for armoured formations in the Arab armies. Following the Camp David Accords and a degree of rapprochement between Israel, Egypt and the governments of other Arab states, modern Western armour has again become commonplace within Arab arsenals. The American M60 and the British Chieftain and Challenger, for example, have equipped frontline units of the Royal Jordanian Army, the Royal Saudi Land Force and the Egyptian Army. By the 1990s, those Arab nations which joined the coalition that expelled the army of Saddam Hussein from Kuwait were equipped, to a great extent, with Western tanks.

▼ **Upgunned Shermans**
Upgunned IDF M-50 Shermans gather in the Sinai Desert, before the beginning of the Six Day War, 1967.

Arab–Israeli War
1948

Although armoured forces played a relatively minor role in the war for Israeli independence, it was readily apparent to military commanders of both sides that future confrontations in the Middle East would involve tanks on a grand scale.

ON 16 OCTOBER 1948, ISRAELI TANKS attacked Egyptian positions in the vicinity of Lod Airport near Tel Aviv. Two Cromwells were destroyed by enemy fire, 10 ancient Hotchkiss H-35s were rendered useless due to mechanical failure or fell into anti-tank ditches and a single Sherman did not engage the Egyptians at all. It was an inauspicious beginning for the armoured command of the Israeli Defence Forces. Arab armour fared little better. Outgunned and outnumbered, the Israelis faced a loose confederation of Arab opponents, whose armies failed to coordinate their offensive efforts and paid the price in lost opportunities.

Fight for survival

On 20 May 1948, Syrian forces had attacked the Israeli kibbutz at Degania near the Sea of Galilee. The militia defending the settlement were reportedly armed only with rifles and automatic weapons, a single British-made PIAT (Projector, Infantry Anti-Tank) shoulder-fired weapon and makeshift Molotov cocktails. The superior Syrian force included at least 18 tanks and armoured cars. During the action, five tanks penetrated Israeli defences but quickly ran into trouble. Two of the French-built Syrian tanks were taken out by a combination of the PIAT and Molotov cocktails. A third tank, this one a Renault R35, was stopped by a Molotov cocktail. It remains in the grounds of the kibbutz today as a monument to the fighting that took place there.

Although the Arab armies failed to press their advantage in firepower and numbers on several occasions, they had recognized the importance of armour early. On the eve of hostilities in 1948, the Egyptian Army fielded a handful of American Sherman and British Crusader and Matilda tanks, nearly 300 armoured Bren gun carriers and a few Marmon-Herrington, Staghound and Humber armoured cars. At least one light tank battalion, consisting of seven tanks, and an armoured reconnaissance battalion of 35 armoured vehicles had been formed.

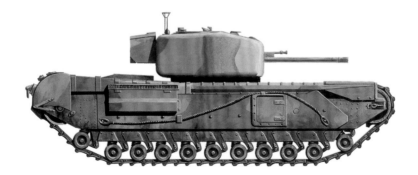

▲ Infantry Tank Mk IV Churchill IV

Israeli Defence Forces / 8th Armoured Brigade

The Churchill Mk IV infantry tank was the most numerous of more than a dozen variants of the versatile chassis produced by the British initially during World War II. Israel inherited, purchased or refurbished a handful of British tanks prior to 1950.

Specifications

Weight: 39.62 tonnes (39 tons)	Speed: 25km/h (15.5mph)
Length: 7.44m (24ft 5in)	Range: 193km (120 miles)
Width: 2.74m (9ft)	Armament: 1 x 57mm (2.24in) 6pdr OQF
Height: 3.25m (10ft 8in)	gun, plus 2 x 7.92mm (0.31in) Besa MGs (1
Engine: 261.1kW (350hp) Bedford	coaxial and 1 ball-mounted in hull front)
12-cylinder petrol	Radio: n/k

Lebanese forces contributed a single armoured battalion of six tanks and four armoured cars to the war, while the Iraqi Army dispatched 47 tanks plus mechanized infantry formations. The Trans-Jordanian Arab Legion, the best trained of all the Arab forces, included motorized infantry but only about a dozen Marmon-Herrington armoured cars. Syrian forces consisted of a battalion of 45 French Renault R35 and R39 tanks along with a battalion of armoured cars.

A core of 10 Hotchkiss H-39 tanks equipped the first armoured formation of the Israeli Defence Forces. Designated the 8th Armoured Brigade, it also included jeeps and half-tracks. The Hotchkiss tanks were grouped into a single company, while the half-tracks were employed as armoured personnel carriers and the jeeps were formed into an assault company.

During the fighting around the town of Lydda and during the 'Ten Days' battles that followed, Moshe Dayan, the future commander of the Israeli Defence Forces and later the nation's defence minister, commanded one of these jeep units, which had been designated the 89th Mechanized Assault Battalion.

At Lydda, Dayan reportedly led his jeeps into the town, firing rapidly. It was the 89th Battalion which formed the post-independence core of Israel's armoured forces.

By the end of the war for independence, the Israeli Defence Forces included more than 100,000 troops, the 7th and 8th Armoured Brigades (the former a new armoured formation) and several artillery regiments. The 8th had been designated as 'armoured' for morale purposes as much as anything else. At best, it lacked the training, experience and equipment to exert a decisive presence in itself on the battlefield. Its mixed bag of antiquated tanks was to be reorganized and upgraded over time; however, its contribution to the successful defence of Israel in 1948 must be described in total as limited.

Although the tank was not a decisive factor in the Arab–Israeli War of 1948, its mere presence did influence the course of events. Tanks would grow in number and importance during the years to come. Firepower and technology improved. Tactics were refined. Plans of attack and defence were formulated, discarded and redrawn. Decades of conflict were to come, and the tank would take centre stage.

HQ

Israeli Defence Forces, Tank Company, 1948

The first armoured formation fielded by the Israeli Defence Forces consisted of 10 elderly French Hotchkiss H-39 tanks dating from the 1930s. The tanks were arranged in three platoons of three each with one headquarters tank and constituted the sole tank formation of the 8th Armoured Brigade. Several of the H-39s were lost during the 1948 war due to enemy action and mechanical breakdowns.

Platoon 1 (3 x Hotchkiss H-39 light tanks)

Platoon 2 (3 x Hotchkiss H-39 light tanks)

Platoon 3 (3 x Hotchkiss H-39 light tanks)

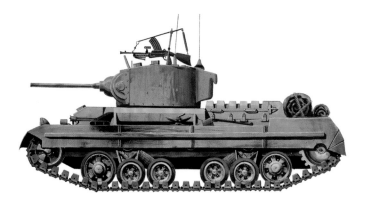

Specifications

Crew: 3

Weight: 17.27 tonnes (17 tons)

Length: 5.89m (19ft 4in)

Width: 2.64m (8ft 8in)

Height: 2.29m (7ft 6in)

Engine: 97.73kW (131hp) AEC 6-cylinder diesel

Speed: 24km/h (15mph)

Range: 145km (90 miles)

Armament: 1 x 40mm (1.57in) 2pdr OQF gun,
    plus 1 x coaxial 7.92mm (0.31in) Besa MG

Radio: n/k

▲ **Infantry Tank Mk III Valentine I**

Israeli Defence Forces / 8th Armoured Brigade

Obsolete by the end of World War II, the British Valentine tank had equipped some frontline units of the British Army and had been abandoned after the conclusion of the war. Its assault gun variant, the Archer, was deployed by Egyptian forces during the Suez Crisis.

Suez Crisis
1956

In a joint operation with Great Britain and France to secure the Suez Canal, the Israeli Defence Forces seized the Sinai Peninsula. While its armour played an increasing role, major strategic and tactical shortcomings were revealed.

POLITICAL ACTION AND REACTION resulted in a preemptive joint military strike against Egypt by Great Britain, France and Israel in the autumn of 1956. Following the controversial arms deal with the Soviet Union in 1955, which resulted in the delivery of heavy and medium tanks and self-propelled assault guns to Egypt, the government of President Gamal Abdel Nasser recognized the communist regime of the People's Republic of China and followed quickly with a declaration that Egypt would nationalize the Suez Canal. Nasser's aggressive stance directly threatened the interests of the European powers in the Middle East and posed a military threat to Israel, which had also endured continual terrorist incursions from Arab territory.

Operation Musketeer

When British Royal Marine commandos landed at Port Said, west of the Suez Canal, and both

IDF, 1956	
Brigades	**Strength**
Infantry	11
Para	1
Armoured	3
TOTAL	15

French and British airborne troops parachuted into Egyptian territory, they were accompanied by armoured units. The Centurions of the 6th Royal Tank Regiment supported No. 40 and No. 42 Commandos, and elements of the 1st and 5th Royal Tank Regiments also participated, while a squadron of AMX-10 light tanks advanced with the 1st Parachute Regiment of the French Foreign Legion. Meanwhile, Israeli armour was to coordinate with the British and French, mounting a push into the Sinai Peninsula with approximately 200 tanks.

HQ

Israeli Defence Forces, Tank Company, 1956

Through the mid-1950s, France was the primary supplier of arms to Israel. Among the armoured vehicles utilized by the Israeli Defence Forces was the AMX-13 light tank, originally equipped with a 75mm (2.9in) cannon and later upgunned to 90mm (3.5in) and 105mm (4.1in) weapons. The Israeli tank company at the time of the Suez Crisis included up to 12 AMX-13s and a headquarters tank.

Platoon 1 (3 x AMX-13 light tanks)

Platoon 2 (3 x AMX-13 light tanks)

Platoon 3 (3 x AMX-13 light tanks)

▲ AMX-13 Light Tank

Israeli Defence Forces / 27th Armoured Brigade

The oscillating turret of the French AMX-13 light tank proved a disappointment in combat conditions. The innovative design of the AMX-13, originally conceived as an air-transportable armoured vehicle, also featured an automatic loading system of revolver-type cartridges.

Specifications

Crew: 3

Weight: 15,000kg (33,000lb)

Length: 6.36m (20ft 10.3in)

Width: 2.5m (8ft 2.5in)

Height: 2.3m (7ft 6.5in)

Engine: 186kW (250hp) SOFAM 8-cylinder petrol

Speed: 60km/h (37mph)

Range: 400km (250 miles)

Armament: 1 x 75mm (2.9in) gun, plus 1 x 7.62mm (0.3in) MG

Radio: n/k

ORGANIZATION: IDF ARMOURED BRIGADE, 1956

☐ IDF Armoured Brigade
☐ HQ

▷ 1 Arm Btn
☐ HQ

| 1 | 2 | 3 | Mec | Rec | SP | Mot |

▷ 2 Arm Btn
☐ HQ

| 1 | 2 | 3 | Mec | Rec | SP | Mot |

▷ 3 Arm Btn
☐ HQ

| 1 | 2 | 3 | Mec | Rec | SP | Mot |

IDF ARMOURED BRIGADE, 1956

Type	Number	Vehicle	Strength
Headquarters	–	–	–
Armoured Btn	3	–	–
Armoured Coy	3	Medium tank	13
Mechanized Coy	1	M3 half-track	n/k
Recce Platoon	1	Jeep	7
SP Artillery Bat	1	M7 Priest Howitzer	4
Motorized Coy	1	–	–

Operation Kadesh

At the time of the Suez Crisis, as the affair came to be known, the Israeli Defence Forces' armour consisted primarily of about 200 World War II-era M4 Sherman tanks of American manufacture, 100 French-designed AMX-13 light tanks and roughly 60 examples of the 105mm (4.1in) self-propelled *Obusier automoteur de 105 Modèle* 5, essentially the 105mm (4.1in) weapon mounted on the AMX-13

chassis. The Egyptian Army was equipped with the Soviet T-34/85, an upgunned version of the original T-34 with an 85mm (3.4in) cannon; M4 Shermans in their original US configuration along with some that had been modified by the British; the Soviet SU-100 self-propelled gun; the Archer self-propelled variant of the British Valentine tank with a 76mm (3in/17-pounder) cannon; and at least 200 Soviet-designed BTR 152 armoured troop carriers. Total Egyptian armoured strength was estimated at more than 1000 vehicles.

The Israelis undertook Operation Kadesh to eliminate the terrorist incursions, secure their borders, lift the quarantine of the port of Eilat which had been imposed by the Egyptians and degrade the fighting capabilities of the burgeoning Egyptian Army, which had only recently accepted delivery of nearly 300 Soviet-designed tanks of Czech manufacture. The armoured corps of the Israeli Defence Forces had been subjected

▲ **M3 Mk. A Half-track**

Israeli Defence Forces / 10th Infantry Brigade

Based on the M5 half-track personnel carriers built by the International Harvester Company, Israeli half-tracks were all designated M3, even M2/M9 variants. The Mk A APCs are identified as IHC M5s by the use of RED-450 engines. Israeli half-track vehicles of World War II-manufacture remained in service into the 1970s.

Specifications

Crew: 2 plus 11 passengers

Weight: 9.3 tonnes (9.15 tons)

Length: 6.34m (20ft 10in)

Width: 2.22m (7ft 3in)

Height: 2.69m (8ft 10in)

Engine: 109.5kW (147hp) IHC RED-450-B

6-cylinder

Speed: 72km/h (45mph)

Range: 320km (200 miles)

to great scrutiny following the 1948 war. Its command structure was reorganized, and it was determined that armoured strength would be a key element in future military confrontations. Still, the 7th Armoured Brigade constituted the army's only standing tank force. Emphasizing speed and firepower, the evolving Israeli armoured doctrine called for tanks that were capable of rapid mobility and able to seek out and destroy enemy forces. While armour had its proponents within the Israeli military establishment, a philosophical controversy as to its actual role persisted, creating confusion among commanders in the field.

Meanwhile, the Israeli effort to upgrade its M4 Sherman medium tanks is indicative of the initiative to improve available armoured vehicles in response to the threat of Egyptian T-34 and IS-3 tanks. The M-50/51 programme resulted in a formidable tank known as the Super Sherman. The purchase of the French AMX-13 had placed in Israeli hands the powerful 75mm (2.9in) CN 75-50 cannon, which had been patterned after the German 75mm (2.9in) KwK 42 L70 as utilized in the Panther medium tank during World War II. Israeli engineers married the M4 Sherman chassis with the high-velocity French gun and produced a tank with greater

firepower. The first 25 M-50s were delivered to armoured units just days before the commencement of Operation Kadesh.

Mobility in the desert

Operation Kadesh achieved its tactical objectives in approximately 100 hours and was fought entirely between the armies of Israel and Egypt. During the offensive of 29 October to 7 November 1956, Israeli forces occupied the entire Sinai Peninsula from the coast of the Mediterranean to Sharm el-Sheikh, took control of the Gaza Strip and halted 16km (10 miles) from the Suez Canal in accordance with a prearranged agreement with the British and French. They lost only 231 soldiers in the process.

Despite the success of Operation Kadesh, the Israeli military establishment has been criticized for failing to fully appreciate the strength of a combined arms approach to combat. Chief among those held accountable for this shortcoming was Dayan, who only late in the planning assigned any significant role to Israeli armour. Infantry had been considered primary, while tank formations were relegated to a support role.

Armour was not fully integrated into the Israeli battle plan, and wheeled transportation for

▲ T-34/85 Model 1953 Medium Tank

Egyptian Army / 4th Armoured Division, Port Said, Suez Canal, November 1956

An export version of the Soviet-designed T-34/85 medium tank which mounted an 85mm (3.4in) main weapon, the Model 1953 was manufactured in Czechoslovakia. Large numbers of the Model 1953 had been delivered to the Egyptian and Syrian Armies by the time of the 1956 Suez Crisis.

Specifications

Crew: 5	Speed (road): 55km/h (33mph)
Weight: 32 tonnes (31.5 tons)	Range: 360km (223 miles)
Length: 6m (19ft 7in)	Armament: 1 x 85mm (3.4in) ZiS-S-53 cannon,
Width: 3m (9ft 10in)	plus 2 x 7.62mm (0.3in) DT MGs (1 coaxial and
Height: 2.6m (8ft 6in)	1 in the bow)
Engine: 372 kW (493hp) V-2 V12 diesel	Radio: R-113 Granat

mechanized infantry was sorely lacking. During one action, Israeli tank commanders became so confused that friendly fire erupted and one formation knocked out eight of the other's nine tanks. Israeli armoured forces were deployed piecemeal and their tactics proved deficient. By the third day of Operation Kadesh, for example, the 7th Armoured Brigade had been divided into three task groups. Each of these was oriented in a different direction and unable to support the other.

No large-scale tank-versus-tank battles occurred during Operation Kadesh. However, an Israeli attack at Umm Qatef was ordered forward without tank support. The Israeli commander on the scene had decided that an attack was too risky without armour, and the nearest tanks were several hours away. Dayan, however, insisted that an attack be carried out immediately. In the event, several Israeli half-tracks were destroyed by Egyptian Archer self-propelled guns, and the Egyptians held their ground.

The lessons learned in the Sinai would be put to good use in the years to come. The Israeli Defence Forces eventually adopted a strategy of large armoured formations attacking swiftly and achieving deep penetrations of enemy lines.

EGYPTIAN ARMY TANK BRIGADE, 1956			
Type	Number	Vehicle	Strength
Headquarters	–	truck	1
AA Company	1	S-60 57mm gun	3
Tank Btn	2		
Headquarters	1	T-34/85 MBT	1
Tank Company	3	T-34/85 MBT	3
Mechanized Btn HQ	1		
Headquarters	1	BTR-152	1
Mech Infantry Coy	3	BTR-152	2
Heavy Weapons Coy	1	81mm mortar	1
		57mm ATG	1
Assault Gun Btn HQ	1	truck	1
		SU-100 assault gun	4

ORGANIZATION

▷ Egyptian Tank Brigade

☐ HQ

| 1 | 2 | AA | Mec | Alt |

▲ **SU-100 SP Gun**

Egyptian Army / 4th Armoured Division, Port Said, Suez Canal,
November 1956

The SU-100 self-propelled gun was developed by the Soviet Union during World War II and remained in service with Arab armies in the Middle East until the 1970s. Modifications for service in the desert resulted in the SU-100M variant.

Specifications

Crew: 4

Weight: 31.6 tonnes (69,665lbs)

Length: 9.45m (31ft)

Width: 3m (10ft)

Height: 2.25m (7.38ft)

Engine: 370kW (500hp) V-2-34 12-cylinder
4-stroke diesel

Speed: 48km/h (30mph)

Range: 320km (200 miles)

Armament: 100mm (3.9in) D-10S gun

Radio: R-113 Granat

Six Day War
1967

Following a series of preemptive air strikes, Israeli tanks and warplanes devastated Arab armour and altered the perceived balance of power in the Middle East.

BY THE MID-1960S, yet another armed confrontation between Israel and its Arab neighbours appeared inevitable. Egyptian president Nasser had closed the Strait of Tiran, compelled United Nations peacekeepers to vacate the Sinai Peninsula and remilitarized the region. An apparent build-up of Egyptian forces on the Israeli frontier had been accompanied by bellicose public statements as well.

In the meantime, Israeli military leaders had continued to revise their plans for battle. The air force would provide a primary means of offensive operations, while the armoured corps would become the foremost element of Israeli Defence Forces ground operations. Although little is known of the specifics of Egyptian armoured doctrine, or of that

SYRIAN ARMOURED BRIGADE, 1967			
Type	Number	Vehicle	Strength
Armoured Btn	3		
Headquarters	1	T-54/T-55 MBT	1
Tank Company	3	T-54/T-55 MBT	3
Mechanized Btn	1		
Headquarters	1	BTR-152	1
Mechanized Coy	3	BTR-152	2
Heavy Weapons Coy	1	HMG in BTR-152	2
		82mm mortar	1

ORGANIZATION: SYRIAN ARMOURED BRIGADE, 1967

Syrian Armoured Brigade

HQ

1 Arm Btn — HQ — 1 2 3
2 Arm Btn — HQ — 1 2 3
3 Arm Btn — HQ — 1 2 3

Mec Btn — HQ — 1 2 3 Hv

▲ **T34/85 Model 1953 Medium Tank**

Syrian Army / 44th Armoured Brigade, Golan Heights, 1967

Made in Czechoslovakia, this Model 1953 T-34/85 includes a Soviet-manufactured DShK 12.7mm (0.5in) heavy anti-aircraft machine gun mounted on the turret ring. During the Six Day War, Syrian armour took serious losses from Israeli aircraft. The inscription reads, 'Al Shaheed Hormuz Yunis Butris'.

Specifications

Crew: 5

Weight: 32 tonnes (31.5 tons)

Length: 6m (19ft 7in)

Width: 3m (9ft 10in)

Height: 2.6m (8ft 6in)

Engine: 372 kW (493hp) V-2 V12 diesel

Speed (road): 55km/h (33mph)

Range: 360km (223 miles)

Armament: 1 x 85mm (3.4in) ZiS-S-53 cannon, plus 1 x DShK 12.7mm (0.5in) turret-mounted anti-aircraft HMG and 2 x 7.62mm (0.3in) DT MGs (1 coaxial and 1 in the bow)

Radio: R-113 Granat

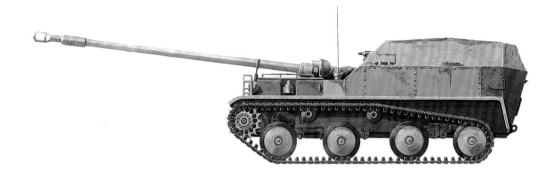

▲ ASU-57 SP Gun

Egyptian Army / 7th Infantry Division, Sinai, Rafah, 1967

Lightly armed and armoured, the ASU-57 assault gun was originally intended as a support weapon for Soviet airborne formations. Its low silhouette and high speed improved survivability on the battlefield. The 57mm (2.24in) high-velocity gun offered a high rate of fire and excellent armour-penetration capabilities.

Specifications

Crew: 3	Engine: 41kW (55hp) M-20E four-cylinder petrol
Weight: 3300kg (7260lb)	Speed: 45km/h (28mph)
Length: 4.995m (16ft 4.7in)	Range: 250km (155 miles)
Width: 2.086m (6ft 10in)	Armament: 1 x 57mm (2.24in) CH-51M gun, plus
Height: 1.18m (3ft 10.5in)	1 x 7.62mm (0.3in) anti-aircraft MG
	Radio: n/k

ISRAELI ARMOURED BRGIGADE, 1967			
Type	Number	Vehicle	Strength
Headquarters	–		
Armoured Btn	2	Centurion/M48A1	50
Reconnaissance Coy	1	jeeps with 106mm recoilless rifles	6
Mechanized Btn	1	M3/5 half-track	n/k
SP Artillery Btn	1	M3 120mm mortar on half-tracks	12

of other Arab states such as Syria and Lebanon, it is reasonable to assume that battlefield tactics followed those of the Soviet armoured doctrine developed for potential combat against NATO forces in Western Europe.

Preemptive strike

The Israelis, on the other hand, rationalized that the preemptive strike, an offensive blow as a defensive measure, offered the best chance for victory. Thus on 5 June 1967, Israel launched a series of major air strikes against the air forces of Egypt, Syria and Jordan, destroying most of the Arab aircraft on the ground. In practice, the strikes were instrumental in the ensuing success of Israeli ground operations.

Without adequate air cover, Arab armour was battered from above. In turn, Israeli tanks destroyed

hundreds of enemy armoured vehicles, although the theory of armoured prominence was resisted in some command circles. In less than a week of fighting, more than 300 Egyptian tanks, one-third of the entire Egyptian armoured force, were captured. The remainder was virtually wiped out. The Royal Jordanian Army lost 179 tanks, and the Syrian Army suffered 118 tanks destroyed. In total, it is estimated that the Israelis destroyed 600 Arab tanks. Fewer than 700 Israeli soldiers were killed, and Israeli armoured losses were minimal.

Tank power

More than 2500 tanks took part in the Six Day War, with the Israelis deploying their ageing Super Shermans, the French AMX-13s and those British Centurions which were still operational. However, in addition to improvising and maintaining their older tanks, the Israelis had obtained some new armoured fighting vehicles. An historic arms deal with West Germany had resulted in the delivery of the American M48A2 Patton tank, armed with a 90mm (3.5in) main gun. Later known as the Magach series, the American M48s and successor M60s that entered service with the Israelis were modernized on a continual basis, fitted with heavier weapons, better engines and improved armour.

Israeli forces also captured a large number of Jordanian M48s during the Six Day War, and many of these were incorporated into the ranks of the Israeli Armoured Corps.

During the decade following the 1948 war, the United States had rebuffed several Israeli overtures for the purchase of arms. On the eve of the Six Day War, however, a direct appeal from Israeli prime minister Golda Meir finally resulted in a continuing flow of weapons from the United States to Israel. In 1966, the British government offered Israel the opportunity to purchase obsolete Centurion tanks

and to participate in the development of the new Chieftain main battle tank. Although this partnership lasted only three years and was terminated largely due to an outcry from several Arab nations, the Israelis put the Centurions to good use and gained invaluable knowledge in tank design.

When the Six Day War erupted, the Israeli Magach contingent consisted of the M48A1 and M48A2 Patton tanks, some of which had been modified by the ordnance corps of the Israeli Defence Forces

▲ **IS-3 Heavy Tank**

Egyptian Army / 7th Infantry Division, Sinai, Rafah, 1967

With its 122mm (4.8in) cannon, the Soviet-designed IS-3 heavy tank proved formidable in desert action. At Rafah during the Six Day War, IS-3s destroyed several M48A2 Patton tanks of the Israeli Defence Forces' 7th Armoured Brigade.

Specifications

Crew: 4	Speed: 40km/h (25mph)
Weight: 45.77 tonnes (45.05 tons)	Range: 185km (115 miles)
Length: 9.85m (32ft 4in)	Armament: 1 x 122mm (4.8in) D-25T gun,
Width: 3.09m (10ft 2in)	plus 1 x 12.7mm (0.5in) DShK HMG on AA
Height: 2.45m (8ft)	mount and 1 x coaxial 7.62mm (0.3in) DT MG
Engine: 447kW (600hp) V-2-JS V12 diesel	Radio: 10R (when fitted)

Specifications

Crew: 5	Speed: 37km/h (23mph)
Weight: 46 tonnes (45.27 tons)	Range: (road) 220km (136.7 miles),
Length: 9.18m (30ft 1in)	(terrain) 80km (49.7 miles)
Width: 3.07m (10ft 1in)	Armament: 1 x 152mm (6in) ML-20S howitzer;
Height: 2.48m (8ft 1in)	1 x 12.7mm (0.5in) DShK HMG on AA mount
Engine: 447kW (600hp) V-2 diesel	Radio: 10RF (when fitted)

▲ **ISU-152 Heavy SP Assault Gun**

Egyptian Army / 6th Mechanized Division, Sinai, 1967

The Soviet-designed ISU-152 heavy assault gun was available in relatively small numbers during the Six Day War and often deployed with the anti-tank companies that were organic to the armoured brigades of the Egyptian Army.

with the 105mm (4.1in) L7 gun, a powerful AVDS 1790a diesel engine, and better communications equipment.

In addition to the American M48s which were deployed by the Jordanians, the Arab arsenal included a large number of the World War II-era T-34/85 tanks and SU-100 self-propelled guns. May of these were Czech-built Model 1953s supplied following the 'Czech Arms Deal' of 1955. By this time, the T-54/55 series of Soviet tanks, first developed in the late 1940s, had been incorporated into an Egyptian armoured force, which had deployed them slowly

Specifications

Crew: 5

Weight (without blade): 31.6 tonnes (67,000lb)

Length: 6.06m (19ft 9in)

Width: 2.62m (8ft 7in)

Height: 2.74m (9ft)

Engine: 312kW (425hp) Chrysler A57
30-cylinder petrol

Speed: 40km/h (25mph)

Range: 161km (100 miles)

Armament: 1 x 105mm (4.1in) howitzer M4,
plus 1 x coaxial 12.7mm (0.5in) Browning
M2HB MG

Radio: n/k

▲ **Sherman M4 Dozer**

Israeli Defence Forces / 7th Armoured Brigade, Sinai, 1967

The Israeli Defence Forces upgunned many of its M4A3 Sherman tanks with the 105mm (4.1in) howitzer M4 and fitted a few with the M1 bulldozer blade. The M4 also incorporated an improved horizontal volute spring suspension.

▲ **M-51 Isherman**

Israeli Defence Forces / 7th Armoured Brigade / 2nd Battalion / 4th Company

A joint development of French and Israeli engineers, the M-51 Isherman incorporated the superb French 105mm (4.1in) CN 105 F1 gun into the original turret of the M4A1 Sherman tank, which had originally mounted a 75mm (2.9in) cannon. The tank also had installed a US-made Cummins diesel engine and wide-track HVSS suspension. The M-51 was capable of knocking out the T-34 variants and T-55 MBTs employed by Syria and Egypt.

Specifications

Crew: 5	Speed: n/k
Weight: 39 tonnes (42 tons)	Range: 270km (168 miles)
Length (hull): 5.84m (19ft 2in)	Armament: 1 x 105mm (4.1in) CN 105 F1 gun,
Width: n/k	plus 2 x 7.62mm (0.3in) MG (1 coaxial and
Height: n/k	1 hull-mounted)
Engine: 338kW (460hp) Cummins V8 diesel	Radio: n/k

after the 1956 Sinai fighting. By 1967, the Egyptians had received nearly 300 T-54/55 tanks along with IS-3M heavy tanks and the amphibious PT-76. A large number of the T-54/55s were allocated to the 4th Armoured Division, which had been decimated in the Sinai. The ISU-152 self-propelled gun, another Soviet World War II design, remained in service with Arab forces in limited numbers.

Enter Israel Tal

The officer to whom the revised Israeli armoured doctrine of the Six Day War is primarily attributed is General Israel Tal, who had served as chief of the Israeli Armoured Corps from 1964 to 1967. Tal was a veteran of the 1948 war, had served as a brigade commander in the Sinai in 1956 and had come to the conclusion that heavy tanks, such as the American Pattons and British Centurions, served Israel's battlefield purpose better than the light French alternatives such as the AMX-13 and AMX-30. Tal reasoned that the heavier armour of the Patton and Centurion afforded greater crew survivability; these tanks also carried larger-calibre weapons. Although they sacrificed some speed, these tanks could work in conjunction with infantry and artillery to reduce fixed fortifications and rapidly penetrate enemy lines. These same tanks would ultimately close with enemy armour and fight decisive battles on a grand scale. Tal emphasized superior training, including superb gunnery skills.

Unlike in earlier Arab–Israeli combat, tank-versus-tank battles were frequent during the Six Day War, and the weaknesses of several tanks, including the M48, were exposed. Although the 90mm (3.5in) guns of the Jordanian Pattons had greater range than

the guns of the Israeli Super Shermans, the M48s proved vulnerable due to their external auxiliary fuel tanks. Once the Israelis discovered this design flaw, numerous Jordanian M48s were put out of action. On 5–6 June 1967, Generals Avraham Yoffe and Ariel Sharon led Israeli armoured forces against the Egyptians at Abu Ageila. The Israeli force consisted of dozens of Centurion and Super Sherman tanks mounting the 105mm (4.1in) French CN 105 F1 gun and a number of AMX-13s with 90mm (3.5in) cannon. Opposing them were 66 Egyptian T-34/85s and 22 SU-100s. Sharon attacked the Arab force from multiple points, destroying 40 AFVs and losing 19 in the fighting.

During the brief but decisive action of the Six Day War, the Israeli Defence Forces occupied 109,000 square kilometres (42,000 square miles) of territory, including the Sinai Peninsula, the West Bank of the Jordan River and, in the north, the Golan Heights. The Old City of Jerusalem had come into Jewish possession for the first time in 2000 years. The Israelis also controlled the strategically vital Suez Canal.

Although armoured forces had contributed significantly to the stunning Israeli victory, the absence of Arab air power had increased the armour's effectiveness on the ground. Combined arms still did not receive the emphasis which the Israelis' own doctrine seemed to demand. Nevertheless, the modern Israeli Defence Forces gained invaluable experience in the deployment of tanks on the battlefield, knowledge of the shortcomings of Arab tanks and an understanding of enhancements which would make their own armoured force one of the finest of its kind in the world.

Yom Kippur War
1973

Intent on reclaiming prestige and territory lost during the Six Day War, Egypt and Syria attacked Israel on two fronts. Following initial successes, however, they were driven back.

THE SURPRISE ASSAULT by the Egyptians across the Suez Canal on 6 October 1973 was in concert with a Syrian strike against Israeli defences in the north on the Golan Heights. Taking the Israelis

completely by surprise, Egyptian troops crossed the canal in small boats, their tanks and armoured vehicles following behind on ferries and pontoon bridges, and pierced the Bar-Lev Line. Israeli commanders had relied on the fixed fortifications of the Bar-Lev Line to repel Egyptian attacks against the Suez Canal and the Sinai Peninsula. They had also counted on armoured formations to hold the Golan Heights with minimal infantry support. Meanwhile, the Egyptians had deployed large numbers of Soviet-made mobile surface-to-air (SAM) missiles. The immediate result was a heavy toll in Israeli aircraft, which had decimated the Arab armoured ranks in the Six Day War of 1967. The Egyptian troops also carried Soviet-made Sagger anti-tank missiles and the RPG-7 shoulder-fired anti-tank weapon, which proved lethal against Israeli tanks. For their part, the Israelis, although they were unprepared for the sudden onslaught on two fronts, quickly recovered. Armed with

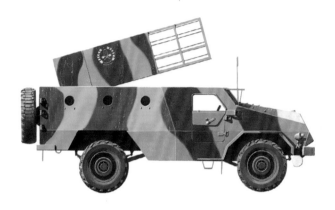

Specifications

Crew: 2
Weight: Not available
Length: 6.12m (20ft)
Width: 2.57m (8ft 5in)
Height: 2.3m (7ft 6in)
Engine: 125kW (168hp) diesel
Speed: 86km/h (54mph)
Range: 800km (500 miles)
Armament: 12 x 80mm (3.15in)
   rocket-launcher tubes
Radio: n/k

▲ **Walid APC rocket launcher**

Egyptian Army / 2nd Infantry Division / 10th Brigade

A variant of the Soviet-produced BTR-152 armoured personnel carrier, the Walid was manufactured in Egypt and exported to other Arab countries. The Walid carried a crew of two and a complement of up to 10 combat infantrymen. Some were fitted with 80mm (3.15in) rocket launchers.

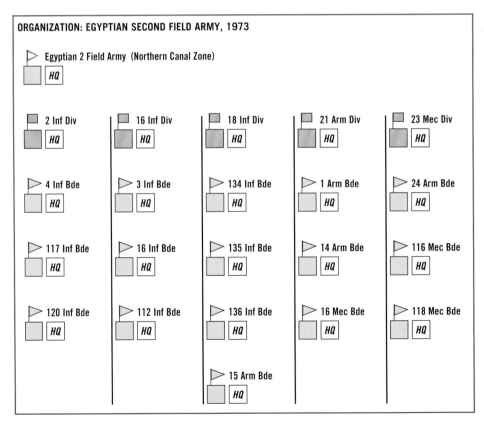

ORGANIZATION: EGYPTIAN SECOND FIELD ARMY, 1973

▷ Egyptian 2 Field Army (Northern Canal Zone)
  HQ

2 Inf Div	16 Inf Div	18 Inf Div	21 Arm Div	23 Mec Div
HQ	HQ	HQ	HQ	HQ
4 Inf Bde	3 Inf Bde	134 Inf Bde	1 Arm Bde	24 Arm Bde
HQ	HQ	HQ	HQ	HQ
117 Inf Bde	16 Inf Bde	135 Inf Bde	14 Arm Bde	116 Mec Bde
HQ	HQ	HQ	HQ	HQ
120 Inf Bde	112 Inf Bde	136 Inf Bde	16 Mec Bde	118 Mec Bde
HQ	HQ	HQ	HQ	HQ
		15 Arm Bde		
		HQ		

▲ Zelda M113 APC

Israeli Defence Forces / 87th Armoured Reconnaissance Battalion /
3rd Company

Incorporating the Toga armour package of perforated steel plates on its front and
sides, the Zelda M113 armoured personnel carrier was an Israeli improvement to
the basic design of the ubiquitous US M113 APC. A command version of the Zelda
was also produced.

Specifications

Crew: 2 + 11

Weight: 12,500kg (27,600lb)

Length: 5.23m (17ft 2in)

Width: 3.08m (10ft 1in)

Height: 1.85m (6ft .8in)

Engine: 158kW (212hp) Detroit Diesel
6V-53T 6-cylinder diesel

Speed: 61km/h (38mph)

Range: 480km (300 miles)

Armament: 1 x 12.7mm (0.5in) MG (2 x 7.62mm/
0.3in) in some configurations

▲ T-34/100 Tank Destroyer

Egyptian Army / 23rd Mechanized Infantry Division / 24th Armoured Brigade

Armed with a 100mm (3.9in) BS-3 anti-tank gun, the T-34/100 was an Egyptian
tank destroyer variant of the Soviet T-34 medium tank. Utilizing the T-34 chassis,
the Egyptians modified the turret with armour plate extensions and added a recoil
mechanism. Lacking the heavier armour protection of more recent tanks, the
T-34/100 was mainly used in a defensive role.

Specifications

Crew: 4

Weight: n/k

Length (hull): 6m (19ft 7in)

Width: 3m (9ft 9in)

Height: n/k

Engine: 372 kW (493hp) V-2 V12 diesel

Speed (road): 55km/h (33mph)

Range: 360km (223 miles)

Armament: 1 x 100mm (3.9in) BS-3
anti-tank gun

Radio: n/k

US-made wire-guided TOW missiles, Israeli troops countered with the destruction of scores of Egyptian and Syrian tanks.

Still, the Yom Kippur War saw major clashes between the main battle tanks of the Israeli Defence Forces and the Egyptian and Syrian Armies. On the eve of the war, the Israelis had indeed intended to mobilize their entire air force along with four armoured divisions and had contemplated a preemptive strike against the Syrians. They were confident that their armoured forces, including the 401st Armoured Brigade, stationed along the Suez Canal and the first unit equipped with the modern American M60 Patton tank, could hold against an Arab thrust. In 1973, the Israeli Armoured Corps consisted of at least 2300 tanks and up to 3000 other armoured vehicles. Israeli armoured formations had been battle-tested during the Six Day War. Their veteran units included the 7th and 188th Armoured Brigades along the Golan Heights.

Israeli tanks in the field included the M48s and M60s of the Magach series, the M-50 and M-51 Super Shermans, the modified British Centurion, which the Israelis called the Sho't, and a large number of T-54/55s that had been captured during the Six Day War and redeployed with Israeli units. Many of the Israeli Magachs and Super Shermans had been upgraded with the British 105mm (4.1in) L7 cannon. An array of self-propelled weapons included the American-made M-109 155mm (6.1in) howitzer. Egyptian forces totalled nearly 1700 tanks, and more than 1000 of these actually crossed the Suez Canal and battled the Israelis in the Sinai in 1973. Armoured personnel carriers of Soviet and Czech manufacture, and self-propelled guns of World War II vintage were also deployed.

The Syrian Army contained more than 1200 tanks. Many of the Arab armoured vehicles were the ageing T-34/85s delivered during the late 1950s; however, the T-54/55 and T-62 main battle tanks (the latter with a 115mm/4.5in main gun) were present in significant numbers, having filled out the depleted Arab armoured formations in the wake of the Six Day War.

Among the Egyptian units that crossed the Suez Canal on 6 October 1973 was the 2nd

ISRAELI ARMY COMMANDERS, OCTOBER 1973	
Name	Command
Maj-Gen David Elazar	CoS General Headquarters
Maj-Gen Israel Tal	Deputy CoS General Headquarters
Maj-Gen Yitzhak Hoffi	GoC Northern Command
Brig-Gen Rafael Eytan	36 Mechanized Division
Maj-Gen Dan Lanner	240 Armoured Division
Maj-Gen Musa Peled	146 Armoured Division
Maj-Gen Yona Ephrat	GoC Central Command
Maj-Gen Shuel Gonen	GoC Southern Command
Brig-Gen Avraham Adan	162 Armoured Division
Maj-Gen Ariel Sharon	143 Armoured Division
Brig-Gen Kalman Magen	252 Armoured Division
Maj-Gen Yeshayahu Gavish	Sinai Command
Maj-Gen B Peled	Air Force
Maj-Gen B Telem	Navy

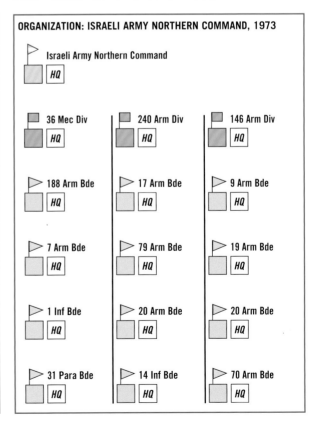

ORGANIZATION: ISRAELI ARMY NORTHERN COMMAND, 1973

Israeli Army Northern Command HQ

36 Mec Div HQ — 240 Arm Div HQ — 146 Arm Div HQ

188 Arm Bde HQ — 17 Arm Bde HQ — 9 Arm Bde HQ

7 Arm Bde HQ — 79 Arm Bde HQ — 19 Arm Bde HQ

1 Inf Bde HQ — 20 Arm Bde HQ — 20 Arm Bde HQ

31 Para Bde HQ — 14 Inf Bde HQ — 70 Arm Bde HQ

Specifications

Crew: 4

Weight: n/k

Length: 6.95m (22ft 10in)

Width: 3.63m (11ft 11in)

Height: 3.27m (10ft 9in)

Engine: 551 kW (750hp) General Dynamics Land
Systems AVDS-1790 series diesel

Speed: n/k

Range: n/k

Armament: 1 x 105mm (4.1in) L7 gun, plus 3 x
7.62mm (0.3in) MGs

Radio: n/k

INSIGNIA

The Israeli Armoured Corps has utilized a series of chevrons, rings, numbers and Hebrew letters for unit designation. In the case of the chevron, a vehicle belonging to a 3rd Company is pictured. Battalion markings were determined by rings around the gun barrel, while platoon and individual tanks were identified by a combination of Hebrew letters and numbers usually painted at the turret rear.

▲ Magach 3 M48 Medium Tank

Israeli Defence Forces / 401st Armoured Brigade / 3rd Battalion / 3rd Company

The Israelis improved the M48 Patton tanks received initially from West Germany and later from the United States with 105mm (4.1in) guns and better diesel engines. M48s lost in the Yom Kippur War were often replaced by M60s.

▲ Sho't Centurion Mk 5

Israeli Defence Forces / 7th Armoured Brigade / 2nd Battalion / 1st Company

Entering service with the Israeli Armoured Corps in 1970, the Sho't was an Israeli variant of the British Centurion tank which had been upgunned with the 105mm (4.1in) L7 gun. Both the Centurion Mk 3 and Mk 5 were upgraded with improved fire control systems and armour as well.

Specifications

Crew: 4

Weight: 5.18 tonnes (4.7 tons)

Length: 7.82m (25ft 8in)

Width: 3.39m (11ft9in)

Height: 3.01m (9ft 10in)

Engine: 480kW (643hp) Continental AVDS-1790-
2A diesel

Speed: 43km/h (27mph)

Range: 205km (127 miles)

Armament: 1 x 105mm (4.1in) L7 gun, plus 1 x
12.7mm (0.5in) ranging MG and
2 x 7.62mm (0.3in) MGs (1 coaxial and 1 on
commander's cupola)

Radio: n/k

Infantry Division, later to be reorganized as the 7th Mechanized Division. Attacking the Bar-Lev Line, the 2nd Division and accompanying formations were supported by more than 800 tanks and took control of the canal, destroying Israeli strongpoints and armoured vehicles in great numbers while losing only 20 of their own tanks.

When the Israelis finally stabilized the front and counterattacked, heavy clashes of armour ensued. On 14 October, the Egyptians committed six of their 26 armoured brigades available in an attempt to claim strategically vital high ground. More than 1000 Egyptian and 800 Israeli tanks engaged in the largest armoured battle since World War II. The Israelis fought in company formation and from prepared positions with the added support of combined arms – artillery, infantry and air support. In a single day, the Egyptians lost 264 tanks, while the Israelis lost only 40. The Israelis seized the momentum and actually crossed the Suez Canal from the east, trapping the Egyptian Third Army.

Golan Heights

The 800 tanks of the Syrian 5th, 7th and 9th Mechanized Infantry Divisions included a large number of T-55 and T-62 models. These hit the Israeli positions along the Golan Heights simultaneously with the Egyptian attack in the Sinai. Only 176 tanks of the Israeli Barak and 7th Armoured Brigades stood between the Syrians and Tel Aviv. At the end of the first day of fighting, the Barak Brigade reported only 15 remaining serviceable tanks. Fighting raged on the heights and in the Valley of Tears. A pair of Israeli Sho't tanks were reported to have stood against 150 Syrian T-55s and T-62s, destroying dozens of them in a 30-hour fight.

In tank-versus-tank combat on the Golan Heights, the Centurion Sho't and other tanks in the Israeli forces were eventually deemed superior to the Arab armour, and within a week the Syrians had lost as many as 1000 tanks. Again, the Israelis seized the initiative and invaded Syria, halting less than 48km (30 miles) from Damascus, the Syrian capital.

They had initially reeled before the Arab onslaught, but during the Yom Kippur War the Israelis demonstrated their ability to adapt older tanks to modern conditions with improved weapons, powerplants and armour protection. Still, their losses in terms of armour were grievous, estimated at well over 1000 tanks. At the end of the Yom Kippur War, the Israeli military establishment was shaken.

IDF, Armoured Reconnaissance Battalion, 1973

Packing substantial firepower, an Israeli armoured reconnaissance battalion during the Yom Kippur War of 1973 consisted of three reconnaissance companies. Each of these included a pair of modified Centurion Sho't tanks with 105mm (4.1in) cannon and three M113 Zelda armoured personnel carriers, with a total capacity of about 100 combat infantrymen.

1 Company (2 x Sho't MBTs; 3 x Zelda M113 APCs)

2 Company (2 x Sho't MBTs; 3 x Zelda M113 APCs)

3 Company (2 x Sho't MBTs; 3 x Zelda M113 APCs)

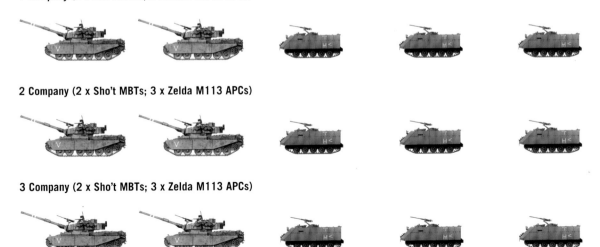

▲ **Soltam Systems L33 155mm SP Howitzer**

Israeli Defence Forces / 188th Armoured Brigade

Distinguished by its large, boxlike turret structure and based on the chassis of
the M4A3E8 Sherman tank, the Soltam Systems L33 mounted a 155mm (6.1in)
cannon. After trials in 1968, the L33 entered production in 1970. The vehicle was
deployed shortly before the Yom Kippur War.

Specifications	
Crew: 8	Engine: 331kW (450hp) Ford GAA V8 petrol
Weight: 41.5 tonnes (40.8 tons)	Speed: 38km/h (24mph)
Length (hull): 5.92m (19ft 5in)	Range: 260km (162 miles)
Width: 2.68m (8ft 9in)	Armament: 1 x 155mm (6.1in) L33 howitzer, plus
Height: n/k	1 x 7.62mm (0.3in) MG
	Radio: n/k

Lebanese Civil War
1975–90

**War-torn Lebanon suffered not only internal strife during 15 years of civil war but also the
intervention of its Arab and Israeli neighbours as well as the terrorism of local insurgent groups.**

FOR YEARS, LEBANON has been wracked by civil war
as paramilitary factions, spurred by nationalism
or religious ardour, vied for control of the country.
Complicating the situation was the presence of
anti-Israeli groups such as the Palestine Liberation
Organization (PLO) and Hezbollah. Syria and
Israel intervened from time to time in the Lebanese
Civil War, with the Israelis attempting to establish
a secure northern border and deter PLO guerrillas
from infiltrating or launching rocket attacks against
settlements near the frontier. Lebanon further provided
a battleground for clashes with Syria, a traditional
enemy of Israel, whose resolve to fight the Jewish state
had been steeled by the separate peace between Israel
and Egypt following the Camp David Accords of 1978.

Attacks by the PLO and other terrorist groups,
along with concern over the growing Syrian presence
in Lebanon, has prompted the Israelis to launch

military operations against Lebanon on several
occasions, including major operations in 1978, 1982
and 2006. In each case, Israeli armour participated.
Intended initially to protect Israel against the armies
of neighbouring Arab states, the Israeli Defence
Forces found themselves often involved in difficult
urban fighting, battling militia armed with anti-
tank weapons and planting improvised explosive
devices (IEDs) along roadways. Counterinsurgency
operations presented particular challenges to Israeli
armour. Close-quarter fighting in narrow streets
diminished the effectiveness of the main battle tank's
manoeuvrability, while the stand-off firepower of a
high-velocity gun was lessened as well.

Armoured development

Through much of the 1970s and into the 1980s, the
Israeli Magach series, based on the American M48

and M60 Patton tanks, served as the backbone of the Israeli armoured forces. These vehicles included the Magach 5 and 6, upgraded with the Blazer armour protection package, the 6B with improved fire control, the 6B Batash with fourth generation passive armour and the Magach 7A and 7C with a thermal sleeve for the 105mm (4.1in) main gun and improved armour configurations.

Following the Yom Kippur War, the Israelis committed to the development of their own main battle tank, comparable to the finest armoured fighting vehicles in the world, including the American Abrams, the German Leopard, the British Chieftain and the Soviet T-72. The result was the Merkava, or Chariot in translation from the Hebrew. The first

Merkava was delivered to the Israeli Defence Forces in 1979, the product of Israeli design, engineering and manufacturing expertise as well as the integration of technology purchased from abroad when necessary.

Merkava and its adversary

General Israel Tal receives much of the credit for the design of the Merkava, which stresses the survivability of the tank's crew, employing entry and exit ports from the rear; it has modern spaced armour, a frontal engine compartment, ammunition stowage to the vehicle's rear and a protective system against nuclear, biological and chemical attack. The latest variant, the Merkava Mk 4, is powered by a General Dynamics GD833 1125kW (1500hp)

Specifications
Crew: 2 + 6
Weight: 3600kg (7900lb)
Length: 5.02m (16ft 5.6in)
Width: 2.03m (6ft 8in)
Height: 1.66m (5ft 5in)
Engine: 89kW (120hp) Chrysler 6-cylinder petrol
Speed: 100km/h (62mph)
Range: 550km (340 miles)
Armament: 1 x 7.62mm (0.3in) MG
Radio: n/k

▲ RBY Mk 1

Israeli Defence Forces / Golani Brigade / 51st Battalion

A light armoured reconnaissance vehicle produced by Israel Aircraft Industries, the RBY Mk 1 has been in service with the Israeli Defence Forces and the armies of other countries since 1975. A variety of machine guns and cannon can be fitted to the vehicle, including a 106mm (4.17in) recoilless rifle. The Israelis have largely replaced it with the RAM 2000.

▲ Rascal

Israeli Defence Forces / Southern Regional Command / 366th Division / 55th Artillery Battalion 'Draken' ('Dragon')

The light, self-propelled Rascal 155mm (6.1in) gun was designed and built by Soltam Ltd. Weighing only 20.3 tonnes (20 tons), the Rascal was the lightest of the Soltam 155mm (6.1in) self-propelled weapons. It was capable of transport by air, truck or rail.

Specifications
Crew: 4
Weight: 19,500kg (43,000lb)
Length (with gun): 7.5m (24ft 7in)
Width: 2.46m (8ft 1in)
Height: 2.3m (7ft 7in)
Engine: 261kW (350hp) diesel
Speed: 50km/h (31mph)
Range: 350km (220 miles)
Armament: 1 x 155mm (6.1in) howitzer

diesel engine. Its 120mm (4.7in) gun is second to none in firepower.

The Soviet-designed T-72 tanks in service with the Syrian Army trace their lineage to the T-62 and the T-54/55. Production of the T-72 was undertaken in 1971. The tank mounts a powerful 125mm (4.9in) 2A46M smoothbore gun, and the basic vehicle is powered by a 585kW (780hp) V12 diesel engine. Several variants of the T-72 have been produced, including the T-72A with improved laser rangefinding

equipment and better optics. The T-72M and T-72M1, export versions of the T-72A, were delivered to Syria and included heavier armour protection for the frontal hull and turret. Estimates of the number of T-72s utilized by the Syrian Army top 1500.

During the periodic fighting in Lebanon, Israeli Merkava and Syrian T-72 tanks have reportedly met on a number of occasions. While each side has claimed that its main battle tank is superior to that of the other, it is well known that Iraqi export

Specifications

Crew: 7

Weight: n/k

Length (hull): 6m (19ft 7in)

Width: 3m (9ft 10in)

Height: n/k

Engine: 372 kW (493hp) V-2 V12 diesel

Speed (road): 55km/h (33mph)

Range: 360km (223 miles)

Armament: 1 x 122mm (4.8in) D-30 howitzer

Radio: n/k

▲ **T-34/122 SP Howitzer**

Egyptian Army / 7th Mechanized Division, 1975

As the T-34/85 medium tank became obsolete as a main battle tank, the Egyptian Army adapted the chassis to carry a heavy 122mm (4.8in) D-30 howitzer for mobile fire support of its mechanized infantry formations. The howitzer was mounted either in a modified turret or openly. The modification consisted of cutting away the roof and rear parts of the turret, and building a new, larger turret out of sheet armour.

▲ **T-34 with 122mm D-30 SP Howitzer**

Syrian Army / 1st Armoured Division / 58th Mechanized Brigade, Lebanon, 1982

The Syrian Army adapted the heavy D-30 122mm (4.8in) howitzer to the T-34 medium tank chassis and produced a self-propelled weapon with an open platform for the crew operating the gun. When the vehicle was in motion, the platform folded.

Specifications

Crew: 7

Weight: n/k

Length (hull): 6m (19ft 7in)

Width: 3m (9ft 10in)

Height: n/k

Engine: 372 kW (493hp) V-2 V12 diesel

Speed (road): 55km/h (33mph)

Range: 360km (223 miles)

Armament: 1 x 122mm (4.8in) D-30 howitzer

A Syrian T-55 halts beside the road in the much fought-over Golan Heights, sometime in the 1970s.

versions of the T-72 were decimated by coalition forces during the Gulf War of 1991 and the US-led invasion of Iraq in 2003. Although the Israelis acknowledged that they did sustain the loss of some Merkavas against the Syrians, they also asserted that none of the tanks' crewmen were killed in action.

Street fighting

While direct confrontations between Israeli and Syrian tanks have been common enough in southern Lebanon, the counterinsurgency operations of the Israeli Defence Forces required modifications to existing armoured fighting vehicles. Claims that no Merkava crewmen were killed in earlier battles could not hold true during the 2006 Lebanon War.

The Israeli Merkava tanks battled Hezbollah guerrillas armed with modern anti-tank missiles, such as the Russian A-14 Komet and RPG-29 Vampir. Projectiles penetrated the armour of at least five Merkavas. Improvised explosive devices also proved hazardous. The lessons learned fighting in the streets of Lebanese towns off and on for more than a decade resulted in the addition of a removable V-shaped underbelly armour package along with other improvements.

The Merkava LIC, a variant of the Mk 3 BAZ and Mk 4 tanks, is specifically designed for urban warfare, otherwise known as 'low intensity conflict'. The Merkava LIC includes a turret-mounted 12.7mm (0.5in) machine gun for close-in fire support and protection against infantry. The weapon is fired from within the tank, avoiding the exposure of the crewmen to small-arms fire. A camera facing to the tank's rear provides the driver with a more complete view of the vehicle's close surroundings, particularly valuable in an urban setting,. A strong steel mesh protects vulnerable areas of the tank, such as exhaust tubes, optical equipment and ventilation structures, against the attachment of explosives.

▲ **T-34/85M Medium Tank**

Palestine Liberation Army, 1980

Also known as the Model 1969, the T-34/85M actually incorporated some components of the later Soviet T-54/55 tank, including similar road wheels, external auxiliary fuel tanks, night driving and vision equipment and improved communication gear.

Specifications

Crew: 5	38.88-l diesel
Weight: 32 tonnes (31.5 tons)	Speed (road): 55km/h (33mph)
Length: 6m (19ft 7in)	Range: 360km (223 miles)
Width: 3m (9ft 10in)	Armament: 1 x 85mm (3.4in) ZiS-S-53 cannon; 2
Height: 2.6m (8ft 6in)	x 7.62mm (0.3in) DT MGs (bow and coaxial)
Engine: 433kW (581hp) Model V-55 12-cyl.	Radio: R-123

▲ **Khalid Main Battle Tank**

Royal Jordanian Land Forces, 1990

The Khalid main battle tank is based on a late production model of the British Chieftain tank, which includes specifications particular to the requirements of the Jordanian military, such as a 900kW (1200hp) Condor diesel engine and fire control specialization. In November 1979, Jordan placed an order with the UK manufacturers for 274 Khalid MBTs for delivery from 1981. Alterations carried out since the Khalid entered service with the Jordanian Army have included modifications of sights and stowage to allow for the carrying and firing of the Royal Ordnance 120mm (4.7in) APFSDS-T ammunition.

Specifications

Crew: 4

Weight: 58,000kg (127,890lb)

Length (hull): 6.39m (21ft 10in)

Width: 3.42m (11ft 7in)

Height: 2.435m (9ft 11in)

Engine: 900kW (1200hp) Perkins Engines Condor
 V12 1200 12-cylinder diesel

Speed: 48km/h (30mph)

Range: 400km (248.5 miles)

Armament: 1 x 120mm (4.7in) L11A5 gun,
 plus 2 x 7.62mm (0.3in) MGs

Radio: n/k

Iran–Iraq War
1980–88

Border disputes and struggles to gain preeminence among the nations of the Persian Gulf spurred Saddam Hussein's Iraq to attack Iran.

During the decade from 1968 to 1978, the Baathist regime in Iraq purchased hundreds of tanks, self-propelled guns and support vehicles from the Soviet Union and France. In 1973 alone, the Iraqis ordered 400 T-55 and T-62 tanks. This was followed by an order for 600 T-62s three years later. By 1980, the Soviets had delivered.

In 1978, the French delivered 100 AMX-30B tanks and 100 VCR-6 armoured personnel carriers equipped with anti-tank missile systems to Iraq. Meanwhile, US arms shipments to the military machine of the Shah of Iran neared $1.5 billion between 1950 and 1970. Replacement parts, including engines for the latest Patton series main

battle tank, the M60, were reported to have been supplied by Israel.

When Saddam Hussein attacked Iran in 1980, the Iraqi Army numbered nearly 200,000 men and 2200 tanks. Confident of victory, his armoured spearheads attacked areas where only company-sized Iranian armoured units were available to defend. Eventually, however, the steady Iraqi advance was halted. Throughout the 1970s, Iraq had purchased large quantities of T-55, T-62 and T-72 main battle tanks from the Soviet Union as well as more than 500 BTR-50 and BTR-60 armoured personnel carriers. By 1976, more than 1000 Soviet-built tanks had been delivered to Iraq. This trend continued

▶ **Iranian armour**

A Soviet-built T-72 main battle tank in Iranian colours stops by the roadside during the Iran–Iraq War of the 1980s.

during the eight-year war with Iran, and by 1990 Iraq had made good its losses and even augmented its armoured force to 5700 tanks.

Post-revolutionary Iran, on the other hand, had isolated itself from the rest of the world, and much of the armoured force at its disposal lacked spare parts or trained maintenance personnel. In the Iranian arsenal were American-made M47 and M48 Patton tanks, British Chieftain Mk 5 main battle tanks and light armoured vehicles of US, British and Soviet manufacture. With the ascent of the Ayatollah Khomeini in 1979, an order with Britain for the Shir Iran 2 tank was cancelled. This design was subsequently developed by the British into the new Challenger tank. In 1979, the Iranian Army fielded five organized armoured divisions and several independent armoured formations attached to infantry units. Nearly 200 of its tanks were Shir

Iran 1 variants of the Mk 5 Chieftain, shipped from Britain prior to the overthrow of the Shah. During the Iran–Iraq War, the People's Republic of China emerged as a major supplier of arms to both belligerents, including copies of Soviet armoured vehicles, and along with North Korea remained a primary post-war supplier to Iran.

Neither Iran nor Iraq employed sustainable armoured doctrine to any great extent during the war. Neither chose to utilize tank formations in manoeuvre, opting to dig tanks into revetments and employ them as artillery pieces. As stationary

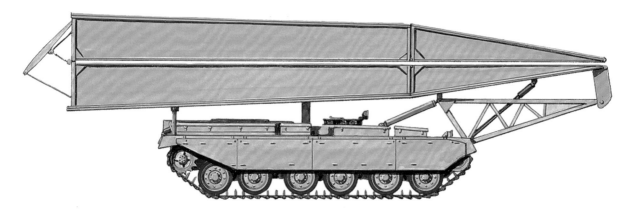

Specifications

Crew: 3	Engine: 559kW (750hp) Leyland L60 12-cylinder
Weight: 53.3 tonnes (117,500lb)	multi-fuel
Length: 13.74m (45ft 9in)	Speed: 48km/h (30mph)
Width: 4.16m (13ft 8in)	Range: 400km (250 miles)
Height: 3.92m (12ft 10in)	Armament: None

▲ **Cheftain AVLB**

Iranian Army / 92nd Armoured Division

Based on the chassis of the Chieftain Mk 5 tank, the AVLB (Armoured Vehicle Launched Bridge) bridging tank was a component of a large order placed by the Imperial Iranian Army in 1971. Delivery of 707 Chieftains, including main battle tanks and several variants, was completed in early 1978.

targets, they were often easily dispatched by anti-tank weapons. The ill-trained crewmen of both sides struggled to implement the technology of their weapons. Therefore gunnery was poor and fire control systems were underutilized. Maintenance was virtually non-existent in many cases.

Fourth largest army

An inflexible Iraqi command structure and an apparent unwillingness on the part of Saddam Hussein's generals to commit substantial armoured forces to a decisive battle hampered Iraqi combat effectiveness and contributed to the prolonged war of attrition. Iraq maintained an edge in tanks, acquiring upgraded export versions of the T-72 by 1987. In spite of

staggering losses, the Iraqi Army had swelled to 1.7 million men that year, including five armoured divisions, each with an armoured brigade and a mechanized brigade, and three fully mechanized divisions consisting of at least one armoured brigade and two brigades of mechanized infantry. The elite Presidential Guard Force included three more armoured brigades. Saddam Hussein's army had grown to the fourth largest in the world – a force with which an international coalition would soon contend.

The Iranian advantage was in sheer weight of numbers. Human wave attacks were a common Iranian offensive tactic. Each side was reported to have used chemical weapons. The estimated death toll for both combatants was well above 200,000.

Specifications

Crew: 3 + 9

Weight: 7 tonnes (15,400lb)

Length: 4.57m (14ft 11.8in)

Width: 2.49m (8ft 2in)

Height: 2.03m (6ft 8in)

Engine: 108kW (145hp) Peugeot PRV 6-cylinder
  petrol

Speed: 100km/h (62mph)

Range: 800km (500 miles)

Armament: 1 x 7.62mm (0.3in) MG

Radio: n/k

▲ **Panhard VCR Armoured Personnel Carrier**

Iraqi Army / 1st Mechanized Division

Developed in France at the request of the Iraqi government, the Panhard VCR was an armoured personnel carrier capable of transporting a complement of nine infantrymen. The vehicle was also developed as a platform for turrets capable of launching anti-tank guided missiles, following the purchase of these by Iraq.

Specifications

Crew: 1 + 12

Weight: 13 tonnes (28,600lb)

Length: 6.15m (20ft 2in)

Width: 2.59m (8ft 6in)

Height: 2.09m (6ft 10.3in)

Engine: 158kW (212hp) Detroit Diesel 6V-53N
  6-cylinder diesel

Speed: 90km/h (56mph)

Range: 850km (528 miles)

Armament: 1 x 12.7mm (0.5in) HMG, plus
  1 x 7.62mm (0.3in) MG

Radio: n/k

▲ **EE-11 Armoured Personnel Carrier**

Iraqi Army / 9th Armoured Division

Utilized by both Iraq and Iran, the EE-11 Urutu was designed, manufactured and exported by Brazil in the early 1980s. The EE-11 is capable of carrying up to 12 combat infantrymen and has proven comparable to better known, more costly designs.

Chapter 6

Post-Cold War Conflicts

The absence of Cold War has not ushered in an era of absence of conflict. On the contrary, the main battle tank, its complementary armoured fighting vehicles and the mechanized infantry who man them have maintained a preeminent role in combat operations on land. Just as control of the air and sea have long been essential for victory in war, the missions of taking and holding ground are accomplished only in the context of the defeat of an enemy army. The presence of the tank and armoured fighting vehicle projects the capability of an armed force to accomplish such a task.

◀ **Main battle tank**
A US Army M1A1 Abrams from Apache Troop, 5 Cavalry, 2nd Brigade Combat Team (BCT), 1st Cavalry Division moves out to rejoin the fight after refuelling during a combat operation in Fallujah, Iraq, during Operation Iraqi Freedom.

From Gulf War to Afghanistan

Turning their tanks against guerrilla tactics and insurgency warfare, great armed coalitions have committed to the continuing struggle for dominance in the Middle East and Central Asia.

WHILE THE THREAT of a Cold War-type confrontation between major powers has diminished sharply, the demands for military intervention to maintain an uneasy peace or to dislodge the armies of an aggressor who has unlawfully seized the territory of a neighbour have been steady during the last quarter of a century. Such has been the case with the Gulf War and in the intervention by NATO in Afghanistan, the Balkans and elsewhere. During the same period, the peacekeeping forces of the United Nations have deployed around the world, including the Middle East, the Balkans and the Horn of Africa.

Gulf War

When Saddam Hussein of Iraq sent his army into Kuwait on 2 August 1990, the civilized world met force with force. The invasion of Kuwait was the second unprovoked military offensive undertaken by Saddam Hussein in a decade. In 1980, he had taken advantage of unrest in neighbouring Iran and invaded that country, leading to a prolonged, devastating and bloody eight-year war. During that time, the Baathist dictator continued to build the capacity of his armed forces to wage war. By 1990, the Iraqi Army had grown to the fourth largest in the world. Iraq's armed forces were made up of a large contingent of infantry, Fedayeen irregular troops and an armoured capability spearheaded by the T-54/55 and T-72 tanks manufactured in the Soviet Union and the Eastern European client states of the Soviet Bloc during the 1980s.

Invasion of Iraq

More than a decade later, in 2003, a second armed coalition, led by the United States and Great Britain, invaded Iraq and toppled the repressive regime of Saddam Hussein. US Abrams and British Challenger main battle tanks were instrumental in the drive across hundreds of kilometres of desert to the Iraqi capital of Baghdad and the key port city of Basra respectively. During operations in the southern city of Nasiriyah, images of the tanks and the US Marine AAV7 amphibious infantry fighting vehicle

▲ **Outgunned**

An Iraqi T-55 main battle tank burns after being knocked out by tanks from the British 1st Armoured Division during Operation Desert Storm, 1991. The outdated T-55 proved no match for the latest technology in the Coalition's armoury.

▲ **Soviet hardware**
Iraqi troops pass by in a BMP-1 amphibious tracked infantry fighting vehicle, 2006, during a mission in support of Operation Iraqi Freedom.

were beamed worldwide. In Basra, the Challenger 2 tanks of the British 7th Armoured Brigade were instrumental in capturing the city and maintaining an uneasy peace in the aftermath.

Afghanistan

Meanwhile, the rise of Islamic fundamentalism has threatened to destabilize much of the Arab world and establish conservative regimes in the Middle East and Central Asia. The Taliban has fought a guerrilla war in the mountainous terrain of Afghanistan, boldly seizing large areas of the country. Financed also by the illicit drug trade, the Taliban has openly supported the terrorism of al-Qaeda.

While overwhelming military might is somewhat neutralized by the conduct of low-intensity counterinsurgency warfare, the armour protection of the main battle tank and the armoured fighting vehicle offers an offensive capability to suppress small-arms fire and advance rapidly over favourable terrain. One of the greatest hazards to armoured operations during the recent fighting in Iraq and Afghanistan has been the improvised explosive device (IED). Guerrilla fighters have engineered powerful explosives, often with discarded ordnance such as old landmines and artillery shells. Buried alongside roadways or directly in the anticipated path of an armoured vehicle or truck, the IED may be detonated by contact pressure as tyres or tracks roll forward, or by remote control

with such readily available devices as the common cell phone. In response, NATO vehicles such as the US M2/M3 Bradley fighting vehicle, the Humvee and the British Warrior have been reinforced with appliqué armour to protect crewmen and passengers. Main battle tanks have been fitted with additional armour protection and with armament and defence packages specifically designed to withstand the blast of a roadside bomb or to defeat guerrilla forces in a close-quarter, urban battle where the ability to fire and manoeuvre is limited and civilian populations may be threatened.

Global demands

During United Nations peacekeeping operations and the efforts of NATO forces to quell ethnic violence, particularly in the Balkans and East Africa, major armoured contingents from the United States, Great Britain and other nations of Europe and the Middle East have deployed to these troubled areas. These forces' armoured cars, infantry fighting vehicles and armoured fighting vehicles have proved essential for maintaining security for military and civilian areas, while providing rapid mobility in rugged terrain.

Gulf War – Coalition forces
1991

Trained and prepared for a war against the forces of the Warsaw Pact on the plains of northern Europe, major Coalition armoured assets from the United States and Great Britain entered combat in the desert.

IN RESPONSE TO THE IRAQI INVASION of Kuwait, an armed Coalition of 29 nations mounted an offensive effort on a scale not seen since World War II in an effort to liberate the tiny Arab state. A massive logistical undertaking ensued, as Coalition forces were concentrated from around the globe, many coming from bases in Europe and half a world away in the United States. Operation Desert Shield involved the movement of hundreds of thousands of personnel and millions of tonnes of equipment to staging areas in Saudi Arabia and other Middle East nations.

Primary among the engines of war brought to bear were the main battle tanks and armoured fighting vehicles of the Coalition forces. These included the American M1A1 Abrams, the British Challenger and the French AMX-30, designed and built for a confrontation against the Warsaw Pact in Europe but destined for a confrontation with the Soviet-designed T-72M main battle tanks and armoured vehicles of the Iraqi Army and its elite Republican Guard divisions.

Abrams arrival

When the US 24th Infantry Division and its mechanized units reached Saudi Arabia in the autumn of 1990, its equipment included the first Abrams tanks in theatre. Many of these were the initial configuration of the M1. Eventually, more than 1800 examples of the Abrams tank were deployed during the Gulf War, and more than 800 field modifications were made to upgrade to the M1A1, which bore the brunt of the tank-versus-tank fighting between US and Iraqi forces.

The development of the M1 Abrams may be traced to the late 1960s, more than two decades prior to the vehicle seeing its first combat in 1991. It entered service in 1980 as a replacement for the ageing M60 Patton tanks then in use with the US Army. However, some Patton upgrades, primarily the M60A1 and M60A3, were engaged during the

▲ **M2 Bradley Infantry Fighting Vehicle**

US Army / 24th Mechanized Infantry Division / 3rd Armoured Cavalry Regiment
The 450kW (600hp) eight-cylinder Cummins VTA-903T diesel engine was capable of delivering road speeds of 64km/h (40mph), and the heavily armed M2 Bradley infantry fighting vehicle proved particularly adept at desert warfare.

Specifications

Crew: 3 + 6	Speed: 64km/h (40mph)
Weight: 22,940kg (50,574lb)	Range: 483km (300 miles)
Length: 6.55m (21ft 6in)	Armament: 1 x 25mm (1in) Bushmaster Chain
Width: 3.61m (11ft 9in)	Gun, plus 2 x TOW missile launchers and
Height (turret roof): 2.57m (8ft 5in)	1 x 7.62mm (0.3in) MG
Engine: 450kW (600hp) Cummins VTA-903T	Radio: n/k
turbocharged 8-cylinder diesel	

Gulf War. The early Abrams incorporated several improvements over the M60, including better crew survivability, with ammunition stored as far from crew areas as possible and subsequently a blast door in the turret bustle, which separated ammunition from the crew compartment. Additionally, specialized blow-out armour was designed to distribute the impact of an explosion to further minimize casualties. Composite armour similar to the British Chobham was also installed. Early M1 tanks were armed with the 105mm (4.1in) M68 rifled cannon; however, as the M1 programme went into full production, the decision was made to upgun the tank with the M256 120mm (4.7in) smoothbore cannon, adapted for the

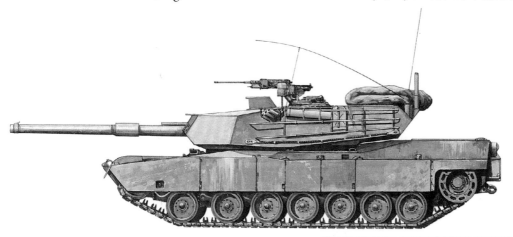

▲ M1A1 Abrams Main Battle Tank

US Army / 1st Armoured Division / 3rd Armored Brigade

The M1A1 Abrams main battle tank dominated the Gulf War battlefield and revealed the extent to which its FLIR (forward-looking infrared) sights could be effective at night. The M1A1 could fix and destroy Iraqi targets often before the opponent was aware of its presence.

Specifications

Crew: 4	AGT 1500 gas turbine
Weight: 57,154kg (126,024lb)	Speed: 67km/h (42mph)
Length (over gun): 9.77m (32ft 3in)	Range: 465km (289 miles)
Width: 3.66m (12ft)	Armament: 1 x 120mm (4.7in) M256 gun; 1 x
Height: 2.44m (8ft)	12.7mm (0.5in) MG; 2 x 7.62mm (0.3in) MGs
Engine: 1119.4kW (1500hp) Textron Lycoming	Radio: n/k

▲ M60A3 Patton Medium Tank

US Marine Expeditionary Force / 1st Tank Battalion

The M60A3 variant of the Patton tank series was deployed to the Gulf and featured improvements such as the latest in APFSDS (armour-piercing fin-stabilized discarding sabot) ammunition, laser rangefinding equipment, smoke dischargers, gun stabilization and thermal imaging night sights.

Specifications

Crew: 4	1790-2A V12 turbocharged diesel
Weight: 52,617kg (51.8 tons)	Speed: 48km/h (30mph)
Length (over gun): 9.44m (31ft)	Range: 500km (311 miles)
Width: 3.63m (11ft 11in)	Armament: 1 x 105mm (4.1in) M68 gun; 1 x
Height: 3.27m (10ft 8in)	12.7mm (0.5in) HMG; 1 x 7.62mm (0.3in) MG
Engine: 559.7kW (750hp) Continental AVDS-	Radio: n/k

Abrams from the Rheinmetall gun which equipped the German Leopard 2 main battle tank.

Nearly 3300 M1s were built during the first five years of production, and by 1986 the M1A1 upgrade programme included a more sophisticated NBC (nuclear, biological and chemical) defence suite, upgraded armour protection and improvements to the tank suspension. Throughout its service life, one of the most controversial components of the Abrams has been its 1120kW (1500hp) gas turbine engine. A fierce debate as to the adoption of the gas turbine or a more traditional diesel engine had concluded with the former winning out. Its power-to-weight ratio resulted in greater power without appreciable added weight; however, the engine was a voracious consumer of fuel, presenting a logistical challenge. In numerous configurations, the M1 Abrams main battle tank has been exported to Saudi Arabia, Egypt, Australia and Kuwait.

Bradley breakthrough

Both the infantry (M2) and cavalry (M3) variants of the Bradley fighting vehicle compiled impressive combat records during the Gulf War. Having entered service in 1981, the Bradley had survived at least 15 years of controversial, scandal-ridden development. The Bradley mounted a McDonnell Douglas M242 25mm (1in) chain gun, capable of penetrating the

thin skins of Iraqi BMP-1 armoured vehicles, along with the effective TOW anti-tank missile system. It had a crew of three and also transported a squad of six combat infantrymen.

British behemoth

The road to deployment for the British Challenger tank had been somewhat circuitous by the time of the Gulf War. The Challenger had been originally designed for export to Iran as the Shir Iran 2 main battle tank, but the order for delivery was promptly cancelled in 1980 after the regime of the Shah had been overthrown by the Islam-inspired Iranian revolution. The cooperative MBT-80 tank programme had failed in Britain and Germany, and the Shir Iran 2 project was adapted for use by the British Army as the Challenger, which was eventually expected to replace the Cold War-era Chieftain. The decision was made following consideration of the purchase of either the American Abrams or the German Leopard 2.

The Challenger mounted the L11A5 120mm (4.7in) gun, carried over from the Chieftain, and employed advanced composite Chobham armour, which was named for the location of the Fighting Vehicle Research and Development Establishment where the material was developed. The armour itself had come about in an effort to improve tank

▲ **Challenger 1 Main Battle Tank**

British Army / 1st Armoured Division / 7th Armoured Brigade

The Challenger 1 main battle tank employed innovative Chobham armour and a powerful 120mm (4.7in) main gun during the 1991 Gulf War. Its service life was somewhat limited, and by 2000 it had been replaced by the heavily redesigned Challenger 2.

Specifications

Crew: 4	Speed: 55km/h (35mph)
Weight: 62,000kg (136,400lb)	Range: 400km (250 miles)
Length (gun forward): 11.56m (35ft 4in)	Armament: 1 x 120mm (4.7in) L11A5 gun,
Width: 3.52m (10ft 8in)	plus 2 x 7.62mm (0.3in) MGs and 2 x smoke
Height: 2.5m (7ft 5in)	dischargers
Engine: 895kW (1200hp) liquid-cooled diesel	Radio: Long range, directional communications
	system with satellite relay capabilities

▲ **Desert Storm**

A British Challenger 1 main battle tank waits by the Basra–Kuwait Highway near
Kuwait City following the retreat of Iraqi forces during Operation Desert Storm. In
the background are British armoured personnel carriers and a wrecked
garbage truck.

survivability against a new generation of ammunition and anti-tank weapons. Offering equivalent protection to much greater thicknesses of rolled homogeneous steel, Chobham was to prove effective against the modern APFSDS (armour-piercing fin-stabilized discarding sabot) ammunition, although most of the ammunition available to Iraqi forces was of older HEAT (high-explosive anti-tank) types.

The Challenger also retained the armour side skirts of the Chieftain and much of its predecessor's suspension. The powerplant consisted of an 895kW (1200hp) V12 diesel engine. Modifications resulted in a total of four variants, or marks, being produced. The Challenger served as the primary British main battle tank during the 1991 Gulf War, and its performance was exemplary. Only with the development of the Challenger 2 did the Gulf War tank assume the designation of Challenger 1.

More than 400 Challenger 1 tanks were built; the first of them had been delivered to the British Army in 1983, initially to the Royal Hussars. By 2000, the majority of the Challenger 1 models had been retired from active service with the British Army. The Jordanian Army purchased 288 upgraded Challenger 1 tanks from Great Britain and placed them in service as the Al Hussein.

Lethal efficiency

While the 1991 Gulf War cannot firmly establish the dominance of the Coalition armoured forces over those of the Warsaw Pact, it is known that in the event the Iraqi tanks were no match for their opponents. True enough, the Iraqis utilized export variants of the Soviet main battle tanks, failed to maintain their equipment to its highest degree of efficiency and were denied the latest in ammunition and technological upgrades. Coalition tanks outranged their Iraqi opponents substantially and were regularly able to destroy targets at stand-off distances. Still, the greatest disparity between the armoured forces was determined to be the level of training and combat efficiency of the tank crews themselves. US and British tank crews had trained for endless hours, the Americans becoming quite familiar with the execution of the AirLand Battle Doctrine initially formulated for combat in Europe but equally effective in the deserts of the Middle East. Coalition tank crews worked in coordinated and effective combat teams, including mechanized infantry, armour and armoured cavalry with tactical air support.

Combined with the high level of combat-readiness exhibited by the Coalition armoured forces, the superior technology of the M1A1 Abrams and the Challenger were devastating. During the Gulf War, the Challenger was credited with the destruction of approximately 300 Iraqi tanks and armoured vehicles without a single loss to enemy fire. The M1A1 Abrams amassed a similar record. For example, during the battle of 73 Easting, the US 3rd Brigade, 1st Infantry Division destroyed 60 Iraqi tanks and 35 armoured fighting vehicles. At Medina Ridge, nearly 100 Iraqi armoured vehicles were destroyed. Only 18 Abrams tanks were lost during the Gulf War, and the majority of these were due to incidents of friendly fire.

▲ Centurion AVRE

British Army / Royal Armoured Corps / 2nd Royal Tank Regiment

The chassis of the Centurion main battle tank provided the platform for a number of variants. During Operation Desert Storm, the Centurion AVRE (Armoured Vehicle Royal Engineers) mounted a 165mm (6.5in) demolition gun and was often equipped with a dozer blade.

Specifications

Crew: 5	Speed: 34.6km/h (21.5mph)
Weight: 51,809kg (113,979lb)	Range: 177km (110 miles)
Length: 8.69m (28ft 6in)	Armament: 1 x 165mm (6.5in) demolition gun,
Width: 3.96m (13ft)	plus 2 x 7.62mm (0.3in) MGs (1 coaxial, 1
Height: 3m (9ft 10in)	anti-aircraft)
Engine: 484.7kW (650hp) Rolls-Royce Meteor	Radio: n/k
Mk IVB 12-cylinder petrol	

Specifications

Crew: 1	Engine: 100kW (134hp) V-8 water-cooled petrol
Weight: 3050kg (6710lb)	Speed: 105km/h (65.6mph)
Length: 4.67m (15ft 4in)	Range: 748km (465 miles)
Width: 1.79m (5ft 11in)	Armament: 2 x 7.62mm (0.3in) MGs
Height: 2.03m (6ft 8in)	

▲ SAS Land Rover

British Army / 22nd Special Air Service / A Squadron

The long-serving SAS Land Rover was deployed with British SpecialAir Service units during Operation Desert Storm, one of its primary missions being the transport of SAS teams deep behind enemy lines on search-and-destroy missions against mobile Iraqi Scud missile sites.

4th Dragoon Regiment, 1991

The standard French armoured regiment of the Gulf War included a company of AMX-10P infantry combat vehicles and a complement of 18 AMX-30 main battle tanks arranged in a headquarters detachment and three squadrons. The AMX-30 had been produced since the mid-1960s and mounted a 105mm (4.1in) main gun. It also served with the armies of Saudi Arabia, Spain, Qatar and Iraq.

HQ (3 x AMX-30 MBT)

Armoured Squadron 1 (5 x AMX-30 MBTs: 1 HQ + 4)

Armoured Squadron 2 (5 x AMX-30 MBTs: 1 HQ + 4)

Armoured Squadron 3 (5 x AMX-30 MBTs: 1 HQ + 4)

Mechanized Infantry Company (6 x AMX-10P ICV)

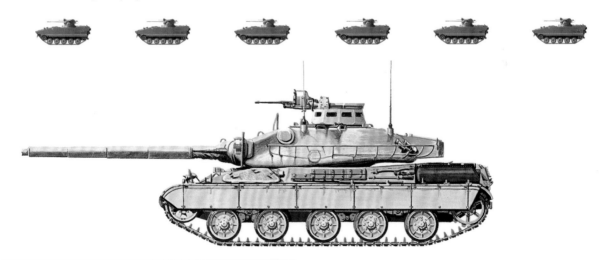

▲ AMX-30 Main Battle Tank

French Army / Sixth Light Armoured Division / 4th Dragoon Regiment

In addition to its main armament, the French AMX-30, developed by GIAT, also mounted a powerful 20mm (0.79in) autocannon. Many of the French tanks deployed during Desert Storm were the AMX-30B with an improved transmission and engine performance, as well as the capability of firing updated ammunition.

Specifications

Crew: 4	12-cylinder diesel
Weight: 35,941kg (79,072lb)	Speed: 65km/h (40mph)
Length: 9.48m (31ft 1in)	Range: 600km (373 miles)
Width: 3.1m (10ft 2in)	Armament: 1 x 105mm (4.1in) gun; 1 x 20mm
Height: 2.86m (9ft 4in)	(0.79in) cannon; 1 x 7.62mm (0.3in) MG
Engine: 537kW (720hp) Hispano-Suiza	Radio: n/k

Gulf War – Iraqi forces
1991

Although Saddam Hussein had built the Iraqi Army into the fourth largest in the world, its inferior equipment and inadequate training were incapable of withstanding the Coalition air and ground assaults.

B Y 1990, THE IRAQI ARMY included both infantry and armoured formations that had been hardened by eight years of costly combat with neighbouring Iran. Saddam Hussein had continued to import main battle tanks of Soviet design, particularly the T-72M and its sub-variants, manufactured in the Soviet Union and in the Warsaw Pact nations of Poland and Czechoslovakia.

Armed with the 125mm (4.9in) 2A46M smoothbore gun, the T-72M mounted formidable firepower. Its powerplant consisted of a 585kW (780hp) 12-cylinder diesel engine, and its improved models were equipped with ceramic composite and steel appliqué armour.

Early T-72 export models were specifically designed for the Middle East market, and initial deliveries of the T-72M to Iraq were undertaken in 1980 soon after the war with Iran broke out. During the subsequent decade, the Iraqi armoured force

INSIGNIA

The red triangle insignia was the emblem of the elite Republican Guards divisions of the Iraqi Army. During Operation Desert Storm, Republican Guards armoured formations were devastated by Coalition tanks during battles such as Medina Ridge on 27 February 1991.

mirrored the organizational structure of Western armies, particularly that of the British. Tactically, it was influenced by Soviet advisors who had been offered to instruct Iraqi crews in the operation of the T-72M.

During the Gulf War, the Iraqi armoured force included the mechanized *Tawakalna* Division and the *Medina* and *Hammurabi* Armoured Divisions of the elite Republican Guard, and the 3rd *Saladin* Division of the regular army. Organizationally, these

▲ **T-55 Main Battle Tank**

Iraqi Army / Tawakalna Division (Mechanized)

The Iraqis modified the T-55 with more armour plating, the addition of 160mm (6.3in) mortars and an observation mast. Some Iraqi T-55s had been fitted with a 105mm (4.1in) main gun, converting this antiquated tank into a tank killer capable of firing armour-piercing rounds. The *Tawakalna* Division suffered heavy losses of AFVs at the Battle of 73 Easting on 26 February, 1991 – the first ground defeat of a Republican Guard unit.

Specifications

Crew: 4	Speed: 48km/h (30mph)
Weight: 39.7 tonnes (39 tons)	Range: 400km (250 miles)
Length (hull): 6.45m (21ft 2in)	Armament: 1 x 100mm (3.9in) D-10T gun, plus 1
Width: 3.27m (10ft 9in)	x 12.7mm (0.5in) DShK AA MG mounted on turret
Height: 2.4m (7ft 10in)	and 2 x 7.62mm (0.3in) DT MGs
Engine: 433kW (581hp) V-55 12-cylinder	Radio: R-130

▶ **Defunct**
An abandoned Iraqi T-72 main battle
tank remains on a battlefield after
Coalition forces claimed the area
during Operation Desert Storm.

included several hundred
tanks each, and total
Iraqi armoured strength
during the Gulf War
was estimated at more
than 3500 main battle
tanks with approximately
one-third of them T-72 export variants. While
the Republican Guard divisions received the most
modern equipment, a number of older T-55s and
T-62s, as well as Chinese-built Type 59 and Type
69 tanks, were fielded.

The Type 59 and Type 69 were among the first
main battle tanks developed in China, and these
were known to have been exported to Iraq during
the early 1980s. Based upon the Soviet T-54 and
components of the T-62, which had been captured
during the brief Sino-Soviet border conflict of 1969,
these tanks primarily mounted 105mm (4.1in)
main guns, although some were reported with
160mm (6.3in) mortars and even 125mm (4.9in)
cannon. Some examples that survived the Gulf War
remained in service into the twenty-first century.

Air assault

Although the Iraqi armoured formations were
indeed a force to be reckoned with, the Coalition
air offensive that preceded the ground assault
in early 1991 substantially degraded the combat
efficiency of the Iraqis. When the ground phase of
Operation Desert Storm commenced, estimates of
the destruction wrought against Iraqi tank capability
ran as high as 40 per cent.

Tactical Coalition air support from fixed-wing
and rotary aircraft was also substantial, including
the devastating fire of the AH-64 Apache and the
AH-1 Cobra attack helicopters. In contrast, Iraqi air
assets were neutralized early in the campaign, and
although some Soviet-made attack helicopters may
have been available for service, they played no
significant role in the war.

Technological trap

Given that the T-72M deployed by the Iraqi Army
during Operation Desert Storm was the export
version of the main battle tank, the latest in Soviet
technology was unavailable to Saddam Hussein.
In fact, the bulk of the T-72 variants sold to Iraq
during the mid-1980s and beyond may have been
manufactured in Poland and Czechoslovakia.

Although automated to a certain extent, the tank's
acquisition and destruction of targets included
several manual steps. Laser rangefinding and infrared
sighting equipment were installed on the most recent
Iraqi T-72s; however, the most current T-72M1 was
at least a decade behind its Coalition adversaries
in technological capabilities. Iraqi tactics had been
influenced by the war with Iran, during which enemy
forces sometimes amassed human wave attacks.
These were often repulsed by Iraqi artillery, which
devastated large formations of exposed infantry but
also resulted in a great dependence on artillery by
the Iraqi Army.

The lack of adequate training further reduced
the combat capabilities of the Iraqi tank crews,
which often attempted to compensate for their
shortcomings by fighting from prepared revetments
or dug-in positions, presighting their weapons to
certain distances and failing to coordinate their
efforts. Total Iraqi losses in tanks and armoured
vehicles during the Gulf War were staggering,
including at least 3000 tanks and up to 2800 other
armoured vehicles, most of which were Soviet-
designed BMP-1 amphibious infantry fighting
vehicles, which had been developed in the mid-
1960s and carried up to eight combat infantrymen.

The Balkans independence wars

Josip Broz Tito, the communist strongman who had held Yugoslavia together since World War II, died in 1980. The fracture of the unified country ensued, with low-intensity guerrilla warfare erupting during a wave of unrest.

A S THE SIX REPUBLICS OF THE FORMER YUGOSLAVIA asserted independence, the Yugoslav People's Army attempted to maintain control of the disintegrating country. While their armoured forces might intimidate separatists in certain situations, it was apparent that guerrilla warfare would lessen the effectiveness of tanks and armoured vehicles. Therefore during fighting in Slovenia, Bosnia and Herzegovina, and Kosovo, Yugoslav and later Serbian armoured forces were utilized to varying degrees.

While the Yugoslav armed forces included a number of Cold War-era T-55 main battle tanks and other vehicles, the M-84, designed in the late 1970s and manufactured under licence in communist Yugoslavia, was also fielded. The M-84 was a variant of the Soviet-designed T-72 and entered service in 1984; more than 600 examples of the tank were built before production ceased in 1991. The 125mm (4.9in) 2A46 smoothbore gun was identical to that of the T-72, but the Yugoslavs made some modifications of their own to the tank, including providing a more powerful 750kW (1000hp) engine, a domestically produced computerized fire control system and composite armour. During the late 1980s, a number of M-84s were also exported to Kuwait by the Yugoslav government.

Realizing that their limited resources included few tanks and armoured vehicles, the separatist leaders for the most part engaged in clandestine operations meant to discourage the central Yugoslav government in Belgrade from interfering with the formation of independent states. The few tanks available to these forces included American-built M4 Shermans and Soviet T-34s, relics of World War II vintage.

▲ **Fire practice**
Members of the 2nd Guards Brigade of the Croatian Defence Council (HVO) Army fire a 12.7mm (0.5in) machine gun mounted on a T-55 main battle tank, during a three-day exercise. Armed forces in the former Yugoslavia mainly use upgraded Soviet-era hardware, including the evergreen T-55.

However, anti-tank weapons such as the Soviet RPG-7 and the German shoulder-fired Armbrust were also employed by guerrilla forces, while landmines were sown in great quantities.

NATO air and ground forces intervened during the Kosovo War in 1999, numerous nations contributing infantry and armoured units to the operation. The German-manufactured Leopard 1 main battle tanks of Danish forces deployed during the intervention were reported to have taken part in combat for the first time against Yugoslav forces. The Leopard 1 mounted a 105mm (4.1in) L7A3 rifled gun of British origin. Its armour protection was up to 70mm (2.76in) thick on its front glacis and turret.

During the independence wars waged in the early 1990s, the Yugoslav People's Army lost scores of tanks to guerrilla activity, while many more were captured and placed in service with the armies of the newly independent states. An estimated 80 M-84s and other tanks were destroyed or captured during the fighting with Slovenian separatists, and during the Battle of Vukovar approximately 100 Serbian tanks and armoured vehicles were destroyed by mines and Croatian troops firing rocket-propelled grenades. The Croatians captured nearly 150 tanks, many of them T-55s, during a series of engagements collectively known as the Battle of the Barracks during the autumn and winter of 1991.

Peacekeeping forces
1991–99

The endeavour to maintain world peace prevailed upon the armoured forces of numerous countries across the globe as political factions vied for control, and centuries-old ethnic tensions revived armed conflict.

THE ARMOURED FORCES of numerous NATO countries have recently been called upon in several instances to effect peace, enforce the mandates of the United Nations or protect civilian populations from atrocities. During the final decade of the twentieth century, peacekeeping forces were deployed to the Balkans, Cambodia, El Salvador, Mozambique, Rwanda, Somalia and other locations across the globe. In many cases, the armoured forces deployed with United Nations peacekeepers were instrumental in accomplishing the assigned tasks.

Patrolling large security zones and areas of territory is a requisite assignment for peacekeeping forces, and armoured cars and fighting vehicles have proved well suited to such duties. A variety of armoured vehicles, including the German Marder, the British Warrior, the US M2 Bradley and the Russian BMP-1 have

▲ **US Army intervention**
Soldiers from the US 10th Mountain Division sit atop their MG-armed Humvees in Bosnia during peacekeeping operations in 2005.

this sort of service. The British Alvis FV 107 Scimitar is representative of those armoured vehicles which have served in the Balkans. One of several such vehicles developed by the Alvis company, the Scimitar mounts a 30mm (1.18in) L21 RARDEN cannon that may be fired in automatic or single-round mode, along with a coaxial 7.62mm (0.3in) machine gun or L94A1 chain gun. Its thin armour plating of up to 12.7mm (0.5in) is effective against small-arms fire and shell fragments but vulnerable to larger-calibre weapons. Other than its powerful armament, the distinctive advantage of the FV 107 Scimitar is speed. Capable of reaching 80km/h (50mph) on the road, the Scimitar is a mobile enforcer and an effective scouting and patrol vehicle.

Humvee

Another well-known vehicle deployed with peacekeeping forces is the US-made High Mobility Multipurpose Wheeled Vehicle, popularly known as the Humvee. Although it was never intended as a frontline fighting vehicle, the Humvee has evolved into a light scouting or armoured car platform, mounting such diverse weaponry as the M2 12.7mm (0.5in) heavy machine gun or the M220 TOW anti-tank missile. The Humvee has been produced in at least 17 variants and is also utilized as a towing vehicle for light artillery or as an ambulance. Its eight-cylinder diesel engine is capable of delivering

speeds of up to 144km/h (90mph); up to 105km/h (65mph) in the case of an armoured variant. During the deployment of US forces to Somalia

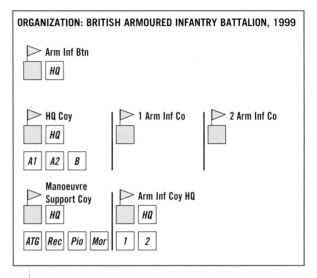

BRITISH ARMOURED INFANTRY BATTALION, 1999	
AFVS	Strength
Warrior IFV	57
Javelin ATGW	12
FV432 APC	21
Recce AFV	8
Personnel (all ranks)	741

▲ FV510 Warrior Infantry Fighting Vehicle

British Army / 1st Armoured Division / 7th Armoured Brigade

The FV510 Warrior infantry fighting vehicle has been in service with the British Army since the 1980s, and more than 1000 units have been produced. Its troop capacity of seven combat-ready soldiers is complemented by a 30mm (1.18in) L21A1 cannon and a 7.62mm (0.3in) machine gun for close support.

Specifications

Crew: 3 + 7

Weight: 25,700kg (56,540lb)

Length: 6.34m (20ft 10in)

Width: 3.034m (10ft)

Height: 2.79m (9ft 2in)

Engine: 410kW (550hp) Perkins V8 diesel

Speed: 75km/h (46.8mph)

Range: 660km (412 miles)

Armament: 1 x 30mm (1.18in) RARDEN cannon, plus 1 x 7.62mm (0.3in) coaxial MG and 4 x smoke dischargers

Radio: Currently Bowman (originally Clansman)

in December 1992, the Humvee became one of the most recognized symbols of United Nations and NATO forces in the field. Practical experience in Somalia, particularly during the low-intensity guerrilla fighting which took place around the capital city of Mogadishu, made it readily apparent that the Humvee was vulnerable to rocket-propelled grenades, to some small arms and to powerful landmines and improvised explosive devices.

Although relatively few casualties were sustained among Humvee crewmen, an armoured upgrade programme was initiated for the base vehicle. Field

British Army, Armoured Infantry Battalion (1999)

The modern British armoured infantry battalion consists of three armoured infantry companies comprising 14 FV510 Warrior infantry fighting vehicles each, along with a battalion command Warrior vehicle. Transport capability is approximately 300 fully equipped combat troops. Lighter units, designated as mechanized infantry, are deployed in wheeled fighting vehicles such as the Saxon, manufactured since the mid-1980s by GKN Defence.

Battalion HQ

Armoured Infantry Company 1 (14 x Warrior IFV)

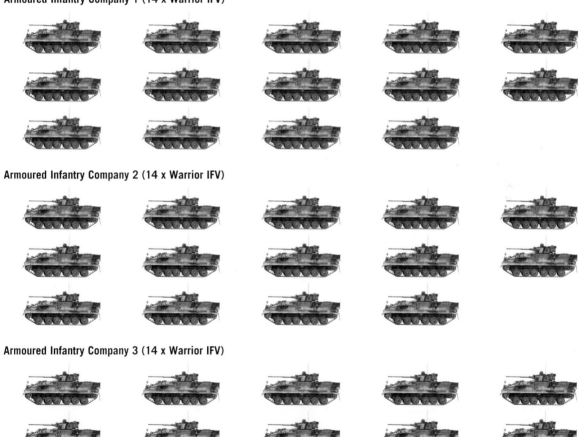

Armoured Infantry Company 2 (14 x Warrior IFV)

Armoured Infantry Company 3 (14 x Warrior IFV)

modification kits have been issued and installed on many of these. Since 1996, the armoured version of the Humvee, the M1114, has also been in production and has been deployed to the Balkans and the Middle East. The M1114 includes a more powerful turbocharged engine, air conditioning, an armoured passenger area and shatter-resistant glass.

Escape from Mogadishu

Perhaps the most enduring episode of the United Nations peacekeeping effort during the 1990s involved the US raid into Mogadishu to attempt the capture of a renegade Somali warlord. During the ensuing firefight, US Rangers suffered several casualties, while helicopters were shot down by rocket-propelled grenades. The incident, popularized in the book and film *Black Hawk Down*, ended with the Rangers evacuating their positions in Mogadishu following an 18-hour ordeal.

The evacuation was accomplished with the assistance of Pakistani and Malaysian peacekeeping forces stationed nearby. The Pakistanis assembled a relief column, which included the venerable M48 Patton tank and the Condor armoured personnel carrier. The Pakistani tanks provided covering fire, while troops deployed from the Malaysian Condors to assist the Rangers.

Designed by the German company Thyssen Henschel, the Rheinmetall Condor was a wheeled 4x4 vehicle with a capacity of up to 12 combat infantrymen. It was armed with a 20mm (0.79in) cannon and a secondary 7.62mm (0.3in) machine gun. During the rescue operation in Mogadishu,

a Condor was struck by a round from a rocket-propelled grenade, killing one soldier.

Balkan bombardment

United Nations and NATO involvement in the Balkans included a large contingent of armoured forces opposed to tank formations of the Yugoslav People's Army and later Serbian forces. The UN and NATO forces included variants of the German Leopard 1 and 2 tanks under the flags of several nations, including Canada, Denmark and Italy; the French Leclerc main battle tank; the American M1A1 Abrams and its variants; and the British Challenger 1.

Confronting the generally inferior T-55 and M-84 tanks of the Yugoslav forces, these modern tanks provided heavy firepower and security for NATO and United Nations installations, while also safeguarding the civilian population. Another primary objective was to prevent the Yugoslav Army from redeploying its forces, particularly its armour, into secured areas.

Although the Leopard 2 has seen little combat during its service life, it has gone into harm's way in Kosovo and in Afghanistan. It continues to be regarded as one of the finest main battle tanks in the world. A considerable modernization of the Leopard 1, which had been developed during the 1960s, the Leopard 2 had a main armament upgrade with the Rheinmetall 120mm (4.7in) L55 smoothbore gun, while its 1120kW (1500hp) V12 twin turbodiesel engine is capable of delivering a respectable 72km/h (45mph) on the road. Its armour is a composite of steel, ceramic, tungsten and plastic.

▶ **Véhicule Blindé Léger (VBL)**
Anti-tank Vehicle

French Army / 3rd Mechanized Brigade

Operating with the French Army since 1990, the VBL anti-tank vehicle combines mobility and firepower. Capable of a top road speed of 95km/h (59mph), it mounts a variety of weapons systems, including the medium-range MILAN anti-tank missile and the short-range ERYX missile unit.

Specifications

Crew: 2 or 3

Weight: 3550kg (7828lb)

Length: 3.87m (12ft 8in)

Width: 2.02m (6ft 7in)

Height: 1.7m (5ft 7in)

Engine: 78kW (105hp) Peugeot XD3T 4-cylinder turbo diesel

Speed: 95km/h (59mph)

Range: 600km (370 miles)

Armament: 1 x MILAN ATGM launcher, plus 1 x 7.62mm (0.3in) GPMG

Radio: VHF system with two PR4G radios, an HF System with one SSB radio for long range and a radio/intercom system for the crew

▲ FV107 Scimitar Light Tank

British Army / Royal Horse Guards and First Dragoons

Often designated as either a light tank or an armoured fighting vehicle, the FV107 is also ideal for reconnaissance with its combination of speed and firepower. Its crew of three has provided valuable intelligence during several deployments, along with direct infantry support.

Specifications

Crew: 3

Weight: 7800kg (17,160lb)

Length: 4.8m (15ft 9in)

Width: 2.24m (7ft 4in)

Height: 2.1m (6ft 11in)

Engine: 142kW (190hp) Jaguar 4.2-litre petrol

Speed: 80km/h (50mph)

Range: 644km (402 miles)

Armament: 1 x 30mm (1.18in) RARDEN cannon, plus 1 x 12.7mm (0.5in) MG

Radio: Clansman VRC 353

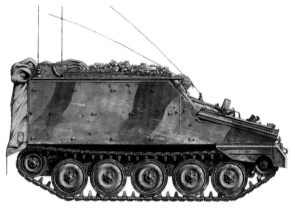

Specifications

Crew: 6

Weight: 14,300kg (31,500lb)

Length: 5.7m (18ft 8in)

Width: 2.67m (8ft 9in)

Height: 1.92m (6ft 3in)

Engine: 186kW (250hp) SOFAM 8Gxb 8-cylinder petrol

Speed: 60km/h (37mph)

Range: 350km (220 miles)

Armament: None

Radio: 4 x radios (various)

◀ FV105 Sultan CVR(T)

British Army / 1st Mechanized Brigade / 2nd Royal Tank Regiment

A command and control vehicle deployed with British Army units, the FV105 Sultan carries a crew of up to six and provides mobile space for radio equipment as well as tactical planning. Developed in the late 1970s, it is based on the chassis of the Alvis FV101 Scorpion.

▲ Dingo APC

German Army / 13th Mechanized Infantry Division

Developed by Krauss-Maffei Wegmann during the mid-1990s, the Dingo armoured personnel carrier is a multi-purpose vehicle deployed primarily by the German Army and capable of transporting troops, supplies and equipment, or combat casualties. The Dingo also serves in a reconnaissance and light air defence role. The Dingo has been used for patrol and transport missions by German forces during peacekeeping missions in Kosovo and Macedonia.

Specifications

Crew: 5 to 8

Weight: 8.8–11.9 tonnes (8.6–11.7 tons)

Length: 5.45m (17ft 10.56in)

Width: 2.3m (7ft 6in)

Height: 2.5m (8ft 2.4in)

Engine: 160kW (215hp) diesel

Speed: 90km/h (56mph)

Range: 1000km (621 miles)

Armament: 1 x 7.62mm (0.3in) MG

Radio: n/k

Specifications

Crew: 5	Engine: 492kW (660hp) Cummins V8 diesel
Weight: 45,000kg (99,225lb)	Speed: 55km/h (34 mph)
Length: 7.2m (23ft 8in)	Range: 240km (150 miles)
Width: 3.4m (11ft 2in)	Armament: 1 x 155mm (6.1in) howitzer, plus
Height: 3m (9ft 10in)	1 x 12.7mm (0.5in) MG
	Radio: n/k

▲ **AS-90 SP Gun**

British Army / 3rd Regiment Royal Horse Artillery

Developed during the mid-1980s and built by the Vickers company, the AS-90 self-propelled gun mounts the 155mm (6.1in) L39 gun atop its tracked chassis. Entering service in 1993, the AS-90 replaced the 105mm (4.1in) equipped Abbot and M109 self propelled guns then in service.

Former Yugoslav forces
1991–99

The break-up of the former Yugoslavia during the 1990s resulted in the formation of armed forces in those autonomous states which emerged, following a series of wars spurred largely by ancient ethnic animosity and territorial ambitions.

DURING FOUR YEARS OF FIGHTING from 1991 to 1995, the armoured vehicles of the Yugoslav People's Army, including the Soviet-made T-54/55 main battle tank and the M-84 tank, a variant of the widely produced Soviet T-72 which was manufactured in Yugoslavia, were pitted against militias, guerrilla forces and paramilitary units in the provinces of Bosnia, Slovenia and Croatia, while the central government in Belgrade came under the increasing influence of Serbia and its despotic leader Slobodan Milosevic.

On the eve of the collapse of the Socialist Federal Republic of Yugoslavia, the nation possessed a potent array of armoured vehicles, although some had certainly reached the age of functional obsolescence. With the brigade as its largest operational unit, the Yugoslav People's Army possessed several armoured and mechanized infantry formations, including more than 1600 tanks. While the number was impressive, the most advanced tank of the Yugoslav People's

Army was most likely its own licence-built M-84 clone of the Soviet T-72. Several hundred armoured personnel carriers were available for service; however, many of these were also of inferior quality due to age and poor maintenance. Regardless, these weapons found continued use in the armed forces of the independent nations that had once been part of the greater Yugoslavia.

During the Ten-Day War for Slovenian independence, few tanks were available to counter the armoured formations of the Yugoslav People's Army; however, the reality of the situation dictated that the Yugoslavs deploy their forces warily. The threat of anti-tank weapons such as the RPG-7 and German Armbrust was ever-present, while landmines and improvised explosive devices were a favoured weapon of the irregular forces. An estimated 20 Yugoslav tanks were destroyed and more than 40 captured during the brief conflict. Afterwards, the government of Slovenia, and in turn its armed forces, assumed control of all Yugoslav military equipment within Slovenian borders.

Some Croatian forces were reported to have utilized both the American M4 Sherman and the Soviet T-34, both of which traced their roots to the 1930s. The Croats executed a series of offensive actions known as the Battle of the Barracks during late 1991 and captured large stockpiles of light weapons, as well as artillery pieces and a significant number of all-important armoured vehicles. At one barracks alone, the attackers secured more than 70 T-55 tanks and nearly 90 armoured personnel carriers of various types.

During the protracted Battle of Vukovar, more than 100 Yugoslav T-55 and M-84 tanks besieged the Croatian city but suffered serious losses to anti-tank missiles, mines and the diminished effect of armoured firepower in urban conditions. A great variety of armoured personnel carriers, fighting vehicles, self-propelled guns and light tanks were utilized by both sides. Throughout more than three years of fighting in Bosnia alone, the warring factions deployed an estimated 1200 tanks of various types.

Among the most common armoured vehicles in the formations of the Yugoslav People's Army and those of the later independent states were the Soviet-

Specifications

Crew: 3 + 7	Engine: 193kW (260hp) V8 diesel
Weight: 13,600kg (23,000lb)	Speed: 90km/h (56mph)
Length: 7.65m (25ft 1in)	Range: 600km (370 miles)
Width: 2.9m (9ft 6in)	Armament: 1 x 14.5mm (0.57in) KPVT MG, plus
Height: 2.46m (8ft .8in)	1 x 7.62mm (0.3in) coaxial PKT MG

▲ BTR-80 Armoured Personnel Carrier

Yugoslav People's Army / 1st Guards Mechanized Division

The BTR-80 armoured personnel carrier entered production during the 1980s and was based on previous designs such as the BTR-70. The Soviets had modified the hull of the BTR-80 to allow greater traverse for its two machine-gun mounts.

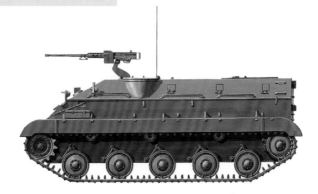

▲ M-60P Tracked Armoured Personnel Carrier

Slovenian Army / 10th Motorized Battalion

Produced in Yugoslavia, the M-60P armoured personnel carrier is fully tracked and capable of transporting up to 10 combat infantrymen. Its troop compartment is cramped due to the necessity to store ammunition, and its armament consists of a pair of machine guns.

Specifications

Crew: 3 + 10	Engine: 104kW (140hp) FAMOS 6-cylinder diesel
Weight: 11,000kg (24,300lb)	Speed: 45km/h (28mph)
Length: 5.02m (16ft 5in)	Range: 400km (250 miles)
Width: 2.77m (9ft 1in)	Armament: 1 x 7.62mm (0.31in) M53 MG
Height: 2.39m (7ft 10in)	Radio: n/k

designed BTR-80 and its predecessors. Production of the wheeled 8X8 BTR-80 was undertaken in the mid-1980s to replace the older BTR-60 and BTR-70 vehicles. However, these remained in service throughout the fighting in the Balkans, as well as the BTR-152, BTR-40 and BTR-50.

The BTR-80 had been used extensively by the armed forces of the Soviet Union and Russia. Manned by a crew of three, its troop-carrying capacity is up to seven fully loaded combat infantrymen. Its main

armament is a 14.5mm (0.57in) machine gun, which may be used for infantry support or in defence against low-flying aircraft. Its top road speed is 80km/h (50mph).

The Yugoslavs produced their own armoured personnel carrier, which they had deployed to mechanized units in large numbers by 1990. The M-60P was originally based upon the chassis of an artillery prime mover and was manned by a crew of three with capacity for up to 10 combat troops. Its

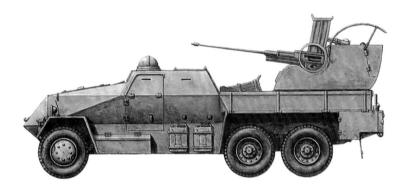

▲ M53/59 Praga SP Anti-aircraft Gun
Yugoslav People's Army / 51st Mechanized Brigade

Dating to the 1950s, the M53/59 Praga self-propelled anti-aircraft gun fielded twin 30mm (1.18in) cannon atop the Praga six-wheeled truck chassis. The gun could also be removed from the truck and operated independently. The crew of four was protected during relocation by an armoured compartment.

Specifications

Crew: 2 + 4	Engine: 82kW (110hp) Tatra T912-2
Weight: 10,300kg (22,660lb)	6-cylinder diesel
Length: 6.92m (22ft 8in)	Speed: 60km/h (37mph)
Width: 2.35m (7ft 9in)	Range: 500km (311 miles)
Height: 2.585m (8ft 6in)	Armament: 2 x 30mm (1.18in) guns

Specifications

Crew: 2 + 17	Engine: 82kW (110hp) ZIL-123 6-cylinder
Weight: 8950kg (19,690lb)	Speed (road): 75km/h (47mph)
Length: 6.83m (22ft 4.9in)	Range: 780km (485 miles)
Width: 2.32m (7ft 7.3in)	Armament: 1 x 7.62mm (0.3in) MG
Height: 2.05m (6ft 8.7in)	

▲ BTR-152 Wheeled APC
Yugoslav People's Army

More than 200 Soviet-made BTR-152, BTR-40 and BTR-50 armored personnel carriers were available to the Yugoslav People's Army when the civil war broke out in the early 1990s. All of these had been purchased from the Soviet Army in the 1960s and 1970s.

defence against attacking infantry was provided by the M53 7.92mm (0.31in) machine gun, a Yugoslav version of the venerable German MG 42. A variant of the vehicle, the M-60PB, mounted a pair of 82mm (3.2in) recoilless rifles.

Another armoured personnel carrier, built in Yugoslavia during the 1970s, was available in large numbers to all contending forces. At the beginning of hostilities, the Yugoslav People's Army possessed more than 400 examples of the M-980, which transported eight infantrymen and mounted either the Soviet AT-3 anti-tank missile or a 20mm (0.79in) cannon.

In addition to the elderly M4 Sherman, M47 Patton and T-34 tanks, and even some 100 American M3 half-tracks, pressed into service during the Balkan Wars, the Czech-manufactured M53/59 Praga anti-aircraft gun, mounted on a wheeled vehicle and first manufactured in the 1950s, was deployed by the Yugoslavs. The LVRS M-77 Oganj was a multiple-launch rocket system first developed in Yugoslavia during the late 1960s. The Cold War veteran PT-76 light amphibious tank, once seen in great numbers in the Soviet Red Army, was also utilized in the Balkans.

▲ **M-80 Mechanized Infantry Combat Vehicle (MICV)**
Serbian Land Forces / 17th Mechanized Battalion
Conceived as an improvement to the M-980 armoured vehicle, which had been produced in large numbers, the M-80 mounts anti-tank missiles or a 30mm (1.18in) cannon. It entered production in 1980 and has been produced in several variants.

Specifications

Crew: 3 + 7	turbo diesel
Weight: 13,700kg (30,200lb)	Speed: 60km/h (37mph)
Length: 6.4m (20ft 11in)	Range: 500km (310 miles)
Width: 2.59m (8ft 5in)	Armament: 2 x Yugoslav Sagger ATGWs or 1 x
Height: 2.3m (7ft 6in)	30mm (1.18in) cannon; 1 x 7.62mm (0.3in) MG
Engine: 194kW (260hp) HS-115-2 8-cylinder	Radio: n/k

The Caucasus
1991–PRESENT

Following the demise of the Soviet Union, the region of the Caucasus has been the focus of armed conflict involving the military forces of Russia and the former Soviet republic of Georgia, as well as counterinsurgency operations in Chechnya.

THE DEMANDS OF MODERN COMBAT have required that the Russian military continue to develop and modernize its armoured fighting vehicles during the last 20 years. The continuing unrest in Chechnya and its low-intensity counterinsurgency war, as well as the need for upgraded weapons systems to maintain some semblance of parity with the West, have given rise to the T-90 main battle tank.

In production since the mid-1990s, the T-90 is based on the design of the T-72, one of the most widely produced tanks in history. The survivor of a challenge from the Soviet-era holdover T-80U, the T-90 incorporates a 125mm (4.9in) smoothbore gun that is also capable of firing anti-tank guided missiles. Its main armament and some of its target acquisition equipment were borrowed from the

T-80U. Powered by a 12-cylinder, 630kW (840hp) engine, the T-90 is capable of a top road speed of 65km/h (40mph), comparable to Western main battle tanks. Its armour protection consists of steel, aluminum and plastic composite, reinforced by Kontakt explosive reactive armour that diminishes the penetrating capability of modern ammunition, and electronic counter-measures that include jamming equipment to ward off anti-tank guided missiles.

Infantry support

Numerous weapons systems that originated in the former Soviet Union have been retained or improved by Russian engineers. Among these are the BMP-2 and BMP-3 infantry fighting vehicles. By the mid-1970s, Soviet designers had become aware of the deficiencies of their BMP-1 infantry fighting vehicle, which had proved vulnerable to even 12.7mm (0.5in) machine-gun fire during service with Egyptian forces during the Yom Kippur War of 1973. The BMP-2 entered production in the Soviet Union after 1980 with improved armour protection and is armed with the 9M113 Konkurs anti-tank missile system and a 30mm (1.18in) 2A42 autocannon, complemented by a 7.62mm (0.3in) machine gun for close defence. Its troop-carrying capacity is up to seven combat infantrymen.

Specifications
Crew: 2
Weight: 3470kg (7650lb)
Length: 5.8m (19ft)
Width: 2.32m (7ft 7in)
Height: 2.44m (8ft)
Engine: 1 x 85kW (113hp) ZMZ-66 eight-cylinder diesel
Speed: 90km/h (56mph)
Range: 800km (500 miles)
Armament: N/A

▲ GAZ-66 Truck
Russian Ground Forces

Produced from 1966 to 1999, the GAZ-66 is a 4x4 vehicle used for engineering, troop transportation, and even as a mobile nuclear-biological-chemical (NBC) contamination centre.

▲ T-72B Main Battle Tank
Russian Ground Forces / 5th Guards Tank Division

Entering production in 1985, the new T-72B included a new main gun, sights and fire control system. It is also capable of firing 9M119 Svir guided missiles, has additional appliqué armour on the front of the hull, and has a more robust 630kW (840hp) engine.

Specifications
Crew: 4	Speed: 60km/h (37.5mph)
Weight: 38,894kg (85,568lb)	Range: 570km (356 miles)
Length: 9.53m (31ft 4in)	Armament: 1 x 125mm (4.9in) D-81 smoothbore
Width: 4.75m (15ft 7in)	gun; 1 x 12.7mm (0.5in) air defence HMG and
Height: 2.29m (7ft 4in)	1 x 7.62mm (0.3in) coaxial MG
Engine: 630kW (840hp) V-84 liquid-cooled four-stroke multi-fuel diesel	Radio: R-713 radio

Specifications

Crew: 3 + 7

Weight: 14,600kg (32,120lb)

Length: 6.71m (22ft)

Width: 3.15m (10ft 4in)

Height: 2m (6ft 7in)

Engine: 1 x 223kW (300hp) Model UTD-20
6-cylinder diesel

Speed: 65km/h (40.6mph)

Range: 600km (375 miles)

Armament: 1 x 9M113 AT-missile launcher, plus
1 x 30mm (1.18in) cannon and 1 x 7.62mm
(0.3in) coaxial MG

Radio: R-173, R-126 and R-10

▲ **BMP-2 Infantry Fighting Vehicle**

Russian Ground Forces / 131st Motor Rifle Brigade

The amphibious BMP-2 infantry fighting vehicle was developed in the Soviet Union during the 1980s and is armed with anti-tank missiles and a 30mm (1.18in) autocannon. It carries up to seven soldiers in its troop compartment.

▲ **BTR-90 Infanty Fighting Vehicle**

Russian Ground Forces / 201st Motor Rifle Division

In use only with the Russian armed forces, the BTR-90 infantry fighting vehicle was seen publicly for the first time in 1994. Carrying a troop complement of nine soldiers, the vehicle is armed with a 30mm (1.18in) autocannon, a 30mm (1.18in) grenade launcher, anti-tank guided missiles and a 7.62mm (0.3in) machine gun.

Specifications

Crew: 3 + 9

Weight: 17,000kg (37,500lb)

Length: 7.64m (25ft)

Width: 3.2m (10ft 6in)

Height: 2.97m (9ft 9in)

Engine: 157kW (210hp) V8 diesel

Speed: 80km/h (50mph)

Range: 600km (370 miles)

Armament: 1 x 30mm (1.18in) 2A42 cannon, plus 1 x automatic grenade launcher, 4 x AT-5 Spandrel ATGWs, 1 x 7.62mm (0.3in) coaxial PKT MG

Radio: n/k

Specifications

Crew: 3 + 7

Weight: 18,700kg (18.4 tons)

Length: 7.2m (23ft 7in)

Width: 3.23m (10ft 7in)

Height: 2.3m (7ft 7in)

Engine: 373kW (500bhp) UTD-29 6-cylinder diesel

Speed: 70km/h (43mph)

Range: 600km (373 km)

Armament: 1 x 100mm (3.9in) 2A70 rifled gun, plus 1 x 30mm (1.18in) 2A72 autocannon and 3 x 7.62mm (0.3in) PKT MGs

Radio: R-173

▲ **BMP-3 Infanty Fighting Vehicle**

Russian Ground Forces / 2nd Guards Tamanskaya Motor Rifle Division

The latest generation of the Soviet and Russian BMP series of infantry fighting vehicles, the BMP-3 debuted in 1987. Its 100mm (3.9in) gun doubles as an anti-tank missile launcher, and the vehicle also mounts a 30mm (1.18in) autocannon for close infantry support.

Although the BMP-2 has remained on active duty, a successor, the BMP-3 amphibious infantry fighting vehicle, entered service with the Red Army in 1987. Equipped with the 30mm (1.18in) autocannon, the 2A70 100mm (3.9in) gun/missile launcher system and three 7.62mm (0.3in) machine guns for added protection against infantry or tank killer squads employing shoulder-fired missiles, the BMP-3 is one of the most heavily armed infantry fighting vehicles in the world.

In addition to fighting terrorists and separatists in Chechnya, the Russian Federation's armed forces have fought with neighbouring Georgia as recently as 2008. During the South Ossetia War, the Georgian Army was reported to have lost at least 70 T-72 tanks and more than a dozen armoured personnel carriers, many of which were captured by the Russians and remained in good working order. Both sides are known to have deployed the aged T-54/55 and variants of the T-72, while the Russians also committed the T-62.

Specifications

Crew: 4	Speed: 60km/h (37.5mph)
Weight: 38,000kg (83,600lb)	Range: 570km (356 miles)
Length: 9.33m (28ft 6in)	Armament: 1 x 105mm (4.1in) gun, plus 1 x
Width: 3.37m (10ft 4in)	12.7mm (0.5in) coaxial HMG and 1 x 7.62mm
Height: 2.3m (7ft)	(0.3in) coaxial MG
Engine: 544kW (730hp) V12 diesel	Radio: (external) YRC-83, (crew) VIC-8

▲ T-80 Main Battle Tank

Russian Ground Forces / 4th Guards Kantemirovskaya Tank Division

Similar in design to the preceding T-64, the T-80 was deployed to the Soviet Red Army in 1976. During the First Chechen War, the tank performed poorly due to a lack of explosive reactive armour. Numerous variants remain in service in Russia and with armies of other former Soviet republics.

▲ T-90 Main Battle Tank

Russian Ground Forces / 5th Guards Tank Division

The T-90 main battle tank combines elements of its predecessors, the T-80 and the T-72, particularly the T-72BM and T-80U variants. The T-90 main armament is a 125mm (4.9in) smoothbore gun, which is also capable of firing anti-tank guided missiles. The T-90A saw combat action during the 1999 Chechen invasion of Dagestan. According to Moscow Defence Brief, one T-90 was hit by seven RPG anti-tank rockets but remained in action.

Specifications

Crew: 3	Speed: 65km/h (40mph)
Weight: 46,500kg (102,532lb)	Range: 650km (400 miles)
Length (hull): 6.86m (22ft 6in)	Armament: 1 x 125mm (4.9in) 2A46M Rapira
Width: 3.37m (11ft 1in)	3 smoothbore gun; 1 x 12.7mm (0.5in) anti-
Height: 2.23m (7ft 4in)	aircraft HMG; 1 x 7.62mm (0.3in) co-axial MG
Engine: 630kW (840bhp) V-84MS 12-cylinder	Radio: n/k
multi-fuel	

Iraq and Afghanistan

2003–PRESENT

Toppling the repressive regime of Saddam Hussein in Iraq and battling the Taliban in Afghanistan have placed demands upon the world's most advanced armoured vehicles.

WHEN THE US-led armed Coalition invaded Iraq in the spring of 2003, the objective was to remove a bloody dictator from power and neutralize the supposed threat of weapons of mass destruction. Advancing on the Iraqi capital of Baghdad and securing the port city of Basra were major challenges, particularly when confronted with an armed enemy force of more than 500,000 army, Republican Guard and fanatical Fedayeen paramilitary personnel.

As in the Gulf War of 1991, speed and overwhelming firepower would once again dictate the progress of the war on the ground. However, this time a lengthy air campaign did not precede the commencement of land operations, and within hours Coalition troops and tanks, particularly those based in Kuwait, had crossed the frontier into Iraq.

The M1A1 and M1A2 Abrams main battle tanks made up the bulk of the US heavy armour during the Iraq War, each an improved version of the original M1 Abrams. While a number of the early M1s were upgraded to the M1A1 in the field during the Gulf War of 1991, the M1A2 variant went into production in 1992. A number of existing tanks were also upgraded to the M1A2.

Mounting the same main gun as the M1A1, the reliable 120mm (4.7in) M256 adaptation of the Rheinmetall smoothbore originally utilized in the German Leopard 2 main battle tank, the M1A2 contained extensive upgrades, with an independent thermal viewer and weapons control for the tank commander along with enhanced navigation and radio equipment. Designated the M1A2 SEP (System Enhancement Package), a sub-variant includes FBCB2 (Force XXI Battlefield Command Brigade and Below) communications capabilities, improvements to the engine cooling system, digital maps and upgraded armour that incorporates depleted uranium.

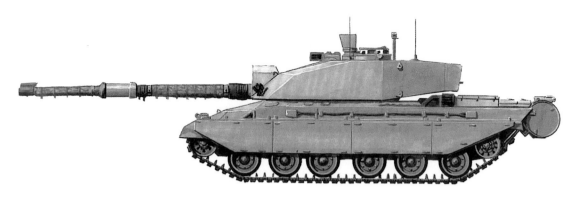

Specifications

Crew: 4	Range: 400km (250 miles)
Weight: 62,500kg (137,500lb)	Armament: 1 x 120mm (4.7in) L30A1 gun, plus
Length: 11.55m (35ft 4in)	2 x 7.62mm (0.3in) MGs and 2 x smoke rocket
Width: 3.52m (10ft 8in)	dischargers
Height: 2.49m (7ft 5in)	Radio: Long range, directional communications
Engine: 895kW (1200hp) liquid-cooled diesel	system with satellite relay capabilities
Speed: 57km/h (35.6mph)	

▲ **Challenger 2 Main Battle Tank**

British Army / 1st Armoured Division / 7th Armoured Brigade

The Challenger 2 main battle tank entered service with the British Army in 1998 and has compiled an impressive combat record. Armed with a 120mm (4.7in) rifled gun and equipped with the latest armour protection and electronics, it is expected to serve well into the twenty-first century.

IRAQI REPUBLICAN GUARD, 2003	
Unit	Strength
Tank Brigade:	2
Tank Battalions	3
Mechanized Infanty Battalion	1
Motorized Special Forces Company	1
Engineering Company	1
Reconnaissance Platoon	1
Medium Rocket Launcher Battery	1
Mechanized Infantry Brigade	1
Mechanized Infantry Battalions	3
Tank Battalion	1
Anti-tank Company	1
Motorized Special Forces Company	1
Engineering Company	1
Reconnaissance Platoon	1
Medium Rocket Launcher Battery	1
Divisional Artillery Brigade	1
Self-propelled Artillery Battalions (155mm SP)	3
Self-propelled Artillery Battalions (152mm SP)	2
Self-propelled Artillery Battalions (122mm SP)	2
Divisional Units	
Motorized Special Forces Battalions	3
Reconnaissance Battalion	1
Anti-tank Battalion	1
Engineer Battalion	1

The British Challenger 2 main battle tank includes few of the components of the Challenger 1 and is armed with the 120mm (4.7in) L30A1 gun, which replaces the earlier L11 weapon of the Challenger 1. Protected by second-generation Chobham armour, the Challenger 2 fields the latest in digital fire control, thermal imaging and computerization. An armoured recovery variant and a bridging vehicle have been developed using its chassis.

Combat lethality

During the 2003 Iraq War, the T-72M and older Iraqi tanks that had survived the Gulf War once again proved no match for the modern Coalition main battle tanks. During the inter-war years, the Iraqis had been able to acquire some tanks to replace their heavy losses from 1991, including the Chinese Type 59 and Type 69, upgraded versions based on the old Soviet T-54/55 with 125mm (4.9in) guns and additional armour.

Relatively few Abrams tanks were lost to enemy action; some were disabled by mines, roadside bombs or roving anti-tank squads of Fedayeen carrying shoulder-fired missiles. Friendly-fire incidents were also reported. According to British sources, no Challenger 2s were lost to enemy action, and one tank withstood multiple hits from rocket-propelled grenades and a MILAN anti-tank missile.

Both tanks performed extremely well, and most of the losses in the field occurred during the occupation of Iraq which followed the actual invasion. Indicative of their superb tank-versus-tank performance was

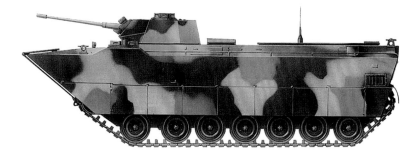

▲ **Advanced Amphibious Assault Vehicle (AAAV)**

US Marine Corps / I Marine Expeditionary Force

Designed as a replacement for the ageing AAV-7A1 amphibious assault vehicles in use by the US Marine Corps for more than 30 years, the AAAV, also known as the Expeditionary Fighting Vehicle, is scheduled for deployment by 2015 with a troop capacity of 17 Marines and a main armament of the 30mm (1.18in) or 40mm (1.57in) MK44 cannon.

Specifications

Crew: 3 + 17

Weight: 33,525kg (73,922lb)

Length: 9.01m (29ft 7in)

Width: 3.66m (12ft)

Height: 3.19m (10ft 6in)

Engine: 2015kW (2702hp) MTU MT883

12-cylinder multi-fuel

Speed: 72km/h (45mph)

Range: 480km (300 miles)

Armament: 1 x 30mm (1.18in) Bushmaster II cannon, plus 1 x 7.62mm (0.3in) MG

Radio: n/k

the rapid destruction of seven T-72s by M1A2s with no losses to the Americans during a battle on the outskirts of Baghdad.

Perhaps the most highly criticized armoured vehicle deployed by the US during the Iraq War was the AAV-7A1 tracked amphibious assault vehicle. One of the fiercest battles of the invasion took place at the city of Nasiriyah as Iraqi forces contested bridges across the Euphrates River. Troops of the 1st Marine Division were heavily engaged, and several of their AAVs were destroyed by rocket-propelled

grenades while the vehicles also proved vulnerable to some small-arms fire.

The AAV was conceived to replace the prior generation of amphibious vehicles used by the US Marine Corps and entered service during the early 1980s. Its distinctive boat-shaped bow and high profile are easily recognizable, and its troop complement of 25 combat soldiers is among the largest of any similar vehicle in the world. Its armament includes the M242 25mm (1in) Bushmaster chain-fed autocannon, with a maximum rate of fire of 225 rounds per minute, as

▲ M1114 High Mobility Multipurpose Wheeled Vehicle (HMMWV)
US Army / 3rd Infantry Division
The versatile HMMWV, popularly known as the Humvee, has been in service with US forces since the mid-1980s. Its armour protection has been upgraded with field kits, while a more heavily protected production version has also been introduced.

Specifications
Crew: 1 + 3
Weight: 3870kg (8375lb)
Length: 4.457m (14ft 7in)
Width: 2.15m (7ft)
Height: 1.75m (5ft 8in)
Engine: 101kW (135hp) V8 6.21 air-cooled diesel
Speed: 105km/h (65.6mph)
Range: 563km (352 miles)
Armament: Various, including machine guns, grenade launchers and surface-to-air missile (SAM) launchers
Radio: AN/VRC-12

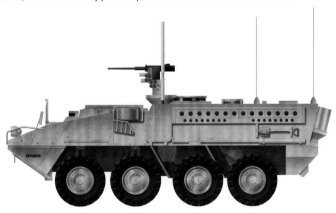

Specifications

Crew: 2 + 9	Engine: 260kW (350hp) Caterpillar C7
Weight: 16.47 tonnes (16.2 tons)	Speed: 100km/h (62mph)
Length: 6.95m (22.92ft)	Range: 500km (310 miles)
Width: 2.72m (8.97ft)	Armament: 1 x 12.7mm (0.5in) M2 MG
Height: 2.64m (8.72ft)	Radio: n/k

▲ IAV Stryker Armoured Personnel Carrier
US Army / 2nd Infantry Division / 4th Stryker Brigade
The eight-wheeled Stryker armoured fighting vehicle entered service with the US Army in 2002 and carries up to nine soldiers. Its mobility and protection have been instrumental during operations in Iraq. Its weapons systems are remotely controlled from inside the vehicle.

well as a 12.7mm (0.5in) machine gun and a 40mm (1.57in) grenade launcher.

Afghanistan intervention

Since 2001, US, British and subsequently NATO forces have been involved in the effort to end Taliban rule, quell the subsequent insurgency and destroy the al-Qaeda terror network in Afghanistan. While heavy armour has been utilized to project firepower, particularly during heavy fighting for control of cities and urban areas, mountainous terrain has limited its mobility, often confining the main battle tank to roads and areas clear of mines and improvised explosive devices.

Light armoured vehicles such as the M2/M3 Bradley fighting vehicle, the Humvee and the Land Rover Wolf utility vehicle have proved their value as patrol and rapid response vehicles. The Land Rover

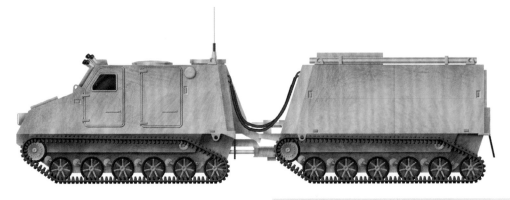

▲ BVS 10 Viking Armoured Personnel Carrier

British Army / Royal Marines / Armoured Support Group

A collaborative design effort between Britain and Sweden, the BVS 10 entered service with the Royal Marines in 2005. Fully amphibious, the vehicle carries up to four soldiers in its front vehicle and up to eight in the trailer. It is protected by specialized armour and mounts a light machine gun.

Specifications

Crew: (front car) Driver + 4 passengers; (rear car) 8 passengers
Weight: 10,600kg (23,369lb)
Length: 7.5m (24ft 7in)
Width: 2.1m (6ft 10.7in)
Height: 2.2m (7ft 2.5in)
Engine: 183kW (250bhp) Cummins 5.9l in-line

6-cylinder turbo diesel
Speed: (road) 50km/h (31mph); (cross country) 15km/h (9.3mph); (water) 5km/h (3.1mph)
Range: 300km (186 miles)
Armament: Capacity for 1 x 12.7mm (0.5in) Browning HMG or 1 x 7.62mm (0.3in) MG
Radio: n/k

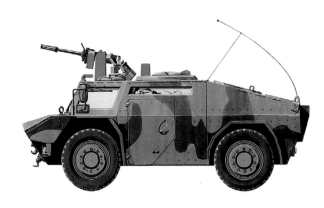

Specifications

Crew: 3
Weight: 7900kg (17,400lb)
Length: 5.72m (18ft 9in)
Width: 2.49m (8ft 2in)
Height: 2.18m (7ft 1.8in)
Engine: 179kW (240hp) Deutz diesel
Speed: 115km/h (71mph)
Range: 860km (530 miles)
Armament: 1 x 12.7mm (0.5in) MG or 1 x 7.62mm (0.3in) MG or 1 x 40mm (1.57in) grenade launcher
Radio: n/k

▲ LGS Fennek

German Army / 13th Mechanized Infantry Division

The LGS Fennek light armoured reconnaissance vehicle is currently deployed by the German and Dutch Armies and has served recently in Afghanistan. Its speed and light armour have proven optimal for scouting and patrol duties, although rocket-propelled grenades and improvised explosive devices have damaged vehicles in the field.

Wolf has been a mainstay of the British forces in both Iraq and Afghanistan, carrying up to six soldiers. The Wolf traces its lineage to the company's light truck and transport vehicles of the World War II period.

The US Army's Stryker series of infantry fighting vehicles is destined to play a greater role in Afghanistan. The vehicle was already well known for its deployment to Iraq, and the first Stryker unit arrived in Afghanistan in 2009. Developed from earlier Canadian and Swiss armoured vehicle designs, the Stryker entered service with the US Army in 2002 to complement the older M2/M3 Bradleys. Conceived as a method of introducing combat troops to the battlefield rapidly, the Stryker carries up to nine soldiers and is armed with a 12.7mm (0.5in) machine gun or 40mm (1.57in) grenade launcher mounted in the Protector M151 remote weapons station, which may be operated from the relative safety of the vehicle's interior.

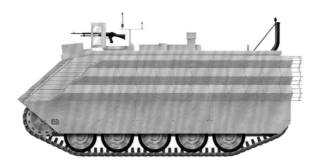

▲ FV 430 Bulldog Armoured Personnel Carrier
British Army / 1st Armoured Division / 7th Armoured Brigade

The FV 430 Bulldog entered service with British forces in Iraq and Afghanistan late in 2006 in response to the hazards posed by rocket-propelled grenades and improvised explosive devices. Equipped with an extensive reactive armour package, it also carries a remote-controlled 7.62mm (0.3in) machine gun.

Specifications

Crew: 2 + 10
Weight: 15.3 tonnes (15 tons)
Length: 5.25m (17ft 2.6in)
Width: 2.8m (9ft 2.3in)
Height: 2.28m (7ft 5.8in)
Engine: 179kW (240hp) Rolls-Royce K60 multi-fuel
Speed: 52km/h (32mph)
Range: 580km (360 miles)
Armament: 1 x 7.62mm (0.3in) MG, plus 2 x 3-barrel smoke dischargers
Radio: n/k

Specifications

Crew: 2 + 4
Weight: 17,000kg (38,000lb)
Length: 5.91m (19.41ft)
Width: 2.74m (9.0ft)
Height: 2.64m (8.67ft)

Engine: 243kW (330hp) Caterpillar C-7 diesel
Speed: 105km/h (65mph)
Range: 966km (600 miles)
Armament: Optional remote weapons station

▲ Mastiff PPV (Protected Patrol Vehicle)
British Army / 1st Armoured Division / 7th Armoured Brigade

The Mastiff PPV is the British variant of the basic Cougar armoured fighting vehicle built by Force Protection Inc. Acquired by both the British and US Armies, the Cougar is designed specifically to safeguard against mines and improvised explosive devices. The Mastiff entered service with British forces in 2007.

Chapter 7

Modern Developments

Technology has never stood still, and the development of modern armoured vehicles is indicative of this. Indeed, during the last decade the pace of progress may even have quickened as both preeminent and emerging nations have committed to the continuing modernization of their armoured forces and to participation in the lucrative arms export industry. The latest generation of main battle tanks and armoured vehicles is characterized by an array of sophisticated offensive and defensive systems, increasing firepower while improving target acquisition, battlefield communication and armour protection. Although technology continues to advance, the human element remains the prime mover for the successful employment of armoured doctrine. A capable commander and crew combined with the basics of speed, armour protection and firepower remain likely to win the day.

◀ **Fording feline**
The Leopard 2 main battle tank is one of the best modern tanks in service. Besides Germany, its operators include Austria, Denmark, the Netherlands, Spain and Sweden.

Europe

1991–PRESENT

Numerous European nations have undertaken development of armoured vehicles, or expanded their production, particularly in the areas of main battle tanks, infantry fighting vehicles and self-propelled artillery.

WHILE THE BRITISH CHALLENGER 2 and the German Leopard 2 main battle tanks remain preeminent among modern European main battle tank designs, France, Poland, Italy and others have entered their own main battle tanks into production in recent years. European nations have proved innovative in tank design since the beginning – consider the German and British machines of World War I and the speed and firepower of the *Wehrmacht* panzers of World War II. During the late 1950s, Sweden produced the turretless Stridsvagen 103, which reduced production expense and performed favourably in head-to-head testing against its contemporaries. France introduced the oscillating turret with the AMX-10.

Since its deployment during Operation Iraqi Freedom and to Bosnia and Kosovo, the Challenger 2 has continued to undergo refinement. According to the Ministry of Defence, numbers of main battle tanks and their role are changing within the military, including the consolidation of several armoured squadrons and the allocation of one armoured regiment to focus primarily on reconnaissance. The Challenger Lethality Improvement Programme is currently in progress and includes the possible replacement of the 120mm (4.7in) L30 rifled gun with the 120mm (4.7in) Rheinmetall L55 smoothbore, which is common to the German Leopard 2. Enhanced NBC (nuclear, biological and chemical) defences are also being evaluated.

Meanwhile, the Challenger 2E emerged in response to the necessity of fighting and maintaining combat efficiency in extreme climates and is intended for the export market. Competing directly with the Leopard 2 and other main battle tanks for purchase contracts, the Challenger 2E was produced from approximately 2002 to 2005. Extensive trials took place in the deserts of the Middle East, and the Challenger 2E remains equipped with the 120mm (4.7in) L30 rifled gun. However, its combat prowess was augmented by a battlefield communications and management system that allows for the tracking of multiple targets simultaneously and

▲ **Pandur Armoured Personnel Carrier**

Austrian Army / 4th Mechanized Infantry Brigade

The Pandur armoured personnel carrier was developed in the 1980s by Steyr-Daimler-Puch Spezialfahrzeug and transports up to 12 infantrymen. Weapons systems include heavy machine guns and up to a 105mm (4.1in) cannon. A turreted version reduces troop capacity to six. The Pandur II has supplanted the Pandur I in recent years.

Specifications	
Crew: 2 + 8	6-cylinder turbo diesel
Weight: 13,500kg (29,800lb)	Speed: 100km/h (60mph)
Length: 5.7m (18ft 8in)	Range: 700km (430 miles)
Width: 2.5m (8ft 2in)	Armament: 1 x 12.7mm (0.5in) HMG; 2 x 3 smoke
Height: 1.82m (5ft 11in)	grenade launchers; various other configurations
Engine: 179kW (240hp) Steyr WD 612.95	Radio: n/k

provides enhanced acquisition and ranging. Thermal sights were improved for both the commander and gunner, while the commander may also operate the turret independently. The engine was upgraded with the 1125kW (1500hp) Europack MTU 883 diesel.

Leap of the Leopard

The most recent variant of the Leopard 2, the 2A6, was the first of the German tanks to mount the longer 120mm (4.7in) L55 smoothbore gun. An auxiliary engine has been added in the 2A6 along with

air conditioning and enhanced protection against landmines, with some of these tanks designated 2A6M. The German Army began upgrading more than 200 of its frontline tanks to the 2A6 configuration in 2000, and the first deliveries of production 2A6s occurred the following year. Another variant of the 2A6, the 2E, offers greater armour protection and was developed in a cooperative effort by German and Spanish engineers. Still another variant, the Leopard PSO, includes combat survivability systems designed for urban warfare.

Specifications

Crew: 4	four-stroke 12-cylinder diesel
Weight: 59,700kg (131,616lb)	Speed: 72km/h (45mph)
Length: 9.97m (32ft 8in)	Range: 500km (311 miles)
Width: 3.5m (11ft 6in)	Armament: 1 x 120mm (4.7in) L55 smoothbore
Height: 2.98m (9ft 10in)	gun, plus 2 x 7.62mm (0.3in) MGs
Engine: 1119kW (1500hp) MTU MB 873	Radio: SEM 80/90 digital VHF

▲ Leopard 2A6 MBT

German Army / 10th Armoured Division

The Leopard 2A6 main battle tank is the most recent variant of the vehicle which entered service with the German Army in 1979. The older 120mm (4.7in) main weapon in previous versions was replaced with the 120mm (4.7in) L55 smoothbore gun.

▲ Renault VBC 90

French Gendarmerie Armoured Squadron

Designed in France for the export market, the wheeled VBC 90 tank destroyer entered production during the early 1980s; however, export sales were limited to the government of Oman, and the French Gendarmerie took delivery of 28 vehicles.

Specifications

Crew: 3	turbo diesel
Weight: 13,500kg (29,800lb)	Speed: 92km/h (57mph)
Length (gun forwards): 8.8m (28ft 10in)	Range: 1000km (620 miles)
Width: 2.5m (8ft 2in)	Armament: 1 x 90mm (3.5in) gun; 1 x 7.62m
Height: 2.55m (8ft 4in)	(0.3in) coaxial MG; 1 x 7.62mm; 2 x 2 smoke
Engine: 164kW (220hp) Renault MIDS 06.20.45	grenade launchers

Throughout its service life, the Leopard 2 has remained a popular export tank. The armies of Denmark, the Netherlands, Greece, Canada, Portugal, Spain and Switzerland are among those fielding the main battle tank today. It has been deployed in the Balkans and to Afghanistan, engaging in notable firefights with Taliban and guerrilla forces.

Leclerc and Ariete

The first production main battle tank designed and manufactured in France in more than 30 years is the Leclerc. Although the early development of a new tank had begun in the 1970s, the Leclerc did not enter production until 1990. France and the United Arab Emirates worked in partnership on the tank and share the expense of development and production.

Replacing the aged AMX-30 in French armoured formations and in the armed forces of the United Arab Emirates, the Leclerc was not intended for major export or a lengthy production run, and fewer than 1000 were built by the time production ceased in 2008. France now has over 400 Leclercs in service and the United Arab Emirates Army over 380, delivered in 2004. The Leclerc has been deployed to Kosovo and with peacekeeping forces in Lebanon; however, it has yet to see substantial combat.

With the Leclerc, French engineers initially rejected the British Chobham armour and developed their own protection package by the 1990s. Emphasis has been on armour protection with composite steel and titanium sandwiching non-explosive and non-energetic reactive armour (NERA). Active counter-measures include a top speed of 71km/h (44mph) for rapid relocation and evasion, along with the Galix defence system that utilizes infrared screening rounds, smoke grenades and anti-personnel weapons against attacking infantry.

The Italian firms Iveco Fiat and OTO Melara combined efforts to develop the C1 Ariete main battle tank, which has been deployed with the nation's armed forces since the mid-1990s. The Ariete is armed with a 120mm (4.7in) OTO Melara smoothbore cannon and protected by a classified composite armour thought to be comparable to that of contemporary main battle tanks. Its 932kW (1250hp) V12 turbocharged engine is capable of delivering a top speed of more than 65km/h (41mph). The tank is equipped with modern target acquisition and sighting equipment, allowing effective operations day or night. Active defences include smoke grenade dischargers and the RALM laser warning receiver, which sounds an alarm when the tank is 'painted' by hostile target acquisition systems. To date, the C1 Ariete has equipped only the four armoured battalions of the Italian Army, and it is scheduled for an engine upgrade as part of an overall performance

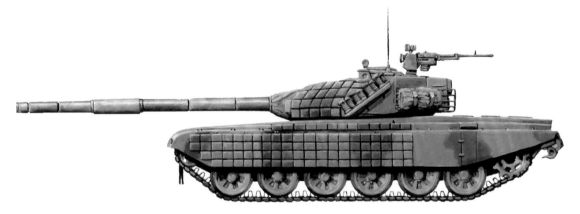

▲ **PT-91 Main Battle Tank**

Polish Land Forces / 1st Mechanized Division 'Warsaw'

A Polish variant of the export version of the ubiquitous T-72 main battle tank, the PT-91 Twardy (Resilient) entered service with the Polish Land Forces during the mid-1990s as both a production vehicle and an upgrade of existing tanks.

Specifications

Crew: 3	supercharged diesel
Weight: 45,300kg (99,886lb)	Speed: 60km/h (38mph)
Length (hull): 6.95m (22ft 10in)	Range: 650km (405 miles)
Width: 3.59m (11ft 9in)	Armament: 1 x 125mm (4.9in) gun; 1 x 12.7mm
Height: 2.19m (7ft 2in)	(0.5in) HMG; 1 x 7.62mm (0.3in) MG
Engine: 634kW (850bhp) S-12U V12	Radio: n/k

enhancement programme. Approximately 200 tanks have been produced, and the tank was deployed to Iraq in 2004.

Infantry fighting vehicles

The German Marder, which entered service in 1971 and is currently being retired in favour of the Puma, was the first infantry fighting vehicle designed and developed by a NATO country for the specific purpose of transporting troops to a combat area and providing direct fire support for their operations. It was followed by the British Warrior and the American M2/M3 Bradley. The infantry fighting vehicle has remained significant

▲ Leclerc Main Battle Tank

French Army / 6th-12th Cuirassier Regiment

The Leclerc's main armament is the GIAT CN120-26 120mm (4.7in) smoothbore cannon, which is compatible with most common NATO ammunition. The powerplant is a 1125kW (1500p) eight-cylinder engine.

Specifications

Crew: 3	Speed: 71km/h (44mph)
Weight: 54.5 tonnes (117,000lb)	Range: 550km (345 miles)
Length (gun forwards): 9.87m (30ft)	Armament: 1 x 120mm (4.7in) GIAT CN120-
Width: 3.71m 11ft 4in)	26/52 gun; 1 x 12.7mm (0.5in) coaxial MG; 3 x 9
Height: 2.46m (7ft 6in)	smoke dischargers
Engine: 1 x 1125.5kW (1500hp) SAEM UDU V8X	Radio: 2 x frequency hopping radio sets
1500 T9 Hyperbar 8-cylinder diesel	

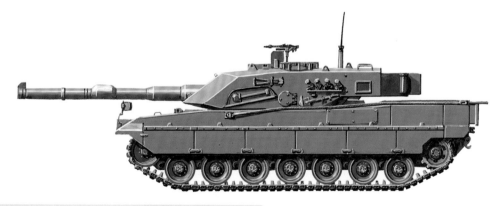

Specifications

Crew: 4	Speed: 66km/h (41.3mph)
Weight: 54,000kg (118,800lb)	Range: 600km (375 miles)
Length: 9.67m (29ft 6in)	Armament: 1 x 120mm (4.7in) gun, plus
Width: 3.6m (11ft)	2 x 7.62mm (0.3in) MGs (1 coaxial,
Height: 2.5m (7ft 7in)	1 anti-aircraft) and 2 x 4 smoke dischargers
Engine: 932kW (1250hp) IVECO FIAT MTCA V12	Radio: n/k
turbocharged diesel	

▲ C1 Ariete Main Battle Tank

Italian Army / 31st Tank Battalion

The C1 Ariete main battle tank was deployed to the Italian Army in the mid-1990s and has proved comparable in armour protection and firepower to contemporary tanks of other nations. The Ariete mounts a 120mm (4.7in) smoothbore gun and a pair of 7.62mm (0.3in) machine guns.

in supporting infantry operations and providing protection to troops on the ground, while the type has also performed well in a reconnaissance role.

Given the need for scout, reconnaissance and patrol types, several European nations have developed their own light armoured vehicles. These have been deployed with NATO and United Nations peacekeeping forces in the Middle East and the Balkans and proved popular on the thriving export market. A new generation of self-propelled artillery

has also emerged during the last decade as many NATO countries replace their ageing US-made M109 weapons systems.

The German Panzerhaubitze 2000 entered production in 1998 and mounts a 155mm (6.1in) L52 gun developed by Rheinmetall, and more than 400 are in use with the armed forces of Germany, Italy, the Netherlands and Greece. A European contemporary is the British AS-90, in service since 1993 and mounting the 155mm (6.1in) L31 cannon.

▲ Centauro Tank Destroyer

Italian Army / Aosta Mechanized Brigade

The wheeled Centauro tank destroyer mounts a 105mm (4.1in) gun and two 7.62mm (0.3in) machine guns. It has seen extensive deployment to the Balkans, Somalia, Iraq and Lebanon. Combining speed and firepower, the Centauro has excelled in convoy escort and infantry support roles as well.

Specifications

Crew: 4	Speed: 108km/h (67mph)
Weight: 25,000kg (55,100lb)	Range: 800km (500 miles)
Length (with gun): 8.55m (28ft 6in)	Armament:1 x 105mm (4.1in) gun, plus
Width: 2.95m (9ft 8in)	2 x 7.62mm (0.3in) MGs (1 coaxial,
Height: 2.73m (8ft 11.5in)	1 anti-aircraft) and 2 x 4 smoke grenade
Engine: 388kW (520hp) Iveco MTCA 6-cylinder	launchers
turbo diesel	Radio: n/k

Specifications

Crew: 3 or 4	4-cylinder diesel
Weight: 3200kg (7100lb)	Speed: 120km/h (75mph)
Length: 4.86m (15ft 11in)	Range: 500km (300 miles)
Width: 1.78m (5ft 1in)	Armament: 1 x Oerlikon KAD-B17 20mm (0.79in)
Height: 1.55m (5ft 1in)	gun in T 20 FA-HS turret
Engine: 71kW (95hp) Fiat Model 8144.81.200	

▲ OTO Melara R3 Capraia Armoured Reconnaissance Vehicle

Italian Army

The OTO Melara R3 Capraia armoured reconnaissance vehicle enables its three- or four-man crew to assess enemy strength and positions. Its armour is effective against most small arms, and the vehicle mounts a variety of weapons, including a 20mm (0.79in) Oerlikon.

▲ **Wheeled tank destroyer**
An Oto Melara Centauro tank destroyer is put through its paces somewhere in the Italian countryside.

The Middle East and Asia
1991–PRESENT

Although the emerging nations of the Middle East and Asia have utilized armoured vehicles of other nations, their development of indigenous armour has accelerated in recent years.

THE ISRAELI DEFENCE FORCES have developed into one of the most efficient and experienced fighting forces in the world, and the Merkava main battle tank has become symbolic of their prowess. From the IDF perspective, the Merkava series was born of necessity. Following the Six Day War of 1967, Great Britain and France discontinued the supply of some weapons to Israel. Therefore, the Israeli military establishment determined that the nation would become as self-reliant as possible in terms of modern military hardware. The development of a main battle tank became a priority.

Designed by Israeli Military Industries and manufactured by IDF Ordnance, the Merkava Mk 1 entered service in 1979. Since then, successive upgrades, or marks, have been introduced. Each of these has been involved in combat operations against

paramilitary factions such as the Palestine Liberation Organization and Hezbollah.

Israeli armoured doctrine has long stressed the survivability of tank crews, reasoning that a confident crew, assured that its survival is likely, will assert itself more boldly in the face of an enemy. True enough, the Merkava design has reflected this philosophy and marked a radical departure from conventional configurations. The main battle tank's diesel engine and fuel tanks were located forward to provide additional protection for the crew in the event of hull penetration. Furthermore, the turret was positioned somewhat towards the rear.

Merkava MBT
The experience with the Merkava Mk 1 during the 1982 incursion into Lebanon resulted in the

upgraded Merkava Mk 2, which included improved fire control and urban warfare equipment specifically designed for low-intensity confrontations. The later Merkava Mk 3 entered service in 1989 and mounted the 120mm (4.7in) MG251 smoothbore cannon adapted from the popular Rheinmetall design, an upgrade from the original 105mm (4.1in) L7 gun.

Most recently, the Merkava Mk 4, which includes the latest in urban warfare fittings, a much improved powerplant consisting of a 1125kW (1500hp) General Dynamics GD833 diesel engine and

modular composite armour whose standards remain classified, entered service in 2004. The Merkava Mk 4 also incorporates the Trophy Active Protective System, which raises an alarm when the tank is 'painted' by enemy laser rangefinding equipment, identifies the likely point of impact and selects appropriate counter-measures.

The Merkava Mk 4 was heavily engaged against Hezbollah militia during the 2006 Lebanon War, and some critics have claimed that it proved extremely vulnerable to anti-tank missiles. However,

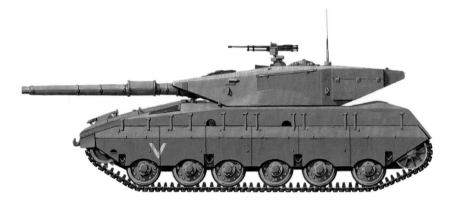

Specifications

Crew: 4
Weight: 55,898kg (122,976lb)
Length: 8.36m (27ft 5.25in)
Width: 3.72m (12ft 2.5in)
Height: 2.64m (8ft 8in)
Engine: 671kW (900hp) Teledyne Continental AVDS-1790-6A V12 diesel
Speed: 46km/h (28.6mph)
Range: 500km (310 miles)
Armament: 1 x 120 mm (4.7in) MG253 cannon, plus 1 x 7.62mm (0.3in) MG
Radio: n/k

▲ **Merkava Mk 4 MBT**

Israeli Defence Forces / 401st Armoured Brigade, Israeli occupied territories, 2004

The Merkava main battle tank was the first armoured vehicle of its kind developed and manufactured in Israel. Since the 1980s, the Merkava has served as the frontline main battle tank of the Israeli Defence Forces, while older Magach tanks remain in service.

▲ **Arjun Main Battle Tank**

Indian Army / 67th Armoured Regiment, 2005

The development of the Arjun main battle tank was undertaken in the 1970s by India's largest defence contractor, the Defence Research and Development Organization. However, setbacks in its design and testing phases resulted in lengthy delays in Arjun production, which was not begun in earnest until early in the twenty-first century. The tank mounts a 120mm (4.7in) rifled main gun.

Specifications

Crew: 4
Weight: 58 tonnes (127,600lb)
Length: 9.8m (32ft 2in)
Width: 3.17m (10ft 5in)
Height: 2.44m (8ft)
Engine: 1044kW (1400hp) MTU MB 838 Ka 501 water-cooled diesel
Speed: 72km/h (45mph)
Range: 400km (250 miles)
Armament: 1 x 120mm (4.7in) gun, plus 1 x 7.62mm (0.3in) MG
Radio: n/k

its combat record has validated the primary maxim of crew survivability, and more than 500 are currently in service.

Meanwhile, the government of India had embarked on the development of the Arjun main battle tank during the early 1970s; however, serious delays and political circumstances relegated the tank to a lower priority and it did not enter production until 2004. Needless to say, numerous technological upgrades

from the original version were necessary before trials with the Indian Army and acceptance into full production.

Traditionally, India had been a major arms purchaser from the Soviet Union, and this trend continued with the T-72 and later models such as the T-90. Mounting a 120mm (4.7in) rifled gun, the Arjun is being equipped with sophisticated fire control and rangefinding equipment, while its primary

▲ Al-Khalid Main Battle Tank

Pakistani Army / 6th Armoured Division

A joint venture between Pakistan and the People's Republic of China, the Al-Khalid entered service with the Pakistani Army in 2001. The tank's design is based on the Chinese Type 90, itself an amalgamation of both Soviet and Western technology. Its main armament is a 125mm (4.9in) smoothbore gun. A current upgrade programme is under way.

Specifications

Crew: 3

Weight: 47,000kg (103,617lb)

Length: 10.07m (33ft)

Width: 3.5m (11ft 6in)

Height: 2.435m (7ft 11in)

Engine: 890kW (1200hp) KMDB 6TD-2 6-cylinder diesel

Speed: 72km/h (45mph)

Range: 450km (992 miles)

Armament: 1 x 125mm (4.9in) smoothbore gun, plus 1 x 12.7mm (0.5in) external AA MG and 1 x 7.72mm (0.303in) coaxial MG

Radio: n/k

Specifications

Crew: 4

Weight: 45.5 tonnes (100,327lbs)

Length: 6.89m (22ft 7in)

Width: 3.35m (11ft)

Height: 2.76m (9ft 1in)

Engine: 1 x 620kW (831hp) MTU 90 diesel

Speed: 60km/h (38mph)

Range: 600km (380 miles)

Armament: 1 x 104mm (4.1in) gun; 2 x 7.62 (0.3in) MGs; 4 x smoke dischargers

Radio: n/k

▲ OF 40 Mk2 Main Battle Tank

Union Defence Force (United Arab Emirates), 1990

Designed for the export market during the late 1970s, the OF 40 main battle tank was a joint venture between Otobreda and Fiat. Incorporating some features of the German Leopard 1 main battle tank, its performance nevertheless proved disappointing. The United Arab Emirates has taken delivery of 36 OF-40s since 1981. These were the mainstay of the Union Defence Force until the late 1990s, when the UEA began taking delivery of Leclerc main battle tanks.

APFSDS (armour-piercing fin-stabilized discarding sabot) ammunition is produced indigenously in India.

Egyptian effort

Long an arms customer of the Soviet Union, Egypt has, interestingly, pursued an upgrade of the vintage T-54/55 main battle tank. Following evaluation of an upgraded T-54, which had been modified in the United States, the T-54E, better known as the Ramses II, was accepted into Egyptian production as late as 2004. In a curious blend of once adversarial Cold War technology, the Ramses II shares a common gun, the 105mm (4.1in) M68 rifled cannon, with the American M60A3 Patton export tanks already deployed with the Egyptian Army. Its powerplant, a 677kW (908hp) turbocharged diesel, is also quite similar to that of the M60A3. Laser fire control equipment, an improved communication system, armour skirting and updated NBC defences are in place. An estimated 400 Ramses II tanks were to be in service with the Egyptian Army when the project was completed.

Specifications

Crew: 4

Weight: 45,800kg (101,972lb)

Length: 9.9m (32ft 6in)

Width: 3.27m (10ft 8in)

Height: 2.4m (7ft 11in)

Engine: 677kW (908hp) TCM AVDS-1790-5A turbocharged diesel

Speed: 72km/h (45mph)

Range: 600km (373 miles)

Armament: 1 x 105mm (4.1in) M68 rifled gun, plus 1 x 12.7mm (0.5in) M2HB HMG and 1 x 7.62mm (0.3in) coaxial MG

Radio: n/k

▲ Ramses II

Egyptian Army / 36th Independent Armoured Brigade

A modernization of the Soviet T-54/55 main battle tank introduced a half-century ago, the Ramses II incorporates modern technology from the United States, such as an improved gun (the 105mm/4.1in M68 rifled canon), better target acquisition equipment and a high-performance engine.

▲ Fahd APC

Egyptian Army / 23rd Independent Armoured Brigade

In service since 1986, the Fahd APC was designed to fit the requirements of the Egyptian military. It replaced older APCs in Egyptian service, such as the Soviet BTR-40. The Fahd consists of a Mercedes-Benz LAP 1117/32 truck chassis fitted with an armoured body. More than 1400 are in Egyptian service, with hundreds also employed by the militaries of Libya, Kuwait and Bangladesh.

Specifications

Crew: 2 + 10

Weight: 10,900kg (24,000lb)

Length: 6m (9ft 8in)

Width: 2.45m (8ft 4in)

Height: 2.1m (6ft 10in)

Engine: 125kW (168hp) 6-cylinder diesel

Speed: 90km/h (56mph)

Range: 800km (500 miles)

Armament: None as standard

Radio: n/k

South Africa
1980–PRESENT

During the twenty-first century, South Africa has leveraged its experience battling guerrillas across rugged terrain to develop several light armoured vehicles and a main battle tank.

FOR YEARS, THE ARMOURED FORCES of South Africa fielded the Semel main battle tank, adapted from the British Centurion of the early Cold War years. By the late 1970s, development of the Olifant was well under way, and the tank entered full production by the end of the decade. With 172 Olifant tanks in service, the South Africans have continually upgraded the vehicle. The initial upgrade, the Olifant Mk 1B of the early 1990s, was already in progress when the first production tanks were delivered. Equipped with the 105mm (4.1in) L7 gun, the Olifant Mk 1B utilized a hand-held laser rangefinder for target acquisition.

An extensive modernization programme was initiated with a contract to BAE Land Systems in 2003. The Olifant Mk 2, which entered service in 2007, features a new 675kW (900hp) turbocharged V12 diesel engine, a vastly improved turret that allows the tank to fire on the move, thermal sights and integral laser rangefinding equipment, modular armour, and the ability to mount either a 105mm (4.1in) or 120mm (4.7in) smoothbore gun.

Safety and speed

South Africa's state-run arms manufacturer, Armscor, has embarked on a concentrated effort to increase sales, which contracted in recent years but were ironically robust during the United Nations Security Council embargo on the nation's trade during the era of apartheid. Forays into the global arms export market have been primarily characterized by the development of armoured cars and light reconnaissance vehicles.

The wheeled G6 Rhino self-propelled howitzer has been in production since 1987 and is operated by the armed forces of Oman and the United Arab Emirates

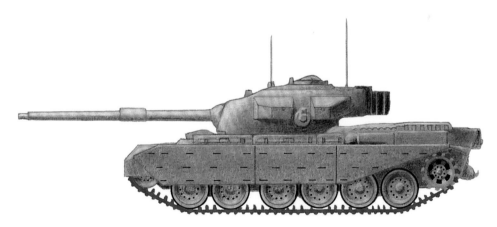

▲ **Olifant Mk 1A Main Battle Tank**

South African Army / 1st Tank Regiment

The Olifant Mk 1A main battle tank entered service with the South African armed forces during the late 1970s and was rapidly supplanted by the Mk 1B. The accuracy of its 105mm (4.1in) L7 rifled cannon was enhanced by laser rangefinding equipment which was hand operated by a crewman. Later upgrades have significantly improved the tank's performance.

Specifications

Crew: 4	Speed: 45km/h (28.1mph)
Weight: 56,000kg (123,200lb)	Range: 500km (313 miles)
Length: 9.83m (30ft)	Armament: 1 x 105mm (4.1in) gun, plus
Width: 3.38m (10ft 4in)	2 x 7.62mm (0.3in) MGs (1 coaxial, 1 anti-
Height: 2.94m (8ft 11in)	aircraft) and 2 x 4 smoke dischargers
Engine: 559kW (750hp) V12 air-cooled	Radio: n/k
turbocharged diesel	

as well. Mounting a powerful 155mm (6.1in) gun, the Rhino has been used in combat during the prolonged South African Border War and may well have inspired Iraq to develop similar heavy mobile weapons, which did not enter production but were reported to mount 210mm (8.3in) cannon. A modified G6 turret has also been fitted to the T-72 and Arjun main battle tanks.

The development of the Ratel infantry fighting vehicle arose due to difficulties in procuring replacement parts and new vehicles due to the arms embargo of the apartheid era. Since the 1970s, variants of the wheeled Ratel have mounted a variety of weapons, such as 7.62mm (0.3in) machine guns, anti-tank mines and even a 90mm (3.5in) cannon, thus expanding the

capabilities of the vehicle from a basic reconnaissance type to a direct fire support platform and a 'battle taxi' carrying six infantrymen. Continuing development of armoured vehicles has proved profitable for South African manufacturers. Given the high risk of landmines and improvised explosive devices, the RG-31 Nyala 4x4 troop carrier produced by Land Systems OMC has been described as one of the finest mine-protected vehicles in the world. Capable of transporting six infantrymen, the RG-31 is in use with the armed forces of at least eight countries, including the United States, Canada and France, and is classified by the US military as an MRAP (Mine Resistant Ambush Protected) vehicle.

Specifications
Crew: 4
Weight: 28,000kg (61,700lb)
Length: 7.09m (23ft 3in)
Width: 2.9m (9ft 6in)
Height: 2.8m (9ft 2in)
Engine: 420kW (563hp) diesel
Speed: 120km/h (75mph)
Range: 700km (430 miles)
Armament: 1 x 76mm (2.9in) gun; 1 x 7.62mm
   (.3in) coaxial MG, plus 1 x 7.62mm (.3in
   turret-mounted MG
Radio: n/k

▲ **Rooikat 76 Armoured Car**

South African Army / 8th Reconnaissance Battalion

In service since 1990, this highly mobile, South African-made armoured car was designed for combat reconnaissance and seek-and-destroy operations, as well as combat support and anti-guerrilla actions. It can be fitted with either a 76mm (2.9in) or a 105mm (4.1in) cannon.

Specifications
Crew: 3 + 6
Weight: 19,000kg (41,887lb)
Length: 7.212m (23ft 4in)
Width: 2.526m (8ft 3in)
Height: 2.915m (9ft 7in)
Engine: 210kW (282bhp) 6-cylinder
in-line diesel
Speed: 105km/h (65mph)
Range: 860km (534 miles)
Armament: 1 x 90mm (3.5in) gun, plus
3 x 7.62mm (0.3in) MGs
Radio: n/k

▲ **Ratel 20**

South African Army / 61st Mechanized Infantry Battalion Group

In service with the South African military for more than 30 years, the Ratel armoured fighting vehicle is slated for replacement by the Patria armoured modular vehicle of Finnish manufacture. The Ratel has proved adept at both troop transport and fire support, armed with machine guns, anti-tank missiles and cannon.

Brazil
1991–PRESENT

More than 30 Brazilian manufacturers of armoured cars and fighting vehicles have found a ready market across the globe as low-intensity conflicts are prosecuted.

WHILE SOARING SALES raised Brazil to the sixth largest exporter of arms in the world, the nation's own fleet of armoured personnel carriers is currently being upgraded by a foreign company. The Italian firm Iveco has been engaged to produce a new six-wheeled armoured personnel carrier capable of transporting up to 11 soldiers and mounting a 30mm (1.18in) cannon or 12.7mm (0.5in) machine gun, which may be incorporated into a remote turret of Israeli manufacture.

Meanwhile, the Brazilians have been recognized for their EE-3 Jararaca armoured fighting vehicle of the 1980s and the EE-9 Cascavel armoured car, which has been operated by at least 17 countries and mounts an imposing 90mm (3.5in) cannon. Both vehicles were manufactured by the now-defunct Engesa defence contractor. During the 1980s, Engesa also produced prototypes of a main battle tank, the EE-T1 Osorio, to carry either a 105mm (4.1in) or 120mm (4.7in) gun, but it never reached production.

Specifications
Crew: 3
Weight: 5500kg (12,100lb)
Length: 4.12m (13ft 6.2in)
Width: 2.13m (6ft 11in)
Height: 1.56m (5ft 1.4in)
Engine: 89kW (120hp) Mercedes-Benz OM 314A
4-cylinder turbo diesel
Speed: 100km/h (60mph)
Range: 750km (470 miles)
Armament: 1 x 12.7mm (0.5in) Browning M2 HB
HMG as standard

▲ **EE-3 Jararaca**

Brazilian Army / 17th Mechanized Cavalry Regiment

A light armoured reconnaissance vehicle, the EE-3 Jararaca is powered by an 89kW (120hp), four-cylinder Mercedes-Benz diesel engine and mounts a 12.7mm (0.5in) machine gun for close defence. Variants mounted 20mm (0.79in) and heavier cannon or the MILAN anti-tank missile system.

▲ **EE-9 Cascavel**

Brazilian Army / 13th Armoured Infantry Battalion

The long service life of the EE-9 Cascavel has been marked by numerous variants and upgrades, and it is expected to continue for at least another decade. The most common, the Cascavel III, mounts a 90mm (3.5in) cannon of Belgian design and manufactured under licence.

Specifications
Crew: 3
Weight: 13,400kg (29,542lb)
Length: 5.2m (17ft 1in)
Width: 2.64m (8ft 8in)
Height: 2.68m (8ft 10in)
Engine: 158kW (212hp) Detroit Diesel 6V-53N
6-cylinder water-cooled
Speed: 100km/h (62mph)
Range: 880km (547 miles)
Armament: 1 x 90mm (3.5in) gun, plus
2 x 7.62mm (0.3in) MGs (1 coaxial,
1 anti-aircraft)
Radio: n/k

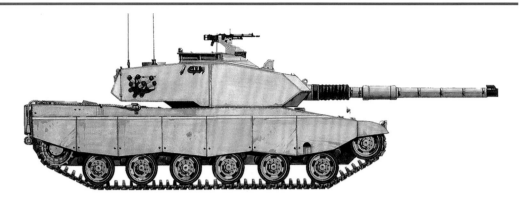

▲ **Engesa EE-T1 Osorio**

Brazilian prototype

The Osorio main battle tank project eventually led to the bankruptcy of the Engesa company, particularly after Iraq, one of its primary clients, ceased orders for armoured vheicles and Saudi Arabia opted to purchase the US M1A1 Abrams tank. The prototype Osorio mounted either a 120mm (4.7in) smoothbore or 105mm (4.1in) rifled gun.

Specifications	
Crew: 4	Speed: 70km/h (43.5mph)
Weight: 39,000kg (85,800lb)	Range: 550km (342 miles)
Length: 9.995m (32ft 9.5in)	Armament:1 x 105mm (4.1in) or 1 x 120mm
Width: 3.26m (10ft 8.3in)	(4.7in) gun, plus 1 x 7.62mm (0.3in) MG
Height: 2.371m (7ft 9.3in)	Radio: n/k
Engine: 745kW (1000hp) 12-cylinder diesel	

The Far East
1995–PRESENT

The nations of the Far East have embarked on programmes of armoured vehicle development for their own armed forces and export to other nations during the twenty-first century.

ALTHOUGH ITS EARLIEST TANK designs were based solidly on Soviet technology, the People's Republic of China has begun to develop its own main battle tanks and armoured fighting vehicles, primarily funded by the manufacturing conglomerate China North Industries Corporation (NORINCO), and manufactured for the People's Liberation Army and for export purposes.

The latest generation of Chinese main battle tank, the Type 96, reached the army in the late 1990s and improved on the performance of previous main battle tanks such as the Type 88 and its predecessors, the Type 59 and 69, which were generally copies of the Soviet T-54/55. The Type 96 represents an improvement over previous Chinese designs, particularly in its powerplant, a 750kW (1000 hp) diesel with acceptable performance, outclassing previous engines whose problems had plagued Chinese engineers for decades. The Type 96 also incorporates modular explosive reactive armour and

a distinctive turret, which closely resembles those of many Western tanks rather than the rounded 'frying pan' look of older Soviet-inspired models.

The Type 96 mounts the 125mm (4.9in) smoothbore cannon, which has become standard on later model main battle tanks of Russian and Chinese manufacture. Its secondary armament consists of a pair of 7.62mm (0.3in) machine guns, and more than 1500 are currently in service with the People's Liberation Army.

In recent years, China has also entered the export market, selling a number of its Type 90 tanks to Pakistan for further joint development as the Al-Khalid. The Chinese military establishment had declined to adopt the Type 90 as its primary tank during the 1980s; however, its relative ease of manufacture and reasonable cost made it ideal for the cooperative venture. A notable 'second generation' Chinese tank is the Type 85, which was built by NORINCO and debuted in 1988.

The most advanced Chinese main battle tank is the Type 99, which was developed originally as the Type 98 during the 1990s and was seen publicly during the National Day parade in 1999. The Type 99 closely resembles Western contemporaries, utilizing sloped armour and a powerful 1125kW (1500hp) diesel engine. Through several variations, its capabilities have improved to rival those of the US Abrams, British Challenger and German Leopard tanks. It main armament includes 125mm (4.9in), 140mm (5.5in), or 155mm (6.1in) smoothbore guns, which are controlled by thermal and laser rangefinding equipment. A battlefield control system has also been installed, while the tank is protected by explosive reactive armour and a laser defence system that initiates a series of responses when the vehicle is identified by enemy targeting equipment.

Asian colossus

In recent years, the People's Liberation Army doctrine of combined arms has somewhat redefined the role of tanks and armoured fighting vehicles. In 2006, the army unveiled a reorganized mechanized infantry division equipped to fight as an independent battle group. The Type 92 wheeled infantry fighting vehicle and Type PL02 assault gun are expected to be key elements in the rapid mobility of these mechanized infantry formations. The Type 92 is armed with anti-tank rockets, a grenade launcher or a flamethrower.

The PL02 assault gun mounts a 100mm (3.9in) cannon. The world's largest land military force, the People's Liberation Army is highly mechanized and is estimated to include nine armoured divisions, 12 independent armoured brigades and 27 mechanized or motorized infantry divisions. More than 10,000 tanks of various configurations are either deployed with active units or available in reserve.

North Korean nemesis

The secretive North Korean Chonma-ho upgrade to the Soviet-built T-62 main battle tank has produced an estimated 1200 vehicles, although their combat efficiency is somewhat questionable. It is known that the tanks mount 115mm (4.5in) or 125mm (4.9in) smoothbore cannon and are powered by a 563kW (750hp) diesel engine. The Chonma-ho debuted with North Korean forces in 1992, and a new North Korean main battle tank is reported in production. However, detail on this vehicle remains scarce.

The threat of military action by its communist neighbour to the north has prompted South Korea to remain vigilant and to develop its own main battle tank in recent years. Although the South would be confronted with overwhelming numbers of communist soldiers and armoured vehicles, it is possible that superior combat efficiency and technology might bolster defences against North Korean aggression.

▲ **Dragoon Amphibious Armoured Vehicle**

Royal Thai Army

Produced by US company General Dynamics in the 1980s, the Dragoon is based on the automotive components of the US Army's M113 APC. It is completely amphibious, and is propelled in water by its wheels at a speed of 4.8km/h (3mph), while three drain pumps remove water entering through the doors.

Specifications

Crew: 3 + 6	Speed: 116km/h (72mph)
Weight: 12,700kg (28,000lb)	Range: 1045km (650 miles)
Length: 5.89m (19ft 4in)	Armament: 1 x 90mm (3.4in) KEnerga gun; 1 x
Width: 2.44m (8ft)	7.62mm (0.3in) coaxial MG
Height: 2.8m (9ft 3in)	Radio: n/k
Engine: 223kW (300hp) diesel	

Although the South Korean Army has long depended on equipment manufactured in the United States and on the presence of American troops to deter North Korean military action, the South Koreans have manufactured the K1 main battle tank and its successor, the K1A1, since 1985. Based largely on the American M1 Abrams design, the tank is built in South Korea by Hyundai. The K1 was originally armed with the Korean-built KM68A1

105mm (4.1in) gun. Notable differences from the Abrams were its powerplant, the 900kW (1200hp) 10-cylinder diesel MTU-871 Ka-501 engine, and its weight of 51.8 tonnes (51 tons), making it lighter than the M1. US technology was prevalent in the K1, including thermal sights, laser rangefinding and composite armour whose characteristics remain classified. Illustrating the globalization of arms technology, the K1A1, deployed to the South Korean

▲ Type 85 Main Battle Tank

People's Liberation Army / 12th Armoured Division

The Type 85 main battle tank was introduced in 1991 and constituted an improvement over the previous Type 80, which had been based on the Soviet T-54/55. Later models included more powerful engines and modular armour. Some Type 85s were manufactured in Pakistan under licence.

Specifications

Crew: 3	Speed: 57.25km/h (35.8mph)
Weight: 41,000kg (90,200lb)	Range: 500km (312 miles)
Length: 10.28m (31ft 5in)	Armament:1 x 125mm (4.9in) gun; 1 x 12.7mm
Width: 3.45m (10ft 6in)	(0.5in) anti-aircraft HMG; 1 x 7.62mm (0.3in)
Height: 2.3m (7ft)	coaxial MG; 2 x smoke grenade launchers
Engine: 544kW (730hp) V12 diesel	Radio: Type 889B

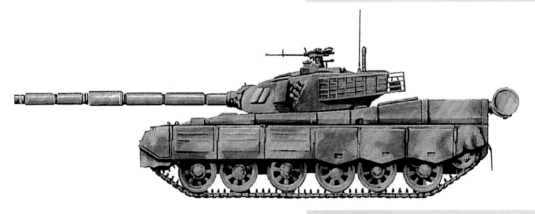

▲ Type 90-II

People's Liberation Army / 3rd Armoured Division

The Type 90-II main battle tank included an attempt to upgrade the powerplant of previous models with disappointing results, and the engine was replaced with a diesel of Ukrainian design. An export variant was purchased by Pakistan as the basis for the Al-Khalid main battle tank.

Specifications

Crew: 3	Speed: 62.3km/h (39mph)
Weight: 48,000kg (105,822lb)	Range: 450km (249 miles)
Length: 10.1m (33ft 1in)	Armament: 1 x 125mm (4.9in) smoothbore gun,
Width: 3.5m (11ft 6in);	plus 1 x 12.7mm (0.5in) external anti-aircraft
Height: 2.2m (7ft 2in)	MG and 1 x 7.62mm (0.3in) coaxial MG
Engine: 895kW (1200hp) Perkins CV12-1200 TCA 12-cylinder diesel	Radio: n/k

Army in 2001, mounts the 120mm (4.7in) KM256 smoothbore, a licensed version of the US M256, which, in turn, is a licensed production model of a German Rheinmetall weapon. The K1A1 includes a reconfigured turret and upgraded target acquisition systems. Its armour protection is enhanced with a composite designated as KSAP (Korean Special Armour Plate).

Black Panther

While the K1 and K1A1 main battle tanks may be sufficient to oppose the technology fielded by the North Koreans, the South Korean military establishment is producing a complementary tank, the K2 Black Panther, which is intended to supplement the existing modern tanks in the armed forces while replacing those elderly tanks of the US Patton series, which have been in service for decades. Nearly 400 examples of the new tank are scheduled for production. The Black Panther implements a substantial amount of South Korean technology, which in part provided the impetus for the project, begun in the mid-1990s. Prohibitively expensive, the K2 has incorporated the contributions of at least 11 South Korean defence contractors and showcases some of the nation's most advanced military systems. The primary armament of the Black Panther is a 120mm (4.7in) L55 smoothbore gun with automatic

loading system, capable of firing modern APFSDS ammunition manufactured in South Korea. The tank is powered by a 1125kW (1500hp) 12-cylinder diesel engine. Its advanced technology includes global positioning equipment, sophisticated battlefield management capabilities through computerized command and control apparatus, a battlefield management and communication system that allows one tank to share real-time information with others in formation, and radar warning and jamming defences.

The army of the Republic of Korea fields nearly 6000 armoured vehicles, including approximately 3000 tanks, half of which are the modern K1 and K1A1. Its troop strength is roughly 520,000, the sixth highest in the world.

Japan's new generation

The Japanese Type 10 main battle tank is slated as the successor to the Type 74 and Type 90 main battle tanks currently in service with the nation's defence forces. As the Type 74, a contemporary of the German Leopard 1 and the US M60 Patton main battle tanks, and the Type 90, which was fielded more than 20 years ago, continue to be upgraded and their service lives extended, the Type 10 marks an impressive advance in the capabilities of Japanese land forces. Production of the Type 10 is scheduled

▲ **Type 87 SPAAG**

Japan Ground Self-Defense Force / 2nd Combined Brigade

The Type 87 self-propelled anti-aircraft gun mounts a pair of radar-directed 35mm (1.38in) autocannon. Developed during the 1980s as a replacement for the outmoded American M42 Duster, the Type 87 has a chassis by Mitsubishi, while its weapons, similar to the Swiss Oerlikon, were produced by Japan Steel Works.

Specifications

Crew: 3	diesel
Weight: 36,000kg (79,400lb)	Speed: 60km/h (37mph)
Length: 7.99m (26ft 2in)	Range: 500km (310 miles)
Width: 3.18m (10ft 5in)	Armament: 2 x 35mm (1.38in) autocannon
Height: 4.4m (14ft 5in)	Radio: n/k
Engine: 536kW (718hp) 10F22WT 10-cylinder	

Specifications

Crew: 3	10-cylinder diesel
Weight: 50,000kg (110,250lb)	Speed: 70km/h (43mph)
Length: 9.76m (32ft)	Range: 400km (250 miles)
Width: 3.43m (11ft 4in)	Armament: 1 x 120mm (4.7in) gun; 1 x 12.7mm
Height: 2.34m (7ft 11in)	(0.5in) HMG; 1 x 7.62mm (0.3in) MG
Engine: 1118kW (1500bhp) Mitsubishi 10ZG	Radio: n/k

▲ **Type 90 Main Battle Tank**

Japan Ground Self-Defence Force / 7th Armoured Division

Mounting a licence-built version of the German Rheinmetall 120mm (4.7in) smoothbore gun with an automatic loading system, the Japanese Type 90 main battle tank entered service in 1990 and nearly 350 examples were built. Its armour protection and target acquisition equipment were comparable to Western tanks of the same generation.

to commence in 2010, and its design phase was undertaken during the 1990s. The tank is expected to mount a 120mm (4.7in) smoothbore main weapon manufactured by Japan Steel Works Ltd and capable of firing standard NATO ammunition. Its sloped modular armour and profile are similar to those of the German Leopard 2 or the French Leclerc main battle tanks, and its armour protection is a composite structure of ceramic, steel and other components. It is powered by a 900kW (1200hp) 8-cylinder diesel

engine, and at approximately 40.6 tonnes (40 tons) is somewhat lighter than contemporary main battle tanks of other nations.

Currently, the Japan Ground Self-Defense Force deploys approximately 1000 Type 90 and Type 74 tanks. It includes one armoured division and nine infantry divisions and totals about 150,000 troops. The primary combined arms unit is the brigade, which incorporates mechanized infantry and armoured elements.

Australian armour

The Royal Australian Armoured Corps has recently provided manpower to NATO and Coalition forces in Iraq and Afghanistan as well as during the unrest in East Timor, Rwanda and Somalia. It is equipped with the American M1A1 Abrams main battle tank and includes British Land Rover reconnaissance

◄ **Type 90 MBT**

With its vertical front, sides and rea, the turret of the Japanese Type 90 is similar to that of the Leopard 2.

vehicles and the US M113 armoured personnel carrier. The Bushmaster wheeled armoured vehicle is manufactured in Australia under licence from Timoney Technology of Ireland. The Bushmaster underwent trials with the Australian Army in the late 1990s, and more than 800 units have been built to date. Capable of transporting up to nine combat infantrymen, the vehicle mounts 5.56mm (0.22in) and 7.62mm (0.3in) machine guns for close defence. Lightly armoured, the Bushmaster is nevertheless considered effective against mines and improvised explosive devices. Several armoured cavalry regiments deploy the Bushmaster, as does the Royal Australian

Air Force and the armies of Great Britain and the Netherlands.

Besides the major powers of Asia–Pacific, other regional players maintain modern armoured forces. The Malaysian Army has purchased a number of Polish PT-91M main battle tanks and fields infantry vehicles and tank destroyers of Turkish, South African and Brazilian manufacture. The Royal Thai Army includes an armoured division, a cavalry division and five independent tank battalions equipped with the British-made Scorpion light tank. The army of Myanmar has more than 100 T-55 and T-72 tanks and at least 1000 armoured infantry vehicles.

▲ **Bionix 25**

Singapore Armed Forces / 5th Infantry Brigade

The first production model of the Bionix armoured personnel carrier, the Bionix 25 has been manufactured since 1996. Developed in Singapore to replace the M113 vehicle of US design, it is capable of transporting up to seven infantrymen. The Bionix 25 is armed with the M242 Bushmaster 25mm (1in) cannon.

Specifications

Crew: 3 + 7

Weight: 23,000kg (50,700lb)

Length: 5.92m (19ft 5in)

Width: 2.7m (8ft 10in)

Height: 2.53m (8ft 4in)

Engine: 354kW (475hp) Detroit Diesel Model 6V-92TA

Speed: 70km/h (43mph)

Range: 415km (260 miles)

Armament: 1 x 25mm (1in) Boeing M242 cannon; 2 x 7.62mm (0.3in) MGs (1 coaxial, 1 turret-mounted); 2 x 3 smoke grenade launchers

Radio: n/k

▲ **Warthog**

Singapore Armed Forces / UK Ministry of Defence, delivery 2010

The Warthog variant of the Bronco all-terrain tracked carrier was jointly developed by Singapore Technologies Kinetics and the Defence Science & Technology Agency for the Singapore Armed Forces. The fulfilment of an order for the Warthog by the British Ministry of Defence is under way. Slated to replace the Viking carrier, the Warthog transports up to 10 infantrymen and features slat armour and anti-mine reinforcement.

Specifications

Crew: (front car) 4; (rear car) 8

Weight: 18 tonnes (17.7 tons)

Length: 8.6m (28ft 2.5in)

Width: 2.3m (8ft 2.4in)

Height: 2.2m (7ft 2.5in)

Engine: 261kW (350hp) Caterpillar 3126B

Speed: (road) 65km/h (40mph);

(water) 5km/h (3.1mph)

Range: n/k

Armament: 1 x 7.62mm (0.3in) MG or 1 x 5.56mm (0.22in) MG

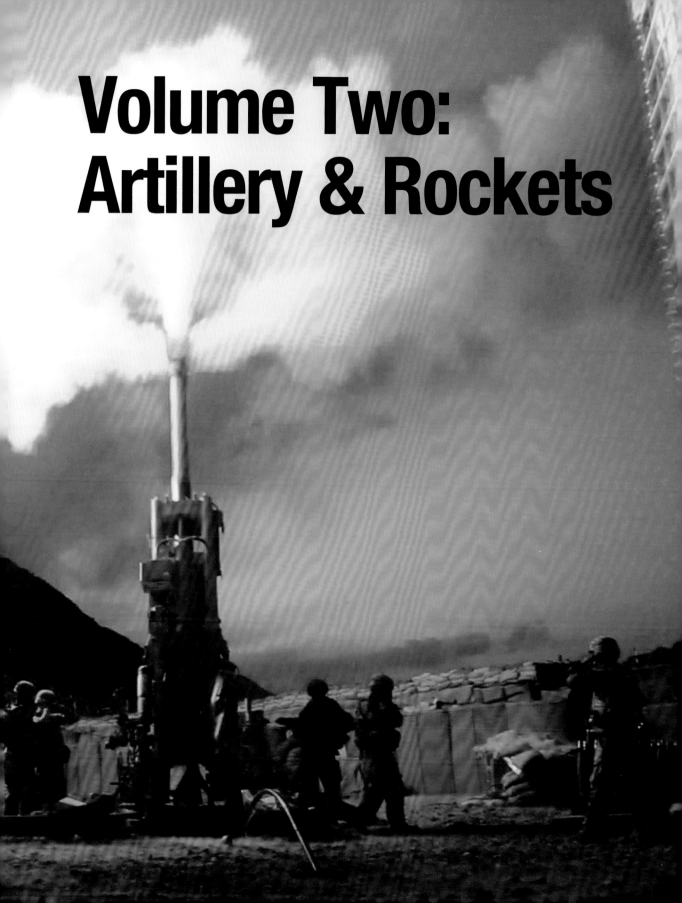

Volume Two:
Artillery & Rockets

Introduction

For centuries, artillery has demonstrated the
capability to change the course of history. Its
evolution through modern times has maintained
the potential to dominate the battlefield in a
tactical sense and to bring nations to the brink
of destruction or the negotiating table as an
instrument of strategic diplomacy. Conventional,
nuclear, biological and chemical weapons,
guided munitions and smart systems continue
to keep artillery relevant during the conflicts
of the twenty-first century. Although some have
theorized that the days are over when artillery
will dominate the battlefield landscape, a
student of recent history need only observe the
nature of combat since the end of World War II.
Artillery has not only exerted influence on
the ground; it has stretched into the sky and
beyond the horizon.

◀ **Infantry support**
Gunners with the US 31st Regimental Combat Team fire a 75mm (2.95in) recoilless rifle in support of
infantry units directly across the valley, somewhere in Korea, June 1951.

THE END OF WORLD WAR II marked a watershed in modern history. Weapons systems were modernized, upgraded and invented with astonishing rapidity. While the repercussions of the war itself are still being felt on a global scale, these advances in arms and armament have themselves become influencers during the last half-century and will continue as such in the future. The idea and application of artillery was altered perhaps more than any other weapon type as a result of the massive conflict of 1939–45.

Flash and fire

With a flash and a detonation of unprecedented destructive power, the nuclear age was born. With a cloud of smoke and flame, hurtling towards the stratosphere, the ballistic missile came into being. These awesome events have shaped the development and influence of artillery on the course of political and military events far beyond the ability of most to comprehend. Artillery, therefore, is at centre stage in modern military thinking. Civilian leaders and

▲ **Mobile nuclear threat**
Mounted on top of light tracked launchers, Soviet FROG-5 missiles are unloaded from a massive transport aircraft. Precursor of the more numerous FROG-7, the FROG-5 strategic missile was first deployed in the early 1960s. Its 503kg (1100lb) nuclear warhead had a range of 32km (20 miles).

military commanders must consider its potential impact on the outcome of battle more so than ever before. The introduction of artillery shells tipped with nuclear warheads; air defence missiles which control the skies for hundreds of kilometres around them; anti-tank projectiles capable of defeating the most advanced armoured vehicles; and intercontinental ballistic missiles packing such devastating power that they could destroy civilization as we know it in a matter of minutes – all give reason for analysts and observers to pause.

The prospect of devastating chemical and biological weapons has been sufficient to send troops to war around the world, while such capabilities at the disposal of terrorist organizations could place the lives of millions in peril.

Power and potential

'An artillery barrage is a terrifying thing,' wrote author Erich Maria Remarque in his classic *All Quiet on the Western Front*. While the image of a soldier huddled in a shell crater in the midst of the no man's land moonscape during World War I is familiar enough, such a scene has often been repeated. As General George S. Patton Jr noted at the end of World War II, there was no question in anyone's mind as to how the war was won. It was the artillery which made the difference.

During the modern era, technology and ingenuity – and indeed the flow of armed conflict itself – have not altered the conclusion that artillery is a deciding factor in the course of a fight. Prolonged air bombardment may well soften the resolve of an enemy to resist; however, the 1991 Gulf War and Operation Iraqi Freedom which followed a decade later were prosecuted to final victory by troops advancing on the ground, preceded by sustained artillery bombardment and accompanied by towed, self-propelled, air-defence and anti-tank artillery

▼ **Big gun raid**
A column of M109A2 155mm (6.1in) self-propelled howitzers of the US 29th Field Artillery Regiment drive through the town of Donje Caparde, Bosnia and Herzegovina, in the Zone of Separation, during a patrol in support of Operation Joint Endeavour, April 1996.

capable of engaging and defeating a mechanized and determined enemy.

While the complexity of artillery has increased substantially since 1945, the capabilities of artillery have grown exponentially. Not only is its destructive capacity unequalled in military history but artillery is also able to go more places, engage a greater variety of targets and displace more quickly than ever before. The introduction of lighter materials facilitates airlift and rapid deployment. The refinement of the laser, sophisticated radar and integrated fire-control systems results in astonishing accuracy. The well-trained and motivated soldier manipulates an offensive and defensive system of awesome complexity and immense destructive force. The future of the entire planet is placed in the hands of a relative few.

Considering a forward focus, the future of artillery as a tactical weapon seems assured, while its strategic implications are unlikely to diminish. From high-tech futuristic engagements between modern armies to the suppression of terrorist guerrillas ensconced in mountainous hideaways, artillery exerts its force today and will do so tomorrow with saturation and precision. In truth, modern artillery has assumed an authoritative role in both peace and war. Today, for those who are aware of its capabilities, the silence of artillery is as deafening as its roar.

Chapter 8

Cold War Europe, 1947–91

With the end of World War II, the map of Europe
was redrawn. Spheres of influence and differing world views
resulted in a face-off between two armed camps along a
closed border between East and West – and the drama
was to last half a century. For the armed forces of each, the
organization and firepower of modern artillery would shape
combat doctrine and serve to heighten the tension of the
Cold War. A new generation of technologically advanced
conventional artillery – towed, self-propelled, airmobile or
specifically designed for air defence – outfitted the ranks
of modern armies, while strategic and tactical artillery
capable of delivering nuclear warheads raised the
stakes in a global contest of wills.

◀ Show of strength

Red Army 2S3 (M1973) self-propelled guns take part in a parade in Moscow's Red Square, sometime
during the 1980s. Developed as a response the US Army's M109, the 2S3 provided highly mobile fire
support for motorized rifle and tank divisions.

Introduction

The Cold War in Europe presented specific offensive and defensive requirements for both NATO and Warsaw Pact forces, resulting in the refinement of strategic and tactical doctrines.

WHILE ARTILLERY is theoretically utilized in coordination with air assets and manoeuvring ground troops to gain victory on the battlefield, one US Army field manual states that aggressive employment of artillery may in itself serve as the decisive element in the defeat of enemy ground forces in certain circumstances, particularly when an aggressor assumes the offensive.

'Artillery theory employs the concept of fire strike, which is a severe and intense bombardment by all artillery weapons to defeat the enemy without the use of ground troops,' it reads. 'Artillery fires are laid down with such weight, volume, and accuracy that the artillery fire itself is an offensive.'

At the outset of the Cold War, it was apparent to Western military strategists that the potential to be on the receiving end of such a devastating utilization of offensive firepower was very real. The Soviet Red Army was by far the most capable military force on the European continent. Should the word be given, the tremendous artillery capability of the Red Army might devastate US and other troop concentrations in Western Europe, resulting in catastrophically high casualties and a loss of combat efficiency from which the defenders could not recover.

For a relatively brief period, the trump card for the West was the exclusive nuclear capability of the United States. Demonstrated with telling

▲ **Towed tank killers**
East German MT-LB tracked prime movers tow T12 (2A19) anti-tank guns on manoeuvres somewhere in Eastern Europe.

◀ **Popular model**
The Czech-built DANA 152mm (6in) self-propelled gun was cheap to manufacture and easy to maintain. First entering service in 1981, by 1994 over 750 units had been produced.

effect against the Japanese cities of Hiroshima and Nagasaki in World War II, the nuclear edge was a perceived advantage for the US even though the number of atomic bombs available was either limited or zero and their delivery against Soviet targets would certainly be problematic. By the summer of 1949, even this perceived advantage for the US military had evaporated. Although the North Atlantic Treaty Organization (NATO) had been formed in the West for collective defence against Soviet aggression, that August the Soviets successfully detonated a plutonium bomb. The nuclear arms race was on.

While the superpowers expended billions of dollars and roubles to gain the upper hand with strategic nuclear arms, developing successive generations of intercontinental ballistic missiles (ICBMs) with multiple warheads, varied methods of delivery and destructive capabilities many times that of the bombs which had brought Japan to its knees in 1945, the issue of armies facing one another across hostile borders in Western Europe remained. Tension had heightened to a dangerous level even before 1950, with the Soviet blockade of Berlin and the subsequent airlift. The former allies had reached the brink of a shooting war less than three years after their defeat of Nazi Germany.

Tactical nuclear weapons

For both the United States and the Soviet Union it seemed likely that a strategic nuclear exchange

would follow the initiation of ground combat in Europe. The armed force which achieved the upper hand more swiftly on the European battlefield might at least dictate the future of the continent, or what was left of it. Therefore, the development of tactical nuclear weapons became a priority for the armies of both NATO and the Warsaw Pact, which was formed by the Soviet Union and its satellite states of Eastern Europe in the spring of 1955.

While some military planners envisioned a war in Europe which would rival the scope of World War II in terms of troops and materiel involved, there was no doubt that both conventional artillery and tactical nuclear weapons delivered by means of artillery would be employed. The prospect for victory would be determined by the effectiveness of the first nuclear strikes and the capability of the manoeuvring ground troops to exploit the advantage gained.

Without doubt, the most logical strategy for NATO forces in Europe was that of tactical nuclear defence. In such a scenario, the artillery and the air forces of the NATO powers would serve as the delivery system for these nuclear weapons. Conventional weapons, such as tanks along with self-propelled guns and mechanized infantry, would subsequently assume the mobile offensive or maintain a strong defensive line to block the westward advance of Warsaw Pact forces.

During World War II, the Soviets had already demonstrated that their doctrine of massed conventional artillery could serve as an effective precursor to offensive operations. Tactical nuclear weapons would serve only to enhance the power of the Red Army to strike first, while the defensive capabilities of Red Army artillery were also well known. For both NATO and the Warsaw Pact one conclusion was inescapable. On the tactical level, artillery would serve as the weapon of decision on the ground. On the strategic plane, ICBMs might render the entire exercise moot.

Early Soviet artillery
1945–70

The Red Army possessed tremendous artillery assets at the close of World War II and began to modernize with missiles, radar-directed weapons and heavier guns in the coming years.

THE SPECTACULAR SOVIET COUNTERATTACK at Stalingrad, which eventually surrounded and annihilated the German Sixth Army, was preceded by a devastating artillery barrage. Massed cannon and howitzers wreaked havoc on German positions and enabled a rapid advance by Red Army ground troops.

This established success continued to dictate the offensive doctrine of Soviet military planners during the early years of the Cold War as they employed the proven Model 1942 76.2mm (3in) field gun in both an anti-tank and infantry support role and the 152mm (6in) gun-howitzer variants, which were capable of firing a 43.5kg (96lb) shell more than 17,000m (19,000 yards), among their standard field artillery weapons.

By 1955, the Red Army had deployed its first nuclear-capable artillery piece, the 152mm (6in) D-20 gun-howitzer, which eventually replaced the Model 1937 152mm (6in) weapon and could fire rocket-assisted ammunition up to 29,992m (32,800 yards). Developed by the F. Petrov Design Bureau, the D-20 could fire conventional shells at a rate of up to six per minute in a burst mode or one per minute

at a sustained rate. It remains in use around the world today and has been built under licence as the Type 66 in the People's Republic of China.

As nuclear field artillery gained in importance, the development of missiles followed suit, and in the mid-1950s the Soviet Union took the lead in surface-to-air missile (SAM) deployment with the S-25 Berkut, or Golden Eagle, which was known to NATO as the SA-1 Guild. The first operational guided-missile system in the world, the SA-1's development was authorized in the summer of 1950. Besides the SAMs, the system included early-warning and targeting radar, fighter aircraft and Tupolev early-warning planes. As such, the coordination of the system was truly groundbreaking in modern warfare.

By the spring of 1955, batteries of SA-1 missiles were deployed in defensive positions around Moscow, while a companion, the mobile SA-2 Guideline missile, was also in the field. In the early 1960s, a supply of SA-1s was shipped to North Korea. Subsequent Soviet surface-to-air missiles were to gain notoriety defending the cities of Hanoi and Haiphong during the Vietnam War and in the

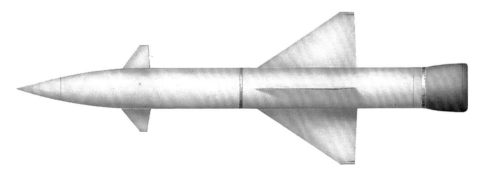

▲ S-25 Berkut (SA-1 Guild)

Soviet Air Defence Force, 1957

The S-25 Berkut, or SA-1 Guild in NATO nomenclature, was the first surface-to-air missile in the world to become operational. The SA-1 combined target-acquisition and early-warning radar and was based on a German design of World War II. The system was primarily deployed in defence of the Soviet capital of Moscow.

Specifications

Configuration: single, liquid-fuel rocket motor	Diameter: 700mm (27.5in)
Deployment: launch site	Launch weight: 3500kg (7716lb)
Length: 12m (39ft 4in)	Range: 40km (24.8 miles)
	Launch preparation time: 5 minutes

arsenals of Egypt and other Arab nations during the wars with Israel in 1967 and 1973.

Coordinated firepower

In the support of offensive operations, Soviet military doctrine stressed the importance of coordinated artillery action involving several tenets. These included continuous reconnaissance by ground, air and instrument capabilities; concentrated artillery support in the direction of the main attack; coordination of massed conventional artillery fires, nuclear missile attacks and air strikes; acquisition of targets for artillery, tactical air support and nuclear fire means; strong anti-tank reserves at regiment and higher levels; and continuous close coordination between all combat levels.

The Soviets stressed continuous fire support from artillery, and necessarily this meant that mobility

was a key component of the offensive. Artillery supporting the initial advance was expected to displace and follow the front-line battalions and regiments on a pre-planned basis. Theoretically, the ability of substantial artillery to keep pace with infantry posed problems which were solved at the lowest operational level with man-portable mortars or light towed weapons such as the 82mm (3.2in) PM-37 and PM-41 mortars. The PM-37 was capable of firing up to 30 rounds of high explosive per minute. Its 11.5kg (25.3lb) shell had a maximum range of 3040m (3325 yards), and due to its success on the battlefield, the PM-41, which was easier to manufacture, was introduced.

The heavier towed infantry mortar which was prevalent with the Red Army of the early Cold War was the 160mm (6.3in) M1943, which had been the heaviest weapon of its type utilized by

▶ 85mm M1939 anti-aircraft gun

Soviet Army / 20th Air Defence Regiment, 1960

The longevity of the 85mm (3.3in) M1939 anti-aircraft gun was remarkable, spanning four decades from 1939 into the 1970s. The weapon was adept in both anti-aircraft and anti-tank roles and was utilized in later versions of the T-34 medium tank and the SU-85 self-propelled gun. It was widely exported and equipped units of the Egyptian and North Vietnamese armies.

Specifications

Crew: 4	Weight: 3057kg (6000lb)
Calibre: 85mm (3.3in)	Range: 7620m (25,000ft)
Elevation: - 2 degrees to + 82 degrees	Muzzle velocity: 800m/sec (2625ft/sec)

◀ 160mm M1943 mortar

Soviet Army / 27th Guards Motorized Rifle Division, 1970

A heavy, breechloading mortar which was towed by a light truck or personnel carrier, the 160mm (6.3in) M1943 was deployed in brigades of 32 mortars, each brigade consisting of four battalions with eight weapons apiece. The heavy recoil of the weapon was absorbed by an internal system and a substantial baseplate.

Specifications

Crew: 4	Weight: 1170kg (2580lb)
Calibre: 160mm (6.3in)	Range: 5150m (5630 yards)
Elevation: + 45 degrees to + 80 degrees	Muzzle velocity: 245m/sec (804ft/sec)

▲ BM-24 multiple rocket launcher

Soviet Army / 54th Artillery Regiment, 1955

Introduced in the early 1950s, the BM-24 introduced slight improvements over the BM-13 multiple launch rocket system, which gained fame as the 'Stalin Organ' during World War II. Artillery and motorized infantry regiments of the Red Army fielded the BM-24, which was mounted atop a 6X6 truck and was later replaced by the BM-21.

Specifications

Crew: 6

Calibre: 240mm (9.45in)

Rocket length: 1.18m (46.45in)

Rocket weight: 112.5kg (248lb)

Range: 10,300m (11,265 yards)

Rate of fire: 2 rds/sec

System combat weight: 9200kg (10.14 tons)

Specifications

Crew: 3

Weight: 3300kg (7260lb)

Length: 4.995m (16ft 4.7in)

Width: 2.086m (6ft 10in)

Height: 1.18m (3ft 10.5in)

Engine: M-20E 41.25kW (55hp) 4-cylinder
  gasoline

Speed: 45km/h (28mph)

Road range: 250km (155 miles)

Armament: 1 x 57mm (2.2in) gun

▲ ASU-57 SP gun

Soviet Army / 78th Guards Airborne Division, 1969

Designed to be parachuted with a rocket-assisted apparatus into combat in order to support Red Army airborne divisions, the ASU-57 was an excellent design which remained in service with Soviet forces for more than 20 years. Although the weapon was light, using the engine of an automobile and with a welded aluminium hull construction, its firepower augmented the ability of airborne troops to sustain combat operations.

Specifications

Crew: 7

Weight: 50,167kg (110,600lb)

Engine: V-12-5 525kW (700hp) diesel

Armament: 1 x 420mm (16.5in) mortar

▲ 2B1 Oka self-propelled mortar

Soviet Army, not deployed, 1957

The Oka self-propelled mortar was an experimental 420mm (16.5in) mortar which was found to have numerous shortcomings, including a recoil which damaged drive sprockets, gears and mountings, a low rate of fire and continuing maintenance issues. Its development was abandoned by 1960 as resources were diverted to the production of tactical ballistic missiles.

the Red Army during World War II. The M1943 was originally an upgunned version of the 120mm (4.7in) mortar; however, it was quickly determined that a breechloading weapon would be necessary since the weight of the projectile at 40.8kg (90lb) was too great for infantrymen to lift and load from the muzzle at a reasonable rate. As a breechloader, the M1943 could fire up to ten rounds per minute with a range of 5150m (5630 yards).

Even with advances in the mobility of surface-to-air missiles, the Soviets depended on anti-aircraft guns to provide the necessary defence against enemy planes. Among their finest guns of this type was the 85mm (3.3in) M1939, developed on the eve of World War II but unavailable in large numbers until 1942. The M1939 proved a versatile weapon and also equipped

later versions of the famed T-34 medium tank and the SU-85 self-propelled assault gun. M1939 crews were issued both anti-aircraft and anti-tank ammunition, and the weapon had an effective range against enemy planes of 7620m (25,000ft) while its muzzle velocity of 800 metres per second (2625 feet per second) was a key element in its effectiveness against armour. The M1939 remained in service with numerous armed forces into the 1970s.

The largest towed artillery piece fielded by the Red Army during the Cold War was the 180mm (7.1in) S-23 gun, which made its debut in 1954. Capable of firing nuclear ammunition, the S-23 had a range of 30,000m (32,808 yards) with conventional shells and up to 43,000m (47,025 yards) with rocket-assisted ammunition.

Soviet Mortar Battery (part of Motorized Infantry Battalion), 1968

The Soviet motorized infantry battalion deployed in Eastern Europe at the height of the Cold War included a battery of 120mm (4.7in) mortars composed of three sections of two weapons each. The 120mm (4.7in) mortar was indicative of the Soviet philosophy of treating mortars as artillery weapons for close infantry support. The 120mm (4.7in) mortar could be fired by dropping the round down the muzzle or by trip wire. Additional equipment included reconnaissance armoured personnel carriers and trucks to transport infantry and communications gear and personnel.

Battery HQ (1 x field car, 1 x APC)   **Reconnaissance (1 x APC)**   **Communications (1 x truck)**

Section (2 x 120mm/4.7in mortar, 2 x truck)

Section (2 x 120mm/4.7in mortar, 2 x truck)

Section (2 x 120mm/4.7in mortar, 2 x truck)

Soviet ICBMs
1950–89

Soviet tactical nuclear missiles comprised potentially the most damaging threat to NATO forces in Western Europe, and were sometimes deployed on mobile launchers. By the mid-1960s, the Soviet Union had deployed intercontinental ballistic missiles (ICBMs) and developed a series of intermediate-range missiles which could degrade NATO nuclear capabilities in Europe.

MEDIUM-RANGE NUCLEAR MISSILES deployed by the Soviets during the Cold War were capable of striking vital NATO installations and population centres throughout Western Europe. Prior to the implementation of treaties limiting such missiles, the Soviet arsenal contained as many as 550 weapons of this type, and they provided the primary offensive nuclear threat to NATO and the West in Europe. Medium-range ballistic missiles (MRBMs) typically included weapons with ranges of 300km (190 miles) to 3500km (2175 miles) and were classified between intermediate-range ballistic missiles (IRBMs) and tactical missiles, with strategic ICBMs right at the top.

Soviet research into medium-range ballistic missiles began in earnest in the early 1950s, and by the end of the decade the R-12 Dvina, known to NATO as the SS-4 Sandal, had been deployed in the Eastern Bloc. Although early design efforts had been centred around shorter-range engines and overall aerodynamics and in-flight stability, the liquid oxygen which powered these earlier engines was replaced by a nitric acid oxidizer in combination with kerosene as a fuel source. The SS-4 played a significant role in the early years of the Cold War, with the capability of delivering warheads up to 2.3 megatons with devastating results.

▲ **R-12 Dvina (SS-4 Sandal)**

Soviet Army / 24th Guards Division, 1960

The SS-4 Sandal medium-range ballistic missile entered service with Soviet forces on 4 March 1959 and constituted the bulk of the Soviet nuclear threat to Western Europe. The SS-4 was powered by a single-stage liquid-fuelled rocket engine and was manufactured by the Yuzhmash factory in the Ukraine. The deployment of the SS-4 precipitated the Cuban Missile Crisis of October 1962.

Specifications

Configuration: single-stage, liquid fuel	Launch weight: 27,000kg (59,536lb)
Deployment: launch pad or silo	Range: 2000km (1250 miles)
Length: 22.4m (73ft 6in)	Launch preparation time: 1-3 hours
Diameter: 1.65m (5ft 5in)	

▲ **R-14 Chusovaya (SS-5 Skean)**

Soviet Army / 24th Guards Division, 1961

The R-14 intermediate-range ballistic missile increased the range of the SS-4 substantially and was the first Soviet ballistic missile to have implications of near worldwide range. First observed by the West in 1964, it was estimated that the SS-5 had been in service for several years. The SS-5 is believed to have entered production in the spring of 1961, and it was launch-capable from hardened silos, pads or mobile systems.

Specifications

Configuration: single-stage, liquid fuel	Launch weight: 60,000kg (118,100lb)
Deployment: mobile, launch pad or silo	Range: 3500km (2175 miles)
Length: 25m (82ft)	Launch preparation time: 2 hours
Diameter: 2.44m (8ft)	

According to Soviet sources, the SS-4 was deployed in March 1959, and it was first seen by Western observers during the autumn of the following year. In October 1962, it was the deployment of the SS-4 to Cuba which precipitated the Cuban Missile Crisis. The range of the SS-4, which was estimated at 2000km (1250 miles), placed numerous major American cities within range of Soviet-built nuclear warheads. President John F. Kennedy imposed a naval blockade of the island, and negotiations were eventually successful in defusing the confrontation. However, it may be reasonably concluded that the crisis brought the superpowers closer to a nuclear exchange than at any other time in the history of the Cold War.

By the mid-1960s, the longer-range R-14 Chusovaya, or SS-5 Skean, had been deployed by the Soviet strategic rocket forces. Its hydrazine and nitrogen tetroxide propellant boosted its range to 3500km (2175 miles), while the blast yield remained sizeable at up to two megatons. Production of the SS-5 commenced in April 1961, and continued for nearly a decade.

ICBM research was very successful, and some estimates stated that the Soviets had deployed significant numbers of these weapons in hardened silos by 1960. In fact, the US Central Intelligence Agency (CIA) once asserted that up to 500 Soviet ICBMs would be operational by 1963. In the spring of 1961, the construction of at least two sites which would facilitate the development and testing of Soviet ICBMs was detected following the authorization of a solid-fuel missile with a range of up to 12,000km (7456 miles) in the autumn of 1959.

Arms race

A nuclear arms race which was to last more than 30 years ensued, with the destructive capabilities of such weapons steadily increasing. Numerous systems were developed, deployed, and then dismantled by treaty. Even so, the Russian Federation maintains a substantial nuclear arsenal today, and in retrospect

▶ **UR-100 (SS-11 Sego)**

Soviet Army / 28th Missile Division, 1967

More than 1400 variants of the UR-100 intercontinental ballistic missile were deployed by the Soviet Union from 1966 to 1976. The UR-100 was a single-stage liquid-fuelled missile which made up the majority of the Soviet nuclear inventory for more than 20 years; however, it was rarely seen in public. The UR-100 was improved on several occasions, with variants produced with decoy warheads to ward off anti-missile defences and with multiple re-entry vehicles.

Specifications

Configuration: single-stage, liquid fuel	Launch weight: 48,000kg (47.24 tons)
Deployment: silo	Range: 10,600km (6650 miles)
Length: 19m (62ft 4in)	Launch preparation time: 3 minutes
Diameter: 2.4m (7ft 10in)	

▲ **RT-2 (SS-13 Savage)**

Soviet Army / 7th Guards Missile Division, 1969

Seen in public for the first time in 1965 and deployed in 1969, the RT-2, known to NATO as the SS-13 Savage, joined the SS-16 system as the first solid-propellant ICBMs in the Soviet inventory. Development of the SS-13 had begun in 1959, and testing was conducted from 1966 to 1968. The missile was modified several times, and its most common warhead yield was 600 kilotons. The SS-13 remained in service for two decades and was eventually replaced by the SS-25 Topol.

Specifications

Configuration: three-stage, solid fuel	Launch weight: 34,000kg (33.46 tons)
Deployment: silo	Range: 8000km (4970 miles)
Length: 20m (65ft 7in)	Launch preparation time: 3-5 minutes
Diameter: 1.7m (5ft 7in)	

there is little doubt that the tremendous expense of ICBM and intermediate-range missile development and maintenance adversely affected the economy of the Soviet Union and hastened its downfall.

Among the first operational Soviet ICBMs to be deployed in significant numbers was the RT-2, or SS-13 Savage in NATO nomenclature. The design of the SS-13 was completed in 1963, the missile was successfully test-fired in late 1966 and the system was deployed by the end of 1968. Modified several times, the basic SS-13 was capable of delivering a single warhead with a yield of up to one megaton, although Western sources placed the yield somewhat higher. The SS-13 remained in service for 20 years, the last of the missiles being dismantled and replaced by the SS-25 Topol in the mid-1990s.

In the West, the greatest threat was without doubt the development of the R-36 series of ICBMs. These missiles were also utilized in the Soviet space programme, and their continuing improvement, culminating in the R-36M, labelled the SS-18 Satan by NATO, was cause for alarm among Western analysts due to a perceived first-strike capability. The first missile of the R-36 series, the SS-9 Scarp, appeared in the mid-1960s, while the SS-18 was tested in the early 1970s with more than 50 deployed by 1977.

SS-18 Satan

The SS-18 was capable of delivering a single warhead of up to 20 megatons, and SS-18 variants were also configured for MIRV (multiple independent re-entry vehicles). It was these variants which caused such consternation in the West, as the estimated MIRV capacity of the SS-18 was up to ten warheads of 550 to 750 kilotons. Theoretically, the MIRV-equipped

▲ R-36 (SS-9 Scarp)

Soviet Army / 28th Guards Missile Division, 1970

The comparatively massive Soviet R-36 intercontinental ballistic missile fairly startled Western observers. Designated the SS-9 Scarp, the missile entered service in underground silos in the mid-1960s and displayed tremendous range and accuracy, while its nuclear payload and number of warheads increased steadily with successive versions. Some NATO analysts believed the SS-9 provided the Soviets with first-strike capability.

Specifications

Configuration: three-stage, liquid fuel	Launch weight: 190,000kg (87 tons)
Deployment: silo	Range: 12,000km (7456 miles)
Length: 36m (118ft)	Launch preparation time: 5 minutes
Diameter: 3.1m (10ft 2in)	

▲ R-36M (SS-18 Satan)

Soviet Army / 62nd Rocket Division, 1975

The MIRV-capable SS-18 Satan caused great concern in the West with its potential first-strike capability. The heaviest ICBM in the world, the SS-18 was one of several missiles in the R-36 series which originated in the 1960s. Capable of carrying a conventional 20-megaton warhead, the SS-18 was modified several times, with the MIRV variant appearing in 1970. The R-36M, which was deployed in late 1975, was theoretically capable of destroying Western missiles in their silos. In the early 1990s, more than 300 R-36M launch sites were known to NATO. The SS-18 was transported in a launch container and loaded into the silo.

Specifications

Configuration: two-stage, liquid fuel
Deployment: silo
Length: 37m (121ft 3in)
Diameter: 3.2m (10ft 4in)
Launch weight: 220,000kg (216.5 tons)
Range: 16,000km (10,000 miles)
Launch preparation time: unknown

SS-18 could destroy contemporary US missiles before they could be readied to launch.

Treaty reductions

By the late 1980s, the United States and the Soviet Union had conducted negotiations intended to reduce the number and types of nuclear missiles in their respective arsenals. The Intermediate-Range Nuclear Forces Treaty was concluded in 1987 and banned most cruise missiles and ground-launched intermediate ballistic missiles with ranges of 500km (310 miles) to 5500km (3418 miles). With the signing of the treaty, the SS-4 and SS-5 components of the Soviet nuclear complement were disarmed at the Lesnaya Missile Elimination Facility. The last of the SS-4s, 149 missiles, were disassembled in May 1990.

▲ MR-UR-100 Sotka (SS-17 Spanker)

Soviet Army / 28th Missile Division, 1983

The SS-17 Spanker, designated by the Soviets as the MR-UR-100 Sotka, was a MIRV-capable ICBM which was intended as a replacement for the outdated SS-11 missile. The SS-17 was a cold-launch system, which ignited the liquid propellant of the first stage once the missile had been launched from its silo by a gas generator. More than 260 SS-17s had been deployed by the early 1980s. By the early 1990s these missiles were dismantled under treaty.

Specifications

Configuration: two-stage, liquid fuel
Deployment: silo
Length: 24.4m (80ft)
Diameter: 2.5m (8ft 3in)
Launch weight: 65,000kg (63.97 tons)
Range: 11,000km (6835 miles)
Launch preparation time: unknown

▲ UR-100N (SS-19 Stiletto)

Soviet Army / 60th Missile Division, 1985

Intended as a replacement for the earlier silo-launched SS-11 ICBM, the SS-19 utilized an onboard computer to improve accuracy. It was also larger than the SS-11 and was transported in a launch cylinder which was then inserted into the silo. Research on the SS-19 was begun in 1974, and by the early 1980s more than 350 were in service. Contrary to previous treaty terms, the missiles may be rearmed with MIRV warheads. More than 130 SS-19 missiles remain active with the armed forces of the Russian Federation.

Specifications

Configuration: two-stage, liquid fuel
Deployment: silo
Length: 27.3m (85ft 6in)
Diameter: 2.5m (8ft 3in)
Launch weight: 78,000kg (76.78 tons)
Range: 10,000km (6200 miles)
Launch preparation time: unknown

▲ RSD-10 Pioneer (SS-20 Saber)

Soviet Army / 60th Missile Division, 1985

Known to NATO as the SS-20 Saber, this mobile intermediate-range ballistic missile was in service from 1976 to 1988 and could target and destroy most major NATO bases or cities in Western Europe, complementing strategic SS-18 missiles with a first-strike capability of their own. In 1979, at least 14 operational SS-20 launchers had been identified, and nearly 700 missiles were eventually constructed to replace the SS-4 and SS-5 systems. These were dismantled in the early 1990s as a result of treaty agreements.

Specifications

Configuration: two-stage, solid fuel
Deployment: mobile
Length: 16.4m (53ft 9in)
Diameter: 1.4m (55in)
Launch weight: 13,000kg (12.8 tons)
Range: 5000km (3100 miles)
Launch preparation time: continual readiness

Early NATO artillery
1947–70

NATO forces depended largely on artillery of World War II-vintage during the early years of the Cold War in Europe; however, some light weapons were developed along with nuclear-capable systems.

WITH THE DEVELOPMENT of the Cold War, the NATO troops opposing the Red Army were at a distinct disadvantage in terms of numbers, including troops, tanks and artillery. During the brief period of the US nuclear monopoly, such a deficiency seemed less significant to a degree; however, when the Soviet Union became a nuclear power in 1949 it was readily apparent to military planners in the West that tactical, intermediate and long-range nuclear capability was of the utmost importance to ensure the balance of power and provide not only defensive capabilities to forces in Western Europe but also sufficient strength to act as a deterrent to possible Soviet aggression.

Such a necessity was acutely realized with the Berlin crisis of the late 1940s and the outbreak of the Korean War in 1950. Throughout the course of the Cold War, the United States deployed 15 infantry and armoured divisions and five armoured cavalry regiments to Western Europe. Each of these was equipped with a variety of conventional artillery weapons suited for specific purposes. Along with the forces of other NATO countries, the US Army relied on the 105mm (4.1in) M2A1 howitzer, the M114 155mm (6.1in) howitzer, the M1 240mm (9.45in) howitzer, the M2 Long Tom 155mm (6.1in) gun and the M115 203mm (8in) howitzer for primary firepower during the early years of the Cold War.

Classic Light Gun

By the late 1960s, the British Army was developing its own L118 105mm (4.1in) gun, which was commonly referred to as the 'Light Gun'. Designed to replace various types in service with the British Army since World War II, the Light Gun was designed by the Royal Armament Research and Development Establishment at Fort Halstead, Kent, and was capable of firing up to eight rounds per minute to a range of 17,200m (18,810 yards). As the Light Gun began to appear in greater numbers, older models such as the venerable 25-pounder, the Italian OTO Melara Mod 56 pack howitzer, the 105mm (4.1in) L5 pack howitzer, and a number of aging 75mm (2.95in) weapons were retired.

▲ **3.7in RCL Gun**

British Army / 1st Battalion, Green Howards, 1958

The 3.7in (94mm) RCL Gun had its origins during World War II but did not see service during that conflict. A later variant of 120mm (4.7in) was also issued to NATO troops in Europe. The recoilless rifle used a system of jets to the rear which counterbalanced its recoil, allowing the carriage to be relatively lightweight.

Specifications

Crew: 3-5	Weight: 170kg (375lb)
Calibre: 94mm (3.7in)	Range: 2000m (2185 yards)
Elevation: - 5 degrees to + 10 degrees	Muzzle velocity: 1000m/sec (3280ft/sec)

The 155mm (6.1in) FH-70 towed artillery piece, which was developed in the 1960s and reached front-line units in Western Europe more than a decade later, was the result of collaborative efforts between British, West German and, later, Italian engineers. Intended as a replacement for the M114, the FH-70 was served by a crew of eight, fired at a sustained rate of three to six rounds per minute and reached an

Specifications

Crew: 3-4	Weight: 5150kg (5.06 tons)
Calibre: 40mm (1.57in)	Range: 3500m (3834 yards)
Elevation: - 4 degrees to + 90 degrees	Muzzle velocity: 1005m/sec (3300ft/sec)

▲ **40mm Bofors L/70 anti-aircraft gun**
British Army / 16th Light Air Defence Regiment Royal Artillery, 1963
The Swedish Bofors 40mm L/70 anti-aircraft gun was an improvement over the previous 40mm (1.57in) weapon with a longer barrel which increased the weapon's rate of fire. Introduced in the 1950s, the gun was transported aboard a similar carriage to that of its predecessor and was sold widely.

29 Commando Light Regiment Royal Artillery, 1962

The typical organization of light artillery regiments of the British Army during the early 1960s included three batteries of four 105mm (4.1in) pack howitzers. The most prevalent pack howitzer then in service with the British Army was the Italian OTO Melara Mod 56, which was originally designed for use by mountain troops. For ease of transport, the Mod 56 could be broken down into a dozen components and loaded aboard pack animals.

8 'Alma' Battery (4 x 105mm/4.1in pack howitzers)

79 'Kirkee' Battery (4 x 105mm/4.1in pack howitzers)

145 'Maiwand' Battery (4 x 105mm/4.1in pack howitzers)

effective range of 30,000m (32,808 yards) depending on the type of ammunition used.

While a new generation of conventional artillery had taken on added importance, older weapons such as the 3.7in (94mm) RCL Gun maintained an important role with infantry units of the British Army in Europe. The weapon had been developed in Britain by the Broadway Trust and dated to World War II but did not enter service during that conflict.

The original version, which fired a 'wallbuster' shell containing plastic explosive, was later supplanted by a 120mm (4.7in) gun which was issued during the Cold War. The Swedish 40mm (1.57in) Bofors L/70 was also delivered to armed forces around the world during the 1950s and equipped NATO anti-aircraft units. An improved version of the famed World War II anti-aircraft weapon, this variant included a longer barrel which effectively doubled the weapon's rate of fire and accommodated a larger round.

Early nuclear weapons

Among the early nuclear weapons deployed with NATO forces to Western Europe was the MGR-1 Honest John, which was tested in 1951 and entered service two years later. The Honest John was used in conjunction with several launchers and delivered conventional high-explosive rounds, chemical

weapons such as Sarin nerve gas and tactical nuclear warheads up to 30 kilotons. Although the Honest John rocket was fin-stabilized, its accuracy was suspect when firing chemical or high-explosive rounds. As precision guided systems were introduced, production ceased in 1965. More than 7000 were manufactured, and the Honest John continued in service with the armed forces of numerous countries until the mid-1980s.

The Davy Crockett recoilless rifle was developed during the late 1950s to fire the M388 tactical nuclear weapon. The Davy Crockett is perhaps more accurately described as two weapons systems, one which utilized the M28 102mm (4in) and a second which used the M29 155mm (6.1in) gun. The weapon's rather ungainly appearance belied its potential destructive power: the M29, for example, could project the M388 out to a distance of four kilometres (2.5 miles).

The warhead itself weighed 23kg (51lb) and delivered a blast equivalent to around 20.3 tonnes (20 tons) of TNT. Originally intended as a stopgap weapon, the Davy Crockett was deployed with detachments of infantrymen who would target Soviet tanks and infantry and destroy them while contaminating the surrounding area with radiation for up to two days, during which NATO forces could deploy and react to an attack in strength.

▲ **MGR-1 Honest John**

US Army / Eighth Army Field Artillery Detachment, 1961

The MGR-1 Honest John was the first surface-to-surface missile in the US arsenal capable of firing a nuclear warhead. Tested in 1951 and deployed to Western Europe in 1953, the Honest John could also deliver conventional or chemical weapons. The MGR-1 was transported in three sections which were rapidly assembled just prior to firing.

Specifications

Calibre: 762mm (30in)

Rocket length: 7.57m (24ft 10in)

Rocket weight: 1950kg (4300lb)

Range: 36.8km (23 miles)

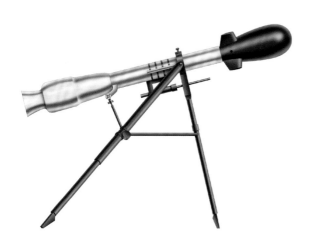

US Army / 55th Infantry Platoon, 82nd Airborne Division, 1964

The M29 Davy Crockett recoilless rifle weapon system was one of two which fired the nuclear M388 projectile. Whereas the M28 utilized a 102mm (4in) gun to project the weapon, the M29 used a 155mm (6.1in) rifle. One of the smallest nuclear weapons of the Cold War, the Davy Crockett was deployed to infantry units and was to be used in delaying actions against Soviet formations.

Specifications

Crew: 3	Weight: 34.5kg (76lb)
Diameter: 280mm (11in)	Range: 4km (2.5 miles)
Length: 787mm (31in)	

Western self-propelled guns
1947–90

Countering the firepower and mobility of the Warsaw Pact forces, self-propelled guns were designed to accompany NATO infantry across the rolling countryside of Northern Europe during combat.

A VARIETY OF SELF-PROPELLED GUNS supported NATO ground capabilities during the Cold War in Europe, providing mobile firepower in opposition to the early SU-76 and SU-85 weapons which appeared in the Warsaw Pact order of battle along with heavier guns such as the ISU-152, which was prominent in the suppression of the 1956 uprising against the communist government of Hungary. Under the US Army ROAD (Reorganization Objective Army Division) structure, infantry, armoured and mechanized divisions might each include attached or organic self-propelled artillery units, while the role of the self-propelled artillery was not only to provide fire support for infantry formations but also to add punch to the armoured cavalry regiments which were tasked with reconnaissance and combat roles.

Early NATO self-propelled guns included the 105mm (4.1in) M7 Priest, which initially appeared with US forces in the spring of 1942, and the M41 Gorilla, which debuted in 1945. The M41 mounted the 155mm (6.1in) M1 howitzer atop the chassis of the M24 Chaffee light tank. Powered by twin Cadillac 44T24 V8 gasoline engines generating a combined 165kW (220hp), the M41 had a maximum range of 160km (100 miles). Fewer than 300 were built. The M7 was powered by the nine-cylinder Continental R-975 412.5kW (550hp) gasoline engine and served into the late 1950s, seeing action during the Korean War.

One of the longest-lived basic designs of the Cold War era is the US M109, which was developed from the early 1950s as a replacement for the M44, which was active from 1953 until about 1962. The M109 entered service in the 1960s and was equipped with a 155mm (6.1in) main weapon capable of firing tactical nuclear ammunition. At the time of writing, more than 4000 variants of the M109 remain in service with the armed forces of more than 30 countries. The M109 had also replaced the M108 105mm (4.1in) howitzer, which was developed during the early 1960s and withdrawn from service by the middle of the decade. Sharing some common components with the M109 and the M113 armoured personnel carrier, the M108 was served by a crew of five with an operational range of 360km (224 miles).

The M110 203mm (8in) howitzer was the largest Cold War weapon of its kind in the US arsenal. Its heavy firepower was often assigned to the divisional level in battalion strength and also in battalions at the higher corps and army levels. Powered by a General Motors 8V71T supercharged diesel engine which generated 304kW (405hp), the vehicle had an impressive range of 523km (325 miles).

Specifications

Crew/capacity: 10

Weight: 6,812kg (15,020lb)

Length: 6.4m (20ft 9in)

Width: 2.29m (7ft 6in)

Height: 2.75m (9ft 1in)

Engine: 2 x 101kW (136 hp) Bedford 3500 cc engine

Speed: 47.5km/h (30mph)

Road range: 322km (200 miles)

Armament: n/a

▲ **Bedford Traclat**
Prototype, 1945

The Traclat (Tracked Light Artillery Tractor) was based closely on the German World War II-era SdKfz 7 artillery tractor. Designed to tow a 24 pdr field gun, it could travel at 48 km/h (30 mph) up a 1 in 30 gradient.

1st Regiment Royal Horse Artillery, British Army of the Rhine (BAOR), 1989

As the Cold War began, the 1st Regiment of the Royal Horse Artillery served in Palestine supporting anti-terrorist operations. Amid the growing threat from the Soviet Red Army, the regiment redeployed to Germany during the early 1950s with the 20th Armoured Brigade, 6th Armoured Division. During the 1950s, the regiment had been armed with the M44 155mm (6.1in) self-propelled howitzer, a US design which was later supplanted by the M109. In 1989, prior to being refitted with the AS-90 self-propelled gun, the regiment was equipped with the durable and long-serving Abbot 105mm (4.1in) self-propelled howitzer.

Regiment (24 x Abbot 105mm/4.1in SP howitzers)

▲ **MK61 SP howitzer**

French Army / II Corps, Germany, 1957

The 105mm (4.1in) MK61 self-propelled howitzer was a variant of the AMX-13 light tank, constructed with its enclosed turret atop the AMX-13 chassis. Developed concurrently with the AMX-13, it was eventually supplanted by the 155mm (6.1in) GCT self-propelled gun.

Specifications

Crew: 5

Weight (approx): 16,500kg (36,382lb)

Length: 6.4m (30ft)

Width: 2.65m (8ft 3.3in)

Height: 2.7m (8ft 10.3in)

Engine: 186.4kW (250hp) SOFAM 8Gxb

  8-cylinder petrol

Speed: 60km/h (37.3mph)

Road range: 350km (217.5 miles)

Armament: 1 x 105mm (4.1in) gun, plus

  2 x 7.5mm (0.295in) MGs

▲ **Canon de 155mm Mk F3 Automoteur**

French Army / II Corps, Germany, 1964

Constructed on a modified AMX-13 light tank chassis, the Mk F3 155mm (6.1in) self-propelled gun is the smallest of its kind ever produced. Designed in the early 1950s as a replacement for older US-made M41 self-propelled guns, the Mk F3 entered service with the French Army a decade later.

Specifications

Crew: 2

Weight: 17,410kg (38,304lb)

Length: 6.22m (20ft 5in)

Width: 2.72m (8ft 11in)

Height: 2.085m (6ft 10in)

Engine: 186kW (250hp) SOFAM 8Gxb 8-cylinder

  petrol

Speed: 60km/h (37mph)

Road range: 300km (185 miles)

Armament: 1 x 155mm (6.1in) gun

In response to the NATO requirement for a standard 105mm (4.1in) weapon, the British Abbot was developed by Vickers in the early 1950s. The Abbot mounted the 105mm (4.1in) gun atop a modified FV430 chassis which accommodated the fully rotating turret and the rear housing of the main weapon. The Abbot entered service in 1965 and was replaced more than 20 years later by the M109 and another Vickers system, the AS-90. With a crew of six, an operational range of 390km (240 miles) and a

top speed of 47.5km/h (30mph), the Abbot was well suited for close infantry support.

The MK61, an early French self-propelled howitzer, was a variant of the AMX-13 light tank constructed with an enclosed turret and mounting a 105mm (4.1in) main weapon. The MK61 was intended to be airmobile and possibly used in support of airborne troops. By the 1970s, it had been replaced by the GCT 155mm (6.1in) gun, which was also sold to the armed forces of Saudi Arabia and Iraq.

Western ICBMs
1946–90

The development of tactical, intermediate-range and intercontinental ballistic missiles in the West was undertaken as a deterrent to Soviet military aggression and to maintain some balance of power in Europe.

SOON AFTER THE END OF WORLD WAR II, it was apparent in the West that a nuclear arsenal capable of defending the member countries of the NATO alliance was essential to the strategic defence doctrine which was employed to deter Soviet territorial expansion around the globe and to counter the numerical superiority of Warsaw Pact conventional forces poised to strike Western Europe.

Incorporating the research and development of rocket engines which had resulted in the successful launch of the V-2 rocket by the Germans during World War II, the United States advanced its early research into long-range ballistic missiles under the auspices of Project Paperclip. The country's defence establishment committed to the deployment of long-range nuclear missiles which could target cities in the Soviet Union from the continental United States while also continuing to research tactical missile systems and heavy bombers capable of delivering nuclear weapons. In time, these systems would include long-range ICBMs which could reach targets thousands of kilometres away.

Strategic nuclear umbrella

For the half-century of the Cold War, the nuclear doctrine of the United States – and as a follow-on

that of NATO – rested upon the 'triad' of land-based ICBMs, long-range heavy bombers such as the B-52 Stratofortress which could deliver nuclear weapons, and submarine-launched ICBMs. This strategic doctrine was developed in the early 1950s, and the first operational US ICBM, the Atlas D, was placed in service at Vandenberg Air Force Base, California, in the autumn of 1959. Within two years, the US Air Force could report three squadrons of an updated Atlas E missile located in a least four sites across the country.

In 1955, the Titan programme was undertaken as a successor to the Atlas ICBM. The resulting Titan I missile was rapidly improved with the Titan II, a mainstay of the US ICBM complement into the 1980s. The Titan II was test-fired in December 1961 and placed in service two years later. It initially carried one nine-megaton W-53 nuclear warhead with a range of 15,000km (9300 miles). At any given time, more than 50 were stationed in silos and could be launched within 60 seconds.

By the mid-1960s, the US had deployed at least 1000 Atlas, Titan and Minuteman I and Minuteman II missiles with a like number of warheads. Meanwhile, the British government, in cooperation with the United States, briefly pursued the Blue

▲ Titan II ICBM

US Air Force / 308th Strategic Missile Wing, 1962

The Titan missile programme was undertaken in the mid-1950s and rapidly developed the Titan I ICBM. The Titan II, which was more accurate over a greater distance with a heavier nuclear payload, was tested in 1961 and became operational in 1963. Dozens were placed in silos in the Midwestern United States, fuelled and ready for launch, for the next 20 years. The Titan II also served as a launcher for the NASA (National Aeronautics and Space Administration) manned space flight programme.

Specifications

Configuration: two-stage, liquid fuel

Deployment: silo

Length: 29.9m (98ft)

Diameter: 3.05m (10ft)

Launch weight: 99,792kg (98.21 tons)

Range: 15,000km (9300 miles)

Launch preparation time: 60 seconds

Streak missile, a medium-range weapon which could complement the ongoing US ICBM programme. This endeavour was undertaken in 1955 and abandoned five years later. The US attempted to develop an air-launched nuclear missile, named Skybolt, but this project was rendered impractical with the advent of submarine-launched ballistic missiles.

The early Titan and Minuteman missile systems were operational simultaneously during the early 1960s and were placed on alert during the Cuban Missile Crisis of October 1962. At the end of that year, the US strategic ICBM arsenal totalled over 200 warheads; however, most of these were configured with the Atlas missile system, which was rapidly being outclassed by both US technology and rising Soviet capabilities.

Indicative of US missile development at the height of the Cold War was the Minuteman programme, which was undertaken in the late 1950s. Even as the Minuteman I reached operational status, the upgrade to Minuteman II was in progress. Under the Minuteman Force Modernization Program, the upgrade included an improved guidance system, heavier second stage, longer range and greater

survivability in the event of a Soviet first strike. The payload of the MIRV-capable Minuteman II was increased to the 1.2-megaton W-56 nuclear warhead, while the missile could reach targets as far away as 13,000km (8100 miles).

The modern US strategic nuclear arsenal consists solely of the Minuteman III missile, following the retirement of the Peacekeeper missile, popularly known as the MX, of which only about 50 were built. The LGM-30G Minuteman III reached deployment in 1970, and plans to decrease the maximum load of three warhead re-entry vehicles to one have been considered during the post-Cold War era. The total US strategic ICBM force is estimated at 500 Minuteman III missiles today.

The SSBS S3 missile marked a second generation of French intermediate-range ballistic missiles. Its development was undertaken in 1973 to replace the aging S2, and deployment began during the early 1980s. By 1984, a total of 18 hardened sites were in service to complement the concurrent MSBS submarine-launched missile programme. Each SSBS S3 carried a 1.2-megaton nuclear warhead with a range of 3500km (2175 miles).

▲ **SSBS S3**

French Army / 1st Strategic Missile Group, 1980

With a more powerful second stage engine and advanced re-entry vehicle, the SSBS S3 missile improved on the S2 design and entered service with the French armed forces in 1980. The weapon carried a 1.2-megaton nuclear warhead and was launched from hardened silos located in the Plateau d'Albion region of France. By the mid-1990s, the French government had announced that it would dismantle all land-based nuclear missiles, relying on submarines and bombers for nuclear deterrence.

Specifications

Configuration: two-stage, solid fuel
Deployment: silo
Length: 13.7m (44ft 11in)
Diameter: 1.5m (60in)
Launch weight: 25,800kg (25.39 tons)
Range: 3500km (2175 miles)
Launch preparation time: unknown

▲ **LGM-30F Minuteman II**

US Air Force / 447th Strategic Missile Squadron, 1965

Improving on the navigation system, range and nuclear payload of the Minuteman I missile, the Minuteman II was the result of the Minuteman Force Modernization Program of the early 1960s. Better accuracy was provided by an onboard computer which could provide data for multiple targets. The Minuteman II was supplanted by the design's third generation, the Minuteman III, in the 1980s.

Specifications

Configuration: three-stage, solid fuel	
Deployment: silo	Launch weight: 31,746kg (31.24 tons)
Length: 18.2m (69ft 8in)	Range: 12,500km (7770 miles)
Diameter: 1.84m (6ft)	Launch preparation time: 30 seconds

Early Western air defence missiles
1947-70

The threat of Soviet air interdiction on the battlefield and long-range Soviet bombers carrying nuclear payloads led NATO to develop missile systems with the latest technology.

WITH THEIR AIR DEFENCE missile programmes in their infancy, both the United States and the Soviet Union leveraged their own technology while appropriating advances by German scientists who had previously worked under the Nazi regime. The missile systems themselves might potentially be utilized as replacements for heavy air defence artillery, which was often inaccurate and difficult to transport. By the time NATO was formed in 1949, the US and Great Britain were well on their way to the deployment of operational air defence missiles.

Evolving NATO doctrine included the deployment of missile systems to protect major cities in Western Europe and North America, while air defence in depth theorized that attacking Warsaw Pact aircraft would be required to run a gauntlet of fire. Coordinated NATO air defence included fighter aircraft, surface-to-air missiles and anti-aircraft guns. Attacking aircraft would first be located by early-warning radar and then engaged by fighter planes and long-range missiles. In response to the radar, enemy pilots would be required to fly low to avoid detection, making them vulnerable to shorter-range missiles fired from both mobile and hard sites, as well as effective anti-aircraft guns which would engage the aircraft at lower altitude.

NATO air defence planners believed strongly that somewhat redundant systems and defence in depth would take a toll on any Warsaw Pact pilot's ability to execute his mission. If the enemy plane was not destroyed outright, the pilot would be required to maintain readiness to take evasive action throughout his mission. Further, action taken to avoid or exploit the weaknesses of one defensive system would likely expose the enemy aircraft to another.

Intercontinental cordon

In the case of the strategic-bombing threat, missiles were deployed as a last line of defence around major cities. As early as 1944, the United States

▲ **Test fire**
A Thunderbird missile is launched somewhere from British soil. The Thunderbird was design for medium-range air defence.

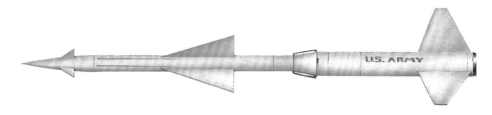

Specifications

Configuration: two-stage, solid then liquid fuel	Launch weight: 1114kg (2455lb)
Deployment: site-launched	Range: 40km (25 miles)
Length: 10.62m (34ft 10in)	Launch preparation time: immediate
Diameter: 305mm (12in)	

▲ **Nike Ajax**

US Army / 3rd Battalion, 71st Air Defense Artillery, 1959

The first surface-to-air guided missile in service with an active army, the Nike Ajax was controlled by a computer which directed and detonated the missile based on data from two radar systems, one with a guiding beam and another which tracked the target. The Ajax was relatively short-ranged at 40km (25 miles).

▲ **MIM-14 Nike Hercules**

US Army / 2nd Battalion, 52nd Air Defense Artillery, 1965

Used for a time in concert with the Ajax and sharing a number of the same components, the MIM-14 Hercules was a distinct improvement, with an increased speed of Mach 3.5 and a much greater range than the first-generation Ajax. The Hercules, which was also nuclear-capable, entered service in 1958 and was deployed to several NATO countries as an upgrade to the Ajax.

Specifications

Configuration: two-stage, solid fuel	Launch weight: 4720kg (10,405lb)
Deployment: site-launched	Range: 155km (96 miles)
Length: 12.5m (41ft)	Launch preparation time: immediate
Diameter: 800mm (31.5in)	

had undertaken the Nike project, and by the end of 1953 the Nike Ajax became the first weapon of its kind to enter service with an active military force. In December of that year, Nike Ajax units were positioned around Washington DC, replacing hundreds of anti-aircraft guns. The missile delivered warheads of up to 81kg (179lb) with a maximum range of 40km (25 miles). The first successful test-firing of the Ajax occurred in 1951 when a Boeing B-17 Flying Fortress bomber drone was destroyed. The Ajax remained in service with air defence units until the mid-1960s.

Components of the Ajax system were expensive to manufacture and were also utilized in the next generation of Nike project missiles, designated the MIM-14 Hercules, which was deployed beginning in the spring of 1958. Aside from positions protecting US cities and intercontinental ballistic missile sites, the Hercules was also posted to Western Europe and the Far East. Its effective range was more than

double that of the Ajax at 155km (96 miles), while the system was also capable of delivering a nuclear warhead of up to 20 kilotons. The Hercules often worked in tandem with the MIM-23 HAWK system, which was developed in the early 1950s and has remained in use for decades.

British air defence missile development was active during the 1940s with the English Electric Thunderbird, which was under development as a high-altitude interceptor system as early as 1949. The first missile designed and produced for the British Army, the Thunderbird entered service in 1959 and equipped heavy air defence regiments of the Royal Artillery or designated squadrons of the Royal Air Force. It delivered a high-explosive warhead to a maximum range of 75km (46 miles). Another primary air defence missile of British and NATO forces was the Bristol Bloodhound, which had a range of 80km (50 miles). It entered service in 1958 and remained active into the 1990s.

▲ Bristol Bloodhound Mark 1

Royal Air Force / No. 242 Squadron, 1959

Entering service in 1958, the Bristol Bloodhound was fired from fixed positions and intended initially to protect squadrons of Royal Air Force V Bombers deployed at eight sites in Britain. The Bloodhound was improved several times and easily recognized with its distinctive quartet of external boosters. The missile carried a high-explosive warhead with a proximity fuse. The last battery in British service was retired in 1991.

Specifications

Configuration: external booster	Launch weight: 2270kg (5000lb)
Deployment: site-launched	Range: 80km (50 miles)
Length: 8.46m (27ft 9in)	Launch preparation time: immediate
Diameter: 546mm (27.5in)	

▲ English Electric Thunderbird

British Army / 457th Heavy Air Defence Regiment, Royal Artillery, 1963

Development of the Thunderbird surface-to-air missile was undertaken by English Electric Corporation in 1949, and the system entered service with the Royal Artillery in 1959. The Thunderbird was intended to replace heavy anti-aircraft guns such as the 94mm (3.7in) weapons which were prevalent among British units during World War II. Large tail fins and short wings stabilized the missile, which could be detonated with a proximity fuse or on command.

Specifications

Configuration: external booster	Launch weight: unknown
Deployment: site-launched	Range: 75km (46 miles)
Length: 6.35m (20ft 10in)	Launch preparation time: immediate
Diameter: 527mm (20.75in)	

Specifications

Configuration: two-stage, solid fuel
Deployment: site launched
Length: 6m (19ft 8in)
Diameter: 400mm (15.75in)
Launch weight: 400kg (882lb)
Range: 30km (19 miles)
Launch preparation time: unknown

▲ RSD 58 SAM

Swiss Air Force / Ground Based Air Defence, 1961

An early surface-to-air missile developed in 1947 by the Oerlikon and Contraves companies, the RSD 58 entered service with the Swiss, Italian and Japanese armed forces following the conclusion of testing in 1952. Sliding rear fins stabilized the missile in flight and corrected its path along a radar beam which guided it to within lethal distance of the target. A radio-triggered proximity fuse detonated the warhead.

Late Warsaw Pact artillery
1970–89

The need for direct fire support for ground troops in Europe led to the development of Soviet artillery capable of keeping pace with advancing infantry and concentrating decisive firepower, while Soviet client states produced their own variants of some Red Army weapons.

THE PRINCIPLES OF SOVIET combined-arms doctrine as understood by Western analysts during the 1970s included several interdependent concepts such as mobility and high rates of combat operations; concentration of main efforts and creation of superiority in forces and means over the enemy at the decisive place and at the decisive time; surprise and security; combat activeness; preservation of the combat effectiveness of friendly forces; conformity of the goal; and coordination. Particularly in the cases of mobility and coordination, modern artillery would be a key element in any Red Army or Warsaw Pact combat operation in Western Europe.

During World War II, the Red Army had demonstrated its ability to coordinate self-propelled, field and heavy artillery with offensive movement, concentrating where necessary. As the Cold War dragged on, heavy guns such as the 122mm (4.8in) D-30 were deployed during the 1960s and widely exported. Older weapons, including the 152mm

(6in) D-1 howitzer, remained in service into the 1980s. Heavy mortars of 120mm (4.7in) and 160mm (6.3in) were deployed with smaller infantry units, their plunging fire expected to eliminate fixed targets or disrupt infantry assaults. Mobile rocket launchers such as the BM-21 system, which was mounted atop a 6X6 truck, were continually improved during the 1960s as well. With the advent of tactical nuclear weapons, the artillery took on the additional responsibility of a delivery system for these, and missiles such as the FROG (Free Rocket Over Ground) series were deployed.

Wielding the hammer

At the height of the Cold War, Soviet Marshal of Artillery G.E. Peredelsky wrote, '… artillery has become the basis of firepower of the ground forces. It has the decisive role of creating the preponderance of power over the enemy which frequently determines the outcome of the battle.'

▲ **2S3 (M1973) 152mm SP gun-howitzer**

Soviet Army / 6th Guards Separate Motor Rifle Brigade, 1981

Introduced to the Red Army in 1973, the 2S3 (M1973) 152mm (6in) self-propelled gun-howitzer replaced the older D-20 system in artillery regiments of Soviet and Warsaw Pact forces to provide fire support for tank and motorized rifle regiments.

Specifications

Crew: 6	Speed: 55km/h (34mph)
Weight: 24,945kg (54,880lb)	Road range: 300km (186 miles)
Length: 8.4m (27ft 6.7in)	Armament: 1 x 152mm (6in) gun, plus
Width: 3.2m (10ft 6in)	1 x 7.62mm (0.3in) anti-aircraft MG
Height: 2.8m (9ft 2.25in)	Radio: n/k
Engine: 388kW (520hp) V12 diesel	

To that end, the development of a new generation of Soviet weapons, with a late emphasis on self-propelled artillery, was undertaken in earnest during the mid-1960s. The 152mm (6in) 2S3 Akatsiya, or Acacia, known in the West as the M1973, had been designed largely in response to the appearance of the US-made M109 self-propelled howitzer.

The main weapon of the 2S3 was mounted atop a modified chassis similar to that of the SA-4 surface-to-air missile. Its development was authorized in 1967, and it entered service six years later. By the

1980s, Western intelligence sources estimated that front-line Soviet armoured and mechanized infantry divisions stationed in East Germany included a battalion of 2S3s, usually totalling 18 vehicles, in their organic artillery regiments. Near the end of the decade, this number had increased to as many as three battalions and up to 54 of the self-propelled guns.

The 2S4 Tyulpan, or Tulip, was first identified by Western observers in 1975 and mounts a 240mm (9.45in) mortar designed to be particularly effective against fortified and fixed targets. Deployed with Red Army troops to Afghanistan, the 2S4 remains the

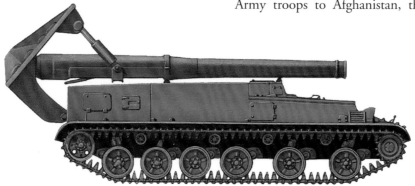

▲ **2S4 (M1975) self-propelled mortar**

Soviet Army / 5th High Powered Artillery Brigade, 1979

Derived from the chassis of the GMZ minelaying combat vehicle, the 2S4 Tyulpan, or Tulip, mounts a 240mm (9.45in) breechloading mortar, the largest weapon of its kind currently in service. The Tyulpan was first identified by NATO observers in 1975 and is capable of firing laser-guided or nuclear ammunition.

Specifications

Crew: 9

Weight: 30,481kg (30 tons)

Length: 8.5m (27ft 10in)

Width: 3.2m (10ft 6in)

Height: 3.2m (10ft 6in)

Engine: 390kW (520hp) V-59 diesel

Speed: 62km/h (38.53mph)

Road range: 420km (261 miles)

Armament: 1 x 240mm (9.45in) mortar

Specifications

Crew: 4

Weight: 13,800kg (13.58 tons)

Speed: 63km/h (39.15mph)

Road range: 550km (342 miles)

Armament: 1 x 120mm (4.7in) mortar

Rate of fire: 8 rounds per minute

▲ **SPM-85 PRAM 120mm self-propelled mortar**

Czech People's Army / 7th Artillery Division, 1983

Adapted from the chassis of the versatile Soviet-designed BMP-1 amphibious tank, the SPM-85 PRAM was deployed with the Czech People's Army in the early 1980s. Its 120mm (4.7in) mortar is capable of firing up to 40 rounds in five minutes or a maximum of 70 rounds in ten minutes. The weapon has also been reported as highly mobile. It may also be equipped with anti-tank guided missiles.

largest self-propelled mortar in service in the world. Although its rate of fire is extremely low at one round per minute, it has proven to be an effective weapon.

In the early 1980s, the Czechoslovak armed forces deployed the self-propelled SPM-85 PRAM 120mm (4.7in) self-propelled mortar, mounted on the adapted chassis of the Soviet-designed BMP-1 amphibious tank. With an impressive rate of fire, 18 to 20 rounds per minute, the highly mobile SPM-85 was allocated to mechanized infantry units to provide accurate fire against targets at a distance of up to 8000m (8750 yards).

172nd Artillery Regiment, Red Army, Rudelstadt, German Democratic Republic, 1989

The composition of the 172nd Artillery Regiment of the Soviet Red Army is indicative of the emphasis placed on firepower and mobility during the later years of the Cold War. The combination of the BM-21 rocket launcher and 2S3 Akatsiya with its 152mm (6in) D-22 howitzer L/27 provided the ability to saturate enemy positions with area fire and follow up with self-propelled artillery which could provide direct support. In both cases, the weapons systems were mobile and able to displace in a relatively short period of time in order to accompany mechanized infantry during an advance.

Regiment (48 x 2S3 SP artillery, 18 x BM-21 rocket launchers)

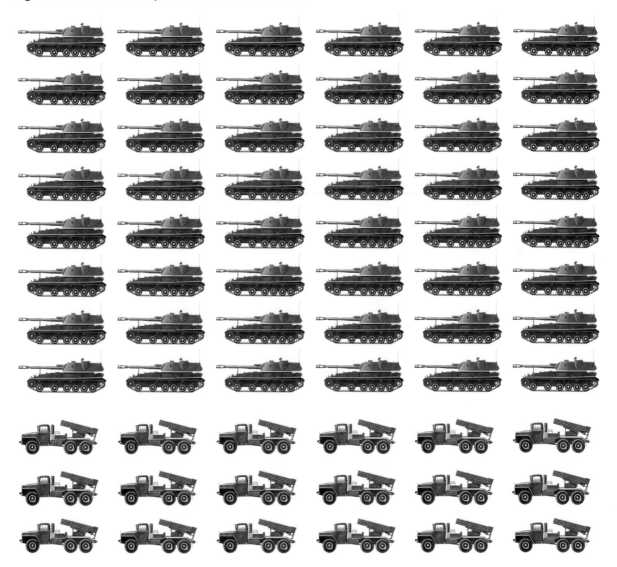

Soviet theatre missiles
1950–89

Western intelligence sources observed the development of Soviet missile technology from the late 1940s and correctly judged that the progress achieved was largely based upon the work of German scientists relocated to the Soviet Union following World War II.

THE SOVIETS ACTIVELY pursued cruise-missile capabilities based on the German V-1 design. During the mid-1950s, it was believed that the majority of Soviet nuclear delivery would be by heavy bombers flying one-way missions. However, at the same time no less than four separate programmes for the development of what came to be known as the Scud family of intermediate-range missiles was detected.

Scud squad

Smaller nuclear weapons were often mounted on the tracked ISU-152 chassis, which was a variant of the heavy JS-3 tank chassis produced late in World War II. The initial mobile-launched nuclear-capable missiles produced in the Soviet Union were designated R-11 through R-17 and known to NATO as the Scud series. The R-17 Elbrus, or SS-1C Scud B, was representative of Soviet capabilities during the 1950s and 1960s. The R-17 programme was undertaken in 1958 as an improvement to the

R-11 and utilizing a more powerful kerosene and nitric acid single-stage liquid-propellant rocket. The first successful launch of the R-17 occurred in 1961, and the missile had entered service by 1964. It was capable of delivering high-explosive, chemical or nuclear warheads exceeding 50 kilotons.

Scud technology has been exported to numerous countries, and the system has also been copied and produced under licence. Modified Iraqi Scud missiles were fired on Israel and inflicted the highest number of Coalition casualties during the Gulf War of 1991. The Scud threat was taken so seriously by Coalition commanders that special forces units were dropped in enemy territory to seek out and destroy the mobile launchers.

Tactical leap

Among the unguided rocket systems which were widely deployed by Warsaw Pact forces was what NATO designated the FROG (Free Rocket Over Ground) series of mobile launchers. The last of

▲ R-17 Elbrus (SS-1C Scud B)

Soviet Army / 8th Guards Artillery Brigade, 1970

The best known of the Soviet tactical ballistic missiles, the R-17 Elbrus, a member of the Scud family to NATO observers, has served as a component of the Soviet arsenal since the 1960s and has been exported to more than 30 countries. An improvement over the R-11 missile, the R-17 was larger and included an improved guidance system.

Specifications

Configuration: single-stage, liquid fuel	Launch weight: 6300kg (13,888lb)
Deployment: mobile	Range: 280km (173 miles)
Length: 11.25m (36ft 11in)	Launch preparation time: 1 hour
Diameter: 850mm (33.5in)	

▼ TR-1 Temp (SS-12 Scaleboard)

Soviet Army / 3rd Shock Army Surface-to-Surface Missile Brigade, 1982

The TR-1 Temp, known to NATO as the SS-12 Scaleboard, was a mobile intermediate ballistic missile originally intended to replace the Scud. The SS-12 entered service in 1969 and was rarely seen by Western observers due to the fact that it was mobile and deployed from a container which opened only when the weapon was to be fired. The weapon remained with the Red Army during its service life and was never sold to other countries.

these, the Luna M, or FROG-7, was mounted atop the modified ZIL-135 8x8 truck which included a transporter, erector and launcher apparatus, and made its operational debut in 1965. The FROG-7 rocket warhead weighed 550kg (1200lb) and could reach targets as far away as 70km (43 miles). Its mobility was an advantage on the battlefield, allowing for displacement following firing and providing a greater chance of survivability by avoiding retaliatory action.

The FROG-7 could be made ready to launch within 30 minutes and was capable of delivering high-explosive, chemical or tactical nuclear weapons. It has been exported to numerous countries, some of which have modified the system to extend its range and payload.

Specifications

Configuration: single-stage, liquid fuel

Deployment: mobile

Length: 12m (39ft 4in)

Diameter: 1m (39in 4in)

Launch weight: 9700kg (9.55 tons)

Range: 900km (555 miles)

Launch preparation time: 15 minutes

▲ OTR-23 Oka (SS-23 Spider)

Soviet Army / 6th Motorized Rifle Brigade, 1981

By the end of the 1970s, the aging SS-1C Scud-B mobile missile had become obsolete and was replaced by the OTR-23 Oka, or SS-23 as it was known to NATO. The SS-23 was intended to suppress NATO tactical nuclear weapons, which Soviet analysts assumed would be employed early in a military confrontation in Western Europe to neutralize Warsaw Pact superiority in conventional arms and personnel. The OTR-23 was transported on a wheeled launcher and capable of firing within approximately five minutes.

Specifications

Configuration: single-stage, solid fuel

Deployment: mobile

Length: 7.5m (24ft 7in)

Diameter: 900mm (2ft 11in)

Launch weight: 29,465kg (29 tons)

Range: 400km (250 miles)

Launch preparation time: 5 minutes

▼ Luna M (FROG-7)

Soviet Army / 11th Surface-to-Surface Missile Battalion, 1980

Although the Soviet FROG (Free Rocket Over Ground) system was first deployed during the late 1950s, the FROG-7 appeared in 1965 and was still in active service with the Red Army a quarter-century later. The FROG-7 is carried atop an 8X8 transporter-erector-launcher vehicle. Its single-stage solid-fuel rockets are unguided and may carry nuclear, chemical or high-explosive weapons.

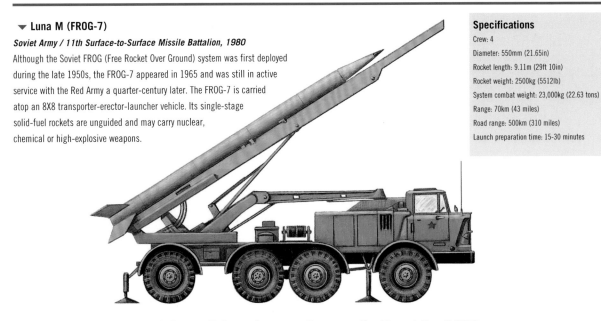

Specifications

Crew: 4

Diameter: 550mm (21.65in)

Rocket length: 9.11m (29ft 10in)

Rocket weight: 2500kg (5512lb)

System combat weight: 23,000kg (22.63 tons)

Range: 70km (43 miles)

Road range: 500km (310 miles)

Launch preparation time: 15-30 minutes

4th SSM Battalion, Red Army, Erfurt, German Democratic Republic, 1989

The typical Red Army FROG-7 battery of the late Cold War era was equipped with a headquarters battery and a pair of firing batteries, each equipped with two transporter-erector-launcher vehicles and long-range meteorological radar. The FROG-7b was an improved version capable of carrying cargo ordnance which could distribute bomblets or anti-personnel mines. The unguided nature of the FROG series resulted in a fairly inaccurate result; however, its longevity is testament to its filling a significant tactical role on the battlefield.

**Battalion
(4 x FROG-7)**

SSM Brigade, Red Army (Western Group of Forces (WGF), Western TVD, Neubrandenburg, German Democratic Republic, 1989

The Red Army intermediate-range ballistic-missile brigade of the 1980s consisted of a complement of 18 mobile OTR-23 Oka missile launchers. The Oka included an 8X8 truck with an operational range of 500km (310 miles). Each Oka was capable of firing conventional high-explosive fragmentation, chemical or nuclear warheads. The Oka, which could be readied to fire in five minutes or less, was designed to neutralize NATO command-and-control centres, and other high-priority theatre targets.

Brigade (18 x SS-23)

Warsaw Pact air defence
1965–90

Soviet and Warsaw Pact air defence stressed a cooperative effort between aircraft, surface-to-air missiles and anti-aircraft guns to provide comprehensive defence in depth against enemy attack.

SATURATING THE SURROUNDING air space from low to high altitude was the objective of Soviet ground air defence during the Cold War. Heavy reliance was placed on surface-to-air missiles, mobile and capable of reacting to any threat within minutes. At greater range, fighter aircraft would engage enemy planes, while effective mobile anti-aircraft guns would provide a short-range layer of fire, theoretically building a wall of defence for Red Army and Warsaw Pact ground forces against air attack. Military planners further equipped infantry units with shoulder-fired missiles, such as the SA-7 Grail, for use against low-flying fixed-wing aircraft and helicopters.

Curtain of steel

Early warning and rapid intervention by air defences were considered essential to maintaining control of the air. At the height of the Cold War, large Warsaw Pact Army or Front (Army Group) formations were protected against air attack by the SA-2 Guideline and SA-4 Ganef missile systems, which could engage enemy aircraft at long range.

Each tank or motorized infantry division of the Red Army included an organic air defence regiment equipped with either anti-aircraft guns or surface-to-air missiles. Rarely, if ever, were these systems intermingled. Therefore, a typical air defence regiment might deploy four batteries of six S-60 57mm (2.2in) guns for a complement of 24; five batteries of four mobile 2K12 Kub surface-to-air missiles, known to NATO as the SA-6 Gainful, for a total of 20 launchers; or five batteries of four mobile 9K33 Osa surface-to-air missiles, designated as the SA-8 Gecko by NATO command, for a total of 20 launchers. The SA-6 entered service in 1970 and was intended for low- to medium-altitude air defence with a range of up to 24km (15 miles). The SA-8 provided low-altitude and short-range missile defence. The Gecko was deployed in 1972, and

▲ **9K33 Osa (SA-8 Gecko)**

Soviet Army / 21st Motorized Rifle Division, 1983

Initially identified in the West in 1976, the SA-8 Gecko mobile anti-aircraft missile was the first weapon of its kind to mount its own engagement radar on the same vehicle which transported the missile, the 6X6 9K33 transporter-erector-launcher. The SA-8 delivers a 19kg (42lb) high-explosive fragmentation or proximity-fused warhead. By 1980, an improved SA-8B Mod 1 carried up to six missiles.

Specifications

Configuration: single-stage, solid fuel	Launch weight: 130kg (287lb)
Deployment: mobile	Range: 15km (9.3 miles)
Length: 3.15m (19ft 4in)	Launch preparation time: 5-minute reload
Diameter: 210mm (8.26in)	

▲ **2K12 Kub (SA-6 Gainful)**
Soviet Army / 30th Guards Motorized Rifle Division, 1988

Designed to protect Warsaw Pact ground forces from air attack, the SA-6 Gainful utilizes a solid-fuel rocket booster to achieve speeds in excess of Mach 1.5. Its high-explosive proximity-fused warhead claimed an alarmingly high number of Israeli aircraft during the 1973 Yom Kippur War, and the SA-6 has become one of the most widely used systems of its type in the world. To date, at least 20 countries have fielded the system.

Specifications

Configuration: single-stage, solid fuel
Deployment: mobile
Length: 5.7m (18ft 9in)
Diameter: 335mm (13.2in)
Launch weight: 600kg (1323lb)
Range: 20km (13 miles)
Launch preparation time: 15 minutes

7th Air Defence Regiment, Red Army, Zeithan, German Democratic Republic, 1989

Stationed in East Germany near the end of the Cold War, the Red Army's 7th Air Defence Regiment was equipped with the SA-6 Gainful mobile air defence missile system. Regiments such as the 7th, equipped with missiles, were further complemented by units which employed anti-aircraft guns. Together these constituted an in-depth air defence system. Each carrier transported four missiles in firing position. The vehicle acquisition radar was effective at a distance of 20km (12.5 miles).

Regiment (20 x SA-6)

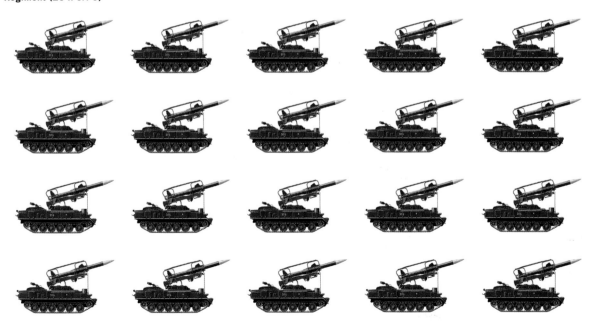

its maximum missile range was estimated at 15km (9.3 miles). Both the SA-6 and SA-8 systems remain widely used.

Each air defence regiment was further augmented by an additional platoon of ZSU-23-4 anti-aircraft guns. The ZSU-23-4 was proved effective during the Vietnam War and the Arab–Israeli wars of 1967 and 1973. The system mounted four 23mm (0.9in) guns, each with an effective rate of fire of 1000 rounds per minute. These were often deployed in defence of the SA-6 and SA-8 launchers. In addition, the SA-9 Gaskin close-support anti-aircraft system was utilized as a last echelon of defence. The SA-9 mounted four infrared homing missiles atop an amphibious scout car. Airborne units utilized the SA-7 Grail and the light, airmobile ZSU-23-2 organized in batteries of six with up to 36 vehicles per division.

Late Western artillery
1970–91

Artillery components of NATO forces in Western Europe were counted on to resist the advance of Warsaw Pact forces during a ground offensive, buying time for deliberation on the use of nuclear weapons.

ACKNOWLEDGING THE NUMERICAL superiority of Soviet and Warsaw Pact forces in Europe, NATO nevertheless devised a cooperative defensive programme to resist the advance of enemy forces in the event of a ground war. There is little doubt that a decisive outcome in favour of NATO forces on the ground would have required the use of nuclear weapons at least on a tactical scale. To that end, the early Cold War saw the deployment of low-level weapons such as the M28/29 Davy Crockett system, which utilized a 102mm (4in) gun or 155mm (6.1in) recoilless rifle to discharge a shell armed with a 23kg (51lb) nuclear warhead.

While the nuclear alternative was difficult even to contemplate since Soviet retaliation was virtually assured, it remained a reality. In addition, the improvement of conventional artillery was undertaken with vigour by the 1970s, resulting in several improved systems which were deployed with NATO armed forces in Western Europe and indeed with armies around the world.

Organizational changes among the various armies which made up the NATO forces also occurred. The typical structure of a US Army Division during the early to mid-Cold War period included a divisional artillery component comprising four artillery battalions. Three of these usually contained up to three batteries of 105mm (4.1in) howitzers, each containing four guns for a complement of 36; the fourth battalion had three batteries of four 155mm (6.1in) howitzers, totalling 12.

Shoot and scoot

By the 1990s, the US Army had reorganized several times, with the motorized and light divisional concepts arranged for rapid deployment but with sufficient firepower to defeat enemy formations which included substantial armoured assets. Modern US divisions maintain an organic divisional artillery component together with a separate air defence

▲ **LARS training**
West German troops man a LARS multiple rocket launcher during winter manoeuvres. Armed with 36 rockets, the weapon was designed for rapid concentration of fire on designated targets.

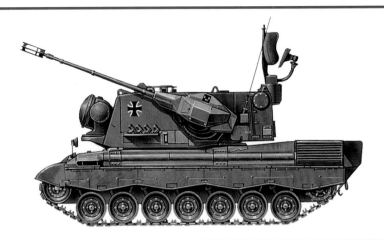

▲ Flugabwehrkanonenpanzer (Flakpanzer) Gepard

German Army / 11th Flak Regiment, 1988

Deployed primarily to provide air defence for armoured formations, the Gepard utilizes high-explosive and armour-piercing ammunition fired from a pair of 35mm (1.38in) autocannon mounted externally from the crew compartment to avoid the introduction of gases into a confined space. The Gepard employs both acquisition and tracking radar which feed data to an onboard computer system to control the guns.

Specifications

Crew: 4	Engine: 623kW (830hp) 10-cylinder MTU MB 838
Weight: 47,300kg (104,060lb)	Ca M500 multi-fuel
Length: 7.68m (25ft 2in)	Speed: 65km/h (40mph)
Width: 3.27m (10ft 9in)	Road range: 550km (342 miles)
Height: 3.01m (9ft 10in)	Armament: 2 x 35mm (1.38in) utocannon

▲ SIDAM-25 self-propelled anti-aircraft gun

Italian Army / 4th Air Defence Regiment, 1987

The SIDAM-25, developed by the Italian firm of OTO Melara, mounts four 25mm (0.98in) Oerlikon cannon guided by laser rangefinding equipment and a fire-control computer. The SIDAM-25 includes a complete turret system mounted atop the chassis of the M113 armoured personnel carrier. It has also been modified to fire the French Mistral surface-to-air missile.

Specifications

Crew: 3	
Weight: 14,500kg (14.27 tons)	Engine: 161kW (215hp) 6-cylinder Detroit Diesel
Length: 4.86m (20ft)	Speed: 65km/h (40mph)
Width: 2.69m (8ft 10in)	Road range: 500km (310 miles)
Height: 1.83m (6ft)	Armament: 4 x 25mm (1in) Oerlikon cannon

artillery battalion. As the exigencies of combat demanded greater mobility, the development of light, airmobile field artillery and self-propelled systems for both ground support and anti-aircraft defence became priorities. Among the prerequisites for modern mobile fire-support systems is the 'shoot and scoot' capability, which allows the weapon to deploy, acquire targets, fire its ordnance, displace and then assume a favourable firing location before enemy counterbattery fire or any other response can be brought to bear.

By the 1990s, the principal weapons deployed with a direct fire support battalion of the US Army, particularly one working within a brigade combat team, would often include the M119 105mm (4.1in) howitzer, a towed weapon which was actually designed by Royal Ordnance Factories of Great Britain as the L118/L119 Light Gun.

1st Flak Regiment, German Army, Federal Republic of Germany, 1989

Flak regiments of the German Army were often detailed to provide close anti-aircraft defence against enemy fixed-wing aircraft and helicopters. Coordinating with missile defences and other guns, the Gepard SP anti-aircraft gun was capable of firing a combined 1100 rounds per minute from its radar-directed 35mm (1.38in) autocannons. The turret is mounted on the chassis of the Leopard 1 main battle tank. Although the Gepard has been upgraded several times, it is scheduled for replacement by a new system in the coming years.

Regiment (36 x Flakpanzer Gepard)

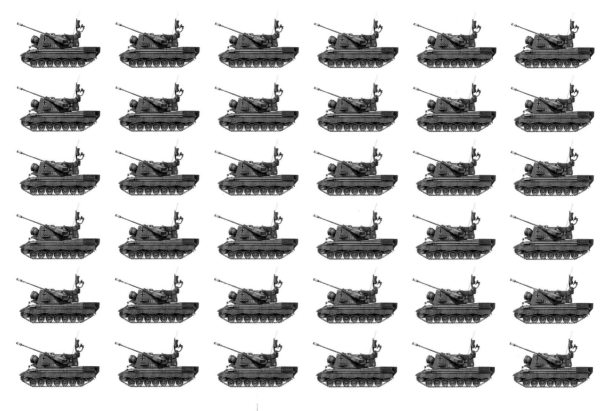

Specifications

Crew: 5

Weight: 20,000kg (19.7 tons)

Length: 4.86m (15ft 11in)

Width: 2.69m (8ft 10in)

Height: 2.16m (7ft 1in)

Engine: 159kW (212hp) 6-cylinder Detroit Diesel

Speed: 66km/h (41mph)

Road range: 483km (300 miles)

Armament: 1 x 120mm (4.72in) mortar; 1 x 7.62mm (0.3in) MG

▲ M113A1G PzMrs (Panzermörser)

German Army / 7th Panzer Artillery Regiment, 1988

Utilized by the German Army as a light reconnaissance vehicle, the M113A1G is a converted version of the US M113 armoured personnel carrier, designed to carry a 120mm (4.72in) mortar in the troop compartment. The mortar is fired directly out of an open space in the rear of the hull roof. Specialized versions are often used for forward air control or artillery observation.

▲ **LARS II MLRS**

German Army / 11th Rocket Artillery Battalion, 1988

Entering service with the German Army in 1970, the LARS (Light Artillery Rocket System) has been largely replaced by the MLRS and MARS (Mittleres Artillerie Raketen System) systems more common in NATO usage. The LARS II entered service in 1980 and is capable of firing high-explosive fragmentation ammunition as well as a cargo warhead which distributes anti-tank mines. The system is fired from inside the cab of the transporter.

Specifications

Crew: 3

Rocket diameter: 110mm (4.33in)

Rocket length: 2.263m (7ft 5in)

Rocket weight: 35kg (77.16lb)

System combat weight: 17,480kg (17.2 tons)

Range: 14,000m (15,310 yards)

Rate of fire: 36 rounds in 18 seconds

12th Rocket Artillery Battalion, German Army, Federal Republic of Germany, 1989

The LARS II multiple launch rocket system was portable atop a wheeled 6X6 MAN high-mobility-truck chassis and was designed to deliver heavy fire support to NATO ground troops. It was capable of delivering 36 rockets in 18 seconds or firing a cluster warhead which distributed anti-tank mines. Rocket artillery battalions of the German Army each had 16 LARS II systems, all 209 LARS IIs in service having been upgraded from an earlier configuration. Retired from the Germany Army by 1998, the system is still in use with numerous countries.

Battalion (16 x LARS II)

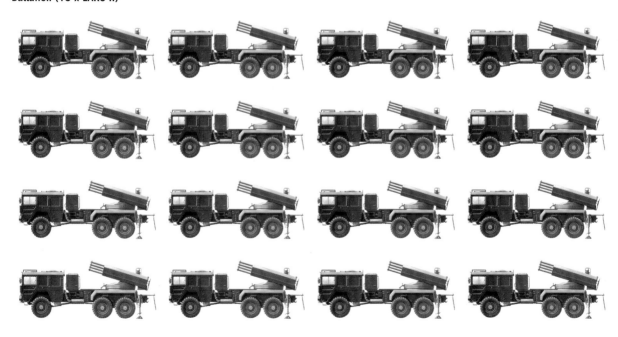

With a maximum rate of fire of eight rounds per minute for three minutes, the M119 is capable of a sustained rate of fire of three rounds per minute for up to 30 minutes. Its light weight makes the weapon ideal for transport by air and for operations in company with fast-moving infantry formations. Light formations such as airborne units have fielded the L118/L119 in batteries of six guns.

The M198 155mm (6.1in) gun-howitzer is a primary weapon of general support artillery battalions. Introduced in the late 1970s as a replacement for the M114 of World War II vintage, the M198 is capable of firing at a maximum range of more than 29,992m (32,800 yards) with ammunition assisted by rocket propulsion, and 17,800m (19,685 yards) with conventional high-explosive ammunition. Further, the M198 is nuclear-capable and was intended to provide NATO forces with the modern tactical nuclear punch which had become a priority with the onset of the Cold War a generation earlier. The M198 has a sustained rate of fire of two rounds per minute and can reach up to four rounds per minute during maximum exertion. It is served by a crew of nine.

Early in the 1990s, the British firm of BAE Land Systems began research on yet another improved

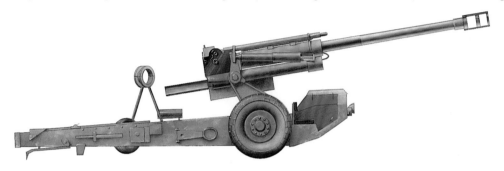

▲ **155mm SB-155/39 towed howitzer**
Spanish Army / 17th Artillery Regiment, 1983

The Spanish government's armament factory, known as Empresa Nacional Santa Barbara, developed the 155mm (6.1in) SB-155/39 towed howitzer during the late 1970s and equipped some artillery units with the weapon during the following decade. The SB-155 is a split-trail howitzer, which, with its disengagement of the wheels and use of a firing pedestal in action, provides more stability when firing.

Specifications

Crew: 8	Weight: 9500kg (9.35 tons)
Calibre: 155mm (6.1in)	Range: 24,700m (27,010 yards)
Elevation: - 3 degrees to + 70 degrees	Muzzle velocity: 800m/sec (2625ft/sec)

C Battery, 94th Field Artillery Battalion, US Army, Europe, 1989

The typical field artillery battalion of the US Army in NATO service in Western Europe included a complement of eight M109A3 self propelled guns. The M109A3 was one in a series of upgrades to the original M109 series originated in the 1950s and included as many as 27 improvements such as an upgraded rammer and recoil system for the main weapon, a redesigned bustle to carry an additional 22 rounds of ammunition, redesigned hatches and an improved hydraulic system.

Battery (8 x M109A3 SP guns)

155mm (6.1in) howitzer. Designated the M777, it has equipped numerous units of the British armed forces and is slated to replace the M198 batteries of the US Army and Marine Corps. Weighing 4082kg (9000lb), it has components of lightweight titanium, which contributed to its original name – the Ultralightweight Field Howitzer (UFH). The M777 is easily moved by truck or helicopter and delivers heavy firepower at a rate of five rounds per minute. Its rocket-assisted ammunition can reach out to 30km (18.6 miles).

The primary self-propelled artillery component of NATO forces has long been the US-produced M109 155mm (6.1in) howitzer, which was originally designed in the 1950s and upgraded

Specifications

Configuration: single-stage, liquid fuel

Deployment: mobile

Length: 6.1m (20ft)

Diameter: 560mm (22in)

Launch weight: 1290kg (2850lb)

Range: 120km (75 miles)

Launch preparation time: unknown

▲ **M548 with MGM-52 Lance missile**

US Army / 44th Air Defense Battalion, 1970

The US Army utilized a modified M548 cargo carrier, designated the M752, as a platform both for the transport and firing of the MGM-52 Lance missile. The Lance missile was capable of firing conventional and nuclear warheads with a yield of up to 100 kilotons. A chemical delivery option was considered but abandoned by 1970. The system was withdrawn from Western Europe following the Intermediate-Range Nuclear Forces Treaty of 1987.

Specifications

Crew: 3

Weight: 54,430kg (119,746lb)

Length: 7.674m (25ft 2in)

Width: 3.632m (11ft 11in)

Height: 4.611m (15ft 2in)

Engine: 563kW (750hp) Continental
    AVDS-1790-2D diesel

Speed: 48 km/h (30mph)

Road range: 500km (311 miles)

Armament: 2 x 40mm (1.57in) L/70 Bofors guns

▲ **M247 Sergeant York SPAAG**

US Army / Prototype

In response to the successes of Soviet self-propelled anti-aircraft guns, the US Army embarked on the development of a replacement for its M42 Duster and MIM-72 Chaparral air defence systems in the mid 1970s. The M247 Sergeant York self-propelled anti-aircraft gun mounted a pair of 40mm (1.57in) Bofors L/70 guns atop the chassis of the M48 main battle tank. The M247 was plagued with problems, and only 50 were built. Most of these were used as targets on ordnance ranges. The programme was scrapped in 1985.

on numerous occasions. The latest variant of the M109, the M109A6 Paladin, is the product of a lengthy improvement programme for the venerable system and includes improved Kevlar-based armour protection, greater range and accuracy for its main weapon and an upgraded powerplant. By the end of the 1990s, more than 1000 of the M109A6 were in the hands of US forces or pending delivery.

Both British and German designers, however, embarked on their own development programmes while fielding M109 variants. A series of joint efforts undertaken in the 1970s between the British, Germans and Italians to produce a mutually acceptable self-propelled gun, designated the SP70, had collapsed for various reasons. Therefore, the British Ministry of Defence authorized the development of a self-propelled weapon during the mid-1980s to replace the M109 system, the ageing FV433 Abbot and in some cases the towed FH-70 155mm (6.1in) gun in regiments of the Royal Artillery

Field Artillery Regiment, British Army, 1989

The standard field artillery regiment of the British Army of the Rhine deployed in Western Europe consisted of three batteries of towed FH-70 155mm (6.1in) howitzers, each with three guns. Transportation was provided by the Land Rover reconnaissance vehicle. The FH-70 was a joint design undertaken by Britain, Germany and Italy, and the weapon was eventually assigned as a direct infantry support gun after original plans to equip medium artillery regiments were changed.

Battery (1 x Land Rover [Recon], 3 x FH-70 155mm/6.1in Howitzers)

Battery (1 x Land Rover [Recon], 3 x FH-70 155mm/6.1in Howitzers)

Battery (1 x Land Rover [Recon], 3 x FH-70 155mm/6.1in Howitzers)

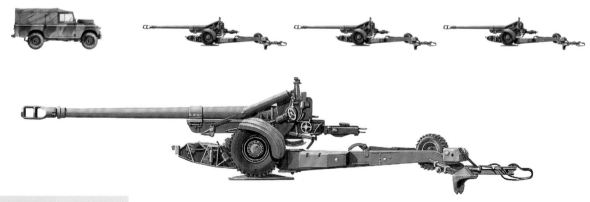

Specifications

Crew: 8

Calibre: 155mm (6.1in)

Elevation: - 4.5 degrees to + 70 degrees

Weight: 9300kg (9.15 tons)

Range: 24,700m (27,010 yards)

Muzzle velocity: 827m/sec (2713ft/sec)

▲ **FH-70 towed howitzer**

British Army / 101st Northumbrian Regiment Royal Artillery, 1991

During the late 1960s, Britain, Germany and Italy embarked on a cooperative effort to design a close infantry support towed artillery piece. The split-trail carriage of the FH-70 provides a stable platform in action, while the gun is capable of firing a variety of high-explosive and rocket-assisted ordnance. The gun entered service in 1978 and utilizes an auxiliary power unit to relocate short distances. Its sustained rate of fire is three to six rounds per minute.

and the Royal Horse Artillery. The result was the AS-90, mounting a 155mm (6.1in) L31 gun and powered by a 495kW (660hp), eight-cylinder Cummins diesel engine. Entering service in 1993, the AS-90 was designed as a complete vehicle, rather than the marriage of a turret and gun which could be mounted atop an existing tank hull, and utilizes the latest in Chobham anti-missile armour protection.

Meanwhile, German engineers worked to develop the PzH 2000, which mounted the Rheinmetall 155mm (6.1in) L52 gun atop a chassis based on that of the Leopard 1 main battle tank and built by Krauss-Maffei Wegmann. The PzH 2000 is capable

of firing up to 60 shells in 12 minutes, and its operational range is 420km (261 miles). The PzH 2000 design placed the engine and transmission forward of the crew compartment to provide greater protection against penetrating projectiles and boasts the latest in composite armour.

An integral component of NATO artillery, particularly in heavy field artillery brigades at corps level within the US Army, is the M270 Multiple Launch Rocket System (MLRS). The M270 entered service in 1983 and is capable of delivering up to 12 rockets in less than one minute. The German Army has operated a rocket system called MARS, which is

▲ GDF-C03

Swiss Army / Artillery Battalion 54, 1992

The Oerlikon-Bührle company produced the GDF-C03 as a mobile air defence system to protect rear areas, including production facilities, marshalling yards, and command and control centres. The system mounts twin 35mm (1.38in) Oerlikon cannon and is either tracked or wheeled. The tracked version is based on a modified M113 armoured personnel carrier chassis, while the wheeled variant employs the HYKA 4X4 vehicle.

Specifications

Crew: 3	Engine: 161kW (215hp) 6-cylinder
Weight: 18,000kg (39,600lb)	GMC 6V-53T diesel
Length: 6.7m (22ft)	Speed: 45km/h (28mph)
Width: 2.813m (9ft 3in)	Road range: 480km (297 miles)
Height: 4m (13ft 2in)	Armament: 2 x 35mm (1.38in) Oerlikon cannon

▶ Oerlikon GAI-B01

Swiss Army / Mechanized Infantry Battalion 29, 1995

Mounted on a tripod-shaped platform, the GAI-B01 20mm (0.79in) anti-aircraft gun includes the Oerlikon 20mm (0.79in) cannon. It is also a capable ground-defence weapon. Simple to deploy and operate, the GAI-B01 uses no hydraulic power. Elevation is cranked with a hand wheel, and traverse is controlled by the feet of the gunner. The weapon may be transported easily aboard a truck or trailer and is in use by armed forces around the world.

Specifications

Crew: 3	Weight: 405kg (892lb)
Calibre: 20mm (0.79in)	Range: 1500m (4920ft)
Elevation: - 5 degrees to + 85 degrees	Muzzle velocity: 1100m/sec (3609ft/sec)

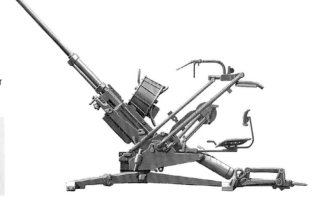

based on MLRS. Development of an improved US battlefield rocket system, HIMARS (High Mobility Artillery Rocket System), was begun in 1996.

Air defence was a further priority with NATO forces, and during the 1960s the US marked off air defence artillery as a separate command from the field artillery. A variety of self-propelled anti-aircraft guns provided close air defence for NATO armour, troops and command-and-control centres. Among the most widely used of these is the German Flakpanzer Gepard (Cheetah), which was developed in the 1960s and deployed by 1970. The Gepard mounts a pair of 35mm (1.38in) autocannon atop the chassis of the Leopard 1 main battle tank. Its

radar-controlled guns work in tandem with teams of infantrymen using the shoulder-fired Stinger anti-aircraft missile, designed to shoot down low-flying fixed-wing aircraft and helicopters.

The Italian firm of OTO Melara produced another effective close air defence weapon in the SIDAM-25, which incorporates four Oerlikon 25mm (0.98in) guns, each capable of firing up to 570 rounds per minute, atop the adapted chassis of the ubiquitous M113 armoured personnel carrier. The effectiveness of the SIDAM-25, however, is limited due to its lack of radar. Its laser rangefinding equipment is efficient during periods of good weather.

▲ **Bandkanon**

Swedish Army / Södra Skånska Regiment, Sweden, 1981

The 155mm (6.1in) Bandkanon self-propelled artillery vehicle was developed by Bofors in the early 1960s and combined the chassis of the Stridsvagn 103 with the heavy cannon. The system entered service with the Swedish Army in 1967.

Specifications

Crew: 5	Engine: 1 x 179kW (240hp) Rolls-Royce diesel;
Weight: 53,000kg (116,600lb)	1 x 224kW (300hp) Boeing gas turbine
Length: 11m (36ft 1in)	Speed: 28km/h (17.4mph)
Width: 3.37m (11ft 0.7in)	Road range: 230km (143 miles)
Height: 3.85m (12ft 7.5in)	Armament: 1 x 155mm (6.1in) gun, plus
	1 x 7.62mm (0.3in) anti-aircraft MG

Self-propelled artillery battalion, Sweden, 1985

Organized in two battalions of 12 vehicles originally, the basic Swedish self-propelled artillery formation later changed to three battalions of eight vehicles. The Bandkanon was at one time one of the heaviest self-propelled artillery vehicles in the world; however, only 26 were built. Its development was undertaken in 1960, and the vehicle entered service in the middle of the decade. The Bandkanon is noteworthy as the world's first fully automatic self-propelled artillery weapon. Its ammunition was stored in clips of 14 rounds.

Battalion (8 x Bandkanons SP artillery)

Western theatre missiles
1970–90

Among the most prominent of the theatre nuclear missiles in the Western inventory is the BGM-109 Tomahawk cruise missile.

THE MOBILE, NUCLEAR-CAPABLE Tomahawk eventually was configured for launch by land, sea and air; however, only the submarine-launched version remains active today. The ground-launched nuclear Tomahawk and its launch apparatus were scheduled to be dismantled due to treaty agreements between the US and the Soviet Union during the late 1980s, and this was accomplished with the removal of all 200-kiloton W-80 nuclear warheads by 1992.

The Tomahawk armed with a conventional 454kg (1000lb) warhead has been utilized during recent conflicts and has proved a remarkably versatile and accurate weapon.

The MGM-31 Pershing intermediate-range ballistic missile was also a factor in the move towards nuclear disarmament during the Cold War. Developed during the late 1950s and deployed to Western Europe and the Korean peninsula soon

56th Pershing II Brigade, US Army, Schwäbisch-Gmünd, Federal Republic of Germany, 1989

Typical of the field artillery formations under the control of the US Army Missile Command in Western Europe was the 56th Pershing II Brigade with a complement of more than 100 mobile Pershing II intermediate-range ballistic missiles. The Pershing II utilized the HEMTT prime mover for launching, which included a crane for assembly and a generator to provide power to the erector and launcher. It carried a nuclear warhead of up to 400 kilotons.

1–9th Field Artillery Battalion (36 x Pershing II)

2–9th Field Artillery Battalion (36 x Pershing II)

4–9th Field Artillery Battalion (36 x Pershing II)

after, the Pershing I was mounted atop the tracked M474 transporter-erector-launcher vehicle. Its warhead was either conventional or the nuclear W-50 with a yield of up to 400 kilotons.

Following an upgrade to the original Pershing, designated the Pershing IA, specifications were issued in 1973 for yet another improved missile. The Pershing II was intended, along with nuclear-capable Tomahawk cruise missiles, to counter the Soviet deployment of the SS-20 Saber intermediate-range ballistic missile. The Pershing II was mounted aboard the HEMTT prime mover, which included

a crane to facilitate assembly. The terms of the Intermediate-Range Nuclear Forces Treaty of 1987 resulted in the dismantling of the Pershing series and the SS-20 by the early 1990s.

▲ **BGM-109 Tomahawk**

US Air Force / 11th Bomb Squadron, 1982

Originally designed for the US Navy, the BGM-109G Gryphon variant of the Tomahawk cruise missile, known as a GLCM (Ground-Launched Cruise Missile), became a primary ground-launched nuclear weapon of NATO forces in Western Europe before treaty limitations ended its nuclear capability with the removal of its 200-kiloton W-80 warheads by 1992. The Tomahawk has been deployed with a 454kg (1000lb) conventional warhead since and remains a notably successful sea-launched system. Onboard guidance capability has enhanced the accuracy of the Tomahawk.

Specifications

Configuration: solid-fuel booster, turbofan
Deployment: mobile
Length: 6.4m (21ft)
Diameter: 530mm (20in)
Launch weight: 1443kg (3181lb)
Range: 2500km (1555 miles)
Launch preparation time: 20 minutes

Specifications

Configuration: two-stage, solid fuel
Deployment: mobile
Length: 10.61m (34ft 10in)
Diameter: 1m (39.5in)
Launch weight: 4600kg (10,141lb)
Range: 1800km (1118 miles)
Launch preparation time: 15 minutes

▲ **MGM-31 Pershing II**

US Army / 41st Field Artillery Regiment, 1983

Reaching operational status in Western Europe in 1983, the Pershing II intermediate-range ballistic missile carried a nuclear warhead of five to 50 kilotons and was intended to engage military targets in the event of armed conflict with Warsaw Pact forces, although its improved range theoretically brought the Soviet capital of Moscow within striking distance of highly mobile launchers located in West Germany. Preceded by the Pershing I and IA, the third-generation Pershing II missiles were dismantled along with Soviet SS-20 intermediate-range missiles as a result of the Intermediate-Range Nuclear Forces Treaty of 1987.

French missile development concentrated on short- and intermediate-range systems such as the SSBS and Pluton. The Pluton, a mobile-launch system mounted atop the chassis of the AMX-30 tank, was capable of carrying conventional warheads and nuclear payloads of up to 25 kilotons. It was a short-range weapon and its operational reach of 120 km (75 miles) was meant for targets inside France or West Germany. Conceived as a replacement for the US Honest John system, the Pluton was lightweight and highly mobile. It entered service in 1974 and was operational for nearly 20 years before it left service in the mid-1990s, scheduled to be replaced by the Hadès system.

▲ **Pluton**

French Army / 3rd Artillery Regiment, 1976

Mounted atop the chassis of the AMX-30 tank, the Pluton tactical nuclear missile entered service with the French Army in 1974, and a total of 42 launchers were produced and fielded in artillery regiments of six launchers each. A 15-kiloton warhead was to be used on the battlefield, while a 25-kiloton warhead was meant for more distant targets. Targeting assistance was provided by an airborne drone.

Specifications

Configuration: two-stage, solid fuel	Launch weight: 2423kg (5342lb)
Deployment: mobile	Range: 120km (75 miles)
Length: 7.64m (26ft 1in)	Launch preparation time: unknown
Diameter: 650mm (25.6in)	

Western air defence missiles
1970–90

Coordinated air defences presented a challenge for NATO military planners as cooperation among member nations was achieved with advancing technology and systems.

AS WESTERN NATIONS independently pursued modern air defence systems based on the deployment of anti-aircraft guns, missiles and aircraft, it became apparent to NATO leaders that without coordination such endeavours would be more costly and would, in time, result in a more vulnerable military posture in Western Europe. When the alliance was formed in 1949, research had been ongoing to develop surface-to-air-missile defence capabilities; however, these efforts sometimes produced redundant systems or missile command-and-control structures which were unable to communicate with one another.

By the 1970s, NATO member nations had determined that should such conditions continue control of vital air space would be in peril in the event of an attack by Warsaw Pact forces. Therefore, an integrated air defence system was initiated and ultimately placed under the control of the NATO Air Defence Committee, which would assume responsibilities for promoting cooperation among member nations.

While missile technology continued to advance, the alliance established the NATO Air Defence Ground Environment as a component of a comprehensive system with sites stretching from Turkey in the eastern Mediterranean to Scandinavia. Early-warning and tracking would enable coordinated interception of hostile planes by aircraft, surface-to-air missiles and anti-aircraft guns. Such a scenario is based on the rapid exchange of intelligence and the ability to bring assets to bear across national boundaries and great distances unhindered by communications difficulties or incompatible equipment.

Mobility, quick reaction, range and reliability have figured prominently in the development of

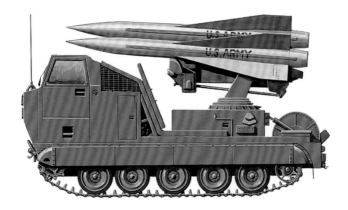

Specifications

Configuration: two-stage, solid fuel
Deployment: mobile
Length: 5.12m (16ft 9in)
Diameter: 356mm (14in)
Launch weight: 626kg (1380lb)
Range: 40km (25 miles)
Launch preparation time: 5 minutes

▲ M727 HAWK

US Army / Test Platoon, Fort Bliss, Texas, 1969

The M727 HAWK (Homing All the Way Killer) was the short-lived self-propelled version of the system which combined the modified M548 tracked vehicle with the MIM-23 HAWK surface-to-air missile. Although the 'SP HAWK', as it was commonly called, was discontinued by August 1971, the missile itself was not phased out of service with the US Army and Marine Corps until 2002. The HAWK, which underwent several operational upgrades, was primarily transported and fired from the M192 triple missile launcher. HAWK batteries remain in service with the armed forces of numerous nations.

Specifications

Configuration: single-stage, solid fuel
Deployment: mobile
Length: 2.87m (113in)
Diameter: 127mm (5in)
Launch weight: 88.5kg (195lb)
Range: 4000m (4375 yards)
Launch preparation time: 5 minutes

▲ M48 Chaparral FAADS

US Army / 44th Air Defense Battalion, 1988

The M48 self-propelled Chaparral surface-to-air missile combined the M548 tracked launch vehicle with a variant of the AIM-9 Sidewinder air-to-air missile. With the failure of the Mauler programme, a joint effort with Great Britain, the US developed the Chaparral, which was deployed in 1969 and was in service for the next 30 years. Several upgrades kept the Chaparral in service, and one of these was target-acquisition equipment borrowed from the FIM-92 Stinger missile. Originally, the Chaparral launcher was simply pointed towards the target to allow the missile to lock on. Later, it was capable of all-weather operation.

air defence missiles deployed by NATO countries. Among the most common of these during the Cold War years were the US-built MIM-23 HAWK and MIM-72 Chaparral missiles.

Development of the HAWK began in 1952 as the US Army considered options for a medium-range surface-to-air missile. Within five years, test-firing and evaluation had been completed, and the system was deployed by the end of the decade. The mobile HAWK is transported, positioned and launched with the M192 towed launcher, and a self-propelled version, the M727, was configured utilizing a modified M548 tracked vehicle. This variant was tested in 1969 but proved impractical and was abandoned in the summer of 1971.

The HAWK has undergone numerous upgrades over the years, including improved navigation, targeting and all-weather capabilities. Its basic 54kg (119lb) high-explosive warhead has been

proved effective against Soviet-manufactured aircraft, particularly during the Arab–Israeli wars of 1967 and 1973, while heavier warheads have been successfully installed. The fragmentation warheads have been improved for use against incoming ballistic missiles as well.

Although the HAWK was retired from active service with the US Army and Marine Corps by 2002, it remains a primary air defence weapon with the armed forces of more than 20 nations, and its adaptability and service life of nearly half a century are truly remarkable. More than 40,000 are believed to have been manufactured.

The MIM-72 Chaparral entered service with the US Army in 1969 as an adaptation of the successful AIM-9 Sidewinder air-to-air missile. The self-propelled Chaparral utilizes the M730 transport vehicle, which is a modification of the M548 and a direct descendant of the M113 armoured personnel

▶ **Roland surface-to-air missile**

German Army / 54th Artillery Regiment, 1978

Developed jointly by France and Germany, the Roland surface-to-air missile series included the Roland I, which operated during favourable weather conditions, the all-weather Roland II, and the Roland III with improved thermal sighting and laser rangefinding. The Roland variants were mounted either on the chassis of the French AMX-30 main battle tank or the German Marder infantry fighting vehicle and also on wheeled vehicles. The Roland entered service with the French Army in 1977 and with the German Army in 1978.

Specifications

Configuration: two-stage, solid fuel
Deployment: mobile
Length: 2.4m (94.5in)
Diameter: 1160mm (6.3in)
Launch weight: 63kg (139lb)
Range: 6.2km (3.9 miles)
Launch preparation time: unknown

▲ **Bofors RBS-70 MANPADS**

Swedish Army / Life Grenadier Regiment, 1979

Developed as a low-cost short-range man-portable air defence missile, the Bofors RBS-70 MANPADS entered service with the Swedish military in 1977 and remains deployed today. The RBS-70 launch system includes a seat for the soldier operating the weapon, and instructions on target acquisition are received through radar signals, which are then processed by a combat control terminal computer. The RBS-70 employs a laser-activated proximity fuse to destroy its target.

Specifications

Configuration: two-stage, solid fuel	Launch weight: 15kg (33lb)
Deployment: man-portable	Range: 5km (3 miles)
Length: 1.32m (52in)	Launch preparation time: immediate
Diameter: 106mm (4.17in)	

Intended to work in tandem with the M163 Vulcan anti-aircraft gun, the original Chaparral was fired manually and required an interval for the missiles to lock onto their targets by identifying exhaust heat.

Two significant upgrades to the missile occurred in the late 1970s with the addition of FLIR camera technology for improved capability in adverse weather conditions; a smokeless motor which allowed better visibility after firing and helped to conceal the launcher location; and an improved target-acquisition apparatus borrowed from the shoulder-fired FIM-92 Stinger anti-aircraft missile. The service life of the Chaparral extended into the late 1990s.

The British Rapier system, which is fired from fixed launch sites or the tracked M548, is one of the longest-serving weapons of its kind in the world. The Rapier entered service in 1971 and was considered a viable air defence system in 2010. The primary air

defence weapon of the British Army, it has essentially replaced other missiles and most anti-aircraft guns in the British arsenal.

A joint effort between France and Germany in the early 1960s produced the Roland surface-to-air missile, which was later improved with all-weather capabilities but endured a lengthy testing period and was not deployed by either nation's armed forces until 1977. Although the Roland and the improved Roland II were never produced in large numbers due to delays during evaluation and rising costs, the US did make a notable purchase of the system in 1975. This attempt to deploy a modified Roland in front-line air defence artillery units, however, met with failure due to difficulties in technology transfer and increasing expense. Fewer than 30 modified Roland missiles were produced.

Specifications

Configuration: single-stage, solid fuel
Deployment: mobile
Length: 2.93m (9ft 7in)
Diameter: 156mm (6.14in)
Launch weight: 85kg (187lb)
Range: 8.5km (5.3 miles)
Launch preparation time: 5 minutes

▲ **Crotale EDIR**

French Army / 3rd Air Defence Squadron, 1991

Originally designed during the 1950s in France for the armed forces of South Africa where it was named 'Cactus', the Crotale EDIR (Infrared Differential Ecartometry) short-range air defence missile has been mounted on a wheeled chassis as well as that of the AMX-30 main battle tank. The Crotale launcher holds up to eight missiles which utilize radar, electro-optical and infrared equipment for target acquisition and tracking. Production of the modernized Crotale NG began in 1990, incorporating the launcher and radar in one vehicle.

Light Air Defence Battery (Tracked Rapier), British Army, 1989

The British Army light air defence battery was composed of an FV432 command vehicle, a variant of the FV430 infantry fighting vehicle, and a complement of six tracked Rapier surface-to-air-missile launchers. The development of the Rapier was subsequent to the failure of the Mauler programme, a joint effort with the United States. The Rapier entered service in 1971 and remains active today. Its longevity is due in large part to its rapid response time and versatility as a radar- and laser-guided missile which is deployed atop mobile M548 launchers or from fixed positions. It has essentially replaced all other missiles and guns in air defence roles with the British Army.

Battery (1 x FV432 command APC, 6 x Tracked Rapier SAM)

Soviet–Afghan War
1979–89

The firepower of Soviet artillery was often negated by rugged terrain and the persistent, low-technology campaign waged by the guerrilla forces in Afghanistan.

FOR A DECADE, the Soviet Union waged a costly, unsuccessful war against the Muslim Mujahideen in Afghanistan. The mechanized might and heavy weaponry of the Red Army were often frustrated by the hit-and-run tactics of guerrilla fighters who struck at convoys and military installations swiftly and then melted away into the rugged countryside. Mountainous terrain, inhospitable desert, and tactics which proved ineffective in counter-insurgency warfare made pursuit and decisive action problematic for Soviet forces. However, when the guerrillas appeared in significant numbers or were caught in the open, the superior firepower and modern technology of the Red Army was telling.

Stinging the Hind

One of the most effective weapons deployed by the Soviets in Afghanistan was the large, yet agile, Mil Mi-24 Hind helicopter gunship, which was in country from the very start. The Mi-24 was heavily armed with a combination of rockets and machine guns and capable of carrying up to eight fully equipped combat infantrymen. Swift airmobile operations supported by the Mi-24 took their toll on the Mujahideen until the United States government intervened with a programme to arm the guerrillas.

The most significant weapon appropriated for the Afghan guerrillas was the shoulder-fired FIM-92 Stinger air defence missile. The Mujahideen possessed few effective anti-aircraft guns, and it was the Stinger which mounted an appreciable challenge to Soviet mastery of the air. With an effective ceiling of approximately 3000m (10,000ft), the Stinger could be fired from distances as great as five kilometres (three miles) from its target, utilizing heat-seeking sensors to lock on. Perhaps one of the greatest advantages of the weapon was its ease of transport and the fact that little or no training was needed to operate it. One defence analyst commented, 'The missile's complexity can be accommodated by almost any potential user nation or group.'

The first shipment of 300 Stinger missiles arrived in Afghanistan in 1986, and this was followed by another 700 the next year. During their first action, the Stingers were reported to have shot down three Mi-24s. They are credited with destroying at least 275 Soviet fixed-wing aircraft and helicopters before the Red Army withdrawal in 1989.

While such a turn of events appears remarkable, it must be noted that the improved air defence capability of the guerrillas made the war effort more costly for the Soviets and was probably the primary reason for the decision to abandon the effort to prop up a weak Marxist government in Kabul.

Specifications

Configuration: two-stage, solid fuel

Deployment: man-portable

Length: 1.52m (60in)

Diameter: 70mm (2.75in)

Launch weight: 10.1kg (22.25lb)

Range: 5000m (3.1 miles)

Launch preparation time: 8 seconds

▲ **FIM-92 Stinger**

Mujahideen guerrilla forces, 1986

Years of research and development were committed to the FIM-92 Stinger shoulder-fired surface to-air missile, which replaced the US Army's first such weapon, the Redeye. The Stinger continues to utilize infrared homing equipment which locks onto a target's heat source; however, its capability is enhanced by ultraviolet detection as well. The Stinger is armed with an impact-fused high-explosive fragmentation warhead which weighs three kilograms (6.6lb). Supply of the weapon to the Mujahideen in Afghanistan hastened the Soviet withdrawal in 1989.

Heavy Red Army hardware

When the Soviet Red Army invaded Afghanistan in 1979, its operational doctrine had been formulated to fight a war against a traditional NATO foe on the rolling terrain of Western Europe. Therefore, military planners maintained a tradition of dependence on massed artillery and close ground support by aircraft. Traditionally, the Red Army considered artillery a primary weapon of decision on the battlefield; however, the acquisition of targets of high value was difficult due to the nature of counter-insurgency warfare.

The missions of the artillery were nevertheless those of direct and indirect support for manoeuvre elements but also to block escape routes of guerrillas during search-and-destroy missions and to cover the withdrawal of Soviet forces when the decision had been made to disengage. During such withdrawal movements, the Soviets learned to direct fire well beyond the suspected positions of the Mujahideen and walk the fire backwards towards their own troops until it was judged that sufficient covering fire had been laid to suppress the small arms of

▲ 122mm D-30 2A18 howitzer

Soviet Army / 108th Motorized Rifle Division, 1980

Developed in the early 1960s as a replacement for the aging M1938 howitzer, the 122mm (4.8in) D-30 was a common element of the Soviet units engaged in Afghanistan and deployed in Europe during the Cold War. The D-30 mounts the 2A18 howitzer, which is the same weapon used on several self-propelled assault guns. Its wide, three-piece trail separates when the weapon is deployed to provide a stable firing platform. The weapon is capable of firing a variety of ordnance, including high-explosive fragmentation and laser-guided shells.

Specifications

Crew: 7

Calibre: 122mm (4.8in)

Elevation: - 7 degrees to + 70 degrees

Weight: 3150kg (6945lb)

Range: 15,400m (16,840 yards)

Muzzle velocity: 690m/sec (2264ft/sec)

Specifications

Crew: 6

Calibre: 23mm (0.9in)

Elevation: - 10 degrees to + 90 degrees

Weight: 950kg (2094lb)

Range: 2000m (6560ft)

Muzzle velocity: 970m/sec (3182ft/sec)

▲ ZU-23-2 towed anti-aircraft cannon

Soviet Army / 56th Separate Airborne Assault Brigade, 1983

Mounting twin 23mm (0.9in) 2A14 autocannon, the ZU-23-2 was developed in the late 1950s to replace the 14.5mm (0.57in) heavy machine gun in an air defence role and remains in service with the armed forces of more than 20 nations today. Intended for use against low-flying aircraft, it is also effective against light armoured vehicles. When the weapon is deployed, its wheeled carriage folds rapidly underneath, allowing it to get into action quickly.

▲ **Firing range**

Red Army soldiers practice firing the D-30 122mm (4.8in) howitzer. First entering service in the early 1960s, the D-30 became the mainstay of many armies during the Cold War period, proving superior to the US-produced 155mm (6.1in) M114 as well as virtually every piece in the 105mm (4.1in) class. The gun is still used today in some developing countries, and has been deployed in the war in Afghanistan by the Afghan National Army.

the guerrillas. Artillery officers maintained control of their weapons most of the time; however, on rare occasions the officers of infantry units were given the authority to order fire support in critical situations.

While the firepower of artillery may indeed have a telling and decisive effect on a stationary enemy which maintains a defined, continuing front, the Mujahideen guerrillas did not oblige. Analysts have noted that the lack of ground manoeuvre and close combat actions taken by the Soviets facilitated the longevity and eventual victory of the guerrilla forces.

Throughout the course of the war, Soviet commanders in Afghanistan recognized the flaw

in this policy and attempted to compensate. One tactic employed by the Red Army was the artillery ambush. Motion detectors were distributed to pick up the sounds of passing insurgent groups or vehicles, and contacts were often followed by heavy fire from 122mm (4.8in) D-30 field howitzers. The self-propelled 2S1 122mm (4.8in) and 2S9 120mm (4.7in) howitzers were often deployed in support of short-duration operations, while truck-mounted rocket launchers such as the BM-21 and BM-27 were frequently used to saturate fixed enemy positions. Still, a lack of light infantry and the difficulties inherent in the manoeuvrability of mechanized infantry hampered ground operations.

In turn, the reliance on artillery continued, and by the end of the war more than 400 artillery pieces and mortars had been lost.

Workhorse

The 122mm (4.8in) D-30 howitzer proved to be a workhorse among towed artillery weapons used by the Red Army in Afghanistan. The D-30 entered service in the mid-1960s as a replacement for the M1938 howitzer, which had been in production until 1955. The weapon is similar in design to an earlier howitzer produced during World War II for the German Army by Czechoslovakia's Skoda works. An interesting feature is its split trail, which divides into three stabilizing legs to assist with the absorption of recoil in action.

The Soviets considered mortars and anti-tank weapons to be artillery and as a matter of course integrated artillery personnel into mechanized infantry units to operate them. When engaged with Mujahideen in mountainous terrain, Soviet commanders often found that the 82mm (3.2in) Vasilek mortar, with its high trajectory and plunging fire, was more effective than the howitzer. This was particularly true when engaging enemy forces in caves or ravines.

One effective method of engagement was to fire the laser-guided Smel'chak, or Daredevil, round against guerrilla positions which might otherwise require a direct assault by infantry. The Smel'chak

was fired by the massive 240mm (9.45in) 2S4 self-propelled mortar, nicknamed the Tyulpan, or Tulip, and known to NATO as the M1975. One battery of 2S4s engaged a Mujahideen stronghold in a deep gorge at a distance of nearly 2400m (2625 yards). After firing conventional high-explosive rounds for ranging, a single Smel'chak was loosed at the target. The resulting direct hit destroyed the guerrilla position.

The BM-21 and BM-27 multiple rocket launchers are direct descendants of the famed BM-13 Katyusha rocket system which gained notoriety during World War II. The BM-21 is mounted atop the Ural 375D 6X6 truck and carries 40 122mm (4.8in) rockets, which may be fired at a rate of two rounds per second. The BM-21 entered service in 1964 and is relatively accurate for an unguided rocket system. It remains a front-line fire-support weapon with the armed forces of more than 50 nations.

The BM-27 multiple rocket launcher appeared in the late 1970s, and its 16 tubes fire a variety of 220mm (8.7in) rockets, including high-explosive fragmentation and chemical warheads, from atop the chassis of the ZIL-135 8X8 launch vehicle. Its crew of four is capable of preparing the system to fire or displacing it within three minutes. The BM-27 was often used in Afghanistan to distribute anti-personnel mines in order to contain the movements of guerrillas during offensive sweeps by infantry units.

▶ **82mm Vasilek Mortar**

Soviet Army / 5th Guards Motorized Rifle Division, 1981

The 82mm (3.2in) Vasilek mortar, or Cornflower, was conceived as a weapon which could provide both the plunging fire of a mortar and the flatter trajectory of field artillery. Developed in the early 1970s, it was utilized by mechanized infantry units of the Soviet Red Army in Afghanistan. The Vasilek could be loaded either from the breech or muzzle and was most often towed, although it has been seen fixed to a light vehicle. It remains in use with some airborne units but has largely been replaced by the 120mm (4.7in) mortar.

Specifications

Crew: 4	Range: 4720m (5162 yards)
Calibre: 82mm (3.2in)	Muzzle velocity: 270m/sec (890ft/sec)
Elevation: - 1 degree to + 85 degrees	
Weight: 632kg (1393lb)	

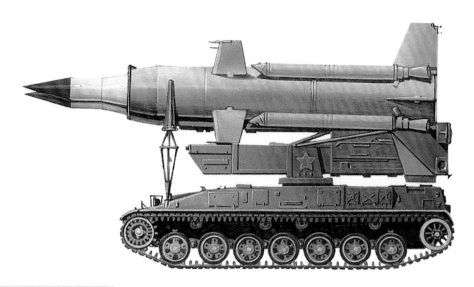

Specifications

Configuration: two-stage; kerosene, solid fuel

Deployment: mobile

Length: 9m (29ft 6in)

Diameter: 800mm (31.5in)

Launch weight: 2500kg (5511lb)

Range: 55km (34 miles)

Launch preparation time: 10 minutes

▲ **2K11 Krug (SA-4 Ganef)**

Soviet Army / 8th Guards Surface-to-Air Missile Brigade, 1988

A large ramjet missile powered by kerosene and solid fuel, the SA-4 Ganef long-range air defencemissile was deployed with the Red Army in the early 1960s. Mounted atop the GM-123 transporter-erector-launcher, the SA-4 was in service briefly with Soviet forces in Afghanistan. The missile is guided initially by acquisition radar and radio signals, before the SA-4 onboard radar locks onto the target, and the proximity fuse is detonated when range has closed sufficiently. Several nations, including the Czech Republic, Hungary and Bulgaria, operate the system today.

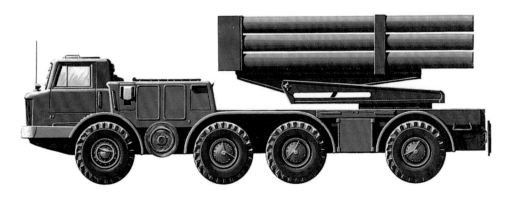

▲ **BM-27 Uragan multiple rocket launcher**

Soviet Army / 201st Motorized Rifle Division, 1983

Entering service with the Red Army during the early 1970s, the BM-27 Uragan multiple launch rocket system includes the wheeled ZIL-135 8X8 mobile launcher along with 16 tubes which fire 220mm (8.7in) rockets. The weapon is highly mobile and can be prepared for relocation in three minutes. Reloading of the full complement of missiles requires 20 minutes.

Specifications

Crew: 4

Calibre: 220mm (8.7in)

Rocket length: 4.83m (15ft 10in)

Rocket weight: 260kg (573lb)

System combat weight: 18,144kg (40,000lb)

Range: 25,000m (15.5 miles)

Rate of fire: 1 round per second

Falklands War: British forces
1982

When British forces moved to retake the distant Falkland Islands from Argentina, light infantry supported by artillery played a pivotal role in the success of the operation.

IN THE SPRING OF 1982, British forces engaged those of Argentina to reassert their nation's sovereignty over the Falkland Islands, a remote cluster of rocky land thousands of kilometres from Britain itself. Logistics presented an immediate challenge, not to mention the air, naval and ground strength of the Argentinian forces to be confronted. British transport vessels sailed almost halfway around the world to facilitate the establishment of a beachhead at San Carlos Water.

Due to the nature of the conflict, including distance, terrain and available support units, it became apparent that light infantry supported by mobile field and air defence artillery along with a relative few light armoured vehicles could exert the proper force to execute the mission. Success on the ground, however, was dependent on control of the air and the supporting presence of the Royal Navy, which could contribute air assets and provide resupply. Partially due to the fact that the navy could remain on station for a somewhat short duration, speed was of the essence.

The long march

When British forces landed at San Carlos, they included troops of 3 Commando Brigade, Royal Marines, and the army's 5 Infantry Brigade. The artillery and surface-to-air assets deployed included 29 Commando Regiment, Royal Artillery, which included three six-gun batteries (7, 8, 70) of the 105mm (4.1in) L118 Light Gun, and 148 Commando Forward Observation Battery, Royal Artillery. The Commando Air Defence Troop carried 12 Shorts Blowpipe surface-to-air missiles, while T Battery, 12 Air Defence Regiment, was armed with the Rapier surface-to-air missile. Also there were 105mm (4.1in) L118 Light Guns of 4 Field Regiment, Royal Artillery, as were the surface-to-air missiles of Blowpipe Troop, 43 Air Defence Battery.

▲ **Preparing to fire**
British Army personnel prepare to fire an L118 Light Gun. Although lacking a heavy punch, the L118 proved to be a useful and adaptable gun in adverse conditions, especially the kind of soft terrain British forces encountered in the Falkland Islands.

The Light Gun proved to be a mobile and versatile weapon during the Falklands War, although the wet, marshy conditions often resulted in challenges for displacing and relocating the weapons. During prolonged fire-support missions, it was not unusual for recoil to cause the howitzer to move more than 2.5m (eight feet) from its original location. Innovative measures were taken to further secure the weapon in its correct position. A total of five batteries, including 30 L118s, were deployed by British forces in the Falklands. Their accurate fire was essential to victory in several sharp clashes during the march to the capital at Stanley.

One British soldier fighting at the Battle of Two Sisters remembered, 'There were three [Argentinian] machine guns, and we brought down constant and effective salvoes of our own artillery fire onto them directly, 15 rounds at a time. There would be a pause, and they'd come back at us again. So we had to do it a second time, all over their positions.'

In preparation for the assault of 2 PARA at Wireless Ridge, Light Guns fired 6000 rounds

Specifications

Crew: 6

Calibre: 105mm (4.1in)

Elevation: - 5.5 degrees to + 70 degrees

Weight: 1860kg (4100lb)

Range: 15,070m (16,480 yards)

Muzzle velocity: 617m/sec (2024ft/sec)

▲ **L118 Light Gun**

British Army / 29 Commando Regiment Royal Artillery, 1982

The L118 Light Gun was introduced to the British Army in 1976 as a replacement for the Italian OTO Melara Mod 56 105mm (4.1in) pack howitzer and became the standard light artillery weapon of the British Army. The Light Gun is served by a crew of six and has a rate of fire of six to eight rounds per minute. Although heavier than the Mod 56, it is airmobile or movable overland by a one-ton Land Rover vehicle.

97 Battery Royal Artillery, Falklands Islands, 1982

During the Falklands War of 1982, 97 Battery Royal Artillery was equipped with six 105mm L118 Light Guns. The battery was one of five which supported British ground operations from San Carlos Water to the final victory at Stanley. The weapons were airlifted by helicopter and often towed by the Land Rover 101 vehicle, which had been designed as the prime mover for both the L118 and the Rapier air defence missile. The L118 proved decisive during several engagements with accurate, sustained fire against Argentinian forces entrenched in positions on high ground.

Battery (6 x 105mm/4.1in L118 Light Guns)

of 105mm (4.1in) ammunition. As the battles around Stanley progressed, the guns were known to have fired up to 400 rounds per day in support of ground forces.

The Light Gun had been developed in the early 1970s and had entered service with the British Army by 1976 as a replacement for the Italian-made OTO Melara Mod 56, a pack howitzer which could be quickly disassembled and transported with light infantry and airborne units. Based somewhat on the design of the older 25-pounder gun, the L118 was heavier than the Mod 56; however, it provided increased range which had been a prerequisite for the new design and was still airmobile due to improvements in lift aircraft. The L118 has further been deployed to the Balkans and the Middle East.

The performance of the Blowpipe and Rapier air defence missiles in the Falklands has been criticized. The Blowpipe had been developed in the early 1970s

and entered service in 1975. Often, a two-man team would operate the Blowpipe, although one soldier could manage and would have an interval of roughly 20 seconds to sight a target and fire. Nearly 100 of the missiles were fired during the campaign, and the official report of the action stated that only nine of these struck their targets. However, further scrutiny disputed even this claim, and it has been reported that only two aircraft were hit, one of these a British Harrier jump jet.

The Rapier missile entered service in 1971, and with improvements it has since replaced most other air defence systems, missiles or guns, in the British Army. After-action reports from the Falklands indicated disappointing initial results. Only 14 hits had supposedly been confirmed with six probables. However, later studies firmly attributed only one shoot-down – an Argentinian A-4 Skyhawk fighter-bomber – to the Rapier.

▲ Rapier surface-to-air missile

British Army / 12 Air Defence Regiment, 1982

The Rapier surface-to-air missile entered service with the British Army in 1971, initially to replace the older English Electric Thunderbird. However, as the air defence requirements of NATO forces evolved, the Rapier took on a larger role and has become the primary air defence weapon of British forces. During favourable weather conditions, the missile is guided by infrared tracking, while the Blindfire tracking and guidance radar allows for use in inclement weather.

Specifications

Configuration: two-stage, solid fuel
Deployment: fixed or mobile
Length: 2.24m (88.2in)
Diameter: 133mm (5.25in)

Launch weight: 42kg (94lb)
Range: 7.25km (4.5 miles)
Launch preparation time: 6 seconds

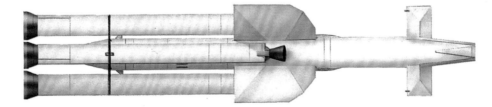

Specifications

Configuration: two-stage; solid-fuel booster & liquid-fuel sustainer
Deployment: shipboard
Length: 6.1m (20ft)

Diameter: 409mm (16.1in)
Launch weight: 2384kg (5256lb)
Range: 58km (36 miles)

▲ Seaslug surface-to-air missile

Royal Navy / HMS Antrim (Destroyer), 1982

The Seaslug missile was introduced to the Royal Navy for shipboard air defence in 1961 and continued in service for 30 years. The missile was deployed during the Falklands War, and at least one incident of its firing was documented. The Seaslug was known as an accurate missile with a probable hit rate of better than 90 per cent. It was guided by radar and carried a 135kg (297lb) warhead.

▲ **Blowpipe MANPADS**

British Army / Air Defence Troop, 3 Commando Brigade, 1982

The man-portable Blowpipe air defence missile entered service with the British Army in 1975 and was retired a decade later. It includes the launch tube containing the missile and an attached sighting unit. The entire apparatus is then aimed and fired from the shoulder. While aiming is assisted through infrared optics, the operator steers the missile to its target by means of a thumb-operated lever. Its 2.2kg (4.85lb) warhead is detonated by proximity fuse.

Specifications

Configuration: two-stage, solid fuel	Launch weight: 11kg (24.5lb)
Deployment: man-portable	Range: 3500m (3825 yards)
Length: 1.4m (55.1in)	Launch preparation time: 20 seconds
Diameter: 76.2mm (3in)	

Falklands War: Argentinian forces
1982

Firing from advantageous positions on high ground, Argentinian artillery performed well during the defence of the Falkland Islands.

AS THE ELITE TROOPS of Britain's 3 PARA assaulted Mount Longdon on the night of 11 June 1982, the soldiers came under intense and accurate fire from Argentinian artillery. For two days, the paras hung on grimly to their hard-won gains, having lost 19 men to artillery and small-arms fire and then another four as the relentless bombardment continued. The artillery fire from the defenders of Mount Harriet and Two Sisters was equally intense that night. The following night on Mount Tumbledown two more British soldiers were killed by Argentinian artillery, and the guns maintained an incessant bombardment of the attacking British at Wireless Ridge throughout the hours of darkness.

Artillery played a major role for both the Argentinians and the British during the brief but bitter war for control of the Falkland Islands. By the time British forces had overcome major logistical challenges to reach the remote islands in force, the Argentinians had moved substantial military assets to the small, rocky archipelago they referred to as the Malvinas.

The heaviest concentration of Argentinian firepower was with the 3rd Artillery Group and the 4th Airborne Artillery Group, which each fielded at least 18 105mm (4.1in) OTO Melara Mod 56 pack howitzers, which were of Italian manufacture and originally intended to equip mountain troops of the Italian Army. In addition, the 3rd Artillery Group contained four 155mm (6.1in) Model 1977 howitzers. Much of this artillery was situated in or near the capital of Stanley for defensive purposes and due to the fact that the heavier artillery was difficult to transport across the marshy terrain. The 601st Anti-Aircraft

ARGENTINA: ARTILLERY UNITS STATIONED IN THE FALKLANDS, 1982			
Unit	Commander	Equipment	Strength
3rd Artillery Group (GA3), 3rd Infantry Brigade	Lt-Col Martín A. Balza	105mm OTO Melara Mod 56 howitzer 155mm Model 1977 howitzer	18 4
4th Airborne Artillery Group (GA4), 4th Airborne Brigade	Lt-Col Carlos A. Quevedo	105mm OTO Melara Mod 56 howitzer	18

Artillery Group was armed with Roland and Tigercat surface-to-air missiles, the Oerlikon GDF-001 35mm (1.38in) twin cannon, the 30mm (1.2in) Hispano Suiza Hs-831 machine gun, and other light weapons.

Flash and thunder

Argentinian artillery was often located in strong positions along ridges and on high ground which guarded the British route of march. Light mortars and recoilless rifles were placed in order to funnel advancing British troops into the lines of fire of entrenched Argentinian soldiers with their rifles and machine guns. During the bitter clash at Goose Green, troops of the Argentinian 25th Independent

Motorized Infantry Regiment held up British attempts to capture Darwin Ridge for several hours as an officer directed the fire of three 105mm (4.1in) guns and 120mm (4.7in) mortars against the attackers. Argentinian forward observers had been able to track the progress of the British advance and call in accurate coordinates for the gunners. The resulting fire inflicted several casualties on the airborne soldiers of 2 PARA, while British artillery was in action, firing more than 1000 rounds in support of the difficult advance and finally compelling the Argentinians to abandon their positions and surrender at Goose Green.

Although the OTO Melara Mod 56 was a weapon with a long history, it had not been intended for

▶ OTO Melara 105mm Mod 56

Argentinian Army / 3rd Artillery Group, 1982

The 105mm (4.1in) OTO Melara Mod 56 pack howitzer remains in service half a century after its initial delivery to the Italian armed forces as a light, easily transportable weapon for mountain infantry. The Mod 56 may be dismantled into 12 component pack loads to facilitate movement through rugged country. A versatile weapon, the Mod 56 may be used with a high trajectory to provide plunging fire support for infantry movements or on a flat trajectory in defensive positions against advancing armoured vehicles.

Specifications

Crew: 6	Weight: 1273kg (2806lb)
Calibre: 105mm (4.1in)	Range: 11,100m (12,140 yards)
Elevation: - 7 degrees to + 65 degrees	Muzzle velocity: 416m/sec (1345ft/sec)

4th Airborne Artillery Group (GA4), 4th Airborne Brigade, Falkland Islands, 1982

Participating primarily in the defence of Stanley, the Falklands capital, the 4th Airborne Artillery Group fielded 18 105mm (4.1in) OTO Melara Mod 56 pack howitzers. The Mod 56 was the most numerous field artillery weapon in Argentinian service during the Falklands War and proved a capable and versatile weapon in the hands of Argentinian artillerymen, providing direct fire against advancing British forces during their push from San Carlos in the spring of 1982. These 105mm (4.1in) weapons were heavily engaged at Goose Green, Mount Longdon, Wireless Ridge and other locations.

Airborne Artillery Group (18 x OTO Melara 105mm/4.1in Mod 56 pack howitzer)

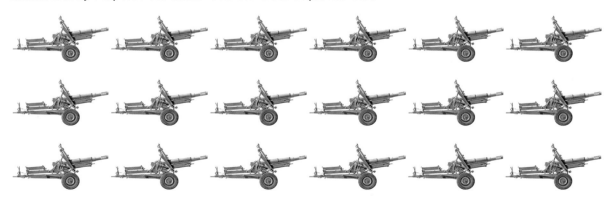

a prolonged engagement. Given the rocky terrain across the Falklands, this 105mm (4.1in) weapon was well suited to holding high ground and bringing fire on enemy troops engaged in a direct assault against the well-prepared Argentinian positions. As mentioned above, the Mod 56 had been developed 30 years earlier as a pack howitzer for mountain troops. The weapon was appreciated by light infantry and airborne units because of its welcome firepower since it was often the heaviest weapon available to such troops and could be wrestled into position by the soldiers with relative ease due to its light weight.

The Mod 56 could be disassembled into 12 components and carried by the soldiers themselves or by pack animals. Cross-country transport was often accomplished by light vehicles towing the weapon or by carrying the gun inside the modified troop compartment of an armoured personnel carrier. It was also light enough to be lifted by helicopter and transported by air as a single piece. Licence copies of the Mod 56 have been produced in China and Great Britain, where it is known as the L5.

The heaviest-calibre field piece engaged during the Falklands War, the Model 1977 howitzer, was based on an original French design, the 155mm (6.1in) SP Gun F3, a self-propelled weapon. The Argentinians removed the gun from its original tracked mounting and placed it on a carriage with a split trail. During the mid-1970s, the Argentinian Army had sought to replace its aging M114 155mm (6.1in) howitzers, which dated from World War II. Backed by the military junta which had previously taken control of

the Argentinian government, the modification of the Model 1977 to the army's specifications was done in concert with the purchase of substantial quantities of weapons and ammunition from numerous countries.

The Model 1977 was primarily engaged in the defence of the mountains and ridges around Stanley and proved to be the only real land-based artillery counter to the accurate gunfire from warships of the Royal Navy. Fewer than ten of the Model 1977s were in action in the Falklands, and these were transported by aircraft to the islands as the British steadily advanced across East Falkland.

Missile threat

The Tigercat surface-to-air missile was, ironically, a British weapon which was a land-based version of the Royal Navy's Sea Cat air defence missile. The Sea Cat was outdated by the early 1980s and had been replaced by the Sea Dart and Sea Wolf systems on some warships; however, it was still widely used. The Tigercat was a mobile variant which was mounted on a triple launcher. Only one kill was claimed by the Sea Cat during the Falklands War, and more than 80 of the missiles were reported to have been launched. No Tigercat kills were confirmed.

The Argentinians had positioned their Roland missiles at fixed launch points in defence of the airport at Stanley. At least four launchers had been purchased during the late 1970s, and these were captured by the British with the surrender of the Argentinian garrison. Eight of ten Roland missiles deployed were fired, and one British Hawker Sea

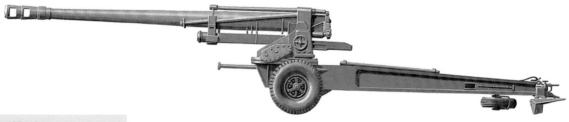

Specifications

Crew: 6

Calibre: 155mm (6.1in)

Elevation: - 10 degrees to + 67 degrees

Weight: 8000kg (7.87 tons)

Range: 22,000m (24,060 yards)

Muzzle velocity: 765m/sec (2510ft/sec)

▲ **155mm Model 1977 howitzer**

Argentinian Army / 3rd Artillery Group, 1982

An Argentinian adaptation of the French self-propelled 155mm (6.1in) F3 gun, the Model 1977 included the barrel of the French weapon mounted on a split-trail carriage. In preparation for firing, the wheels were raised and a firing pedestal lowered in order to provide a stable platform. During the Falklands War, the weapon proved too heavy for easy transport across marshy terrain and was engaged primarily in the defence of Stanley.

Harrier fighter-bomber was shot down by a Roland on 1 June 1982. A joint venture between France and Germany, the Roland had become operational by 1977 and was considered a modern, effective weapon during the Falklands War.

In addition to the Roland and Tigercat missiles, the Argentinians had purchased a number of the French Exocet anti-ship missiles, which could be fired from mobile launchers on land, from on board ship and from aircraft. It was the Exocet which inflicted significant losses on the Royal Navy during the Falklands War. An Exocet hit the destroyer HMS *Sheffield*, inflicting damage which later caused the warship to sink, and also damaged the destroyer HMS *Glamorgan*. A pair of Exocets struck the 15,240-tonne (15,000-ton) Cunard roll-on/roll-off container vessel *Atlantic Conveyor*, causing it to sink five days later. The Exocet became the most recognized weapon of the Falklands War and remains in wide use today. It entered service with the French Navy in 1979, and its basic version carries a 165kg (360lb) warhead. The missile skims the surface of the water at 315m (1030ft) per second and locks onto its target with radar.

Specifications

Crew: 4

Calibre: 35mm (1.38in)

Elevation: - 5 degrees to + 92 degrees

Weight: 6400kg (6.3 tons)

Range: 4000m (13,125 yards)

Muzzle velocity: 1175m/sec (3855ft/sec)

▲ **Oerlikon GDF-001 35mm twin cannon**

Argentinian Army / 601st Anti-Aircraft Artillery Group, 1982

The Swiss-manufactured medium-range Oerlikon GDF-001 35mm (1.38in) air defence gun is a twin mounted weapon deployed atop a wheeled carriage which splits into a four-legged platform for firing. It is fed by an automatic loading system of seven-round clips. The Oerlikon has been in service for many years and forms the Skyguard air defence system when operated in tandem with the Sparrow air defence missile.

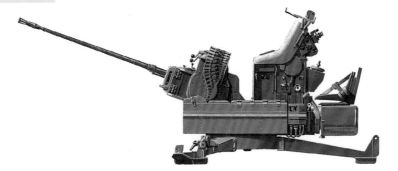

Specifications

Crew: 4

Calibre: 20mm (0.79in)

Elevation: - 5.5 degrees to + 83.5 degrees

Weight: 1650kg (3637lb)

Range: 2000m (6560 yards)

Muzzle velocity: 1050m/sec (3445ft/sec)

▲ **Rheinmetall MK 20 Rh 202 autocannon**

Argentinian Army / 601st Anti-Aircaft Artillery Group, 1982

Transported atop a two-wheeled trailer, the 20mm (0.79in) twin guns of the Rh 202 are positioned on a power mounting which can be removed from the trailer and stabilized on a base of three outstretched legs. With a rate of fire of up to 1000 rounds per minute, its close-support capabilities were critical to the Argentinian defences around the airport at Stanley during the Falklands War.

Chapter 9

The Korean War, 1950–53

The Cold War erupted into a bloody conflict,
which is still unresolved to this day, when North Korean
troops crossed the 38th parallel on 25 June 1950, in an
attempt to unify the Korean peninsula under communist
rule. Although rumours of war had circulated far and wide,
the defending South Korean Army was ill-prepared to
stem the tide of tanks and troops unleashed by the North.
Following a United Nations resolution which authorized
intervention, a US-led coalition embarked on the arduous
task of preserving the pre-war status quo. Initially, neither
side could call upon artillery support as needed; however, as
the war dragged on, heavy guns gained a prominent role.

◀ **Fire in the hole**
Men of the 31st Heavy Mortar Company fire their M2 107mm (4.2in) mortar at an enemy position west of
Chorwon, Korea, in early 1953.

Introduction

The Korean War eventually lapsed into a stalemate reminiscent of the trench warfare on the Western Front during World War I, and the firepower of artillery contributed to the deadlock. The frequent use of big guns caused the conflict to become known as 'the artillery war'.

LESS THAN FIVE YEARS after the end of World War II, the prospect of another catastrophic conflict was all too real. North and South Korea were at war, and the forces of numerous countries had joined the fighting either through United Nations mandate or to protect their own national interests. Unlike any previous conflict in world history, however, the Korean War was prosecuted under the ominous prospect of a nuclear cloud, an apocalyptic exchange of weapons so powerful that humankind might destroy itself.

The world had entered the Nuclear Age, and the research and development of atomic weapons was proceeding. Both the United States and the Soviet Union possessed the atomic bomb, and along with strategic considerations there was experimentation into the feasibility of artillery capable of firing tactical nuclear weapons. By the mid-1950s, nuclear-capable artillery was a reality, and US shells as small as 155mm (6.1in) were tipped with nuclear warheads.

In Korea, however, conventional artillery of World War II vintage remained the order of the day. Supplied by the Soviets, the North Korean Army possessed relatively few artillery pieces or self-propelled guns. When the Chinese People's Liberation Army joined the conflict in the autumn of 1950, the same was true. Although field artillery and heavy guns were scarce among the Chinese formations, there was no shortage of manpower. In the South, the Republic of Korea Army was both undermanned and underequipped. Rushed from bases in Japan, the first US forces to reach Korea under the UN flag were woefully understrength as well.

Dash to Seoul

When the North Koreans attacked, their armoured spearheads, including up to 150 of the formidable Soviet-built T-34 medium tanks, which had gained lasting fame on the Eastern Front in World War II, advanced along a traditional invasion route towards the South Korean capital of Seoul. The North

Koreans had assembled seven infantry divisions, up to 90,000 combat troops, for the assault. Their progress was rapid.

Opposing the North Koreans, the South Koreans were armed primarily with American weapons. Infantry units were equipped with small arms and some 60mm (2.36in) and 81mm (3.19in) mortars, while the artillery was organized into 22 battalions structured in seven field artillery groups of two battalions each along with an additional eight independent battalions. None of these units possessed any guns heavier than 105mm (4.1in).

The first American artillery unit on the ground in Korea was designated Detachment X and included 33 officers and soldiers of the 507th Antiaircraft Artillery Battalion, which arrived four days after the shooting had begun. A mobile unit equipped with 40mm (1.57in) guns, the 507th accounted for a couple of enemy aircraft, and on 30 June the US government authorized the deployment of two full combat divisions to Korea.

Artillery war

For both the UN and the communist forces, the Korean War presented significant challenges to artillery and mechanized operations. Difficult terrain, which included rugged mountains, undulating hills and swift rivers, was complicated by extremes of climate, with the tremendous heat of summer and sub-zero temperatures in winter. Nevertheless, as the war intensified and the numbers of troops committed continued to grow, artillery units on both sides began to play a more prominent role in the fighting.

In spite of the impediments to mobility, heavy guns were often massed together to break up enemy attacks. Close-quarters, hand-to-hand fighting sometimes prompted soldiers to call artillery fire down upon their own positions.

Although the employment of artillery might prove decisive on a tactical level, it was not capable of dictating the overall outcome of the conflict. In the event, the artillery fire control and precision of

▲ **Night mission**

A night-time view showing a salvo being fired by the 1st Rocket Battery, 11th Marine Regiment, somewhere in the Marines' front-line sector, April 1953.

the United Nations forces were often countered by the sheer weight of numbers of Chinese and North Korean troops engaged.

As the cost of war climbed and neither side sought a widening of the conflict beyond conventional weapons, it became apparent that a negotiated ceasefire would be required to stop the bloodshed. The peace talks at Panmunjom eventually resulted in a tenuous armistice, and the presence of artillery on the battlefield had been instrumental in the result.

United Nations forces
1950–53

Led by the armies of the United States and the British Commonwealth, the armed forces of the United Nations deployed artillery in significant numbers to stem the communist tide in Korea.

FIGHTING AT THE HOOK in the summer of 1953, one US Marine Corps gunner with Battery A, 1st Battalion, 11th Marine Regiment, remembered firing all night long in support of the embattled US 25th Infantry Division. On that particular night, the battery fired in barrage rather than volley, with only an occasional check of target coordinates. Incoming enemy artillery rounds kept most of the crews under cover, and the position was hot. Only two Marines at a time operated the guns. An occasional 155mm (6.1in) round from US Army artillery to the rear fell short, adding to the hazard and the din of combat.

From May to June 1953, the 11th Regiment, which consisted of a total of 72 guns, both 105mm (4.1in) and 155mm (6.1in), fired more than 120,000 rounds. While peace talks were ongoing, so was the business of war. The 105mm (4.1in) howitzer M2A1 was the backbone of the US artillery which served during the Korean War. More than 8500 had been produced during World War II, and the weapon's powerful round coupled with a range of more than 11km (12,200 yards) made it a valuable asset to front-line soldiers in Korea. Along with the 105mm (4.1in) weapon, the 75mm (2.9in) M1A1 pack

howitzer was well suited for the difficult terrain of Korea, while the 155mm (6.1in) M1 (also designated M114) and M3 howitzers, the 155mm (6.1in) M2 Long Tom cannon and the 240mm (9.45in) M1 and 203mm (8in) M115 howitzers were also among the variety of US artillery pieces deployed to Korea.

During three years of combat, more than 60 artillery battalions of the US Army and Marine Corps saw service in Korea. The standard US Army division was equipped with three battalions of the light 105mm (4.1in) howitzer for close fire support and a single battalion of 155mm (6.1in) guns at the divisional level. These were capable of reaching targets at distances of up to nearly 15km (16,000 yards). At the height of the Korean War, four additional US infantry divisions were each given access to another battalion of 155mm (6.1in) weapons, while a pair of combined-arms regimental combat teams each included a battalion of 105s.

Corps artillery in Korea served as something of a large unit fire brigade, dispatched to wherever support was needed, either offensively or defensively. These corps units most often included a battalion of the M7 self-propelled 105mm (4.1in) gun,

▶ **Ordnance ML 3in Mortar**

1st Commonwealth Division / 29th Infantry Brigade, 1951

The remarkable longevity of the 3in mortar (actually 3.2in/81.2mm in calibre) is testament to its durability on the battlefield. This standard British infantry support weapon was developed in the late 1920s, improved with a sturdier barrel which lengthened its effective range and served for four decades until replaced by the modern L16 81mm (3.19in) mortar in the mid-1960s.

Specifications

Crew: 2	Weight: 50.8kg (112lb)
Calibre: 81.2mm (3.2in)	Range: 2560m (2800 yards)
Elevation: + 45 degrees to + 80 degrees	Muzzle velocity: 198m/sec (650ft/sec)

nicknamed Priest during World War II because of its high gun ring; four battalions of 155mm (6.1in) guns, some of which were also self-propelled; a battalion of 203mm (8in) howitzers; and an observation battalion. The mammoth 240mm (9.45in) howitzer appeared late in the war and was assigned to the artillery complements of IX and X Corps. The number of guns in a battery varied with the size of the weapon. Six guns completed a battery of 105s or 155s, while a 203mm (8in) battery consisted of four guns, and two guns were included in a 240mm (9.45in) battery.

Early arrival

The first US field artillery unit in Korea was a portion of the 52nd Battalion, consisting of Battery A with six

▲ 40mm Bofors L/60 anti-aircraft autocannon

US Army / 507th Antiaircraft Artillery Battalion, 1950

Of Swedish lineage, the 40mm (1.57in) Bofors L/60 entered service in 1929, and sales to foreign nations began slowly. However, the gun, which became one of the most famous in the history of modern warfare, later sold briskly. By 1941, numerous European countries and the United States had adopted it. The weapon was reliable and versatile, either towed, self-propelled or aboard ship.

Specifications

Crew: 3–4

Calibre: 40mm (1.57in)

Elevation: -5 degrees to + 90 degrees

Weight: 1981kg (4568lb)

Range: 1525m (5000ft)

Muzzle velocity: 823m/sec (2700 ft/sec)

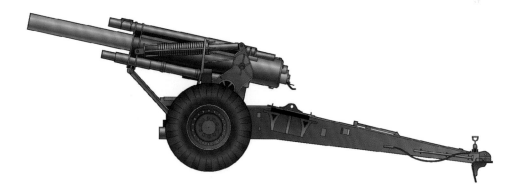

▲ M114 155mm howitzer

Eighth United States Army / 11th Field Artillery Battalion, 1952

Originally deployed during World War II and designated the M1 howitzer, the M114 155mm (6.1in) weapon remains in service today. More than 4000 were produced during World War II and more than 10,000 before production ceased in 1953. The weapon was also mounted on the chassis of the M24 Chaffee light tank and designated the M41 self-propelled howitzer.

Specifications

Crew: 11

Calibre: 155mm (6.1in)

Elevation: - 2 degrees to + 63 degrees

Weight: 5600kg (12,000lb)

Range: 14,600m (16,000 yards)

Muzzle velocity: 563m/sec (1847ft/sec)

105mm (4.1in) howitzers and half of the battalion's headquarters and service batteries. This unit was ordered to support a small force under the command of Lieutenant-Colonel Charles B. Smith, which included slightly less than three companies of infantry whose heaviest weapons were the 75mm (2.9in) recoilless rifle and the 107mm (4.2in) chemical mortar.

As the North Korean juggernaut rolled towards them on the morning of 5 July 1950, the 105s opened up on a column of enemy T-34s. Accounts vary as to precisely how much armour-piercing ammunition was available to the US artillerymen; however, all would agree that the number was less than ten rounds. Accurately firing their guns at the oncoming communist armour, the gunners of the 52nd Battalion were dismayed to see their high-explosive rounds glancing harmlessly off the steel hulls of the tanks. When the gunners did use their armor-piercing rounds, they managed to destroy the lead T-34 with a direct hit. A second tank was disabled by a hit to the chassis which resulted in a thrown tread. The North Koreans did not

▲ **75mm M1A1 pack howitzer**

Eighth United States Army / 5th Ranger Infantry Company Airborne, 1952

Developed in the 1920s, the 75mm (2.9in) M1A1 pack howitzer could be disassembled rapidly and transported by mules across mountainous terrain. It could be dropped by parachute and provided airborne and light infantry units with much-needed firepower. Nearly 5000 were manufactured during World War II, and the weapon was in service until the 1960s.

Specifications

Crew: 6	Weight: 607.4kg (1339lb)
Calibre: 75mm (2.9in)	Range: 8787m (9610 yards)
Elevation: - 5 degrees to + 45 degrees	Muzzle velocity: 381m/sec (1250ft/sec)

Specifications

Crew: 7	Speed: 42km/h (26mph)
Weight: 26.01 tonnes (25.6 tons)	Road range: 201km (125 miles)
Length: 6.02m (19ft 9in)	Armament: 1 x 105mm (4.1in) M1A2 howitzer,
Width: 2.88m (9ft 5in)	plus 1 x 12.7mm (0.5in) HMG on 'pulpit' AA
Height: 2.54m (8ft 4in)	mount
Engine: 298kW (400hp) Continental R975 C1	

▲ **105mm Howitzer Motor Carriage (HMC) M7**

Eighth United States Army / 300th Armoured Field Artillery Battalion, 1952

Nicknamed the Priest by British troops due to the prominent machine-gun ring atop the chassis, which resembled a pulpit, the M7 105mm (4.1in) howitzer provided mobile artillery support for infantry.

halt, however, and overran the American positions. The following day, Lieutenant-Colonel Smith could muster only about 250 officers and soldiers. At least 150 men, including 15 soldiers of the 52nd Field Artillery, had been killed, wounded or captured.

Although the mission of Task Force Smith had been realistically only to slow the North Koreans down rather than stop the offensive in its tracks, a resulting lesson of its defeat became readily apparent. More artillery of all calibres would be needed, along with an ample supply of both high-explosive and armor-piercing shells.

Often enough, UN artillerymen were required to fight as infantry during the Korean War. This

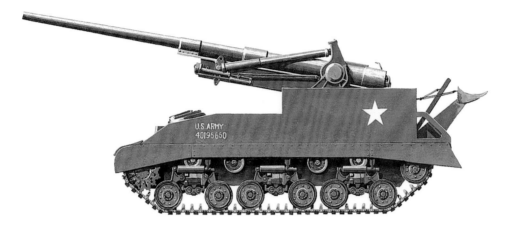

Specifications

Crew: 8
Weight: 40.64 tonnes (40 tons)
Length: 9.04m (29ft 9in)
Width: 3.15m (10ft 4in)
Height: 2.69m (8ft 10in)

Engine: 295kW (395hp) Continental 9-cylinder radial petrol
Speed: 39km/h (24mph)
Road range: 161km (100 miles)
Armament: 1 x 155mm (6.1in) M1A1 gun

▲ 155mm Gun Motor Carriage (GMC) M40

Eighth United States Army / 937th Field Artillery Battalion, 25th Infantry Division, 1951

Introduced late in World War II, the US M40 Gun Motor Carriage was built atop the modified chassis of the M4A3 Sherman tank. Its 155mm (6.1in) cannon provided mobile heavy artillery support for infantry.

Specifications

Crew: 7
Calibre: 280mm (11in)
Elevation: + 55 degrees
Weight: 77,383kg (170,600lb)
Range: 32km (20 miles)
Muzzle velocity: 762m/sec (2500ft/sec)

▼ M65 Atomic Cannon

Eighth United States Army, 1953

Nicknamed Atomic Annie, the M65 atomic cannon was test-fired in 1953 and delivered with US forces to both Europe and the Far East during the Cold War. During the first and only test of a nuclear shell fired from a cannon, the result was the detonation of a Type W-9 15-kiloton warhead at a distance of 11.3km (seven miles).

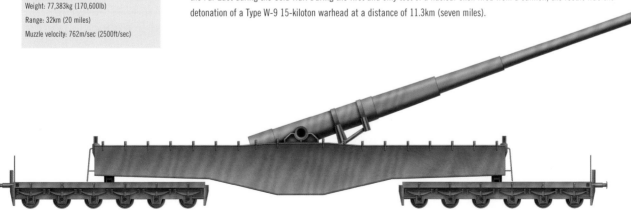

situation occurred for two main reasons. First, due to their lack of organic artillery, communist forces, particularly the Chinese, targeted UN artillery positions and observation posts for early seizure during offensive action. Second, sheer weight of numbers often required the artillerymen to directly defend themselves. Communist infantry was ordered to close with the enemy quickly, causing the artillerymen to cease their devastating fire for fear of hitting their own men.

Commonwealth forces

As part of the 1st Commonwealth Division, the artillery of the British Army and other nations also fought bravely during the Korean War. Several of the 25-pounder (87.6mm/3.45in) guns of 162 Battery, 16th Field Regiment, Royal New Zealand Artillery, fired 300 shells each in a single night during the Battle of Kapyong. At the Battle of the Imjin River in the spring of 1951, the 25-pounders of the 45th Field Regiment, Royal Artillery, and the 107mm (4.2in) mortars of the 170th Heavy Mortar Battery supported the 29th Infantry Brigade and the tanks of the 8th Hussars in a desperate bid to slow down a Chinese offensive. Other British artillery pieces of the Korean War included the 17-pounder (76.2mm/3in) gun, which had developed as the best Allied anti-tank gun of World War II, and the 140mm (5.5in) howitzer.

Numerous other countries fielded artillery batteries during the Korean War in response to the call to arms by the United Nations. One American gunner witnessed the destruction of a battery of Turkish 105mm (4.1in) guns. In the middle of an artillery duel, the Turkish gunners had not safely disposed of their used powder charges, piling them up in close proximity to the weapon while in action. When a direct hit from a North Korean shell destroyed all six of the Turkish guns and killed their crews, the discarded powder charges ignited as well, vaporizing the attached motor transport and ammunition stores.

As in many previous wars, it was often the artillery which inflicted the greatest number of casualties. During the Korean War, the superiority of UN artillery often spelled the difference between victory and defeat. The US and British weapons performed admirably amid harsh conditions, while forward observers risked their lives, often in exposed positions, to direct accurate fire on large concentrations of enemy troops. The US and Commonwealth artillery units were, quite possibly, the most proficient in the world at their craft. The Americans, in particular, had recognized their deficiencies in artillery between the world wars, working to perfect their tactics and improve their weapons with telling effect.

NKPA/PLA
1950–53

Both the North Korean People's Army and the Chinese People's Liberation Army relied on the Soviet Union for heavy weapons. Abandoned Japanese guns from World War II were also utilized by the communists during the Korean War.

ON 29/30 OCTOBER 1950, the 27th British Commonwealth Brigade and the 3rd Battalion, Royal Australian Regiment, fought a savage battle with strong North Korean forces at Chongju. Leading the advance of UN troops into North Korea and toward the mouth of the Yalu River, the British, Australians and supporting M4 Sherman tanks of the US 89th Tank Battalion were slowed by the infantry, tanks and self-propelled guns of the North Koreans.

In the gathering darkness, the North Koreans counterattacked with T-34 medium tanks mounting 76.2mm (3in) cannon and SU-76 self-propelled assault guns, which were similarly armed. Several times, the UN force was in danger of being overrun as North Korean soldiers penetrated their line and had to be systematically hunted down and killed. The communist tanks and self-propelled guns, however, were more problematic. Although the British and

Australian soldiers were able to knock out several of the armoured vehicles with shoulder-fired 88mm (3.5in) bazooka rockets, several North Korean units reached within ten metres (33ft) of the UN perimeter before mortar and 105mm (4.1in) artillery fire forced them to retire. Six rounds from a North Korean gun actually landed near the headquarters of the 3rd Battalion, Royal Australian Regiment, killing the commanding officer.

Soviet surplus

Although their effort failed, the North Koreans had skilfully employed their Soviet-built armoured vehicles, both types of which had been proven effective on the battlefields of the Eastern Front during World War II. The T-34 had become a legend, while the SU-76 had earned a reputation as a durable platform for the ZiS-3 76.2mm (3in) field gun. The SU-76 was second only to the T-34 in number of vehicles produced during World War II. As the Korean War progressed, both would become available to the North Koreans in greater numbers.

With the opening of hostilities, the North Korean People's Army had approximately 90,000 troops massed near the border with the South. Throughout the course of the Korean War, at least ten infantry divisions, an armoured brigade and a brigade of mechanized infantry took part in the fighting. The standard North Korean infantry division

was triangular in configuration and similar to the arrangement of a US division. Its three infantry regiments comprised three battalions which were supported by one battalion of 122mm (4.8in) howitzers and two battalions of 76.2mm (3in) field guns, each of Soviet manufacture. Anti-tank units and self-propelled artillery were also assigned at varying times. A relative few heavy 152mm (6in) howitzers were also in service.

The North Koreans suffered from a lack of artillery throughout the war, and at times their efficiency was poor. Even as their infantry and tanks rolled swiftly across the 38th parallel, the artillery of the North Korean 2nd Infantry Division was roughly handled by counterbattery action from South Korean artillery, which enjoyed a distinct advantage in fire control and accuracy. The 2nd Division artillery was unable to accompany the infantry during the initial offensive, and its losses were not made good until the following spring when it was withdrawn for training and to prepare newly arrived 76.2mm (3in) guns for use in the field.

Although the 4th Infantry Division had been responsible for the decimation of US Task Force Smith in the opening days of the war and continued its march on Seoul, outflanking and isolating South Korean units and elements of the US 24th Infantry Division, its combat efficiency eroded quickly as casualties mounted. Its divisional artillery

▲ **SU-76M SP assault gun**

North Korean People's Army / 105th Armoured Brigade

Second only to the T-34 in production during World War II, the SU-76M was the main production variant of the widely used self-propelled 76.2mm (3in) assault gun. The assault gun was based on the obselete T-70 chassis. Large numbers of these were used by communist forces in Korea.

Specifications	
Crew: 4	Engine: 2 x 52kW (70hp) GAZ 6-cylinder petrol
Weight: 10.8 tonnes (10.6 tons)	Speed (road): 45km/h (28mph)
Length: 4.88m (16ft)	Road range: 450km (280 miles)
Width: 2.73m (8ft 11.5in)	Armament: 1 x 76.2mm (3in) gun, plus
Height: 2.17m (7ft 1.4in)	1 x 7.62mm (0.3in) MG

component was reduced to a paltry 12 guns during the first six weeks of fighting.

Chinese mobilisation

Threatened by the advance of United Nations forces towards the Yalu River in the autumn and winter of 1950, the People's Republic of China responded with a veritable torrent of infantry, attacking sometimes in human waves which sent the enemy forces reeling southwards. The People's Liberation Army, like its North Korean counterpart, lacked strong organic artillery for much of the Korean War. When communist Chinese forces entered the conflict, their government had only months earlier declared victory over the Nationalists, whom they

had fought for years with only a brief respite during which their primary adversary had been the invading Japanese during World War II.

Those Chinese formations designated 'armies' were roughly equivalent in manpower to a US corps and included troop strength of up to 8500 men organized in three divisions. Their equipment, however, was either generally inferior or nonexistent. It has been reported that the typical Chinese army could field fewer than 40 artillery pieces of 76mm (3in) or larger in 1950. In some instances, the heaviest weapon available was the Soviet-made 120mm (4.7in) M1938 mortar.

Chinese industrial capacity was exceptionally low during the Korean War, and it is estimated

▲ 76.2mm Field Gun M1942 (ZiS-3)

North Korean People's Army / 2nd Artillery Regiment, 1950

The M1942 was one of the most famous field guns to emerge from World War II, and more than 100,000 examples of this 76.2mm (3in) weapon were produced in the Soviet Union from 1941 to 1945. Design work was undertaken in 1940, and it was manufactured in greater numbers than any other field artillery weapon of the Red Army. Stalin himself referred to the 76.2mm (3in) M1942 as a masterpiece.

Specifications

Crew: 7	Weight: 1116kg (2460lb)
Calibre: 76.2mm (3in)	Range: 13,300m (14,545 yards)
Elevation: - 5 degrees to + 37 degrees	Muzzle velocity: 680m/sec (2230ft/sec)

▲ 152mm Howitzer M1943 (D-1)

North Korean People's Army / 5th Artillery Regiment, 1951

By combining the carriage of the 122mm (4.8in) M1938 howitzer and the barrel of the 152mm (6.1in) M1938 howitzer, Soviet weapons designers were successful in an attempt to speed up artillery production during World War II. The result was the 152mm Howitzer M1943 (D-1), which features a distinctive muzzle brake on the barrel to assist the carriage in dealing with the recoil. The weapon was exported widely to Soviet client states.

Specifications

Crew: 8	Weight: 3600kg (7937lb)
Calibre: 152.4mm (6in)	Range: 12,400m (13,560 yards)
Elevation: - 3 degrees to + 63.5 degrees	Muzzle velocity: 508m/sec (1666ft/sec)

that enough heavy equipment – including field and self-propelled artillery – to equip 20 divisions was purchased from the Soviet Union. Meanwhile, the communists attempted to compensate for their lack of artillery via adapted tactics. Attacking in overwhelming numbers or at night minimized the effectiveness of United Nations artillery. Infiltrators slipped through enemy lines and emerged at predetermined times to attack artillery emplacements and command-and-control centres. Tunnels and bunkers were sometimes dug into hillsides to escape UN bombardment, and when the barrage lifted, the soldiers emerged to confront the attackers. If the high ground was taken, the communists disengaged, returning to their bunkers.

Then, if the effort was coordinated properly, North Korean or Chinese artillery would shell the United Nations soldiers in their exposed positions, forcing their withdrawal.

Today, the Korean peninsula remains a flashpoint of hostility between North and South. The United States maintains a contingent of approximately 29,000 troops in South Korea, including up to six air defence and field artillery battalions with the latest in sophisticated weaponry such as the MLRS multiple launch rocket system. By comparison, the North Korean People's Army is estimated to possess at least 2500 towed artillery pieces, 3500 self-propelled guns, and 4400 multiple launch rocket systems.

◀ ZPU-2 Type 58 anti-aircraft artillery

People's Liberation Army / 112th Mechanized Infantry Division, 1953

The People's Liberation Army of China fielded the ZPU-2 Type 58 heavy machine gun in the 1950s as an air defence weapon. A copy of the Soviet 14.5mm (0.57in) machine gun, it was deployed during the Korean War and with North Vietnamese and Viet Cong forces during the Vietnam War. A twin-barrelled weapon, the ZPU-2 was towed on a two-wheeled carriage. Its wheels were removed to place it in its firing position on a stabilized three-pronged platform.

Specifications

Crew: 5	Weight: 621kg (1369lb)
Calibre: 14.5mm (0.57in)	Range: 1400m (1531 yards)
Elevation: - 15 degrees to + 90 degrees	Muzzle velocity: 995m/sec (3264ft/sec)

▶ 120mm M1938 mortar

North Korean People's Army / 4th Infantry Division, 1950

Often towed by a light vehicle, the 120mm (4.7in) M1938 mortar could also be carried by infantry to provide close support. The weapon was fired either by a lanyard or by dropping the round down the muzzle and was deployed in combat during the Korean War and later in Vietnam. For many North Korean and Chinese infantry units, it was their heaviest weapon.

Specifications

Crew: 4	Weight: 280kg (617lb)
Calibre: 120mm (4.7in)	Range: 6000m (6560 yards)
Elevation: + 45 degrees to + 80 degrees	Muzzle velocity: 272m/sec (892ft/sec)

Chapter 10

Vietnam, 1959–75

One of the longest wars in human history,
the Vietnam conflict actually traced its origins to a curious
blend of Marxist theory and fervent nationalism, which
was championed by a charismatic leader, Ho Chi Minh.
During the course of the war, the North Vietnamese Army
became a highly skilled fighting force, proficient in the use
of Soviet-made artillery, while Viet Cong guerrillas in the
South conducted raids and kept the French and then the
Americans off balance. For their part, the armies of these
traditional powers were confronted with a new kind of
war. Strategy and tactics were modified, and the role of
artillery was adapted to the changing circumstances of
unconventional battle against a determined enemy.

◀ 'The thing'
Designed as multibarrel rapid fire tank killer, the M50 Ontos (Ancient Greek for 'the thing') proved to be
an excellent close fire support weapon for the US Marine Corps in Vietnam. It mounted six M40 106mm
(4.17in) recoilless rifles, which could be fired in rapid succession.

Introduction

As early as 1959, the government of the United States had determined that the spread of communism in Southeast Asia must be contained. France had vacated Indochina, its former colonial possession, and an increasing American military presence was undertaken.

B Y THE TIME AMERICAN advisers were on the ground with South Vietnamese forces, the ranks of the North Vietnamese Army and the Viet Cong guerrillas included combat veterans who had resolved to unite their country whatever the cost. Experts in hit-and-run tactics, fighting when and where they chose, communist insurgents would strike in ambush and then melt into the dense jungle before heavy firepower could be brought to bear against them. North Vietnamese troops were instructed to close swiftly with their enemy, hold tightly to his belt, and prevent US artillery from inflicting heavy casualties due to the risk of friendly fire.

Mobility and firepower

The terrain of Vietnam, with its flat coastal areas, Mekong Delta, dense jungle of the Central Highlands, and extensively irrigated rice paddies and farmland, presented obstacles to the free movement of artillery by both communist forces and the US and South Vietnamese armies. Towed and self-propelled artillery were utilized by each, but often these weapons were restricted in their areas of operation. Towed artillery, for example, was often unable to follow infantry on the

ground. Therefore, airmobile artillery, light enough to be transported by helicopter, was deemed a viable alternative by US military planners. The light 75mm (2.9in) pack howitzer and M1A2 (also designated the M101) and M102 105mm (4.1in) howitzers were moved by air in support of infantry operations.

Although US artillery had performed superbly during World War II and again during the Korean War, traditional tactics were also deemed ineffective in prosecuting a war against guerrilla forces and an organized army which had learned its lesson on the value of artillery during years of fighting against the French. In Vietnam, there was no defined front line. Therefore, offensive operations were frequently conducted by relatively small units which were dispersed across a wide area.

Traditional US doctrine rarely dictated direct artillery support by a unit smaller than a battalion, which generally consisted of three batteries. In Vietnam, each battery was placed within range of the other in order to provide mutual support for one another in case any of them were threatened. These batteries would then coordinate with the infantry battalions which were on the move. Fire control was

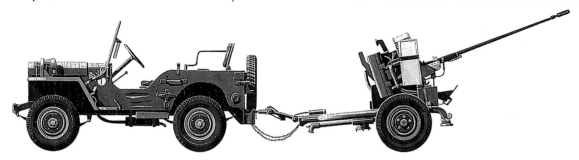

▲ **20mm Tarasque (53 T2) towed anti-aircraft gun**

French Far East Expeditionary Corps / 1st Colonial Far East Anti-Aircraft Artillery, 1953

Mounting the F1 20mm (0.79in) cannon, the Tarasque is a towed, single-barrelled anti-aircraft weapon developed for the French Army as a light gun which could be easily transported and deployed. From towing to deployment the elapsed time for an experienced crew is as little as 20 seconds. The weapon has also proven effective against ground targets.

Specifications

Crew: 3	Weight: 650kg (1433lb)
Calibre: 20mm (0.79in)	Range: 2000m (6560ft)
Elevation: - 8 degrees to + 83 degrees	Muzzle velocity: 1050m/sec (3445ft/sec)

▲ **Heavy howitzer**
The mobile M107 howitzer could provide long-range fire support at distances of up to 30 kilometres (18 miles).

pushed down from the battalion level to the battery commander in tactical situations. At times, a single battery was required to split into sections, and in such cases fire control followed to suit the lowest operational level.

Often, the heavy guns of the US divisional artillery, such as the 155mm (6.1in) and 203mm (8in) weapons, were employed in support situations where they were most needed. However, the great distances covered and the need to provide support to several dispersed units at one time potentially lessened the effectiveness of the artillery at the divisional level.

Inexperienced forces

As US forces prepared to leave Vietnam in the early 1970s, an aggressive programme of 'Vietnamization' was enacted in order to train and equip units of the South Vietnamese Army to defend themselves against the communists. The experience of Vietnamization as it relates to artillery may be considered a microcosm

of the comprehensive effort. At the end of 1970, a total of 1116 guns had been delivered to the South Vietnamese Army.

Extensive training had already taken place. However, the crucial element of time was working against both the South Vietnamese and their American instructors. It became the rule rather than the exception for South Vietnamese gunners to observe Americans servicing artillery rather than stepping into a hands-on role. On several occasions, the inexperienced South Vietnamese were unable to utilize their artillery effectively, and during the communist Easter Offensive of 1972, dozens of artillery pieces were abandoned to the enemy.

The North Vietnamese artillery during the Vietnam War included field weapons such as the proven Soviet 76.2mm (3in) gun of World War II design and the heavier 105mm (4.1in), 130mm (5.1in), and 152mm (6in) weapons, which were known for their considerable range and durability. Soviet-made 60mm (2.36in), 82mm (3.2in) and 120mm (4.7in) mortars were complemented by 57mm (2.2in) and 82mm (3.2in) recoilless rifles. Later in the war, 122mm (4.8in) rockets were commonly used.

US/ARVN forces
1959–75

Firepower and mobility were key elements of the US and South Vietnamese artillery deployment during the Vietnam War. Mutual support of infantry and field artillery units proved critical.

SOON AFTER US TROOPS began to arrive in Vietnam in significant numbers, it became readily apparent that they would be fighting a different kind of war – one without defined lines of battle or enemy positions which might be easily identified and attacked. Infantry tactics were refined with the concept of air mobility and other innovations, and supporting artillery followed suit.

Mobility was acknowledged as a critical element for success against an insurgency, particularly due to the fact that the enemy was resourceful, familiar with the countryside and usually chose the time and place of a confrontation. Counterinsurgency efforts required much larger numbers, with a preferred ratio of as many as ten US and South Vietnamese troops for every Viet Cong guerrilla, in order to reconnoitre areas for evidence of insurgent activity, to find and fix targets and to provide sufficient security. Mobile artillery was essential in bringing firepower to bear against an elusive enemy; however, mobile units were also potentially exposed to ambush or counterattack.

Typically, each brigade of US combat infantry sent to Vietnam was to be supported by two battalions of field artillery, one ordered in direct fire support of the infantry while the other provided an umbrella of area coverage or joined in as needed to leverage offensive operations or break up enemy attacks. During the course of the war, an extensive training programme was established to instruct South Vietnamese soldiers in the proper coordination and utilization of artillery assets. The results of this component of the Vietnamization programme were mixed at best. Although the South Vietnamese did perform well at times, their lack of training contributed to poor performance in the field. Therefore, the lion's share of the artillery in combat during the Vietnam War was fired and maintained by experienced US troops.

Mutual support

US and ARVN (Army of the Republic of Vietnam; the South Vietnamese Army) infantry rarely ventured outside the range of covering artillery, while it was evident that artillerymen were ill-equipped for or ill-disposed to defending themselves in the event of a direct attack by communist troops on their positions. In hostile country, both forward-positioned artillery and infantry

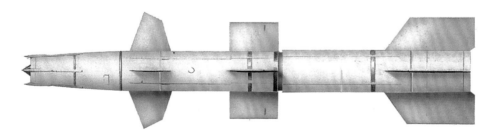

▲ **Talos surface-to-air missile**

US Navy / USS **Long Beach** *(Cruiser), 1966*

Talos was one of the first surface-to-air missile systems to be mounted aboard warships of the US Navy. Its development was undertaken in the late 1940s, and the system was in use until 1979. The Talos missile rode a radar beam towards its target and then engaged a radar homing system to reach the target. A variant was deployed in Vietnam to attack enemy SAM missile sites.

Specifications

Configuration: two-stage, kerosene fuel	Launch weight: 3450kg (7105lb)
Deployment: US Navy cruisers	Range: 120km (75 miles)
Length: 6.78m (22ft, 3in)	Launch preparation time: unknown
Diameter: 762mm (30in)	

could be vulnerable to an enemy which could mass substantial force and attack from virtually any direction.

Whether airlifted or transported on the ground, artillery and infantry required mutual support. Therefore, strong positions which accommodated both infantry and artillery were established in combat zones throughout Vietnam. Such positions came to be known as fire bases. Several considerations went into the selection of a fire base location, including the ability of the artillery to support manoeuvring infantry and the proximity of other field artillery, located at nearby fire bases within range of the subject location or at the divisional level to assist with fire support if necessary. Some of the most ferocious combat of the Vietnam War erupted with the defence of these forward positions.

AIR DEFENCE ARTILLERY UNITS IN VIETNAM, 1967			
Duster	Attached	Based	Area of operation
1st Battalion, 44th Artillery	Battery G, 65th Artillery (M55) Battery G, 29th Artillery (Searchlight)	Dong Ha Da Nang	Phu Bai in the south to Con Thien in the north and Khe Sanh in the west
5th Battalion, 2nd Artillery	Battery D, 71st Artillery (M55) Battery I, 29th Artillery (Searchlight)	Long Binh	North of Saigon
4th Battalion, 60th Artillery	Battery E, 41st Artillery (M55) Battery B, 29th Artillery (Searchlight)	Qui Nhon An Khe Tuy Hoa	

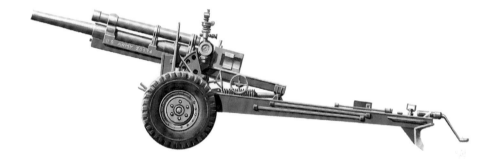

▲ M2A1 105mm Howitzer

US Army / 1st Battalion, 21st Field Artillery Regiment, 1966

Appearing in greater numbers than any other US artillery weapon of the Vietnam War, the 105mm (4.1in) M2A1 howitzer had already been battle-tested during World War II and in Korea. Its high rate of fire and ease of operation endeared the weapon to the artillerymen who served it. The M2A1 remains active today with the armed forces of numerous countries.

Specifications
Crew: 6
Calibre: 105mm (4.1in)
Elevation: - five degrees to + 66 degrees
Weight: 2030kg (4475lb)
Range: 11,200m (12,248 yards)
Muzzle velocity: 472m/sec (1548ft/sec)

Field Artillery Battery, United States Army, 1969

The US Army field artillery battery of the Vietnam era typically included four to six 105mm (4.1in) M2A1 howitzers. The howitzer is noted for its short barrel and steep firing angle, and in Vietnam these weapons served as critical direct fire support for infantry. The M2A1 was airmobile, facilitating the penetration of infantry units into hostile territory and the establishment of forward fire bases. During the course of the Vietnam War, the M2A1 was gradually replaced by the lighter 105mm (4.1in) M102.

5 x 105mm/4.1in Howitzer M2A1

The surrounding terrain and weapons available dictated the organization of the fire base. Infantry drew a close perimeter around the artillery firing positions to defend against large assaults and infiltrators. Usually 105mm (4.1in) and 155mm (6.1in) guns, in batteries of six, would be placed in a star formation, with five of the guns at each point of the star and the sixth in the centre. Other formations, depending on the number and calibre of the guns involved, included the box or diamond. Typically these were used with four-gun batteries of 203mm (8in) or 175mm (6.9in) weapons.

Base camp protection

Other positions, housing headquarters elements larger than the size of a battalion, were known as base camps. These were also protected by artillery, which often fired at distant targets to prevent enemy troops from closing with the command centre. Common missions also included firing on call when requested by manoeuvring infantry, disrupting enemy lines of supply and reinforcement, and direct fire against attacking enemy formations.

A variety of artillery was deployed by the United States in Vietnam, and though it had been in service for three decades, the 105mm (4.1in) M1A2 howitzer, which was later also designated the M101, continued to serve as the backbone of the American field artillery. First developed during the 1930s at

the recommendation of a review board which identified weaknesses in the performance of US artillery during World War I and the dependence on weapons produced in France and Great Britain, the M101 was virtually unchanged from its appearance in World War II. It provided a high rate of fire in direct support of infantry movement and was also supplied to the South Vietnamese forces in large numbers. Light enough to accompany infantry in the field, the M1A2/M101 could also be airlifted to forward positions.

In March 1966, the US began to deliver the improved M102 howitzer to front-line units in Vietnam, and elements of the 21st Field Artillery were the initial recipients of the weapon meant to replace the aging M101. Although it was initially received with scepticism by the veteran gunners who had come to love the M101, the M102 was cheaper to produce. Weighing approximately 1.52 tonnes (1.5 tons), it was considerably lighter and easier to transport, particularly by air, than its predecessor. The maximum rate of fire for the M102 was an impressive ten rounds per minute, while its sustained rate of fire was up to three rounds per minute at a range of 11,500m (12,576 yards).

The 155mm (6.1in) howitzer was fielded in the towed configuration as the M114A1 or deployed as the self-propelled M109. Although the towed version was considered past its prime, it did deliver

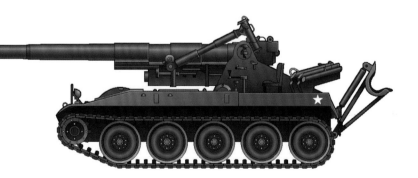

▲ M107 175mm SP gun

US Army / 8th Battalion, 4th Field Artillery Regiment, 1967

The M107 175mm (6.9in) self-propelled gun was often the heaviest weapon engaged in artillery support during the Vietnam War. Its heavy calibre and long range were utilized in area fire support missions and against command-and-control centres. The weapon was sometimes criticized due to perceived inconsistent accuracy at long range.

Specifications

Crew: 13	Engine: 302kW (405hp) General Motors 8V71T
Weight: 28,304kg (62,400lb)	diesel
Length: 6.46m (21ft 2in)	Speed: 80km/h (50 mph)
Width: 3.15m (10ft 4in)	Road range: 725km (450 miles)
Height: 3.47m (11ft 4in)	Armament: 1 x 175mm (6.9in) gun

▲ M109 155mm SP howitzer

Specifications

Crew: 6

Weight: 23,723kg (52,192lb)

Length: 6.612m (21ft 8.25in)

Width: 3.295m (10ft 9.75in)

Height: 3.289m (10ft 9.5in)

Engine: 302kW (405hp) Detroit Diesel

Model 8V-71T diesel

Speed: 56km/h (35mph)

Road range: 390km (240 miles)

Armament: 1 x 155mm (6.1in) howitzer, plus

1 x 12.7mm (0.5in) AA HMG

1st Infantry Division / 1st Squadron, 4th Cavalry Regiment, 1967

The M109 self-propelled howitzer, mounting a 155mm (6.1in) main weapon, was first delivered to the US Army in 1962 and served in numerous armoured formations throughout the Vietnam War, adding heavy artillery capability to combined-arms operations.

3rd Battalion, 13th Field Artillery Regiment, Fire Support Base 'Stuart', June 1969

Deployed in forward positions such as fire-support bases, field artillery battalions sometimes combined a complement of 18 self-propelled M109 155mm (6.1in) howitzers organized in three batteries and a single battery of towed 105mm (4.1in) M2A1 howitzers. The mobile M109 was sometimes able to provide heavy, direct fire support for infantry. Meanwhile, the towed 105s offered a protective umbrella of artillery coverage to units within range. In turn, infantrymen guarded the fire-base perimeter against ground attack.

Battery A (M109 SP howitzers)

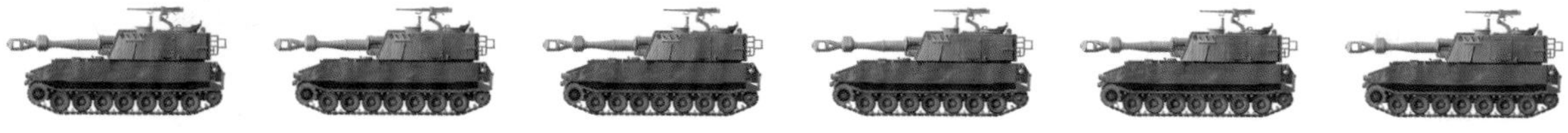

Battery B (M109 SP howitzers)

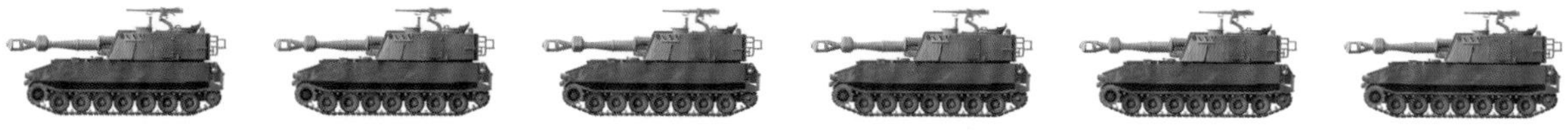

Battery C (M109 SP howitzers)

Battery D (105mm/4.1in howitzers)

effective supporting fire and was called upon at times to participate in direct fire against enemy formations. Surprisingly, it was light enough for air transport. However, it was far less manoeuvrable than the self-propelled M109, which could provide powerful direct fire support on the spot. With a crew of six, the operational range of the M109 was 390km (240 miles). The most widely used self-propelled howitzer in the world in the 1960s, the M109's 155mm (6.1in) weapon could fire a heavy projectile 14,600m (15,967 yards). It was powered by a Model 8V-71T 302kW (405hp) Detroit diesel engine.

Larger self-propelled artillery, such as the M107 175mm (6.9in) gun and the M110 8in (203mm) howitzer were the most powerful weapons of their kind deployed by the US to Vietnam. The maximum range of the M107's heavy weapon was 33,000m (36,089 yards), and it shared a common chassis with the M110, which fired up to an effective range of 17,000m (18,591 yards). The M107 and M110 were both powered by a 302kW (405hp) eight-cylinder General Motors diesel engine. The M108 105mm (4.1in) self-propelled gun was developed in the early 1950s and believed too light to effectively support infantry in Vietnam. However, some of these weapons were supplied to a few units and fired in general area support missions.

US air defence artillery consisted of several weapons systems. The M42A1 Duster mounted twin 40mm (1.57in) Bofors cannon and a 7.62mm (0.3in) machine gun atop the chassis of the M41 Walker Bulldog light tank. The main weapons could fire at a cyclical rate of 120 rounds per minute to a ceiling of 5000m (16,404ft). The M55 Quad 50 was known to both friend and foe as the Whispering Death and consisted of a quadruple mount of four Browning M2 .50-caliber (12.7mm/0.5in) machine guns with a rate of fire up to 1500 rounds per minute. These weapons were sometimes called upon to deliver direct fire against enemy ground forces. The effect was predictably devastating.

The M168 Gatling gun was mounted atop the chassis of the M113 armoured personnel carrier, designated the M163 Vulcan Air Defense System and deployed to Vietnam; however, the system proved less than satisfactory in jungle conditions and its high silhouette was particularly vulnerable to communist rocket-propelled grenades (RPGs).

The HAWK (Homing All the Way Killer) anti-aircraft missile system, developed during the early 1950s, was deployed to Vietnam with several battalions of four batteries each. Its mobile configuration was mounted on a trailer with a hard point holding three missiles in position. In addition to field, heavy and air

▲ **M110A2 SP howitzer**

15th Field Artillery Regiment / Battery A, 7th Battalion, 1969

The M110 self-propelled howitzer was the largest weapon of its kind in the US arsenal during the Vietnam era. The 203mm (8in) main weapon of the M110A2 was distinguished from the M110A1 model by its double-baffle muzzle brake.

Specifications

Crew: 5	Engine: 302kW (405hp) Detroit Diesel V8
Weight: 28,350kg (62,512lb)	Speed: 56km/h (35mph)
Length: 5.72m (18ft 9in)	Road range: 520km (325 miles)
Width: 3.14m (10ft 4in)	Armament: 1 x 203mm (8in) howitzer
Height: 2.93m (9ft 8in)	Radio: n/a

defence artillery, infantry units were armed with mortars and recoilless rifles, while aerial rocket artillery also came into its own in Vietnam. The 69.85mm (2.75in) rockets were often mounted in pods of 48 aboard helicopters and provided tremendous ground support.

US and South Vietnamese artillery units were severely tested on a number of occasions. During the siege of Khe Sanh, artillery reinforcements were flown in regularly. At the height of the battle, nearly 50 artillery pieces, mostly the ubiquitous M101 105mm

(4.1in), and up to 100 six-barrel Ontos mounted or single 106mm (4.17in) recoilless rifles were engaged. East of Khe Sanh, 175mm (6.9in) artillery at Camp Carroll also joined in the effort to hold the base against repeated communist attacks which occurred over an 11-week period while the base itself was under relentless fire from North Vietnamese artillery. During the bitter struggle at Khe Sanh, US Marine artillerymen fired nearly 159,000 rounds in defence of the base, which was later abandoned.

▲ M56 Scorpion SP gun

US Army / 101st Airborne Division, 1968

Designed as a light, airmobile anti-tank gun which packed the offensive firepower of a tank, the M56 was manufactured by Cadillac from 1953 to 1959. Introduced to Vietnam with the 82nd and 101st Airborne Divisions, the M56 proved a disappointment in action as the chassis was insufficient for the recoil of the main 90mm (3.5in) gun.

Specifications

Crew: 4	Engine: 150kW (200hp) Continental 6-cylinder
Weight: 7000kg (15,400lb)	petrol
Length: 5.84m (19ft 2in)	Speed: 45km/h (28mph)
Width: 2.577m (8ft 5in)	Road range: 225km (140 miles)
Height: 2.067m (6ft 9in)	Armament: 1 x 90mm (3.5in) gun

Specifications

Crew: 3	Engine: 108kW (145hp) General Motors
Weight: 8640kg (19,051lb)	302 petrol
Length: 3.82m (12ft 6in)	Speed: 48km/h (30mph)
Width: 2.6m (8ft 6in)	Road range: 240km (150 miles)
Height: 2.13m (6ft 11in)	Armament: 6 x 106mm (4.17in) recoilless rifles;
	4 x 12.7mm (0.5in) M8C spotting rifles

▲ Rifle, Multiple 106mm, Self-propelled, M50 Ontos

1st Marine Division / 1st Anti-Tank Battalion, 1969

An airmobile tank destroyer, the M50 Ontos was lightly armoured but offered heavy firepower with six 106mm (4.17in) recoilless rifles and was utilized primarily as an infantry-support weapon in Vietnam. The M50 was withdrawn from service by the mid-1970s.

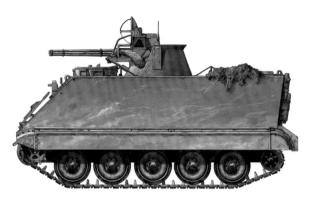

▲ M167 Vulcan Air Defense System (VADS) towed short-range anti-aircraft gun

US Army / 82nd Airborne Division, 1970

Designed for easy transport by air, road or rail, the M167 Vulcan Air Defense System (a towed version of the M163) was deployed with US forces for nearly 30 years. Its six-barrel, 20mm (0.79in) M168 Gatling gun was well suited to defence against low-flying enemy aircraft. The system was guided by radar, and targeting was accomplished via fire-control computer.

Specifications

Crew: 4	Weight: 1569kg (3458lb)
Calibre: 20mm (0.79in)	Range: 1200m (3935ft)
Elevation: - 5 degrees to + 80 degrees	Muzzle velocity: 1030m/sec (3380ft/sec)

▲ M163 Vulcan Air Defense System (VADS)

US Army / 5th Battalion, 2nd Artillery, 1969

The self-propelled version of the Vulcan Air Defense System, the M163 combined the 20mm (0.79in) Gatling gun with the chassis of the M113 armoured personnel carrier. These units were designed for either anti-aircraft or ground-defence duties, and their rate of fire could be adjusted depending on the type of target.

Specifications

Crew: 4	Engine: 161kW (215hp) Detroit 6V-53 6-cylinder
Weight: 12,310kg (27,082lb)	diesel
Length: 4.86m (15ft 11in)	Speed: 67km/h (42mph)
Width: 2.85m (9ft 4in)	Road range: 482.8km (300 miles)
Height: 2.736m (9ft 11in)	Armament: 1 x 20mm (0.79in) M168 Gatling gun

Specifications

Crew: 6	Engine: 373kW (500hp) Continental AOS-895-3
Weight: 22,452kg (49,394lb)	6-cylinder air-cooled petrol
Length: 6.35m (20ft 10in)	Speed: 72.4km/h (45mph)
Width: 3.225m (10ft 7in)	Road range: 161km (100 miles)
Height: 2.847m (9ft 4in)	Armament: 2 x 40mm (1.57in) anti aircraft guns,
	plus 1 x 7.62mm (0.3in) MG

▲ M42 SP anti-aircraft gun

3rd Marine Division / 1st Battalion, 44th Artillery Regiment

The self-propelled M42 Duster anti-aircraft gun was developed during the 1950s and deployed to Vietnam in response to disappointing results from early anti-aircraft missile systems. The 40mm (1.57in) guns of the M42 also proved outstanding in an infantry-support role.

North Vietnamese Army (NVA)
1964–75

Supplied by both the Soviet Union and the People's Republic of China, North Vietnamese military leaders understood the capabilities of efficient artillery and utilized it to its fullest wherever possible.

AS THE UNITED STATES escalated its military involvement in Vietnam, the communist forces under General Vo Nguyen Giap had been at war for years. Giap's veterans remembered the stunning victory of the Viet Minh against the French airhead at Dien Bien Phu in 1954. Their memories were of a systematic reduction of the French capacity to resist and that this had been achieved in large part by the concentrated, sustained fire of artillery.

Taking control of the high ground surrounding the French positions, the communists had manhandled heavy artillery into the surrounding hills and pounded the French without ceasing. When he realized that his own guns were in no position to reply effectively, the French artillery commander committed suicide.

Soviet style

Through combat experience, the North Vietnamese were well aware of the power of artillery and respected the devastating potential of American guns. Therefore, when possible, they positioned their own guns just outside the range of the American weapons. While the US 105mm (4.1in) and 155mm (6.1in) weapons reached out to 11,200m (12,248 yards) and 14,600m (16,000 yards) respectively, the Soviet-made 130mm (5.1in) and 152mm (6in) guns had longer ranges at 14,995m (16,399 yards) and 31,000m (33,902 yards). Thus the North Vietnamese guns were often able to take US and South Vietnamese positions under fire with little concern for counterbattery activity.

Until the mid-1960s, the North Vietnamese Army depended heavily on infantry weapons such as mortars and recoilless rifles. Although these remained significant and were actually included in North Vietnamese and Viet Cong artillery units on a limited basis, access to heavier weapons increased. Older model guns, some dating to the French colonial period and the Japanese occupation during World War II, were replaced or augmented by the 76.2mm (3in) field piece, and guns of 85mm (3.3in), 100mm (3.9in), 122mm (4.8in) and larger calibre. North Vietnamese artillery regiments were generally equipped with 36 guns, including at least 24 guns or howitzers of up to 105mm (4.1in) and as many as 12 130mm (5.1in) or 152mm (6in) weapons.

Captured hardware

The North Vietnamese and Viet Cong training programmes also included lessons on the operation of captured US artillery pieces. The use of rockets increased steadily as the war progressed. These included Soviet 122mm (4.8in) and 140mm (5.5in) and Chinese 107mm (4.2in) weapons. Each of these was ideally suited for attacking large targets, although it became imperative for the shooters to scoot away quickly since US observers might pinpoint the exhaust trails of the rockets and call for retaliatory fire.

A North Vietnamese training manual explained that the 'main purpose of firing rockets is to attack objectives of large area, usually 400 meters by 400 meters, such as enemy strongholds, airfields, storage areas, or towns and to support the infantry and to attack distant objectives that may affect the combat mission of the infantry.'

One North Vietnamese officer who was taken prisoner commented during interrogation that the rockets were to be used in 'hit-and-run tactics adhering to the principles of guerrilla warfare. No more than five rounds were to be fired from a single tripod launcher … and evacuation from the scene could usually be accomplished within five minutes.'

Ke Sahn

Such was the case on numerous occasions as Viet Cong infiltrators launched rockets against such major US installations as Da Nang air base and the forward combat base at Khe Sanh near the Laotian border. During the 77-day siege of Khe Sanh from

January until April 1968, North Vietnamese guns pounded the US positions on an almost daily basis. Often this artillery fire was from communist guns situated across the Laotian frontier. At Khe Sanh, the North Vietnamese undoubtedly believed that a victory on the scale of Dien Bien Phu was within reach. Artillery had proven decisive 14 years earlier, and the pounding of Khe Sanh and US Marine positions in the surrounding hills was relentless. Estimates of the number of North Vietnamese shells of all calibres fired at Khe Sanh top 11,000. During one eight-hour period, more than 1300 shells, mostly 130mm (5.1in) and 152mm (6in), were fired.

▲ **Type 54-1 SP 122mm gun**

North Vietnamese Army / 304th Division, 1972

Based on a modified chassis of the YW-31 armoured personnel carrier and mounting a variant of the Soviet 122mm (4.8in) howitzer developed during the 1930s, the Type 54-1 SP 122mm (4.8in) gun was supplied to the North Vietnamese Army in limited numbers. The weapon was used in support of infantry attacks, providing mobile direct fire.

Specifications

Crew: 7	Engine: 192kW (257hp) Deutz 6150L 6-cylinder
Weight: 15.4 tonnes (34,000lb)	diesel
Length: 5.65m (18ft 6in)	Speed: 56km/h (35mph)
Width: 3.06m (10ft)	Road range: 500km (310 miles)
Height: 2.68m (8ft 9in)	Armament: 1 x 122mm (4.8in) howitzer

Specifications

Crew: 5	System combat weight: varied
Calibre: 132mm (5.2in)	Range: 8500m (9300 yards)
Rocket length: 1.42m (53.9in)	Rate of fire: multiple in 7–10 seconds
Rocket weight: 42.5kg (93.7lb)	

▲ **BM-13 Katyusha rocket launcher**

North Vietnamese Army / 4th Regiment Rocket Battalion, 1968

Of World War II vintage, the Soviet-built BM-13 rocket launcher was a platform for the famous Katyusha rocket which was prominent on the Eastern Front. The majority of the BM-13 systems were mounted atop ZiS-6 6X4 trucks. Several later variants of the famous system were produced in the coming decades.

Anti-Aircraft Battery, North Vietnamese Army, 1970

The standard North Vietnamese Army self-propelled anti-aircraft battery included four ZSU-57-2 guns mounting twin 57mm (2.2in) cannon. The first Soviet weapon of its type to see combat on a large scale since World War II, the ZSU-57-2 fired at a sustained rate of 70 rounds per minute. Later replaced by the ZSU-23-4, the system was widely exported to Warsaw Pact countries and Soviet client states in the Middle East and Africa.

Battery (4 x ZSU-57-2 SP anti-aircraft guns)

Air defence curtain

Although the SAM 1 and SAM 2 surface-to-air missiles received a lot of attention in the Western media, light anti-aircraft weapons were responsible for shooting down far more US aircraft than the high-profile missiles. At Khe Sanh, the light-weapons fire was so intense that resupply aircraft were forced to drop materiel by parachute and maintain altitude rather than risk a landing.

Among the most lethal anti-aircraft weapons in the North Vietnamese order of battle were the ZSU-57-2 and ZSU-23-4 self-propelled guns. The former mounted a pair of 57mm (2.2in) cannon atop the chassis of the T-54 tank, while the ZSU-23-4 Shilka was a quadruple mount of 23mm (0.9in)

cannon. Meant to replace the older ZSU-57-2, the Shilka incorporated the modified chassis of the PT-76 amphibious tank.

During the war, the North Vietnamese and Viet Cong also deployed large numbers of 37mm (1.45in) anti-aircraft guns, of both Soviet and Chinese manufacture, along with the 14.5mm (0.57in) ZPU-4 heavy machine gun, which was effective against low-flying helicopters.

The Vietcong were also supplied with the Chinese-built Type 63 anti-aircraft gun. Mounting twin 37mm (1.45in) guns on the hull of a T-34 tank, the Type 63 proved inneffective as the gun had to be manually elevated and loaded: a severe drawback against fast, low-flying aircraft.

Specifications

Crew: 6	Engine: 372kW (493hp) V-2 V12 diesel
Weight: n/k	Speed: 50km/h (31mph)
Length: 5.9m (19ft 7in)	Road range: 300km (186 miles)
Width: 3m (9ft 10in)	Armament: 2 x 37mm (1.45in) Type 63 AA guns,
Height: 2.6m (8ft 6in)	plus 1 x 7.62mm (0.3in) DT MG

▲ **Type 63 SP anti-aircraft gun**

North Vietnamese Army / 24th Viet Cong Anti-Aircraft Battalion, 1966

Combining the chassis of the Soviet T-34 medium tank and an open turret with a pair of 37mm (1.5in) anti-aircraft cannon, this Chinese-produced self-propelled anti-aircraft weapon was mediocre at best. During the 1960s, the Type 63 was supplied to both North Vietnamese Army and Viet Cong guerrilla forces.

Chapter 11

Cold War in Asia

The phenomenon of the Cold War shaped
the formation and government of nations across the globe
for half a century. The power vacuum created at the end of
World War II gave rise to movements of self-determination,
and the Third World was born. Developing nations in Asia
and elsewhere shook off the yoke of colonial rule, often
through bloody, prolonged military conflict. They settled
old scores and vied for possession of rich natural resources.
National armies and guerrilla forces were supplied by the
superpowers and utilized weapons abandoned by Allied
and Japanese forces following World War II. Prominent
among these were field guns, heavy artillery
and air defence weapons.

◀ **Barrage gun**
The 155mm (6.1in) L/45 Type 89 towed artillery gun was built in China to serve the needs of both the
People's Liberation Army and the export market. It was based on Western technology, being similar to the
Austrian GHN-45 and firing a Western-standard calibre shell.

Introduction

Artillery, more than any other weapon system, offered the armies of Asian nations the ability to alter the course of a battle and even an entire war.

A N IRRESISTIBLE TIDE of armed conflict swept the continent of Asia during the latter half of the twentieth century. Nationalism, ideology, religious fervour and the global ambitions of the Soviet Union and the United States contributed to instability in the region. With the ascent of its communist regime in 1949, the People's Republic of China gained a prominent role in the geopolitical future of the continent as well.

Spheres of influence, control of natural resources, the security of national borders, ethnic tensions and the abstract ideals of freedom versus totalitarianism made Asia a tinderbox and a proving ground for modern weapons systems developed by the superpowers and other arms-exporting nations. The proliferation of nuclear and chemical weapons in the region increased the likelihood of open war, which erupted with regularity, and in some cases remains unresolved to this day.

Proxies and projectiles

Among the detritus of World War II lay hundreds of thousands of abandoned artillery pieces and millions of rounds of ammunition. Often, Japanese forces which were vacating the Asian continent turned their weapons over to Allied authorities or local governments or simply walked away from them. Allied weapons had also been abandoned far and wide. These provided the seeds of the artillery corps of new national armies, guerrilla forces and militias.

Soon enough, these weapons, particularly examples of the venerable Japanese Type 35 75mm (2.9in) gun, were in action on the Korean peninsula in the 1950s and during the Vietnam conflict which persisted for 30 years after the eviction of the Japanese from Indochina. Simultaneously, advancing technology enhanced the mobility and accuracy of heavy guns, while radar-controlled air defence artillery proved deadly, and tactical missiles of various types were introduced.

Driven by the perceived exigencies of the Cold War, the United States and the Soviet Union embarked upon a calculated programme of arms sales and support for their proxy nations and fighting forces in Asia. The US was intent on curbing the spread of communism, while the Soviets took advantage of a volatile blend of previously repressed nationalism and Marxist philosophy to expand the limits of their influence. The ubiquitous Soviet-made 76.2mm (3in) field gun, produced in greater numbers than any other artillery piece in World War II, remains active to this day and was supplied to Soviet clients in great numbers, while the 152mm (6.1in) gun-howitzer was also in common use. The US 105mm (4.1in) M2A1 howitzer was a workhorse in Asia for decades, as vast quantities were exported to the armies of friendly countries.

By the 1980s, a report published by the US Central Intelligence Agency disclosed the magnitude

▲ **Type 75**

The Type 75 multiple rocket launcher mounts 32 130mm (5.1in) rockets on top of the hull of a Type 73 armoured personnel carrier. Introduced in the mid 1970s, in the early twenty-first century the Japanese armed forces were still operating more than 60 of these vehicles.

▲ **Indian WMD**

Prithvi truck-mounted missiles are paraded on India's Republic Day. The Prithvi was India's first indigenously developed ballistic missile. First test-fired in 1988, it is not a particularly sophisticated missile, incorporating propulsion technology from the Soviet SA-2 surface-to-air missile.

of the Cold War involvement of the superpowers, including their arms sales on the Asian continent. In 1980 alone, the report stated, the Soviet Union had supplied $7 billion in military aid, particularly arms, to Third World countries, while more than 50,000 Soviet military advisers had been deployed around the world to instruct the recipients in the efficient use of these weapons.

Although the report had been generated by the CIA, the United States was also active in the global arms trade along with most of the developed countries of Eastern and Western Europe. A black market in arms thrived in Asia, particularly with the rise of insurgencies, civil war and revolution.

Elsewhere in Asia, the People's Republic of China slowly weaned itself away from dependence on Soviet artillery and embarked on a programme of developing

and producing its own such weapons, some of which were nearly identical to original Soviet designs. Territorial disputes between Muslim Pakistan and predominantly Hindu India boiled over into major conflicts twice during the Cold War, pitting large quantities of US and Soviet weaponry against each other; and some of the largest land battles since World War II took place between the Pakistani and Indian armies.

Meanwhile, the Shah of Iran was deposed, and the Islamic fundamentalist power structure which succeeded him came into bloody conflict with the Baathist regime of Saddam Hussein of Iraq. Large quantities of artillery, both towed and self-propelled, were engaged, and widespread reports of the use of chemical weapons were confirmed. Many of these lethal weapons were delivered by modified artillery shells.

China

1950–PRESENT

The People's Republic of China fields the largest army in the world and contains numerous artillery divisions assigned to group armies, as well as unattached artillery regiments of various types.

ONE OF THE PRE-EMINENT NUCLEAR POWERS on the world stage, the People's Republic of China was actively involved in military operations in Southeast Asia during the Cold War, intervening on behalf of North Korea during the bitter Korean War; fighting periodically with neighbouring Vietnam during border disputes and for control of the Spratly and Paracel islands in the South China Sea; and clashing with the Soviet Union on its northern border during the late 1960s.

During the Cold War, the People's Liberation Army evolved significantly, from a low-technology force which had conducted human-wave assaults during the Korean War to a high-tech mechanized army competing for global arms sales and fielding weapons systems, including artillery, on a par with those of other nations. Following the victory of Mao's communist forces over the Nationalists of Chiang Kai-shek in 1948, the Chinese depended largely on Soviet weapons and equipment, particularly systems which had been produced in great quantities during World War II.

Gradually, however, Chinese engineers began to develop their own designs and to modify and adapt their own weapons as needed. For example, the Type 63 self-propelled anti-aircraft gun married the chassis of the famed Soviet T-34 medium tank with an open turret and a pair of 37mm (1.45in) cannon.

By the 1980s, the Chinese Harbin First Machinery Building Group Ltd, previously known as state-run 674 Factory, was producing such weapons as the Type 83 self-propelled 152mm (6in) gun-howitzer, a combination of the towed Type 66 artillery piece and the Type 321 artillery chassis.

The Type 89 155mm (6.1in) field gun-howitzer, also known as the PLL01, was based on an original design known as the CG-45 by Gerald Bull's Space Research Corporation. The Type 89 was introduced in 1987 and was the first Chinese field gun to utilize the Western standard 155mm (6.1in) shell rather than the Soviet standard 122mm (4.8in) projectile. Its existence was originally noted by Western observers during the Chinese National Day military parade in 1999, and while only a relative handful of them are confirmed to have been built, it is known that towed and truck-mounted versions are operational.

Early artillery

Among the earlier light artillery systems manufactured by the Chinese was the Type 63 107mm (4.2in) rocket launcher, which was introduced in 1963. The towed weapon comprised a dozen rocket tubes and provided intense direct fire support to infantry regiments in the field in companies of six units, which were attached to field artillery battalions. Spurred by the need to produce

▶ **Type 63 107mm multiple rocket launcher**

People's Liberation Army / 121st Infantry Division, 1965

In service with the People's Liberation Army for over 30 years, the Type 63 107mm (4.2in) multiple rocket launcher was manufactured in large numbers and proved to be a durable and versatile weapon. Requiring three minutes to reload, its rate of fire is 12 rounds in seven to nine seconds.

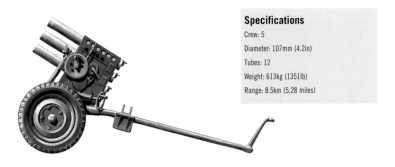

Specifications

Crew: 5

Diameter: 107mm (4.2in)

Tubes: 12

Weight: 613kg (1351lb)

Range: 8.5km (5.28 miles)

▲ CSS-1 ballistic missile

PLA / 51 Base / 806 Brigade, 1965

China's first home-developed ballistic missile, the Dongfeng-2, known to NATO as the CSS-1, was undertaken by the Chinese Academy of Launch Vehicle Technology in the late 1950s. A variant, the Dongfeng-2A, was successfully launched in June 1964. The weapon was withdrawn from service by the 1980s.

Specifications

Configuration: single-stage, liquid fuel
Deployment: believed road-mobile on towed
trailer
Length: 20.61m (67ft 7in)

Body diameter: 1.65m (5ft 5in)
Launch weight: 31,900kg (31.4 tons)
Range: believed 1250km (776.71 miles)
Launch preparation time: 120–180 inutes

▲ CSS-2 ballistic missile

PLA / 51 Base / 810 Brigade, 1975

A single-stage intermediate-range ballistic missile, the CSS-2 is known to the Chinese as the Dongfeng-3. Designed specifically to bring US military bases in Southeast and East Asia within range of the Chinese nuclear arsenal, the Dongfeng-3 entered service in 1971 and was improved in the early 1980s. Some of these missiles have been conventionally armed, and the missile's nuclear payload is up to 3000 kilotons.

Specifications

Configuration: single-stage, liquid fuel
Deployment: launch pad and road mobile
Length: 21.2m (69ft 6in)
Diameter: 2.25m (7ft 5in)

Launch weight: 64,000kg (63 tons)
Range: 2500km (1553.43 miles)
Launch preparation time: 120–180 inutes

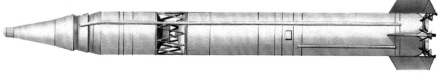

▲ CSS-3 ballistic missile

PLA / 55 Base / 814 Brigade, 1984

The CSS-3, or Dongfeng-4, intermediate-range ballistic missile entered service with the Second Artillery Corps of the People's Liberation Army in the early 1980s. The missile carries a warhead of up to 3000 kilotons, and it is estimated that up to 20 of them are currently deployed in China. The Dongfeng-4 rocket was used to send China's first satellite into orbit in 1970.

Specifications

Configuration: two-stage, believed liquid fuel
Deployment: silo and semi-mobile (towed trailer)
Length: 28m (91ft 10in)
Diameter: 2.25m (7ft 4in)

Launch weight: 82,000kg (80.7 tons)
Range: 4750km (2951.51 miles)
Launch preparation time: 3–5 hours (mobile);
2–3 hours (silo)

▲ CSS-4 ballistic missile

PLA / 54 Base / 801 Brigade, 1980

A two-stage intercontinental ballistic missile, the CSS-4 is known in China as the Dongfeng-5. Requirements for an ICBM capable of reaching targets in North America were issued by the Chinese government in 1965, and the first test flight was conducted in September 1971. The weapon carries a single 3000-kiloton warhead. Three bases are known to house the Dongfeng-5, each with up to ten missiles.

Specifications

Configuration: two-stage, liquid fuel
Deployment: silo or launch pad
Length: 33m (108ft 3in)
Diameter: 3.4m (11ft 2in)

Launch weight: 183,000kg (180.1 tons)
Range: 12,000km (7456 miles)
Launch preparation time: 3–5 hours (launch
pad); 1–2 hours (silo)

its own weaponry and to take advantage of arms sales to other countries, the Chinese government has supported investment in private ventures, such as China North Industries Corporation, known as NORINCO in the West, to develop and produce modern weapons systems. Established in 1980 and rigidly controlled by the country's Commission on Science, Technology and Industry for National Defence, NORINCO manufactures anti-aircraft, anti-missile and other artillery systems.

Specifications

Crew: 5	Speed: 56km/h (35mph)
Weight: 32,000kg (70,560lb)	Road range: 450km (280 miles)
Length: 6.1m (20ft)	Armament: 1 x 155mm (6.1in) WAC-21 howitzer,
Width: 3.2m (10ft 6in)	plus 1 x 12.7mm (0.5in) anti-aircraft MG
Height: 2.59m (8ft 6in)	Radio: n/k
Engine: 391.4kW (525hp) diesel	

▲ **155/45 NORINCO SP howitzer**

People's Liberation Army / 1st Armoured Division, 1997

The NORINCO-designed PLZ 155/45 self-propelled howitzer was conceived in the early 1990s for the Chinese armed forces and the export market. Its 155mm (6.1in) howitzer was modified by Chinese designers from an Austrian weapon. The vehicle also mounts a 12.7mm (0.5in) anti-aircraft machine gun and grenade launchers.

PLA Self-Propelled Artillery Battalion, 1997

The People's Liberation Army self-propelled artillery battalion consists of 18 gun-howitzers divided into three companies of six weapons each. The primary function is infantry support, although a combined-arms strategy is emerging. The firepower of the 155mm (6.1in) guns is also available in numerous unattached armoured regiments; however, organic motorized infantry support is considered to be lacking and may cause undue vulnerability to armoured vehicles and artillery on the battlefield.

1 Company (6 x 155mm/45 SP howitzers)

2 Company (6 x 155mm/45 SP howitzers)

3 Company (6 x 155mm/45 SP howitzers)

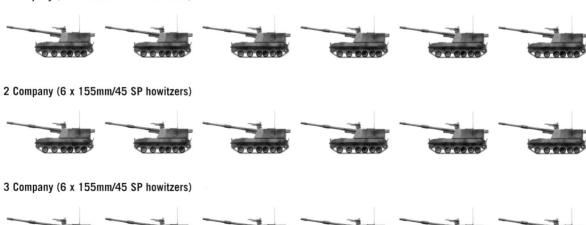

The People's Liberation Army grew in numbers and strength through the 1980s, and by 1989 it was estimated to include up to 35 army groups with 118 infantry, 13 armoured, 17 artillery and 16 anti-aircraft artillery divisions. These were augmented by a large number of support regiments and battalions, many of which included field and anti-aircraft artillery. The armoured divisions often included self-propelled assault and artillery weapons as well.

In the late 1990s, the army was restructured, with a number of People's Liberation Army units being transferred to the People's Armed Police, which had been created in 1983, or relegated to the equivalent of Category B or 'national guard' status. At the same time, a doctrine of combined arms was instituted, revising an old system in which an army division included approximately 12,000 soldiers and contained an organic artillery regiment and anti-aircraft artillery battalion along with an armoured regiment and three infantry regiments. The new arrangement included 'group armies' of four divisions totalling nearly 180,000 troops and containing artillery support at appropriate levels. With the new alignment, the combined number of artillery divisions in the People's Liberation Army was reduced from 33 to eight.

Specifications

Crew: 4

Calibre: 130mm (5.1 inch)

Weight: 14,000kg (13.77 tons)

Rocket length: 1.063m (41.85in)

Rocket weight: 32.80kg (72.3lb)

Warhead: high-explosive fragmentation;
  14.73kg (32.47lb)

Range: 10,115m (11,060 yards)

▲ **Type 70 multiple launch rocket system**

People's Liberation Army / 112th Mechanized Infantry Division, 1980

The 19-barrel, 130mm (5.1in) Type 70 multiple launch rocket system mounted on the Type YW 531 armoured personnel carrier provides intense close support for People's Liberation Army infantry over a reasonably large coverage area. The mount above the crew compartment is rotated and elevated to fix the target area. The Type 70 was replaced by the Type 89 as recently as 1990.

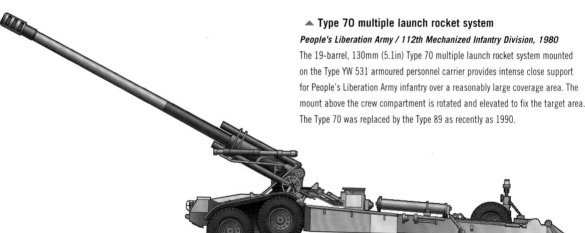

Specifications

Crew: 5

Calibre: 155mm (6.1in)

Weight: 12,000kg (11.8 tons)

Range: 39km (24.23 miles)

Rate of fire: 2–4 rounds per minute

▲ **Type 89 155mm towed howitzer**

People's Liberation Army / 118th Artillery Division, 1996

Developed during the 1980s as a variant of an original design by Gerald Bull's Space Research Corporation, the Type 89 155mm (6.1in) towed howitzer incorporated the standard NATO shell rather than the 122mm (4.8in) Warsaw Pact ordnance and was evidence of a temporary warming in Chinese relations with the West. An auxiliary power unit provides limited self-propulsion.

Recognizing the necessity of obtaining nuclear defensive capability, the People's Republic of China began the development of strategic missiles in 1956, and late in the following year a core group of 600 military personnel began training and development in the deployment of nuclear weapons. As early as 1960, the Chinese nuclear programme had undergone several organizational revisions. Nevertheless, the first successful test-firing of a nuclear-capable missile occurred in October 1963, followed in June 1964 by the launch of the short-

The emblem of the People's Liberation Army is used across all branches of the Chinese armed forces, including the army, navy, air force, artillery and reserve units.

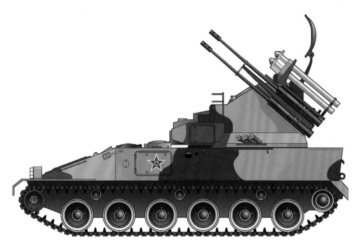

Specifications
Crew: 3
Weight: 22,861kg (22.5 tons)
Length: 6.71m (22ft)
Armament: 4 x 25mm (0.98in) cannon;
 MANPAD missiles
Range: guns – 2.5km (2734 yards);
 missiles – 6km (6562 yards)
Rate of fire: gun – 3200 rounds per minute

▲ **Type 95 SPAAG**

People's Liberation Army / 116th Mechanized Infantry Division, 2004

The Type 95 self-propelled anti-aircraft gun provides the backbone of division-level mobile anti aircraft defence for the People's Liberation Army. Its four 25mm (0.98in) cannon or MANPAD missiles are controlled by a relatively basic radar tracking system. The Type 95 was initially an attempt to produce a weapon equivalent to the performance of the Soviet ZSU-23-4 Shilka and entered service in the late 1990s. Its tracked chassis is common to numerous other vehicles.

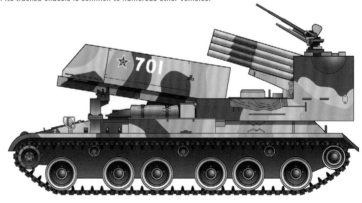

Specifications
Crew: 5
Calibre: 122mm (4.8in)
Number of tubes: 40
Rocket length: 2870mm (9ft 5in)
Rocket weight: 67kg (147.71lb)
System combat weight: 30,000kg
 (29.5 tons) estimated
Range: 30km (28.64 miles)
Rate of fire: 40 rounds in 20 seconds

▲ **Type 89 multiple launch rocket system**

People's Liberation Army/ 124th Motorized Infantry Division, 1998

Entering service with the People's Liberation Army in 1990, the 40-tube, 122mm (4.8in) Type 89 multiple launch rocket system was developed by the China North Industries Group. Its rocket tubes are mounted atop the Type 321 utility chassis. The Type 89, which also served as a replacement for the Type 70, included improvements such as nuclear, biological and chemical defences and automatic loading operations. The weapon may be reloaded in three minutes.

▲ **Type 81 122mm rocket launcher**

People's Liberation Army / 123rd Infantry Division, 1997

Developed from the Soviet BM-21 Grad system, the Type 81 multiple rocket launcher entered service with the People's Liberation Army in 1982. The weapon can be reloaded in eight minutes, and its 40 rocket tubes fire projectiles carrying warheads of 18.3kg (40lb). Outstanding performance led to the Type 81 being deployed from corps level to division and then to artillery battalions attached to motorized infantry units. It replaced the older Type 70.

PLA Artillery Battalion, 1997

The Chinese version of the highly successful Soviet BM-21 Grad close-support multiple launch rocket system, the Type 81 was deployed to motorized infantry divisions of the People's Liberation Army during the 1980s. The Grad has been acknowledged as the most widely used system of its kind in the world, and the Type 81 provides concentrated firepower against fixed targets and infantry concentrations, delivering 122mm (4.8in) rockets from 40 tubes. The Type 81 was originally derived from examples of the Grad captured from North Vietnamese forces in 1979.

Battalion (18 x Type 81 rocket launchers)

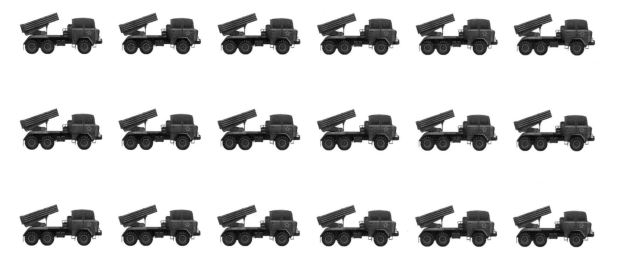

range Dongfeng-1 missile, a licensed copy of the Soviet SS-2 Sibling.

On 1 July 1966 China's strategic nuclear force was placed under the control of the somewhat euphemistically named Second Artillery Corps. Successive generations of ballistic missiles have improved range and payload. The Dongfeng-5, known in NATO nomenclature as the CSS-4, is a two-stage intercontinental ballistic missile which can deliver a 3200kg (7055lb) three-megaton thermonuclear warhead at a maximum range of 10,000 to 12,000km (6214 to 7456 miles), placing the Western United

Specifications

Crew: 6–7

Calibre: 122mm (4.8in)

Number of tubes: 40

Rocket length: 2870mm (9ft 5in)

Rocket weight: 66.8kg (147.27lb)

System combat weight: 15,532kg (15.3 tons)

Range: 20km (12.43 miles)

Rate of fire: 40 rounds in 20 seconds

States and most of Western Europe within range. As recently as 2008, it was estimated that up to 30 Dongfeng-5 missiles were deployed in three brigades, each with six to ten missiles.

Although the number of nuclear warheads currently in the Chinese arsenal is unknown, the tally is well into the hundreds. The Second Artillery Corps is controlled by the Chinese Central Military Commission and headquartered at Qinghe near the capital city of Beijing, while the warheads are dispersed among six missile divisions supported by security, technical and communications regiments. These divisions are based in the main military regions throughout the vast country, including Shenyang, Qimen, Kunming, Luoyang, Huaihua, Xining and Baoji. The total number of personnel assigned to the Second Artillery Corps is believed to exceed 215,000.

PLA II ARTILLERY CORPS (2009)				
Unit	Cover Designator	Province	City/Region	Equipment
51 Base	96101 Unit	Liaoning	Shenyang	
806 Brigade	96111 Unit	Shaanxi	Weinan (Hancheng)	DF-31A (CSS-9)
810 Brigade	96113 Unit	Liaoning	Dalian (Jinzhou)	DF-3A (CSS-2)
816 Brigade	96115 Unit	Jilin	Tonghua	DF-15 (CSS-6)
822 Brigade	96117 Unit	Shandong	Laiwu	DF-21C (CSS-5)
?	96623 Unit	Shandong	Laiwu	Support
52 Base	96151 Unit	Anhui	Qimen (Huangshan)	
807 Brigade	96161 Unit	Anhui	Chizhou	DF-21 (CSS-5)
811 Brigade	96163 Unit	Anhui	Huangshan (Qimen)	DF-21 (CSS-5)
815 Brigade	96165 Unit	Jiangxi	Jingdezhen (Leping)	DF-15B (CSS-6)
817 Brigade	96167 Unit	Fujian	Yongan	DF-15 (CSS-6)
818 Brigade	96169 Unit	Guangdong	Meizhou	DF-15 (CSS-6)
819 Brigade	96162 Unit	Jiangxi	Ganzhou	DF-15 (CSS-6)
820 Brigade	96164 Unit	Zhejiang	Jinhua	DF-15 (CSS-6)
?	96172 Unit	Anhui	Huangshan (Qimen)	Support
Signal Regiment	96173 Unit	Jiangxi	Jingdezhen	Signal
Factory	96174 Unit	Anhui	Huangshan (Xiuning)	Maintenance
53 Base	96201 Unit	Yunnan	Kunming	
802 Brigade	96211 Unit	Yunnan	Jianshui	DF-21 (CSS-5)
808 Brigade	96213 Unit	Yunnan	Chuxiong	DF-21 (CSS-5)
821 Brigade	96215 Unit	Guangxi	Liuzhou	DH-10
?	96217 Unit	Guizhou	Qingzhen	?
?	96219 Unit	Yunnan	Kunming	?
54 Base	96251 Unit	Henan	Luoyang	
801 Brigade	96261 Unit	Henan	Lingbao	DF-5A (CSS-4)
804 Brigade	96263 Unit	Henan	Luanchuan	DF-5A (CSS-4)
813 Brigade	96265 Unit	Henan	Nanyang	DF-31A (CSS-9)
55 Base	96301 Unit	Hunan	Huaihua	
803 Brigade	96311 Unit	Hunan	Huaihua (Jingzhou)	DF-5A (CSS-4)
805 Brigade	96313 Unit	Hunan	Huaihua (Tongdao)	DF-4 (CSS-3)
814 Brigade	96315 Unit	Hunan	Huaihua (Huitong)	DF-4 (CSS-3)
824 Brigade	96317 Unit	Hunan	Shaoyang (Dongkou)	?
?	96321 Unit	Hunan	Shaoyang (Dongkou)	Support
56 Base	96351 Unit	Qinghai	Xining	
809 Brigade	96361 Unit	Qinghai	Datong	DF-21 (CSS-5)
812 Brigade	96363 Unit	Gansu	Tianshui	DF-31A (CSS-9)
823 Brigade	96365 Unit	Xinjiang	Korla	DF-21 (CSS-5)
Training Unit	96367 Unit	Qinghai	Delingha	-
Training Unit	96367 Unit	Xinjiang	Ruowu	-
22 Base	96401 Unit	Shaanxi	Baoji	Logistics support

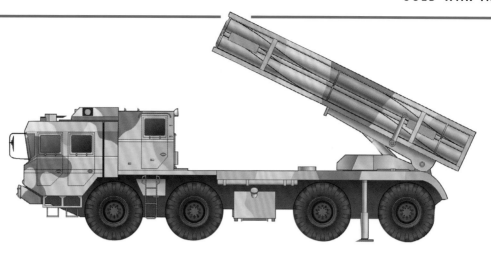

Specifications

Crew: 4

Weight: 38,555kg (37.9 tons)

Rocket weight: 840kg (1852lb)

Range: 130km (80.78 miles)

Reloading time: 20 minutes

▲ **AR1A multiple launch rocket system**

People's Liberation Army / 113th Infantry Division, 2010

Initially demonstrated in 2009, the AR1A multiple launch rocket system was developed from the earlier A-100, which was never adopted by the People's Liberation Army. Its 300mm (11.8in) rockets are contained in ten launching tubes. A full salvo is discharged in 60 seconds. Designed to saturate ground targets, the AR1A is similar to the Russian 9A52-2T Smerch. Carried atop an 8X8 truck chassis, the system is reloaded with an exchange of preconfigured pods.

India and Pakistan in conflict

1965–PRESENT

At odds for decades, these South Asian rivals have fought for control of the Kashmir region and accused one another of inciting rebellion and supporting terrorist organizations.

DURING THE WARS BETWEEN INDIA AND PAKISTAN in 1965 and 1971, artillery played a key role on the battlefield. Supported by US advisers, Pakistani artillery was massed in support of Operation Grand Slam in 1965, enabling Pakistani infantry to break through Indian lines behind a heavy barrage, although neither side possessed adequate firepower for a decisive victory. Pakistani artillery was distributed across two infantry divisions and also comprised one independent brigade of two heavy regiments and three medium regiments plus one each of light anti-aircraft artillery and field artillery. The 7th Division Artillery consisted of two field regiments, the 27th and the 2nd, along with a locating battery, while the 12th Division Artillery consisted of three additional regiments.

Indian artillery had been dispersed across a relatively great distance and was unable to reply with concentrated effect. When Indian ground forces counterattacked, the Pakistani artillery was superbly handled and thwarted the Indian advance on more than one occasion. It has been said that the commander of a Pakistani artillery brigade attached to the IV Army Corps achieved a reputation as an outstanding gunnery officer.

By the outbreak of the 1971 war, the Pakistani Army had organized its 1st Armoured Division's mobile artillery into four regiments of self-propelled guns, a light anti-aircraft regiment plus numerous field artillery and anti-aircraft artillery battalions assigned as needed. The 11th Infantry Division was supported by two field and two medium regiments and a heavy artillery regiment. Future Pakistan president Pervez Musharraf served as a lieutenant of artillery with the 16th Self-Propelled Field Regiment of the 1st Armoured Division.

During the Battle of Assal Uttar in September 1965, a Pakistani offensive was blunted by Indian forces; however, this was due in part to superior Indian tactical manoeuvring and the inept handling of Pakistani armour. Pakistani artillery, including at one point up to 140 massed guns, was of greater range and firepower than the 106mm (4.17in) recoilless rifles, 75mm (2.9in) pack howitzers and 120mm (4.7in) mortars available to the Indians.

While tensions have continued to smoulder, India and Pakistan have modernized their artillery capabilities steadily. Today's Indian Army includes two artillery divisions, an artillery brigade attached to each of its 18 infantry divisions and a total of nearly 200 regiments of field artillery. Primary towed weapons include 105mm (4.1in) light field guns; the Soviet-made 122mm (4.8in) D-30, 130mm (5.1in) M-46 and modified 155mm (6.1in) M-46; as well as the 155mm (6.1in) Bofors FH-77B. Air defence capabilities include more than 12 regiments of surface-to-air missiles plus flak regiments fielding such proven guns as the ZSU-23-4 Shilka.

In response to India's purchase of the Russian 9A52-2T Smerch ground-support rocket system, Pakistan was reported to have procured at least a battalion of the Chinese AR1A, totalling 36 launchers, and is considering manufacturing the modern multiple launch rocket system under licence. Both nations also possess nuclear missiles.

Specifications

Crew: 8	Weight: 4000kg (3.93 tons)
Calibre: 75mm (2.9in)	Effective ceiling: 8565m (28,000ft)
Elevation: - 5 degrees to + 85 degrees	Muzzle velocity: 840m/sec (2755ft/sec)

▲ 75mm Bofors Model 29
Indian Army / 312th Air Defence Brigade, 1965

Similar in design to the German 88mm (3.5in) Flak 18, which served in multiple roles in World War II, the Swedish-manufactured Bofors Model 29 anti-aircraft gun preceded the 88mm (3.5in) weapon by several years. However, several German designers were working in Sweden at the time the weapon was developed. It was exported to numerous countries and remains in service in limited numbers today.

▲ Ordnance BL 5.5in Medium Gun Mk 2
Pakistani Army / 12th Medium Artillery Regiment, 1965

Manufactured first in 1942 as an improvement over the 60-pounder cannon then in service, the 5.5in (140mm) gun was distinguishable by the characteristic horns alongside the barrel, which were components of the spring support for the gun's weight. Serving with British forces for more than 40 years, it was retired in the early 1980s; however, the weapon remains active with the Pakistani Army today.

Specifications

Crew: 10

Calibre: 140mm (5.5in)

Elevation: - 5 to + 45 degrees

Weight: 6190kg (6.09 tons)

Range: 14,813m (16,200 yards)

Muzzle velocity: 510m/sec (1673ft/sec)

Specifications

Crew: 5

Calibre: 155mm (6.1in)

Elevation: - 3 degrees to + 50 degrees

Weight: 11,500kg (11.32 tons)

Range: 22,000m (24,050 yards)

Muzzle velocity: 774m/sec (2450ft/sec)

▲ **FH-77 155mm field howitzer system**

Indian Army / 261st Artillery Brigade, 1971

A truly modern field howitzer of Swedish manufacture, the FH-77 was designed in the early 1980s and utilizes hydraulic power generated by an auxiliary engine system for short-distance movement and to assist in numerous operations, such as loading and ramming, elevating the weapon and lowering the trailing wheels. More than 400 are said to be in service with the modern Indian Army.

Japan
1960–PRESENT

Since the end of World War II, the scope of the Japanese armed forces has been limited and largely dependent upon the United States for support in the event of significant hostilities.

IMMEDIATELY FOLLOWING WORLD WAR II, the Japanese nation was forbidden to rearm or to raise a standing army of any consequence. However, as war erupted on the Asian continent, it became apparent to the United States that Japan might serve as a valuable ally and continuing base of operations against the spread of communism. Indeed, from bases in Japan, the United States has, over the years, preserved a Cold War balance of power with the Soviet Union, opposed the aggression of North Korea and staged military assets to Vietnam.

Although the Japanese Ground Self-Defence Force maintains limited manpower and levels of equipment, its weapons are modern and, in many cases, of Japanese design and manufacture. Strictly controlled through a series of National Defence Program Outlines, the number and types of weapons to be deployed are modified periodically. As of 1976, a total of 1000 artillery pieces were in the Japanese arsenal. This number has been reduced by ten per cent since then, while the number of self-propelled

artillery pieces and vehicles used in the transport of artillery was decreased by 30 per cent, from 900 to 600, in 2005. Eight anti-aircraft artillery groups with surface-to-air-missile capabilities are also maintained.

The latest organizational changes in the Japanese Ground Self-Defence Force were accompanied by a restructuring from divisional to brigade alignment. Prior to the organizational change, an infantry division was usually supported by an artillery regiment of four battalions, each with two batteries of howitzers, and a reserve battalion of four batteries. Each battery typically fielded four guns. Mechanized divisions included an air defence battalion and a field artillery regiment. The current organization consists of a single artillery brigade with three groups and two air defence brigades with three groups.

Towed artillery includes the 155mm (6.1in) FH-70 howitzer, while self-propelled models include the Japanese Type 75 and Type 95 155mm (6.1in) guns and the US MLRS rocket system. Together with several armoured vehicles, the Japanese have

Specifications

Crew: 3
Weight: 36,000kg (79,400lb)
Length: 7.99m (26ft 2in)
Width: 3.18m (10ft 5in)
Height: 4.4m (14ft 5in)
Engine: 536kW (718hp) 10F22WT 10-cylinder
 diesel
Speed: 60km/h (37mph)
Road range: 500km (310 miles)
Armament: 2 x 35mm (1.38in) autocannon

▲ Type 87 SPAAG

Japan Ground Self-Defence Force, 1993

Completed in 1987, this self-propelled anti-aircraft gun combines the
Type 74 tank chassis with the Oerlikon 35mm twin cannon.

Specifications

Crew: 3
Calibre: 130mm (5.1in)
Elevation: 0 to + 50 degrees
Weight: 18,695kg (18.4 tons)
Length: 5.8m (19ft)
Range: 15,000m (16,404 yards)
Engine: 224kW (300hp) Mitsubishi 4ZF diesel
Speed: 53km/h (33mph)

▲ Type 75 multiple launch rocket system

Japan Ground Self-Defence Force / 1st Artillery Brigade, 1984

The Type 75 multiple launch rocket system was developed by the Aerospace Division of Nissan Motor Company during
the mid-1970s. Its 130mm (5.1in) rockets are carried in a boxlike frame of 30 barrels, which is mounted on the
chassis of the Type 73 armoured personnel carrier. More than 60 remained in service two decades after deployment.

▲ Type 81 Tan-SAM

Japan Ground Self-Defence Force / 2nd Anti-Aircraft Artillery Brigade, 1988

Developed by the Toshiba Corporation, the Type 81 Tan-SAM went into design in 1966. The system was originally deployed
in 1981 and has undergone several upgrades. Its 160mm (6.3in) radar-controlled missiles replaced the outmoded 75mm
(2.9in) M51 and 37mm (1.5in) M15A1 anti-aircraft systems while complementing the shoulder-fired FIM-92 Stinger and
MIM-23 HAWK missiles. The Type 81 battery, or firing unit, includes a fire-control vehicle capable of tracking two targets
simultaneously and two launching vehicles.

Specifications

Crew: 15
Missile weight: 100kg (220.46lb)
Missile length: 2.7m (8ft 10in)
Range: 10km (6.21 miles)
Warhead: 9.2kg (20.3lb)

developed notable weapons systems such as the Type 87 self-propelled anti-aircraft gun and the Type 75 multiple launch rocket system. The radar-directed 35mm (1.38in) autocannon of the Type 87 replaced the 1960s-vintage US-made M42 Duster, while the Type 75 was designed to provide close support for infantry. The Type 81 Tan-SAM complements shoulder-fired and heavier platform-launched anti-aircraft missiles and was designed by the Toshiba Corporation.

Singapore
1965–PRESENT

The tiny Republic of Singapore has developed into a manufacturer of modern artillery, and its weapons are in demand around the world.

WHEN THE REPUBLIC OF SINGAPORE gained independence in 1965, its armed forces consisted of only two infantry regiments; however, the newly formed government solicited assistance from Israel and patterned its modern armed forces in similar fashion to the Israeli Defence Forces. Today, the Singapore Armed Forces (SAF) comprises more than 72,000 active personnel and over 300,000 reservists. The SAF includes two artillery battalions and an air defence artillery battalion assigned at the divisional level.

Among the primary artillery weapons of the SAF are the French 105mm (4.1in) GIAT LG-1 towed light howitzer and the FH-88 and FH-2000 155mm (6.1in) howitzers, both of which were designed by engineers in Singapore. The FH-88 was designed in the early 1980s and has been delivered to the Indonesian armed forces as well, while the FH-2000 variant is a product of Singapore Technologies Corporation which entered service in 1993 and was field-tested in New Zealand.

Self-propelled weapons fielded include the 155mm (6.1in) SSPH Primus and the 155mm (6.1in) SLWH Pegasus, both developed in Singapore. The Pegasus entered service in the autumn of 2005 and is intended eventually to replace the LG-1, while the Primus was introduced in 2004 and was developed following an extensive survey of US, British, Japanese and Russian types. In 2007, Singapore ordered at least 18 units of the US HIMARS (High Mobility Artillery Rocket System), and deliveries began in 2009. One notable aspect of the sale was the absence of unguided rockets in the deal, as Singapore apparently is intent on deploying the first fully GPS-guided HIMARS unit known to exist.

▲ 155mm ODE FH-88

Singapore Armed Forces / 21st Artillery Division, 1992

Ordnance Development and Engineering of Singapore developed five prototypes of the FH-88 beginning in 1983, and production of the service model was undertaken four years later. The first howitzer designed in Singapore for the republic's own army, the FH-88 has been a successful replacement for the Soltam M-71. The FH-2000 was a later upgrade of the original production model.

Specifications

Crew: 8

Calibre: 155mm (6.1in)

Elevation: - 3 degrees to + 70 degrees

Weight: 12,800kg (12.59 tons)

Range: 19,000m (20,780 yards)

Muzzle velocity: 765m/sec (2510ft/sec)

Chapter 12

The Middle East and Africa

The Middle East and the continent of Africa
have been torn by strife for centuries. The rise and fall of
mechanized armies have brought regime change, the births
of nations, guerrilla warfare and civil turmoil. Throughout
these periods of unrest, the firepower and range of artillery
have been deciding factors in the course of events. The
outcome on the battlefield dictates the tenor of negotiations
and overtures for peace. Artillery provides a decided edge
in the continuation of diplomacy by other means, as armed
conflict has been described by some. Its mere presence, let
alone its utilization, may tip the military
and political balance.

◀ **SP bombardment**
An Israeli M107 self-propelled howitzer fires on Syrian positions somewhere near the Golan Heights,
October 1973.

Introduction

As European colonialism waned, independent Arab states and the Jewish nation of Israel armed for the series of conflicts which would define the modern era in the Middle East.

THE NATION OF ISRAEL came into being with a declaration of independence on 14 May 1948, and almost immediately it was attacked by neighbouring Arab states. The conflict had deep roots, stretching back more than 2000 years, and the United Nations endorsement of the partition of Palestine sparked a renewal of old antagonisms. While the Arab nations of Egypt, Syria, Iraq, Lebanon and Trans-Jordan had raised standing armies with some degree of mechanization, the fledgling Israeli Defence Forces (IDF) began its storied history as the Haganah, a makeshift, underequipped militia organization facing an enemy which was attacking from several directions.

Elementary artillery

Many of the heavy weapons utilized by both the Arab and Israeli armed forces during the war of 1948 had been abandoned or relinquished to local military control by Allied or Axis forces following World War II. Common among the Arab forces were the British Bren Gun Carrier; the French Lorraine 38L chassis which often mounted a small artillery piece, anti-tank gun or machine gun; and the light British 2-pounder and 6-pounder anti-tank weapons. Armoured vehicles included the Marmon-Herrington armoured car, often mounting the 2-pounder gun with a secondary Browning .30-cal (7.62mm) or .50-cal (12.7mm) machine gun.

The Trans-Jordanian Arab Legion entered the war with at least 7000 soldiers grouped in infantry and mechanized infantry brigades and two fully mechanized brigades with armoured cars and artillery. Its heaviest weapon was the venerable British 25-pounder gun, with a complement of at least four organized into a single battery. The legion's armoured car troop fielded 12 Marmon-Herrington vehicles.

The two brigades of the Egyptian Expeditionary Force included a hotchpotch of pre-World War II French tanks of Hotchkiss and Renault manufacture, the British Matilda and Crusader types and even a few German Mark IV panzers. Its mechanized infantry complement included nearly 300 Bren Gun

Carriers capable of towing light artillery pieces; a variety of armoured cars such as the Humber Mk III and Mk IV; and the Loyd Carrier, which often towed a 6-pounder anti-tank gun.

The Syrian Army of 1948 was noted for its complement of 65mm (2.6in) mountain guns carried on the Lorraine 38L chassis – which in effect produced a makeshift self-propelled artillery piece – and for the anti-aircraft or anti-tank 25mm (0.98in) gun mounted atop the Bren Gun Carrier. Its few artillery pieces were also remnants of the French colonial presence in the Levant and included

▲ **Soviet mortar**
Amir El Hassan (foreground), prime minister of Yemen, examines a Soviet-supplied 82mm Model 1941 mortar captured from the Egyptian Army during the North Yemen Civil War, 1962–70.

▲ **Mobile launcher**

Afghan irregulars man a Soviet-built BM-21 rocket launcher, probably captured after the withdrawal of Soviet troops in 1989. The BM-21 is highly mobile: a trained crew can emplace the system and have it ready to fire in three minutes, and packed up and ready to move in two minutes if encountering counter-battery fire.

75mm (2.9in) and 105mm (4.1in) models. Most of these were well-worn Vichy weapons, which had served pro-Axis forces during the Allied offensive operations of 1941.

The Bren Gun Carrier, or Universal Carrier, was produced in Great Britain from 1934 to 1960, and during that time more than 113,000 were manufactured. The tracked vehicle had originally been intended to transport infantry and support weapons such as heavy machine guns and mortars which were too large to be man-portable. Early models mounted the .303-cal (7.7mm) Bren light machine gun or the Boys 0.55in (13.97mm) anti-tank rifle, and even the British 3in (actually 3.2in/81.2mm) mortar. The carrier was protected by seven to ten millimetres (0.28–0.39in) of armour and powered by a 64kW (85hp) Ford V-8 petrol engine. Its crew of two was often complemented by a contingent of onboard infantrymen. In time, the Bren Gun Carrier was employed by artillery units as the prime mover for the 6-pounder gun, and this was the case with Syrian forces in Palestine.

The Haganah had its origins in the 1920s during the British mandate in Palestine, and by the time of the 1948 war its brigades included British Cromwell and Valentine tanks and the French Hotchkiss H39. Among its most versatile weapons were the numerous variants of the US-built M3 half-track. The M3 was deployed in mechanized infantry units in a troop carrier role, with heavy machine guns or mortars in a modified troop compartment to provide direct infantry fire support, or with a 75mm (2.9in) or 90mm (3.54in) gun used in an artillery or anti-tank function. The British-manufactured Daimler armoured car and a number of improvised mobile weapons, such as the machine-gun-equipped jeep called the Negev Beast, equipped Haganah units.

Along with light weapons of European and US manufacture, the Israelis also utilized the 81mm (3in) Davidka, or Little David, mortar. Only six of these were known to have seen service; however, their presence was considered a tribute to the resourcefulness of the Haganah and its determination to stand up to the vastly superior Arab forces arrayed against it.

Suez Crisis to Six Day War
1956–67

From the Suez Crisis to the Six Day War, the armed forces of the Middle Eastern nations grew in power and performance. The emergence of the Cold War further precipitated the export of modern artillery and other technology to a global hotspot.

INTERNATIONAL TENSIONS grew exponentially with the rise of nationalism and communism around the world, and with the intricacies of politics armed confrontation became an almost inevitable consequence. High-stakes bargaining for the financing of the Aswan Dam resulted in a breakdown of negotiations between Egypt and the Western democracies. When the Egyptian government recognized the People's Republic of China and nationalized the Suez Canal in 1956, Britain, France and Israel responded militarily. This was followed in 1967 by Israel's lightning pre-emptive strike at the start of the Six Day War, during which IDF armour and artillery were skilfully handled and Israel gained

control of the Golan Heights on the Syrian frontier and wrested the entire Sinai Peninsula from Egypt.

Egyptian forces had been substantially augmented by the addition of Soviet-manufactured artillery and the licensed production of rocket systems. Among the most common of the mobile artillery organic to Egyptian Army units were the SU-100 and Archer 17-pounder self-propelled guns. The SU-100 had been developed by the Soviets late in World War II and deployed extensively during the last year of the war. Its 100mm (3.9in) D10S gun was initially installed in an enclosed turret on the chassis of the T-34/85 medium tank and later the chassis of the T-54/55 tank.

▲ **Archer SP gun Dug In**
An Egyptian Army Archer 17 pdr SP gun lies abandoned close to a railway line at Rafah, Sinai, during the Suez Crisis, 1956.

The lighter Archer 17-pounder was of British manufacture and combined the chassis of the Valentine tank and the QF 17-pounder (76mm/3in) gun. Introduced in the autumn of 1944, the Archer was an open-topped gun due to the narrow Valentine chassis, which resulted in the recoil of the weapon into the driver's compartment. Its low silhouette and rear-mounted gun allowed the Archer to lie in ambush, fire at an approaching enemy and make its escape with a minimum of manoeuvre.

Among the towed artillery prevalent at the time of the Suez Crisis and the Six Day War a decade later were the French-designed 155mm (6.1in) Howitzer Model 1950 and the Soviet-built 152mm (6in) Howitzer M1943, better known as the D-1. The Model 1950 was utilized by both Arab and Israeli forces during the period and was one of the first newly manufactured weapons of its kind to emerge on the international arms market following World War II. Its four-wheeled carriage was towed behind a half-track or large truck, and the howitzer was also modified by the Israelis to fit the chassis of the M4 Sherman medium tank, resulting in the M50 self-propelled assault gun.

The D-1 was the result of a need to expedite Soviet artillery production at the height of World War II and comprised the larger 152mm (6in) howitzer mounted on the light carriage of the 122mm (4.8in) M1938 weapon. As a result, Soviet designers had to fit a large muzzle brake on the gun to decrease the recoil. One of the most enduring artillery pieces of the Cold War era, the D-1 served into the 1980s with the armed forces of several Arab nations and was exported around the world.

▲ Walid APC rocket launcher

Egyptian Army / 2nd Infantry Division / 10th Brigade, Abu Ageila, Sinai, 1967

A variant of the Soviet-produced BTR-152 armoured personnel carrier, the Walid was manufactured in Egypt and exported to other Arab countries. The Walid carried a crew of two and a complement of up to ten combat infantrymen. Some were fitted with 80mm (3.15in) rocket launchers.

Specifications

Crew: 2	Speed: 86km/h (54mph)
Weight: not available	Road range: 800km (500 miles)
Length: 6.12m (20ft)	Armament: 12 x 80mm (3.15in)
Width: 2.57m (8ft 5in)	rocket-launcher tubes
Height: 2.3m (7ft 6in)	Radio: n/k
Engine: 125kW (168hp) diesel	

◄ 155mm Howitzer Mle 1950

Egyptian Army / 53rd Artillery Battery, 1967

A post-war French design, the Mle 1950 155mm (6.1in) howitzer remained in service with the armed forces of numerous countries into the 1990s. The weapon features a recoil system of individual cylinders arranged around the barrel in order to provide rapid cooling during sustained action. The stable firing platform consists of a pedestal which is lowered in the carriage centre along with the two legs of a split trail.

Specifications

Crew: 5	Weight: 8100kg (7.97 tons)
Calibre: 155mm (6.1in)	Range: 18,000m (19,685 yards)
Elevation: - 4 degrees to + 69 degrees	Muzzle velocity: 650m/sec (2133ft/sec)

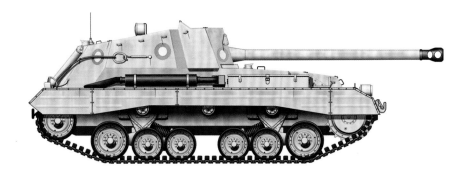

Specifications

Crew: 4	Engine: 123kW (165hp) GMC M10 diesel
Weight: 18.79 tonnes (18.5 tons)	Speed: 24km/h (15mph)
Length: 6.68m (21ft 11in)	Road range: 145km (90 miles)
Width: 2.64m (8ft 8in)	Armament: 1 x 76mm (3in) 17pdr OQF,
Height: 2.24m (7ft 4in)	plus 1 x 7.7mm (0.303in) Bren MG

▲ **Archer 17pdr SP gun**

Egyptian Army / 4th Armoured Division, Port Said, Suez Canal, November 1956

The open-turret self-propelled-gun variant of the British Valentine tank, the Archer tank destroyer was deployed by the Egyptian Army during the Suez Crisis. Its 17-pounder (76mm/3in) gun was effective against Israeli armoured vehicles in the Sinai.

94th Anti-Tank Battery, Egyptian Army, 1956

Typical of an Egyptian Army anti-tank battery at the time of the 1956 Suez Crisis, the 94th fielded a complement of nine Archer 17-pounder self-propelled anti-tank guns. The Archer was manufactured by the British firm of Vickers, and fewer than 700 were actually constructed. Although it was somewhat lighter than other self-propelled artillery in service at the time, the Archer proved adept at fire and manoeuvre. Its 17-pounder (76mm/3in) main gun was powerful enough to engage Israeli M4 Sherman tanks from camouflaged positions and then displace rapidly.

Battery (9 x Archer SP guns)

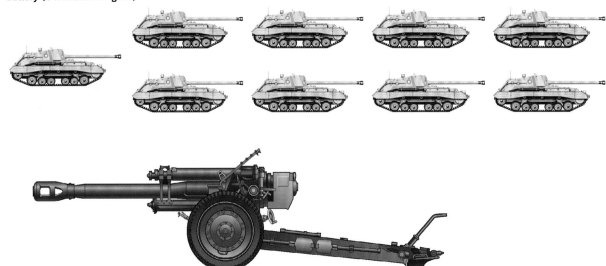

▲ **152mm Howitzer M1943 (D-1)**

Syrian Army / 42nd Mechanized Brigade, 1967

One of the longest-serving field artillery weapons in modern history, the 152mm (6in) M1943 howitzer combined the two-wheeled carriage of the 122mm (4.8in) M1938 howitzer with the barrel of the heavier 152mm (6in) howitzer. Its large muzzle brake minimized destabilizing recoil during long periods of operation. The product of Soviet manufacturing expediency during World War II, the M1943 served with the armed forces of numerous Warsaw Pact and Soviet client states into the 1990s.

Specifications

Crew: 8

Calibre: 152mm (6in)

Elevation: - 3 degrees to + 63.5 degrees

Weight: 3600kg (7937lb)

Range: 12,400m (13,560 yards)

Muzzle velocity: 508m/sec (1666ft/sec)

Yom Kippur War
1973

Coordinated weapons technology initially gave the Egyptian and Syrian armed forces the upper hand. However, Israeli forces rallied to stem the Arab bid to regain control of territory lost in 1967.

WHEN EGYPTIAN FORCES breached the Bar-Lev Line and took Israeli commanders by surprise in October 1973, their well-coordinated capabilities of air and ground defences provided a decided edge during the opening days of the conflict. A centrepiece of the Egyptian tactics was the employment of air defence artillery, ground artillery and man-portable anti-tank missiles. Although the Israeli Defence Forces rallied in the later weeks of the war, the Egyptians had taught the world a lesson in the employment of complementary capabilities of multiple weapons systems.

Integral to the Egyptian offensive was the ingenuity of using high-pressure water hoses which blasted exits for infantry and armoured units through the high sand berms on the eastern bank of the Suez Canal. Once across in force, the Egyptian infantry pierced the Bar-Lev Line and took on the counterattacking Israeli tanks with the potent 9K11 Malyutka anti-tank missile, known to NATO forces as the AT-3 Sagger.

The effectiveness of the Sagger came as a rude shock to the Israelis and accounted for heavy losses in Israeli armour during the three-week war. Specially trained in the use of anti-tank weapons, including the AT-3 and the RPG-7 rocket-propelled grenade, tank-killer teams were among the first Egyptian troops across the Suez Canal, assisting in the capture of isolated posts along the Bar-Lev Line.

Sagger power

The Sagger was an MCLOS (Manual Command Line Of Sight) man-portable missile which was developed in the Soviet Union in the early 1960s and entered service with the Red Army by the autumn of 1963. Weighing 10.9kg (24.3lb), the light missile system was wire-guided and controlled by the operator, who corrected the path to the target with a joystick. The shaped warhead was capable of penetrating the armour of Israeli M48 tanks and other fighting vehicles at distances of up to 3000m (3280 yards).

While the Sagger was an initial shock to the Israelis, it was determined that the operator was able to maintain control of the missile within only 4.6m (15ft) of the firing point. Therefore, as the Yom

▲ **AT-3 Sagger**

Egyptian Army / 3rd Mechanized Infantry Division, 1973

The MCLOS 9K11 Malyutka anti-tank missile was known to NATO as the AT-3 Sagger. This man-portable wire-guided missile is one of the most widely produced and exported systems of its kind in the world and destroyed a number of Israeli armoured vehicles during the Yom Kippur War of 1973.

Specifications

Configuration: single-stage, shaped charge	Launch weight: 10.9kg (24.3lb)
Deployment: man-portable	Range: 3000m (3280 yards)
Length: 860mm (33.86in)	
Diameter: 125mm (4.92in)	

64th Artillery Brigade, Syrian Army, 1973

During the Yom Kippur War of 1973, the Syrian Army's 64th Artillery Brigade fielded both the towed and self-propelled variants of the 122mm (4.8in) D-30 howitzer which had been developed by the Soviet Union in the early 1960s. The Syrian conversion of the D-30 to a self-propelled weapon set the howitzer atop the chassis of the T-34 medium tank. Firing from prepared positions, the towed D-30 proved to be an outstanding anti-tank weapon. Large numbers of these guns remain in service today.

Brigade (54 x 122mm/4.8in D-30 howitzers; 18 x 122mm/4.8in D-30 SP Howitzers)

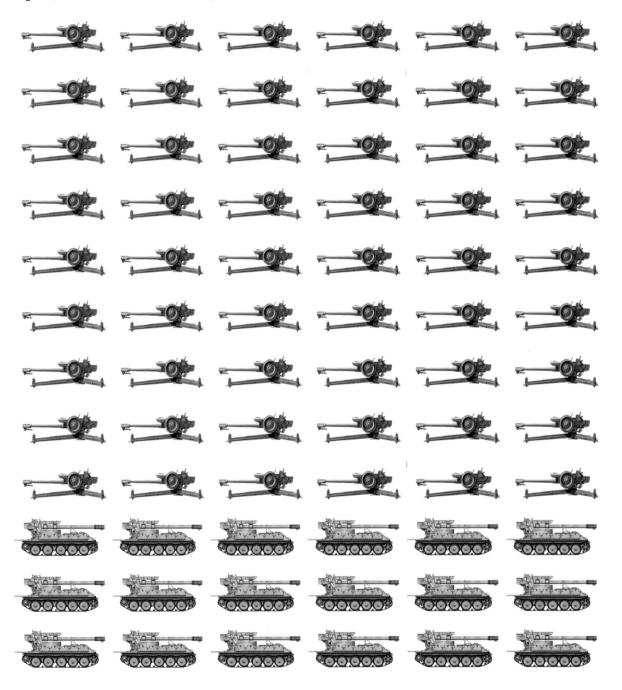

Kippur War progressed, Israeli tanks and infantry concentrated their fire on the position of the Sagger operator, forcing him to displace rapidly and alter the course of the missile. In the intervening time, however, estimates of the number of Israeli vehicles destroyed by the Sagger range from 800 to more than 1000, with the higher figure possibly including vehicles which were disabled and returned to service.

When the Egyptian infantry was forced on the defensive, the troops typically deployed adjacent to dug-in positions with the Sagger at the ready. Advancing Israeli tank crews were well aware of the prowess of the Sagger after the first few days of the Yom Kippur War, and its mere presence altered their method of attack. Israeli armoured doctrine emphasized rapid movement; however, the Sagger

▲ ZSU-23-4 SPAAG

Egyptian Army / 2nd Infantry Division / 51st Artillery Brigade, 1973

With radar-directed quad-mounted 23mm (0.9in) autocannon, the ZSU-23-4 self-propelled anti-aircraft vehicle, commonly called the Shilka, was attached to numerous Egyptian armoured brigades during the Yom Kippur War. Along with surface-to-air missiles, they accounted for a number of low-flying Israeli aircraft.

Specifications

Crew: 4	Engine: 210kW (280hp) V-6R diesel
Weight: 19,000kg (41,800lb)	Speed: 44km/h (27mph)
Length: 6.54m (21ft 5in)	Road range: 260km (162 miles)
Width: 2.95m (9ft 8in)	Armament: 4 x 23mm (0.9in) AZP-23
Height (without radar): 2.25m (7ft 4in)	anti-aircraft cannon
	Radio: n/k

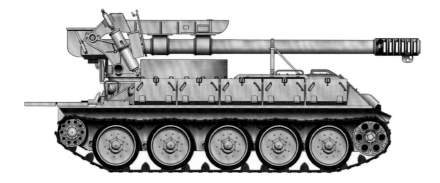

▲ T-34 with 122mm D-30 SP howitzer

Syrian Army / 64th Artillery Brigade, 1973

With its turret removed, the chassis of the World War II-vintage T-34 medium tank provided a stable platform for the 122mm (4.8in) D-30 self-propelled howitzer of the Syrian Army during the Yom Kippur War. In order to keep pace with advancing mechanized infantry units and provide much-needed supporting fire, the Syrians adapted the two Soviet weapons into a capable system.

Specifications

Crew: 7	Engine: 372kW (493hp) V-2 V12 diesel
Weight: n/k	Speed (road): 55km/h (33mph)
Length (hull): 6m (19ft 7in)	Road range: 360km (223 miles)
Width: 3m (9ft 10in)	Armament: 1 x 122mm (4.8in) D-30 howitzer
Height: n/k	

required a more cautious approach. Infantry was deployed to take out the Sagger positions, exacting a toll in both time and lives.

At the Battle of the Chinese Farm, elements of General Ariel Sharon's 143rd Armoured Division encountered stiff resistance and lost approximately 70 of its 250 tanks in one night of savage fighting on 15 October. During the fighting around the Suez Canal as Egyptian forces attempted to disengage,

a single tank-killing team of the Egyptian 19th Infantry Division was reported to have destroyed at least nine Israeli tanks with Sagger missiles.

In the air, the dominance of the Israeli Air Force, which had decimated Egyptian armour and infantry concentrations during the Six Day War of 1967, was challenged by the combination of Soviet-made surface-to-air missiles and rapid-firing self-propelled air defence guns allied with modern radar detection

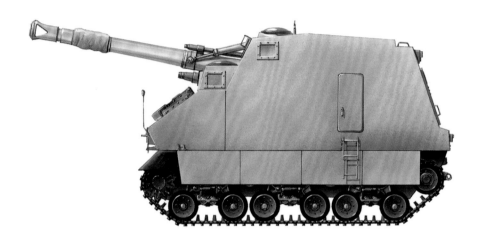

▲ **Soltam Systems M68 155mm SP howitzer**

Israeli Defence Forces / 17th Armoured Brigade, 1973

The Soltam Systems 155mm M-68 gun-howitzer is mounted in the forward part of the superstructure and has an elevation of +52°, a depression of -3° and a total traverse of 60°.

Specifications

Crew: 8	Engine: 331kW (450hp) Ford GAA V8 petrol
Weight: 41.5 tonnes (40.8 tons)	Speed: 38km/h (24mph)
Length (hull): 5.92m (19ft 5in)	Road range: 260km (162 miles)
Width: 2.68m (8ft 9in)	Armament: 1 x 155mm (6.1in) L33 howitzer, plus
Height: n/k	1 x 7.62mm (0.3in) MG

▲ **Soltam Systems M-68 155mm howitzer**

Israeli Defence Forces / 75th Armoured Infantry Battalion, 1973

Based on an earlier Finnish design, the Soltam M-68 155mm (6.1in) howitzer was mounted on a four-wheeled carriage. The wheels at the forward end of each trail leg moved in order for the weapon to be positioned for firing. To stabilize the platform, spades were pounded into the ground and then locked in place.

Specifications

Crew: 8	Weight: 8000kg (7.87 tons)
Calibre: 155mm (6.1in)	Range: 22,000m (24,060 yards)
Elevation: - 10 degrees to + 67 degrees	Muzzle velocity: 765m/sec (2510ft/sec)

systems. The Soviet 2K12 Kub air defence missile, known to NATO as the SA-6 Gainful, was a state-of-the-art surface-to-air missile system at the time of the Yom Kippur War. Development of the SA-6 was undertaken in the summer of 1958, and the system was deployed to units of the Red Army by 1970.

Mounted on a tracked chassis which carried a triple launcher and sophisticated radar codenamed Straight Flush by NATO, the SA-6 took a heavy toll on Israeli aircraft, particularly the American-built A-4 Skyhawk and F-4 Phantom. In response to the deadly success of the SA-6 batteries, Israeli aircraft adopted a tactic of flying low, beneath the trajectory of the radar. In doing so, however, the Israeli aircraft were engaged by the self-propelled ZSU-57-2 and highly effective ZSU-23-4 Shilka anti-aircraft guns of the Egyptian Army.

The Shilka

The ZSU-23-4 Shilka, named for a river in southeastern Russia, consists of a quadruple battery of 23mm (0.9in) radar-directed autocannon mounted on a modified chassis similar to that of the PT-76 amphibious tank and the SA-6 air defence missile. The ZSU-23-4's combined rate of fire is up to 4000 rounds per minute, creating a veritable curtain of fire against low-flying aircraft. Developed in the late 1950s, the Shilka was produced in large numbers from the early 1960s to the 1980s, and many of these weapons were placed in service with the armed forces of Soviet client states. At least five

Israeli Phantoms were shot down by the ZSU-23-4 during one fighter sweep against mobile SA-6 sites on 7 October 1973.

The Shilka had been designed as a replacement for the older ZSU-57-2, which mounted a pair of 57mm (2.2in) autocannon. Although the 57mm (2.2in) guns were of heavier calibre, the ZSU-57-2's combined rate of fire was approximately 240 rounds per minute, substantially lower than that of the Shilka. The ZSU-57-2 was the first self-propelled air defence gun produced in substantial numbers by the Soviet Union. Nicknamed Sparka, or Pair, it proved considerably less effective than its successor during the Yom Kippur War.

The Israeli Defence Forces countered Egyptian self-propelled artillery with the Soltam L33 155mm (6.1in) howitzer, which mounted the potent L33 barrel atop the chassis of the American-designed M4A3E8 'Easy Eight' Sherman tank. This self-propelled howitzer was easily distinguished by its high silhouette and boxlike turret which held eight crewmen. The Soltam M-68 155mm (6.1in) towed howitzer, meanwhile, was designed and built in Israel, entering service with the IDF in 1970. With a range of 22,000m (24,060 yards), it provided much-needed firepower which slowed advancing Egyptian and Syrian troops during the critical opening days of the Yom Kippur War. Based on a pair of Finnish designs from the early 1960s, the M-68 underwent firing trials in 1968 and was later upgraded to the M-71, which featured a longer barrel.

Specifications

Configuration: two-stage, solid fuel	Diameter: 370mm (14.5in)
Deployment: fixed and mobile	Launch weight: 626kg (1380lb)
Length: 5.12m (16ft 9in)	Range: 40km (25 miles)

▲ **MIM-23 HAWK surface-to-air missile**

Israeli Air Force / Southern Air Defence Regiment, 1973

At the outbreak of the Yom Kippur War, the Israeli Air Force had acquired up to 12 batteries of the US-made MIM-23 HAWK surface-to-air missile. Deployed in 1960, the HAWK is still in use as a medium-range air defence missile system. HAWK (Homing All the Way Killer) missiles have also been mounted on mobile tracked vehicles by the Israelis.

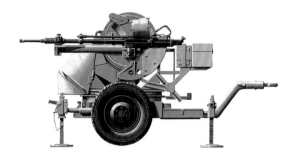

▲ **TCM-20 AA gun (Hispano-Suiza HS.404)**

Israeli Defence Forces / 14th Infantry Brigade, 1973

Basically, the Israeli TCM-20 served during the Yom Kippur War as an updated version of the US towed twin-mount .50-calibre (12.7mm) Browning air defence machine gun. The TCM-20's updated armament consists of two 20mm (0.79in) Hispano-Suiza cannon mounted on a two-wheeled carriage which is easily towed by a light vehicle.

Specifications

Crew: 3	Weight: 1350kg (2976lb)
Calibre: 20mm (0.79in)	Range: 2000m (6560ft)
Elevation: - 10 degrees to + 90 degrees	Muzzle velocity: 844m/sec (2770ft/sec)

Lebanon
1982–2006

Various factions vied for control of Lebanon for several years, and civil war devastated the country. The artillery of the Israeli and Syrian armies and the indiscriminate rocket attacks by insurgents became symbolic of the nation's suffering.

A S CIVIL WAR WRACKED LEBANON beginning in the mid-1970s, neighbouring countries were inexorably drawn into the conflict. While control of the country was at stake, old antagonisms came to the fore, with the Palestine Liberation Organization (PLO) openly inciting unrest between Christian and Muslim militia groups and in turn provoking Israel and Syria to military action. During the same period, the Hezbollah terror organization was founded by Islamic extremists and Palestinian nationalists supported by the government of Iran.

During periods of unrest, the Israeli Defence Forces have invaded or occupied portions of Lebanon, most notably during the 1982 offensive which evicted the Palestine Liberation Organization from the country. Israeli involvement stemmed largely from continuing terror and guerrilla rocket and infiltration attacks against settlements in northern Israel from havens in southern Lebanon. These operations were often backed by the PLO and later by Hezbollah. At the height of its strength in Lebanon, the PLO fielded up to 200 artillery pieces and rocket launchers in the country, organized into seven artillery battalions.

Antagonism old and new

At various times, the Syrian Army deployed at least 200 tanks and artillery pieces, including as many as 19 batteries of air defence missiles such as the SA-6 Gainful, in the region of the Bekaa Valley, while the Israeli Defence Forces committed more than 1200 tanks and armoured personnel carriers along with supporting field artillery and defence units. Numerous paramilitary forces, both Christian and Muslim, numbered in the thousands, and throughout the course of the war these groups were allied with one another, betrayed those alliances, and fought in a confusing tangle of allegiances during which thousands of civilians were killed, wounded or made homeless. While artillery fire is often a deciding factor in the outcome of a battle, during the Lebanese Civil War, it was sometimes employed indiscriminately by several factions against civilian targets which were suspected of harbouring guerrilla fighters or as an instrument of terror in its own right.

Among the most prominent artillery weapons employed by the Syrian Army, the PLO and other forces in Lebanon were the Soviet-made 130mm (5.1in) M1954 and 152mm (6in) field artillery pieces and the BM-21 truck-mounted rocket launcher. Also known as the M-46, the 130mm (5.1in) M1954 was an aging weapon at the time of the Lebanese Civil War but was no less effective. Its crew of eight was capable of firing six rounds per minute under standard combat conditions, eight rounds in burst mode and five rounds in a sustained engagement. Its effective range of 27.5km (17 miles) with unassisted ammunition provided a weapon which could be used against Israeli forces and other targets at a considerable distance. The People's Republic of China has manufactured a copy of the M-46 under licence for a number of years and designated it the Type 59-1.

The 152mm (6in) M1955 D-20 towed gun-howitzer was introduced to the Red Army in 1955 as a nuclear-capable long-range field artillery weapon.

Its crew of eight could fire up to six rounds per minute in burst situations and one round per minute during sustained combat operations. Its range with conventional ammunition was approximately 17.4km (11 miles). Manufactured by the People's Republic of China as the Type 66, the D-20 was the first Soviet field artillery piece to employ a semi-automatic vertical sliding wedge breech block.

A descendant of the original BM-13 Katyusha rocket launchers of the World War II era, the BM-21 Grad 122mm (4.8in) rocket launcher entered service in 1964 and is still in widespread use today. It consists of 40 tubes and is mounted atop the 6X6 Ural 375D truck chassis. With a rate of fire of two rounds per second and a maximum range of 40km (25 miles), the BM-21 battery is capable of saturating a large area of territory and disrupting troop concentrations and armoured formations. Its crew of five can deploy the system into firing position in as little as three minutes, while the reload time is approximately ten minutes. In a barrage situation, all 40 rockets may be airborne in as little as 20 seconds.

While the launchers themselves have been utilized by the PLO and the Syrian Army, guerrilla organizations such as Hamas or Hezbollah have

Specifications

Crew: 7	Engine: 372kW (493hp) V-2 V12 diesel
Weight: n/k	Speed (road): 55km/h (33mph)
Length (hull): 6m (19ft 7in)	Road range: 360km (223 miles)
Width: 3m (9ft 10in)	Armament: 1 x 122mm (4.8in) D-30 howitzer
Height: n/k	

▲ **T-34 with 122mm D-30 SP howitzer**

Syrian Army / 1st Armoured Division / 58th Mechanized Brigade, Lebanon, 1982

This artwork shows the Syrian 122mm (4.8in) D-30 SP howitzer in winter camouflage and in firing position. The crew's firing platform unfolded from the side of the tank chassis. When the vehicle was in motion, the platform folded back.

been known to fire the same 122mm (4.8in) rocket used with the BM-21 from improvised tubes during attacks on Israeli settlements.

Battleship bombardment

The United States became involved in the Lebanese Civil War during the early 1980s as United Nations peacekeepers and multinational forces were introduced to the war-torn country. Frequently these troops were the targets of suicide bombers and insurgent activity. In October 1983, a pair of truck bombings hit a US Marine Corps barracks and a French military installation in the Lebanese capital of Beirut, killing nearly 300 servicemen. Syrian and Druze artillery shelled Christian positions routinely, while the Christians responded in kind and often enough instigated the duels as well. US aircraft attacked Syrian artillery emplacements on several occasions in retaliation for Syrian air defence missiles having been fired against US and French planes.

The 406mm (16in) guns of the battleship USS *New Jersey* fired for the first time on hostile positions near the Lebanese capital on 14 December 1983. On 8 February 1984, the *New Jersey* conducted the heaviest naval bombardment of shore targets since the Korean War, firing 300 406mm (16in) shells at positions occupied by the Syrian Army and its allied Druze militia. After-action reports indicated that at least 30 of these massive shells destroyed a Syrian command post, killing at least one general, reported

to have been the commander of all Syrian forces in Lebanon, and several senior staff officers.

During their numerous incursions into Lebanon, the Israeli Defence Forces have adapted their use of armour and mechanized infantry to the rigours of urban combat while also utilizing artillery fire to suppress the small arms and rockets of guerrilla forces and to duel with Syrian guns. Along with the M-50 self-propelled assault gun, the Israelis deployed their Soltam M-68 155mm (6.1in) artillery and the M-71, an improved version of the M-68 which incorporated not only a longer barrel but also a compressed-air-driven rammer which facilitated rapid loading and firing under combat conditions. The Israelis also modified the chassis of the M4 Sherman tank to carry a number of artillery pieces, including the 155mm (6.1in) L39, a longer version of the L33 gun.

Israeli-made self-propelled artillery

Along with using US-made artillery such as the M109 self-propelled howitzer and the M107 175mm (6.9in) self-propelled gun, the Israelis developed their own self-propelled artillery. In the mid-1980s, the Soltam company experimented with a 155mm (6.1in) self-propelled howitzer known as the Sholef, or Gunslinger, which mounted the heavy weapon atop the modified chassis of the Merkava main battle tank; however, the 45.7-tonne (45-ton) vehicle never entered production. During the 1982

▲ **Rascal light SP howitzer**

Israeli Defence Forces / Southern Regional Command / 366th Division /
55th Artillery Battalion 'Draken' ('Dragon'), 1990

The light self-propelled Rascal 155mm (6.1in) howitzer was designed and built by Soltam Ltd. Weighing only 20.3 tonnes (20 tons), the Rascal was the lightest of the Soltam 155mm (6.1in) self-propelled weapons. It was capable of transport by air, truck or rail.

Specifications	
Crew: 4	Engine: 261kW (350hp) diesel
Weight: 19,500kg (43,000lb)	Speed: 50km/h (31mph)
Length (with gun): 7.5m (24ft 7in)	Road range: 350km (220 miles)
Width: 2.46m (8ft 1in)	Armament: 1 x 155mm (6.1in) howitzer
Height: 2.3m (7ft 7in)	

Lebanon invasion, the MAR-290 was deployed, with four 290mm (11.4in) rocket tubes capable of firing high-explosive fragmentation or cluster ammunition.

The Soltam Rascal light self-propelled 155mm (6.1in) howitzer is contemporary with the Sholef but much lighter at 20.3 tonnes (20 tons) and easily transported by air. The barrel is mounted on a hydraulic turntable at the rear of the chassis, which adds to the Rascal's stability. In preparation for firing, the Rascal deploys two hydraulically operated spades. Its 36 rounds of ammunition are stored externally.

An innovative infantry weapon of the period is the Soltam 120mm (4.7in) mortar. Adopted by the US Army in the early 1990s, the Soltam 120mm is capable of firing a maximum of 16 rounds per minute or four rounds in a sustained environment. Operated by a crew of four or five, the weapon is either towed or mounted on a light vehicle.

▲ **Soltam 120mm Mortar**

Israeli Defence Forces / Golani Infantry Brigade, 1982

A heavy infantry mortar which is often towed on a two-wheeled carriage, the Soltam 120mm (4.7in) mortar has been accepted by several armies, including that of the United States, as a replacement for lighter weapons. Its fin-stabilized ammunition provides accurate plunging fire against enemy positions. Deployment is rapid and involves first tipping the trailer so that the baseplate drops to the ground, and then lifting the tube.

Specifications

Crew: 5	Weight: 231kg (510lb)
Calibre: 120mm (4.7in)	Range: 6500m (7100 yards)
Elevation: + 43 degrees to + 85 degrees	Muzzle velocity: 310m/sec (1017ft/sec)

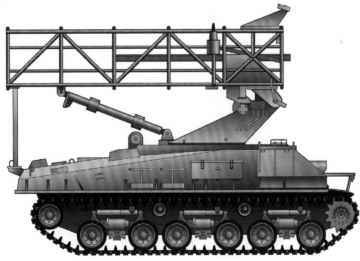

▲ **MAR-290**

Israeli Defence Forces / 211th Armoured Brigade, 1982

An improved version of an Israeli-built copy of the Soviet BM-24 multiple launch rocket system, the MAR-290 consists of four 290mm (11.4in) backward-facing rocket tubes mounted on the modified chassis of the M4 Sherman tank. Its combat debut occurred during the 1982 Israeli invasion of Lebanon, and the weapon is capable of firing high-explosive fragmentation or cluster ammunition.

Specifications

Crew: 4	System combat weight: 29,465kg (29 tons)
Calibre: 290mm (11.4in)	Range: 22km (24,059 yards)
Rocket length: 5.45m (17ft 10in)	Rate of fire: 4 rockets in 10 seconds
Rocket weight: 600kg (1322lb)	

▲ **Fire support**

An Israeli M109A6 self-propelled howitzer bombards positions in Lebanon from
northern Israel during the 2006 Lebanon War.

▲ **M109 SP howitzer**

Israeli Defence Forces / 212th Artillery Regiment / 405th Artillery Battalion /
2nd Platoon, 2006

The US 155mm (6.1in) M109 self-propelled howitzer was developed in the early
1950s and has been upgraded on numerous occasions to include automatic fire
control, an improved gun mount, a longer barrel and improved explosive reactive
armour protection. More than 4000 have been manufactured, and the weapon
today is fielded by the armed forces of more than 30 nations.

Specifications

Crew: 6	Engine: 302kW (405hp) Detroit Diesel
Weight: 27.9 tonnes (27.5 tons)	Model 8V-71T diesel
Length: 6.61m (21ft 8.25in)	Speed: 56km/h (35mph)
Width: 3.26m (10ft 9.75in)	Range: 390km (240 miles)
Height: 3.29m (10ft 9.5in)	Armament: 1 x 155mm (6.1in) howitzer

Iran–Iraq War
1980–88

A horrific war of attrition developed between neighbouring countries following the invasion of Iran by Saddam Hussein's Iraq. Both sides fired ballistic missiles, and the horror of chemical weapons was revealed to the world.

W HEN PRE-EMPTIVE AIR STRIKES hit bases of the Iranian Air Force and troops of the Iraqi Army surged across the frontier with the Islamic Republic, Saddam Hussein had hoped for a quick victory. However, the two nations became locked in a bloody war of attrition with each gaining the upper hand temporarily. Neither, in the end, was able to overcome the other decisively.

Although the Iraqi military had been professionally trained, somewhat modernized and augmented with equipment purchased from a number of nations, and prepared for war, the Iranian force which confronted it possessed equipment, including field artillery and a small number of self-propelled guns, of US manufacture which had been sold to Iran under the regime of the Shah. As the war dragged on, it became apparent that the Iraqis did possess towed and self-propelled artillery in greater numbers than the Iranians, whose armoured vehicles and

infantry were often at a decided disadvantage on the battlefield. However, the sheer weight of Iranian infantry numbers countered the Iraqi advantage in heavy equipment.

At the outset of hostilities, the Iranian Army deployed four independent artillery groups and an air defence command of four HAWK missile battalions. Iranian towed artillery included the US- manufactured M2A1 105mm (4.1in) and M114 155mm (6.1in) howitzers. Self-propelled artillery included the M107 175mm (6.9in) self-propelled gun and the M108 203mm (8in) self-propelled howitzer. At the height of its capability, Iranian artillery numbered approximately 5000 guns of various types.

In 1980, the Iraqi Army could muster more than 7300 towed and self-propelled artillery pieces, some of which had been in service for more than 30 years. Among the towed pieces were the Italian OTO Melara 105mm (4.1in) Mod 56 pack howitzer,

▲ **Canon de 155mm Mle F3 Automoteur**

Iraqi Army / 5th Mechanized Division, 1980

During the Iran–Iraq War, the Iraqi military received 85 examples of this French self-propelled artillery weapon. The gun, also known as the GCT 155mm (6.1in), went into production in 1977, and more than 400 were constructed by the mid-1990s. With a maximum rate of fire of eight rounds per minute and upgraded nuclear, biological and chemical defences, it was one of the most modern self-propelled guns of the Iran–Iraq War.

Specifications

Crew: 4	Engine: 540kW (720hp) Hispano-Suiza 110
Weight: 41,949kg (92,288lb)	12-cylinder multifuel
Length: 10.25m (33ft 7.5in)	Speed: 60km/h (37mph)
Width: 3.15m (10ft 4in)	Range: 450km (280 miles)
Height: 3.25m (10ft 8in)	Armament: 1 x 155mm (6.1in) cannon

the Soviet 152mm (6in) D-20 Model 1955 and 122mm (4.8in) D-30 developed in the 1960s, the US M114, and the Type 59-1, a Chinese copy of the Soviet 130mm (5.1in) M1954 gun. Among the self-propelled artillery in the Iraqi arsenal were the Soviet 122mm (4.8in) 2S1 and 152mm (6in) 2S3 howitzers along with a relative few examples of the American M109.

The Iraqi Army was also equipped with Soviet tactical surface-to-surface FROG (Free Rocket Over Ground) missiles, AT-3 Sagger and AT-4 Spigot anti-tank missiles, and the French MILAN anti-tank missile. Several rocket-launcher systems, including the ubiquitous Soviet BM-16 and BM-21 truck-mounted systems, were also available. The Iraqi ballistic-missile inventory included the Soviet Scud B and a modified Scud known as the Al Hussein, with increased range. Iran responded to Iraqi Scud attacks against Tehran with its own launches of Scud missiles purchased from Syria and Libya directed towards Baghdad. By the end of the war, Iraq had expended more than 500 standard and Al Hussein Scuds, while the Iranians had fired more than 170.

The bull's eye

While the war with Iran was under way, Canadian engineer Gerald Bull was employed by the government of Iraq to produce a generation of

IRANIAN ARTILLERY UNITS, 1980	
Unit	Base
11th Independent Artillery Group	Khuzestan, Iran
22th Independent Artillery Group	Khuzestan, Iran
44th Independent Artillery Group	Khuzestan, Iran
55th Independent Artillery Group	Khuzestan, Iran
4 HAWK missile battalions	Khuzestan, Iran

artillery weapons with great range and the capability of firing conventional, chemical and nuclear weapons. Among the most prominent of the Bull guns developed for the Iraqis and utilized during the war with Iran were approximately 300 new 155mm (6.1in) weapons similar in design to the GC-45, which Bull had developed in the 1970s for several nations, primarily Austria and South Africa. The GC-45 was considered one of the finest weapons of its kind in the world, with a maximum range of 39,600m (24.6 miles) and maximum and sustained rates of fire of five and two rounds per minute respectively. Reports have surfaced that in 1985 Austria shipped 200 of these guns, designated the GHN-45, through Jordan to Iraq for use in the war. By the time of the 1991 Gulf War, these guns were still worrisome to the Coalition partners.

Bull was also commissioned to design two self-propelled guns, the 210mm (8.27in) Al Fao and the

Specifications

Crew: 6

Weight: 28,100kg (61,820lb)

Length: 8.48m (27ft 10in)

Width: 3.27m (10ft 9in)

Height: 2.75m (9ft)

Engine: 388kW (520hp) Model V-54 V12 diesel

Speed: 50km/h (31mph)

Road range: 420km (260 miles)

Armament: 2 x 57mm (2.2in) anti-aircraft guns

▲ **ZSU-57-2 SPAAG**

Iraqi Army / 113th Infantry Brigade, 1980

The ZSU-57-2 originally entered service with the Soviet Red Army in World War II and was later modified to fit the chassis of the T-54 main battle tank. Mounting a pair of 57mm (2.2in) anti-aircraft cannon, the weapon produced a sustained rate of fire of approximately 70 rounds per minute per gun. Its excellent mobility and range contributed to its service longevity into the 1990s.

155mm (6.1in) Majnoon. Although the Al Fao was first seen in public in Baghdad in 1989, neither is known to have entered service with the Iraqi Army. The Al Fao is a similar design to the South African G6 howitzer and has been estimated to weigh 48.8 tonnes (48 tons). Its range of 56,000m (35 miles) is astonishing, particularly considering that its rate of fire is four rounds of 109kg (240lb) ammunition per minute. Most troubling is the capability of the Al Fao to fire chemical rounds containing sarin, mustard or phosgene gases.

Chemical consternation

On numerous occasions during the war with Iran, Saddam Hussein demonstrated a ruthless willingness to use chemical weapons. These deadly weapons of mass destruction were delivered by Scud missiles, aerial bombs, or artillery shells. Series G nerve agents and Series H blister agents were both used. The US Central Intelligence Agency estimated in 1991 that Iran had suffered at least 50,000 casualties due to chemical weapons during the war; however, other estimates exceed 100,000.

In battle, the Iraqis integrated chemical weapons into their defensive schemes. Often, chemical shells would be fired at Iranian troop concentrations and artillery emplacements to disrupt the progress of large Iranian infantry attacks and supporting fire. Offensively, the Iraqis fired conventional high-explosive fragmentation shells at distant targets, while hitting Iranian forward positions, command-and-control centres and marshalling areas near the front line with chemical shells. Iraqi aircraft dropped bombs filled with mustard gas and tabun, a highly toxic nerve agent, and it was also reported that spray devices were affixed to helicopters to disperse chemicals over a wide area of the battlefield.

In March 1986, Javier Pérez de Cuéllar, Secretary General of the United Nations, accused the Iraqis of using chemical weapons in direct violation of the 1925 Geneva Protocol. Although Saddam Hussein continued to deny their use, the evidence began to mount, and independent reports confirmed thousands of casualties. Particularly horrific was the apparent use of nerve gas on the civilian population of the Kurdish town of Halabjah in northeastern Iraq.

Man versus machine

In mid-1982, control of the Iranian military was vested in the country's Islamic clergy. In turn, massive human-wave attacks were ordered against entrenched Iraqi troops and artillery. The results were predictable as Iranian soldiers, many of them as young as nine and as old as 50, were slaughtered. The Iraqis also flooded low-lying areas to impede the progress of Iranian tanks. However, in most instances the combat-effectiveness of tanks on both sides was limited due to the preference of commanders for digging the vehicles in and employing them primarily as artillery.

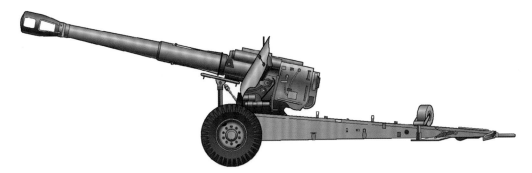

▲ **152mm Towed Gun-Howitzer M1955 (D-20)**

Iraqi Army / 12th Armoured Division, 1980

The Model 1955 152mm (6in) D-20 gun-howitzer was developed in the Soviet Union just after World War II and entered service with the Red Army by the mid-1950s. Intended as a replacement for the 152mm (6in) Model 1937 howitzer, the D-20 featured a split-rail carriage and maximum rate of fire of up to six rounds per minute. The gun was also mounted on a tracked chassis to produce the 2S3 self-propelled assault weapon.

Specifications

Crew: 8

Calibre: 152mm (6in)

Elevation: - 5 degrees to + 63 degrees

Weight: 5700kg (12,566lb)

Range: 17.4km (11 miles)

Muzzle velocity: 650m/sec (2132ft/sec)

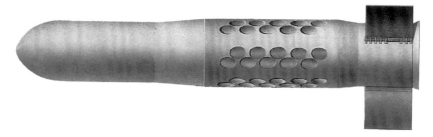

▲ **Dragon ATGM**

Islamic Republic of Iran Army / 30th Infantry Brigade, 1981

Developed in the United States as a shoulder-fired wire-guided anti tank missile, the Dragon was designed in the mid-1960s and entered service with the US Army in 1975. Designed specifically to eliminate Soviet main battle tanks, the weapon could be fired by a single soldier and was used effectively against Iraqi armour during the war of 1980–88.

Specifications	
Configuration: two-stage, hollow charge	Diameter: 292mm (11.5in)
Deployment: man-portable	Launch weight: 14.57kg (32.1lb)
Length: 1154mm (45.4in)	Range: 1000m (1094 yards)

Middle East today
1990–PRESENT

In this volatile region, the military forces of numerous nations have continued to arm and equip with vast amounts of artillery. Although many of these systems have been in service for decades, they remain lethal.

THE PROLIFERATION of artillery throughout the armies of Middle Eastern countries and in the hands of guerrilla and militia organizations has contributed to the instability of the region during the past quarter-century. Following the bloody war with Iran, Saddam Hussein's Iraq embarked on a substantial programme of rearmament, purchasing equipment and technology from numerous countries and posing a threat to neighbouring nations such as tiny Kuwait, which Iraqi forces invaded in August 1990. Countering the Iraqi threat, moderate Arab nations such as Saudi Arabia and Egypt modernized the artillery components of their land forces as well. While each of these remained primarily dependent on foreign technology, some organic modifications to existing systems did occur as each country sought to complement its existing arsenal.

Among the major purchases made by the Iraqis were the American M198 155mm (6.1in) towed and the M109 155mm (6.1in) self-propelled howitzers; the GHN-45 155mm (6.1in) towed howitzer designed by

Canadian engineer Gerald Bull and sold to Iraq via Austria; and the modern French GCT 155mm (6.1in) self-propelled gun. The GCT 155mm was developed in the early 1970s, and Saudi Arabia was the first nation to deploy the weapon after accepting deliveries in the 1980s. Iraq quickly followed suit, purchasing 85 of the GCTs during the Iran–Iraq War. Many of these remained in service with the Iraqi Army into the next decade, and more than 400 were manufactured by the French by 1995. Developed as a replacement for the F3 155mm (6.1in) gun, the GCT provided better armour protection for the four-man crew, enhanced night-vision technology, protection against nuclear, chemical and biological weapons, and an automatic loading system.

The artillery capabilities of the Royal Saudi Land Forces have been substantially improved in recent years with the introduction of more than 300 examples of the US M109A6 Paladin 155mm (6.1in) self-propelled howitzer. The Paladin constitutes a substantial upgrade to earlier versions of the M109,

▲ AMX-13 DCA

Royal Saudi Land Forces / 10th Mechanized Brigade, 1990

Developed in response to the French Army's need for a self-propelled air defence gun, the AMX-13 DCA entered service with the French Army in 1969. Its twin 30mm (1.2in) Hispano-Suiza cannon were mounted on the chassis of the AMX-13 light tank, with the three-man crew protected by an enclosed turret of cast steel. The same turret was later mounted on the AMX-30 tank chassis, and these were also purchased by Saudi Arabia.

Specifications

Crew: 3	Engine: 187.5kW (250hp) SOFAM Model 8Gxb
Weight: 17,200kg (37,840lb)	8-cylinder petrol
Length: 5.4m (17ft 11in)	Speed: 60km/h (37mph)
Width: 2.5m (8ft 2in)	Range: 300km (186 miles)
Height: 3m (9ft 10in)	Armament: 2 x 30mm (1.2in) cannon

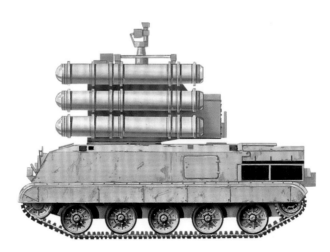

▲ Shahine SAM

Royal Saudi Air Defence Forces / Dhahran Battery, 1991

The Shahine air defence missile system combines the chassis of the French AMX-30 main battle tank and a variant of the French Crotale air defence missile. Seventeen mobile batteries of the Royal Saudi Air Defence Forces were equipped with the Shahine in the 1990s, and other Crotale missiles were posted in static firing positions.

Specifications

Crew: 3	Engine: 517.5kW (690hp) Hispano-Suiza 110
Weight: 38,799kg (85,554lb)	12-cylinder multifuel
Length: 6.59m (21ft 7.4in)	Speed: 65km/h (40mph)
Width: 3.1m (10ft 2in)	Range: 600km (370 miles)
Height: 5.5m (18ft)	Armament: 6 x Crotale SAMs

which date to the late 1950s. The M109A6 includes upgraded armour protection, fire direction control and quicker displacement.

Several hundred M198 and FH-70 155mm (6.1in) field howitzers were acquired by the Saudis during the early 1980s to equip the army's five artillery battalions. The M198 entered service with the US Army in 1979, and a well-trained crew of nine is capable of a maximum rate of fire of four rounds per minute. Although the armed forces of the United States and Great Britain have been replacing their M198s with the Global Combat Systems M777 howitzer, the M198 remains widely used by Middle Eastern countries. The FH-70 entered service in 1978 and was a joint venture between Germany, Italy and the United Kingdom. Its crew of eight can fire as many as six 155mm (6.1in) rounds per minute to a maximum range of 30km (32,808 yards).

Israeli ignition

The modern Israeli Defence Forces remain true to their fundamental doctrine of armour-heavy striking power. However, the lessons of the 1973 Yom Kippur War have influenced the thinking of Israeli commanders to the extent that artillery, both towed and self-propelled, has evolved into a major component of battlefield operations. Israeli tanks had been largely unsupported by self-propelled artillery during the 1973 war, and losses against Egyptian tank-killer units armed with man-portable missiles had been exceptionally high. Since then, Israeli artillery has played a key role in the fighting in southern Lebanon against Syrian and guerrilla forces.

Fielding at least 15 armoured and nine mechanized infantry brigades, the Israelis have augmented their artillery capabilities in recent years with the acquisition of updated US M109 155mm (6.1in) self-propelled howitzers while maintaining their older M-71 towed howitzers and other systems as well. More recent additions include the ATMOS 2000 152mm (6in) and Rascal 155mm (6.1in) self-propelled howitzers.

At the same time, the Israeli military has invested in nuclear-capable weaponry, including field artillery and surface-to-surface missile systems such as the Jericho, which originated during the early 1960s as a joint effort between the Israeli government and the French firm of Dassault. The most recent of the Jericho series, the Jericho III, is reportedly a three-stage, solid-propellant ballistic missile with a range of up to 11,500km (7180 miles) and a nuclear payload of a single warhead of 750kg (1653lb) or three smaller MIRV warheads. Potentially, the Jericho brings the entire Middle East within range of Israeli nuclear weapons.

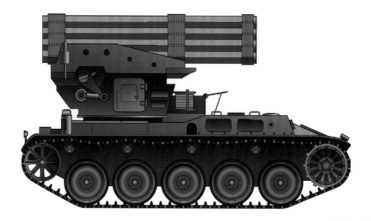

▲ **AMX-13/LAR160 MLRS**

Israeli Defence Forces / 334th Artillery Battalion, 1993

The AMX-13/LAR multiple launch rocket system incorporates the chassis of the French AMX-13 light tank with the LAR 160 rocket launcher. The LAR 160mm (6.3in) rocket is typically carried in pods of 13 and can be adapted to other platforms such as trucks, light armoured vehicles or trailers. The LAR 160 rocket is fin-stablilized and powered by solid propellant. It may be carried by helicopters to provide long-range fire support to airborne and light infantry units.

Specifications

Crew: 6

Calibre: 160mm (6.3in)

Rocket length: 3477mm (11ft 5in)

System combat weight: 16,765kg (16.5 tons)

Range: 45km (49,213 yards)

Rate of fire: unknown

▲ Palmaria SP howitzer

Libyan Army, 1992

Developed solely for the export market, the OTO Melara Palmaria 155mm (6.1in) self-propelled howitzer included an automatic loading system. The heavy weapon was mounted on the chassis of the OF 40 main battle tank. The first prototypes were built in the late 1970s. Production commenced in 1982 and ceased in the early 1990s.

Specifications

Crew: 5	Engine: 559kW (750hp) 8-cylinder diesel
Weight: 46,632kg (102,590lb)	Speed: 60km/h (37mph)
Length: 11.474m (37ft 7.75in)	Road range: 400km (250 miles)
Width: 2.35m (7ft 8.5in)	Armament: 1 x 155mm (6.1in) howitzer, plus
Height: 2.874m (9ft 5.25in)	1 x 7.62mm (0.3in) MG

▲ G6 Rhino 155mm SP howitzer

United Arab Emirates Union Defence Force, 1997

The G6 155mm (6.1in) self-propelled howitzer is an autonomous system with a 700km (435-mile) vehicle fuel range. Developed in South Africa by Denel Land Systems, the G6 is in service with the South African Army (43 systems) and has also been exported to the United Arab Emirates (78 systems) and Oman (24 systems). The crew members are protected against landmines, gunfire and bombardment fragments.

Specifications

Crew: 6	Engine: 391kW (525hp) diesel
Weight: 47,000kg (103,600lb)	Speed: 90km/h (56mph)
Length (chassis): 10.2m (33ft 4.3in)	Road range: 700km (435 miles)
Width: 3.4m (11ft 2in)	Armament: 1 x 155mm (6.1in) cannon
Height: 3.5m (11ft 6in)	

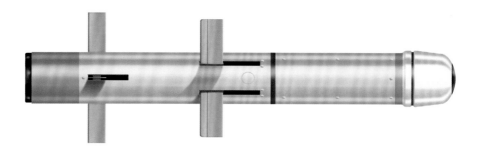

Specifications

Configuration: single-stage, solid fuel

Deployment: man-portable or light vehicle

Length: 1670mm (5ft 6in)

Diameter: 170mm (6.7in)

Launch weight: 4.3kg (9.5lb)

Range: 25,000m (82,000ft)

Launch preparation time: 30 seconds

▲ **Spike AT missile**

Israeli Defence Forces / Golani Brigade, 1998

A man-portable anti-tank missile incorporating fire-and-forget technology, the Spike entered service with the Israeli Defence Forces in 1997. While the missile is line-of-sight oriented, some variants are also capable of targeting through fire-and-observe guidance. The missile carries a tandem HEAT (high-explosive anti-tank) warhead and is powered by a solid-fuel rocket. It is also mounted on light vehicles.

Wars in Africa
1960–2000

Since 1960, Africa has been wracked by more than 20 civil wars, far more than any other continent on the planet. Ethnic strife, territorial ambitions and political strongmen have fuelled the flames of unrest.

THE WAR-TORN CONTINENT OF AFRICA has been the modern scene of locally driven civil war, battles for control of natural resources and the settling of centuries-old tribal and ethnic accounts. Since 1960, major conflicts have been fought in Rwanda, Congo, Somalia, Sudan, Liberia, Burundi and Angola among others, while millions of civilians and paramilitary and military personnel have been killed or made homeless, suffering the twin spectres of starvation and disease in the wake of war. In 1998, at least 11 major armed conflicts were in progress on the continent simultaneously.

Proxy wars

The rise of the Third World created a power vacuum on the African continent, facilitating a surge of nationalism and unrest. Often enough, foreign nations have exacerbated these conflicts through ideological proxy wars or attempts to extend their own influence through puppet governments. Former colonial powers have funnelled arms and equipment to rebel warlords, to legitimate governments fighting for survival and to oppressive regimes bent on crushing opposition.

Outside suppliers

From 1950 to 1989, the United States alone supplied $1.5 billion to various governments and political or military factions in Africa. In 1991, a total of $4.5 million in military hardware was shipped by the US to the government of what was then the nation of Zaire. Soviet military advisers and Cuban troops participated in the long-lasting civil war in Angola. During each of the wars on the African continent, various old and new artillery systems have been primary dealers of death and destruction.

Angolan Civil War
1975–2002

In a confusing tangle of alliances and ideologically charged confrontations, a 27-year civil war in Angola did not end before at least 500,000 people were killed and the superpowers had been drawn into a developing proxy war.

LONG A COLONIAL POSSESSION of Portugal, Angola became an independent nation in the autumn of 1974, and civil war broke out shortly thereafter. The communist-backed ruling party, the MPLA (Popular Movement for the Liberation of Angola), and its military wing, the FAPLA (People's Armed Forces for the Liberation of Angola), opposed the anti-communist UNITA (National Union for the Total Independence of Angola). These were the principal warring factions, and during the course of the fighting the Soviet Union, the United States, Cuba and the neighbouring African countries of Zaire, Mozambique and South Africa were drawn either directly into the fighting or provided material support to one side or the other. United Nations efforts to bring about peace were continually frustrated, and civilian populations were often caught in the crossfire. Three distinct periods of fighting were punctuated by brief intervals of peace, and from 1994 to 1998 the United Nations invested more than $1.6 billion to maintain a peacekeeping force in the country.

During the Angolan Civil War, numerous heavy artillery bombardments were experienced, and many of these were conducted by regular army and paramilitary groups. Soviet military aid to Marxist forces in the country topped $1 billion in 1986,

while Fidel Castro's Cuba not only supplied arms and equipment but also introduced combat troops to the conflict. As the war dragged on, Cuban troop strength approached 40,000. At the same time, the United States sent millions of dollars in aid to UNITA, along with advanced weapons such as the shoulder-fired FIM-92 Stinger air defence missile.

Angola became nothing short of an arms marketplace during the war as numerous countries sold military aircraft, missiles, small arms and artillery to the warring factions. UNITA was known to have purchased a number of FROG (Free Rocket Over Ground) missile systems from North Korea. The Soviet-designed FROG-7 entered service in the mid-1960s and consists of a transporter-erector-launcher atop the wheeled 8X8 ZIL-135 platform. The missile itself packs a 550kg (1200lb) high-explosive warhead with a range of up to 90km (56 miles).

Cold War calamity
Both East and West considered the Angolan Civil War a contest of political and armed will. Angola would prove to be a prime example of proxy warfare with political and ideological prestige at stake for the major powers. The Battle of Cuito Cuanavale in early 1988 proved to be the largest battle on the

Specifications

Configuration: single-stage, solid fuel

Deployment: mobile

Length: 3.15m (19ft 4in)

Diameter: 210mm (8.26in)

Launch weight: 130kg (287lb)

Range: 12km (7.5 miles)

Launch preparation time: 4 minutes

▲ **9K33 Osa (SA-8 Gecko)**

Cuban Revolutionary Armed Forces / Revolutionary Army Command SAM Brigade, 1988

The 9K33 Osa surface-to-air missile, known as the SA-8 Gecko to NATO personnel, is a single-stage solid-fuel low-altitude surface weapon developed in the Soviet Union and deployed in 1972. It was the first mobile air defence system to deploy missiles and onboard radar on the same platform, which includes the 9A33 amphibious 6X6 transporter-erector-launcher. Nicknamed Land Roll by NATO, the sophisticated radar of the SA-8 system allows tracking of multiple targets and minimizes the effects of jamming by electronic countermeasures.

African continent since the World War II fight at El Alamein in far-off Egypt. Both sides claimed a victory; however, the result was indecisive.

Concerned with its border security, the government of South Africa opted to intervene militarily in Angola on several occasions. Among the weapons deployed by the South African Defence Force was the relatively new G5 155mm (6.1in) howitzer, produced in South Africa and based initially on the design of the Gerald Bull GC-45. A lengthy development and modification phase was conducted in the late 1970s, and the G5 entered service with the South African armed forces in 1982. Its eight-man crew could fire at a sustained rate of three rounds per minute, and the weapon was also exported to Iran, Iraq, Malaysia and Qatar.

The South West African Territorial Forces, formed in 1980 under the control of the South African Defence Force, mounted the US-manufactured M40

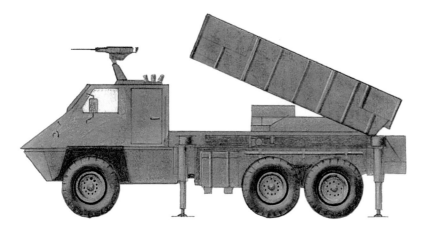

Specifications

Crew: 3
Calibre: 180mm (7.1in)
Rocket length: 4.2m (13ft 9in)
Rocket weight: 152kg (335lb)
System combat weight: 10,000kg (22,046lb)
Range: 16,000m (17,500 yards)
Rate of fire: 450–550rpm/cyclic

▲ **ASTROS II MLRS**

FAPLA / Mechanized Infantry Brigade Artillery Battalion, 1987

The ASTROS II MLRS (multiple launch rocket system) was developed in Brazil by defence contractor Avibrás and entered service with the Brazilian Army in 1983, while also being exported to several countries. Capable of firing rockets of 127mm (5in), 180mm (7.1in) and 300mm (11.8in), the ASTROS utilizes the Tectran Enginharia 10-ton 6X6 wheeled chassis mounting the AV-LMU launcher. Depending on the rocket loaded, the launcher's maximum capacity is from four to 32 missiles. Specifications here are for the 180mm (7.1in) SS-40 rocket.

Specifications

Crew: 4
Calibre: 300mm (11.8in)
Rocket length: 4.85m (15.91ft)
Rocket weight: 645kg (1422lb)
System combat weight: 17,273kg (17 tons)
Range: 68km (42.25 miles)
Rate of fire: unknown

▲ **Avibrás X-40**

FAPLA / Mechanized Infantry Brigade Artillery Battalion, 1976

The predecessor of the ASTROS II MLRS, the Brazilian Avibrás X-40 was a single-stage solid-fuel free flight rocket launcher mounted on the chassis of the Bernardini X1A1 light tank. The X-40 was a cumbersome system. Target acquisition, launching sequence and reloading were time-consuming functions. The X-40 was eventually retired from service in the 1990s.

106mm (4.17in) recoilless rifle atop a variety of 4X4 vehicles including the Toyota Land Cruiser and the Land Rover Defender. The M40 had been developed in the mid-1950s as a replacement for the earlier M27 105mm (4.1in) recoilless rifle. While it is generally referred to as 106mm (4.17in), the M40 is actually also a 105mm (4.1in) weapon. The slight variation in the name was to avoid confusion with other 105mm (4.1in) ammunition which was not compatible with the weapon. Used extensively in Vietnam, it was eventually replaced in the anti-tank role by missiles such as the BGM-71 TOW.

Marxist forces in Angola deployed a variety of Soviet Bloc-supplied towed artillery, and despite its age the 130mm (5.1in) M1954 was among the best. Developed during the mid-1950s as a replacement for older pre-World War II weapons, the M1954 served with FAPLA forces along with the 122mm (4.8in)

D-30 field howitzer of 1960s origin. Officially called the M-46 by the Soviets, the M1954 was light enough for reasonable mobility in the jungles and grasslands of Angola, while its sustained rate of fire of six rounds per minute and maximum rate of eight rounds per minute were formidable. With a maximum range of up to 37.8km (23.5 miles) with performance-assisted ammunition, it is capable of taking opposing forces under fire at a great distance. Although the Soviet Army replaced the M-46 with the 152mm (6in) 2A36 Giatsint B in the late 1970s, the older weapon is still in use around the globe.

In the air

To defend against South African aircraft, the Cuban forces in Angola were equipped with the Soviet-made 9K33 Osa, or Wasp, a potent air defence missile with an effective range of up to 12km (7.5 miles)

▲ **Toyota Land Cruiser with 106mm recoilless rifle**

South West African Territorial Forces / 201st Infantry Battalion 1980

The all-terrain Toyota Land Cruiser was an ideal mobile mount for the US-manufactured 106mm (4.17in) recoilless rifle, an effective anti-tank weapon deployed by the South West African Territorial Forces. The 106mm (4.17in) recoilless rifle was developed during the mid-1950s as a replacement for the older M27 weapon and was later supplanted by anti-tank missiles such as the BTM-71 TOW system.

Specifications

Crew: 3

Calibre: 105mm (4.1in)

Elevation: - 17 degrees to + 65 degrees

Weight: 209.5kg (462lb)

Range: 1350m (1476 yards)

Muzzle velocity: 503m/sec (1650ft/sec)

Specifications

Crew: 8

Calibre: 130mm (5.1in)

Elevation: - 2.5 degrees to + 45 degrees

Weight: 7700kg (16,975lb)

Range: 27.5km (17 miles) unassisted

Muzzle velocity: 930m/sec (3051ft/sec)

▲ **130mm Towed Field Gun M1954 (M-46)**

FAPLA / Mechanized Infantry Brigade Artillery Battalion, 1975

The 130mm (5.1in) towed field gun, known to the Soviets as the M-46 and to NATO as the M1954, is a durable field artillery piece which is still in service with numerous nations after half a century. The M-46 proved a stable firing platform and relatively manoeuvrable towed artillery piece during the Angolan Civil War, and its large numbers were augmented with examples of the newer 122mm (4.8in) D-30 weapon.

and delivering a high-explosive warhead of 19kg (42lb). Known to NATO as the SA-8 Gecko, this missile entered service with the Red Army in 1972 and was produced for nearly a decade. Its 9A33 6X6 wheeled transporter-erector-launcher carries sophisticated radar which allows the tracking of two missiles simultaneously fired at the same target. A full Gecko battery includes four 9A33 vehicles along with two 9T217 transporter vehicles carrying additional missiles.

Brazilian rockets

One of the most effective weapons of the MPLA was of Brazilian manufacture, and the country became one of the leading arms exporters in the world during the 1980s. The ASTROS II MLRS (multiple launch rocket system) entered service in 1983 with the Brazilian Army and rapidly became the most profitable weapons system sold by its manufacturer, the Avibrás

company. Prior to the deployment of the ASTROS II (ASTROS stands for Artillery Saturation Rocket System), Avibrás had marketed the X-40 300mm (11.8in) mobile rocket system, which comprised a single-stage solid fuel rocket launcher mounted atop the chassis of the Bernardini X1A1 light tank.

The ASTROS II consists of the AV-LMU launcher atop the Tectran Enginharia 10-ton 6X6 truck, while rockets of 127mm (5in), 180mm (7.1in) and 300mm (11.8in) are compatible with the system. A full ASTROS II battery consists of six launcher vehicles, six ammunition resupply vehicles and a fire-control vehicle. At the battalion level, command-and-control centres are capable of directing up to four batteries.

FAPLA Mechanized Infantry Brigade artillery elements, 1986

The artillery component of the FAPLA mechanized infantry brigade included HQ and field artillery observation personnel along with a pair of batteries equipped with the 122mm (4.8in) D-30 field howitzer and 76mm (3in) ZIS-3 field gun, the latter a Soviet anti-tank gun dating from World War II. The Soviet-made BM-21 multiple launch rocket system was capable of saturating an area with high-explosive 122mm (4.8in) rockets, while the 120mm (4.7in) mortar team provided plunging fire against hardened enemy positions and troop concentrations. FAPLA operational units were organized similarly to the Soviet Red Army, although the term brigade may be misleading. FAPLA mechanized infantry brigades were smaller versions of the Red Army mechanized infantry regiments.

HQ (1 x truck)   **Field Artillery Observation (1 x truck)**

Artillery Battery (2 x 122mm/4.8in D-30 howitzers, 2 x trucks)

Artillery Battery (2 x 76mm/3in ZIS-3 guns, 2 x trucks)

MLR Battery (2 x BM-21 rocket launchers)   **Mortar Battery (1 x 120mm/4.7in mortar unit, 1 x truck)**

Cuban Motor Rifle Regiment artillery element, 1986

At its height during the late 1980s, Cuban military strength in Angola neared 40,000 troops. The artillery element of a Cuban Revolutionary Armed Forces motor rifle regiment included three artillery batteries, each consisting of a single 122mm (4.8in) D-30 field howitzer along with a pair of BM-21 truck-borne multiple launch rocket systems. The well-equipped Cuban forces brought modern anti-tank missiles such as the AT-3 Sagger and air defence missiles such as the SA-8 Gecko to Angola as well. These were typically organic to infantry battalions, as were the self-propelled FROG-7 surface-to-surface missile and the heavy 120mm (4.7in) mortar.

HQ (1 x truck)   **Field Artillery Observation (1 x truck)**

1 Battery (1 x 122mm/4.8in D-30 howitzer, 1 x truck, 2 x BM-21 rocket launchers)

1 Battery (1 x 122mm/4.8in D-30 howitzer, 1 x truck, 2 x BM-21 rocket launchers)

1 Battery (1 x 122mm/4.8in D-30 howitzer, 1 x truck, 2 x BM-21 rocket launchers)

South Africa
1970–PRESENT

The South African Artillery Formation has participated in territorial actions in Angola and Namibia and as a peacekeeping force in Central Africa.

SINCE ITS INVOLVEMENT IN the Angolan Civil War, the South African Defence Force has maintained a modern complement of weaponry, including the 155mm (6.1in) G5 towed and 155mm (6.1in) G6 self-propelled howitzers, the 40-barrel 127mm (5in) Bateleur MLRS (multiple launch rocket system), the M5 120mm (4.7in) mortar and smaller infantry support weapons.

The South African Artillery Formation is organized as a regular component consisting of the artillery school and the composite 4 Artillery Regiment at Potchefstroom, an airborne artillery battery with the 44 Parachute Regiment located at Bloemfontein and an artillery mobilization centre. Designated as reserve, seven artillery regiments are maintained at cadre strength. Reports currently indicate that a full deployment of the South African Artillery Formation would be a difficult task due to a lack of manpower and the fact that some reserve artillery personnel have been pressed into service as infantry peacekeepers in Central Africa. The 10 Air Defence Regiment is maintained as a separate force.

Contemporary firepower

The primary towed weapon of the South African Artillery Formation is the 155mm (6.1in) G5

howitzer, which has been in service for nearly 30 years and has undergone several improvements during that time. The weapon was designed by the South African firm of Denel Land Systems during the late 1970s. Based on Gerald Bull's GC-45 howitzer, the original 45-calibre version has been upgraded to a 52-calibre weapon designated the G5 2000.

SP version

A self-propelled version of the G5, the G6 Rhino, entered production in the late 1980s and is mounted on a heavy, wheeled 6X6 chassis. The Rhino has been praised for its outstanding mobility, which reduces the effectiveness of enemy

▲ G5 howitzer (Armscor)

South African Artillery Formation / Natal Field Artillery, 1985

The G5 howitzer was developed during the late 1970s by Denel Land Systems, a former arms manufacturing facility of the Armscor company. The G5 incorporated much of the design of the GC-45 howitzer, which had been developed by Canadian engineer Gerald Bull. The G5 is adapted to fire conventional ammunition or an extended-range type with stabilizing fins. Its crew of eight soldiers is capable of a sustained rate of fire of three rounds per minute. An updated G5, designated the G5 2000, made its debut in 2002.

Specifications

Crew: 8

Calibre: 155mm (6.1in)

Elevation: - 3 degrees to + 75 degrees

Weight: 13,750kg (13.56 tons)

Range: 30,000m (32,810 yards)

Muzzle velocity: 897m/sec (2942ft/sec)

Artillery Battery, 61st Mechanized Infantry Battalion, South African Defence Force, 1988

At this time a typical South African Defence Force artillery battery consisted of either two G5 155mm (6.1in) howitzers (with two trucks) or two 120mm (4.7in) M5 mortars. Some artillery batteries were equipped with both, and which weapon was used depended on the task the battery was asked to carry out. The 61st Mechanized Infantry Battalion served under the command of the 82nd Mechanized Brigade in 1988.

Artillery Battery (2 x G5 155mm/6.1in howitzers, 2 x M5 120mm/4.7in mortars, 4 x trucks)

counterbattery fire, and the protection which the armoured hull affords the crew of six against anti-tank mines.

Reports indicate that Denel embarked on the development of a light 105mm (4.1in) howitzer, the G7, in 1995 and that the weapon has undergone extensive tests and modifications related to its weight. A self-propelled version of the G7 was tested jointly with the US Army following a partnership between Denel and General Dynamics Land Systems. The General Dynamics LAV III armoured

vehicle chassis and the G7 gun mount produced a light, air-transportable self-propelled weapon which may outfit units of the American Stryker Brigade. The towed version of the G7 is served by a crew of five and is capable of a sustained rate of fire of six rounds per minute. Its effective range is up to 32km (20 miles) – a long reach for a weapon of its calibre. An even more advanced version of the G7 is planned under a contract designated the Advanced Multirole Light Artillery Gun Capability (AMLAGC) programme.

Specifications

Crew: 6

Weight: 47,000kg (103,600lb)

Length (chassis): 10.2m (33ft 4.3in)

Width: 3.4m (11ft 2in)

Height: 3.5m (11ft 6in)

Engine: 391kW (525hp) diesel

Speed: 90km/h (56mph)

Road range: 700km (430 miles)

Armament: 1 x 155mm (6.1in) cannon

▲ **G6 Rhino 155mm SP howitzer**

South African Army / 8th Mechanized Infantry Battalion, 1997

The wheeled G6 Rhino self-propelled howitzer has been noted for its excellent mobility and protection against anti-tank mines. It has a crew of six, and its 155mm (6.1in) L52 cannon is intended for direct mechanized infantry fire support as well as the protection of advancing tank columns.

▲ **Valkiri multiple launch rocket system**

South African Army / 61st Mechanized Infantry Battalion, 1982

Patterned after the highly successful Soviet-designed BM-21 MLRS (multiple launch rocket system), the Valkiri was introduced to the South African Army in 1982 and deployed to Angola. The system consists of a 4X4 light truck mounting 24 127mm (5in) rocket tubes in three rows of eight. The solid-fuel fin-stabilized rockets carry a pre-fragmented proximity-fused warhead, and reloading time is ten minutes. Another version of the Valkiri, the Mk II or Bateleur, mounts a total of 40 127mm (5in) tubes.

Specifications

Crew: 2

Calibre: 127mm (5in)

Rocket length: 2.68m (8ft 9in)

Rocket weight: 53.5kg (118lb)

System combat weight: 6400kg (14,110lb)

Range: 22,700m (14.1 miles)

Rate of fire: 24-second full salvo

Chapter 13

Modern Conflicts, 1991–2010

Firepower, manoeuvrability and accuracy
of fire are as crucial to victory on the modern battlefield as
they were in the conflicts of centuries past, and no other
weapon delivers the tactical or strategic advantage that
is provided by artillery. With the potential to dominate the
modern battlefield, artillery remains a primary component
of combined-arms doctrine. Whether towed, self-propelled
or man-portable, artillery has evolved with technologically
advanced delivery systems and with munitions which may
be guided to distant targets with pinpoint accuracy.
From shoot and scoot to fire and forget, these weapons
deliver devastating fire and increase the survivability
of the operator.

◀ **Guns across the desert**
A US Marine Corps (USMC) gun crew from Mike Battery, 4th Battalion, 14th Marines, fire an M198 155mm
(6.1in) howitzer at targets near Camp Fallujah, Iraq, 2007.

Introduction

Modern artillery incorporates continuing innovation in the designs of weapons and ammunition with unprecedented precision guidance and stand-off capabilities to destroy targets at long range.

GLOBAL UNREST is a reality in the modern world. Conflicts from the Balkans to Southeast Asia, the Horn of Africa, the Middle East and the Indian sub-continent require a response which is mobile, rapid and decisive. Terrorist and insurgent activity combined with the continuing threat of violence from rogue states such as Iran and North Korea compel other nations to maintain the ability to react swiftly if necessary.

On the move

Lightweight, airmobile guns provide the power behind the deployment of light infantry formations which are capable of rapid movement. In contrast, the movement of tanks and armoured vehicles may be a ponderous task. Therefore, when time is of the essence it is artillery that is adapted to support an armed intervention on the most efficient and mobile basis. While artillery remains a principal component of combined arms in both offensive and defensive

scenarios, it does present the commander with the option of a lone response. Artillery may fire from a distance without the necessity of engaging troops or air support. On the offensive, artillery may be used to blast a gap in an opposing line or to suppress enemy fire against advancing troops, protecting flanks for formations on the move and shifting forward at a pace which is conceivably more rapid than that maintainable by armour, particularly when the latter is required to deploy in difficult terrain or confined space. On the defensive, meanwhile, artillery is a game changer when brought to bear against an enemy counterattack or in the defence of fixed positions. In counterbattery operations, it prevents enemy artillery from hitting marshalling areas or command-and-control centres. Gaining the upper hand on the battlefield allows freedom of movement, and artillery establishes the base from which other ground operations may exploit the enemy's weakness.

▲ **Field howitzer**

British soldiers fire an M777 155mm (6.1in) howitzer at Taliban fighting positions in the Sangin district from an undisclosed forward operating base in the Helmand Province of Afghanistan, April 2007.

▲ **MLRS test-firing**

An MLRS test-fires somewhere near Tikrit, Iraq, 2005. The unitary-guided multiple launch rocket system is the latest addition to the US Army's artillery arsenal and is designed to minimize collateral damage.

Advocates of both rocket and towed artillery point out that each has become lighter and more battlefield-efficient than its predecessors, while even lighter self-propelled artillery is in some cases fit for rapid ground deployment. One component of firepower with favourable mobility involves the introduction of lightweight titanium in the construction of field artillery.

Strong and durable, titanium has replaced heavier materials in the construction of the M777 155mm (6.1in) howitzer. The introduction of the material was a key element of the response of the Global Combat Systems division of defence contractor BAE Systems to the demands of modern ground combat.

Designated originally as an 'ultralight' field howitzer, the M777 is roughly 42 per cent lighter at just over 4000kg (9000lb) than the M198 towed howitzer which it is designated to replace. With an effective striking arc of up to 40km (25 miles) with extended-range ammunition, the M777 entered service in 2005 and has equipped units of the US, Canadian and Australian armed forces.

Its airmobile transport capability has made the M777 an ideal heavy support weapon during the wars in Iraq and Afghanistan, equipping the artillery batteries of many light infantry and airborne units. During one engagement against Taliban forces in Afghanistan, a pair of Canadian M777s inflicted serious casualties on the enemy while firing only a few rounds. Among the sophisticated ammunition used by modern artillery systems are high-explosive fragmentation and improved conventional munitions (ICMs), which are often used for area bombardment; anti-personnel flechette projectiles; HEAT (high-explosive anti-tank) munitions; smoke shells; cluster munitions which scatter smaller bomblets across the battlefield; and ADHPM (artillery-delivered high precision munitions).

The M982 Excalibur artillery shell, developed by US defence contractor Raytheon Missile Systems and the Swedish BAE Systems Bofors, has been battle-tested with outstanding results. Fired from such platforms as the M777 155mm (6.1in) field howitzer and the 155mm (6.1in) M109A6 Paladin self-propelled howitzer during action in Iraq, the Excalibur is an extended-range shell which utilizes folding fins to assist in gliding to its target. Precision is achieved through a GPS system which guides the shell with astonishing accuracy.

Reports from Iraq indicate that the Excalibur shell was utilized in the summer of 2007 and 92 per cent of Excalibur rounds landed within four metres (13ft) of the intended target. The use of Excalibur not only improves the results of the artillery fire and allows it to function in a close-support role but also limits collateral damage in populated areas.

Gulf War
1990–91

Deployed over great distances and in a harsh climate, artillery proved decisive in numerous engagements during the war to liberate Kuwait from Saddam Hussein's Iraqi forces.

WHEN THE IRAQI ARMY invaded tiny Kuwait on 2 August 1990, a multinational coalition was assembled in response, and a tremendous logistical undertaking which lasted several months resulted in the most impressive assemblage of military power in the air and on land and sea in the history of warfare. Following an intense aerial bombardment of several weeks, the Coalition ground forces launched a lightning 100-hour land campaign which led to the rout of the Iraqi forces. Often, artillery took centre stage as the Coalition military commanders executed their battle plan.

During Operation Desert Shield, as the build-up was called, and the following Operation Desert Storm, modern artillery and state-of-the-art military technology were on full display. Along with towed and self-propelled guns and howitzers which are capable of inflicting tremendous damage with concentrated fire, anti-tank missiles, anti-aircraft systems, free-flight rockets and intermediate-range ballistic missiles were utilized during the fighting. In addition, embryonic anti-ballistic-missile technology made its combat debut during Operation Desert Storm, providing a glimpse of the future of missile defence technology.

With the advent of computerized fire direction and lighter, more efficient artillery, the world witnessed a spectacular display of firepower and accuracy during Operation Desert Storm. Half a century after World War II, the ranging of field artillery during a live-fire situation had improved from approximately six minutes to as little as 15 seconds. Even in the harshest of desert climates, with the continuing problems of sand, wind and extreme heat, the barrels of field weapons were known to fire as many as 500 rounds in as little

▲ **Out of commission**
An Iraqi ZSU-23-4 self-propelled anti-aircraft gun lies damaged by the roadside – probably hit by air attack – following Operation Desert Storm.

as four hours without appreciably degrading the efficiency of the barrel or supporting equipment.

Effective deployment

Both the Coalition forces and the Iraqi Army faced significant challenges in terms of the deployment and effective usage of artillery during Desert Storm. For the Iraqis, there is no question that some modern and highly effective weapons systems were available, including the infamous Scud missile, the Soviet-made 122mm (4.8in) 2S1 and 152mm (6in) 2S3 self-propelled howitzers and proven towed artillery such as the 155mm (6.1in) GHN-45 and G5 howitzers. The 122mm (4.8in) D-30 field howitzer had entered service with Soviet forces more than 25 years earlier but remained a viable system. However, the array of weapons acquired by Saddam Hussein, either captured during the 1980–88 war with Iran or purchased through the international arms market, created inconsistencies in training for artillery units as operational instructions were often in foreign languages such as English or Chinese, and compatible ammunition was often difficult to procure.

The challenges inherent in Coalition warfare during Desert Storm contributed to incidents of casualties by friendly fire and confusion among the artillery forces of different nations. Nevertheless, while Iraqi artillery often outranged its Coalition counterpart, the relentless air campaign which preceded the ground phase of the Gulf War, superior fire control and superb training made Coalition artillery deadly and efficient in support of ground action. The Patriot anti-ballistic missile system produced debatable results against the Iraqi Scud but provided analysts with valuable data on the performance of the system during live combat conditions. In the final analysis, there is no rigorous testing programme or research protocol which can totally simulate the conditions of combat. The truest measure of the effectiveness of any artillery system remains combat itself.

The reliance placed on artillery by Coalition forces is readily apparent in the number and types of units engaged. At the height of its deployment for Operation Desert Storm, the Coalition had amassed more than 3800 artillery pieces of 100mm (3.9in) or greater with at least 600 of these self-propelled and the remainder towed. Multiple launch rocket systems such as the US MLRS totalled approximately 800 mobile launchers, and at least 100 tactical surface-to-surface missile launchers were in theatre on the eve of the ground offensive which commenced in January 1991.

Coalition forces
1991

Highly trained and specialized artillery units provided Coalition forces with a decided edge in performance over the Iraqi Army during the Gulf War.

WHEN EGYPTIAN REPORTER Nabila Megalli of the Associated Press telephoned the Khafji Beach Hotel on 30 January 1991, she was seeking confirmation of an Iraqi report that tactical surface-to-surface missiles had set fire to nearby oil refineries. The voice on the other end of the telephone line spoke Arabic, but the accent was distinctive. An Iraqi soldier informed the reporter that the Saudi border town of Khafji had been occupied by Iraqi troops. 'We are with Saddam, with Arabism,' shouted one soldier. A second taunted, 'See you in Jerusalem!'

When it was indeed realized that Iraqi forces had crossed the frontier between Saudi Arabia and Iraq under cover of darkness and executed the lone Iraqi ground offensive of the Gulf War, Saudi and US ground commanders conferred as to the best way to dislodge the invaders. Huey Cobra helicopter gunships, Harrier jump jets and A-10 Warthog ground-attack aircraft destroyed up to 35 Iraqi tanks and scores of armoured personnel carriers with Hellfire anti-tank missiles, while Coalition self-propelled and field artillery units swung into action.

The Iraqi advance had swept past a pair of US Marine reconnaissance teams which managed to remain undetected and called in an artillery fire mission on the occupying Iraqis. Miraculously, all

12 of the trapped Marines survived the battle and managed to avoid being killed by their own artillery.

The heavy gun section of the 3rd Marine Regiment and the artillery of the 1st Battalion, 12th Marines, worked over Iraqi positions for two days. Then, on the third day, Saudi artillery took over. One Marine observer remembered, 'The Saudis insisted that it was their sector and their responsibility, so they wanted to fire their artillery.'

Self-propelled sledgehammer

The Saudis utilized the self-propelled M109A2 155mm (6.1in) howitzer, a variant of the original M109 which had been developed in the early 1950s, deployed in 1963 and continually upgraded for more than 40 years. The M109A2 contained 27 improvements to the early M109 which were designated RAM (Reliability, Availability, Maintainability). These included the introduction of the M185 cannon and the M178 gun mount along with the ability to install the M140 sight-alignment device, plus better ballistic protection for the panoramic telescope. The M109A2 also included increased ammunition storage capacity, improving the load of 155mm (6.1in) ammunition from 28 shells to 36.

OPERATION DESERT STORM: COALITION GROUND FORCES		
Numbers of Artillery	Aug 1990	Dec 1990
Artillery 100mm (3.9in)+	3820	3750
(self-propelled)	620	550
(towed)	3200	3200
Multiple rocket launchers	790	800
SSM launchers	100	100

OPERATION DESERT STORM: US ARTILLERY UNITS	
Corps	Brigade
XVIII Corps	18th FA Bde
	212th FA Bde
	196th FA Bde
VII Corps	210th FA Bde
	42nd FA Bde
	75th FA Bde
	142nd FA Bde

The earliest version of the M109 was initially utilized in combat with US forces during the Vietnam War and with Israeli mobile formations during the Yom Kippur War of 1973. During Desert Storm, variants of the M109 were fielded by US, British and Saudi forces.

▲ M109 SP howitzer

Royal Saudi Land Forces / 17th Mechanized Brigade, 1991

The M109 155mm (6.1in) self-propelled howitzer is one of the longest-lived platforms of its kind in military history. Its development began in the United States in 1952, and its latest variant, the M109A6 Paladin, remains in service although heavily re-engineered. During the 1991 Gulf War, units of the regular Saudi Army and of the Saudi National Guard operated the M109A2, which remains in service with the Royal Saudi Land Forces today.

Specifications

Crew: 6

Weight: 23,723kg (52,192lb)

Length: 6.612m (21ft 8.25in)

Width: 3.295m (10ft 9.75in)

Height: 3.289m (10ft 9.5in)

Engine: 304kW (405hp) Detroit Diesel 8V-71T

Speed: 56km/h (35mph)

Road range: 390km (240 miles)

Armament: 155mm (6.1in) howitzer

▲ **Dug-in launchers**
Saudi Arabian troops man an ASTROS II MLR prior to the start of Operation Desert Storm. The ASTROS II was used by both Saudi and Iraqi forces during the conflict.

The ground game

The towed 155mm (6.1in) M198 and the 105mm (4.1in) M102 field howitzers were workhorses of the Gulf War. Introduced in 1979 as a replacement for the M114, the M198 has a maximum range of more than 29,992m (32,800 yards) with rocket-assisted ammunition, while standard high-explosive rounds reach distances of 17,800m (19,685 yards). With a sustained rate of fire of two rounds per minute and a maximum rate of four rounds per minute, the M198 is served by a crew of nine. Representative of a generation of late Cold War artillery, it is also nuclear-capable. During 14 years of production from 1978 to 1992, more than 1600 were built. Although it is gradually being replaced by the lighter M777 155mm (6.1in) howitzer, the M198 remains in active service with the US Army and US Marine Corps, as well as the armed forces of Australia, Thailand and other countries.

Rocket reaction

Advanced technology in free-flight surface-to-surface rocket systems was demonstrated during the Gulf War by the M270 Multiple Launch Rocket System (MLRS). A fully mobile, self-contained platform, the MLRS displays awesome firepower, with a battery potentially delivering up to 8000 M77 explosive rounds into a target area approximately 550m by 275m (600 yards by 300 yards) in as little as 45 seconds. Its shoot-and-scoot capability allows the MLRS to rapidly displace, reducing the effectiveness of enemy counterbattery fire.

The MLRS was developed as a joint venture by the United States, Germany, France and Great Britain during the 1970s. The US M270 MLRS system entered service in 1983, and its M269 launcher-loader module typically carries a variety of rockets up to 227mm (8.94in) in diameter. A single launcher fires missiles at a rate of 12 per minute or two in 20 seconds. Capable of firing both guided and unguided munitions, the MLRS's effective rocket range is approximately 42km (26.1 miles), while ballistic missiles may reach out to 300km (186 miles). Each M269 pod contains six rockets or a single guided missile such as the US ATACMS (Army

Tactical Missile System), a surface-to-surface missile with a diameter of 610mm (24in) and a length of four metres (13ft), which delivers a high-explosive warhead of up to 227kg (500lb) or cluster munitions. The MGM-140 ATACMS was first used in combat during Operation Desert Storm, when at least 32 were fired by the M270 MLRS.

Patriot parallax

Perhaps the most publicized weapon of the Gulf War was the MIM-104 Patriot surface-to-air missile system, which gained fame in defence of Coalition installations and Israeli cities against attacks by Iraqi Scud missiles. Although originally known as the SAM-D programme and conceived not only as an anti-ballistic missile (ABM) but also as a replacement for the HAWK and Nike Hercules anti-aircraft missiles, the Patriot's continuing development has concentrated on the ABM role. Research on ABM technology began in the United States during the 1960s; however, it was not until 1975 that the forerunner of the modern Patriot underwent testing and field evaluation. In 1976, the SAM-D programme was officially renamed the

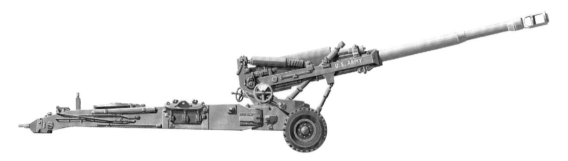

▲ **M198 155mm howitzer**

US Army / 18th Field Artillery Brigade, 1991

Production of the 155mm (6.1in) M198 field howitzer began in 1978, and the weapon was designated to replace the World War II-era M114 weapon. The M198 provided a 155mm (6.1in) medium artillery platform which could be airlifted and could fire at greater range than its predecessor. The M198 remains in service with numerous countries although it is being replaced by the M777 system.

Specifications

Crew: 9	Weight: 7163kg (7.05 tons)
Calibre: 155mm (6.1in)	Range: 18,100m (19,795 yards)
Elevation: - 5 degrees to + 72 degrees	Muzzle velocity: 684m/sec (2244ft/sec)

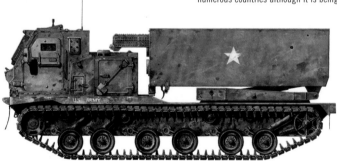

▲ **M270 Multiple Launch Rocket System (MLRS)**

US Army / 42nd Field Artillery Brigade / 27th Regiment / 1st Battalion, 1991

The M270 Multiple Launch Rocket System deploys the MLRS rocket, which was developed as a joint venture between the United States, Great Britain, Germany and France. The M270 entered service in 1983, and more than 1300 have been produced. The MLRS proved valuable in preliminary bombardment of fixed Iraqi positions prior to the launching of the ground phase of the 1991 Gulf War. Its chassis is an adapted version of the M2 fighting vehicle.

Specifications

Crew: 3	System combat weight: 25,191kg (55,420lb)
Calibre: 227mm (8.94in)	Range: 42km (26.1 miles)
Rocket length: 3.94m (12ft 11in)	Rate of fire: 12 rounds/min
Rocket weight: 308kg (679lb)	

Patriot Air Defense Missile System. The weapon was not used in live combat until 15 years later during the Gulf War of 1991.

In the late 1980s, the Patriot programme was expanded to include anti-ballistic missile capabilities. Improvements to the system in recent years include computer technology and software upgrades along with improved radar and missile design and guidance. Patriot has appeared in several variants, including the PAC-2, which is powered by a solid-fuel rocket engine and has a range of 160km (100 miles) and a weight of 900kg (1984lb). The missiles are fired from pods mounted atop the M860 trailer which is towed by the M983 HEMTT Dragon Wagon. The Patriot can be prepared to fire from mobile configuration in about 45 minutes.

Scud destroyers?

While controversy still surrounds the quality of the Patriot's performance during the Gulf War, it does appear that some incoming Scud missiles were intercepted. More than 40 documented Scud launches were engaged by Patriots during the course of the war, and the deployment of the system in protection of Israeli cities helped prevent Israel from entering the conflict against Iraq. Repeatedly, the Iraqis launched Scuds against targets in Kuwait, Saudi Arabia and Israel, and some feared that these might deliver chemical or even low-level nuclear warheads. It is known that combat pilots of the Israeli Air Force remained on full alert, sometimes sleeping in their cockpits.

In assessing the impact of the Scud attacks, Major General Ya'acov Lapidot, who directed the Israeli military police, recalled, 'It emerged that the Scud missiles were armed with only conventional warheads. There were 17 launchings in all, with 41 missiles having been fired at primarily urban-civilian targets … About 10,000 homes were damaged … About 40,000 persons were affected by the attacks. In terms of indirect injury, 10 persons died as a result of suffocation, although we had attempted to instruct the population in the proper use of the gas masks. The rate of cardiac failure and premature births rose, as did the level of psychological stress.'

An error in the Patriot system may have prevented its interception of the Scud which struck a barracks housing members of the US Army 14th Quartermaster Detachment at Dhahran, Saudi Arabia, on 25 February 1991, killing 28 soldiers.

11th Air Defence Artillery (ADA) Brigade, US Army, 1991

Providing theatre ballistic missile defence against Iraqi Scud attacks, the US Army's 11th Air Defence Artillery Brigade deployed a complement of 12 MIM-104 Patriot anti-ballistic missile batteries during the Gulf War of 1991. Development of the Patriot had begun in the 1960s, and the forerunner of the modern system had undergone testing by 1975; however, the technology was still in its relative infancy when Patriot batteries were deployed during Operation Desert Storm. Powered by a solid-fuel rocket motor, the Patriot is guided by radar which homes the missile in on its target, while a proximity fuse detonates the high-explosive fragmentation warhead. The actual rate of successful Patriot-versus-Scud engagements during Desert Storm remains a point of debate.

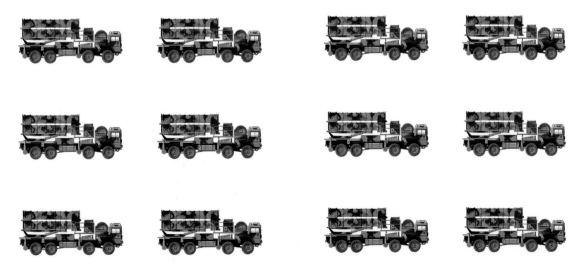

An investigation into the incident determined that the Patriot's internal timekeeping system had lost approximately one-third of a second during 100 hours of deployment on alert status. The result was an incorrect positioning of the incoming Scud. When the speed of the Scud is considered, the miscalculation proves significant – up to 600m (656 yards) – and the subsequently calculated firing solution sent the Patriot on an errant path.

Anti-armour options

During the Gulf War, US and other Coalition troops were armed with several anti-tank guided missiles, some of which had been specifically designed to defeat the armour of the Soviet T-54/55 and T-62 tanks which were fielded by the Iraqi Army.

The M47 Dragon was common among US ground troops, offering a lightweight and mobile medium-range defence with a warhead of 5.4kg (11.9lb) which was capable of penetrating armour

up to 500mm (19.6in) thick. The Dragon was a shoulder-fired, wire-guided missile which was in service with the US military from 1975 to 1995 and was later replaced with the FGM-148 Javelin. Its effective range was up to 1000m (3300ft), and the combined missile and launcher weighed only 10.9kg (24lb).

The excellent performance of Coalition artillery during Operation Desert Storm also identified areas for improvement during future cooperative military ventures. Upgraded communications were deemed imperative to improve accuracy and reduce the number of friendly-fire incidents, while continually advancing technology in target acquisition and fire direction was considered a priority.

Additionally, the number of weapons systems encountered in the Iraqi arsenal indicated that the capabilities of systems from many countries, rather than simply those of Soviet origin, had to be recognized and evaluated.

Iraqi Army
1991

By the time his forces invaded Kuwait in 1990, Saddam Hussein had fought a bloody war with Iran, made good his losses and reconstituted one of the largest armies in the world.

ON PAPER THE IRAQI ARMY which fought the multinational coalition during the 1991 Gulf War appeared formidable – and in some aspects of its military prowess that was the case. However, the tactical execution of the strategic decision to seize and occupy Kuwait presented considerable problems for the Iraqi forces, not the least of which were the operational capabilities of the equipment deployed and the quality and extent of the training Iraqi soldiers had undergone prior to the Kuwaiti adventure.

Mismatch

In the event, the Iraqi Air Force was no match for Coalition air assets. Iraqi armour proved inferior on the battlefield, with the majority of its T-54/55, T-62 and T-72 main battle tanks destroyed in armour-versus-armour clashes with the superior M1A1 Abrams main battle tank and other types belonging to the

Coalition armies. The fighting spirit and quality of Iraqi infantry proved lacklustre in most cases, although some Republican Guard units put up a spirited resistance. For the most part, Iraqi conscripts were eager to surrender to Coalition ground forces following a sustained aerial bombardment of several weeks.

Likewise, Iraqi artillery performance was adversely affected by the relentless Coalition air campaign, which degraded the artillery's combat-effectiveness. Training was apparently inadequate, and Iraqi artillerymen were also faced with the requirements of operating something of a jumble of field artillery, rocket systems and missiles of Soviet, Chinese, US, Brazilian and other manufacture.

The quality and quantity of appropriate ammunition also proved problematic for the Iraqis, with antiquated types proving inadequate for the ranges and fire-support missions required to slow down the Coalition ground juggernaut.

▶ **Spoils of war**

An Iraqi FROG-7 system lies abandoned following the end of Operation Desert Storm.

Missile capability

Although Coalition commanders maintained a healthy respect for all types of Iraqi artillery capabilities, it was the potential destructive power of missile and rocket systems which caused the greatest angst, and these indeed delivered the heaviest blows dealt by Saddam's forces. Although it had already been in service for decades, the Soviet BM-21 mobile rocket launcher posed a threat to Coalition infantry concentrations. A single truck-mounted BM-21 was capable of firing 18 122mm (4.8in) high-explosive rockets at a rate of two rounds per second, while a typical BM-21 battery could lay 35,560kg (35 tons) of explosives in a target area 27.4km (17 miles) distant in the brief span of only 30 seconds. The Iraqi Army was known to possess numerous BM-21 batteries, as well as the Brazilian ASTROS II MLRS.

In the air defence role, the Iraqis possessed a variety of light machine guns and cannon of Eastern Bloc manufacture. These were seen lighting up the dark sky over the Iraqi capital of Baghdad on the first night of the Gulf War, 17 January 1991. However, the display laid bare a serious defensive weakness. US Tomahawk cruise missiles launched from warships and submarines in the Gulf and the Red Sea hit command-and-control centres in Baghdad, disrupting communications and disabling much of the Iraqi fire-control capacity.

Perhaps the most menacing of Iraqi air defence missiles was the Soviet-designed Isayev S-125, known in NATO circles as the SA-3 Goa. On the third day of the war, an SA-3 shot down a US F-16 fighter-bomber over Baghdad, and its pilot was captured. The SA-3 entered service with Soviet forces in 1963 to engage enemy aircraft at low altitude and had been upgraded on several occasions. The Iraqis also possessed a limited number of SA-9 and SA-13 air defence missiles. The mobile FROG-7 missile launcher

▲ **FROG-7**

Iraqi Army / 6th Nebuchadnezzar Mechanized Division, 1991

Developed during the mid-1960s as an upgrade to the original FROG 1 mobile tactical missile system, the FROG-7 single-stage, solid-fuel rocket is carried aboard a wheeled 8X8 chassis which mounts a transporter-erector-launcher. Fin-stabilized and unguided, the rocket is capable of carrying high-explosive, chemical or nuclear warheads.

Specifications

Crew: 4

Calibre: 550mm (21.65in)

Rocket length: 9.11m (29ft 10in)

Rocket weight: 2500kg (5512lb)

System combat weight: 23,000kg (22.63 tons)

Range: 70km (43.5 miles)

Road range: 500km (310 miles)

Launch preparation time: 15–30 minutes

was expected to resist Coalition ground forces with its free-flight, fin-stabilized rocket which carried a 550kg (1200lb) warhead to a range of 70km (43 miles). The FROG-7 entered service with Red Army forces in 1965 and was initially nuclear-capable. During the Gulf War, Coalition domination of the air resulted in the destruction of numerous FROG-7 launchers prior to the commencement of the ground campaign.

Scud scare

By far the most successful weapon system of the Gulf War for the Iraqi armed forces was the mobile SS-1 Scud B theatre ballistic missile. Designed in the Soviet Union during the early 1960s, the Scud B was exported to the Middle East in large numbers. Iraqi modifications to the original weapon included a longer-range version known as the Al Hussein,

which could reach out to 645km (400 miles). During the course of the Gulf War, more than 40 Scuds were fired at Israeli cities, while others targeted civilian and military areas in Kuwait and Saudi Arabia.

The total number of Scud launches neared 200. The early Scud was mounted on an 8X8 wheeled chassis which supported a transporter-erector-launcher system. Its range was roughly 280km (173 miles), and its conventional or nuclear warhead weighed up to 985kg (2172lb).

Attacks by Iraqi Scuds nearly brought Israel in to the Gulf War and troubled the Coalition leadership to the extent that Scud-hunting teams of special forces personnel were deployed deep into the Iraqi desert to find the mobile launchers. Hundreds of sorties by tactical aircraft were also initiated to seek out and destroy the Scud platforms.

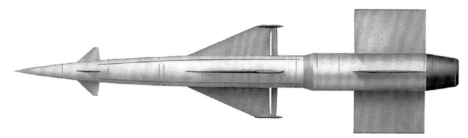

▲ S-125 (SA-3 Goa)

Iraqi Army / 145th Surface-to-Air Missile Brigade, 1991

The Soviet-designed Isayev S-125 surface-to-air missile, designated the SA-3 Goa by NATO, traced its lineage to the mid-1950s and the early days of air defence missile technology. The SA-3 went into production in 1959 and equipped units of the Red Army by 1963. Powered by a solid-fuel motor, the missile was lifted by a booster rocket which then fell away, and the warhead was guided to its target by a radar beam.

Specifications

Configuration: two-stage, solid fuel	Launch weight: 950kg (2094lb)
Deployment: mobile or fixed	Range: 30km (18.5 miles)
Length: 6.7m (22ft)	Launch preparation time: reload 15 minutes
Diameter: 450mm (17.7in)	

Specifications

Configuration: single-stage, liquid fuel	Launch weight: 6300kg (13,888lb)
Deployment: mobile	Range: 280km (173 miles)
Length: 11.25m (36ft 11in)	Launch preparation time: 1 hour
Diameter: 850mm (33.5in)	

▲ SS-1 Scud B

Iraqi Army / Independent Operation, 1991

The Scud B variant of the Soviet SS-1 theatre ballistic missile debuted in the mid-1960s in response to a directive to improve deployment time. Older SS-1 designs required fuelling after the missile had been erected into its firing position. The Scud B was mounted on a wheeled 8X8 chassis, and its mobility challenged Coalition forces during the Gulf War of 1991. The extended-range Al Hussein variant was among several types which had been modified by the Iraqis.

NATO air defence
1991–PRESENT

Focused on countering aircraft and ballistic missiles, NATO air defence capabilities have been tested in numerous regional conflicts around the globe.

D URING AN ERA of supersonic attack aircraft, ballistic missiles capable of speeds greater than Mach 2, heavily armed helicopters and tank-killing planes flying low and slow over the battlefield, NATO air defence capabilities require more versatility today than ever before. At theatre level, the MIM-104 Patriot anti-ballistic missile system continues to be refined, and a new generation of the Patriot and similar weapons is taking shape. From the soldier's perspective, the lightweight, man-portable FIM-92 Stinger missile provides a daunting air defence capability for the individual soldier or squad with boots on the ground.

From either perspective, state-of-the art systems and extensive training have proved their worth. In the case of the Patriot, although theory and conjecture have surrounded its performance during the 1991 Gulf War, its mere presence in theatre reduced the potential for armed intervention by Israel and bolstered the confidence of the civilian populations in areas which had been targeted by Iraqi Scud B missiles. The FIM-92 Stinger, on the other hand, was instrumental in compelling the Soviet Union to withdraw its forces from Afghanistan during the late 1980s and remains a battle-tested weapon.

Intercontinental engagement
The land-based nuclear intercontinental ballistic missile (ICBM) defence of the United States is trusted to the Minuteman III, a three-stage, solid-fuel missile with a range of up to 13,000km (8100 miles), which was developed during the late 1960s and is expected to remain in service, pending upgrades, until at least 2025. The Minuteman is complemented by the submarine-launched Trident missile and other munitions which are delivered by aircraft. Its MIRV (multiple independent re-entry vehicle) capability allows several nuclear warheads to impact targets independently, and its heaviest warhead is the W-87 with an estimated yield of up to 475 kilotons.

The reliance on the Minuteman III came as a result of the START II treaty negotiated between the United States and Russia during the early 1990s. Although START II was never formally enacted, the decision was made to deactivate the LGM-118 Peacekeeper missiles which were then in the US arsenal. Following nearly 15 years of research by defence contractors Boeing, Martin Marietta, Denver Aerospace and TRW, approximately 50 Peacekeepers had been deployed by the mid-1980s in response to an array of MIRV-capable Soviet ICBMs. Popularly known as the MX missile, the Peacekeeper MIRV

▲ **Starstreak**
British Army / 12th Regiment Royal Artillery, 1999
The versatile Starstreak surface-to-air missile is fired from the shoulder, from wheeled Land Rover vehicles, or from a launcher fixed to the roof of the Alvis Stormer armoured fighting vehicle. Introduced in 1997 to replace the Javelin missiles then in service with the British Army, the Starstreak actually fires three submunitions, called darts. These are detonated by a delayed fuse.

Specifications

Configuration: two-stage, solid fuel	Launch weight: 16.82kg (37.08lb)
Deployment: man-portable, mobile or fixed	Range: 7km (4.4 miles)
Length: 1.4m (55in)	
Diameter: 127mm (5in)	

carried up to ten re-entry vehicles bearing the W-87 nuclear warhead, which was originally a weapon of 300 kilotons and was later increased.

While the reasons for the deactivation of the Peacekeeper were numerous, among the most compelling were its somewhat disappointing range of 9600km (6000 miles) and its per-unit cost of roughly $70 million. The last of the LGM-118 missiles was dismantled during the autumn of 2005, and as many as 500 W-87 warheads originally intended for Peacekeeper missiles may, in fact, be transferred to the longer-range Minuteman III.

Mobile air defence

While the HAWK system has been a mainstay of NATO air defence for decades, mounted at fixed sites or towed on trailers, the shoulder-fired, wheeled or tracked Starstreak surface-to-air missile provides a close-in additional deterrent to air attack. Deployed by the British Army in 1997, the Starstreak was developed by Thales Air Defence Limited, and the missile is guided to the target by a triangular laser pattern emitted from the launch unit. The weapon actually fires three warheads powered by a two-stage, solid-fuel rocket booster, and the trio of submunitions is detonated by a delayed fuse when the projectile reaches the target. Each submunition, referred to as a dart, weighs 900g (1.98lb). Intended to replace the Javelin missile, the Starstreak weighs 16.82kg (37.08lb).

The tracked version of the Starstreak consists of the Alvis Stormer armoured fighting vehicle chassis with a launcher carrying eight missiles fixed to the roof and internal storage of 12 additional rounds. The Stormer has an operational range of 640km (800 miles), and the Starstreak missile itself is effective at a range of up to seven kilometres (4.4 miles).

Since its introduction in 1971, the Rapier missile has been a mainstay of British air defence and serves as the primary weapon of its kind today, replacing

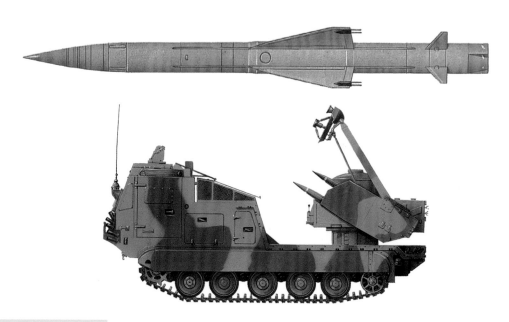

Specifications

Configuration: two-stage, solid fuel
Deployment: fixed or mobile
Length: 2.24m (88.2in)
Diameter: 133mm (5.25in)
Launch weight: 42kg (94lb)
Range: 7250m (4.5 miles)
Launch preparation time: 30 seconds

▲ **Tracked Rapier**

British Army / 22 Air Defence Regiment / 11 Air Defence Battery, 1993

The tracked Rapier surface-to-air missile system was developed in response to a request from the government of the Shah of Iran in the late 1970s. However, with the overthrow of the Shah's regime the vehicles were subsequently purchased by the British Army. The tracked Rapier mounts the missile launcher atop the modified M548 cargo carrier version of the M113 armoured personnel carrier. The Rapier reaches a speed of Mach 2.2 and carries a high-explosive armour-piercing warhead.

other gun and missile systems in their entirety. In the region of 25,000 Rapier missiles have been manufactured, as well as some 600 launchers, and the system is expected to remain in place until 2020.

Rapier is fired from fixed sites and mobile tracked launchers. Its two-stage rocket powers a semi-armour-piercing warhead at a speed of Mach 2.2, and an all-weather version of the Rapier includes the Blindfire radar guidance system. The tracked Rapier incorporates the launcher atop the modified M548 cargo carrier version of the M113 armoured personnel carrier.

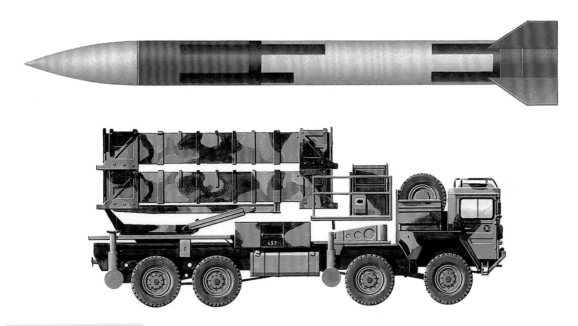

Specifications

Configuration: solid-fueled rocket
Deployment: fixed or mobile
Length: 5.31m (17ft 5in)
Diameter: 41cm (16in)
Launch weight: 900kg (2000lb)
Range: 160km (100 miles)
Time of flight: 9 seconds – 3.5 minutes

▲ MIM-104 (GE) Patriot

US Army / 35th Air Defense Brigade / 1st Battalion, 1991

The MIM-104 Patriot anti-ballistic missile entered service with the US military in 1981 following extensive research and development which dated to the 1960s. The Patriot achieved notoriety during the 1991 Gulf War and was originally intended to defend against enemy aircraft as well as missiles. Powered by a solid-fuel rocket motor, the missile has an effective range of 160km (100 miles). Its high-explosive fragmentation warhead weighs 73kg (160lb) and is detonated by a proximity fuse.

▲ LGM-118 Peacekeeper

US Air Force / 400th Missile Squadron, 2003

Popularly known as the MX missile, the LGM-118 Peacekeeper ICBM was deployed in limited numbers by the mid-1980s in response to the Soviet Union's fielding of multiple MIRV-capable ICBMs. Following the negotiations which resulted in the START II treaty, the US began dismantling its Peacekeepers even though the treaty was not enacted. Today, US land-based ICBM missile defence rests with the Minuteman III system.

Specifications

Configuration: four-stage, solid and liquid fuel
Deployment: silo
Length: 21.6m (70ft 10in)
Diameter: 2.34m (7ft 8in)
Launch weight: 88,450kg (87 tons)
Range: 9600km (6000 miles)
Launch preparation time: under 30 inutes est.

Balkans conflicts
1991–95

Fuelled by nationalistic fervour, war raged in the Balkans, a region torn by ethnic strife, during the early 1990s, and artillery took a heavy toll in military and civilian lives.

WHEN THE FORCES OF CROATIA AND BOSNIA and Herzegovina opposed the Serbian Army in the summer of 1995, each side was able to muster nearly 600 artillery pieces of various types, including field guns, self-propelled howitzers, air defence weapons and rocket launchers. The LVRS M-77 Oganj MLRS was one of a relative few weapons deployed during the Balkan unrest of the early 1990s which were actually designed and manufactured in the former Yugoslavia. The development of the weapon, which included a 6X6 FAP 2026 wheeled flatbed truck and a launcher which held 32 128mm (5in) rockets, was undertaken by a Yugoslav mechanical engineer who also served as the chief operating officer of the artillery department of the country's military technical institute.

First seen in public in 1975, the rocket launcher was also produced in a later variant, the Oganj 2000 ER, which was capable of firing the Soviet-designed BM-21 Grad rocket from a bank of 50 122mm (4.8in) tubes. Croatian forces also modified the Oganj to fire the 122mm (4.8in) rocket and named the weapon the M-91 Vulkan.

Another Eastern European weapon produced outside the Soviet Union, the M53/59 Praga self-propelled anti-aircraft gun was deployed by the Yugoslav People's Army and appeared to be something of a battlefield anachronism in the 1990s. A Czech design of the late 1950s, the weapon mounted a pair of 30mm (1.2in) autocannon atop the chassis of the Praga V3S 6X6 truck. Mounted at the back of the truck bed, the cannon were fed by 50-round belts, and the vehicle usually carried up to 900 rounds of ammunition.

The M53/59 possessed no radar, and the guns were aimed visually, limiting their use to daylight and favourable weather conditions. Although the weapon is functionally obsolete as an anti-aircraft platform, it may still play a role in the armed forces of underdeveloped nations, since the penetrating power of the 30mm (1.2in) round is effective against light armoured vehicles and infantry. When the Czech military brought in the Soviet self-propelled ZSU-57-2 57mm (2.2in) anti-aircraft gun for testing against the M53/59, they actually preferred the performance of their own weapon and declined further Soviet deliveries.

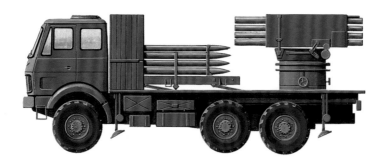

▲ **LVRS M-77 Oganj MLRS**

Serbian Army / 2nd Land Force Brigade

Mounting 32 tubes for launching 128mm (5in) rockets, the LVRS M-77 Oganj proved a devastating weapon system during the Yugoslav Wars. Introduced in 1975 following several years of development in Yugoslavia, it is still in use today with the Serbian armed forces.

Specifications	
Crew: 5	Engine: 191kW (256hp) 8-cylinder diesel
Weight: 22,400kg (49,400lb)	Speed: 80km/h (50mph)
Length: 11.5m (37ft 7in)	Road range: 600km (370 miles)
Width: 2.49m (8ft 2in)	Armament: 32 + 32 x M-77 or M-91 rockets, plus
Height: 3.1m (10ft 2in)	1 x 12.7mm (0.5in) HMG

▲ **Running repairs**

US Army soldiers of Alpha Battery, 1st Battalion, 6th Field Artillery, 1st Infantry Division (Mechanized), attached to Camp McGovern, Bosnia and Herzegovina, replace worn-out track pads on an M109 SP howitzer during Operation Joint Guard, July 1997.

Both Serbian and Croatian forces maintained substantial inventories of Soviet-made surface-to-air missiles, and among the most readily available was the Lavochkin OKB S-75, commonly referred to in NATO circles as the SA-2 Guideline. By the 1990s, the SA-2 was getting on in years. Its development began in the early 1950s, and it had reached Red Army artillery units by 1957. It gained notoriety for its shooting-down of an American U-2 spy plane piloted by Francis Gary Powers in 1960, an event which spawned a major dispute between the superpowers. The SA-2 was later supplied to North Vietnam to provide some protection against devastating raids by US bombers against the North Vietnamese capital of Hanoi and the major port

city of Haiphong. China also produced the missile, designating it the HQ-1 and HQ-2.

In the hands of the Serbian and Yugoslav armies, the SA-2 posed a serious threat to NATO aircraft flying combat or patrol missions in the Balkans. Its operational range was up to 45km (29 miles), and its radar guidance delivered a 200kg (441lb) high-explosive fragmentation warhead.

In the mid-1990s, when elements of the British Army deployed with NATO forces they were equipped with the 155mm (6.1in) AS-90 self-propelled gun, which was designed and manufactured by Vickers Shipbuilding and Engineering as a replacement for the army's aging complement of 155mm (6.1in) M109 and 105mm (4.1in) Abbot self-propelled howitzers.

Following the failed SP70 gun programme of the 1980s, the development of the AS-90 accelerated, and the weapon was introduced in 1993. Mounting the NATO-compatible 155mm (6.1in) L31 gun, it is capable of firing three rounds in a ten-second burst, six rounds per minute for up to three minutes or two rounds per minute for the duration of one hour.

A Turret Controlled Computer (TCC) provides the technology which facilitates the rapid-fire burst.

The AS-90 (Artillery System for the 90s) equips two regiments of the Royal Horse Artillery and three regiments of the Royal Artillery. Its operational range is 420km (261 miles), and its autonomous navigation and gun-laying systems allow it to fight without external visual aids. Nearly 200 examples of the AS-90 were produced between 1992 and 1995, and in 2002 approximately half of these were upgraded from a 39-calibre barrel to a longer 52-calibre barrel.

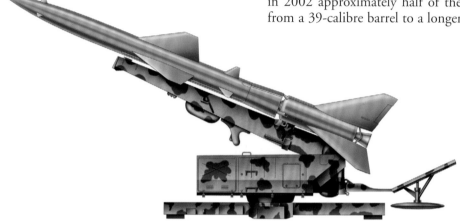

▲ Lavochkin OKB S-75 (SA-2 Guideline)

Serbian Army / 21st Kordun Corps Artillery Battalion, 1995

The Soviet-designed Lavochkin OKB S-75 surface-to-air missile was known to NATO as the SA-2 Guideline. An early Soviet air defence missile, the SA-2 remains in operation with upgrades after half a century and equipped units of several armies during the Balkan conflicts of the 1990s. Mounted on a trailer, the rail-launched missile was towed into firing position and guided to its target by radar.

Specifications

Configuration: two-stage, solid and liquid fuel	Launch weight: 2300kg (5071lb)
Deployment: mobile	Range: 45km (29 miles)
Length: 10.6m (34ft 9in)	Launch preparation time: 8-hour radar set-up
Diameter: 700mm (27.6in)	

▲ AS-90 SP gun

British Army / 3rd Regiment Royal Horse Artillery, 1995

Developed during the mid-1980s and built by the Vickers company, the AS-90 self-propelled gun mounts the 155mm (6.1in) L31 gun atop its tracked chassis. Entering service in 1993, the AS-90 replaced the 105mm (4.1in) Abbot and 155mm (6.1in) M109 self-propelled weapons then in service.

Specifications

Crew: 5	Engine: 492kW (660hp) Cummins V8 diesel
Weight: 45,000kg (99,225lb)	Speed: 55km/h (34mph)
Length: 7.2m (23ft 8in)	Road range: 240km (150 miles)
Width: 3.4m (11ft 2in)	Armament: 1 x 155mm (6.1in) howitzer, plus 1 x
Height: 3m (9ft 10in)	12.7mm (0.5in) MG

War in the Caucasus

1992–PRESENT

Unrest in the Caucasus erupted with the collapse of the Soviet Union and continues today with territorial and ethnic disputes which remain unresolved.

THE TERRIBLE CIVIL WARS and ethnic cleansing which have wracked the region of the Caucasus since the fall of the Soviet Union have been characterized by political turmoil as well as military clashes. Several of these episodes have involved the former Soviet republic of Georgia and the breakaway provinces of South Ossetia and Abkhazia, which have sought independent governments, while forces of the Russian Federation have battled Islamic separatists and Chechen nationalists for years. Throughout these hostilities, civilian, paramilitary and military casualties have been high, particularly due to the use of artillery in shelling both targets of military importance and civilian population centres. Mercenary forces have been hired on several occasions, and the use of landmines has led to the maiming and crippling of thousands.

The South Ossetia War of 1991–92 ended with a tenuous cease-fire in place; however, tensions continued to smoulder. Neither side could muster well-trained and experienced troops, with the Georgian National Guard forming only days before the war began in early 1991. As the fighting wore on, it often degenerated into a contest of armed militia factions vying for control of the region, and the government of Georgia accused the Russian Federation of intervening on behalf of the rebel forces. Georgian government troops deployed Soviet-era equipment, including towed and self-propelled howitzers along with truck-mounted multiple launch rocket systems, and implemented Soviet-style counterinsurgency tactics, with the artillery playing a key role in neutralizing guerrilla activities.

Following the seizure of the Black Sea coastal resort town of Gagra in the autumn of 1992, one of the bloodiest battles between Georgian government troops and Abkhaz militia took place, the latter supported by the militant Confederation of Mountain

◀ **Man-handled mortar**

Russian Army infantry man-handle an 120mm (4.72in) mortar along a road somewhere in Abkhazia as part of a peacekeeping force in 1994, following the end of the Abkhazia War of 1992–93. The pro-Russian region of Abkhazia attempted to break away from Georgia following Georgia's declaration of independence from the old Soviet Union.

Peoples of the Caucasus (CMPC). The fighting at Gagra left hundreds dead and caused relations between Georgia and the Russian Federation to deteriorate rapidly.

One major bone of contention between the Russians and the Georgians was the apparent willingness of the Russians to funnel military hardware and supplies to the Abkhaz forces, including T-72 main battle tanks and BM-21 Grad multiple launch rocket systems. The truck-borne BM-21 is a devastating weapon which the Abkhaz

militia had not possessed prior to its Gagra offensive, and much of the weaponry was apparently funnelled to the rebels through the town of Gudauta on the Black Sea, where Russian forces, including an air defence regiment and a supply unit, were known to be operating.

The mistrust which these early civil wars engendered sowed the seeds of more than a decade of conflict between the Russian Federation and Georgia, culminating in a brief but bitter invasion of Georgia by Russian forces in 2008.

Chechnya
1994–PRESENT

Declaring full independence from Russia, the breakaway province of Chechnya became a battleground in the mid-1990s and again at the end of the twentieth century when Chechen and allied forces invaded the neighbouring republic of Dagestan.

FACTIONAL INFIGHTING erupted in civil war in Chechnya in 1994 as vigorous debate raged over independence from the Russian Federation and threatened regional stability. On the premise of restoring constitutional order, the Russian Army entered Chechnya and embarked on an arduous campaign to subdue separatists under the leadership of former Soviet Air Force general Dzhokhar Dudayev. From the outset, the war was unpopular with the Russian populace, and despite early successes, including the capture of the Chechen capital of Grozny, the Russians found themselves embroiled in a battle with a tenacious insurgency reminiscent of the Afghan debacle of the 1980s.

Conscript confusion

Many of the Russian troops sent to Chechnya were draftees who had little military training. Casualties were high due to landmines, booby traps and the hit-and-run tactics of the Chechens. Predictably, Russian commanders fell back on their superior firepower in the hope of demoralizing the rebels and degrading their ability to fight. Although they exerted control over extensive areas in the valleys and flatlands of Chechnya, the Russians faced serious problems in their effort to clear the rebels from the surrounding mountains. Ambushes were highly effective, actually

destroying heavy Russian armoured columns while they transited the narrow roads and mountain passes. Before a cease-fire ended the fighting in 1996, more than 5000 Russian troops were estimated to have been killed and at least 20,000 wounded, although these numbers are unverified. Meanwhile, casualties among Chechen rebels and civilians may have exceeded 100,000.

The Russians undertook a second invasion of Chechnya in the summer of 1999 following the invasion of neighbouring Dagestan by guerrillas of the Chechen-sponsored Islamic International Peacekeeping Brigade (IIPB). The IIPB consisted of veteran Chechen fighters and Islamic guerrillas from numerous Middle Eastern countries. By the spring of 2000, the Russians had taken control of the Chechen capital at Grozny and re-established direct control over Chechnya. Although large-scale military operations have ceased, a persistent insurgency has remained active in the region for nearly a decade and even expanded into neighbouring areas of Russian territory. Chechen fighters have perpetrated numerous acts of terrorism inside Russia.

Breakaway firepower

On both occasions during which Russian forces have fought Chechen rebels in recent years, they have done so with overwhelming firepower at their disposal. Applying the difficult lessons of Afghanistan and the First Chechen War, Russian commanders often refused to send troops into confined areas where manoeuvre was limited or into urban areas where guerrillas were known to be holed up. Rather, they ranged their artillery on surrounding high ground and called in massive air strikes which obliterated targets but caused widespread collateral damage and killed thousands of Chechen civilians.

Field artillery deployed by the Russian Army included the long-serving 122mm (4.8in) D-30 howitzer and older towed weapons generally of 100mm (3.9in) or 152mm (6in). The D-30 has remained the towed workhorse of the Soviet and subsequently the Russian armed forces for more than 40 years. Based on a World War II-era Czech design for the German Army, the D-30 is capable of firing a high-explosive shell of nearly 22kg (48lb) to a maximum range of 15,400m (16,840 yards).

SP guns

Although the terrain was often a challenge for the Russians, particularly in marshy or rugged areas, the 2S1 M1974 self-propelled howitzer proved adept at fighting across the Chechen landscape in direct support of Russian troops. The amphibious 2S1 mounts the 122mm (4.8in) 2A18 howitzer, the same weapon as the D-30 field howitzer, atop the MT-LB chassis. Although the boatlike bow of the

MT-LB resembles that of the light amphibious PT-76 tank, it is a completely separate design. The 2S1 equipped the armoured divisions and motorized rifle regiments of the Russian Army, and its relatively light weight of 15,700kg (34,540lb) resulted in a favourable ground pressure and greater mobility.

Designated the M1974 by Western sources since it was first seen in a Polish military parade during that year, the 2S1 is known to the Russians as the Gvozdika, or Carnation. Several variants were produced in the Soviet Union, Poland and Bulgaria, with more than 500 of the weapons deployed by the two Soviet client states at one time. Although the 2S1 exhibits excellent road speed at 60km/h (37mph), its light armour makes it susceptible to rocket-propelled grenades and anti-tank weapons.

Rocket systems

The Russian Army deployed two notable rocket systems to Chechnya, the 300mm (11.8in) BM-30 Smerch and 220mm (8.7in) TOS-1 multiple launchers. The largest weapon of its kind in the world, the Smerch, or Tornado, mounts 12 tubes atop the 8X8 wheeled 9A52 vehicle. The Smerch was responsible for much of the heavy bombardment endured by the Chechens, and a full salvo can be released in 38 seconds to saturate an area of 67 hectares (166 acres). The system may be readied to fire in as little as three minutes, while reloading is a 36-minute process.

Specifications

Crew: 4

Calibre: 300mm (11.8in)

Rocket length: 7.6m (24ft 11in)

Rocket weight: 243kg (536lb)

System combat weight: 44,401kg (43.7 tons)

Range: 70km (43.5 miles)

Rate of fire: 12 rounds in 38 seconds

▲ **BM-30 Smerch heavy multiple rocket launcher**

Russian Ground Forces / 136th Motor Rifle Brigade, 1997

The BM-30 Smerch multiple rocket launcher is capable of placing massive firepower over a considerable area. Its bank of 12 300mm (11.8in) rocket tubes is mounted atop the 8X8 9A52 wheeled vehicle, and a full salvo could be fired in as little as 38 seconds. The Smerch was designed in the early 1980s and entered service with the Soviet Army in 1989. A typical battery consists of six launch vehicles and six reloading vehicles carrying an additional 12 rockets each.

The short-range TOS-1 launcher was suspected of having fired thermobaric ammunition against fixed fortifications and in some urban areas during the Chechen wars (TOS is an abbreviation for 'heavy flamethrower system'). The thermobaric warhead contains flammable liquid which is released in a cloud and ignites when in contact with oxygen. The resulting explosion creates a devastating swirl of flame and extreme pressure. Loosing up to 30 rounds in a span of 15 seconds, the weapon consists of a launcher mounted atop the chassis of the T-72 main battle tank. With an effective range of up to 3500m (3828 yards), the TOS-1 was first used in combat in Afghanistan in the early 1980s.

▲ **2S1 M1974 SP howitzer**

Russian Ground Forces / 5th Guards Tank Division, 1996

Mounting a 122mm (4.8in) main gun, the 2S1 Gvozdika (Carnation) self-propelled howitzer has been known in the West as the M1974, referencing the year in which it was first observed in public. Several former Soviet republics maintain the M1974 in their inventories today.

Specifications

Crew: 4	Engine: 179kW (240hp) YaMZ-238V V8
Weight: 15,700kg (34,540lb)	water-cooled diesel
Length: 7.3m (23ft 11.5in)	Speed: 60km/h (37mph)
Width: 2.85m (9ft 4in)	Road range: 500km (310 miles)
Height: 2.4m (7ft 10.5in)	Armament: 1 x 122mm (4.8in) howitzer, plus 1 x
	7.62mm (0.3in) anti-aircraft MG

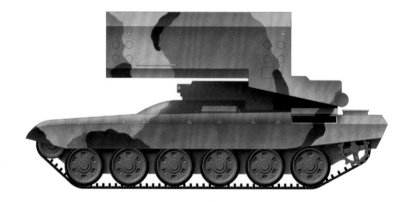

Specifications

Crew: 3	System combat weight: 46,738kg (46 tons)
Calibre: 220mm (8.7in)	Range: 3500m (3828 yards)
Rocket length: unknown	Rate of fire: 30 rounds in 15 seconds
Rocket weight: 175kg (385.8lb)	

▲ **TOS-1 multiple rocket launcher**

Russian Ground Forces / 860th Independent Flamethrower Battalion, 1999

Highly effective against fixed fortifications, the TOS-1 30-barrel 220mm (8.7in) rocket launcher is capable of firing devastating thermobaric ammunition which bursts into flame when its warhead disperses combustible liquid. The TOS-1 was most likely involved in the clearing of landmines during the Chechen wars as well. The system first appeared in combat in Afghanistan during the late 1980s. Its maximum rate of fire is 30 rounds in 15 seconds.

South Ossetian conflict
2008

During less than two weeks of fighting, the former Soviet republic of Georgia lost control of its remaining territory in South Ossetia, defeated by the firepower and mobility of the Russian Army.

IN AUGUST 2008, war broke out for at least the third time in the troubled region of South Ossetia as Georgia sought to assert control over the area. In response to Georgia's offensive, Russian forces were deployed within hours. A four-day battle raged around the city of Tskhinvali as Georgian forces moved forward under a steady artillery barrage from 152mm (6in) field howitzers and 122mm (4.8in) BM-21 Grad multiple launch rocket systems. According to some sources, a Georgian rocket or shell was falling on the city every 15 to 20 seconds.

Russian response

The Russians counterattacked the following day and reportedly fired at least one SS-21 short-range ballistic missile against the Georgian city of Borzhomi, while attack aircraft pounded the Georgian infantry and artillery around Tskhinvali, forcing the Georgians out of the city in the largest battle of the brief conflict. As the tide turned in favour of the Russians, the Georgian forces suffered not only from the

effective fire of Russian artillery and air support but also from flagging morale. Eventually, the Georgians were turned back in disarray, and Russian troops rolled into four cities across the Georgian frontier. Within days, a French-sponsored peace agreement had been reached.

During the course of the short but sharp South Ossetia War, much of Georgia's heavy equipment was disabled. The single Georgian artillery brigade had deployed more than 100 weapons, including 122mm (4.8in) D-30 towed howitzers and the self-propelled 152mm (6in) SpGH DANA, 152mm (6in) 2S3 Akatsiya and 203mm (8in) 2S7 Pion. The Georgians also fired Soviet-made BM-21 and Czech-built R-70 122mm (4.8in) rocket launchers. Russian artillery included the self-propelled 152mm (6in) 2S19 MSTA and the 2S3 along with the BM-21 and the 300mm (11.8in) BM-30 Smerch rocket launchers.

The 2S3 Akatsiya, or Acacia, was designated the SO-152 by its Soviet manufacturers. It is easily distinguishable from the lighter 2S1 because its 152mm

▲ **DANA SP guns**
Two DANA SP howitzers stand at the roadside following the end of hostilities in South Ossetia in 2008.

(6in) howitzer extends well beyond the forward edge of the hull while the shorter 122mm (4.8in) gun of the 2S1 is flush with the edge. The 2S3 was developed in the late 1960s to counter the American 155mm (6.1in) M109 self-propelled howitzer, and it entered service with the Red Army in 1971. Since that time, it has continued to outfit armoured formations of the forces of former Soviet republics while it has been exported to at least a dozen countries.

By the end of the 1980s, Soviet armoured and motorized rifle divisions each contained up to three battalions of the 2S3, totalling as many as 54 weapons. The 2S3 mounts an adapted version of the D-20 towed field howitzer, and the chassis is the modified Objekt 123 tracked vehicle which also powers the 2K11 Krug air defence missile system.

The 152mm (6in) 2S19 MSTA self-propelled howitzer ushered in a new generation of mobile

▲ **2S3 Akatsiya M1973 SP howitzer**

Russian Ground Forces / 20th Guards Motor Rifle Division, 2008

The 2S3 Akatsiya provided direct fire support to Soviet and Russian armoured and motorized rifle divisions. Its heavy gun is fitted atop the shortened chassis of the SA-4 air defence missile system. Equipped with nuclear, biological and chemical defences, improved armour, and night vision equipment, it was usually serviced by a crew of six, two of whom stood behind the vehicle to handle ammunition.

Specifications

Crew: 6	Engine: 390kW (520hp) V12 diesel
Weight: 24,945kg (54,880lb)	Speed: 55km/h (34mph)
Length: 8.4m (27ft 6.7in)	Road range: 300km (186 miles)
Width: 3.2m (10ft 6in)	Armament: 1 x 152mm (6in) howitzer
Height: 2.8m (9ft 2.25in)	

▲ **2S19 MSTA SP howitzer**

Russian Ground Forces / 131st Motor Rifle Brigade, 2008

Development of the 2S19 as a replacement for the aging 2S3 self-propelled howitzer began in 1985, and the weapon entered service with the Soviet armed forces in 1989. Its 152mm (6in) main armament was modified from the 2A65 towed howitzer, and in 2008 the Russians introduced an improved version which incorporated an automatic fire-control system.

Specifications

Crew: 5	Engine: 630kW (840hp) V-84A diesel
Weight: 42,000kg (92,593lb)	Speed: 60km/h (37mph)
Length: 7.15m (23ft 5in)	Road range: 500km (311 miles)
Width: 3.38m (11ft)	Armament: 1 x 152mm (6in) howitzer
Height: 2.99m (9ft 9in)	

armour for the Soviet Union and later the forces of the Russian Federation. Mounting a modified version of the 2A65 152mm (6in) towed howitzer, the 2S19 is capable of firing up to eight rounds per minute. The weapon incorporates the chassis of the modern T-80 main battle tank and the reliable engine of the T-72. Intended as a replacement for the 2S3, it is equipped with an automatic loader, protection against nuclear, biological and chemical weapons, night vision equipment and improved armour protection. The weapon fires high-explosive

fragmentation rounds as well as smoke and chemical shells, and the laser-guided Krasnopol munition. It is also nuclear-capable.

Based on the 8X8 Tatra 813 truck, the 152mm (6in) DANA self-propelled howitzer was introduced by Czech designers in the 1970s and remains active with the armies of Georgia, the Czech Republic, Libya, Poland and Slovakia. During the South Ossetia War, four DANAs of the Georgian forces were reported destroyed by Russian ground-attack aircraft while three were captured. The weapon was meant

▲ **DANA SP howitzer**

Georgian Army / Joint Artillery Brigade, 2008

Developed in Czechoslovakia as a wheeled alternative to the expense of the Soviet 2S3 self-propelled 152mm (6in) howitzer, the DANA incorporated the chassis of the Tatra 813 truck and an enclosed turret mount for the main weapon. The DANA was one of the first artillery systems to introduce an autoloader which could load a shell with the barrel at any elevation.

Specifications

Crew: 4/5	Engine: 257kW (345hp) V12 diesel
Weight: 23,000kg (50,600lb)	Speed: 80km/h (49.71mph)
Length: 10.5m (34ft 5in)	Road range: 600km (375 miles)
Width: 2.8m (9ft 2in)	Armament: 1 x 152mm (6in) gun, plus
Height: 2.6m (8ft 6in)	1 x 12.7mm (0.5in) HMG

▲ **2S7 Pion SP gun**

Georgian Army / Joint Artillery Brigade, 2008

The 203mm (8in) 2S7 Pion self-propelled gun entered service in the mid-1970s with the main armament situated atop the chassis of the T-80 main battle tank and mounted externally. The 2S7 is capable of firing conventional and rocket-assisted ammunition. During the South Ossetia War, the Georgian Army deployed several of these weapons which had been acquired from Ukraine.

Specifications

Crew: 7	Engine: 630kW (840hp) V-46-I V12 diesel
Weight: 47,246kg (46.5 tons)	Speed: 50km/h (31mph)
Length: 10.5m (34ft 5in)	Road range: 650km (404 miles)
Width: 3.38m (11ft)	Armament: 1 x 203mm (8in) howitzer
Height: 3m (9ft 10in)	

to supply the direct fire support needed for infantry operations without the expense of purchasing the 2S3 from the Soviets, and through more than 30 years of service over 750 DANAs have been manufactured.

The heaviest gun deployed to South Ossetia, the 203mm (8in) 2S7 Pion, or Peony, was first seen in the West in 1975 and consists of the hull of the T-80 main battle tank and an externally mounted gun. Its crew

of seven can ready the gun to fire within five minutes and prepare the tracked chassis for displacement with as little as three minutes' notice. Four 203mm (8in) shells are carried aboard the 2S7, while a support vehicle is usually close by with additional rounds. To date, more than 1000 2S7s have been built, and the system has been operated by several former Soviet republics and Eastern Bloc nations.

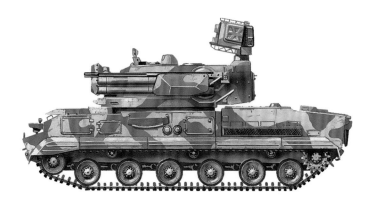

▲ 9K22 Tunguska

Russian Ground Forces / 67th Separate Anti-Aircraft Brigade, 2008

The 9K22 Tunguska air defence weapon incorporates twin 30mm (1.2in) autocannon and the 9M311 air defence missile. Developed in the 1970s as a counter to low-flying tank-destroyer aircraft, the Tunguska entered service with the Red Army in 1982. Its 30mm (1.2in) guns generate a combined rate of fire of up to 5000 rounds per minute, while the semi-automatic command to line of sight (SACLOS), two-stage, solid-fuel missile is detonated by a radio fuse.

Specifications

Configuration: two-stage, solid fuel	Launch weight: 57kg (126lb)
Deployment: mobile	Range: 3500m (11,000ft)
Length: 2.56m (8ft 5in)	Secondary armament: twin 30mm (1.2in) cannon

▲ BM-21 rocket launcher

Russian Ground Forces / 9th Motor Rifle Division, 2008

Developed in the early 1960s as a successor to the original Katyusha multiple rocket launcher of World War II fame, the BM-21 Grad, or Hail, has been in service around the world for nearly 50 years. It mounts a bank of up to 40 122mm (4.8in) rocket tubes, which may be fired at a rate of two rounds per second, atop the Ural 375D 6X6 truck. The weapons carry high-explosive fragmentation, cluster or incendiary warheads.

Specifications

Crew: 4	System combat weight: 13,700kg (13.48 tons)
Calibre: 122mm (4.8in)	Range: 20.37km (12.66 miles)
Rocket length: 3.226m (10ft 7in)	Rate of fire: 2 rounds per second
Rocket weight: 77.5kg (171lb)	

Russian air defence

1992–PRESENT

During the last decade of its existence, the Soviet Union significantly upgraded its short-range air defence missile capabilities, and these types proved their usefulness in later conflicts.

DURING THE 2008 SOUTH OSSETIA WAR, the Russian Air Force was reported to have lost several aircraft. Three of these were Sukhoi Su-25 close-support attack aircraft, while a fourth was a Tupolev Tu-22 strategic bomber. Although it may not be unusual for an air force to sustain losses in combat, the irony of the Ossetia shooting-downs stems from the fact that these planes were most likely lost to air defence missiles initially deployed during the last years of the Soviet Union and fielded by the small Georgian armed forces against the Russians in South Ossetia. Therefore, it must be concluded that the Russians had failed at least in part to develop or maintain countermeasures against the missiles they had inherited.

Gadfly and Gopher

Although these losses in no way threatened Russian air supremacy, they indicated a pronounced gap in the effectiveness of Russian aerial countermeasures and jamming equipment in relation to the improvements which had been incorporated in two air defence missile systems during the late 1970s. These were the 9K37M1 Buk-1M medium-range missile system, identified by NATO as the SA-11 Gadfly, and the 9K35 Strela-10 short-range missile system, known to NATO observers as the SA-13 Gopher. Intended to replace the SA-6 Gainful and SA-9 Gaskin air defence missiles which had been in service since the 1960s, the Gadfly and Gopher missiles entered service with the Soviet armed forces in 1979 at roughly the same time that the tracked 9K22 Tunguska combined missile and 30mm (1.2in) cannon air defence system was entering service as well. This was due in part to a cost-saving initiative.

The sophisticated radar, nicknamed Snow Drift, of the 9K37M1 Buk, or Beech, is capable of tracking up to six individual targets at the same time and engages fixed-wing aircraft, helicopters and cruise missiles.

Specifications

Configuration: single-stage, solid fuel

Deployment: mobile

Length: 5.55m (18ft 2in)

Diameter: 860mm (33.86in)

Launch weight: 690kg (1521lb)

Range: 30km (19 miles)

Launch preparation time: 5 minutes

▲ **9K37M1 Buk-1M (SA-11 Gadfly)**

Russian Ground Forces / 66th Guards Motor Rifle Regiment, 1994

The SA-11 Gadfly, officially known as the 9K37M1 Buk-1M to the Soviets and then the armed forces of the Russian Federation, entered service with the Red Army in 1979 as an eventual replacement for the medium-range SA-6 Gainful air defence missile system. Incorporating numerous improvements, such as advanced radar and guidance systems, the SA-11 is capable of tracking up to six separate targets simultaneously and is effective against fixed-wing aircraft, helicopters and cruise missiles.

Thought to be effective up to 90 per cent of the time, the system is capable of rapid movement, displacing in as little as five minutes. Along with the Snow Drift radar, the system consists of the TELAR (transporter-erector-launcher and radar) vehicle which is a variant of the GM-569 tracked chassis. A standard battalion consists of a command vehicle, six TELAR vehicles, and support vehicles which carry missile reloads. The missile itself is typically a variant of the 9M38 with a high-explosive fragmentation warhead which is detonated by a proximity fuse.

The SA-13 Gopher, known as the 9K35 Strela-10 (Arrow) to the Russians, consists of a modified MT-LB tracked chassis and is capable of firing either the 9M37 missile or the earlier 9K31 mounted by the SA-9 Gaskin air defence system. The missiles are visually aimed and utilize infrared guidance against low-flying targets. Known as Hat Box, the SA-13 radar is situated between two missile pods and provides the range to the target. Four radar antennae are positioned at each corner of the rear deck of the chassis. The 9M37 missile is typically capable of a speed approaching Mach 2. It weighs approximately 40kg (88lb), and it is 2.2m (7ft 3in) in length.

During Operation Desert Storm in 1991, the SA-13 was reportedly responsible for shooting down at least two US low-flying A-10 Thunderbolt 'Warthog' ground-attack aircraft, and it is likely that the system damaged several others. In Kosovo, Serbian forces deployed the SA-13 and were known to have damaged a pair of A-10s.

Great Grumble

The long reach of Soviet air defence missiles was extended in the late 1970s with the introduction of the SA-10 Grumble, officially known as the S-300 missile. The S-300 also spawned subsequent variants, the SA-12 Giant/Gladiator and the SA-20 Gargoyle. The S-300 entered service with Soviet forces in 1978, and the system has undergone a series of upgrades over the last 30 years. It consists of the 5P85-1 vehicle – which is a combined truck and trailer – surveillance and low-altitude radar, and the sophisticated 30N6 fire-control system. A variety of missiles are available depending on the range to the target and each delivers a high-explosive fragmentation warhead weighing up to 150kg (330lb). In 2007, the Russian Federation agreed to sell numerous S-300 systems to the Islamic Republic of Iran; however, the governments of the United States and Israel objected and the sale has not been concluded.

The basic SA-10 was intended to defend major Soviet cities against cruise-missile attack, and during the mid-1980s at least 80 examples of the system were deployed, with many of these forming a defensive cordon around Moscow. Although there is no official record of the SA-10 in combat, it is considered by Western analysts to be a highly capable system. It is fielded by several former Soviet republics and client states today.

▲ **ZRK-BD 9K35 Strela-10 (SA-13 Gopher)**

Russian Ground Forces / 28th Guards Tank Regiment, 1996

The ZRK-BD Strela-10 air defence missile, designated the SA-13 Gopher by NATO, entered service with the Soviet Red Army in 1979 as a short-range, optically aimed and infrared-guided system which was intended to replace the SA-9 Gaskin. The SA-13 was capable of firing both the 9M37 missile which was its primary armament and the 9K31 which originally was fielded with the Gaskin. The SA-13 is mounted atop the modified chassis of the tracked MT-LB vehicle and its operational range is 500km (311 miles). The SA-13 system vehicle is known as a TELAR (transporter-erector-launcher and radar).

Specifications

Configuration: single-stage, solid fuel

Deployment: mobile

Length: 2.19m (7ft 3in)

Diameter: 120mm (4.72in)

Launch weight: 41kg (90lb)

Range: 5km (3.1 miles)

Launch preparation time: 3 minutes

▲ S-300 (SA-10 Grumble)

Russian Ground Forces / 5th Air Defence Brigade, 2003

The S-300 air defence missile, known in NATO nomenclature as the SA-10 Grumble, entered service with Soviet forces in 1978, initially as a defence against cruise missiles although later versions were adapted for use against incoming ballistic missiles. By the mid-1980s, at least 80 of these transporter-erector-launcher vehicles, which include a truck-and-trailer combination designated the 5P85-1, were reportedly in service protecting major Soviet cities. An improved version, the S-400 (NATO SA-21) entered service with Russian forces in 2004.

Specifications

Configuration: single-stage, solid fuel
Deployment: mobile
Length: 7.5m (24ft 7in)
Diameter: 500mm (19.69in)
Launch weight: 1800kg (3968lb)
Range: 200km (124 miles)
Launch preparation time: 5 minute

War in Iraq and Afghanistan
2001–PRESENT

A decade on from the end of the Gulf War, the world was a very different place. Saddam Hussein threatened the use of weapons of mass destruction, and the arduous War on Terror had begun.

THE WAR ON TERROR and the looming threat of weapons of mass destruction compelled an armed coalition, including NATO countries, to commit troops and military hardware to preserve security in the Middle East and elsewhere. Since his army had been defeated decisively during the Gulf War of 1991, Saddam Hussein had rebuilt the Iraqi war machine into an apparent threat to peace in the Middle East once again. Using chemical weapons against the separatist Kurds in northern Iraq and brutally suppressing an uprising in the south around the major port city of Basra, the Iraqi strongman caused growing concern in the West regarding his willingness to plunge the Middle East into another destabilizing war of conquest.

Simultaneously, the horrific events of 11 September 2001 confronted the United States, Great Britain and other nations with the stark reality that Islamic fundamentalism and its accompanying philosophy of Jihad, or holy war, against the West constituted a very real threat to the safety and security of the world.

In response to these dual threats, the armed forces of numerous nations were mobilized in a coalition which moved to quell the menace. From bases in Saudi Arabia, Kuwait, Bahrain, the United Arab Emirates and other locations, logistical planning began in earnest in 2002 as the deadline for Iraq to comply with United Nations resolution 1441 approached. The resolution had set a deadline for Iraq to disclose any and all of its weapons of mass destruction capabilities and allow UN inspectors on the ground inside the country to verify these disclosures. US President George W. Bush had promised to authorize military intervention in Iraq in the event of non-compliance, asserting that Saddam Hussein's unwillingness to comply would trigger the provisions of earlier UN resolutions which were enacted during the Gulf War period.

Beyond Babylon

Although Secretary of State Colin Powell had addressed a plenary session of the UN Security

Council in February 2003 and outlined US concerns and 'evidence' of Iraqi weapons of mass destruction, the discovery of such weapons proved elusive during the actual invasion which followed, calling into question the legitimacy of the invasion. Nevertheless, the record amassed by Saddam Hussein during the years of authoritarian rule by his Baath Party had contributed greatly to his own demise.

Aside from chemical and biological weapons, his nuclear programme was considered a clear threat to Israel, and as early as 1981 the Israelis had bombed a nuclear reactor which was under construction in Iraq and could have potentially produced fuel for a nuclear weapon. During the Iran–Iraq War of the 1980s, Saddam Hussein had enlisted the services of Canadian astrophysicist Gerald Bull, who was widely known for his research into 'super guns', artillery pieces capable of firing shells tipped with nuclear warheads. During the Gulf War, components of such weapons were discovered by Coalition troops and intercepted in transit from various countries.

Two big guns, known as Baby Babylon and Big Babylon, had been under construction in Iraq, with Baby Babylon actually placed in an excavated position

for testing in the summer of 1989. Baby Babylon was impressive enough with a bore of 350mm (13.8in) and a barrel of roughly 52m (170ft) in length. The weapon was installed 145km (90 miles) north of Baghdad at Jabal Hamrayn, and its range was estimated at approximately 668km (415 miles). Big Babylon was conceptualized on a truly gargantuan scale, with a barrel which was 152m (500ft) in length and 1500 tonnes (1476 tons) in weight, and with a bore of one metre (3.3ft). Had Big Babylon become operational, it would have provided further data for Bull's development of an even bigger weapon under his HARP (High Altitude Research Project) programme. One HARP design consisted of a 91m (300ft) barrel weighing 1905 tonnes (1875 tons).

Super guns aside, Coalition and NATO planners respected even the conventional artillery capabilities of the Iraqi Army and acknowledged the difficulty of tracking the rocket launchers, heavy mortars and shoulder-fired weapons of the Al Qaeda and Taliban forces. They were also well aware of the need for air-transportable field artillery and self-propelled guns which could keep pace with advancing infantry during sustained ground campaigns.

▲ **Fire support**

US Army artillerymen calibrate their 105mm (4.1in) howitzer to provide fire support at a forward operating base near Kalsu, Iraq, 2007. The artillerymen are with Alpha Battery, 2nd Battalion, 377th Parachute Field Artillery Regiment.

Iraq
2003

Rapid Coalition movement, supported by field artillery and self-propelled guns, resulted in the reduction of the Iraqi Army and the capture of Baghdad and Basra.

WITH HIS COUNTRY on the brink of invasion, Saddam Hussein's Iraqi Army consisted in part of at least three armoured divisions, three mechanized infantry divisions and 11 infantry divisions. While these formations have been estimated at actually 70 to 80 per cent of their official strength, they still constituted a potent fighting force. Along with more than 2500 assorted field artillery pieces, self-propelled guns, multiple launch rocket systems and surface-to-surface missiles, the Iraqis also possessed substantial man-portable anti-tank weapons and surface-to-air missiles of Soviet origin.

Iraqi air defence
In addition to the Soviet-era ZSU-23-4, ZSU-57-2, M1939 twin 37mm (1.5in) and assorted guns of 85mm (3.3in), 100mm (3.9in) and 130mm (5.1in) calibre, the Iraqis fielded a variety of air defence missiles, including the SA-2, SA-6, SA-9, SA-13 and SA-16. While several of these were carried atop tracked or wheeled transporter-erector-launcher

IRAQI ARMY ARTILLERY, 2003		
Type	**Weapon**	**Strength**
Towed Artillery	105mm (M-56 pack) 122mm (D-74; D-30; M1938) 130mm (M-46; Type 59-1) 155mm (G-5; GHN-45; M114)	1900
Self-propelled Artillery	122mm (2SI) 152mm (2S3) 155mm (M109A1/ A2; AUF-1 (GCT))	200
Multiple Rocket Launchers	107mm 122mm (BM-21) 127mm (ASTROS II) 132mm (BM-13/16) 262mm ('Ababeel-100')	200
Mortars	81mm 120mm 160mm (M1943) 240mm	–
Surface-to-Surface Missiles	FROG (Free Rocket Over Ground) Scud	50 6

▲ **BM-21 rocket launcher**

Iraqi Republican Guard / Hammurabi Armoured Division / 8th Mechanized Brigade, 2003

The Soviet-era BM-21 multiple launch rocket system was prominent among the weapons deployed by Iraqi Republican Guard and regular army divisions during Operation Iraqi Freedom. Although it was highly mobile, the BM-21 proved susceptible to Coalition air power and its performance was average at best when compared with more modern MLRS platforms such as the 127mm (5in) ASTROS II.

Specifications
Crew: 4

Calibre: 122mm (4.8in)

Rocket length: 3.226m (10ft 7in)

Rocket weight: 77.5kg (171lb)

System combat weight: 13,700kg (13.48 tons)

Range: 20.37km (12 miles)

Rate of fire: 2 rounds per second

Specifications

Crew: 4

Weight: 29,750kg (29.28 tons)

Length: 6.19m (20ft 3in)

Width: 3.15m (10ft 3in)

Height: 3.24m (10ft 7in)

Engine: 302kW (405hp) Detroit Diesel

Speed: 56km/h (35mph)

Road range: 405km (252 miles)

Armament: 1 x M126 155mm (6.1in) howitzer

▲ M109A6 Paladin SP gun

US Marine Corps / 1st Marine Expeditionary Force / 11th Marine Regiment, 2003

The standard self-propelled howitzer of the US Army and Marine Corps, the 155mm (6.1in) M109A6 Paladin was the latest of a series of improvements to the M109 design which had entered service more than 40 years earlier. The M109A6 was used exclusively by the US forces and has not been exported to other countries. The Paladin has been described as an all-new system in comparison to earlier M109 variants and incorporates the latest in explosive reactive armour and an internal navigation system.

SP Artillery Battalion, US Army, 2007

The self-propelled artillery battalion of the US Army during Operation Iraqi Freedom incorporated a headquarters and service battery and three firing batteries equipped with a complement of at least 18 M109A6 Paladin 155mm (6.1in) self-propelled howitzers, which were assigned to heavy brigade combat teams and fire brigades. Each Paladin battery consists of a battery headquarters, two firing platoons of three sections and a support platoon. The support platoon includes two ammunition sections; maintenance, supply and food service sections; and platoon headquarters. A battery operations centre provides fire-direction control.

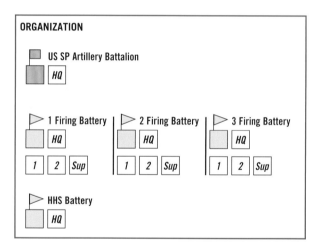

ORGANIZATION

US SP Artillery Battalion
HQ

1 Firing Battery
HQ
1 2 Sup

2 Firing Battery
HQ
1 2 Sup

3 Firing Battery
HQ
1 2 Sup

HHS Battery
HQ

Battery 1 (6 x M109A6 Paladin SP guns)

Battery 2 (6 x M109A6 Paladin SP guns)

Battery 3 (6 x M109A6 Paladin SP guns)

vehicles, the SA-16 Gimlet, as it was designated by NATO, was a man-portable weapon which was known to have shot down a Coalition Panavia Tornado fighter-bomber during the Gulf War. Its light weight of 10.8kg (24lb) allowed for rapid deployment and target acquisition.

Officially known to the Soviets and later the Russian ground forces as the 9K38 Igla, or Needle, the SA-16 entered service in 1981 and was later upgraded to the SA-18 Grouse. Its infrared guidance system, IFF (Identification Friend or Foe) capability and countermeasure resistance combine in a formidable short-range weapon.

Howitzer hammer

Operation Iraqi Freedom was a tour de force for Coalition artillery. One defence analyst observed that it 'proved to be the deciding factor in many of the conflicts – although the enemy artillery outnumbered and outranged the coalition force FA [field artillery]. The FA in Operation Iraqi Freedom was the lowest ratio of artillery pieces to troops in war since before World War I. Artillery fires came at a premium with lines of communication stretched from the Kuwait border to Baghdad ... The magnificent soldier and Marine field artilleryman adapted to changes while rapidly moving great distances, made critical decisions independently in decentralized operations with little or no sleep and executed fire missions with extraordinary precision in constant movements to contact, meeting

engagements and urban operations as part of the most effective joint fires team in history....'

Along with the 155mm (6.1in) M198 towed field howitzer, the 155mm (6.1in) M109A6 Paladin served as the workhorse of US artillery during Operation Iraqi Freedom. Although the M109 had been in service for more than 40 years and undergone numerous upgrades, the Paladin was virtually a new system. Its M126 main weapon could produce a rate of fire of up to four rounds per minute, while the vehicle's extended operational range of 405km (252 miles) allowed it to work closely with front-line troops during offensive operations. Its sophisticated target-acquisition and gun-stabilization equipment allow the Paladin to operate in varied climates and weather conditions, while its crew of four is protected by advanced explosive reactive armour and nuclear, biological and chemical defences.

The M198 equipped units of the US Army and Marine Corps, with one American infantry division's supporting artillery firing nearly 14,000 rounds during the ground campaign. A number of these were precision-guided M898 SADARM submunition sense-and-destroy rounds, which home in on enemy targets, particularly light armoured vehicles and tanks, within a radius of the 155mm (6.1in)

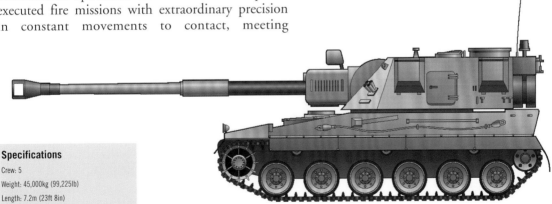

Specifications

Crew: 5

Weight: 45,000kg (99,225lb)

Length: 7.2m (23ft 8in)

Width: 3.4m (11ft 2in)

Height: 3m (9ft 10in)

Engine: 492kW (660hp) Cummins V8 diesel

Speed: 55km/h (34mph)

Road range: 240km (150 miles)

Armament: 1 x 155mm (6.1in) howitzer, plus 1 x 12.7mm (0.5in) MG

▲ **AS-90 SP gun**

British Army / 1st Armoured Division / 7th Armoured Brigade / 3rd Royal Horse Artillery, 2003

Dubbed the AS-90 (Artillery System for the 90s), this 155mm (6.1in) self-propelled gun was developed during the 1980s and entered service in 1993 as a replacement for the aging British complement of M109 weapons. Its crew of five is capable of firing three rounds in a ten-second burst, six rounds per minute for up to three minutes or two rounds per minute for a period of one hour. Manufactured by Vickers Shipbuilding and Engineering, it initially equipped five regiments of the Royal Artillery and the Royal Horse Artillery.

shell which bursts above the target. As Marines cleared the insurgent stronghold of Fallujah, one soldier reported that the M198 had made 'everybody get out of town'.

Fighting alongside the US 1st Marine Expeditionary Force, the British 1st Armoured Division was augmented by the attachment of the 3rd Royal Horse Artillery. For the action, the regiment had increased its complement of AS-90 155mm (6.1in) self-propelled guns to 32. In the event, it provided tactical fire support to four battle groups within the 7th Armoured Brigade and constituted one of the largest formations of artillery assembled by the British Army since World War II.

Along with the US 11th Marine Regiment – an artillery unit – elements of the 3rd Royal Horse Artillery and the 7th Royal Horse Artillery became an effective fighting unit despite inherent challenges such as incompatible communications equipment. As the Coalition forces fought their way through the strategic town of Naseriyah, British guns fired more than 9000 rounds of 155mm (6.1in) ammunition and 13,000 105mm (4.1in) rounds.

Artillery officer Brigadier Andrew R. Gregory praised the performance of the AS-90 and the towed 105mm (4.1in) L118 Light Gun. 'The AS-90 howitzer proved to be robust, versatile and provided the range, accuracy and, when required, significant weight of fire to degrade almost all enemy actions … The L118 light gun also proved its worth, particularly when it was lifted along with sufficient ammunition onto the Al Faw peninsula early in the operation.'

▲ M1045 HMMWV TOW missile carrier

US Army / 3rd Infantry Division / 2nd Brigade, 2003

The M1045 HMMWV is one of several variants of the ubiquitous M998 'Humvee' family of light military vehicles. This HMMWV (High-Mobility Multi-purpose Wheeled Vehicle) mounts the wire-guided TOW anti-tank missile and is equipped with supplemental armour for the protection of its crew. The TOW firing platform is capable of 360-degree traverse to engage enemy armour. Another variant, the M1046, includes the TOW missile launcher and a powered towing winch.

Specifications

Crew: 4	Engine: 112.5kW (150hp) 6.2-litre V8 fuel-injected diesel
Weight: 2359kg (5200lb)	
Length: 4.57m (15ft)	Speed: 89km/h (55mph)
Width: 2.16m (7ft 1in)	Road range: 563km (350 miles)
Height: 1.83m (6ft)	Armament: TOW anti-tank missile

Specifications

Configuration: two-stage, solid fuel
Deployment: fixed or mobile
Length: 2.4m (94.5in)
Diameter: 160mm (6.3in)
Launch weight: 63kg (139lb)
Range: 6.2km (3.9 miles)
Launch preparation time: 8 seconds

▲ Roland surface-to-air missile

Iraqi Army / 5th Mechanized Division / 20th Mechanized Brigade, 2003

The Roland air defence missile was a joint development by France and Germany during the 1960s and has remained in service for decades. The system was also purchased by the US Army and equipped several Iraqi air defence units during both Operation Desert Storm and Operation Iraqi Freedom. Credited with shooting down a US A-10 Thunderbolt ground-attack aircraft during Iraqi Freedom, the Roland was deployed by the Iraqis mounted on the bed of an 8X8 truck or as a self-propelled weapon atop the modified chassis of the AMX-30 main battle tank.

Afghanistan

2001–PRESENT

The War on Terror has focused attention on light, air-transportable artillery systems which maintain critical firepower superiority in rugged terrain.

ALMOST A DECADE OF FIGHTING in Afghanistan has emphasized the need for durable, lightweight artillery which may be airlifted to critical areas and recovered quickly for maintenance and upkeep. The vast mountainous regions of the country often restrict the movement of self-propelled artillery; therefore, towed weapons have retained a signicant role in the fight against the Taliban and Al Qaeda strongholds.

During the war in Afghanistan, US and British forces, as well as contingents of troops from other NATO countries, have deployed the M777 155mm (6.1in) ultralight field howitzer, the GIAT LG-1 and L118 Light Gun 105mm (4.1in) towed howitzers, and self-propelled weapons including the M109A6 Paladin and AS-90 155mm (6.1in) howitzers. Artillery units of the Afghan Army have brought the Soviet-era D-30 122mm (4.8in) towed howitzer into action following extensive training by British forces.

'I'm extremely pleased with what I've seen ...' reported one British officer. 'The ANA [Afghan National Army] are progressing extremely quickly, and you can really see the progress that is being made. This is just an example of how much better the ANA is getting as a fighting force. The advantage of having extra D-30 guns is that we can augment our already existing guns within Afghanistan and particularly in Helmand in the fight against the insurgency in southern Afghanistan.'

A versatile field artillery weapon, the British L118 Light Gun has been in service since the 1970s and widely exported. It was developed by the Royal Armament Research and Development Establishment (RARDE), and production was undertaken in 1975 by the Royal Ordnance Factory, Nottingham. The weapon traces its lineage to the World War II-era QF 25-pounder and replaced the Italian OTO Melara Mod 56 105mm (4.1in) pack howitzer and several small mortars in service with the British Army. A modified version of the L118, the L119A, has been placed in service with the US Army.

British gun crews serving in Afghanistan have nicknamed the L118 the Dragon due to its excellent results in action against the Taliban. The weapon can acquire and engage a target at a distance of

7TH PARACHUTE REGIMENT, ROYAL HORSE ARTILLERY, 2007	
Unit	Strength
F (Sphinx) Parachute Battery	4
G Parachute Battery (Mercer's Troop)	4
H Parachute Battery (Ramsay's Troop)	4
I Parachute Battery (Bull's Troop)	4
Aviation Tactical Group	–
LAD REME	–

7th Parachute Regiment, Royal Horse Artillery, 16th Air Assault Brigade, British Army, 2007

The only parachute artillery regiment of the British Army, the 7th is equipped with the L118 Light Gun. It consists of six batteries and has actively participated in several modern conflicts, including the wars in Afghanistan, Iraq and Kosovo. The 105mm (4.1in) L118 has proved an effective and highly mobile field artillery weapon, particularly when deployed in support of light infantry and airborne units. Serving with the 16th Air Assault Brigade, elements of the 7th Parachute Regiment have deployed the L118 by air and with light ground-transport vehicles. The weapon's maximum rate of fire is up to eight rounds per minute.

Battery (4 x L118 Light Guns)

three kilometres (1.86 miles) within five seconds. An automatic pointing system (APS) allows the gun to be unlimbered and in action within 30 seconds. At 1158kg (4100lb), the L118 is often towed by medium-weight vehicles such as the Land Rover or Humvee or airlifted by Chinook or Wessex helicopter. Its rate of fire is up to eight rounds per minute.

The more powerful M777 155mm (6.1in) howitzer incorporates titanium in its construction which accounts for a considerable reduction in weight compared with predecessors such as the M198 155mm (6.1in) howitzer. The M777 is light enough to be transported by the V-22 Osprey aircraft or the CH-47 Chinook helicopter. On several occasions the M777 has worked in cooperation with tanks and self-propelled artillery, firing at a maximum rate of up to five rounds per minute.

As in Iraq, the M982 Excalibur extended-range guided artillery shell has been used with success in Afghanistan. Fired from the M777, the Excalibur has been quite effective against caves and remote Taliban command or training centres. Sergeant Henry Selzer of the US Army's 173rd Airborne Brigade Combat Team noted that the M777 and Excalibur combination was fired for the first time at Camp Blessing in the Kunar Province of northeast Afghanistan. 'The M777 is designed to be a digitally programmed weapon,' he said. 'The fuse setting was performed by the Enhanced Portable Inductive Artillery Fuse Setter, placed on the tip of the round, sending a digital message containing the coordinate for the round to find.' Captain Ryan Berdiner of C

▲ **M777 155mm Ultralight Field Howitzer**

US Army / 173rd Airborne Brigade Combat Team / 321st Field Artillery Regiment / 3rd Battalion, 2009

The M777 Ultralight Field Howitzer enhances the capabilities of heavy field artillery by providing a lighter and more mobile alternative to the M198 towed howitzer which remains in service with the armed forces of numerous countries. The M777 was developed by BAE Systems' Global Combat Systems Division and entered service with the US Army and Marine Corps in 2005. It has also been deployed by Canadian and Australian artillery units. The M777 utilizes a digital fire-control system similar to that which equips the M109A6 Paladin self-propelled howitzer and is transported by aircraft, helicopter or medium truck.

Specifications

Crew: 5

Calibre: 155mm (6.1in)

Elevation: - 5 degrees to + 70 degrees

Weight: 4182kg (9200lb)

Range: 40km (25 miles)

Muzzle velocity: 827m/sec (2713ft/sec)

▲ **GIAT LG-1 towed howitzer**

Canadian Army / Royal Horse Artillery / 5th Heavy Artillery Regiment, 2006

The French GIAT LG-1 towed howitzer entered service with the Canadian armed forces in 1996 and provides a lightweight, airmobile weapon which is particularly suited to supporting fire in difficult terrain such as NATO troops have encountered in Afghanistan. The LG-1 is capable of an impressive rate of fire of 12 rounds per minute and weighs only 1520kg (3400lb). In mid-2005, the Canadian armed forces embarked on a programme to upgrade their LG-1 complement with an improved muzzle brake and larger carriage tyres.

Specifications

Crew: 5

Calibre: 105mm (4.1in)

Elevation: - 3 degrees to + 70 degrees

Weight: 1520kg (3400lb)

Range: 19.5km (12.1 miles)

Muzzle velocity: 490m/sec (1608ft/sec)

Battery, 3rd Battalion, 321st Field Artillery Regiment, added, 'By using the Excalibur we are mitigating a lot of collateral damage that other rounds may cause. The main purpose of the M777 is that it is more able to help the units in the Korengal Valley by providing more timely and accurate fire.'

The French 105mm (4.1in) LG-1 entered service in the mid-1990s and was specifically designed for rapid deployment. Its light weight of 1520kg (3400lb) reduces the useful life of the barrel; however, the weapon is capable of firing an impressive maximum of 12 rounds per minute. In addition to service in Afghanistan, the LG-1 has been deployed to the Balkans. The gun may be towed by light vehicles such as the Land Rover or Humvee and is also airmobile via parachute drop or delivery. Four guns may be transported in the cargo space of the C-130 transport aircraft. Firing the standard NATO 105mm (4.1in) round, the LG-1 may be taken in and out of service in less than 30 seconds.

Precision rocket

Having initially developed it to improve the accuracy of the M26 rocket, the US military continues to refine the GMLRS (Guided Multiple Launch Rocket System), which is compatible with the existing M270 or HIMARS launchers. Potential vulnerability to a new generation of accurate long-range rocket and artillery ammunition prompted research on the GMLRS, which extends the range of the older M26 to 60km (37.28 miles). The GMLRS currently includes two types of ammunition, the dual-purpose improved cluster munition (DPICM), which carries 404 bomblets, and the M31A1 rocket, with a single 91kg (200lb) high-explosive warhead. Each is guided by a global positioning system with internal measurement unit guidance.

The stated objective of the GMLRS is to provide greater range, more accurate fire and therefore better results with fewer rockets. It also enhances the shoot-and-scoot capabilities of the HIMARS and M270 launchers, which have seen action in both Iraq and Afghanistan. More than 150 GMLRS rockets were fired during Operation Iraqi Freedom, and reports indicate that the system has been in use against the Taliban as well, since its extended range and pinpoint accuracy are capable of striking enemy positions which would be difficult for ground troops to reach in force.

Fire and forget

The ability to displace quickly is a key to the survival of individual soldiers and small operating units which field portable missiles for use against armoured

▲ HIMARS MLRS

US Army / 3rd Field Artillery Regiment / 5th Battalion, 2007

The HIMARS (High Mobility Artillery Rocket System) was deployed for the first time by the US Army in 2005 following a decade of development led by Lockheed Martin Missiles and Fire Control. The system was adopted by the US Marine Corps in 2002. Situated atop a 6X6 truck which is one of the latest in the army's FMTV (Family of Military Tactical Vehicles), the HIMARS carries six high-explosive rockets or a single ATACMS.

Specifications

Crew: 3

Calibre: 227mm (8.94in)

Rocket length: 3.94m (12ft 11in)

Rocket weight: 360kg (675lb)

System combat weight: 10,886kg (24,000lb)

Range: 32km (20 miles)

Rate of fire: 6 rounds in 45 seconds

vehicles and hardened targets. In Afghanistan, the Taliban have been on the receiving end of the FGM-148 Javelin missile, which has been fielded by troops from several NATO countries. Intended as a replacement for the Dragon anti-tank missile, the Javelin was developed by divisions of Raytheon and Lockheed Martin beginning in the late 1980s and entered service in 1996.

During Operation Iraqi Freedom, the Javelin proved deadly against the T-54/55, T-62 and T-72 main battle tanks of the Republican Guard and the Iraqi Army. In Afghanistan, it has performed well against Taliban concentrations in buildings or urban settings as well as caves and mountainous strongholds. The Javelin's fire-and-forget technology allows the operator to immediately displace rather than linger in position to guide the weapon with wire or other means. In soft-launch mode, the missile is fired when ready; however, the rocket propulsion system does not fully engage until the missile reaches some distance from the launch site, minimizing backblast and any tell-tale exhaust signature. Its shaped high-explosive anti-tank (HEAT) warhead weighs 8.4kg (18.5lb) and is detonated by contact.

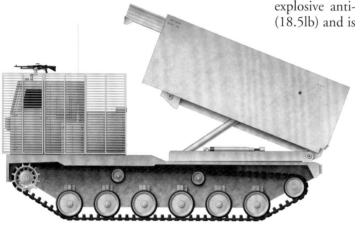

Specifications

Crew: 3

Calibre: 227mm (8.94in)

Rocket length: 3.94m (12ft 11in)

Rocket weight: 90kg (200lb)

System combat weight: 24,756kg (54,578lb)

Range: 60km (37 miles)

Rate of fire: 12 rounds in 60 seconds

▲ **Guided Multiple Launch Rocket System (GMLRS)**

US Army / 3rd Field Artillery Regiment / 5th Battalion, 2007

The GMLRS system provides the US Army and Marine Corps with additional defence against a new generation of precision-guided missiles and artillery shells, while also offering an improved strike capability over the older M26 rocket. The GMLRS includes improved range and economy of force, with fewer rockets required to accomplish a fire mission, while also minimizing collateral damage. Two types of GMLRS ammunition are currently in use, the M31A1 high-explosive projectile and the DPICM (dual-purpose improved cluster munition) which carries more than 400 bomblets.

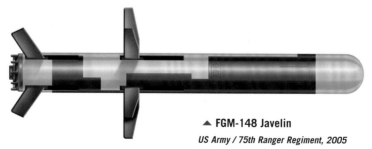

▲ **FGM-148 Javelin**

US Army / 75th Ranger Regiment, 2005

The Javelin anti-tank missile was widely used during Operation Iraqi Freedom and recorded numerous successes against the Soviet-era main battle tanks deployed by the Iraqi forces. The weapon has also been deployed to Afghanistan and utilized against hardened Taliban targets. Its fire-and-forget technology allows the operator to displace quickly and minimizes the exhaust signature of the missile due to its soft launch, which also reduces backblast.

Specifications

Configuration: two-stage, solid fuel	Launch weight: 22.3kg (59lb)
Deployment: man-portable	Range: 2500m (2734 yards)
Length: 1.1m (43in)	Rate of fire: 3 rounds in 2 minutes
Diameter: 127mm (5in)	

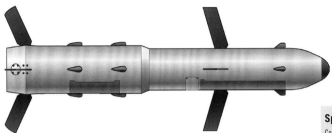

▲ Raytheon Griffin

US Special Operations Command (SOCOM), Afghanistan, 2009

First developed in 2006 and deployed from around 2008, the Griffin is a precision-guided miniature missile designed to support US Special Forces in combat operations. Two versions of the missile have been produced: Griffin A is designed to be launched from aircraft such as the MC-130W Combat Spear Hercules; Griffin B is a tube-launched, forward-firing missile that can be carried by helicopters, unmanned aerial vehicles (UAVs) and ground vehicles such as the Humvee or a light truck. Targets are designated by a controller using a graphic interface with GPS/INS coordinates or direct laser guidance.

Specifications

Configuration: single missile, solid fuel

Deployment: aircraft, UAVs and ground vehicles

Length: 1092mm (43in)

Diameter: 140mm (5.5in)

Launch weight: 15kg (33lb)

Warhead weight: 5.9kg (13lb)

Guidance system: GPS/INS with laser
 terminal homing

Range: unknown

Recent developments
2000–PRESENT

Rapidly advancing technology continues to push the proverbial envelope in terms of the research and development of new artillery systems, while the modern battlefield serves as a proving ground for such weapons.

COOPERATION AMONG NATIONS in the development of new arms and related technology is nothing new. However, with increasing costs and complexity and limited resources such activities may well continue on an unprecedented scale. Although some cooperative ventures have failed in the past, others have been extraordinarily successful. One such endeavour in the sphere of field artillery is the M777 155mm (6.1in) howitzer. Its manufacturer is the British firm BAE Systems, while more than 70 per cent of its components are produced by US contractors and the weapon was tested in the United States at Camp Shelby, Mississippi, with final assembly taking place in the US.

The M777 has become a model of efficiency and was slated to eventually replace the 155mm (6.1in) M198 towed howitzer with the US Army and Marine Corps as well as the 105mm (4.1in) L118 Light Gun in use by British forces, thus providing a viable alternative to a 105mm (4.1in) weapon in terms of mobility while also packing a stronger punch.

Research on the M777 was begun by Vickers in the 1990s, and by 2010 as many as 650 examples of the weapon were expected to be in service with the US armed forces.

Russian response

One of the most advanced and versatile Russian field artillery weapons is the 120mm (4.7in) Nona-K 2B16 towed cannon. Research on the Nona-K was begun in the late 1980s following the Soviet military experience in Afghanistan, and the weapon was eventually produced in a towed and self-propelled version. Firing at a maximum rate of up to five rounds per minute, the Nona-K is capable of sufficient elevation to operate as an anti-tank gun, howitzer or mortar. The towed version is serviced by a crew of five and transported by the UAZ-469 or GAZ-66 4X4 trucks. With a range of 12km (7.46 miles), it weighs 1200kg (2646lb) and fires a variety of ammunition suitable for the varied targets being engaged. The towed Nona-K and its offspring were the product of cooperation between several design bureaux within the former Soviet Union, including the Precision Mechanical Engineering Central Research Institute. To facilitate rapid firing, the gun is equipped with a compressed-air system which clears the barrel and places a new round in the breech.

The self-propelled Nona-K has been produced in both an amphibious wheeled version designated the 2S23 and a tracked variant known as the 2S9. The tracked 2S9 is airmobile and deployed with Russian airborne artillery units. It consists of the 120mm (4.7in) gun in an enclosed turret atop the chassis of the BMD fighting vehicle. Its modern systems include nuclear, biological and chemical weapons safeguards and night-vision equipment.

▲ ADATS

Canadian Army / 4 Air Defence Regiment, 1995

The ADATS (Air Defence Anti-Tank System) entered service with the Canadian Army in 1989 as a combination air-and-armoured-vehicle-defence system mounted atop the modified chassis of the M113 armoured personnel carrier. The Swiss Oerlikon firm developed the system during the early 1980s, and it includes a bank of eight missiles with high-explosive fragmentation warheads which are tracked by electro-optical equipment following target surveillance and acquisition by radar. The missile's effective range is ten kilometres (6.2 miles).

Specifications

Configuration: single-stage, solid fuel

Deployment: mobile

Length: 2.08m (6ft 10in)

Diameter: 152mm (6in)

Launch weight: 51kg (112.5lb)

Range: 10km (6.2 miles)

Launch preparation time: 5 seconds

▲ 76mm Otomatic Air Defence Tank

Italian Army / never entered service

Developed primarily to defend ground troops from attack by helicopter and fixed-wing aircraft, the 76mm (3in) Otomatic Air Defence Tank entered trials during the late 1980s but was never accepted into service as the Italian Army maintains 20mm (0.79in) to 40mm (1.57in) weapons as primary air defence guns. Capable of operating in adverse weather conditions, the system's radar tracked targets to a distance of 15km (9.32 miles).

Specifications

Crew: 4	Engine: 562.5kW (750hp) MTU V10 multifuel
Weight: 47,000kg (46.26 tons)	Speed: 60km/h (37mph)
Length: 7.08m (23ft 3in)	Road range: 500km (310 miles)
Width: 3.25m (10ft 8in)	Armament: 1 x 76mm (3in) gun
Height: 3.07m (10ft 1in)	

Self-propelled successors

In 2002, the United States government cancelled the $11 billion XM2001 Crusader project, which had been intended to produce a replacement for the venerable M109 self-propelled howitzer, particularly its latest incarnation, the M109A6 Paladin. However, the Paladin was deemed sufficient for a time, while research continued under the auspices of the army's Future Combat Systems (FCS) programme. Meanwhile, British designers also abandoned an upgrade of the AS-90 howitzer known as the Braveheart. That project ended due to complications with propelling charges for several rounds which were to be compatible with the long, 52-calibre 155mm (6.1in) main weapon.

Following the failure of the SP70 project – a combined effort between Germany, the United Kingdom and Italy to produce a self-propelled 155mm (6.1in) howitzer during the 1970s – German designers embarked on their own project and produced the highly successful Panzerhaubitze 2000. A joint venture between Krauss-Maffei Wegmann and Rheinmetall, the PzH 2000 (Armoured Howitzer 2000) has been utilized in combat in the Balkans and in Afghanistan.

A Rheinmetall product which has been adopted by several other countries, the 155mm (6.1in) L52 howitzer main gun of the PzH 2000 is well known for an outstanding rate of fire of up to three rounds in nine seconds in burst situations, ten rounds in as little as 56 seconds and a sustained rate of up to 13 rounds per minute. Its chassis is supplied by Krauss-

▲ **SBAT 70 multiple rocket launcher**

Brazilian Army / 1st Artillery Battalion, 1995

Developed by the Brazilian firm Avibrás, the SBAT 70 is designed to fire multiple ordnance against varied targets such as armoured vehicles and troop concentrations. Its bank of 36 tubes is transported by a two-wheeled trailer. Originally conceived as an aircraft rocket, the SBAT 70 was reconfigured as a ground weapon and is operated by a crew of four. It has been offered for export.

Specifications

Crew: 4
Calibre: 70mm (2.75in)
Rocket length: 1.41m (55.5in)
Rocket weight: 11.7kg (29.8lb)
System combat weight: 1000kg (2204lb)
Range: 8500m (9295 yards)
Rate of fire: unknown

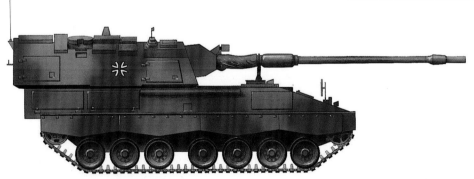

Specifications

Crew: 5	Engine: 745.7kW (1000hp) MTU 881 V12 diesel
Weight: 55,000kg (121,275lb)	Speed: 60km/h (27mph)
Length: 7.87m (25ft 10in)	Road range: 420km (260 miles)
Width: 3.37m (11ft)	Armament: 1 x 155mm (6.1in) L52 gun, plus
Height: 3.4m (11ft 2in)	1 x 7.62mm (0.3in) MG
	Radio: n/k

▲ **Panzerhaubitze 2000**

German Army / 1st Armoured Division

The self-propelled Panzerhaubitze 2000 provides heavy fire support to NATO troops in Afghanistan with its Rheinmetall 155mm (6.1in) L52 gun. The system has been selected by several nations to replace the aging M109 gun. It is operated by the armed forces of Germany, Italy, the Netherlands and Greece.

Maffei Wegmann and incorporates numerous components of the Leopard 1 main battle tank chassis. Wegmann also designed the turret.

Anti-tank tech

In response to a generation of improved main battle tanks, including the Russian T-90, Israeli Merkava, German Leopard 2 and US M1A1 Abrams, sophisticated anti-tank missiles are under development. The Russian 9M133 Kornet was reported in the hands of Hezbollah militants during the Israeli invasion of southern Lebanon in 2006, and its shaped HEAT charge is capable of penetrating up to 1190mm (47in) of armour protection. During one reported engagement, 11 Merkava tanks were damaged by Hezbollah fighters armed with the Kornet, which is usually carried by a two-man crew. The missile is also effective against low-flying aircraft, and has a range of 5000m (5468 yards).

In 2004, the Russian Ground Forces also deployed the AT-15 Springer anti-tank missile, which is officially known as the 9M123. Mounted atop the 9P157-2 tank-destroyer chassis, which is adapted from that of the BMP-3 fighting vehicle, the AT-15 tracks targets with radar and locks on with an onboard laser.

Although the United States cancelled its

LOSAT (Line of Sight Anti-Tank) programme, the Compact Kinetic Energy Missile (CKEM) has been tested extensively, including a live-fire event which occurred in 2006 against a stationary T-72 tank. The CKEM delivers a kinetic energy penetrator warhead at a speed of up to Mach 6.5. The missile weighs 45kg (99lb) and has an estimated range of 10,000m (10,936 yards).

Future fire

In the coming years, more complex and capable artillery systems will emerge. Among those in research and development today, the BAE Systems NLOS (Non-Line-Of-Sight) cannon shows promise. Leveraging technology from the abandoned XM2001 Crusader project, the NLOS will combine the ultimate in shoot-and-scoot capability with light weight and a fully automated target-acquisition, gun-laying and firing system.

British engineers are also currently working on a new generation of artillery ordnance dubbed the ERO/MCS (Extended Range Ordnance/Modular Charge System). The project also includes upfitting the AS-90 self-propelled howitzer with the longer 155mm (6.1in) 52-calibre barrel from the 39-calibre version installed on many of the vehicles, thus extending the howitzer's range from nearly 25,000m (27,000 yards) to 30,000m (33,000 yards). In essence, the project is designed to

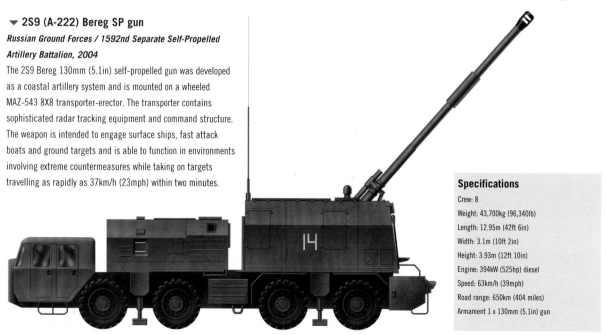

▼ 2S9 (A-222) Bereg SP gun

Russian Ground Forces / 1592nd Separate Self-Propelled Artillery Battalion, 2004

The 2S9 Bereg 130mm (5.1in) self-propelled gun was developed as a coastal artillery system and is mounted on a wheeled MAZ-543 8X8 transporter-erector. The transporter contains sophisticated radar tracking equipment and command structure. The weapon is intended to engage surface ships, fast attack boats and ground targets and is able to function in environments involving extreme countermeasures while taking on targets travelling as rapidly as 37km/h (23mph) within two minutes.

Specifications

Crew: 8
Weight: 43,700kg (96,340lb)
Length: 12.95m (42ft 6in)
Width: 3.1m (10ft 2in)
Height: 3.93m (12ft 10in)
Engine: 394kW (525hp) diesel
Speed: 63km/h (39mph)
Road range: 650km (404 miles)
Armament 1 x 130mm (5.1in) gun

also lengthen the service life of the entire AS-90 weapon system.

Although some military analysts are predicting the demise of artillery as it is known in the traditional sense, the future appears set to contradict that opinion. Considering the nature of modern warfare, it can also be asserted with confidence that the need for firepower delivered in a timely manner and with pinpoint accuracy is greater today than ever before.

Although other weapons such as futuristic aircraft will undoubtedly play an important role in armed conflicts of the twenty-first century, there remains no other force which can dominate a battlefield so thoroughly and on such a sustained basis as artillery.

▲ Caesar 155mm self-propelled artillery system
French Army / 40th Armoured Artillery Regiment, 2008

The French-designed Caesar 155mm (6.1in) self-propelled howitzer is mounted atop a Renault 6X6 truck. Developed by GIAT, the weapon is operated by a crew of five which can be reduced to three if necessary. It is air-transportable by heavy aircraft such as the C-130 or by CH-53 helicopter. The Caesar is also deployed by the Royal Thai Army and entered service in 2003. Saudi Arabia has also purchased a large number of the systems.

Specifications

Crew: 5	Engine: 180kW (240hp) 6-cylinder diesel
Weight: 17,700kg (17.4 tons)	Speed: 100km/h (62mph)
Length: 10m (32ft 10in)	Road range: 600km (373 miles)
Width: 2.55m (8ft 4in)	Armament: 1 x 155mm (6.1in) cannon
Height: 3.7m (12ft 2in)	

Specifications

Crew: 4
Weight: 33,500kg (73,855lb)
Length: 14.1m (46ft 3in)
Width: 3m (9ft 10in)
Height: 3.3m (10ft 10in)
Engine: 255kW (340hp) diesel
Speed: 70km/h (43.5mph)
Road range: 500km (311 miles)
Armament 1 x 155mm (6.1in) cannon

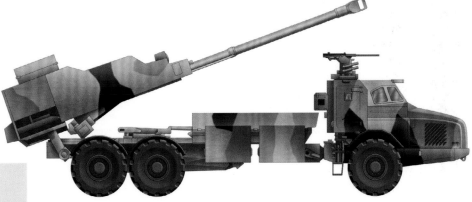

▲ Archer FH77 BW L52 self-propelled howitzer
Swedish Army / to be deployed 2011

BAE Systems Bofors of Sweden developed the Archer FH77 L52, which mounts a 155mm (6.1in) howitzer atop a wheeled 6X6 Volvo A30D chassis. The weapon is served by a crew of up to four. Its burst rate of fire is three rounds in 15 seconds, while its sustained rate is 75 rounds per hour and its intense rate is 20 rounds in two and a half minutes. The Archer is complete with onboard computerized fire-control and gun-laying systems. It is scheduled to enter service in 2011.

Glossary

AA Anti-Aircraft

AAV Assault Amphibian Vehicle. US term for armoured tracked amphibians used by marine corps, formerly called landing vehicle tracked or LVT.

AAVC Assault Amphibian Vehicle, Command. AAV with additional communications fit for unit commanders.

AAVP Assault Amphibian Vehicle, Personnel. Troop-carrying AAV.

ACAV Armoured Cavalry Assault Vehicle. Variant of M113 APC with additional heavy machine guns; used in Vietnam.

ACCV Armoured Cavalry Cannon Vehicle. APC with heavy gun used for fire support.

ACP Armoured Command Post. Armoured vehicle with extra communications gear used by commanders in the field.

Active Armour Armour designed to dynamically thwart incoming warheads. Explosive cassettes containing embedded sensors detect an impacting projectile and explode outwards to decrease its damaging effect on the vehicle.

Ammunition A complete unit of fire, consisting of primer, case, propellant and projectile.

AMR Automitrailleuse de Reconnaissance – scout car (French)

AMX Atelier de construction d'Issy-les-Moulineaux. Primary postwar constructor of French tracked and wheeled AFVs.

AP Armour Piercing. Ammunition designed to penetrate and destroy armoured targets. Term usually reserved for solid shot fired at high velocity.

APAM Anti-Personnel, Anti-Materiel. Dual-purpose round for use against soft targets.

APC Armoured Personnel Carrier. APCs, usually armed with machine guns, generally transport infantry to the battle before the troops dismount to fight on their own.

AR/AAV Armoured Reconnaissance/ Airborne Assault Vehicle

Armour (1) Generic term for all armoured vehicles.

Armour (2) Protection. Armour was originally one material throughout, usually specially hardened steel. Modern armour is a laminated series of layers, which can include metals and related composites (e.g. titanium diboride), ceramics and related composites (e.g. crystal whiskers in a bonded matrix), organic fibres and composites (e.g. woven cloth), and layered and honeycombed combinations of these.

Armoured Car Wheeled vehicle protected by armour.

AT Anti-Tank. Applied to weapons and weapon systems whose primary function is to destroy heavy armour.

AVLB Armoured Vehicle-Launched Bridge. Temporary bridge usually laid down by a converted tank chassis.

AVRE Armoured Vehicle Royal Engineers. British term for combat engineer vehicle.

Ballistics The science of studying projectiles and their paths. Ballistics can be 'interior' (inside the gun), 'exterior' (in-flight), or 'terminal' (at the point of impact).

Blindé French term meaning 'Armoured'

Bore The interior of the barrel of any firearm, forward of the chamber.

BRDM Soviet four-wheeled reconnaissance vehicle.

BTR Soviet/Russian eight-wheeled armoured personnel carrier.

Bullet Projectile fired by small arms and machine guns. Can be anti-personnel or anti-armour. usually solid, but can also be filled – tracer, incendiary, or a combination.

Calibre (1) Internal diameter of gun or bullet or shell expressed in inches (e.g. a .30-calibre machine gun fires bullets 0.3in in diameter), centimetres or millimetres.

Calibre (2) Length of a tank or artillery gun barrel expressed as a multiple of the internal calibre of the weapon.

Carrier Wheeled or tracked armoured vehicle used to transport supplies and ammunition to the front line.

CFV Cavalry Fighting Vehicle. M3 reconnaissance variant of the M2 Bradley infantry fighting vehicle.

CGMC Combination Gun Motor Carriage.

Chassis Lower part of a tank's hull, containing the engine, transmission and suspension and on to which the tracks are attached.

Christie suspension Designed by J. Walter Christie in the 1920s. Independently sprung road wheels on tall, vertical helical springs.

Coaxial Two guns mounted in the same turret or mantlet, rotating together and firing along the same axis.

Composite armour Armour made up from layers of differing materials, offering increased resistance to kinetic, shaped-charge and plastic rounds.

Cupola Armour plated revolving dome on top of the turret.

CVR(T) Combat Vehicle Reconnaissance (Tracked). Scorpion/Scimitar family of armoured vehicles.

CVR(W) Combat Vehicle Reconnaissance (Wheeled). Fox light armoured car.

Depression Angle by which a tank's gun can point below the horizontal. Limited by length of gun inside turret, where the gun is mounted in the turret, and the height of the inside of the turret.

Direct fire Line-of-sight fire directly towards a target, as opposed to indirect fire. Most tanks use direct fire exclusively in battle.

Elevation Angle by which a tank's gun can point above the horizontal – the greater the angle the greater the range.

ERA Explosive Reactive Armour. See Active armour.

ERFB-BB Extended Range Full Bore Base Bleed. An artillery round which uses base bleed to increase range. See BB (Base Bleed).

FAAD Forward Area Air Defense. US term for quick-reacting air-defence systems intended to protect troops in the front line.

FAASV Forward Area Ammunition Support Vehicle. Tracked and armoured supply vehicle used by the US army to resupply forward deployed artillery units.

FAV Fast Attack Vehicle. Light vehicle carrying MGs, cannon, grenade launchers or missiles. Used by Special Forces making raids behind enemy lines.

FCS Fire Control System. Computers, laser rangefinders, optical and thermal sights and gunlaying equipment designed to enable a fighting vehicle to engage the enemy accurately.

Fragmentation Standard anti-personnel explosive technique. Such a device (which could include mines, hand grenades, shells or bombs) is usually made from steel, heavily scored so that when it detonates it will shatter into hundreds of razor-sharp shards.

GMC Gun Motor Carriage. WWII US army name for self-propelled gun, mounted on wheeled, half-tracked or tracked platforms. Also applied to tank destroyers, which were lightly armoured tank hunters armed with powerful guns in open-topped turrets.

GPMG General-Purpose Machine Gun. MG used as both infantry LMG and for sustained fire. Variants adapted as coaxial guns for tanks and as anti-aircraft guns on many different kinds of armoured vehicle.

Hard target Protected target with some immunity to small-arms fire and fragmentation weapons.

HE High Explosive

HEAP High Explosive Anti-Personnel. Dual-purpose HE round which destroys by a combination of blast and anti-personnel effects.

HEAT High Explosive Anti Tank. Tank round or missile with shaped-charge warhead designed to burn through the thickest of armour.

HEP High Explosive Plastic. US term for a tank round that deforms on surface of target before exploding. Designed to send shockwaves through armour flaking off razor-sharp shards into the interior.

Howitzer Artillery piece with short barrel capable of high angle fire. Originally a low-velocity short-range weapon, though modern self-propelled howitzers have a long range. Howitzers are usually used for indirect fire.

Hull Main part of armoured vehicle, comprising chassis and superstructure, onto which tracks/wheels and turret are mounted.

IFCS Integrated Fire Control System. British system developed for the Chieftain tank incorporating target location, rangefinding and gun engagement.

JGSDF Japanese Ground Self Defence Force. Postwar Japanese army, purely defensive in posture.

LARS Light Artillery Rocket System. Multiple rocket system developed for the German Bundeswehr.

Laser Light Amplification by Stimulated Emission of Radiation.

Intense beam of single wavelength light used by the military primarily for rangefinding and target illumination.

LAV Light Armoured Vehicle. Canadian-built wheeled APC based on a Swiss design and used by the US Marine Corps.

LAW Light Anti-armour Weapon. Hand-held rocket launcher giving infantry some short-range anti-armour capability.

Light tanks One of the original classes of tanks. Thinly armoured fast tanks designed primarily for reconnaissance.

LMG Light Machine Gun. Squad support weapon which can often be fired from the gun ports of infantry fighting vehicles.

LRV Light Recovery Vehicle

LVT Landing Vehicle, Tracked. The original amphibious assault vehicles used by the Allies in Europe and the Pacific during World War II. The term continued in use until the 1990s with the LVTP-5 and the LVTP-7, before being replaced by the designation AAV, or Assault Amphibian Vehicle.

Machine Guns Rifle-calibre small arms capable of automatic fire, used as primary or secondary armament of armoured vehicles.

MBT Main Battle Tank. MBTs are the primary tank type of modern armies, and combine characteristics of their medium and heavy tank ancestors.

MICV Mechanized Infantry Combat Vehicle.

MLRS Multiple Launch Rocket System. M270 armoured vehicle capable of firing 12 rockets out to

a range of more than 30km (19 miles).

MRL Multiple Rocket Launcher. Launch platform for unguided artillery missiles.

MRS Muzzle Reference System. Sensor at muzzle of gun which measures barrel wear and sag, correcting aim to make allowance for inaccuracies these can cause.

Muzzle velocity Speed of projectile as it leaves the muzzle. Air friction means velocity drops rapidly once in flight.

Periscope Optical device which enables viewer to see over obstacles. Enables tank crew to look out while remaining protected.

QF or **Quick Firing** Fixed ammunition – cartridge case and projectile joined.

Rate of fire Number of rounds that can be fired in a period of time, usually expressed in rounds per minute.

Reconnaissance Vehicle Mobile Lightly armoured vehicle used for gathering battlefield intelligence.

RMG Ranging Machine Gun. A machine gun coaxial with the main armament. The bullets have the same ballistic performance as the main gun.

RP Rocket propelled. Applied to tank ammunition, artillery rounds and antitank grenades.

RPG Rocket Propelled Grenade Launcher. Soviet-made infantry antitank weapons.

Running gear The transmission, suspension, wheels and tracks of a tank.

Sabot French word for 'wooden shoe', describing the cladding around an APDS round.

SAM Surface-to-Air Missile

Semi-automatic Firearm which fires, extracts, ejects and reloads only once for each pull and release of the trigger.

Shell Hollow projectile normally fired from a rifled gun. Shell can have a number of fillings, including HE, submunitions, chemical and smoke.

Shot Solid projectile, usually armour-piercing.

Sloped Armour Angled armour – projectiles will either ricochet or be forced to penetrate diagonally.

Smoothbore Cannon without rifling, designed to fire unrotated fin-stabilized projectiles.

SP Self-Propelled

SPAAG Self-Propelled Anti-Aircraft Gun system

SPAAM Self-Propelled Anti-Aircraft Missile system

SPAT Self-Propelled Anti-Tank system

SPG Self-Propelled Gun

SPH Self-Propelled Howitzer

Tank Heavily armed and armoured full-tracked fighting vehicle. Originally called tank as a disguise during early development.

Tank Destroyer US army WWII lightly armoured tracked vehicle armed with a powerful gun. Designed to ambush enemy armour.

Thermal imaging Sensor system which detects heat generated by targets and projects it as a TV-style image onto a display screen.

Track Endless belt circling the sprocket, idler, roadwheels and return rollers of a tracked suspension and providing the surface for the wheels to run on.

Trajectory The curved path of a projectile through the air.

Transmission Means by which the power of the engine is converted to rotary movement of wheels or tracks. Transmission can be hydraulic mechanical or electrical.

Traverse The ability of a gun or turret to swing away from the centreline of a vehicle. A fully rotating turret has a traverse of 360 degrees.

Tread Distance between the centrelines of a vehicle's tracks or wheels.

Turret Revolving armoured box mounting a gun. Usually

accommodates commander and other crew.

Velocity The speed of a projectile at any point along its trajectory, usually measured in feet per second or metres per second.

Bibliography

Bidwell, Shelford. *Artillery of the World*. Brassey's, London, 1977.

Clancy, Tom. *Armored Cav: A Guided Tour of an Armored Cavalry Regiment*. Berkley Books: New York, 1994.

Crismon, Fred W. *U.S. Military Tracked Vehicles*. Motorbooks International, Osceola, Wisconsin, 1992.

Crismon, Fred W. *U.S. Military Wheeled Vehicles*. Motorbooks International, 1994.

Department of the Army, United States Army Intelligence and Security Command, United States Army Intelligence and Threat Analysis Center. *Soviet Army Operations*. U.S. Army, Arlington, Virginia, 1978.

Green, Michael & James D. Brown. *M2/M3 Bradley at War*. Zenith Press: Minneapolis, Minnesota, 2007.

Haskew, Michael E. *Artillery from the Civil War to the Present Day*. Metro Books, New York, 2008.

Hogg, Ian. *Tank Killing: Anti-Tank Warfare by Men and Machines*. Sarpedon, New York, 1996.

Hogg, Ian. *Twentieth Century Artillery*. Freidman/Fairfax Publishers, New York, 2000.

Jackson, Robert. *Tanks and Armoured Fighting Vehicles Visual Encyclopedia*. Amber Books Ltd., London, 2009.

Leyden, Andrew. *An After Action Report: Gulf War Debriefing Book*. Hellgate Press, Grants Pass, Oregon, 1997.

Macksey, Kenneth & John H. Batchelor. *Tank: A History of the Armoured Fighting Vehicle*. Charles Scribner's Sons: New York, 1970.

Mossman, Billy C. *United States Army in the Korean War: Ebb and Flow November 1950–July 1951*. Center of Military History United States Army, Washington, D.C., 1990.

Zaloga, Steven. *M1 Abrams vs T-72 Ural: Operation Desert Storm 1991*. Osprey Publishing Ltd.: Oxford, United Kingdom, 2009.

Useful Websites

armchairgeneral.com
army-technology.com
defenseindustrydaily.com
eliteforces.info
enemyforces.net
fas.org
globalsecurity.org

history.army.mil
historyofwar.org
israelnewsagency.com
janes.com
militaryfactory.com
militaryhistoryonline.com
militaryphotos.net

military-today.com
nationmaster.com
o5m6.de
olive-drab.com
orbat.com
sinodefence.com
turretsandtracks.co.uk
wikipedia.org

Index

Page numbers in *italics* refer to illustrations.